The AMERICAN PRESIDENCY

Historical and Contemporary Perspectives

Advisory Editor in Political Science
Roger H. Davidson
Congressional Research Service

The AMERICAN PRESIDENCY

Historical and Contemporary Perspectives

Edited by

HARRY A. BAILEY, JR.
Temple University

JAY M. SHAFRITZ
University of Pittsburgh

The Dorsey Press
Chicago, Illinois 60604

This book was set in Goudy Oldstyle by Arcata Graphics/Kingsport.
The editors were Leo Wiegman, Waivah Clement, and Jane Lightell.
The production manager was Bette Ittersagen.
The designer was Diana Yost.
Malloy Lithographing, Inc. was the printer and binder.

ISBN 0-256-05752-4

Library of Congress Catalog Card No. 87–71354

Printed in the United States of America

1 2 3 4 5 6 7 8 9 0 ML 5 4 3 2 1 0 9 8

Foreword

by R. Gordon Hoxie

The American Presidency: Historical and Contemporary Perspectives will be an enduring work. The editors of this volume, Professors Harry A. Bailey, Jr., and Jay M. Shafritz, masterfully trace the origins and development of the nation's most significant political office. It begins by describing the conditions which demanded radical change. In the decade after the Declaration of Independence of 1776 the United States were not united. This was true even while the war for independence was being waged.

As early as September 1780, more than a year before the decisive Battle of Yorktown, General Washington's twenty-five-year-old aide-de-camp, Alexander Hamilton, had fervently written, "There is only one remedy—to call a convention of all the states." In the ensuing seven years by private letters, speeches, newspaper articles and resolutions he worked strenuously toward his goal.

Patrick Henry refused to accept appointment to the 1787 Philadelphia Convention because he "smelt a rat." As Chief Justice Warren E. Burger observed, the "rat" Henry "smelled was the replacement of the Articles of Confederation with a Constitution creating a strong national government." The closely contested struggle for ratification of the Constitution comes alive in the debate in New York State between Governor George Clinton and Hamilton. The former's opposition to a strong executive is countered by Hamilton's 1788 conception, "Energy in the executive is a leading character in the definition of good government." Such energy, The Federalist No. 70 reminds us, "is essential to the protection of the community against foreign attacks: It is not less essential to the steady administration of the laws."

Professors Bailey and Shafritz perceive the dangers of an imperiled as well as an imperial president. Before the Iran-contra controversy surfaced, they recognized the fragility of presidential leadership. They portray the historical, present, and future presidency as perceived by the Congress, the media, and by presidents themselves; they assess the presidential selection process, executive-legislative relations, the presidency and the courts, executive-bureaucratic relations, the presidential advising and decision-making process, the domestic and the foreign policy presidencies, the presidency and the media, and presidential personalities, and they conclude with perspectives on presidential power.

From the vast array of literature on the presidency, from Clinton, Hamilton, and James Madison in the late eighteenth century to Barber, Edwards, Greenstein, Heclo, Neustadt, Wayne, Wildavsky, and many others today, a wealth of experience, insights, and knowledge is set forth. But beyond this, the editors have skillfully drawn and organized their volume to truly give what their subtitle portrays, "Historical and Contemporary Perspectives." Only two such reasoned scholars could do so, weaving the essays together into a master work.

The presidency, indeed the entire political system which they portray, is going through a difficult, protracted testing period. The work of the Framers of 1787, which was reverently viewed by Washington and Madison as a miracle, was also viewed by them as a great experiment. What they conceived in the separation of powers system, with checks and balances in defense of the freedom for which they had striven, has gone through many severe testing periods, including civil war and desperate depression. But in many ways the testing is more confusing today. Unlike the decades of the 1930s, 1940s, and 1950s of combating depression, engaging in total war, or helping build a new world, the past quarter century has had no unity of purpose. In the 1960s, 1970s, and 1980s, the bureaucracy, political parties, the media and the presidency itself have all undergone vast change. Where Eisenhower could work effectively with recognized congressional leaders, that leadership has been fractured by congressional members, most particularly beginning with those elected in 1974, acting as independent spirits. To those newly elected members, seniority meant little. As early as 1970, political parties, which had been engines of policy from the first presidential administration, had virtually been replaced by numerous interest groups which have fostered their own relationships with members of Congress and of the bureaucracy.

In brief, in domestic and foreign policy, it is a difficult time to lead. There is a need to revitalize political parties, to restore as the Constitutional Framers conceived, a *national* interest paramount to regional and special interest groups.

Both the Congress and the presidency need to put their own institutions in order for effective collaborative roles. What is needed is less rhetoric and more accomplishments, more character and less distrust. Administrative machinery both in the Congress and the presidency are badly in need of overhauling. There should be a meaningful consolidation of congressional committees on the one hand and more effective institutional rather than ad hoc presidential organization on the other. All of this is, of course, easier said than done. As the aged John Adams wrote to the aged Thomas Jefferson, nearly a half century after the Declaration of Independence, "A free government is a complicated piece of machinery the nice and exact adjustment of whose springs, wheels, and weights is not yet well comprehended. . . ." We are still seeking the "exact adjustment" in today's more difficult environment.

As Roger Brown and David Welborn express it in their essay in this volume, ". . . the apparent intractibility of many contemporary public policy problems, the new interest group politics, congressional independence, and a critical watchdog media, among other phenomena, make garnering support for presidential efforts an onerous task." In the final analysis there is no substitute for leadership or statesmanship. As we reflect on the bicentennial of the Constitution and of the principal political office which the Framers created, we are fortunate to have this new volume. Indeed, as we move ahead into the third century of this bold experiment in political principle, organization, and practice, this volume will provide landmarks in our continued quest to "secure the Blessings of Liberty. . . ."

R. G. H.

Preface

The American presidency has become the dominant political institution in the tripartite national government system. Many observers consider it to be the nerve center, not only of the United States, but of the western political world. This has not always been true. The powerful office that is the modern presidency is, essentially, a product of the twentieth century. The earlier nineteenth century presidency was, with few exceptions, hemmed in by the Madisonian system of checks and balances and by a political-economic system that extolled the virtues of limited government. Thus, the role of the presidency in nineteenth-century American political theory was essentially that of carrying out the will of Congress. Andrew Jackson and Abraham Lincoln were outstanding exceptions to the rule.

The modern presidency is a dynamic office performing a variety of roles and exercising a range of powers that the Founders and earlier occupants of the office never anticipated. Today's presidency (the president himself and the Executive Office of the President) is itself a large number of specialized offices with hundreds of employees. It sits astride an enlarged national bureaucracy of over a dozen executive departments and numerous other agencies. The Executive Office of the President as well as this enlarged national bureaucracy were ushered into the governmental framework by the president and Congress working in concert during the New Deal. They expanded with the exigencies of World War II and later with the numerous policies and programs of the Great Society.

Despite the enormous power that has accrued to the presidency through precedent, congressional delegation, and federal court decisions, especially since the turn of the century, considerable constraints limit a president's capacity to achieve policy goals. The modern presidency operates under the limitations of a cabinet whose members often owe their allegiances elsewhere. It also operates under the limitations of a bureaucracy, which officials may and do resist presidential direction; of a more decentralized and recalcitrant Congress; of political parties in decline; and of a political process where party primaries and television are major factors in the calculus of presidential power.

All of these constraints place considerable demands on a president's personality and bargaining skills. A chief executive must mitigate if not overcome them to achieve a modicum of policy goals, both domestic and foreign.

This book attempts to show how the modern president utilizes the office, its powers, and individual personality and bargaining skills to cope with contemporary problems. We proceed on the assumption that a thorough understanding of the modern presidency cannot occur without reference to its history and development. For these reasons, we have included lengthy and comprehensive introductions to each of the chapters that, we believe, clearly place the American presidency in both its historical and contemporary perspectives.

ACKNOWLEDGMENTS

Many people were helpful in various ways in the preparation of this book. We collectively thank all of the authors and publishers for permission to reprint their materials. The following individuals have also earned a special note of thanks: Gloria J. Basmajian, Roger Davidson, David P. Dillard, R. Gordon Hoxie, Albert C. Hyde, Lawrence Korb, Irene Matthews, Aaron S. Neba, J. Steven Ott, and David H. Rosenbloom.

Many experienced instructors of courses on the American presidency were kind enough to review our outline and provide us with invaluable insights. We wish to esepcially acknowledge: Herb Asher, The Ohio State University; Cary R. Covington, University of Iowa; John H. Kessel, The Ohio State University; James Pfiffner, George Mason University; Richard M. Pious, Columbia University; and Lester G. Seligman, University of Illinois.

Harry A. Bailey, Jr.
Jay M. Shafritz

Contents

CHAPTER I

Origins and Creation
of the Presidency

The contemporary American presidency has been strongly influenced by the experiences of a people under colonial and revolutionary governments. The earliest holders of executive power in America were the colonial governors.[1] Many of them incurred widespread enmity because they looked to England and the Crown rather than to the people of their colonies for policy guidance.

After the American Revolution, which lasted from 1775 to 1781 (formal recognition of independence from Great Britain did not come until 1783 with the Treaty of Paris), the framers of state constitutions with a few exceptions (the state of New York, for example) created weak executive branches and strong legislatures. For the country as a whole, the founders created a national government under the Articles of Confederation in 1781. As a major shortcoming, the Articles lacked a central chief executive. For the execution of its decrees, the Confederation Congress became a legislative-executive body.

Experiences with weak executives at the state level and almost no executive at the national level caused many of the leading politicians in the new nation to agitate for a strong central government and for a national chief executive. Among these politicians were James Madison and George Washington of Virginia, Alexander Hamilton of New York, and James Wilson and Benjamin Franklin of Pennsylvania.

Chiefly through the efforts of James Madison, a general convention of the states was called to meet at Annapolis, Maryland, to discuss commercial problems. Delegates from five states (Virginia, Pennsylvania, New York, New Jersey, and Delaware) attended. At this meeting, the delegates announced the calling of a general convention to meet at Philadelphia in May 1787 to revise the Articles of Confederation.

The delegates sent notice of their resolution to the Congress of Confederation and it authorized the federal convention in a resolution adopted February 21, 1787, stating that "on the second Monday in May next, a convention of delegates who shall have been appointed by the several states be held at Philadelphia."[2]

On May 25, 1787, the Convention organized, began its work in earnest, and remained in continuous session until September 17, 1787, with the exception of adjournment for two days over the Fourth of July and another ten days from July 26 to August 6 to allow the Committee on Detail to prepare its report.[3]

1

The fifty-five delegates who assembled in Convention to draw up a new constitution brought with them conflicting viewpoints: some favored a weak chief executive, others favored a strong one.[4] One popular alternative was a plural executive in which executive power would be shared by a council or committee. A second alternative was the single executive who alone would lead an executive branch. But many delegates were fearful that a single executive was the route to despotic government.

Clearly, the framers wanted to avoid the weaknesses of a plural executive or government by committee, which they had experienced under the Articles of Confederation. They were also attempting to preclude the abuses they had endured before the American Revolution under the domination of a king. However, the majority of the framers present desired to provide an executive power capable of penetrating to the remotest parts of the Union not only for enforcing the national laws, but also for the purpose of bringing assistance to the states in the event of emergencies or domestic disorders.[5]

R. Gordon Hoxie's essay examines the origins of and the controversies over the presidency in the constitutional convention. He notes that the founders looked to the example of the New York governorship as a satisfactory model for the federal chief executive. Prior to the convention, the New York governorship commended itself to the founders because Governor George Clinton was able to rout out the remnants of Shays's men who had fled to New York after springing their rebellion in Massachusetts in 1786;[6] during the debate over ratification, Clinton was also able to put down the savage Doctors' Riots in New York City in 1788.[7] Hoxie's essay, "The Presidency in the Constitutional Convention," which provides a fruitful starting point for an understanding of the creation of the presidency, is reprinted here.

James Madison, a leading spokesman for a revision of the Articles of Confederation and a supporter of a strong national executive, was one of Virginia's delegates to the convention; later he would become the fourth president of the United States. Madison's early ideas for the American presidency were, in substance, embodied in the resolutions drawn up by the Virginia delegates and submitted to the Convention on May 29, 1787. These resolutions became known as the Virginia or Randolph Plan because Edmund Randolph had been its nominal author. The Randolph Plan proposed a strong national government; a second plan was known as the New Jersey or Patterson Plan after William Patterson who represented the views of the small states and states' rights advocates.

The debate over the Virginia and New Jersey plans, as well as other proposals submitted by individual delegates[8] or other states, took place in a Committee of the Whole where discussion could be conducted informally. When discussion led to stalemate, the framers made use of committees to work out compromises.

The strong executive advocates were unhappy with the Randolph Plan for specifying an executive elected by Congress; James Wilson of Pennsylvania even suggested direct popular election. When this idea was rejected by most of the delegates, Wilson suggested that the people of the various states choose presidential electors who would then meet and choose the chief executive. When first proposed, this idea received little favor. As the Convention neared a close, however, the Committee on Postponed Matters recommended that a president be chosen by an electoral college. The proposal was eventually adopted by the Convention. In short, as Gregor Reinhard has written, three committees were crucial in the formation of the constitutional presidency: the five-member Committee on Detail, the eleven-member Committee on Postponed Matters, and the final five-member Committee on Style.[9]

In a letter to Thomas Jefferson in France, James Madison summarized many of the views aired in the Convention as well as his own. The letter reviews the great objects of the convention, the debate over whether the executive should be a single person or a plurality, the mode of selection of the president (whether by the people at large, by the executives of the states, or by Congress or some part of it), the duration of executive tenure, reeligibility for election, and the appointment power of the president. Madison's letter is reprinted here.

The Constitution's antagonists, the Antifederalists, felt that the new Constitution granted excessive power to the executive and restored much of the same authority that the people had fought to overthrow. The Antifederalists were particularly incensed at what they saw to be centralist tendencies in the Constitution. Leading Antifederalists included George Mason of Virginia, Elbridge Gerry of Massachusetts, Patrick Henry of Virginia (who, parenthetically, later became a Federalist), and George Clinton of New York.[10]

George Clinton, the governor of New York from 1777 to 1795 and again from 1800 to 1803, opposed the ratification of the Constitution on the grounds that its vagueness left unclear the election of a president and a vice president after the expiration of their first term of four years, since there was no explicit provision for reelection after the expiration of their offices. This could, Clinton thought, result in a president establishing himself in office for life.[11] Clinton also agonized over the absence of any provision in the Constitution for a council that would assist the president while the Senate was in recess. He was distressed, too, that the president was not directly chosen by the people, as was the Governor of New York. And he was disturbed further that the new president would possess the enormous powers of appointment, of receiving ambassadors, of vetoing legislation, and of granting pardons, all without carefully delineated checks upon this power.

Clinton's seven essays in opposition to the Constitution, written under the pseudonym "Cato," were addressed to the voters of New York and published in the *New York Journal* from September 22, 1787, to January 3, 1788. Two of these essays, numbers IV and V dated November 8 and 22, 1787, and addressed "To the Citizens of the State of New York," are reprinted here.

The Antifederalist challenge to the proposed Constitution did not go unopposed. Alexander Hamilton, one of the three New York delegates to the Convention and later the first Secretary of the Treasury under President George Washington, was greatly concerned by the large number of Antifederalist pamphlets that made their appearance in New York soon after the Convention adjourned. In October 1787, Hamilton began publishing articles under the pseudonym "Publius" in the New York newspaper, the *Independent Journal.* [12] In all, eighty-five articles appeared between October 1787 and July 1788 in various New York newspapers. At least fifty of these were the work of Hamilton. James Madison and John Jay wrote the others. In total, *The Federalist Papers* are generally considered the most important work of political theory ever written in the United States, the one product of the American mind that is rightly counted among the classics of political philosophy. Hamilton's support for the presidency was spelled out in eleven of these essays: Federalist numbers 67 through 77.

Hamilton attacked Governor Clinton for his hostility to the Constitution but more generally focused on winning over doubters and hesitant Antifederalists and on defending the doctrine of national ascendancy. More specifically, Hamilton aimed to clearly explain the necessity of various provisions in the Constitution and to assure the fearful that the new government would not trample their liberties.

Hamilton's "Federalist No. 69," reprinted here, was written as an answer to Governor Clinton's charge that the presidency would differ little from the British monarchy. Hamilton clarifies the political differences between the republican executive, with powers of governance under a check and balance system such as the Constitution would provide, and the hereditary monarchy of Great Britain, with virtually unlimited powers of rule.

In a second Federalist paper reprinted here, Number 70, Hamilton continued his analysis and defense of the Constitution's Article II by asserting the merits of a unitary executive and indicating how a strong executive is compatible with republican principles. The plural executive, Hamilton argues, conceals faults and destroys responsibility in that it deprives the people of the capacity to restrain it by public opinion; moreover, it makes it difficult for the people to discover clearly who is guilty of misconduct. Hamilton concludes that a single executive with central and coordinating power is essential to the well-being of the republic and, moreover, this power is more easily confined and held accountable when it is concentrated in the hands of one person.

NOTES

1. Byron R. Abernathy, *Some Persisting Questions Concerning the Constitutional State Executive,* Governmental Research Series no. 23 (Lawrence, Kan.: Governmental Research Center, 1960), p. 2.
2. Max Ferrand (ed.), *The Records of the Federal Convention of 1787,* vol. 1, rev. ed. (New Haven, Conn.: Yale University Press, 1966), p. xi.
3. Ibid.
4. See Alfred H. Kelly and Winfred A. Harbison, *The American Constitution: Its Origins and Development,* 4th ed. (New York: W. W. Norton, 1963), p. 132, and Joseph E. Kallenbach, *The American Chief Executive: The Presidency and the Governorship* (New York: Harper & Row, 1966), pp. 32–33; for an excellent study of the delegates in the

Convention who contributed most to the invention of the presidency, see Donald L. Robinson, "The Inventors of the Presidency," *Presidential Studies Quarterly* 13, no. 1 (Winter 1983), pp. 8–25.

5. Edward S. Corwin, *The President: Office and Powers, 1787–1957* (New York: New York University Press, 1957), p. 10.

6. Shays's rebellion was an armed revolt begun in 1786 by farmers in western Massachusetts seeking relief from debts and possible foreclosure of mortgages.

   Debt-ridden farmers, struck by the economic depression that followed the American Revolution, petitioned the Massachusetts senate to issue paper money and to prevent foreclosure of mortgages on their property and their own imprisonment for debt as a result of high land taxes. When the state senate refused to grant these requests, armed farmers led by Captain Daniel Shays, a bankrupt Revolutionary War officer, forcibly shut down the county courts in Northampton in August 1786 to prevent the judge from hearing mortgage foreclosure cases.

   In September 1786, Shays's men forced the state supreme court at Springfield to adjourn. In December 1787, the rebels attempted to capture the city arsenal at Springfield. Massachusetts Governor James Bowdoin directed Generals Benjamin Lincoln and William Shephard to stop any attack on the arsenal. The farmer rebels were routed by these two elements of the state militia.

   Earlier, Governor Bowdoin had asked Congress to help against the rioters. Under the Articles of Confederation, however, Congress lacked the power to respond. Shays's rebellion is, thus, considered a major factor in the calling of a Constitutional Convention to revise the Articles and a strong argument for ratifying the Constitution once it was drafted.

   For a detailed discussion of the mobs of the American Revolution, see Jules Archer, *Riot! A History of Mob Action in the United States* (New York: Hawthorn Books, 1974), pp. 44–45.

7. The Doctors' Riots occurred in New York City in 1788 when New Yorkers discovered that students of medicine were digging up bodies from graveyards to be dissected for the purpose of learning anatomy.

   A young surgeon at Columbia Hospital displayed a human arm to some children playing nearby and indicated that it belonged to the recently deceased mother of one of the boys. The boy reported this to his father who, in turn, opened the mother's grave to find her body gone. Friends of the family heard the news and marched on the city hospital. As the word spread, hundreds of other angry New Yorkers burst into the hospital, attacked the students, and smashed equipment.

   The Mayor and the Sheriff of New York City went to the hospital; in order to appease the mob, they took the students and their instructors into custody. Later, a second mob broke into the hospital to search for students and doctors. The mob proceeded to the jail when it learned that the students and doctors had been placed there for their own protection. City authorities called a small number of militia for assistance. The cautious militia's guns were seized by the mob and destroyed.

   New York Governor Clinton, the Mayor of New York City, and other leading citizens, including John Jay, accompanied by a new and larger militia, went to the jail to plead with the mob to disperse and return to their homes. The soldiers were met with bricks and stones. Governor Clinton ordered the militia to shoot. Many of the mob were hit; in panic, the mob fled in every direction. For more details on the

Doctors' Riots see Joel Tyler Headley, *Mass Violence in America: Pen and Pencil Sketches of the Great Riots* (New York: Arno Press and New York Times, 1969), pp. 57–65.

8. One plan that did not receive any floor debate was a detailed proposal for a strong national executive submitted by Charles Pinckney of South Carolina. Introduced to the convention on the same day that Randolph presented the Virginia plan, it was simply referred to the Committee on Detail. However, three months later, James Wilson is said to have relied heavily on Pinckney's plan in writing the final draft of the executive article. On this point, see Larry Berman, *The New American Presidency* (Boston: Little, Brown, 1986), pp. 24–25, and Kallenbach, *American Chief Executive*, p. 40, footnote 18. The Pinckney plan continues to be the source of some controversy; see Ferrand, *Records of the Federal Convention*, vol. 3, pp. 565–609, and Robinson, "Inventors of the Presidency," p. 20.

9. Gregor Reinhard, "The Origins of the Presidency," in *The American Presidency: A Policy Perspective from Readings and Documents*, ed. David C. Kozak and Kenneth N. Ciboski (Chicago: Nelson-Hall Publishers, 1985), p. 3.

10. For a more complete look at the ideas of the Antifederalists, see Morton Borden, ed., *The Antifederalist Papers* (East Lansing: Michigan State University Press, 1965); Cecelia M. Kenyon, ed., *The Antifederalist* (Indianapolis: Bobbs-Merrill, 1966); Alpheus T. Mason, *The States Rights Debate: Antifederalism and the Constitution* (Englewood Cliffs, N.J.: Prentice-Hall, 1964); and Cecelia M. Kenyon, "Men of Little Faith: The Antifederalists on the Nature of Representative Government," *William and Mary Quarterly*, 12, no. 2, Third Series (January 1955), pp. 3–43.

11. Clinton's fears were, in retrospect, unwarranted. Although no limit was placed on a president's reeligibility for office by the 1789 Constitution, the two-term tradition soon developed based on the practices of the early presidents, including George Washington, Thomas Jefferson, James Madison, James Monroe, and Andrew Jackson, who limited themselves to two terms. Upon close examination, however, the tradition turns out to be more myth than reality. The American presidential tenure in office has been more nearly a one-term tradition. For the evidence, see Harry A. Bailey, Jr., "Presidential Tenure and the Two-Term Tradition," *Publius* 2 (Fall 1972), pp. 95–106.

12. "Publius," which is Latin for "public man," is the pen name Alexander Hamilton, James Madison, and John Jay used for the series of articles that became the Federalist papers. The authors used this strategy because they were obvious supporters of the Constitution and wished to give their arguments for ratification greater legitimacy. Moreover, it was fashionable in Hamilton's day for gentlemen who wrote to newspapers to use a pen name. In this regard, see George W. Carey, "Publius—A Split Personality?" *Review of Politics* 46, no. 1 (January 1984), pp. 5–22.

1
The Presidency in the Constitutional Convention

R. Gordon Hoxie

THE CONSTITUTIONAL CONVENTION

The Climate

The climate out of which the Constitutional Convention was convened was the severe economic depression of 1785–86 and the related Shays's Rebellion in Massachusetts in 1786. That Fall the Annapolis Convention had issued an invitation to all of the 13 states to send delegates to Philadelphia to consider revisions to the constitution. The Congress sent out a similar request on February 21, 1787. All of the states except Rhode Island sent delegates. In all, 74 delegates were chosen, but only 55 actually participated in the proceedings. The early decision in this convention, held without media access, was to create a new constitution. Thirty-nine signed that instrument, after having been in closed, confidential session, in Independence Hall from May 25–September 17, 1787. By July 1788 the Constitution had been endorsed with scant enthusiasm by 11 state conventions. North Carolina and Rhode Island withheld approval until after the new federal government was placed in operation in the Spring of 1789.

Leading Creators of the Presidency

The Convention was remarkable for the learning and talent of the Framers.

Washington served as the presiding officer. Although he did not play an active role in the deliberations, he was the person who epitomized in the minds of the Framers, the ideal executive. Moreover, his belief in a strong executive was crucial.

James Madison has been referred to with considerable exaggeration as "the father of the Constitution." He was certainly not the father of the presidency. It was Madison who had inspired the convening of the Alexandria and Mount Vernon meetings of March 1785 and the Annapolis Commercial Convention of September 1786, which examined frailties of the Articles of Confederation.

Alexander Hamilton had drafted the report of the Annapolis Convention calling for a Convention to convene in Philadelphia in May, 1787, "to take into consideration the situation of the United States, to devise such further provisions as shall appear to them necessary to render the Constitution . . . adequate to the exigencies of the Union. . . ."[1] Moreover, it was Hamilton, not Madison, who in 1780, had made the first proposal to revise the then constitution, the Articles of Confederation.[2] Hamilton, who preferred the British parliamentary system, contributed most valuably in convening the Convention and in securing the Constitution's ratification.

Madison was the person who took

Source: Presidential Studies Quarterly 15 (Winter 1985). This essay is based upon a lecture delivered at the National Archives, Washington, D.C., April 18, 1984 for the Constitutional Study Group.

most copious notes at the Convention. Moreover, he played a major role in making the principal proposals on the executive, by James Wilson and Gouverneur Morris, acceptable to the majority of the delegates.[3]

Wilson and Morris, the intellectual leaders of the group who conceived the Presidency, are deserving of special attention. Wilson, a native of Scotland, educated at St. Andrews and the University of Edinburgh, had come to Pennsylvania in 1765 at age 23. He studied law under John Dickinson and became one of the most prominent lawyers in America. He came to the Constitutional Convention with a clear notion of what he wanted, a single chief executive elected by the people, for a relatively short term, subject to re-election; the executive would have no advisory council except perhaps a cabinet of his own choosing.

Working closely with Wilson was his fellow Pennsylvania delegate, Gouverneur Morris, a transplanted New Yorker who had graduated from King's College (Columbia) in 1768. Morris had long advocated a strong executive in terms similar to those of Wilson. Morris had been a framer of the New York State Constitution of 1777, which had made the popularly elected New York governor the strongest chief executive in the United States. According to the records of the convention, Morris spoke more often than any other member.

Major Issues

Many major issues confronted the Framers, ranging from the relationships between the federal government and the states to the relationship between the executive, legislative, and judicial branches of the proposed federal government. There were numerous areas of concern for potential despotism on the part of the federal government and of

domination on the part of the large over the smaller states. Some of these concerns, notably the large vs. the small states, almost destroyed the convention. But the matter which took the most time was that of the executive. To grasp this one must understand that the federal government under the Articles of Confederation simply had no executive branch.

Conceptions on the executive branch raised such issues as tenure, a single or a plural executive (i.e., a council), and an executive chosen either by the legislature or the people, or by the state governments (as was the case of the Congress under the Articles of Confederation). The only question more vexing was the representation of large vs. small states. This seemingly irreconcilable issue, caused Washington to lament to Hamilton, July 10, 1787, "I *almost* despair of seeing a favorable issue to the proceedings of the Convention, and do therefore repent having had any agency in the business."[4]

The Great Compromise of July 16th, often referred to as the Connecticut Compromise, salvaged the Convention. By this agreement all of the states would be represented in the lower house according to population, but in the upper house they would all have equal representation. Further assurance was placed in the Constitution that no new state would be "formed by the junction of two or more states, or parts of states, without the consent of the legislatures of the states concerned as well as the Congress." (Another concern of the smaller states, that related to the organization of territories and states from the western lands, had been resolved almost simultaneously by the single most constructive piece of legislation of the old Congress, that is the Northwest Ordinance adopted July 13th, 1787.) Other continuing debates in the Convention concerned such matters as the control of commerce between states and the nature of the executive and the means of executive selection. Indeed, James Wilson termed the matters related to the executive "the most difficult of all on which we have to decide."[5]

Creating the Presidency

The first days, May 25–29, had been devoted to organizing the Convention. Considerations on major resolutions began on May 29th with the Virginia Plan, which encompassed much of which became the constitution. This was presented by the state's governor, Edmund Randolph, who opposed a strong executive. He would have the executive chosen by and subordinate to the legislature. Still, it was a beginning, representing a general recognition that there should be an executive.

Then, on the morning of June 1, Wilson had startled the delegates with his proposal "that the Executive consist of a single person." The venerable, much respected Benjamin Franklin, who preferred a plural executive chosen by the legislature, rose to request clarification. Charles Pinckney of South Carolina proposed a council of state, including the heads of executive departments (like the British Cabinet). Pinckney's proposal for a council and that of Gouverneur Morris failed of adoption because of strong sentiment against overstructuring the executive and against any advisory council. Wilson countered that "a council oftener serves to cover, than prevent malpractice." Hamilton was of similar view in opposing an advisory council.

Nonetheless there was formidable opposition to Wilson's proposal for a single executive. Joining with Franklin and Randolph in opposition were George Mason of Virginia, Roger Sherman of Connecticut and Hugh Williamson of North Carolina. However, after three days of debate, Wilson's motion for a single executive was approved.[6]

It should be noted that at the time the United States determined to have a single executive, Great Britain was moving towards a plural executive of ministers and a prime minister comprising a *governing* cabinet. Significant changes were being made at that time in the British cabinet system. The younger Pitt, then serving as Prime Minister, was going directly to the people for support. This move towards a democratic cabinet system seems to have failed to impress John Adams, who served as the American Minister in London from 1785–1788. Among the Framers only Alexander Hamilton expressed particular interest in an English model.

Selection and Tenure, Separation and Strength

Although the Framers had early arrived at the decision for having an executive and a single one at that, the third major question, on the manner of selection and the tenure of the executive, resisted solution for more than three months. The Virginia, or "large state," plan had called for the election of the executive by the legislature. Most of the delegates adhered to this conception through the hot summer of 1787.

The pre-revolutionary experience had promoted the old Whig doctrine that the executive should be subservient to the legislature. As Charles Corwin wrote, "The colonial period ended with the belief prevalent that the 'executive magistracy' was the natural enemy, the legislative assembly the natural friend of liberty."[7] This view had been reflected both in the state constitutions and in the Articles of Confederation. Roger Sherman expressed the prevailing view in the Constitutional Convention in June 1787 when he termed "the Executive magistracy as nothing more than an institution for carrying the will of the Legislature into effect. . . ."[8]

But there was also a philosophical heritage for a strong and separate executive. This had its roots in the writings of Locke and Montesquieu. Locke, in his *Second Treatise on Government* (1689) had stated, ". . . the good of the society requires that several things should be left to the discretion of him that has the executive power. . . . For the legislators not being able to foresee and provide by laws for all that may be useful to the community, the executor of the laws, having the power in his hands, has by the common law of Nature a right to make use of it for the good of society."[9]

Further, there were many in the Constitutional Convention familiar with Montesquieu's *L'Esprit des lois* (1748), particularly the celebrated separation of powers doctrine which held that the legislative, executive, and judicial parts of government must be kept separate and defended from the intrusion of the other parts. This doctrine was to become basic to the Constitution. James Wilson, who chaired the Committee on Detail, continued to lead the move towards a strong, separate executive. Gouverneur Morris continued to support Wilson's views. Among others they persuaded James Madison to accept the separation of powers doctrine. Both Wilson and Morris, as residents from Pennsylvania, lived in the only state with a unicameral legislature; both distrusted legislative supremacy.

Relatively few of the delegates favored popular election of the President; among them: Wilson, Morris, Madison, Franklin, and Hamilton. The last must come as a surprise to many since Hamilton is portrayed as distrusting the people. They ignore his June 18th address proposing election "by the people, or by a process originating with the people."

Hamilton's critics also overlook his subsequent emphasis in Federalist 77 that the President must have a "due dependence in the people, a due responsibility."

In the light of recent interest in a single six year term, it should be noted that the Framers offered this as a protective device, i.e., a single six or seven year term, when election of the executive by the legislature was being considered. They dropped the single term when considering popular election or election by an electoral college. Wilson, who favored popular election and the opportunity for re-election, noted: "It seems to be the unanimous sense that the Executive should not be appointed by the Legislature, unless he is rendered ineligible a 2d time."[10] Obviously Wilson was being rhetorical, since there was no unanimity on that or any other issue. As Charles Warren pointed out more than a half century ago, "In almost all the votes a long term with no re-election was favored, if the choice of Executive was to be by the Legislature; and a short term with possibility of re-election, if the choice was to be otherwise than by the Legislature. In other words, the views of most of the delegates as to length of term and as to re-election were dependent on the *mode* of election."[11]

Despite the best efforts of Wilson, Morris, and Madison, the proposal for the legislature electing the executive came near to passage. However, Morris proved to be a superb parliamentarian, who avoided defeat while searching for an alternative method of selection. As recently described by Professor William H. Riker, he was "an active and dominating floor leader, whose colleagues respected his abilities, who creatively suggested deals, and who knew how to abandon hopeless positions."[12] Morris believed strongly that "in the strength of the Executive will be found the Strength of America."[13] As a provision for a strong executive, Morris advocated and secured in the Constitution a qualified executive veto, the President's serving in the office of commander in chief, and the President's appointive authority. But he was also instrumental in securing the provision for impeachment for misconduct. Morris became a subject of especial interest to Theodore Roosevelt, who, at age twenty-eight, wrote a biography on his subject. Roosevelt particularly admired Morris's tenacity in combating the view that the legislature should select the executive. The young Roosevelt saw in Morris much of his own future conception of the Presidency. "He [Morris] inclined to regard the President in the light of a tribune chosen by the people to watch over the legislature," Roosevelt wrote, "and giving him the appointing power, he believed, would force him to make good use of it, owing to his sense of responsibility to the people at large, who would be directly affected by its exercise, and who could and would hold him accountable to its abuse."[14]

The Committee of Eleven

Having rather continuously for three months, from June 1 to August 31, debated the nature, the authority, and the means of selection of the executive, the Convention resorted to a committee. (Committees were presumably chosen by delegates voting individually rather than as states.) The so-called Committee of Eleven, chaired by David Brearly, was named on August 31 to resolve "unfinished business." This included the means of selecting the President and the distribution of authority between the Senate and the President. Brearly, the former Chief Justice of the New Jersey Supreme Court, had a proven track record of challenging legislative authority.

Serving with him on the Committee of Eleven were Morris, Madison, Roger Sherman, Pierce Butler, Rufus King, John Dickinson, Nicholas Gilman, Daniel Carroll, and Abraham Baldwin. As such they were all creators of the Presidency.

The Committee of Eleven had to bring in a compromise position between those favoring election by the legislature and those favoring popular election. Their compromise, an electoral college, presumably would satisfy both those for popular and those for legislative selection. The electors were to be chosen in a manner prescribed by state legislatures, which permitted popular elections. But, and this is the point that fooled the Framers, it was believed that "in nineteen cases out of twenty," the matter would have to be referred to the Senate to decide! According to the Committee's proposal, each state would have the same number of electors as it had Senators and Representatives. The person with the highest number of electoral votes would be the President, providing that person received a majority of the electoral votes. And the person with the second highest number would be the Vice President. The Committee, and indeed the Framers, were convinced that there would be so many candidates that in most instances no one would get a majority of the electoral votes. The Committee had proposed that the Senate would then select the President. Only on this point was there opposition to the Committee's report. Morris, the principal spokesman for the Committee, made the compromise, placing this responsibility in the hands of the House of Representatives, rather than the Senate, with the provision that each state have only one vote. In point of fact only on three occasions (1800, 1824, and 1876) did a presidential candidate fail to win a majority of the electoral vote. The tie between Jefferson and Burr in 1800 resulted in the 12th Amendment, requiring separate voting for Presidents and Vice Presidents. The House made the selection in 1800 and 1824. (In the case of 1876, a Commission decided which candidate had the majority of electoral votes.)

With the establishment of the Electoral College, the Convention voted for Presidential terms limited to four years. Morris believed strongly in eligibility for re-election. And no limitation of terms was imposed.

The Committee of Eleven also resolved the issues as to whether the Senate or the President should make treaties and senior appointments. Reporting on September 4, they gave the President the authority "with the Advice and Consent of the Senate" to make treaties and to appoint Supreme Court Justices, ambassadors, and all other officers of the United States whose appointments were not otherwise provided for. On September 7, these matters were accepted by the Convention.

The Committee on Style which placed the Constitution in its final form consisted of Hamilton, William Samuel Johnson, King, Madison, and Morris. The last is generally credited with the most work of the committee which was accomplished between September 8th and 12th. Hence the Constitution was ready for signatures.

Reflections

And so it was that the issues of the executive were finally resolved in a final weekend of skillful negotiation. More time had been consumed on the means of selection of the President than any other matter that came before the Convention. As Riker observed, "It is astonishing that a compromise put together over a weekend to satisfy diverse, parochial, and temporary interests has, with

only slight modification by the Twelfth Amendment, served adequately for two centuries."[15]

Ironically that on which the Framers had labored longest had resulted in the one portion of the Constitution deemed by many as most archaic, the Electoral College. Despite the fact that three Presidents who won a majority of the popular vote were defeated by their rivals in the electoral vote, the system has not served the Nation badly. As Calvin C. Jillson concluded, the system has earned "in the practically minded American political community the conservative presumption against tinkering with a reasonably successful mechanism."[16]

The Constitution was a remarkable achievement by a remarkable group. As John Conway expressed it, "Probably never before or since has there been assembled in North America for political discussion a group of men so intellectually distinguished."[17] Their most remarkable, their most unique creation was the American Presidency. Professor Donald L. Robinson identifies 21 of the 55 Framers as the "inventors of the Presidency." Four of these did not sign the Constitution. Among the signers, there were six who conceived of the Presidency with the essential ingredients it has taken: (1) single executive; (2) no constitutional cabinet or council; (3) popularly elected; (4) broad powers. Those six were Washington, Hamilton, King, Madison, Morris and Wilson.[18] And of those it was principally Wilson and Morris aided by Madison who had created the Presidency. Wilson had been the principal initiator and Morris the principal parliamentarian.

Again, it was Washington and Hamilton, aided by Madison, who in the years 1789–1797 established the foundations, the guiding principals of the Presidency in operation. In the interim, Hamilton, aided by Madison and to a lesser extent by Jay, took up his pen to write the Nation's most distinguished political treatise, *The Federalist,* as an instrument to convince Americans in general and New Yorkers in particular that the Constitution should be ratified. As Madison wrote of Hamilton nearly a half-century later (1831), "If his theory of government deviated from the republican standard, he had the candor to avow it, and the greater merit of co-operating faithfully in maturing and supporting a system which was not his choice."[19]

NOTES

1. Broadus Mitchell, *Alexander Hamilton, Youth to Maturity 1775–1788* (New York: Macmillan, 1957), p. 366.

2. Clinton Rossiter, *Alexander Hamilton and the Constitution* (New York: Harcourt, Brace and World, 1963), pp. 37, 272–74. According to Rossiter, "Hamilton's letter (to James Duane in 1780) was the first clear-cut, responsible appeal for the kind of convention that met at last in 1787."

3. Donald L. Robinson, "The Inventors of the Presidency," *Presidential Studies Quarterly,* XIII, 1, Winter 1983, p. 15.

4. Ibid., p. 8.

5. William H. Riker, "The Heresthetics of Constitution-Making: The Presidency in 1787, with Comments on Determinism and Rational Choice," *The American Political Science Review,* 78, 1, March 1984, p. 2.

6. Calvin C. Jillson, "The Executive in Republican Government: The Case of the American Founding," *Presidential Studies Quarterly,* IX, 4, Fall 1979, pp. 387–388.

7. Edward S. Corwin, *The President: Office and Powers, 1787–1957* (New York: New York University Press, 1957), pp. 5–6.

8. Jillson, op. cit., p. 388.

9. Herman Pritchett, "The President's Constitutional Position," in Rexford G. Tugwell and Thomas E. Cronin (eds.), *The Presidency Reappraised* (New York: Praeger Publishers, 1974), p. 13.

10. Riker, op. cit., p. 9.

11. Charles Warren, *The Making of the Constitution* (Cambridge, Mass.: Harvard University Press, 1928; reprint ed., New York: Barnes and Nobel Inc., 1967), pp. 97–98.

12. Riker, op. cit., p. 14.

13. Robinson, op. cit., p. 15.

14. Theodore Roosevelt, *Gouverneur Morris* (Oyster Bay, N.Y.: Theodore Roosevelt Association, 1975), p. 99.

15. Riker, op. cit., p. 14.

16. Jillson, op. cit., p. 401.

17. John Conway, "Politics, Culture, and the Writing of Constitutions," in Harvey L. Dyck and H. Peter Krosby (eds.), *Empire and Nations* (Toronto: University of Toronto Press, 1969), p. 8.

18. Robinson, op. cit., pp. 8–25.

19. Mitchell, op. cit., p. 412. Although the aged Madison had come to a more generous view of Hamilton, he never came to believe that Hamilton was trustful of a democratic system. Both Jefferson and John Adams had doubtless prejudiced Madison's views.

    The philosophical criticisms which scholars and the public in general have of Hamilton are largely based on his June 18th address before the Constitutional Convention. Regrettably he never wrote out this most important address which has four versions from the notes of other delegates (Madison, Robert Yates, John Lansing, Jr., and Rufus King). Hamilton's *own* notes indicate: "The democracy must be immediately derived from the people." See Harold C. Syrett (ed.), *The Papers of Alexander Hamilton,* IV (New York: Columbia University Press, 1962), pp. 178–211.

2
James Madison to Thomas Jefferson
New York, October 24, 1787

You will herewith receive the result of the Convention, which continued its session till the 17th of September. I take the liberty of making some observations on the subject, which will help to make up a letter, if they should answer no other purpose.

This ground-work being laid, the great objects which presented themselves were (1) to unite a proper energy in the Executive, and a proper stability in the Legislative departments, with the essential characters of Republican Government (2) to draw a line of demarkation which would give to the Central Government every power requisite for general purposes, and leave to the States every power which might be most beneficially administered by them (3) to provide for the different interests of different parts of the Union (4) to adjust the clashing pretensions of the large and small States. Each of these objects was pregnant with difficulties. The whole of them together formed a task more difficult than can be well conceived by those who were not concerned in the execution of it. Adding to these considerations the natural diversity of human opinions on all new and complicated subjects, it is impossible to consider the degree of concord which ultimately prevailed as less than a miracle.

The first of these objects, as respects the Executive, was peculiarly embarrassing. On the question whether it should consist of a single person, or a plurality of co-ordinate members, on the mode of appointment, on the duration in office, on the degree of power, on the re-eligibility, tedious and reiterated discussions took place. The plurality of co-ordinate members had finally but few advocates. Governour Randolph was at the head of them. The modes of appointment proposed were various, as by the people at large—by electors chosen by the people—by the Executives of the States—by the Congress, some preferring a joint ballot of the two Houses—some a separate concurrent ballot, allowing to each a negative on the other house—some, a nomination of several candidates by one House, out of whom a choice should be made by the other. Several other modifications were stated. The expedient at length adopted seemed to give pretty general satisfaction to the members. As to the duration in office, a few would have preferred a tenure during good behaviour—a considerable number would have done so in case an easy & effectual removal by impeachment could be settled. It was much agitated whether a long term, seven years for example, with a subsequent & perpetual ineligibility, or a short term with a capacity to be re-elected, should be fixed. In favor of the first opinion were urged the danger of a gradual degeneracy of re-elections from time to time, into first a life and then a hereditary tenure, and the favorable effect of an incapacity

Source: Excerpted from *The Records of the Federal Convention of 1787,* by Max Ferrand, vol. 3, pp. 131–33, New Haven, Conn.: Yale University Press. Copyright © 1966 by Yale University; © 1911, 1937 by Yale University Press. Reprinted by permission.

to be reappointed on the independent exercise of the Executive authority. On the other side it was contended that the prospect of necessary degradation would discourage the most dignified characters from aspiring to the office, would take away the principal motive to ye faithful discharge of its duties— the hope of being rewarded with a reappointment would stimulate ambition to violent efforts for holding over the Constitutional term—and instead of producing an independent administration, and a firmer defence of the constitutional rights of the department, would render the officer more indifferent to the importance of a place which he would soon be obliged to quit forever, and more ready to yield to the encroachmts. of the Legislature of which he might again be a member. The questions concerning the degree of power turned chiefly on the appointment to offices, and the controul on the Legislature. An *absolute* appointment to all offices—to some offices—to no offices, formed the scale of opinions on the first point. On the second, some contended for an absolute negative, as the only possible means of reducing to practice the theory of a free Government which forbids a mixture of the Legislative & Executive powers. Others would be content with a revisionary power, to be overruled by three fourths of both Houses. It was warmly urged that the judiciary department should be associated in the revision. The idea of some was that a separate revision should be given to the two departments—that if either objected two thirds, if both, three fourths, should be necessary to overrule.

3

To the Citizens of the State of New York

George Clinton
November 8, 1787

Admitting, however, that the vast extent of America, together with the various other reasons which I offered you in my last number, against the practicability of the just exercise of the new government are insufficient to convince; still it is an undesirable truth, that its several parts are either possessed of principles, which you have heretofore considered as ruinous and that others are omitted which you have established as fundamental to your political security, and must in their operation, I will venture to assert, fetter your tongues and minds, enchain your bodies, and ultimately extinguish all that is great and noble in man.

In pursuance of my plan I shall begin with observations on the executive branch of this new system; and though it is not the first in order, as arranged therein, yet being the *chief*, is perhaps entitled by the rules of rank to the first consideration. The executive power as described in the 2d article, consists of a president and vice-president, who are to hold their offices during the term of four years; the same article has marked

Source: "The Letters of Cato," *New York Journal* (November 8 and 22, 1787).

the manner and time of their election, and established the qualifications of the president; it also provides against the removal, death, or inability of the president and vice-president—regulates the salary of the president, delineates his duties and powers; and, lastly, declares the causes for which the president and vice-president shall be removed from office.

Notwithstanding the great learning and abilities of the gentlemen who composed the convention, it may be here remarked with deference, that the construction of the first paragraph of the first section of the second article is vague and inexplicit, and leaves the mind in doubt as to the election of a president and vice-president, after the expiration of the election for the first term of four years: in every other case, the election of these great officers is expressly provided for; but there is no explicit provision for their election in case of expiration of their offices, subsequent to the election which is to set this political machine in motion; no certain and express terms as in your state constitution, that *statedly* once in every four years, and as often as these offices shall become vacant, by expiration or otherwise, as is therein expressed, an election shall be held as follows, &c., this inexplicitness perhaps may lead to an establishment for life.

It is remarked by Montesquieu, in treating of republics, that *in all magistracies, the greatness of the power must be compensated by the brevity of the duration, and that a longer time than a year would be dangerous.* It is, therefore, obvious to the least intelligent mind to account why great power in the hands of a magistrate, and that power connected with considerable duration, may be dangerous to the liberties of a republic, the deposit of vast trusts in the hands of a single magistrate, enables him in their exercise

to create a numerous train of dependents: this tempts his *ambition,* which in a republican magistrate is also remarked, *to be pernicious,* and the duration of his office for any considerable time favors his views, gives him the means and time to perfect and execute his designs, *he therefore fancies that he may be great and glorious by oppressing his fellow-citizens, and raising himself to permanent grandeur on the ruins of his country.* And here it may be necessary to compare the vast and important powers of the president, together with his continuance in office, with the foregoing doctrine—his eminent magisterial situation will attach many adherents to him, and he will be surrounded by expectants and courtiers, his power of nomination and influence on all appointments, the strong posts in each state comprised within his superintendence, and garrisoned by troops under his direction, his control over the army, militia, and navy, the unrestrained power of granting pardons for treason, which may be used to screen from punishment those whom he had secretly instigated to commit the crime, and thereby prevent a discovery of his own guilt, his duration in office for four years: these, and various other principles evidently prove the truth of the position, that if the president is possessed of ambition, he has power and time sufficient to ruin his country.

Though the president, during the sitting of the legislature, is assisted by the senate, yet he is without a constitutional council in their recess; he will therefore be unsupported by proper information and advice, and will generally be directed by minions and favorites, or a council of state will grow out of the principal officers of the great departments, the most dangerous council in a free country.

The ten miles square, which is to become the seat of government, will of course be the place of residence for the president and the great officers of state; the same observations of a great man will apply to the court of a president possessing the powers of a monarch, that is observed of that of a monarch—*ambition with idleness—baseness with pride—the thirst of riches without labor—aversion to truth—flattery—treason—perfidy—violation of engagements—contempt of civil duties—hope from the magistrate's weakness; but above all, the perpetual ridicule of virtue*—these, he remarks, are the characteristics by which the courts in all ages have been distinguished.

The language and the manners of this court will be what distinguishes them from the rest of the community, not what assimilates them to it; and in being remarked for a behavior that shows they are not *meanly born*, and in adulation to people of fortune and power.

The establishment of a vice-president is as unnecessary as it is dangerous. This officer, for want of other employment, is made president of the senate, thereby blending the executive and legislative powers, besides always giving to some one state, from which he is to come, an unjust pre-eminence.

It is a maxim in republics that the representative of the people should be of their immediate choice; but by the manner in which the president is chosen, he arrives to this office at the fourth or fifth hand, nor does the highest vote, in the way he is elected, determine the choice, for it is only necessary that he should be taken from the highest of five, who may have a plurality of votes.

Compare your past opinions and sentiments with the present proposed establishment, and you will find, that if you adopt it, that it will lead you into a system which you heretofore reprobated as odious. Every American Whig, not long since, bore his emphatic testimony against a monarchical government, though limited, because of the dangerous inequality that it created among citizens as relative to their rights and property; and wherein does this president, invested with his powers and prerogatives, essentially differ from the king of Great Britain (save as to name, the creation of nobility, and some immaterial incidents, the offspring of absurdity and locality). The direct prerogatives of the president, as springing from his political character, are among the following: It is necessary, in order to distinguish him from the rest of the community, and enable him to keep, and maintain his court, that the compensation for his services, or in other words, his revenue, should be such as to enable him to appear with the splendor of a prince; he has the power of receiving ambassadors from, and a great influence on their appointments to foreign courts; as also to make treaties, leagues, and alliances with foreign states, assisted by the Senate, which when made become the supreme law of land: he is a constituent part of the legislative power, for every bill which shall pass the House of Representatives and Senate is to be presented to him for approbation; if he approves of it he is to sign it, if he disapproves he is to return it with objections, which in many cases will amount to a complete negative; and in this view he will have a great share in the power of making peace, coining money, etc., and all the various objects of legislation, expressed or implied in this Constitution: for though it may be asserted that the king of Great Britain has the express power of making peace or war, yet he never thinks it prudent to do so without the advice of his Parliament, from whom he is to derive his support, and therefore these powers, in both president and king, are substantially the same: he is the generalissimo of the nation, and of course has the command and control of the army, navy and militia; he is the general conservator of the peace of the union—he may pardon all offences, except in cases of impeachment, and the principal fountain of all offices and employments. Will not the exercise of these powers therefore tend either to the establishment of a vile and arbitrary aristocracy or monarchy? The safety of the people in a republic depends on the share or proportion they have in the government; but experience ought to teach you, that when a man is at the head of an elective government invested with great powers, and interested in his reelection, in what circle appointments will be made; by which means an *imperfect aristocracy* bordering on monarchy may be established.

You must, however, my countrymen, beware that the advocates of this new system do not deceive you by a fallacious resemblance between it and your own state government which you so much prize; and, if you examine, you will perceive that the chief magistrate of this state is your immediate choice, controlled and checked by a just and full representation of the people, divested of the prerogative of influencing war and peace, making treaties, receiving and sending embassies, and commanding standing armies and navies, which belong to the power of the confederation, and will be convinced that this government is no more like a true picture of your own than an Angel of Darkness resembles an Angel of Light.

November 22, 1787

In my last number I endeavored to prove that the language of the article relative to the establishment of the executive of this new government was vague and inexplicit; that the great powers of the president, connected with his duration in office, would lead to oppression and ruin; that he would be governed by favorites and flatterers, or that a dangerous council would be collected from the great officers of state; that the ten miles square, if the remarks of one of the wisest men, drawn from the experience of mankind, may be credited, would be the asylum of the base, idle, avaricious and ambitious, and that the court would possess a language and manners different from yours; that a vice-president is as unnecessary as he is dangerous in his influence; that the president cannot represent you because he is not of your own immediate choice; that if you adopt this government you will incline to an arbitrary and odious aristocracy or monarchy; that the president, possessed of the power given him by this frame of government, differs but very immaterially from the establishment of monarchy in Great Britain; and I warned you to beware of the fallacious resemblance that is held out to you by the advocates of this new system between it and your own state governments.

And here I cannot help remarking that inexplicitness seems to pervade this whole political fabric; certainly in political compacts, which Mr. Coke calls *the mother and nurse of repose and quietness* the want of which induced men to engage in political society, has ever been held by a wise and free people as essential to their security; as on the one hand it fixes barriers which the ambitious and tyrannically disposed magistrate dare not overleap, and on the other, becomes a wall of safety to the community—otherwise stipulations between the governors and governed are nugatory; and you might as well deposit the important powers of legislation and execution in one or a few and permit them to govern according to their disposition and will; but the world is too full of examples, which prove that *to live by one man's will became the cause of all men's misery.* Before the existence of express political compacts it was reasonably implied that the magistrate should govern with wisdom and justice; but mere implication was too feeble to restrain the unbridled ambition of a bad man, or afford security against negligence, cruelty or any other defect of mind. It is alleged that the opinions and manners of the people of America are capable to resist and prevent an extension of prerogative or oppression, but you must recollect that opinion and manners are mutable, and may not always be a permanent obstruction against the encroachments of government; that the progress of a commercial society begets luxury, the parent of inequality, the foe to virtue, and the enemy to restraint; and that ambition and voluptuousness, aided by flattery, will teach magistrates where limits are not explicitly fixed to have separate and distinct interests from the people; besides, it will not be denied that government assimilates the manners and opinions of the community to it. Therefore,

a general presumption that rulers will govern well is not a sufficient security. You are then under a sacred obligation to provide for the safety of your posterity, and would you now basely desert their interests, when by a small share of prudence you may transmit to them a beautiful political patrimony, which will prevent the necessity of their travelling through seas of blood to obtain that which your wisdom might have secured? It is a duty you owe likewise to your own reputation, for you have a great name to lose; you are characterized as cautious, prudent and jealous in politics; whence is it therefore that you are about to precipitate yourselves into a sea of uncertainty, and adopt a system so vague, and which has discarded so many of your valuable rights? Is it because you do not believe that an American can be a tyrant? If this be the case, you rest on a weak basis: Americans are like other men in similar situations, when the manners and opinions of the community are changed by the causes I mentioned before; and your political compact inexplicit, your posterity will find that great power connected with ambition, luxury and flattery, will as readily produce a Caesar, Caligula, Nero and Domitian in America, as the same causes did in the Roman Empire.

4
The Federalist, No. 69
Alexander Hamilton

Proceed now to trace the real characters of the proposed Executive, as they are marked out in the plan of the convention. This will serve to place in a strong

light the unfairness of the representations which have been made in regard to it.

The first thing which strikes our

Source: This essay by "Publius" was originally published in the *New York Packet,* March 14, 1788.

attention is that the executive authority, with few exceptions, is to be vested in a single magistrate. This will scarcely, however, be considered as a point upon which any comparison can be grounded; for if, in this particular, there be a resemblance to the king of Great Britain, there is not less a resemblance to the Grand Seignior, to the khan of Tartary, to the Man of the Seven Mountains or to the governor of New York.

That magistrate is to be elected for *four* years; and is to be re-eligible as often as the people of the United States shall think him worthy of their confidence. In these circumstances there is a total dissimilitude between *him* and a king of Great Britain, who is an *hereditary* monarch, possessing the crown as a patrimony descendible to his heirs forever; but there is a close analogy between *him* and a governor of New York, who is elected for *three* years, and is re-eligible without limitation or intermission. If we consider how much less time would be requisite for establishing a dangerous influence in a single State than for establishing a like influence throughout the United States, we must conclude that a duration of *four* years for the Chief Magistrate of the Union is a degree of permanency far less to be dreaded in that office than a duration of *three* years for a corresponding office in a single State.

The President of the United States would be liable to be impeached, tried, and, upon conviction of treason, bribery, or other high crimes or misdemeanours, removed from office; and would afterwards be liable to prosecution and punishment in the ordinary course of law. The person of the king of Great Britain is sacred and inviolable; there is no constitutional tribunal to which he is amenable; no punishment to which he can be subjected without involving the crisis of a national revolution. In

this delicate and important circumstance of personal responsibility, the President of Confederated America would stand upon no better ground than a governor of New York, and upon worse ground than the governors of Maryland and Delaware.

The President of the United States is to have power to return a bill which shall have passed the two branches of the legislature for reconsideration; and the bill so returned is to become a law if, upon that reconsideration, it be approved by two thirds of both houses. The king of Great Britain, on his part, has an absolute negative upon the acts of the two houses of Parliament. The disuse of that power for a considerable time past does not affect the reality of its existence; and is to be ascribed wholly to the crown's having found the means of substituting influence to authority, or the art of gaining a majority in one or the other of the two houses, to the necessity of exerting a prerogative which could seldom be exerted without hazarding some degree of national agitation. The qualified negative of the President differs widely from this absolute negative of the British sovereign; and tallies exactly with the revisionary authority of the council of revision of this State, of which the governor is a constituent part. In this respect the power of the President would exceed that of the governor of New York because the former would possess, singly, what the latter shares with the chancellor and judges; but it would be precisely the same with that of the governor of Massachusetts, whose constitution, as to this article, seems to have been the original from which the convention have copied.

The President is to be the "commander-in-chief of the army and navy of the United States, and of the militia of the several States, when called into the actual service of the United States. He is to have power to grant reprieves and pardons for offences against the United States, *except in cases of impeachment;* to recommend to the consideration of Congress such measures as he shall judge necessary and expedient; to convene, on extraordinary occasions, both houses of the legislature, or either of them, and, in case of disagreement between them *with respect to the time of adjournment,* to adjourn them to such time as he shall think proper; to take care that the laws be faithfully executed; and to commission all officers of the United States." In most of these particulars the power of the President will resemble equally that of the king of Great Britain and of the governor of New York. The most material points of difference are these:—*First.* The President will have only the occasional command of such part of the militia of the nation as by legislative provision may be called into the actual service of the Union. The king of Great Britain and the governor of New York have at all times the entire command of all the militia within their several jurisdictions. In this article, therefore, the power of the President would be inferior to that of either the monarch or the governor. *Secondly.* The President is to be commander-in-chief of the army and navy of the United States. In this respect his authority would be nominally the same with that of the king of Great Britain, but in substance much inferior to it. It would amount to nothing more than the supreme command and direction of the military and naval forces, as first general and admiral of the Confederacy; while that of the British king extends to the *declaring* of war and to the *raising* and *regulating* of fleets and armies—all which, by the Constitution under consideration, would appertain to the legislature.[1] The governor of New York, on the other hand, is by the constitution of the State vested only with the command of its militia and navy. But the constitutions of several of the States expressly declare their governors to be commanders-in-chief, as well of the army as navy; and it may well be a question whether those of New Hampshire and Massachusetts, in particular, do not, in this instance, confer larger powers upon their respective governors than could be claimed by a President of the United States. *Thirdly.* The power of the President, in respect to pardons, would extend to all cases, *except those of impeachment.* The governor of New York may pardon in all cases, even in those of impeachment, except for treason and murder. Is not the power of the governor, in this article, on a calculation of political consequences, greater than that of the President? All conspiracies and plots against the government which have not been matured into actual treason may be screened from punishment of every kind by the interposition of the prerogative of pardoning. If a governor of New York, therefore, should be at the head of any such

[1] A writer in a Pennsylvania paper, under the signature of TAMONY, has asserted that the king of Great Britain owes his prerogative as commander-in-chief to an annual mutiny bill. The truth is, on the contrary, that his prerogative, in this respect, is immemorial, and was only disputed, "contrary to all reason and precedent," as Blackstone, vol. i. page 262, expresses it, by the Long Parliament of Charles I.; but by the statute the 13th of Charles II. chap. vi., it was declared to be in the king alone, for that the sole supreme government and command of the militia within his Majesty's realms and dominions, and of all forces by sea and land, and of all forts and places of strength, EVER WAS AND IS the undoubted right of his Majesty and his royal predecessors, kings and queens of England, and that both or either house of Parliament cannot nor ought to pretend to the same.—Publius.

conspiracy, until the design had been ripened into an actual hostility he could insure his accomplices and adherents an entire impunity. A President of the Union, on the other hand, though he may even pardon treason when prosecuted in the ordinary course of law, could shelter no offender, in any degree, from the effects of impeachment and conviction. Would not the prospect of a total indemnity for all the preliminary steps be a greater temptation to undertake and persevere in an enterprise against the public liberty than the mere prospect of an exemption from death and confiscation if the final execution of the design, upon an actual appeal to arms, should miscarry? Would this last expectation have any influence at all when the probability was computed that the person who was to afford that exemption might himself be involved in the consequences of the measure, and might be incapacitated by his agency in it from affording the desired impunity? The better to judge of this matter, it will be necessary to recollect that, by the proposed Constitution, the offense of treason is limited "to levying war upon the United States, and adhering to their enemies, giving them aid and comfort"; and that by the laws of New York it is confined within similar bounds. *Fourthly.* The President can only adjourn the national legislature in the single case of disagreement about the time of adjournment. The British monarch may prorogue or even dissolve the Parliament. The governor of New York may also prorogue the legislature of this State for a limited time; a power which, in certain situations, may be employed to very important purposes.

The President is to have power, with the advice and consent of the Senate, to make treaties, provided two thirds of the senators present concur. The king of Great Britain is the sole and absolute representative of the nation in all foreign transactions. He can of his own accord make treaties of peace, commerce, alliance, and of every other description. It has been insinuated that his authority in this respect is not conclusive, and that his conventions with foreign powers are subject to the revision, and stand in need of the ratification, of Parliament. But I believe this doctrine was never heard of until it was broached upon the present occasion. Every jurist[2] of that kingdom, and every other man acquainted with its Constitution, knows, as an established fact, that the prerogative of making treaties exists in the crown in its utmost plenitude; and that the compacts entered into by the royal authority have the most complete legal validity and perfection, independent of any other sanction. The Parliament, it is true, is sometimes seen employing itself in altering the existing laws to conform them to the stipulations in a new treaty; and this may have possibly given birth to the imagination that its co-operation was necessary to the obligatory efficacy of the treaty. But this parliamentary interposition proceeds from a different cause: from the necessity of adjusting a most artificial and intricate system of revenue and commercial laws to the changes made in them by the operation of the treaty; and of adapting new provisions and precautions to the new state of things to keep the machine from running into disorder. In this respect, therefore, there is no comparison between the intended power of the President and the actual power of the British sovereign. The one can perform alone what the other can do only with the concurrence of a branch of the legislature. It must be admitted that, in this instance, the power of the federal

[2] *Vide* Blackstone's *Commentaries,* vol. i. p. 257.— Publius.

Executive would exceed that of any State Executive. But this arises naturally from the sovereign power which relates to treaties. If the Confederacy were to be dissolved it would become a question whether the Executives of the several States were not solely invested with that delicate and important prerogative.

The President is also to be authorised to receive ambassadors and other public ministers. This, though it has been a rich theme of declamation, is more a matter of dignity than of authority. It is a circumstance which will be without consequence in the administration of the government; and it was far more convenient that it should be arranged in this manner than that there should be a necessity of convening the legislature, or one of its branches, upon every arrival of a foreign minister, though it were merely to take the place of a departed predecessor.

The President is to nominate and, *with the advice and consent of the Senate,* to appoint ambassadors and other public ministers, judges of the Supreme Court, and in general all officers of the United States established by law, and whose appointments are not otherwise provided for by the Constitution. The king of Great Britain is emphatically and truly styled the fountain of honour. He not only appoints to all offices, but can create offices. He can confer titles of nobility at pleasure; and has the disposal of an immense number of church preferments. There is evidently a great inferiority in the power of the President, in this particular, to that of the British king; nor is it equal to that of the governor of New York, if we are to interpret the meaning of the constitution of the State by the practice which has obtained under it. The power of appointment is with us lodged in a council composed of the governor and four members of

the Senate chosen by the Assembly. The governor *claims,* and has frequently *exercised,* the right of nomination, and is *entitled* to a casting vote in the appointment. If he really has the right of nominating, his authority is in this respect equal to that of the President and exceeds it in the article of the casting vote. In the national government, if the Senate should be divided, no appointment could be made; in the government of New York, if the council should be divided, the governor can turn the scale and confirm his own nomination.[3] If we compare the publicity which must necessarily attend the mode of appointment by the President and an entire branch of the national legislature with the privacy in the mode of appointment by the governor of New York, closeted in a secret apartment with at most four, and frequently with only two persons; and if we at the same time consider how much more easy it must be to influence the small number of which a council of appointment consists than the considerable number of which the national Senate would consist, we cannot hesitate to pronounce that the power of the chief magistrate of this State, in the disposition of offices, must, in practice, be greatly superior to that of the Chief Magistrate of the Union.

Hence it appears that, except as to the concurrent authority of the President in the article of treaties, it would be difficult to determine whether that magistrate would, in the aggregate,

[3] Candour, however, demands an acknowledgment that I do not think the claim of the governor to a right of nomination well founded. Yet it is always justifiable to reason from the practice of a government, till its propriety has been constitutionally questioned. And independent of this claim, when we take into view the other considerations, and pursue them through all their consequences, we shall be inclined to draw much the same conclusion.— Publius.

possess more or less power than the Governor of New York. And it appears yet more unequivocally that there is no pretence for the parallel which has been attempted between him and the king of Great Britain. But to render the contrast in this respect still more striking, it may be of use to throw the principal circumstances of dissimilitude into a closer group.

The President of the United States would be an officer elected by the people for *four* years; the king of Great Britain is a perpetual and *hereditary* prince. The one would be amenable to personal punishment and disgrace; the person of the other is sacred and inviolable. The one would have a *qualified* negative upon the acts of the legislative body; the other has an *absolute* negative. The one would have a right to command the military and naval forces of the nation; the other, in addition to this right, possesses that of *declaring* war, and of *raising* and *regulating* fleets and armies by his own authority. The one would have a concurrent power with a branch of the legislature in the formation of treaties; the other is the *sole possessor* of the power of making treaties. The one would have a like concurrent authority in appointing to offices; the other is the sole author of all appointments. The one can confer no privileges whatever; the other can make denizens of aliens, noblemen of commoners; can erect corporations with all the rights incident to corporate bodies. The one can prescribe no rules concerning the commerce or currency of the nation; the other is in several respects the arbiter of commerce, and in this capacity can establish markets and fairs, can regulate weights and measures, can lay embargoes for a limited time, can coin money, can authorise or prohibit the circulation of foreign coin. The one has no particle of spiritual jurisdiction; the other is the supreme head and governor of the national church! What answer shall we give to those who would persuade us that things so unlike resemble each other? The same that ought to be given to those who tell us that a government, the whole power of which would be in the hands of the elective and periodical servants of the people, is an aristocracy, a monarchy, and a despotism.

Publius

5
The Federalist, No. 70
Alexander Hamilton

There is an idea, which is not without its advocates, that a vigorous Executive is inconsistent with the genius of republican government. The enlightened well-wishers to this species of government must at least hope that the supposition is destitute of foundation, since they can never admit its truth without at the same time admitting the condemnation of their own principles. Energy in the Executive is a leading character in the definition of good government. It is

Source: This essay by "Publius" was originally published in the *New York Packet*, March 18, 1788.

essential to the protection of the community against foreign attacks; it is not less essential to the steady administration of the laws; to the protection of property against those irregular and high-handed combinations which sometimes interrupt the ordinary course of justice; to the security of liberty against the enterprises and assaults of ambition, of faction, and of anarchy. Every man the least conversant in Roman story knows how often that republic was obliged to take refuge in the absolute power of a single man, under the formidable title of Dictator, as well against the intrigues of ambitious individuals who aspired to the tyranny and the seditions of whole classes of the community whose conduct threatened the existence of all government, as against the invasions of external enemies who menaced the conquest and destruction of Rome.

There can be no need, however, to multiply arguments or examples on this head. A feeble Executive implies a feeble execution of the government. A feeble execution is but another phrase for a bad execution; and a government ill executed, whatever it may be in theory, must be, in practice, a bad government.

Taking it for granted, therefore, that all men of sense will agree in the necessity of an energetic Executive, it will only remain to inquire what are the ingredients which constitute this energy? How far can they be combined with those other ingredients which constitute safety in the republican sense? And how far does this combination characterise the plan which has been reported by the convention?

The ingredients which constitute energy in the Executive are, first, unity; secondly, duration; thirdly, an adequate provision for its support; fourthly, competent powers.

The ingredients which constitute safety in the republican sense are, first, a due dependence on the people; secondly, a due responsibility.

Those politicians and statesmen who have been the most celebrated for the soundness of their principles and for the justice of their views have declared in favour of a single Executive and a numerous legislature. They have, with great propriety, considered energy as the most necessary qualification of the former, and have regarded this as most applicable to power in a single hand; while they have, with equal propriety, considered the latter as best adapted to deliberation and wisdom, and best calculated to conciliate the confidence of the people and to secure their privileges and interests.

That unity is conducive to energy will not be disputed. Decision, activity, secrecy, and dispatch will generally characterise the proceedings of one man in a much more eminent degree than the proceedings of any greater number; and in proportion as the number is increased, these qualities will be diminished.

This unity may be destroyed in two ways: either by vesting the power in two or more magistrates of equal dignity and authority; or by vesting it ostensibly in one man, subject, in whole or in part, to the control and co-operation of others in the capacity of counsellors to him. Of the first, the two Consuls of Rome may serve as an example; of the last, we shall find examples in the constitutions of several of the States. New York and New Jersey, if I recollect right, are the only States which have intrusted the executive authority wholly to single men.[1] Both these methods of destroying the unity of the Executive have their

---

[1] New York has no council except for the single purpose of appointing to offices; New Jersey has a council whom the governor may consult. But I think, from the terms of the constitution, their resolutions do not bind him.—Publius.

partisans; but the votaries of an executive council are the most numerous. They are both liable, if not to equal, to similar objections, and may in most lights be examined in conjunction.

The experience of other nations will afford little instruction on this head. As far, however, as it teaches anything, it teaches us not to be enamoured of plurality in the Executive. We have seen that the Achaeans, on an experiment of two Praetors, were induced to abolish one. The Roman history records many instances of mischiefs to the republic from the dissensions between the Consuls, and between the military Tribunes, who were at times substituted for the Consuls. But it gives us no specimens of any peculiar advantages derived to the state from the circumstance of the plurality of those magistrates. That the dissensions between them were not more frequent or more fatal is matter of astonishment, until we advert to the singular position in which the republic was almost continually placed, and to the prudent policy pointed out by the circumstances of the state, and pursued by the Consuls, of making a division of the government between them. The patricians engaged in a perpetual struggle with the plebeians for the preservation of their ancient authorities and dignities; the Consuls, who were generally chosen out of the former body, were commonly united by the personal interest they had in the defence of the privileges of their order. In addition to this motive of union, after the arms of the republic had considerably expanded the bounds of its empire, it became an established custom with the Consuls to divide the administration between themselves by lot—one of them remaining at Rome to govern the city and its environs, the other taking the command in the more distant provinces. This expedient must, no doubt, have had great influence in preventing those collisions and rivalships which might otherwise have embroiled the peace of the republic.

But quitting the dim light of historical research, attaching ourselves purely to the dictates of reason and good sense, we shall discover much greater cause to reject than to approve the idea of plurality in the Executive, under any modification whatever.

Wherever two or more persons are engaged in any common enterprise or pursuit there is always danger of difference of opinion. If it be a public trust or office, in which they are clothed with equal dignity and authority, there is peculiar danger of personal emulation and even animosity. From either, and especially from all these causes, the most bitter dissensions are apt to spring. Whenever these happen, they lessen the respectability, weaken the authority, and distract the plans and operations of those whom they divide. If they should unfortunately assail the supreme executive magistracy of a country, consisting of a plurality of persons, they might impede or frustrate the most important measures of the government in the most critical emergencies of the state. And what is still worse, they might split the community into the most violent and irreconcilable factions, adhering differently to the different individuals who composed the magistracy.

Men often oppose a thing, merely because they have had no agency in planning it, or because it may have been planned by those whom they dislike. But if they have been consulted, and have happened to disapprove, opposition then becomes, in their estimation, an indispensable duty of self-love. They seem to think themselves bound in honour, and by all the motives of personal infallibility, to defeat the success of what has been resolved upon contrary to their sentiments. Men of upright, benevolent tempers have too many opportunities of remarking, with horror, to what desperate lengths this disposition is sometimes carried, and how often the great interests of society are sacrificed to the vanity, to the conceit, and to the obstinacy of individuals who have credit enough to make their passions and their caprices interesting to mankind. Perhaps the question now before the public may, in its consequences, afford melancholy proofs of the effects of this despicable frailty, or rather detestable vice, in the human character.

Upon the principles of a free government inconveniences from the source just mentioned must necessarily be submitted to in the formation of the legislature; but it is unnecessary, and therefore unwise, to introduce them into the constitution of the Executive. It is here, too, that they may be most pernicious. In the legislature, promptitude of decision is oftener an evil than a benefit. The differences of opinion, and the jarrings of parties in that department of the government, though they may sometimes obstruct salutary plans, yet often promote deliberation and circumspection, and serve to check excesses in the majority. When a resolution, too, is once taken, the opposition must be at an end. That resolution is a law, and resistance to it punishable. But no favourable circumstances palliate or atone for the disadvantages of dissension in the executive department. Here they are pure and unmixed. There is no point at which they cease to operate. They serve to embarrass and weaken the execution of the plan or measure to which they relate, from the first step to the final conclusion of it. They constantly counteract those qualities in the Executive which are the most necessary ingredients in its composition—vigour and expedition, and this without any counterbalancing good. In the conduct of

war, in which the energy of the Executive is the bulwark of the national security, everything would be to be apprehended from its plurality.

It must be confessed that these observations apply with principal weight to the first case supposed—that is, to a plurality of magistrates of equal dignity and authority, a scheme the advocates for which are not likely to form a numerous sect; but they apply, though not with equal, yet with considerable weight to the project of a council, whose concurrence is made constitutionally necessary to the operations of the ostensible Executive. An artful cabal in that council would be able to distract and to enervate the whole system of administration. If no such cabal should exist, the mere diversity of views and opinions would alone be sufficient to tincture the exercise of the executive authority with a spirit of habitual feebleness and dilatoriness.

But one of the weightiest objections to a plurality in the Executive, and which lies as much against the last as the first plan, is that it tends to conceal faults and destroy responsibility. Responsibility is of two kinds—to censure and to punishment. The first is the more important of the two, especially in an elective office. Man, in public trust, will much oftener act in such a manner as to render him unworthy of being any longer trusted than in such a manner as to make him obnoxious to legal punishment. But the multiplication of the Executive adds to the difficulty of detection in either case. It often becomes impossible, amidst mutual accusations, to determine on whom the blame or the punishment of a pernicious measure, or series of pernicious measures, ought really to fall. It is shifted from one to another with so much dexterity, and under such plausible appearances, that the public opinion is left in suspense about the real author. The circumstances which may have led to any national miscarriage or misfortune are sometimes so complicated that, where there are a number of actors who may have had different degrees and kinds of agency, though we may clearly see upon the whole that there has been mismanagement, yet it may be impracticable to pronounce to whose account the evil which may have been incurred is truly chargeable.

"I was overruled by my council. The council were so divided in their opinions that it was impossible to obtain any better resolution on the point." These and similar pretexts are constantly at hand, whether true or false. And who is there that will either take the trouble or incur the odium of a strict scrutiny into the secret springs of the transactions? Should there be found a citizen zealous enough to undertake the unpromising task, if there happen to be collusion between the parties concerned, how easy it is to clothe the circumstances with so much ambiguity as to render it uncertain what was the precise conduct of any of those parties?

In the single instance in which the governor of this State is coupled with a council—that is, in the appointment to offices, we have seen the mischiefs of it in the view now under consideration. Scandalous appointments to important offices have been made. Some cases, indeed, have been so flagrant that ALL PARTIES have agreed in the impropriety of the thing. When inquiry has been made, the blame has been laid by the governor on the members of the council, who, on their part, have charged it upon his nomination; while the people remain altogether at a loss to determine by whose influence their interests have been committed to hands so unqualified and so manifestly improper. In tenderness to individuals, I forbear to descend to particulars.

It is evident from these considerations that the plurality of the Executive tends to deprive the people of the two greatest securities they can have for the faithful exercise of any delegated power: *first,* the restraints of public opinion, which lose their efficacy, as well on account of the division of the censure attendant on bad measures among a number as on account of the uncertainty on whom it ought to fall; and, *secondly,* the opportunity of discovering with facility and clearness the misconduct of the persons they trust, in order either to [effect] their removal from office or their actual punishment in cases which admit of it.

In England, the king is a perpetual magistrate; and it is a maxim which has obtained for the sake of the public peace, that he is unaccountable for his administration, and his person sacred. Nothing, therefore, can be wiser in that kingdom, than to annex to the king a constitutional council, who may be responsible to the nation for the advice they give. Without this, there would be no responsibility whatever in the executive department—an idea inadmissible in a free government. But even there the king is not bound by the resolutions of his council, though they are answerable for the advice they give. He is the absolute master of his own conduct in the exercise of his office, and may observe or disregard the counsel given to him at his sole discretion.

But in a republic, where every magistrate ought to be personally responsible for his behaviour in office, the reason which in the British Constitution dictates the propriety of a council, not only ceases to apply, but turns against the institution. In the monarchy of Great Britain, it furnishes a substitute for the prohibited responsibility of the chief magistrate, which serves in some degree as a hostage to the national justice for his good behaviour. In the American republic it would serve to destroy, or would greatly diminish, the intended and necessary responsibility of the Chief Magistrate himself.

The idea of a council to the Executive, which has so generally obtained in the State constitutions, has been derived from that maxim of republican jealousy which considers power as safer in the hands of a number of men than of a single man. If the maxim should be admitted to be applicable to the case, I should contend that the advantage on that side would not counterbalance the numerous disadvantages on the opposite side. But I do not think the rule at all applicable to the executive power. I clearly concur in opinion, in this particular, with a writer whom the celebrated Junius pronounces to be "deep, solid, and ingenious," that "the executive power is more easily confined when it is ONE";[2] that it is far more safe there should be a single object for the jealousy and watchfulness of the people; and, in a word, that all multiplication of the Executive is rather dangerous than friendly to liberty.

A little consideration will satisfy us that the species of security sought for in the multiplication of the EXECUTIVE is unattainable. Numbers must be so great as to render combination difficult, or they are rather a source of danger than of security. The united credit and influence of several individuals must be more formidable to liberty than the credit and influence of either of them separately. When power, therefore, is placed in the hands of so small a number of men as to admit of their interests and views being easily combined in a common enterprise, by an artful leader it becomes more liable to abuse, and more dangerous when abused, than if it be lodged in the hands of one man;

who, from the very circumstance of his being alone, will be more narrowly watched and more readily suspected, and who cannot unite so great a mass of influence as when he is associated with others. The Decemvirs of Rome, whose name denotes their number,[3] were more to be dreaded, in their usurpation than any ONE of them would have been. No person would think of proposing an Executive much more numerous than that body; from six to a dozen have been suggested for the number of the council. The extreme of these numbers is not too great for an easy combination; and from such a combination America would have more to fear than from the ambition of any single individual. A council to a magistrate, who is himself responsible for what he does, are generally nothing better than a clog upon his good intentions, are often the instruments and accomplices of his bad, and are almost always a cloak to his faults.

I forbear to dwell upon the subject of expense; though it be evident that if the council should be numerous enough to answer the principal end aimed at by the institution, the salaries of the members, who must be drawn from their homes to reside at the seat of government, would form an item in the catalogue of public expenditures too serious to be incurred for an object of equivocal utility. I will only add that, prior to the appearance of the Constitution, I rarely met with an intelligent man from any of the States, who did not admit, as the result of experience, that the UNITY of the executive of this State was one of the best of the distinguishing features of our constitution.

Publius

---

[2] De Lolme.—Publius.

[3] Ten.—Publius.

CHAPTER II

Presidential Views of the Office

In the history of the American presidency, three presidential views of the office have competed for ascendancy at one time or another. Indeed, as we have seen in Chapter I, debate about the proper roles and powers is as old as the Constitutional Convention that created the presidency. The debate since the Convention in 1787 has focused on the statements of presidents themselves and their perspectives on how the duties of the office should be viewed and exercised. The first presidential view addressed here is the executive prerogative view of the presidency, the second is the stewardship view, and the third is the literalist view.

The executive prerogative view of the president's power has its origin in English theorist John Locke's *Second Treatise of Government* (1690). Locke wrote that:

> Where the legislative and executive power are in distinct hands—as they are in all moderated monarchies and well-framed governments—there the good of the society requires that several things should be left to the discretion of him that has the executive power; for the legislators not being able to foresee and provide by laws for all that may be useful to the community, the executor of the laws, having the power in his hands, has by the common law of nature a right to make use of it for the good of the society, in many cases where the municipal law has given no direction, till the legislative can conveniently be assembled to provide for it. Many things there are which the law can by no means provide for; and those must necessarily be left to the discretion of him that has the executive power in his hands, to be ordered by him as the public good and advantage shall require; nay, it is fit that the laws themselves should in some cases give way to the executive power, or rather to this fundamental law of nature and government; viz., that, as much as may be, all members of the society are to be preserved. . . .
>
> This power to act according to discretion, for the public good, without the prescription of the law and sometimes even against it, is that which is called "prerogative"; for since in some governments the lawmaking power is not always in being, and is usually too numerous and so too slow for the dispatch requisite to execution, and because also it is impossible to foresee, and so by laws to provide for, all accidents and necessities that may concern the public . . . therefore there is a latitude left to the executive power to do many things of choice which the laws do not prescribe.[1]

Abraham Lincoln, the sixteenth president of the United States, subscribed to the prerogative view of presidential powers. Upon taking office in March 1861, he responded to the secession of eleven states of the South from the Union (which actually began in December 1860 almost immediately after his election) and the firing upon Fort Sumter in South Carolina in April 1861 by the Confederate forces. Without bothering to call a special session of Congress to seek a declaration of war, Lincoln nonetheless recognized a state of war and ordered a blockade of southern ports.

Lincoln called for volunteers and enlarged the regular army beyond the legal limits. He directed the expenditure of millions of dollars out of the federal treasury for the support of the war in advance of congressional appropriations. He suspended the writ of habeas corpus and ordered the arrest and detention of citizens without trial in violation of the Constitution, and he refused to reinstate the writ of habeas corpus when ordered to do so by Chief Justice Roger Taney.[2] Later during the war, on January 1, 1863, Lincoln issued the Emancipation Proclamation, undercutting Congress, which had claimed the power as its own.

Lincoln thus exercised the prerogative power that John Locke had articulated a century earlier. Lincoln explained in his April 5, 1864, letter to Albert Hodges, editor of the Frankfort, Kentucky, newspaper *Commonwealth* that, "my oath to preserve the Constitution to the best of my ability imposed upon me the duty of preserving by every indispensable means, that government—that nation, of which that Constitution was the organic law. Was it possible to lose the nation and yet preserve the Constitution? By general law, life and limb must be protected, yet often a limb must be amputated to save a life; but a life is never wisely given to save a limb." Lincoln went on to argue "that measures otherwise unconstitutional might become lawful by becoming indispensable to the preservation of the Constitution through preservation of the nation. Right or wrong, I assumed this ground, and now avow it." Lincoln's complete letter is reprinted here under the title, "The Prerogative Theory of the Presidency."[3]

Two twentieth-century presidents were to contribute significantly to the conceptualization of the powers of the presidency. They were Theodore Roosevelt, the twenty-sixth president of the United States (serving from 1901 to 1909), and his successor William Howard Taft, the twenty-seventh president (serving from 1909 to 1913).

At the beginning of the twentieth century, the stewardship approach to presidential power, first expressed in the actions of Andrew Jackson, gained a boost during the tenure of Theodore Roosevelt who, to be sure, behaved in "stewardship" fashion while in office, but articulated this view in his autobiography only after he had left office. In foreign affairs, Roosevelt consulted Congress when he was legally obligated to do so, but in most cases used the executive power to its limits. Roosevelt took the Panama Canal, settled the Alaskan boundary dispute on his own terms, and sent the fleet around the world on a practice cruise without congressional permission. Much of his domestic legislative program was passed by Congress, although when he faced fierce opposition he appealed to the people for support and usually won.

Roosevelt believed strongly that "every executive officer, and above all every executive officer in high position, was a steward of the people bound actively and affirmatively to do all he could for the people. . . ." Roosevelt felt, in sum, that he was free to do as he pleased in that twilight zone lying between the prohibitions of the law and duties required by specific constitutional or statutory enactments. His essay, "The Stewardship Theory of the Presidency" is reprinted here.

William Howard Taft, later appointed Chief Justice of the Supreme Court by President Warren Harding (making him the only person ever to have held both offices), held a strictly literalist[4] view of the presidency.[5] Unlike his predecessor, Theodore Roosevelt, Taft did not subscribe to the stewardship approach to presidential power. Time and again, Taft argued that "there is no undefined residuum of power which he can exercise because it seems to be in the public interest." Taft's basic premise assumed that "the president can exercise no power which cannot be fairly and reasonably traced to some specific grant of power or justly implied and included within such express grant as proper and necessary to its exercise." Taft's essay, "The Literalist Theory of the Presidency," is reprinted here.

NOTES

1. John Locke, *The Second Treatise of Government*, ed. with an introduction by Thomas P. Peardon (New York: The Liberal Arts Press, 1952), pp. 91–92.

2. See *Ex parte Merryman*, 17 Fed. Ces. 144 (1861). Taney was the fifth Chief Justice of the Supreme Court of the United States.

3. For a definitive contemporary textbook interpretation of a president's prerogative powers see Richard M. Pious, *The American Presidency* (New York: Basic Books, 1979), p. 15. See also Thomas Engeman, "Presidential Statesmanship and the Constitution: The Limits of Presidential Studies," *Review of Politics* 44, no. 2 (1982), pp. 266–81.

4. The Taft view of the presidency did not carry over to his view of the role of the U.S. Supreme Court. After serving as president from 1909 to 1913, Taft served as Chief Justice from 1921 to 1930 where he was a "driving judicial activist." On this point, see Henry J. Abraham, *Justices and Presidents: A Political History of Appointments to the Supreme Court* (New York: Oxford University Press, 1974), p. 154.

5. The literalist view of the presidency has alternately been called the "constitutional" or "restricted" view of the presidency. See, for examples, L. Peter Schultz, "William Howard Taft: A Constitutionalist's View of the Presidency," *Presidential Studies Quarterly* 9, no. 4 (1979), pp. 402–14 and Sidney Warren, ed., *The American President* (Englewood Cliffs, N.J.: Prentice-Hall, 1967), pp. 26–27.

6
The Prerogative Theory of the Presidency
Abraham Lincoln

Letter to A. G. Hodges
Executive Mansion, April 4, 1864

My dear Sir: You ask me to put in writing the substance of what I verbally said the other day in your presence, to Governor Bramlette and Senator Dixon. It was about as follows:

"I am naturally antislavery. If slavery is not wrong, nothing is wrong. I cannot remember when I did not so think and feel, and yet I have never understood that the presidency conferred upon me an unrestricted right to act officially upon this judgment and feeling. It was in the oath I took that I would, to the best of my ability, preserve, protect, and defend the Constitution of the United States. I could not take the office without taking the oath. Nor was it my view that I might take an oath to get power, and break the oath in using the power. I understood, too, that in ordinary civil administration this oath even forbade me to practically indulge my primary abstract judgment on the moral question of slavery. I had publicly declared this many times, and in many ways. And I aver that, to this day, I have done no official act in mere deference to my abstract judgment and feeling on slavery. I did understand, however, that my oath to preserve the Constitution to the best of my ability imposed upon me the duty of preserving, by every indispensable means, that government—that nation, of which that Constitution was the organic law. Was it possible to lose the nation and yet preserve the Constitution? By general law, life and limb must be protected, yet often a limb must be amputated to save a life; but a life is never wisely given to save a limb. I felt that measures otherwise unconstitutional might become lawful by becoming indispensable to the preservation of the Constitution through the preservation of the nation. Right or wrong, I assume this ground, and now avow it. I could not feel that, to the best of my ability, I had even tried to preserve the Constitution, if, to save slavery or any minor matter, I should permit the wreck of government, country, and Constitution all together. When, early in the war, General Frémont attempted military emancipation, I forbade it, because I did not then think it an indispensable necessity. When, a little later, General Cameron, then Secretary of War, suggested the arming of the blacks, I objected because I did not yet think it an indispensable necessity. When, still later, General Hunter attempted military emancipation, I again forbade it, because I did not yet think the indispensable necessity had come. When in

Source: From John Nicolay and John Hay, eds., *The Complete Works of Abraham Lincoln*, vol. 10, (New York: Francis D. Tandy Co., 1894), pp. 65–68. This letter to Albert G. Hodges, editor of the Frankfort, Kentucky *Commonwealth* was used as a campaign document in the election of 1864.

March and May and July, 1862, I made earnest and successive appeals to the border States to favor compensated emancipation, I believed the indispensable necessity for military emancipation and arming the blacks would come unless averted by that measure. They declined the proposition, and I was, in my best judgment, driven to the alternative of either surrendering the Union, and with it the Constitution, or of laying strong hand upon the colored element. I chose the latter. In choosing it, I hoped for greater gain than loss; but of this, I was not entirely confident. More than a year of trial now shows no loss by it in our foreign relations, none in our home popular sentiment, none in our white military force—no loss by it anyhow or anywhere. On the contrary it shows a gain of quite a hundred and thirty thousand soldiers, seamen, and laborers. These are palpable facts, about which, as facts, there can be no caviling. We have the men; and we could not have had them without the measure.

"And now let any Union man who complains of the measure test himself by writing down in one line that he is for subduing the rebellion by force of arms; and in the next, that he is for taking these hundred and thirty thousand men from the Union side, and placing them where they would be but for the measure he condemns. If he cannot face his case so stated, it is only because he cannot face the truth."

I add a word which was not in the verbal conversation. In telling this tale I attempt no compliment to my own sagacity. I claim not to have controlled events, but confess plainly that events have controlled me. Now, at the end of three years' struggle, the nation's condition is not what either party, or any man, devised or expected. God alone can claim it. Whither it is tending seems plain. If God now wills the removal of a great wrong, and wills also that we of the North, as well as you of the South, shall pay fairly for our complicity in that wrong, impartial history will find therein new cause to attest and revere the justice and goodness of God. *Yours truly,*

A. Lincoln

7
The Stewardship Theory of the Presidency
Theodore Roosevelt

My view was that every executive officer, and above all every executive officer in high position, was a steward of the people bound actively and affirmatively to do all he could for the people, and not to content himself with the negative merit of keeping his talents undamaged in a napkin. I declined to adopt the view that what was imperatively necessary for the nation could not be done

Source: Reprinted with the permission of Charles Scribner's Sons from *The Autobiography of Theodore Roosevelt,* Centennial Ed., pp. 197–200. Copyright © 1913 Charles Scribner's Sons; renewed © 1941 Edith Carow Roosevelt. Copyright © 1958 Charles Scribner's Sons.

by the President unless he could find some specific authorization to do it. My belief was that it was not only his right but his duty to do anything that the needs of the nation demanded unless such action was forbidden by the Constitution or by the laws. Under this interpretation of executive power I did and caused to be done many things not previously done by the President and the heads of the departments. I did not usurp power, but I did greatly broaden the use of executive power. In other words, I acted for the public welfare, I acted for the commen well-being of all our people, whenever and in whatever manner was necessary, unless prevented by direct constitutional or legislative prohibition. . . .

The course I followed, of regarding the Executive as subject only to the people, and, under the Constitution, bound to serve the people affirmatively in cases where the Constitution does not explicity forbid him to render the service, was substantially the course followed by both Andrew Jackson and Abraham Lincoln. Other honorable and well-meaning Presidents, such as James Buchanan, took the opposite and, as it seems to me, narrowly legalistic view that the President is the servant of Congress rather than of the people, and can do nothing, no matter how necessary it be to act, unless the Constitution explicitly commands the action. Most able lawyers who are past middle age take this view, and so do large numbers of well-meaning, respectable citizens. My successor in office took this, the Buchanan, view of the President's powers and duties.

For example, under my administration we found that one of the favorite methods adopted by the men desirous of stealing the public domain was to carry the decision of the secretary of the interior into court. By vigorously opposing such action, and only by so doing, we were able to carry out the policy of properly protecting the public domain. My successor not only took the opposite view, but recommended to Congress the passage of a bill which would have given the courts direct appellate power over the secretary of the interior in these land matters. . . . Fortunately, Congress declined to pass the bill. Its passage would have been a veritable calamity.

I acted on the theory that the President could at any time in his discretion withdraw from entry any of the public lands of the United States and reserve the same for forestry, for water-power sites, for irrigation, and other public purposes. Without such action it would have been impossible to stop the activity of the land-thieves. No one ventured to test its legality by lawsuit. My successor, however, himself questioned it, and referred the matter to Congress. Again Congress showed its wisdom by passing a law which gave the President the power which he had long exercised, and of which my successor had shorn himself.

Perhaps the sharp difference between what may be called the Lincoln-Jackson and the Buchanan-Taft schools, in their views of the power and duties of the President, may be best illustrated by comparing the attitude of my successor toward his Secretary of the Interior, Mr. Ballinger, when the latter was accused of gross misconduct in office, with my attitude toward my chiefs of department and other subordinate officers. More than once while I was President my officials were attacked by Congress, generally because these officials did their duty well and fearlessly. In every such case I stood by the official and refused to recognize the right of Congress to interfer with me excepting by impeachment or in other constitutional manner. On the other hand, wherever I found the officer unfit for his position, I promptly removed him, even although the most influential men in Congress fought for his retention. The Jackson-Lincoln view is that a President who is fit to do good work should be able to form his own judgment as to his own subordinates, and, above all, of the subordinates standing highest and in closest and most intimate touch with him. My secretaries and their subordinates were responsible to me, and I accepted the responsibility for all their deeds. As long as they were satisfactory to me I stood by them against every critic or assailant, within or without Congress; and as for getting Congress to make up my mind for me about them, the thought would have been inconceivable to me. My successor took the opposite, or Buchanan, view when he permitted and requested Congress to pass judgment on the charges made against Mr. Ballinger as an executive officer. These charges were made to the President; the President had the facts before him and could get at them at any time, and he alone had power to act if the charges were true. However, he permitted and requested Congress to investigate Mr. Ballinger. The party minority of the committee that investigated him, and one member of the majority, declared that the charges were well-founded and that Mr. Ballinger should be removed. The other members of the majority declared the charges ill-founded. The President abode by the view of the majority. Of course believers in the Jackson-Lincoln theory of the presidency would not be content with this townmeeting majority and minority method of determining by another branch of the government what it seems the especial duty of the President himself to determine for himself in dealing with his own subordinate in his own department. . . .

8

The Literalist Theory of the Presidency

William Howard Taft

While it is important to mark out the exclusive field of jurisdiction of each branch of the government, Legislative, Executive and Judicial, it should be said that in the proper working of the government there must be coöperation of all branches, and without a willingness of each branch to perform its function, there will follow a hopeless obstruction to the progress of the whole government. Neither branch can compel the other to affirmative action, and each branch can greatly hinder the other in the attainment of the object of its activities and the exercise of its discretion.

The true view of the Executive functions is, as I conceive it, that the President can exercise no power which cannot be fairly and reasonably traced to some specific grant of power or justly implied and included within such express grant as proper and necessary to

Source: Excerpted from *Our Chief Magistrate and His Powers* by William Howard Taft, pp. 138–45. Copyright © 1916 by Columbia University Press. Reprinted by permission.

its exercise. Such specific grant must be either in the Federal Constitution or in an act of Congress passed in pursuance thereof. There is no undefined residuum of power which he can exercise because it seems to him to be in the public interest, and there is nothing in the Neagle case and its definition of a law of the United States, or in other precedents, warranting such an inference. The grants of Executive power are necessarily in general terms in order not to embarrass the Executive within the field of action plainly marked for him, but his jurisdiction must be justified and vindicated by affirmative constitutional or statutory provision, or it does not exist. There have not been wanting, however, eminent men in high public office holding a different view and who have insisted upon the necessity for an undefined residuum of Executive power in the public interest. They have not been confined to the present generation. We may learn this from the complaint of a Virginia statesman, Abel P. Upshur, a strict constructionist of the old school, who succeeded Daniel Webster as Secretary of State under President Tyler. He was aroused by Story's commentaries on the Constitution to write a monograph answering and criticizing them, and in the course of this he comments as follows on the Executive power under the Constitution:

> The most defective part of the Constitution beyond all question, is that which related to the Executive Department. It is impossible to read that instrument, without being struck with the loose and unguarded terms in which the powers and duties of the President are pointed out. So far as the legislature is concerned, the limitations of the Constitution, are, perhaps, as precise and strict as they could safely have been made; but in regard to the Executive, the Convention appears to have studiously selected such loose and

general expressions, as would enable the President, by implication and construction either to neglect his duties or to enlarge his powers. *We have heard it gravely asserted in Congress that whatever power is neither legislative nor judiciary, is of course executive, and, as such, belongs to the President under the Constitution.* How far a majority of that body would have sustained a doctrine so monstrous, and so utterly at war with the whole genius of our government, it is impossible to say, but this, at least, we know, that it met with no rebuke from those who supported the particular act of Executive power, in defense of which it was urged. Be this as it may, it is a reproach to the Constitution that the Executive trust is so ill-defined, as to leave any plausible pretense even to the insane zeal of party devotion, for attributing to the President of the United States the powers of a despot; powers which are wholly unknown in any limited monarchy in the world.

The view that he takes as a result of the loose language defining the Executive powers seems exaggerated. But one must agree with him in his condemnation of the view of the Executive power which he says was advanced in Congress. In recent years there has been put forward a similar view by executive officials and to some extent acted on. Men who are not such strict constructionists of the Constitution as Mr. Upshur may well feel real concern if such views are to receive the general acquiescence. Mr. Garfield, when Secretary of the Interior, under Mr. Roosevelt, in his final report to Congress in reference to the power of the Executive over the public domain, said:

> Full power under the Constitution was vested in the Executive Branch of the Government and the extent to which that power may be exercised is governed wholly by the discretion of the Executive unless any specific act has been prohibited either by the Constitution or by legislation.

In pursuance of this principle, Mr. Garfield, under an act for the reclamation of arid land by irrigation, which authorized him to make contracts for irrigation works and incur liability equal to the amount on deposit in the Reclamation Fund, made contracts with associations of settlers by which it was agreed that if these settlers would advance money and work, they might receive certificates from the government engineers of the labor and money furnished by them, and that such certificates might be received in the future in the discharge of their legal obligations to the government for water rent and other things under the statute. It became necessary for the succeeding administration to pass on the validity of these government certificates. They were held by Attorney-General Wickersham to be illegal, on the ground that no authority existed for their issuance. He relied on the Floyd acceptances in 7th Wallace, in which recovery was sought in the Court of Claims on commercial paper in the form of acceptances signed by Mr. Floyd when Secretary of War and delivered to certain contractors. The Court held that they were void because the Secretary of War had no statutory authority to issue them. Mr. Justice Miller, in deciding the case, said:

> The answer which at once suggests itself to one familiar with the structure of our government, in which all power is delegated, and is defined by law, constitutional or statutory, is, that to one or both of these sources we must resort in every instance. We have no officers in this government, from the President down to the most subordinate agent, who does not hold office under the law, with prescribed duties and limited authority. And while some of these, as the President, the Legislature, and the Judiciary, exercise powers in some sense left to the more general definitions necessarily incident to fundamental law found in the Constitution, the larger portion of them are the creation of statutory law, with duties and powers prescribed and limited by that law.

My judgment is that the view of Mr. Garfield and Mr. Roosevelt, ascribing an undefined residuum of power to the President is an unsafe doctrine and that it might lead under emergencies to results of an arbitrary character, doing irremediable injustice to private right. The mainspring of such a view is that the Executive is charged with responsibility for the welfare of all the people in a general way, that he is to play the part of a Universal Providence and set all things right, and that anything that in his judgment will help the people he ought to do, unless he is expressly forbidden not to do it. The wide field of action that this would give to the Executive one can hardly limit.

CHAPTER III

Nomination and Election of the President

The quest for the presidency begins quadrennially with a decision by an American citizen that he or she possesses the requisite ambition, desire, and energy necessary to campaign for the office of president, and that he or she meets the constitutional requirements and personal attributes that Americans have historically considered necessary, if not sufficient, for the occupancy of the White House.

The Constitution requires only that a person be a natural-born citizen, thirty-five years of age, and fourteen years a resident of the United States. Naturalized citizens have not usually been considered eligible for the office.[1] In practice, however, the presidents have been white, Protestant males, of northern European ancestry, married with children, highly educated, and well-off financially.[2] There have been exceptions. Al Smith, a Catholic, was the Democratic party's nominee for president in 1928; he lost. John Kennedy, also a Catholic, was the Democratic party's nominee for president in 1960; he won. James Buchanan won the presidency as a bachelor on the Democratic ticket in 1856 and remained a bachelor throughout his term of office. Two divorced persons have been nominated for the presidency, Adlai Stevenson, the Democratic nominee for president in 1952 and 1956 and Ronald Reagan, the Republican nominee for president in 1980 and 1984. Stevenson lost on both occasions; Reagan won both times.

No women, blacks, or Jews have ever become the nominee of their parties for the office of the presidency, although Geraldine Ferraro, a woman of southern European ancestry, became the nominee of the Democratic party in 1984 for the vice presidency. In addition, Jesse Jackson, a black man, presented himself as a serious candidate for the nomination of the Democratic party in 1984 and garnered approximately 20 percent of the delegate votes to the Democratic National Convention. Walter Mondale won the Democratic nomination that year.

The facts that a Catholic once won the presidency, a woman has now been nominated for vice president, a black actively seeks the nomination of his party for president, and a divorced man has been elected to the presidency on two occasions, with no fanfare over the divorce, all indicate a more open nomination process and a more democratic polity. And, as we shall see, the presidential primary system is encouraging greater rank-and-file participation in the selection of the party's nominees. All of this is likely to affect, even more, the traditional personal characteristics required for candidacy.

The campaign for the nomination is sometimes a long process depending upon when candidates decide to begin their drive for the presidency. Some candidates begin their campaigns only months before the quadrennial year in which they seek the nomination; others begin years earlier.

Under the old nominating system, which existed from about 1832 through 1968, the political parties chose presidential nominees through national nominating conventions which were composed of delegates, mostly elected in state party caucuses or conventions, not party primaries. The state party caucuses and conventions were dominated by party activists who could swing their delegation behind the presidential candidate of their choice. This usually resulted in nominating the candidate who had the most popular support and a reasonably good chance of winning the November election.

In 1968, delegates to the Democratic National Convention picked in state caucuses and conventions successfully nominated Vice President Hubert Humphrey for president despite considerable hostility throughout the nation to President Lyndon Johnson's Vietnam policy, which Humphrey had unblushingly embraced. This nomination, though Humphrey did very well in the November race against Richard Nixon, convinced many Democrats, especially the followers of Eugene McCarthy, that the state caucuses and conventions had become unresponsive to the people.

In response to the violent events at the Democratic Convention of 1968 and the loss of the presidency to Richard Nixon, the Democratic Party created two commissions in 1969: the O'Hara Commission on Rules and the McGovern-Fraser Commission on Party Structure and Delegate Selection. Their job was to undertake an "examination of the structures and processes used to select delegates to the National Convention" in order "to give all Democratic voters . . . a full, meaningful and timely opportunity to participate in the selection of delegates, and, thereby, in the decisions of the Convention itself."[3]

The O'Hara and McGovern-Fraser Commissions drafted a number of reform measures which established guidelines for delegate selection and their representation. The reformers provided specifically for:

1. A new vote allocation to the state delegations based mainly on electoral college strength and the Democratic vote in recent elections.

2. The elimination of the unit, or winner-take-all, rule in the Democratic primaries and conventions in favor of a proportional division of a state's convention votes.

3. The inclusion of women, minority groups, and youth (those between eighteen and thirty years old) in the delegations in relationship to their proportions in a state's population.

4. No more than 10 percent of a state's delegation to the national convention to be named by its state committee.

The Republican party, while not under the same pressures as the Democratic party, did, nevertheless, establish the Delegates and Organization Committee, popularly known as the Ginn Committee, for its Chairman Rosemary Ginn, a Missouri National Committeewoman. The reform proposals, much more limited than those of the Democrats, were approved in 1972 by the Republican National Convention for the choice of delegates to its 1976 National Convention. These included:

1. Maximizing grassroots participation by opening the primary and convention systems to all qualified citizens.
2. Requiring each state to seek equal representation between men and women.
3. Requiring each state to seek delegate representation by persons under the age of twenty-five in numerical equity to their voting strength within the state's general population.
4. Informing citizens about how to participate in the nomination process.
5. Eliminating party leaders as ex officio delegates.

Eventually, all of these proposals were approved with the exception of the recommendation for the proportional representation for young people. Missing from the Republican party reforms was any effort to abolish winner-take-all primaries or to make mandatory quotas for representation of population groups in the delegate makeup of the Republican party.[4]

Following the 1972 Democratic National Convention, a new commission under the leadership of Baltimore Councilwoman (now U.S. Senator) Barbara Mikulski was charged with making recommendations for the 1976 election. The major results of this commission's efforts were the replacement of stringent quotas for blacks, women, and youths with nonmandatory affirmative action programs and a ban against open cross-over primaries.

After the 1976 Convention, Morley Winograd, the state chairman of the Michigan Democratic Party, was appointed to head another commission to continue reform recommendations for the 1980 election. The Winograd Commission's recommendations resulted in:

1. Elimination of the loophole primary and the extension of the proportional representation principle to district contests.[5]
2. Increasing the size of the state delegations to accommodate state party and elected officials.
3. Requiring primary states to set filing deadlines for candidates thirty to ninety days before the voting.
4. Continuing the ban on cross-over open primaries established earlier by the Mikulski Commission.

Following the 1980 Convention, the Democratic National Convention created another commission under the leadership of Governor James B. Hunt of North

Carolina to develop rules for the 1984 nomination. The effects of the Hunt Commission's recommendations were:

1. The creation of uncommitted-delegate spots for major party and elected officials, who were called Superdelegates.[6]
2. An end to the ban on the loophole primary, that is, a return to winner-take-all district elections.
3. A shorter three-month primary and caucus season.
4. A weakened delegate-binding rule.
5. The maintenance of a candidate's right to approve delegates.
6. The continued ban on the cross-over primary.

If the McGovern-Fraser Commission was firmly committed to giving all Democratic party members the fullest opportunity to participate in the delegate-selection process, the Hunt Commission appeared equally committed to ensuring "party unity and candidate support," and a "desire to make the nominating convention a meaningful decision-making arena rather than simply a forum for ratifying decisions made in presidential primaries and state caucuses."[7] But what impact have the reforms had on the party system and the conduct of the American presidency?

Jack Walker writes that,

> The target of criticism has shifted from choices per se to the electoral process that produced those choices. A proliferation of primaries, some say, has needlessly prolonged presidential campaigns, given undue importance to television, and put a premium on candidates' style rather than on their past performances or their positions on the issues. Changes in party rules, others note, have destroyed the nominating conventions' prime functions and have gravely diminished the mediating role of political parties in America.[8]

After reviewing the reforms that began with the McGovern Commission, Walker concludes that,

> The reforms of the 1960s and 70s helped to ease the American political system through a period of turmoil. Newly enfranchised groups were absorbed peaceably, sometimes belatedly, into the electorate. While some confusion ensued, the net result has been to make the political process more open. The reformist impulse was both expedient and fundamentally correct.[9]

Robert Nakamura writes that "the debate on the current nominating system centers on the consequences of formal changes in the rules and laws governing it: the formalization of opportunities for participation in the Democratic Party as well as changes like public financing and the increased number of primaries affecting both parties." Nakamura contends that,

> These changes undoubtedly have made the process more permeable and have thereby diminished the power of party elites and enhanced that of the shapers of mass participation such as candidate organizations, direct mail and communications specialists, and the mass media. Critics have faulted this system for replacing party professionals with others

less interested in or less able to select nominees popular with voters and capable of governing if elected.[10]

Nakamura argues that the virtues of the prereform nominating system are often touted, but never explicitly demonstrated. After reviewing, among other things, the realignment that had set in before the reforms, he concludes that there is "no systematic evidence that postreform nominees are more unpopular, amateurish or radical than they would have been without the reforms given the same electoral environment."[11]

Finally, Michael Nelson tells us that "the good old days of party politics . . . just were not that good."[12] Nelson reminds us of James Bryce's classic study, *The American Commonwealth* (1888), in which Bryce states that party pros did have a talent for choosing electable candidates, but that great men are not chosen president precisely because the merits of a president are one thing and those of a candidate another.[13]

Nelson Polsby argues that it is now fashionable to blame the decay of the party on Democratic Party reforms. He asks: Is there a discernible relationship between what has happened in the party system and what has happened to the presidency? To evaluate this question Polsby further asks: Did party reforms change the outcomes in the last three presidential elections? He is persuaded that the reforms did effect the outcomes in the three elections since 1968. Polsby finds that the proliferation of primaries in the delegate selection process was inspired by the McGovern-Fraser Commission reforms (fourteen states adopted primaries after 1968), that in 1972 and 1980 the candidates of the minority party won, and that in 1976 the factional rather than the consensual candidate of the majority party won.

President Carter's victory under such circumstances persuades Polsby that the nomination machinery now permits candidates to emerge and be elected president without coming to terms with a broad coalition. This being so, Polsby argues, a president may never learn how to govern or, if he does, he may do so too late in his term of office. Thus the selection process negatively affects a president's power to govern. Polsby's provocative essay, "Reform of the Party System and Conduct of the Presidency," is reprinted here.

If some party reforms have been instituted about which we may now raise questions, some reforms, especially the proposed abolition of the electoral college, remain to be achieved. Jeane Jordan Kirkpatrick writes,

> Two unrelated principles have inspired most political reforms in this century: the desire to end corruption in politics and the desire to achieve direct democracy with perfect equality for all citizens. . . . The electoral college is conceived by the proponents of its abolition as an offense against the principle of one man, one vote since, given certain assumptions and circumstances, some voters have more significance than others.[14]

As Raymond Tatalovich and Byron Daynes point out, "The framers of the Constitution were not especially concerned about making the president directly accountable to the people."[15] Nevertheless, the American political system has, over the years, driven the presidency to a greater measure of accountability to the citizenry.

But how does the electoral college work to elect a president? On the first Tuesday after the first Monday in November, Americans do not vote directly for presidential nominees, but for a slate of electors who are pledged, but not constitutionally bound, to cast their votes for the candidate receiving a plurality of the popular vote in their state. These electors travel to their respective capitals in December of a presidential election year and cast their ballots with the Secretaries of State of their respective states who then transmit these ballots to the president of the United States Senate.

To win the presidency, a candidate must receive a majority, that is, 270 of the 538 electoral votes. The number of electors is based on the combined numbers of U.S. Senators and Representatives allotted to each state plus the three for the District of Columbia made possible by the Twenty-Third Amendment.

If no candidate wins a majority of the 538 electoral college votes, the U.S. House of Representatives must select the president from among the top three electoral contenders. Each state delegation has only one vote. A majority of the fifty state delegations, that is twenty-six votes, are needed to elect a president.

Supporters of the electoral college argue that, among other good reasons for keeping the electoral college, it works.[16] These same supporters say that the electoral college has only failed in three instances to elect a president: 1800, 1824, and 1876.[17] Even so, they argue, Congress was able to resolve the disputes peaceably.

Critics of the electoral college have charged that it is undemocratic and dangerous. It is undemocratic because it permits candidates to win the presidency without majorities of the popular votes.[18] It is dangerous because it makes uncertain the outcome of a presidential contest whenever the election is thrown into the House of Representatives where the choice must be made from among the three top candidates. This has led to periodic demands by newspaper editors, journalists, public office holders, and political scientists for the abolition of the electoral college.[19]

Richard Watson argues that the electoral college ought to be abolished and direct election instituted in its stead. In his essay, "The Electoral College," taken from his book, *The Presidential Contest* and reprinted here, Watson briefly traces the history of the electoral college, its failures, and some of its near failures, and discusses the several alternatives proposed to reform the electoral college. Watson would not, however, reform the electoral college, he would abolish it. He believes that the continued existence of the electoral college threatens the legitimacy of the American political system.

NOTES

1. See Charles Gordon, "Who Can Be President of the United States: The Unresolved Enigma," *Maryland Law Review* 28, no. 1 (Winter 1968), pp. 1–32.

2. For excellent summaries of the personal characteristics that have been and, to considerable extent, still are required of candidates for and occupants of the office of the president,

see Clinton Rossiter, *The American Presidency* (New York: Harcourt, Brace and World, 1960), p. 201; and Richard A. Watson, *The Presidential Contest*, 2nd ed. (New York: John Wiley & Sons, 1984), pp. 22–23.

3. *Mandate for Reform*, Report of the Commission on Party Structure and Delegate Selection (Washington, D.C.: Democratic National Committee, 1970), pp. 9–10.

4. See Watson, *The Presidential Contest*, p. 14; Stephen T. Wayne, *The Road to the White House: The Politics of Presidential Elections* (New York: St. Martin's Press, 1980), p. 89; and Robert J. Huckshorn, *Political Parties in America* (North Scituate, Mass.: Duxbury Press, 1980), pp. 133–36.

5. Winner-take-all voting had been eliminated for the 1976 election; however, a loophole in party rules permitted states that elected delegates by districts to continue to do so. The result was some winner-take-all votes at the congressional district level.

6. The "Superdelegates" to be chosen by the Democratic members of the U.S. House and Senate and by the state parties were to hold 14 percent of the convention votes. The goal was to return some nomination power to the party regulars who, during the prereform period, had the largest voice in the nomination decision.

7. Raymond Tatalovich and Byron W. Daynes, *Presidential Power in the United States* (Monterey, Calif.: Brooks/Cole Publishing, 1984), p. 55.

8. Jack Walker, "Presidential Campaigns: Reforming the Reforms," *The Wilson Quarterly* 5, no. 4 (Autumn 1981), pp. 88–89.

9. Ibid., p. 101.

10. Robert T. Nakamura, "The Reformed Nominating System: Its Critics and Uses," *PS* 16, no. 4 (Fall 1983), p. 667.

11. Ibid.

12. Michael Nelson, "The Presidential Nominating System: Problems and Prescriptions," in *What Role for Government: Lessons for Policy Research,* ed. Richard Zeckhauser and Derek Leebaert (Durham, N.C.: Duke University Press, 1983), p. 43.

13. Ibid.

14. Jeane Jordan Kirkpatrick, *Dismantling the Parties: Reflections on Party Reform and Party Decomposition* (Washington, D.C.: American Enterprise Institute 1978), p. 24.

15. Tatalovich and Daynes, *Presidential Power*, p. 38.

16. Literature that supports the retention of the electoral college includes: Harry A. Bailey, Jr., "The Electoral College and American Federalism," *Illinois Quarterly* 36, no. 2 (December 1973), pp. 51–62; Judith Best, *The Case against Direct Election of the President: A Defense of the Electoral College* (Ithaca, N.Y.: Cornell University Press, 1975); Martin Diamond, *The Electoral College and the American Idea of Democracy* (Washington, D.C.: American Enterprise Institute, 1977); and John Wildenthal, "Consensus after LBJ: The Role of the Electoral College," *Southwest Review* 53 (Spring 1968), pp. 113–130.

17. There was no popular vote for electors in the election of 1800.

18. Those presidents who won elections without majorities of the popular vote include: John Quincy Adams (1824), Rutherford Hayes (1876), and Benjamin Harrison (1888). The configuration of the popular vote in 1888: 5,447,129 votes for Harrison gave him 233 electoral votes while 5,537,857 for Grover Cleveland gave him only 168 electoral votes. The 1888 election, unlike those of 1824 and 1876, did not require resolution by the Congress.

19. For some representative literature calling for the abolition of the electoral college, see Lawrence D. Langley and Alan Braun, *The Politics of Electoral Reform* (New Haven, Conn.: Yale University Press, 1972); Neil R. Pierce, *The People's President* (New York: Simon and Schuster, 1968); and John Yunker and Lawrence D. Langley, "The Biases of the Electoral College: Who Is Really Advantaged?" in *Perspectives on Presidential Selection,* ed. Donald Matthews (Washington, D.C.: Brookings Institution, 1972).

9
Reform of the Party System and the Conduct of the Presidency

Nelson W. Polsby

I

In this paper, I propose to explore whether there is a discernible relationship between what happens in the U.S. party system and what happens in the conduct of the Presidency. It is an analysis that draws heavily upon the contemporary history of the United States, and on that account alone may encounter disagreement from participants and observers who see things differently. Indeed, some measure not only of disagreement but disagreeableness seems hard to avoid in an area of study where any sort of contribution may easily be mistaken for ammunition in ongoing political controversy. But as much as it would simplify our lives if it were so, whether a causal connection is weak or strong, whether an ascertainable fact is true or false, does not depend on anyone's political sympathies. And so there is room for the sort of discourse in which political scientists sometimes engage, even on an issue like the consequences of party reform.

An ill-tempered quotation from a political activist sets the stage nicely:

It has become fashionable among a certain group of pundits and political scientists to blame the reforms undertaken by the Democratic Party after its 1968 convention for all manner of political ills— declining voter participation, the proliferation of single-issue groups, weak presidential leadership, poor congressional performance, and, above all, the decay of the political party. So great has been the hostility to these reforms, to the reformers who perpetrated them and to the proliferation of presidential nominating primaries that followed in their wake, that one expects any day now to see a book published that blames these reforms, not only for our political ills, but for cancer, heart disease, and falling arches.[1]

It goes beyond my current intentions to explore all the causal connections

[1] Curtis B. Gans, "How the White House Is Won," *Washington Post Book World* (August 12, 1979), p. 10.

Source: From *Problems and Prospects of Presidential Leadership in the Nineteen Eighties;* vol. I, pp. 103–21, edited by James S. Young, 1982, Lanham, Maryland: University Press of America. Copyright © 1982 University Press of America.

that this offhanded display of partisan pique seeks to dismiss but it does seem to me perfectly permissible to ask:

1. Did party reforms change the probable outcomes of the three Presidential elections since they were enacted?
2. Did party reforms have any direct effects on the conduct of the Presidency beyond that?

I believe answers to both questions can be given in the affirmative, but think the grounds for belief in both cases are certainly not so obvious as to command immediate and unanimous assent. Indeed even after these grounds are more thoroughly explored reasonable observers may find ample bases for disagreement about the conclusions. Let us nevertheless see what the case for the affirmative looks like.

In three out of the last four Presidential elections, the minority party has won.[2] The first of these, 1968, can be straightforwardly described as an occasion in which certain short-run forces having to do with the extraordinary saliency of the Vietnam War among Democratic élites caused the majority party to tear itself apart in public. This can be shown, among other ways, by the extremely low public opinion ratings of

the 1968 Democratic nominee after the convention that nominated him. Conventions normally boost the ratings of their nominees.[3]

At that Democratic convention, other forces were set in motion which, it is now frequently argued, have in some degree institutionalized the handicap which hindered the Democratic nominee of 1968, and aided the Republicans in each of the subsequent Presidential elections, two out of three of which resulted in victories for the Republican minority.

It is necessary to invoke a rather complicated chain of causal connections in order to maintain this argument. With apologies to Rube Goldberg, here is at least one account of how the process is supposed to have worked:

1. The 1968 Democratic convention mandated a Reform commission on the selection of delegates for subsequent conventions.
2. This commission, named for its chairmen, George McGovern and Donald Fraser, issued a series of guidelines, which for various reasons became compulsory party legislation.
3. A series of lawsuits established the right of national parties, and their chosen instruments, to place requirements upon state parties with respect to the identities of state party delegates to national party conventions.
4. State party leaders, faced with complex requirements and the threat of exclusion of their state

[2] Compare, for example, the disparities between party identifications as monitored by public opinion surveys and presidential vote:

	Dem. % of Party ID	Dem. % of Pres. Vote	Rep. % of Party ID	Rep. % of Pres. Vote
1968	55	43	33	43
1972	51	38	34	61
1976	52	50	33	48
1980	52	41	33	51

Source: Center for Political Studies, University of Michigan. (Independent leaners included with the party toward which they lean.)

[3] In August of 1968, just before the Democratic convention, Humphrey got 29% of the vote in a Gallup trial heat with Richard Nixon and George Wallace; in early September, he got 31%. On average, candidates jump about 8 points after they are nominated. See *Gallup Opinion Index* Report 183, December 1980.

delegations from national party conventions, drastically changed delegation selection procedures.

5. Primary elections thus became the main instrument for delegate selection. The results of primaries were regarded as sure to pass muster in accordance with national guideline enforcement machinery, and hence assure seating at the national convention.

6. Delegate selection by this method, however, introduces certain distortions into the procedures which, though permissible under the guidelines, nevertheless drastically altered the incentive structure under which the nomination process was conducted.

7. This in turn has led to nominations of candidates unable to command widespread support, and thus has thrown at least two Presidential elections—in 1972 and 1980—to the more ideologically cohesive but numerically smaller minority party.

Not all the steps in this argument are matters of much controversy. Nobody doubts that the McGovern Commission came into being, that it issued guidelines, that its recommendations were incorporated as Democratic party legislation, and that the legality of the centralization of the Democratic party—and consequently also of the Republicans—was secured by recourse to the courts.[4]

Starting at the fourth point in the argument, and increasingly as the argument progresses, objections of various sorts, and the needs for elucidation and further explanation crop up. These demand some attention.

It has, for example, been denied that the undoubted proliferation of primaries in the delegate selection process were inspired by McGovern-Fraser Commission reforms. Two former staff members of the Commission have generated a short list of other possible motives for switching to primary elections.[5] These include a desire on the part of state party leaders to attract the coverage of the national television networks for the purposes of drawing attention to state or regional problems. In addition, there is the simple financial attraction of having a primary, since

> The candidates, their campaigns, and the press who cover them are known to spend a great deal of money in "crucial" primary states.[6]

These authors also mention several states—Texas, North Carolina, Georgia—in which primary elections were instituted because it was believed that such elections were going to be helpful to the favorite son Presidential candidacies of Lloyd Bentsen, Terry Sanford and Jimmy Carter, respectively. They do not describe how or why these primaries were superior to the methods of delegate selection they replaced, from the standpoint of these candidates. In Georgia, for example, prior to the reforms "the entire national convention delegation was chosen by the state party chairman, in consultation with the Demo-

---

[4] For accounts of the reform process, see Byron Shafer, *The Party Reformed: Reform Politics in the Democratic Party 1968–1972* (Ph.D. dissertation, University of California, Berkeley, 1979) and William J. Crotty, *Decision for the Democrats* (Baltimore: Johns Hopkins, 1978). The court cases are *Cousins v. Wigoda*, 419 US 477 (1975), and *Democratic Party v. LaFollette*, 49 US. Law Week 4178 (1981).

[5] Kenneth A. Bode and Carol F. Casey, "Party Reform: Revisionism Revised" in Robert A. Goldwin (ed.), *Political Parties in the Eighties* (Washington: AEI, 1980) pp. 3–19.

[6] Ibid., p. 17.

cratic governor."[7] It is easy to envisage such a system being even more advantageous to a favorite son than a primary. The other reasons given make sense as possible excuses for switching to primary elections at any time; what they do not explain is why all these reasons so suddenly occurred to so many state party leaders all at once, and only after the guidelines had come into being, unless it was because the compulsion of newly instituted guidelines may have suddenly stimulated an interest in publicizing state problems, or in raising money for the tourist industry. Thus the observation of the Winograd Commission of the Democratic Party that

> many states . . . felt that a primary offered the most protection against a challenge at the next convention[8]

does not seem so far-fetched after all. As former McGovern-Fraser Commissioner Austin Ranney said:

> Most of the fourteen states which adopted presidential primaries after 1968 did so as a direct response to the McGovern-Fraser rules. Some decided that primaries were the best way to provide genuine "full, meaningful and timely participation." Others decided that the best way to keep the new national delegate-selection rules from upsetting their accustomed and preferred ways of doing state and local party business would be to establish a presidential primary and thereby split off presidential nomination matters from all other party affairs. And still others calculated that the new rules made caucuses and conventions much more vulnerable than

a primary to being captured by small but dedicated bands of ideologues.[9]

At a decade's remove in time, and with the matter increasingly disputed by political adversaries rather than as a purely academic bone of contention, it may be exceedingly difficult to recover enough of the historical record to nail this point down conclusively. The matter of motivations is at best conjectural, not least on account of the probable existence of mixtures of motives among many actors, and the consequent overdetermination of the result. It is certainly worth a try, however, to ventilate even if we cannot conclusively settle this issue. There is no disputing, at any rate, that primary elections did proliferate as a means of delegate selection between 1968 and 1972. They have continued to do so. There were 17 such elections in 1968, 23 in 1972, 30 in 1976, 34 in 1980.

The claim that primaries as a method for selecting delegates introduces certain kinds of distortion into the process rests on two bases. One has to do with the sorts of participants who dominate primary electorates. The other has to do with the formal properties of choice in primary elections as they are run in the United States, in which outcomes are produced by aggregating the first—and only the first—preferences of voters who spread their selections over a broad field of contenders.

Because primary elections have long been a feature of American state politics, a line of argument that has some claim to venerability in political science establishes the first point. As V. O. Key Jr., one of the ablest of those who have studied the matter, says, "The American political tradition caps decisions made

---

[7] Ibid., p. 10.

[8] Report of the Commission on Presidential Nomination and Party Structure (Morley A. Winograd, Chairman), *Openness, Participation, and Party Building: Reforms for a Stronger Democratic Party* (Washington: Democratic National Committee, January 1978), p. 25.

[9] Austin Ranney, *The Federalization of Presidential Primaries* (Washington, D.C.: AEI, 1978), pp. 2–3.

by popular vote with a resplendent halo of legitimacy."[10] Yet the chapter of Key's book of which this is the first sentence is titled: *Participation in Primaries: The Illusion of Popular Rule.*

Key establishes that in the large number of state primaries which he examined, in several states and over a number of different elections, "the effective primary constituency" is often "a caricature of the entire party following."[11]

Key's major findings—that state primary electorates were unrepresentative of the state electorate, and that candidates frequently needed to mobilize only very small numbers of voters to win—are confirmed for more recent national primary elections, notably by work of Austin Ranney, James I. Lengle, and the Democratic party's own Winograd Commission.[12] Table I gives Winograd Commission findings comparing Democratic primary electorates with Democratic voters in the 1976 election for 13 states.

Consistently, and not only in the instant case, those voters lower down on the socio-economic scale are disproportionately missing from primary electorates.

The second sort of distortion which primary elections promote is harder to describe. It is nevertheless as well founded in the literature of political science as the first, and rests on the seemingly intractable fact that once the number of alternatives available to an electorate gets above two, and so long as only the first choices of voters are counted, there is a lively possibility that the plurality winner of such an election will not be a true majority choice.[13] Two strategic imperatives are thus created: one suggests that it is in the interests of party leaders to restrict and channel choices by primary electorates so that majority sentiment in the general election can be mobilized. The other is that it is in the interests of candidates to put themselves forward into the lottery in large numbers, thus reducing the number of voters necessary for any candidate among them to attract in order to win. The interests of candidates are squarely counterpoised against those of party leaders: party leaders desire the assembly of coalitions, candidates the mobilization of factions.[14]

Key says:

The small size of the blocs of voters necessary to win nominations has a most significant consequence for the nature of the party . . . The direct communion of potential candidates with small groups of voters places enormous difficulties in the way of those party leaders disposed to work beyond the primaries to the general election and to put forward the most appealing slate. Individual politicians with a grasp on a small bloc of voters which can be turned into a primary victory are difficult to discipline or to bargain with. The support of even a weak personal organization, the loyalties and admiration of an ethnic group, a wide acquaintance within a religious group, simple notoriety achieved in a variety of ways, an alliance with an

---

[10] V. O. Key, Jr., *American State Politics* (New York: Knopf, 1956), p. 133.

[11] Ibid., p. 152.

[12] Ranney, op. cit., and Ranney, *Curing the Mischiefs of Faction* (Berkeley: University of California, 1975); James I. Lengle, *Representation and Presidential Primaries: The Democratic Party in the Post-Reform Era* (Ph.D. dissertation, University of California, Berkeley, 1978); Report of the Commission on Presidential Nomination and Party Structure, op. cit.

[13] See Kenneth Arrow, *Social Choice and Individual Values* (New York: Wiley, 1963).

[14] For more on this problem see Nelson W. Polsby, "Coalition and Faction in American Politics: An Institutional View," in Seymour Martin Lipset (ed.), *Emerging Coalitions in American Politics* (San Francisco: Institute for Contemporary Studies, 1978), pp. 103–123.

TABLE I • COMPARISON OF DEMOCRATIC PRIMARY ELECTORATE AND DEMOCRATIC GENERAL ELECTORATE, 1976
(percentage of voters)

	Less than High School Education		Black		Over Age 65		College Degree or Beyond		Income Over $20,000/yr.	
	Primary	General	Primary	General	Primary	General	Primary	General	Primary	General
California	11	27	12	15	9	19	34	17	35	23
Florida	13	30	8	14	23	28	28	17	26	16
Illinois	19	34	15	16	8	17	23	6	25	21
Indiana	21	40	10	11	7	24	13	6	17	11
Massachusetts	12	19	2	3	10	18	36	22	24	24
Michigan	20	30	11	22	11	17	20	10	16	17
New Hampshire	11	18	—	—	6	13	38	18	15	14
New Jersey	12	41	17	26	9	16	35	14	37	19
New York	15	31	15	20	15	14	32	19	32	16
Ohio	15	32	11	17	7	19	25	10	23	17
Oregon	19	18	n.a.	n.a.	23	13	23	20	15	23
Pennsylvania	17	32	8	15	9	15	23	15	20	9
Wisconsin	18	25	3	7	13	19	22	15	n.a.	n.a.

Note: n.a. signifies data are not available.
Source: Democratic Party, Commission on Presidential Nomination and Party Structure, "Openness, Participation and Party Building: Reforms for a Stronger Democratic Party," Washington, D.C., January 25, 1978, pp. 11–13.

influential newspaper—these and a variety of other elements may create power within the narrow circle of people who share control in the politics of the direct primary.[15]

The risk in the general election is that dissatisfied party voters will bolt the party choice. This may happen if they feel deprived of their first choice by a sequence of primary wins by some other candidate or candidates, and/or deprived of their second or even third choice or of any satisfactory choice by the institutionalized lack of a genuine party deliberative process that weighs the expression of second choice opinion, or that juxtaposes pairs of alternatives *seriatim*, or that takes strongly negative feelings of party—or general election—voters into account. In 1972 and again in 1980 something like 30% of voters describing themselves as Democrats evidently deserted the presidential candidate of their party and voted Republican.[16]

The great bulk of the deserters in both years described themselves as dissatisfied with the candidate of their own party, not as ideologically attracted by the Re-

publican candidate.[17] The point is worth underscoring because all three winners—in 1972, 1976, and 1980—have described themselves and been described by their supporters as vested with extraordinary electoral mandates. All behaved as though they thought they had such mandates. None did.[18]

II

The first major proposition of this paper was that the party reforms facilitated the defection of Democratic voters in disgust to the Republican party—twice in numbers sufficient to elect a Republican President—because they have gravely damaged the capacity of the Democratic party to organize a nomination process that can compose the diversity and the differences among party leaders and presidential hopefuls. The evidence is highly plausible, though for the most part indirect. Alternative explanations such as the idea that Democrats defect because they are closet Republicans founder on all sorts of difficulties: the fact that heavy majorities reject Republican positions on most political issues, that Democrats retain the nominal loyalties of more voters than Republicans, that Democratic voters

---

[15] Key, op. cit., pp. 144–145.

[16]   Defection Levels for Democrats
                    1952–1980

Year	To Rep. Cand.	To 3rd Party	Total
1980	26%	4%	30%
1976	18		18
1972	33		33
1968	12	14	26
1964	13		13
1960	16		16
1956	15		15
1952	23		23

Post-1968 mean: 27% Democratic defection.
1952–1968 mean: 18.6% Democratic defection.
Source: The Gallup Opinion Index Report No. 183, December, 1980, pp. 6–7.

[17] See Everett Carll Ladd, "The Brittle Mandate: Electoral Dealignment and the 1980 Presidential Election," *Political Science Quarterly* 96 (Spring 1981), pp. 1–25. Also, Adam Clymer, "Displeasure with Carter Turned Many to Reagan," *New York Times*, November 9, 1980; and *Public Opinion* (December/January 1981), p. 43.

[18] See Nelson W. Polsby, "Interest Groups and the Presidency: Trends in Political Intermediation in America," in Walter Dean Burnham and Martha Wagner Weinberg (eds.), *American Politics and Public Policy* (Cambridge, Mass.: the MIT Press, 1978), pp. 41–52.

outnumber Republicans for all other offices.[19]

The second proposition is even harder to establish by means of straightforward argument. Yet there are features of American government since 1972 which do lend themselves to the conclusion that party reform has had an impact on the conduct of the Presidency beyond electing the candidate of the minority party in 1972 and 1980 and a factional rather than a consensus choice of the majority party in 1976.

Presumably this argument must rest primarily on the conduct of the Carter Presidency, since the Nixon and Reagan presidencies can be set aside as directly attributable to the derangement of electoral results by virtue of the derangement of the nomination process. As more than a few observers have had occasion to remark, the Carter Presidency did have a number of curious features.

The most significant of these no doubt was Mr. Carter's seeming inability to get along with Congress. Outside observers were entitled to view this inability with some amazement. After all, President Carter was a middle-of-the-road Democrat, and during his Presidency the Congress was controlled— overwhelmingly controlled—by the Democratic party.[20] The last previous

time an overwhelmingly Democratic Congress coincided with a Democratic President, after the 1964 landslide election, a bumper crop of new and innovative programs had resulted.[21]

Times had changed on Capitol Hill since the enactment of the Great Society however. Friends of President Carter were quick to point out that important changes had overtaken Congress in the intervening decade and a half, making the task of a President—any President— far more difficult. Congress had democratized its rules, for example, had endured a period of fierce antagonism with President Nixon, had created an enormous staff bureaucracy in part to wage war on the executive branch, and had undergone drastic turn-over in membership so that a majority of members could not hark back to the good old days of Presidential-Congressional cooperation.

In the old days, it was said, (the examples frequently coming from the Kennedy era of 1961–63) a President could strike a bargain with the Congressional leadership, and the leadership could deliver the Congress. Committee chairmen ruled their roosts, and this meant that once a committee chairman committed himself to cooperation with the President, the President's task of assembling a majority in Congress was greatly simplified. By the time of the Carter Presidency (1977–80) the argument goes, committee chairmen had lost their power to the chairmen of subcommittees, and subcommittee chairmanships were dispersed among the multitudes. Instead of cultivating an alliance with twenty senior Congressmen, Presidential legislative liaison had to court 120

---

[19] Ladd, *op. cit.*; Arthur Miller, "What Mandate? What Realignment?" *The Washington Post Outlook* (June 28, 1981); Louis Harris, "No Mandate for a Switch on Social Questions Seen," *Washington Post* (December 4, 1980); George Skelton, "Conservative Mandate for Reagan Contains Limits," *Los Angeles Times* (November 20, 1980); *Public Opinion* (December/January, 1981) pp. 24–25.

[20] The 95th Congress (1977–78) began with 292 Democrats and 143 Republicans (67% Democratic). The 96th Congress (1979–80) had 276 Democrats and 159 Republicans (63.4% Democratic).

[21] Convenient overviews are contained in the *Congressional Quarterly Almanac* 21 (1965), pp. 65–112, and ibid., 22 (1966), pp. 69–130.

subcommittee chairmen, a much more complicated task.[22]

There is a grain of truth in this argument, but no more than a grain. The "good old days" existed only during the brief span of the 89th Congress. And the bad new days of the Carter era were structurally far more favorable to a middle-of-the-road Democratic President than anything Presidents Truman or Kennedy ever saw. Congressional reform devolved power not only downward to subcommittee chairmen but also upward to the House Democratic leadership. Mistakes, ineptitude and Presidential neglect of Congress played a far more significant role in creating the Carter administration legislative record than Carter administration apologists admit. The litany of Presidential mistakes toward Congress was nearly endless: an inability to settle upon legislative priorities, a reluctance to bring Congress into the process of formulating proposals before they arrived, fully blown, on Capitol Hill, a disinclination to interact or bargain directly with Congressmen and a tendency to appeal to a mythical entity known as "the people" presumably over the heads of Congressmen, themselves elected public officials, the vast majority of whom had run well ahead of Jimmy Carter in their home districts.[23]

President Carter's legislative liaison was in the hands of a person totally inexperienced and unknown on Capitol Hill, but this was only the beginning of the problem. The Carter administration could—and eventually did—hire people more experienced in the ways of Con-

gress to join the liaison staff. But for a time many of these people were housed in the White House's East Wing, physically and symbolically removed from the center of Presidential power, and only Frank Moore, their chief, had direct access to the President. The Carter administration ignored the advice of friendly predecessors to establish regular beats for liaison personnel based on the bloc structure of Congress and instead at the beginning established issue specialties for them. This meant that different liaison people would deal with the same Congressman on different issues, and no regular relationship, no orchestration of give and take over the long haul, could easily be established. Worse, Presidential liaison people, allegedly issue specialists, were never tied into the policy formation process in the White House and so were denied both flexibility and credibility in dealing with Congress.[24]

Despite repeated efforts from Congressional leaders to bridge the gap between Capitol and White House, neither President Carter nor his closest aides who actually participated in policymaking made informal acquaintances in Congress. It became common coin on the Hill that Mr. Carter had conceptualized Congress as indistinguishable from the Georgia legislature.[25] Democrats from all parts of the political spectrum—

---

[22] See, e.g., Lance Morrow, "A Cry for Leadership," *Time* (August 6, 1979) pp. 24–28.

[23] In 1976 President Carter ran ahead of just 22 winning Democrats in the House and behind 270. John F. Bibby, Thomas E. Mann, Norman Ornstein, *Vital Statistics on Congress, 1980* (Washington: AEI, 1980), p. 20.

[24] Eric L. Davis, "Legislative Liaison in the Carter Administration," *Political Science Quarterly* 94 (Summer, 1979), pp. 287–301. For a compendium of complaints about Carter's handling of Congress, see Betty Glad, *Jimmy Carter: In Search of the Great White House* (New York: Norton, 1980), pp. 417–427; Haynes Johnson, *In the Absence of Power* (New York: Viking, 1980), pp. 154–168 and *passim*; Dom Bonafede, "Carter's Relationship with Congress—Making a Mountain Out of a 'Moorehill'," *National Journal* (March 26, 1977), pp. 456–463 and "The Tough Job of Normalizing Relations with Capitol Hill," *National Journal* (January 13, 1979), pp. 54–57.

[25] See Haynes Johnson, op. cit., pp. 22, 43.

but most notably those from his own part of the spectrum—began to collect and disburse, like children with bubble-gum cards, a fund of Jimmy Carter stories illustrating his utter lack of interest in listening to Congressional advice, his stubbornness, his parochial insularity. He evidently had no back-channels to Capitol Hill and wanted none, no Congressional cronies, no unofficial sources of information, indeed virtually no friends.

The political resources of such a president were bound to be easily depleted, even among those, undoubtedly a great number, who wished him no particular ill. Given heavy Democratic majorities, the Speaker and the Senate Majority Leader could rally majorities in behalf of a President who could not or would not help himself, but not easily and not often. For since the rise of large Congressional staffs, Congressmen no longer need to take the word of the executive branch on any controverted point if they choose not to. The Congressional party can now, if it chooses to do so, chart its own course with respect to policy fully in possession of adequate intellectual fortification. The capacity to do so, however, operates at least in part independently of the inclination to do so. The development of staff capacity was a Congressional response to the Presidency of Richard Nixon. The use of this capacity when the Presidency was in Democratic hands was a response to the Presidential style of Jimmy Carter.

In order to get a sense of the internal dynamics of the Carter Congresses in relation to the Presidency some historical background is helpful. Essentially, throughout most of the last fifty years, the internal struggle of central importance to Congress has been between liberal Democrats on one hand, and a conservative coalition, encompassing conservative Southern Democrats and

Republicans on the other. Franklin Roosevelt's abortive attempt to purge Congress of conservative Democrats was an early recognition of the capacity of the conservative coalition to hamper the political plans of liberal Democratic presidents.[26] The strength of these two grand coalitions has ebbed and flowed over the years, changing tidally with the results of biennial elections.[27] Both sides have taken what advantages they could from internal rules of Congress pertaining especially in the Senate to freedom of debate, in the House to control over the agenda and in both houses to seniority in committee assignments. And both have interacted strategically with the President—the conservative group mobilizing their strength, when they needed to, around threats of vetoes by conservative presidents, and the liberal group around the pressure of liberal Presidents' programs. The great resources in the hands of the conservative coalition over most of the fifty years have been the seniority of their leaders, and their tactical skill and tenacity. The great resources of the liberal group were

[26] J. B. Shannon, "Presidential Politics in the South, 1938—I," *Journal of Politics* 1 (May, 1939), pp. 146–170, "Presidential Politics in the South 1938—II," *Journal of Politics* 1 (August 1939), pp. 278–300.

[27] See John F. Manley, "The Conservative Coalition in Congress," in Robert L. Peabody and Nelson W. Polsby (eds.), *New Perspectives on the House of Representatives* (Chicago: Rand McNally, 1977), pp. 97–117; James Patterson, *Congressional Conservatism and the New Deal* (Lexington: University of Kentucky Press, 1967); David W. Brady and Charles S. Bullock III, "Coalition Politics in the House of Representatives," in Lawrence C. Dodd and Bruce I. Oppenheimer (eds.), *Congress Reconsidered*, 2nd edition (Washington, D.C.: C. Q. Press, 1981), pp. 186–203; Mack C. Shelley II, "The Conservative Coalition and the President, 1953–1978," a paper delivered at the Southern Political Science Association Annual Meeting, Gatlinburg, Tennessee, November, 1979.

two: numbers, and the claims on the Democratic side of party loyalty.

By 1960, the liberals had the numbers in the Senate, but in the House of Representatives the picture was quite different. The election of 1958 was a Democratic landslide year, sending 283 Democrats to the House. Yet, as Representative Clem Miller, a liberal Democrat from Northern California, pointed out: "The combination of Southern Democrats and Northern Republicans can always squeak out a majority when they want to, and they want to on a great number of significant issues . . . Actually, the Democratic party as non-Southerners define it is a minority in the House."

"There are 160 Northern Democrats and roughly 99 Southern Democrats," Miller figured. "This includes Texas, but does not include the border states . . . which generally cancel each other out. Maryland votes against us, West Virginia with us, Missouri cancels itself out, half liberal, half Southern, and Kentucky, ambivalent, sometimes with us and sometimes against us . . . Begin with a base of 160 Northern Democratic votes. Add to it fifty percent of the (roughly 30) border state Democrats. We are always 15 to 30 votes shy . . ."[28]

So long as the conservative Democrats from the South have a lively option of coalescing on the floor with a mostly united Republican party, efforts to organize the Democratic party in the House by requiring greater party loyalty of such a large minority are bound to come to grief. From 1958 to 1978, however, the strength of this minority within the Democratic party in the House eroded so as to permit effective action in the

Democratic caucus. Meanwhile, liberal Democrats became better organized and better able to mobilize their big battalions as needed.

A slightly different way of doing Clem Miller's arithmetic yields the 20-year comparisons visible in Table II.

Over a 20-year period it was mostly conservative Southern Democrats who lost their seats to Republicans. Outside the South, Democrats, mostly liberal, replaced Republicans. So over the 20-year span the House became more liberal overall, and this trend was accentuated within the Democratic caucus.

And, indeed, the Democratic caucus was the engine of change within the House this last decade. Prodded by its organized liberals, the Democratic Study Group, the Caucus established a subcommittee bill of rights, took power from committee chairmen, deposed chairmen in historic breaches of seniority, put the Speaker in charge of committee assignments in general and of assignments to the Rules Committee in particular.[29]

Some of these changes clearly decentralized power; but some took powers previously dispersed to committees and their chairmen and vested them in the House Democratic leadership, and especially the Speaker. And it was an organ of centralized party leadership, the caucus, that did it.

These observations must be kept in

---

[28] Clem Miller, member of the House: *Letters of a Congressman,* John W. Baker, ed. (New York: Scribners, 1962), pp. 123–124.

[29] On Congressional reforms during the 1970s, see Norman J. Ornstein and David W. Rohde, "Shifting Forces, Changing Rules and Political Outcomes: The Impact of Congressional Change on Four House Committees," in Peabody and Polsby, op. cit., pp. 186–269; Lawrence C. Dodd, "Congress and the Quest for Power," in Lawrence C. Dodd and Bruce I. Oppenheimer (eds.), *Congress Reconsidered,* 1st edition (New York: Praeger, 1977), pp. 269–307; and Roger H. Davidson and Walter J. Oleszek, *Congress Against Itself* (Bloomington: Indiana University Press, 1977).

TABLE II · COALITIONS IN THE HOUSE (1960 and 1980)

	86th Congress 1959–60 Elected 1958	96th Congress 1979–80 Elected 1978
Democrats	280[*]	281
Republicans	152	154
Southern[†] seats	106	108
Conservative Democrats	66	47
Mainstream[‡] Democrats	33[§]	31
Republicans	7	30
Non-Southern Seats		
Democrats	181	203
Republicans	145	124
Democratic Caucus		
Non-South plus		
Mainstream South	214	234
Conservative South	66	47
Conservative Coalition		
Republicans plus		
Conservative Southern		
Democrats	218	201

[*] Three vacancies by the end of the Congress.
[†] Southern seats are seats from 11 states of the old confederacy.
[‡] Mainstream Southern Democrats are those whose CQ Party support exceeds their party opposition scores by at least 2–1.
Sources: 1960 CQ Almanac (Washington: Congressional Quarterly, 1960) pp. 140–141; Congressional Quarterly Weekly Report, January 10, 1981, pp. 82–83.
[§] Includes Speaker Rayburn.

mind in evaluating the claim that Congress is less tractable than heretofore to leadership from a Democratic President. The 20-year record of the institution suggests, rather, enormous gains in the numbers of regular Democratic seats, and a sizeable potential for favorable results for any Democratic President willing to work with the leadership in establishing legislative priorities and strategies. A proliferation of subcommittees means, after all, that leadership is needed in scheduling the orderly consideration of what would otherwise soon become an indigestible log-jam of pro-posals. And with his exclusive right to make appointments to the Rules Committee, the Speaker gained the influence he needed to coordinate traffic headed for the House floor. This influence was denied all Speaker O'Neill's predecessors, reaching back to the revolt against Joseph Cannon at the turn of the century.[30]

[30] For a list of the powers lost by Cannon in the year 1909–10 and not regained in the intervening years, see Guide to the Congress of the United States (Washington, D.C.: Congressional Quarterly, 1971), pp. 42–43, 134–135 and 603.

So it will not do to argue that the undeniably significant changes in the way Congress does business were at the root of difficulties that President Carter had in mobilizing Congressional support for his proposals. Congressional change was not a cause of President Carter's problems with Congress, and more generally in governing. Quite to the contrary, if anything, a hard look at Congress deepens the puzzle of Carter's difficulties. By any reasonable gauge, relations with Congress ought to have been a bright, not a dark spot in President Carter's record. And so, far from being an explanation, Congress and its difficulties with the Carter administration themselves need explaining.

Why did Mr. Carter maintain such unsatisfactory relations with Congress? One explanation, which no doubt gained popularity from the way White House sources reinforced it, was that Mr. Carter believed he owed Congress nothing and could just as effectively as dealing with Congress directly reach out over the heads of Congress and gain the support of the people for his programs.[31] It is easy to see how such delusions might arise: a byproduct of the reform of Presidential nominations has been the removal of members of Congress from the process.[32] The gaining of the nomination is now an exercise in mass persuasion; not so long ago it was far more an exercise in élite persuasion. Not until he was far into his term of office did Mr. Carter give any indication that he understood that for a Demo-

crat to govern successfully required the mobilization not merely of the faction that nominated him but also of the grand coalition that elects and reelects Democrats.

In the pattern of his cabinet appointments an observer could read President Carter's determination to neglect the broad Democratic coalition.[33] Interest groups traditionally tied to the party—most conspicuously labor unions and ethnic groups—were ignored. In office President Carter dedicated himself to high-minded administrative goals: efficiency, uniformity, reduction of waste, zero-base budgeting, comprehensive reform, and finding once and for all solutions to problems.[34] Moreover, he maintained these theoretical commitments to general and far-reaching purposes while separating himself from the piecemeal accommodations of bureaucrats and the narrowly focused desires of interest groups. This poses a fundamental problem. How is it that President Carter found it possible to gratify this theoretical preference in the harsh arena of national politics?

The most satisfactory answer to this, and to all the other puzzles of the Carter presidency I have named, is that Mr. Carter learned the wrong lessons from his long and difficult struggle to achieve the Presidential nomination. These lessons he took with him into the White House and they exercised a profound and lasting influence upon the way he sought to govern.

---

[31] Glad, op. cit., p. 420, and Johnson, op. cit., p. 22.

[32] For figures on the precipitous decline in the direct participation of members of Congress in the nomination process, see "Report of the Commission on Presidential Nomination and Party Structure," op. cit., p. 18.

[33] See Nelson W. Polsby, "Presidential Cabinet Making: Lessons for the Political System," *Political Science Quarterly* 93 (Spring 1978), pp. 15–25.

[34] A discerning article which finds these themes in President Carter's 1976 campaign speeches is Jack Knott and Aaron Wildavsky, "Jimmy Carter's Theory of Governing," *The Wilson Quarterly* 1 (Winter 1977), pp. 49–67.

III

This seems to me a bare outline of the sort of argument that would have to be made in support of the proposition that the party reforms of 1968–72 succeeded so well that they influenced the conduct of the Presidency. There is surely nothing inevitable about the way in which the Carter Presidency took shape. Nevertheless as the nomination machinery has evolved, it has been possible for candidates to emerge and be elected President without coming to terms with the need to build a broad party coalition. Nothing in the processes that screen and winnow candidates compels attentiveness to the field of forces that exists once a newly elected President is faced with the need to govern. He may never learn how to govern, or he may learn too late.

10
The Electoral College
Richard A. Watson

The method of selecting the president was among the most difficult problems faced by the delegates to the Constitutional Convention (Farrand, 1913, p. 160). A variety of plans were proposed, the two most important being selection by the Congress and direct election by the people. The first, based on the practice in most states of having the governor chosen by the legislature, had the backing of a number of delegates, including Roger Sherman of Connecticut. It was eventually discarded because of fear of legislative supremacy, and also because the delegates could not choose between state-unit voting, which favored the small states, and joint action of the two chambers, which benefited the large states with their greater voting power in the House of Representatives. Direct popular election was supported by three of the most influential members of the convention—James Madison of Virginia and James Wilson and Gouverneur Morris of Pennsylvania—but it was considered too democratic by most delegates; as George Mason of Virginia put it, "It would be as unnatural to refer the choice of a proper magistrate to the people as it would to refer a trial of colors to a blind man."

Having decided against both popular election and selection by legislative bodies, the delegates proceeded to adopt an entirely new plan put forth by one of their own committees. The proposal, which some historians believe was based on a method used in Maryland to elect its state senators (Peirce, 1968, p. 430), stated that each state legislature could choose, by whatever means it desired, electors (none of whom could be members of Congress or hold other national office) equal to its total number of senators and representatives in Congress. The individual electors would assemble at a fixed time in their respective state capitals and cast two votes each for

Source: Excerpted material reprinted with permission of Macmillan Publishing Company from *The Presidential Contest* by Richard A. Watson. New York: Macmillan Publishing Company, 1984.

president. These votes were then to be transmitted to Washington, D.C., where they would be opened and counted during a joint session of Congress. Whoever received the largest number of electoral votes would be declared president, provided a majority (one over half) had been obtained; if no candidate received a majority, the House of Representatives, voting by states (one state delegation, one vote), would choose the president from among the five candidates receiving the highest number of electoral votes. After the president was chosen, the person with the next highest number of electoral votes would be declared vice president. If two or more contenders received an equal number of electoral votes, the Senate would choose the vice president from among them.

This complicated procedure reflected certain values and assumptions about human nature that are enunciated in *The Federalist Papers*.[1] As previously mentioned, the Founders felt that the average person did not have the ability to make sound judgments about the qualifications of the various presidential candidates and that therefore this crucial decision should be left to a small group of electors—a political elite who would have both the information and the wisdom necessary to choose the best people for the nation's two highest offices. Since the electors could not be national officeholders with connections to the president, they could approach their task without bias; because they assembled separately in their respective state capitals rather than as a single body, there

would be less chance of their being corrupted or exposed to popular unrest. Moreover, since they were convened for a single purpose and would be dissolved when their task was completed, the possibility of tampering with them in advance or rewarding them with future favors was eliminated.

Philosophy shaped the presidential selection process adopted by the delegates, but so did a recognition of political factors. Lucius Wilmerding (1958, Ch. 8) suggests that some of the delegates did not expect the electors to be entirely insulated from popular preferences. They anticipated that each state's electors would cast one vote for a "native son," a locally popular political figure, and the other for a "continental character," an individual with a national reputation that members of the political elite would be aware of, even though the person might not be well known to the average citizen.[2] It was also expected that after George Washington's presidency the electoral votes would be so widely distributed that few candidates would receive a majority and, therefore, most elections (Mason estimated about nineteen out of twenty) would ultimately be decided by the House of Representatives. The electors would thus serve to "screen" (today we would say "nominate") the candidates, and the House would choose (elect) the president from among them. The large-state/small-state conflict, which was settled by the Connecticut Compromise on the composition of the Senate and House, also arose in the plan the delegates worked out for the selection of the chief executive. In the initial vote by the

---

[1] The particular selection, Number 68, is generally attributed to Alexander Hamilton. It is difficult to determine whether the views expressed represent the attitudes of a majority of the convention delegates or in particular those of Hamilton, who was more of an elitist than most of the others.

[2] Evidence for this assumption is provided by Article II, Section 1 of the Constitution, which states that at least one of the two persons for whom an elector votes must not be an inhabitant of his own state.

electors the large states had the advantage, since the number of each state's votes reflected the size of its House delegation. If no candidate got a majority, the small states were favored in the second selection, since the contingent vote was by states, not by the number of Representatives.

As was true of so many issues decided by the Founders, the method of selecting the president represented a compromise. In addition to resolving the large-state/small-state conflict just discussed, the electoral college device took into account the attitudes of states' rights advocates by allowing the state legislatures to decide how the electors should be chosen. It also held open for those who favored letting the people choose the president the possibility of the electors' actually reflecting the popular vote for the president in their state. As John Roche (1961, p. 810) has pointed out, the intermediate elector scheme gave "everybody a piece of the cake"; however, he also notes that "the future was left to cope with the problem of what to do with this Rube Goldberg mechanism" (p. 811).

Events soon nullified both the philosophical and political assumptions underlying the Founders' vision of the electoral college and forced them to cope with the "Rube Goldberg mechanism." The formation and organization of political parties in the 1790s proceeded so quickly that by the election of 1800 the electors no longer served as independent people exercising their own judgments on candidates' capabilities; instead they acted as agents of political parties and the general public. In 1800 party discipline was so complete that all Republican electors cast their two votes for Thomas Jefferson and Aaron Burr. Although it was generally understood that Jefferson was the Republican candidate for president and Burr for vice president,

the Constitution provided no means for the electors to make that distinction on their ballots. The result was a tie in electoral votes; neither won a majority, and the matter was handed to the House of Representatives for a final decision. Ironically, the Federalists, despite their major defeat in the congressional elections of 1800, still controlled the lame-duck Congress (which did not expire until March 1801) and therefore were in a position to help decide which Republicans would serve as president and vice president. At the urging of Alexander Hamilton, who disagreed with Jefferson on policy matters but distrusted Burr personally, some of the Federalist representatives eventually cast blank ballots, which permitted the Republican legislators to choose Jefferson as president on the thirty-sixth ballot.

One result of this bizarre chain of events was the ratification in 1804 of the Twelfth Amendment, stipulating that electors cast separate ballots for president and vice president. The amendment also provides that if no presidential candidate receives a majority of the electoral votes, the House of Representatives, balloting by states, will select the president by majority vote from among the three (instead of five) candidates who receive the highest number of electoral votes. If no vice presidential candidate receives a majority of electoral votes, similar procedures are to be used by the Senate in choosing between the two persons with the highest number of electoral ballots.

Other changes in the selection of the president followed; however, they did not come by way of constitutional amendments, but as political developments that fit within the legal framework of the electoral college. Thus state legislators, who were granted the power to determine how electors should be chosen, began giving this right to the general electorate. By 1832 all states except South Carolina had done so.

Another matter left to the discretion of the states—how their electoral votes would be counted—soon underwent change. Initially states were inclined to divide the vote by congressional districts; the candidate who won the plurality of the popular votes in each district received its electoral vote, and the remaining two electoral votes (representing the two Senate seats) were awarded to the statewide popular winner. However, legislatures soon began to adopt the "unit" or "general-ticket" rule, whereby all the state's electoral votes went to the candidate who received the plurality of the statewide popular vote. Two political considerations prompted this decision. The state's majority party benefited because it did not have to award any electoral votes to a minority party that might be successful in individual congressional districts. Also, this system maximized the influence of the state in the presidential election by permitting it to throw all its electoral votes to one candidate. Once some states adopted this procedure, others, wanting to maintain their political effect on the presidential contest, felt that they had to follow. As a result, by 1836 the district plan had vanished and the unit system taken its place.[3]

One other major political development of the era changed the nature of the presidential election contest: the elimination on a state-by-state basis of property qualifications for voting. By the early 1840s *white manhood suffrage* was virtually complete in the United States. Therefore the increasing democratization of American political life is reflected in the procedure for choosing the most important public official. Yet the formal

provisions of the electoral college remain the same today as they were in 1804, when the Twelfth Amendment was adopted.

Today these formal provisions provide a strange system for choosing the chief executive. Although most Americans view the system as a popular election, it really is not. When we mark our ballots for a presidential candidate, the vote is actually cast for the electors who are linked with that candidate. In mid-December the state electors associated with the winning candidate (party faithfuls who are chosen in primaries, at conventions, or by state committees) meet in their state capitals to vote. (About one-third of the states attempt by law to bind the electors to vote for the popular-vote winner, but there is some question whether such laws are constitutional.) The results of the electoral balloting are transmitted to Washington, D.C., and on the following January 6 they are counted and the outcome is announced before a joint session of the Congress by the presiding officer of the Senate, who is the incumbent vice president. If, as usually happens, one candidate receives a majority of the electoral votes, the vice president officially declares that candidate to be president, a procedure that has occasionally resulted in some ironic moments. In January 1961 Richard Nixon declared his opponent, John Kennedy, to be president; eight years later another vice president, Hubert Humphrey, declared his political opponent, this time Richard Nixon, as the chief executive!

The electoral college system as it operates today is considered by many students of presidential elections to be not only strange but also grossly unfair and even dangerous.

One major effect of the electoral college is that the election results are decided on a state-by-state basis. The fact that today all jurisdictions except Maine

---

[3] It should be noted that the district plan has been used since then from time to time by a few individual states, most recently by Maine.

utilize the unit or general-ticket system means that all the electoral votes of a state go to the candidate that wins a mere plurality of its popular votes. Thus, in effect, there are fifty separate presidential contests with a winner-take-all principle that puts a premium on a state popular vote victory, no matter how small the margin of that victory may be.

There is also a built-in bias in the electoral college that works to the advantage of certain states over others. As Lawrence Longley (1980) points out, the very small and very large states are benefited by the present system. The small states are advantaged by what he terms the "constant two" votes, that is, the fact that all states, regardless of size, receive two electoral votes that represent their two senators. This factor, plus the additional vote they receive for their House members, means that the smallest states control three electoral votes, even though their population alone might entitle them to just one or two votes. Even more advantaged, however, are the very large states; they benefit from the unit or general-ticket system because all their electoral votes are awarded to their popular vote winner. Thus in 1980 (the last election based on the 1970 census) the popular vote winner in California (Ronald Reagan) received 45 electoral votes, almost 17 percent of the total 270 electoral votes required for election.[4] (See Figure 1 for an illustration of the size of the various states based upon their number of electoral votes for the 1984 election, which will reflect changes occasioned by the 1980 census.)

Longley's analysis further shows that certain groups of voters are advantaged by their residency in the very small and very large states benefited by the electoral college system. Included are those who live in the states in the Far West and, to a lesser extent, in the East. Also benefited are voters who tend to be concentrated in urban areas, both central cities and the suburbs. These include ethnic groups but, interestingly enough, not blacks, because as Longley points out, a large number of them continue to live in the South, which as a region contains a disproportionate number of medium-sized states (those with from 4 to 14 electoral votes), which are presently disadvantaged by the electoral college system.

Finally, as Longley indicates, the electoral college benefits certain kinds of candidates. These include, of course, those of the two major parties that are in a position to win enough popular votes in a state to be awarded its electoral votes. In addition, the college advantages third party candidates who have a regional appeal sufficient to win some states, but it disadvantages those without that regional appeal. Thus in 1948 Dixiecrat presidential candidate, Strom Thurmond, carried 4 states with a total of 39 electoral votes, even though he won only about 2.4 percent of the national popular vote; that same year the Progressive candidate, Henry Wallace, with the same percentage of the nationwide vote, did not carry any state and thus received no electoral votes at all.[5]

The most serious problem relating to the election of the president continues

---

[4] The 270 votes are a majority of the total number of 538 electoral votes; this latter figure arises from the 435 electoral votes representing members of the House of Representatives, the 100 representing the senators from the 50 states, and the 3 electoral votes of the District of Columbia.

[5] It should be pointed out, however, that Wallace may have affected the results of the Truman–Dewey contest in some states; some analysts feel that Wallace's winning 8 percent of the popular vote in New York state probably drained away many votes from Truman, who lost the Empire State to Dewey by a close 45 to 46 percent popular-vote margin.

FIGURE 1 · STATE SIZE BASED ON THE NUMBER OF ELECTORAL VOTES FOR THE 1984 ELECTION

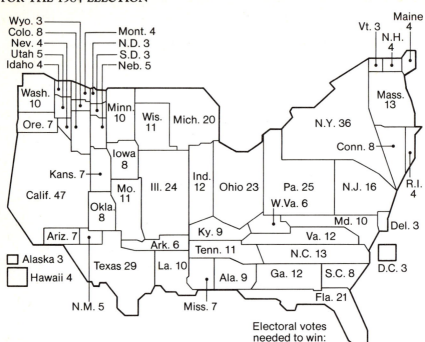

Source: Adapted from Stephen Wayne, *The Road to the White House: The Politics of Presidential Elections* (New York: St. Martin's Press, 1960), Figure 1–1, p. 14.

to be the electoral college. It was devised as a means of allowing knowledgeable elites in the various states to choose a "continential" character, but its essential form remains for an entirely different purpose—to enable rank-and-file voters to select their major public official in a nationwide popular election. The end result of this perversion is a number of abuses associated with our presidential election system.

The electoral college as it operates today violates some of the major tenets of political equality. Not every person's vote really counts the same: the influence one has in the election of the president depends on the political situation

in one's particular state. For many Americans who support a losing candidate in their state, it is as though they had not voted at all, since under the general-ticket system all the electoral votes of a state go to the candidate who wins a plurality of its popular votes. Other citizens who live in populous, politically competitive states have a premium placed on their vote because they are in a position to affect how large blocs of electoral votes are cast. Nor does the electoral college ensure that the candidate who receives the most popular votes will win the presidency: John Quincy Adams in 1824, Rutherford B. Hayes in 1876, and Benjamin Harrison in 1888 went to the White House even though they trailed their respective political opponents, Andrew Jackson, Samuel Tilden, and Grover Cleveland. In 1976 Jimmy Carter almost suffered the same fate: if some 9,000 voters in Hawaii and Ohio shifted their ballots to President Ford, the latter would have edged out Carter in the electoral college, 270–268.

The requirement that a candidate win a majority of the electoral votes or have the election decided by the House of Representatives also violates the idea of political equality. In 1948 Harry Truman defeated Thomas Dewey by over 2 million popular votes, but if some 12,000 people in California and Ohio had voted for Dewey rather than the president, the election would have been thrown into the House of Representatives for a decision. The same thing could have happened in 1960 if some 9,000 people in Illinois and Missouri had voted for Nixon instead of Kennedy, and again in 1968 if about 42,000 persons in Missouri, New Jersey, and Alaska had cast their ballots for Hubert Humphrey instead of President Nixon.[6] Permitting the House of Representatives, voting by states, to select the president of the United States is not consistent with the "one man, one vote" principle.

The 1968 election also illustrates another danger of the electoral college system: an elector need not cast his or her ballot for the candidate who wins the plurality of votes in the elector's state. Had Nixon failed to win a majority of the electoral votes, third-party candidate George Wallace would have been in a position to bargain with him. Wallace could have asked his electors (45)[7] to cast their ballots for Nixon, which would have given the latter enough electoral votes so that the election would not go into the House. Although Wallace's 45 electoral votes would not have been enough to give Humphrey a majority of the electoral votes (even if the latter had carried Missouri, New Jersey, and Alaska), the Alabama governor could have tried to bargain with Humphrey by offering to use his influence with Southern members of the House of Representatives to get them to choose him over Nixon.

These problems have created a great deal of dissatisfaction with the electoral college over the years. The sentiment for changing it has increased recently, particularly in the wake of the above-noted elections of 1948, 1960, 1968, and 1976, in which a switch in votes of a relatively few persons in key states would have sent the selection of the president into the House or immediately changed the result. Yet while there is widespread agreement on the necessity for changing the electoral college, there is marked disagreement over what form that change should take. Five basic plans have been suggested as substitutes for the present system.

The first, known as the *automatic plan*, which would make the least change in the present system, would eliminate the possibility of "faithless electors" by abolishing that office and automatically casting a state's electoral votes for the popular-vote winner in that state. If no candidate received a majority of the

---

[6] In all these elections, persons other than the two major party candidates received electoral votes; therefore, the losing candidates, Dewey, Nixon, and Humphrey, could have carried the above states and still not have had a majority of the electoral votes.

[7] Although Wallace actually earned 45 electoral votes, he received 46 because one elector in North Carolina (which went for Nixon) cast his vote for the Alabama governor. In 1960, 1972, and 1976, single electors in Oklahoma, Virginia, and Washington also did not cast their ballots for the candidates receiving the popular vote plurality in their states.

electoral votes, a joint session of Congress would choose the winner, with each representative and senator having one vote.

The second, known as the *district plan*, proposes that we return to the method that the states used early in our history (and that was recently reinstated by Maine), under which the presidential candidate who won the plurality vote in each House district would receive its electoral vote, with the remaining two electoral votes going to the statewide popular winner. If no candidate received a majority of the electoral votes, senators and representatives, sitting jointly and voting as individuals, would choose the president from the three candidates having the highest number of electoral votes. This plan's major supporters have been members of Congress and private groups from rural areas, such as the American Farm Bureau. If the plan were adopted, the crucial areas would be the politically competitive congressional districts where the two major parties traditionally divide the vote 55 to 45 percent.

A third proposal, known as the *proportional plan*, would divide each state's electoral votes in proportion to the division of the popular vote: a candidate receiving 60 percent of the popular vote in a state would receive 60 percent of its electoral votes. A plan of this nature, introduced by Republican Senator Henry Cabot Lodge of Massachusetts and Democratic Representative Ed Gossett of Texas, passed the Senate in 1950 but failed to be enacted by the House. The plan would eliminate the present advantage of the large states in being able to throw all their electoral votes to one candidate and has therefore been opposed by many of their legislators, including John Kennedy when he was a senator from Massachusetts. One possible consequence of a proportional division of the electoral votes would be a

fairly even split between the two major candidates so that neither would receive a majority; hence there would be a greater likelihood of elections being thrown into Congress for decision.[8]

The fourth plan, *direct popular election* of the president, has picked up major support in recent years, especially since its recommendation in 1967 by a special commission of the American Bar Association. In addition, it has been endorsed by such politically disparate groups as the Chamber of Commerce of the United States and the AFL-CIO. In 1969 the House passed a constitutional amendment providing that the president (and vice president) be elected by a minimum of 40 percent of the popular vote, and if no candidate received so large a vote, that a runoff be held between the two front runners. The Senate failed to pass the amendment, however, despite the efforts of its major sponsor, Birch Bayh, Democrat of Indiana. After Carter's narrow electoral college victory, Bayh introduced the same measure in 1977 but it failed to clear the Congress that year. No such proposal has subsequently been enacted.

A fifth proposal, recently advanced by a research group, the Twentieth Century Fund, is known as the *national bonus plan*. It would award the nationwide popular winner, 102 "bonus" votes (2 for each state plus 2 for the District of Columbia), these extra votes to be added to the electoral votes received under the present state-by-state system. To win the election a candidate would still have to receive a majority of the new total

---

[8] Most of the proportional plans have suggested lowering the winning electoral-vote requirement from a majority to 40 or even 35 percent to avoid the possibility of having the election go to the House. They have also proposed that, if no candidate receives the requisite proportion of electoral votes, the two houses, meeting jointly and voting as individuals, choose the president.

number of electoral votes, 640 (538 + 102), or 321 votes; if no one did, a runoff would be held between the two front runners. Thus the proposal retains the electoral college system but makes the total electoral vote better reflect the nationwide popular vote. It also allows the voters rather than the House of Representatives to make the final choice of the president if no candidate receives a majority of the electoral votes.

In my judgment, the first three plans have serious defects. The automatic plan meets only the problem of the faithless elector and ignores several others: the undue influence of the very small and very large states; the winner-take-all principle by which all the electoral votes of a state go to the candidate who wins a plurality of the popular votes, no matter how narrow that margin may be; and the possibility of a person's winning the presidency even though he trails his opponent in the nationwide popular vote. The district plan would incorporate into the selection of the president the gerrymandering abuses present in elections to the House of Representatives—manipulating of district boundaries (including noncompact, noncontiguous ones) to favor particular political interests. The proportional plan would eliminate the winner-take-all advantage presently enjoyed by the large states but would retain the small-state benefit, because all states, regardless of size, would receive two electoral votes representing their two senators; it also would not prevent the possibility of a minority-vote president.

The last two plans, the direct popular election of the president and the national bonus plan, provide the most promising prospects for reform. The former ensures what none of the other plans can: that the person receiving the largest number of nationwide popular votes will be elected president. The national bonus plan makes it much more likely than does the present system that the popular-vote winner will also obtain a majority of the electoral votes but *does not guarantee it*. However, by retaining elements of the present state-by-state electoral system, the bonus plan incorporates features of federalism that are not present under the direct popular election plan.

In my judgment, both of these plans would be far superior to the present system. Of the two, I prefer the direct popular election because it guarantees that the national popular-vote winner will be chosen as president. While the national bonus system does retain the state-by-state feature of the present system, I feel that sufficient elements of federalism are already contained in our political system through the equal representation of the states in the Senate and in the arrangement of separate state powers and political institutions whose independence is guaranteed from national encroachment by a written constitution. I see no good reason why federalism should also require that states be represented as electoral units in the selection of our only major national official.

I realize that arguments can be made against the direct popular election of the president. One is that it will jeopardize our two-party system. This fear is based on two separate considerations. One is that since the election will depend on a nationwide instead of a state-by-state vote, candidates will no longer need to deal with state political leaders; this factor would weaken these leaders, who have traditionally played such a vital role in American political parties. The second concern, expressed by Alexander Bickel (1968, pp. 14–16), is that direct popular election of the president will encourage minor political parties, freed of the necessity of actually winning state electoral votes, to run and support enough candidates to prevent either major party nominee from winning the necessary 40 percent of the nationwide popular vote. These minor parties would then be in a bargaining position to determine which of the two leading candidates will win in the runoff election.

I believe these fears are unfounded. State party leaders will continue to play a role in presidential nominations. It is even possible that they would become more active in the general election under a popular election system, since all votes that they could muster would count in their candidate's nationwide total. I also think it highly improbable that the winning party candidate would not be able to win 40 percent of the popular vote. As Longley and Braun (1975, Ch. 2) point out, in the presidential elections held since 1824, only Abraham Lincoln in 1860 failed to achieve that proportion (he won 39.8 percent of the vote).[9] If anything, the electoral college system is more vulnerable than a popular election one to minor parties, because in the United States such parties tend to be regional and thus are best able to affect the distribution of electoral votes of individual states. A recent case in point occurred in New York in 1976. If Eugene McCarthy had been able to get on the ballot there, many observers feel, he would have drained away enough popular votes from Carter to allow Ford to carry the state and, with it, enough electoral votes (41) to have won the presidential election.

Another major problem[10] of the direct election system is the effect that its adoption might have on the nomination process. As Austin Ranney (1978, p. 4) suggests, most of the arguments made against the electoral college and in favor of direct national election can also be made against national party conventions and in favor of a direct national primary. Both the electoral college and national conventions violate the one-person, one-vote rule, make it possible to choose a candidate preferred by a minority, and place artificial barriers between the people and their choice of candidates. Although Ranney does not make the point explicitly, it might well be argued that the adoption of the direct election of the president would logically lead in time to a similar enactment of a national primary law: historically, the number of electoral votes a state has has affected the size of its delegation to national conventions. Thus the selection and nomination processes have been linked, and tampering with one might influence the other.

I confess that the last possibility gives me the greatest cause for concern since I do not favor the adoption of a national primary that could further diminish the influence of political leaders in the nomination process. I do feel, however, that the two processes are distinct, and changing one does not necessarily mean altering the other. Moving from the electoral college system to a direct popular election of the president would not

---

[9] Neil Peirce (1968, p. 295) also cites figures compiled by Donald Stokes showing that in 170 gubernatorial elections occurring in the 30 most competitive states between 1952 and 1964 (these contests, of course, were based on the direct popular vote), the winning candidate never received less than 40 percent of the popular vote.

[10] I do not feel that the arguments that the electoral college is desirable because it presently amplifies close popular election outcomes (Diamond 1977,

p. 16) and that direct popular election would increase the possibility of vote fraud (Best 1975, Ch. 6) are significant. Justifying a distortion of the actual election results to create a false mandate seems curious. Moreover, the effects of vote fraud are more likely to be felt at the state than the national level; in 1976, 9,000 false ballots in Hawaii and Ohio could have reversed Carter's electoral victory, but it would have taken almost 100 times that number to have eliminated his 1.7 million nationwide popular plurality.

be nearly so radical a change as abandoning the convention system for a national presidential primary. The first alternative does not significantly change the method of selection or the people participating in the election of the president; it merely changes how the votes are *counted.* However, a change in the presidential nominating system would substitute a whole new method of selection and bring new persons into the process who are not now eligible to vote in presidential primaries. It would also involve developing some new means of choosing vice presidential candidates and of adopting the party platform. It would, it is hoped, be much more difficult to convince political decision-makers to adopt a national primary than to move to a direct popular election of the president. No broad range of groups similar to those favoring the direct election of the president has surfaced to support a national primary; the first was recently passed by the House, and the second has not been given serious consideration by Congress.

In the final analysis, the known defects of the present electoral college system must be weighed against the possible dangers that the direct election of the president might bring, particularly its potential effect on the nomination process. I would be willing to take the gamble associated with change. I cannot see the wisdom of perpetuating an electoral system that in 1976 almost permitted an appointed chief executive, who lost his only presidential election by almost 2 million votes, to remain in office for another term. Our political system, already subject to a great deal of cynicism by the American people, should not have to bear that additional threat to its legitimacy.

REFERENCES

Best, Judith (1975). *The Case Against the Direct Election of the President: A Defense of the Electoral College.* Ithaca, N.Y.: Cornell University Press.

Bickel, Alexander (1968). *The New Age of Political Reform: The Electoral College, the Convention and the Party System.* New York: Harper & Row.

Diamond, Martin (1977). *The Electoral College and the American Idea of Democracy.* Washington, D.C.: American Enterprise Institute.

Farrand, Max (1913). *The Framing of the Constitution of the United States.* New Haven: Yale University Press.

Longley, Lawrence (1980). "Minorities and the 1980 Electoral College." Paper delivered at the annual meeting of the American Political Science Association.

Longley, Lawrence, and Alan Braun (1975). *The Politics of Electoral College Reform.* New Haven: Yale University Press.

Peirce, Neal (1968). *The People's President: The Electoral College in American History and the Direct-Vote Alternative.* New York: Simon and Schuster.

Ranney, Austin (1978). *The Federalization of Presidential Primaries.* Washington, D.C.: American Enterprise Institute.

Roche, John (1961). "The Founding Fathers: A Reform Caucus in Action." *The American Political Science Review,* 55, 799–816.

Wilmerding, Lucius (1958). *The Electoral College.* New Brunswick, N.J.: Rutgers University Press.

CHAPTER IV

The Presidential Advisory System

The federal government grew rapidly during the New Deal period. Because there was little time, or, it was largely believed, inclination for planning, it featured many poorly conceived and poorly implemented organizational designs that were neither economical nor effective. These poor designs often reflected the considerable political conflict between the executive and legislative branches. Both the presidency under Roosevelt and the Congress had deliberately contributed to this problem by establishing programs in new organizations and agencies only with regard to political objectives, as opposed to taking managerial considerations into account. "This persistent struggle over organizational control would be addressed by the Brownlow Committee—which would provide the first formal assessment of government organization from a mangerial perspective."[1] Thus the objective conditions of the New Deal provided President Roosevelt with the logic for an enhanced advisory system or what had become known as the institutional presidency.[2]

The institutional presidency had its beginning with the Budget and Accounting Act of 1921 which created the Bureau of the Budget. President Woodrow Wilson had asked for additional budgetary authority earlier, but it was President Warren Harding who was able to get the bill passed and signed into law.

During his first term in office, Roosevelt had a number of White House assistants and the Bureau of the Budget to assist him in managing the growing bureaucracy.[3] Because the Bureau of the Budget was committed to the traditional principles of public administration, that is, the separation of politics from administration and neutral competence, Roosevelt moved away from relying on the bureau to borrowing personnel from departments and on bringing in selected aides through an appointments strategy.[4]

During his second term, Roosevelt decided that the time had come to develop a solid institutional foundation for presidential leadership. On March 20, 1936, Roosevelt appointed a small group of men—Louis Brownlow, Charles Merriam, and Luther Gulick—to diagnose the manpower support needs of the president and to make appropriate recommendations for the reorganization of the executive branch.

The President's Committee on Administrative Management or the Brownlow

Committee, as it was popularly known, made its report to the president in January 1937. The proposals of the committee were simple and straightforward. Essentially, they combined to say that "the president needs help" and recommended enhanced presidential instruments for management of the executive branch to include special staff persons for the president and presidential authority to redistribute and restructure executive branch agencies subject to congressional veto. The thrust of the Brownlow Report was to enlarge the presidential office, but with the intention of keeping it relatively small. Most of the Brownlow Committee's introduction to its report and its section on "the White House Staff" are reprinted here.

Roosevelt agreed with the committee's report and submitted legislation to Congress in 1938. Congress, however, killed the bill, fearing too much power in the presidency, especially in the wake of Roosevelt's efforts to "pack" the Supreme Court. After considerable acrimony and bargaining, the president resubmitted a modified reorganization bill in early 1939; on April 3 Congress passed the Reorganization Act of 1939.

Under the Reorganization Act, Roosevelt issued his famous Executive Order 8248 of September 3, 1939, establishing an Executive Office of the President and placing within it a White House Office with six personal assistants, the Bureau of the Budget (transferred from the Treasury Department), a Liaison Office for Personnel Management, a National Resources Planning Board, and an Office of Government Reports.[5] It is important to note that this strategy gave the president two types of staff: those in the White House whose services were more political and personal and those in the EOP whose responsibilities were more institutional in nature.[6] Don K. Price points out that the Executive Office of the President "remained suspect in some political circles as a New Deal innovation until it was confirmed as a regular part of the constitutional system by the Hoover Commission Report of 1947–1949."[7]

In its report, the commission called vigorously for increased managerial capacity in the Executive Office of the President through unlimited discretion over presidential organization and staff, a strengthened Bureau of the Budget, an Office of Personnel located in the EOP, and the creation of a staff secretary to provide liaison between the president and his subordinates. In addition, the commission recommended that executive branch agencies be reorganized to permit a coherent purpose for each department and better control by the president. Many of its recommendations were adopted, including the passage of the Reorganization Act of 1949 and the establishment of the Department of Health, Education, and Welfare in 1953.[8] In the main, however, the Executive Office agencies were to help the president but not to have authority in their own right. Second, the EOP staff were not to be in the chain of command between the president and the heads of executive departments. Third, department heads were to be the major line officials and political arms of the president. Finally, the great majority of employees in the institutional staff agencies were to be employed on a merit basis. It was expected that, overall, the EOP would remain a relatively small institution.[9]

Despite the assumptions of the Brownlow Committee that the EOP would remain small, it has increased considerably. Thomas Cronin notes that the EOP began with six top-level assistants in 1939 but has expanded to several offices and over 100 top-level assistants.[10] The growth of the EOP staff is said to have at least three negative consequences for the presidency:

1. It has isolated the president from reality and his critics.
2. It has weakened the cabinet by injecting itself between the president and the cabinet.
3. It is now a policy advocate in its own right.

John Hart examined the Brownlow Committee views of the presidential staff and found that, today, the staff does what Brownlow says they should not do: They display no passion for anonymity, they exercise power on their own account, many attend cabinet meetings with full cabinet status, and many control specific-issue cabinets. In short, Hart argues, the presidential staff has broken loose from Brownlow's constrained *administrative-management* model of staff.

The post-Watergate reformers who would like to curb and control the White House staff, Hart avers, subscribe to a constrained *management-politics* model which assumes that administration at the presidential level cannot be divorced from politics. However, in order to curb the power and politics of the White House staff, the post-Watergate reformers would revive cabinet government.[11] Hart is skeptical that such a revival of cabinet government is possible given the political needs of the modern presidency.

Hart concludes that the Brownlow model still has its uses: it delineates the precise requirements and conditions necessary for nonpolitical staff assistance to the president and spells out that organizational and structural constraints are not sufficient to prevent presidential assistants moving from a confined administrative role to a flexible one. Staff is now a political force and will be constrained only by political forces competing against it. The response to the powerful presidential staff, Hart says, must be political not institutional. His essay, "No Passion for Brownlow: Models of Staffing the Presidency," is reprinted here.

Article II, Section 1 of the U.S. Constitution reads in part, "The executive power shall be vested in a President of the United States of America." Article II, Section 2 reads in part,

> The President . . . may require the Opinion, in writing, of the principal Officer in each of the executive Departments, upon any subject relating to the Duties of their respective Offices . . . and he shall nominate, and by and with the Advice and Consent of the Senate, shall appoint Ambassadors, other public ministers and Consuls, Judges of the Supreme Court, and all other Officers of the United States, whose appointments are not herein otherwise provided for and which shall be established by Law: but Congress may by law vest the appointment of such inferior Officers, as they think proper, in the President alone, in the Courts of Law, or in the Heads of Departments.

A close reading of the Constitution thus reveals that executive responsibility in the American system rests exclusively with the president, that his power is unitary, not collegial. The cabinet is not mentioned in the Constitution, which refers only to executive departments, and it has no formal authority: It does not collectively make decisions. In a few words, the cabinet's institutional legitimacy derives solely from custom and function.[12]

Three executive departments were established by the First Congress in 1789: State, War, and Treasury. An attorney general was also created from the beginning but only as a legal advisor to the president, not as a department head. The attorney general's office achieved department status in 1870. In any event, by 1793 Washington had named all four officers as his cabinet.

Because the cabinet does not share constitutional authority with the president and has no collective decision-making power, each cabinet member derives his or her authority singly from the president and works with him or her directly in planning policy for the particular department.[13] The result is that only inconsequential matters are dealt with in cabinet meetings.

Members of the cabinet, because they have their own department goals to pursue, become rivals for presidential attention, for congressional budgets, and for enabling statutes. The resulting fragmentation hobbles the cabinet's capacity to view government problems from the perspective of the president's own special needs and circumstances.

This fragmentation led, in part, to the creation of the White House Office and the Executive Office of the President. Nevertheless, presidents have, until recently, selected their cabinets on the basis of traditions, trade-offs, and obligations.[14] This selection process guaranteed interest group and congressional input into the selection process, independent standing for a cabinet member who could have some clout in presidential decision-making, and, most of all, considerable political support for a president's policies. In recent years, however, changes in the party system to include state primaries over caucuses to select convention delegates, public financing and mass mailings to reduce the power of party fundraising, and the use of television to appeal to the voters over the ringing of doorbells by party workers have resulted in presidents selecting their cabinets less on the basis of clientele needs and congressional concerns and more to make the executive branch more responsive to the president.

In his "Presidential Cabinet Making: Lessons for the Political System," reprinted here, Nelson Polsby spells out three distinct strategies by which a president may select cabinet officers: clientele, specialist, and generalist. He also discusses why recent presidents have moved from an essentially clientele strategy to a generalist strategy to choose their cabinet officers.

The clientele strategy enhances what Polsby calls the "federalist model of presidential legitimacy," whereas the generalist strategy enhances the presidential model of presidential legitimacy. Polsby sees considerable danger to a president's capacity to govern effectively with the ascendancy of the presidential model. A fundamental problem, says Polsby, is its impact on the kind of cabinet a president selects and the decreased reliance of the political executives on the accumulated expertise of the permanent government.

NOTES

1. Jay M. Shafritz and Albert C. Hyde, eds., *Classics of Public Administration*, 2nd ed. (Chicago: Dorsey Press, 1987), p. 42.

2. The institutionalized presidency is a term used in reference to the Executive Office of the President to include such advisory agencies as the White House Office, the Office of Management and Budget, the Council of Economic Advisers, and the National Security Council. For a full discussion of the concept of the institutionalized presidency, see Robert S. Gilmour, "The Institutionalized Presidency: A Conceptual Clarification," in *The Presidency in Contemporary Context*, ed. Norman C. Thomas (New York: Dodd, Mead, 1975).

3. The president did have a White House staff prior to 1939. In 1933, when Franklin Roosevelt assumed office, the White House staff consisted of thirty-seven persons, nine of whom had professional rank. Three of the nine had key positions known as Secretaries to the President to handle appointments, press, and correspondence. The Bureau of the Budget, albeit in Treasury, was indirectly an arm of the president; it employed thirty-three persons. See Stephen Hess, *Organizing the Presidency* (Washington, D.C.: Brookings Institution, 1976), p. 27.

4. On this point see Terry M. Moe, "The Politicized Presidency," in *The New Directions in American Politics*, ed. John E. Chubb and Paul E. Peterson (Washington, D.C.: Brookings Institution, 1985), p. 248.

5. For the data on the organization of the Executive Office of the President since 1939, see Robert V. Goehlert and Fenton S. Martin, *The Presidency: A Research Guide* (Santa Barbara, Calif.: ABC-Clio, 1985), pp. 244–46; for the executive order itself see *Federal Register* 4 (September 12, 1939), pp. 3864–65.

6. See Hess, *Organizing the Presidency*, p. 39.

7. See Don K. Price, "The Institutional Presidency and the Unwritten Constitution," in *Problems and Prospects of Presidential Leadership in the Nineteen-Eighties*, vol. I, ed. James Sterling Young (Lanham, Md.: University Press of America, 1982), p. 58. For the report of the First Hoover Commission see Commission on Organization of the Executive Branch of the Government, *General Management of the Executive Branch* (Washington, D.C.: U.S. Government Printing Office, 1949).

8. See Jay M. Shafritz, *The Facts on File Dictionary of Public Administration* (New York: Facts on File Publications, 1985), pp. 252 and 253. See Also Edward H. Hobbs, "An Historical Review of Plans for Presidential Staffing," *Law and Contemporary Problems* 21 (Autumn 1956), pp. 683–84.

9. See Price, "The Institutional Presidency and the Unwritten Constitution."

10. See Thomas E. Cronin, "The Swelling of the Presidency," *Saturday Review* 1 (February 1973), pp. 30–36; see also Harold Relyea, "Growth and Development of the President's Office," in *The American Presidency*, ed. David Kozak and Kenneth Ciboski (Chicago: Nelson-Hall, 1984), pp. 105–42.

11. For some of the post-Watergate literature which would revive cabinet government

see Hess, *Organizing the Presidency*, pp. 154, 179, 208–16; The National Academy of Public Administration, *A Presidency for the 1980s* (Washington, D.C.: National Academy of Public Administration, 1980); and Bradley D. Nash with Milton S. Eisenhower, R. Gordon Hoxie, and William C. Spragens, *Organizing and Staffing the Presidency* (New York: Center for the Study of the Presidency, 1980).

12. See Richard Fenno, *The President's Cabinet* (New York: Vintage Books, 1959), p. 17.

13. See R. Gordon Hoxie, "The Cabinet in the American Presidency," *Presidential Studies Quarterly* 14, no. 2 (Spring 1984), especially p. 215.

14. See Hess, *Organizing the Presidency*, p. 180.

11
Report of the President's Committee on Administrative Management
Louis Brownlow, Charles E. Merriam, & Luther Gulick

THE AMERICAN EXECUTIVE

The need for action in realizing democracy was as great in 1789 as it is today. It was thus not by accident but by deliberate design that the founding fathers set the American Executive in the Constitution on a solid foundation. Sad experience under the Articles of Confederation, with an almost headless Government and committee management, had brought the American Republic to the edge of ruin. Our forefathers had broken away from hereditary government and pinned their faith on democratic rule, but they had not found a way to equip the new democracy for action. Consequently, there was grim purpose in resolutely providing for a Presidency which was to be a national office. The President is indeed the one and only national officer representative of the entire Nation. There was hesitation on the part of some timid souls in providing the President with an election independent of the Congress; with a longer term than most governors of that day; with the duty of informing the Congress as to the state of the Union and of recommending to its consideration "such Measures as he shall judge necessary and expedient"; with a two-thirds veto; with a wide power of appointment; and with military and diplomatic authority. But this reluctance was overcome in the face of need and a democratic executive established.

Equipped with these broad constitutional powers, reenforced by statute, by custom, by general consent, the American Executive must be regarded as one of the very greatest contributions made by our Nation to the development of modern democracy—a unique

Source: President's Committee on Administrative Management, *Administrative Management in the Government of the United States, January 8, 1937* (Washington, D.C.: U.S. Government Printing Office, 1937), pp. 1–6.

tion the value of which is as evident in times of stress and strain as in periods of quiet.

As an instrument for carrying out the judgment and will of the people of a nation, the American Executive occupies an enviable position among the executives of the states of the world, combining as it does the elements of popular control and the means for vigorous action and leadership—uniting stability and flexibility. The American Executive as an institution stands across the path of those who mistakenly assert that democracy must fail because it can neither decide promptly nor act vigorously.

Our Presidency unites at least three important functions. From one point of view the President is a political leader— leader of a party, leader of the Congress, leader of a people. From another point of view he is head of the Nation in the ceremonial sense of the term, the symbol of our American national solidarity. From still another point of view the President is the Chief Executive and administrator within the Federal system and service. In many types of government these duties are divided or only in part combined, but in the United States they have always been united in one and the same person whose duty it is to perform all of these tasks.

Your Committee on Administrative Management has been asked to investigate and report particularly upon the last function; namely, that of administrative management—the organization for the performance of the duties imposed upon the President in exercising the executive power vested in him by the Constitution of the United States.

IMPROVING THE MACHINERY OF GOVERNMENT

Throughout our history we have paused now and then to see how well the spirit and purpose of our Nation is working

out in the machinery of everyday government with a view to making such modifications and improvements as prudence and the spirit of progress might suggest. Our Government was the first to set up in its formal Constitution a method of amendment, and the spirit of America has been from the beginning of our history the spirit of progressive changes to meet conditions shifting perhaps more rapidly here than elsewhere in the world.

Since the Civil War, as the tasks and responsibilities of our Government have grown with the growth of the Nation in sweep and power, some notable attempts have been made to keep our administrative system abreast of the new times. The assassination of President Garfield by a disappointed office seeker aroused the Nation against the spoils system and led to the enactment of the civil-service law of 1883. We have struggled to make the principle of this law effective for half a century. The confusion in fiscal management led to the establishment of the Bureau of the Budget and the budgetary system in 1921. We still strive to realize the goal set for the Nation at that time. And, indeed, many other important forward steps have been taken.

Now we face again the problem of governmental readjustment, in part as the result of the activities of the Nation during the desperate years of the industrial depression, in part because of the very growth of the Nation, and in part because of the vexing social problems of our times. There is room for vast increase in our national productivity and there is much bitter wrong to set right in neglected ways of human life. There is need for improvement of our governmental machinery to meet new conditions and to make us ready for the problems just ahead.

Facing one of the most troubled periods in all the troubled history of mankind, we wish to set our affairs in the very best possible order to make the best use of all of our national resources and to make good our democratic claims. If America fails, the hopes and dreams of democracy over all the world go down. We shall not fail in our task and our responsibility, but we cannot live upon our laurels alone.

We seek modern types of management in National Government best fitted for the stern situations we are bound to meet, both at home and elsewhere. As to ways and means of improvement, there are naturally sincere differences of judgment and opinion, but only a treasonable design could oppose careful attention to the best and soundest practices of government available for the American Nation in the conduct of its heavy responsibilities.

THE FOUNDATIONS OF GOVERNMENTAL EFFICIENCY

The efficiency of government rests upon two factors: the consent of the governed and good management. In a democracy consent may be achieved readily, though not without some effort, as it is the cornerstone of the Constitution. Efficient management in a democracy is a factor of peculiar significance.

Administrative efficiency is not merely a matter of paper clips, time clocks, and standardized economies of motion. These are but minor gadgets. Real efficiency goes much deeper down. It must be built into the structure of a government just as it is built into a piece of machinery.

Fortunately the foundations of effective management in public affairs, no less than in private, are well known. They have emerged universally wherever men have worked together for some common purpose, whether through the state, the church, the private association, or the commercial enterprise. They have been written into constitutions, charters, and articles of incorporation, and exist as habits of work in the daily life of all organized peoples. Stated in simple terms these canons of efficiency require the establishment of a responsible and effective chief executive as the center of energy, direction, and administrative management; the systematic organization of all activities in the hands of qualified personnel under the direction of the chief executive; and to aid him in this, the establishment of appropriate managerial and staff agencies. There must also be provision for planning, a complete fiscal system, and means for holding the Executive accountable for his program.

Taken together, these principles, drawn from the experience of mankind in carrying on large-scale enterprises, may be considered as the first requirement of good management. They comprehend the subject matter of administrative management as it is dealt with in this report. Administrative management concerns itself in a democracy with the executive and his duties, with managerial and staff aides, with organization, with personnel, and with the fiscal system because these are the indispensable means of making good the popular will in a people's government.

MODERNIZING OUR GOVERNMENTAL MANAGEMENT

In the light of these canons of efficiency, what must be said of the Government of the United States today? Speaking in the broadest terms at this point, and in detail later on, we find in the American Government at the present time that the effectiveness of the Chief Executive is limited and restricted, in spite of the clear intent of the Constitution to the contrary; that the work of the Executive Branch is badly organized;

that the managerial agencies are weak and out of date; that the public service does not include its share of men and women of outstanding capacity and character; and that the fiscal and auditing systems are inadequate. These weaknesses are found at the center of our Government and involve the office of the Chief Executive itself.

While in general principle our organization of the Presidency challenges the admiration of the world, yet in equipment for administrative management our Executive Office is not fully abreast of the trend of our American times, either in business or in government. Where, for example, can there be found an executive in any way comparable upon whom so much petty work is thrown? Or who is forced to see so many persons on unrelated matters and to make so many decisions on the basis of what may be, because of the very press of work, incomplete information? How is it humanly possible to know fully the affairs and problems of over 100 separate major agencies, to say nothing of being responsible for their general direction and coordination?

These facts have been known for many years and are so well appreciated that it is not necessary for us to prove again that the President's administrative equipment is far less developed than his responsibilities, and that a major task before the American Government is to remedy this dangerous situation. What we need is not a new principle, but a modernizing of our managerial equipment.

This is not a difficult problem in itself. In fact, we have already dealt with it successfully in State governments, in city governments, and in large-scale private industry. Gov. Frank O. Lowden in Illinois, Gov. Alfred E. Smith in New York, Gov. Harry F. Byrd in Virginia, and Gov. William Tudor Gardiner in

Maine, among others, have all shown how similar problems can be dealt with in large governmental units. The Federal Government is more extensive and more complicated, but the principles of reorganization are the same. On the basis of this experience and our examination of the Executive Branch we conclude that the following steps should now be taken:

1. To deal with the greatly increased duties of executive management falling upon the President the White House staff should be expanded.

2. The managerial agencies of the Government, particularly those dealing with the budget, efficiency research, personnel, and planning, should be greatly strengthened and developed as arms of the Chief Executive.

3. The merit system should be extended upward, outward, and downward to cover all non-policy-determining posts, and the civil service system should be reorganized and opportunities established for a career system attractive to the best talent of the Nation.

4. The whole Executive Branch of the Government should be overhauled and the present 100 agencies reorganized under a few large departments in which every executive activity would find its place.

5. The fiscal system should be extensively revised in the light of the best governmental and private practice, particularly with reference to financial records, audit, and accountability of the Executive to the Congress.

These recommendations are explained and discussed in the following sections of this report.

THE PURPOSE OF REORGANIZATION

In proceeding to the reorganization of the Government it is important to keep prominently before us the ends of reorganization. Too close a view of machinery must not cut off from sight the true purpose of efficient management. Economy is not the only objective, though reorganization is the first step to savings; the elimination of duplication and contradictory policies is not the only objective, though this will follow; a simple and symmetrical organization is not the only objective, though the new organization will be simple and symmetrical; higher salaries and better jobs are not the only objectives, though these are necessary; better business methods and fiscal controls are not the only objectives, though these too are demanded. There is but one grand purpose, namely, to make democracy work today in our National Government; that is, to make our Government an up-to-date, efficient, and effective instrument for carrying out the will of the Nation. It is for this purpose that the Government needs thoroughly modern tools of management.

As a people we congratulate ourselves justly on our skill as managers—in the home, on the farm, in business big and little—and we properly expect that management in government shall be of the best American model. We do not always get these results, and we must modestly say "we count not ourselves to have attained," but there is a steady purpose in America to press forward until the practices of our governmental administration are as high as the purpose and standards of our people. We know that bad management may spoil good purposes, and that without good management democracy itself cannot achieve its highest goals.

I. THE WHITE HOUSE STAFF

In this broad program of administrative reorganization the White House itself is involved. The President needs help. His immediate staff assistance is entirely inadequate. He should be given a small number of executive assistants who would be his direct aides in dealing with the managerial agencies and administrative departments of the Government. These assistants, probably not exceeding six in number, would be in addition to his present secretaries, who deal with the public, with the Congress, and with the press and the radio. These aides would have no power to make decisions or issue instructions in their own right. They would not be interposed between the President and the heads of his departments. They would not be assistant presidents in any sense. Their function would be, when any matter was presented to the President for action affecting any part of the administrative work of the Government, to assist him in obtaining quickly and without delay all pertinent information possessed by any of the executive departments so as to guide him in making his responsible decisions; and then when decisions have been made, to assist him in seeing to it that every administrative department and agency affected is promptly informed. Their effectiveness in assisting the President will, we think, be directly proportional to their ability to discharge their functions with restraint. They would remain in the background, issue no orders, make no decisions, emit no public statements. Men for these positions should be carefully chosen by the President from within and without the Government. They should be men in whom the President has personal confidence and whose character and attitude is such that they would not attempt to exercise power on their own account.

They should be possessed of high competence, great physical vigor, and a passion for anonymity. They should be installed in the White House itself, directly accessible to the President. In the selection of these aides the President should be free to call on departments from time to time for the assignment of persons who, after a tour of duty as his aides, might be restored to their old positions.

This recommendation arises from the growing complexity and magnitude of the work of the President's office. Special assistance is needed to insure that all matters coming to the attention of the President have been examined from the over-all managerial point of view, as well as from all standpoints that would bear on policy and operation. It also would facilitate the flow upward to the President of information upon which he is to base his decisions and the flow downward from the President of the decisions once taken for execution by the department or departments affected. Thus such a staff would not only aid the President but would also be of great assistance to the several executive departments and to the managerial agencies in simplifying executive contacts, clearance, and guidance.

The President should also have at his command a contingent fund to enable him to bring in from time to time particular persons possessed of particular competency for a particular purpose and whose services he might usefully employ for short periods of time.

The President in his regular office staff should be given a greater number of positions so that he will not be compelled, as he has been compelled in the past, to use for his own necessary work persons carried on the payrolls of other departments.

If the President be thus equipped he will have but the ordinary assistance that any executive of a large establishment is afforded as a matter of course.

In addition to this assistance in his own office the President must be given direct control over and be charged with immediate responsibility for the great managerial functions of the Government which affect all of the administrative departments, as is outlined in the following sections of this report. These functions are personnel management, fiscal and organizational management, and planning management. Within these three groups may be comprehended all of the essential elements of business management.

The development of administrative management in the Federal Government requires the improvement of the administration of these managerial activities, not only by the central agencies in charge, but also by the departments and bureaus. The central agencies need to be strengthened and developed as managerial arms of the Chief Executive, better equipped to perform their central responsibilities and to provide the necessary leadership in bringing about improved practices throughout the Government.

The three managerial agencies, the Civil Service Administration, the Bureau of the Budget, and the National Resources Board should be a part and parcel of the Executive Office. Thus the President would have reporting to him directly the three managerial institutions whose work and activities would affect all of the administrative departments.

The budgets for the managerial agencies should be submitted to the Congress by the President as a part of the budget for the Executive Office. This would distinguish these agencies from the operating administrative departments of the Government, which should report to the President through the heads of departments who collectively compose his Cabinet. Such an arrangement would materially aid the President in his work of supervising the administrative agencies and would enable the Congress and the people to hold him to strict accountability for their conduct.

12
No Passion for Brownlow: Models of Staffing the Presidency
John Hart

Some forty-five years have elapsed since Franklin Roosevelt's Committee on Administrative Management under the chairmanship of Louis Brownlow gave birth to the Executive Office of the President. The famous passage in its report which argued that 'The President needs help' (President's Committee on Administrative Management 1937:5) was the origin of the vast personal staff that he has at his disposal today—a staff whose growth proceeded unchecked and largely unnoticed until the Vietnam war and the Watergate crisis began to focus attention on its pivotal position in the presidential decision making process.

The dangers inherent in the presidential staff system were recognized by some political scientists long before the crises of the last decade (for the best example see Bailey 1956:31), but generally criticism was muted by the predominance of the strong-presidential-government school of thought during the 1950s and 1960s. Since then, however, the presidential staff, particularly the White House staff, has been seen by many commentators as the major problem of the institutionalized presidency. The criticism took off with George Reedy's expo-

sure of the inner life of the White House as "a mass of intrigue, posturing, strutting, cringing and pious commitment to irrelevant windbaggery . . . designed as the perfect setting for the conspiracy of mediocrity" (1970: xiv). Reedy popularized the idea of the isolation of the president—a president cut off from the realities of the world by a palace guard staff. Other adverse consequences of the growth of the presidential staff were identified by Thomas Cronin in his seminal essay "The Swelling of the Presidency," first published in 1973. In a later revision and extension of that essay, Cronin claimed that "The swelling and continuous expansion of the presidency have reached such proportions that the president's ability to manage has been weakened rather than strengthened. Bigger has not been better. The effectiveness of presidential leadership has not been enhanced by a bloated White House staff," and he concluded by saying that "Today, the president needs help merely to manage his help" (Cronin 1975:118).

Since Reedy and Cronin, criticism of the presidential staff system has broadened in scope and has been accompanied by a variety of proposals for reform (for

Source: Politics 17, no. 2 (1982).

a sample see Hess 1976; Heineman and Hessler 1980; Rose 1980; Heclo 1981; Heclo and Salamon 1981; Nash *et al.* 1980; Szanton 1981). A recent report by a distinguished committee established by the National Academy of Public Administration has encapsulated both the concern and the criticism. Under the chairmanship of Don K. Price and Rocco Siciliano, the National Academy's panel identified eleven major shortcomings of the Executive Office of the President and came to the conclusion that:

> Viewed against the crisis of public management, the Executive Office of the President exhibits weaknesses that demand correction. Inadequacies in that office reduce the ability of our national leadership to pursue coherent and well-considered courses of action. Remedying this situation will not solve all our problems of governing. It *will* represent a large step in the right direction (National Academy of Public Administration 1980:15).

Cronin's reference back to the Brownlow report is fleeting, but nonetheless important for two reasons. Firstly, the linkage between Brownlow and the existing situation might suggest that Brownlow was in some way responsible for the uncontrolled expansion of the presidential staff which, I shall argue, is not the case. Secondly, unlike Cronin, many of the post-Watergate critics of the presidency tend to ignore the origins of the Executive Office of the President. It is, however, well worthwhile looking at what Brownlow proposed in 1937 for, although the modern presidential staff system originated there, in no way can his report be seen as a blueprint for what exists today.

THE BROWNLOW REPORT

On 22 March 1936, President Roosevelt announced the appointment of a three-man committee, composed of Louis Brownlow, Charles Merriam and Luther Gulick, to study the organization of the executive branch with a view to improving presidential management and control. The immediate impulse for reform was, as Clinton Rossiter noted, Roosevelt's "own candid recognition that an otherwise professional performance during his first term in the presidency was being severely hampered by the sheer multiplicity and complexity of his duties and by the want of effective assistance in their discharge" (Rossiter 1949:1207).

On 14 November, Brownlow and Gulick met with Roosevelt and presented him with an outline of the major recommendations of the committee, most of which he approved. With the necessary changes required by the president, the final report was handed over at the beginning of January 1937. It became the basis for the Reorganization Act of 1939 and Executive Order 8248 which finally implemented the Brownlow proposals that survived the legislative battle in Congress.

Brownlow recommended establishing the major managerial units of government, covering budgeting, planning and personnel management in an Executive Office of the President. He also proposed an extension of the merit system in the civil service, consolidation of all government agencies, including the regulatory agencies, into a few large departments and a major reform of the existing system of fiscal accountability. The report also advocated that the president be given up to six executive assistants—a proposal that was to become the basis of the immediate personal staff working for the president in what is now known as the White House Office.

The legislative passage of the Brownlow proposals was stormy and complex (see Polenberg 1966). The reorganization legislation got dragged down with Roosevelt's unpopular court-packing bill and also clashed with counter proposals from a Senate select committee on executive reorganization headed by Senator Byrd and backed by the Brookings Institution.[1] Although the legislation eventually passed the Senate by a narrow margin in March 1938, it was defeated in the House the following month. A much watered-down bill was finally signed into law on 3 April 1939. The proposal to enlarge the president's personal staff was one of the few features of the Brownlow report to survive the legislative process.

The Brownlow report was greeted with both praise and criticism from academics, professional public administrators and politicians. The director of the Public Administration Clearing House, Herbert Emmerich, called it "a beacon on the road to enlightened administration" (Emmerich 1950:90), while Edward S. Corwin thought the report was "thorough goingly Jacksonian" (1957: 96)—the strongest epithet he could muster short of "totalitarian." The academic attack on Brownlow has focussed on the committee's willingness to give Roosevelt the sort of report he wanted—a charge which Brownlow admits and stoutly defends (Brownlow 1949:106)—and on the committee's misguided adherence to the principles of rational organization (see, for example, Schaffer 1962). The political criticism at the time was more concerned with the goal of re-organization (i.e., the traditional argument about reorganization-for-economy as opposed to Roosevelt's reorganization-for-efficiency) and, specifically, with what was seen as a blatant power grab with respect to the president's proposals on the Civil Service Commission, the Auditor-General and the merit system.

The proposal to give the president additional staff assistance was not at the center of the criticism of Roosevelt's reorganization bill and, apart from some journalistic cynicism, was generally accepted from the beginning. The notion of a presidential staff was not, in itself, anything new. Roosevelt already had a press secretary, an appointments secretary and a secretary for political affairs prior to Brownlow (see Roosevelt 1982:48), and a total White House staff of thirty-seven. Brownlow merely recommended an additional six and that largely as a consequence of the other reforms proposed in the report. Furthermore, as Seligman has pointed out, personal staffs are a common characteristic of executive leadership positions in many large-scale organizations (1956: 411). It is interesting to note that although the staffing proposal was the first of the six recommendations in the report, Brownlow listed it last of all and gave it little attention when he discussed the committee's recommendations in his autobiography some years later (1958: 386).

Irrespective of how presidents have used their staffs since, Brownlow defined the role of the six assistants in careful and narrow administrative-managerial terms. The size of the staff was to be limited—"a small number of executive assistants . . . probably not exceeding six," said the report immediately following the statement that "the President needs help."[2] It then went to some lengths to spell out what the aides were not to be and were not to do. "These aides would have no power to make decisions or issue instructions in their own right," wrote Brownlow. "They would not be interposed between the President and the heads of his departments. They would not be assistant presidents in any sense." To use the parlance of the Nixon White House, these six assistants were intended to be senior 'gophers.'" Their function, according to Brownlow, was to assist the president "in obtaining quickly and without delay all pertinent information possessed by any of the executive departments so as to guide him in making his responsible decisions; and then when decisions have been made, to assist him in seeing that every administrative department or agency is promptly informed."

Brownlow placed heavy emphasis on the desired personal characteristics and qualities of the new assistants. "Their effectiveness in assisting the President will be directly proportional to their ability to discharge their functions with restraint. . . . They should be men in whom the President has personal confidence and whose character and attitude is such that they would not attempt to exercise power on their own account." Brownlow then produced the phrase he later came to regret. The presidential assistants, he said, "should be possessed of high competence, great physical vigor and a passion for anonymity."

Brownlow's ideas about the role of the White House staff emerged after discussions he had had with Tom Jones, once deputy to the head of the British cabinet secretariat, Sir Maurice Hankey. Jones had used precisely the same words to describe the attributes of Hankey and had recommended the British secretariat as the model for Brownlow to follow (see Brownlow 1949:105; Brownlow 1958:357; Karl 1963:282). Indeed, Brownlow followed it very closely. His original recommendation was that Roosevelt should establish an administrative secretariat under one executive director, rather than the corps of executive assistants that appeared in the report.[3] He had also proposed that the presidential assistants should be recruited from the executive departments, do a tour of duty in the White House and then return to their former positions. That proposal was included in the report and was analogous to the recruitment system adopted by the British Cabinet Office

where positions in the secretariat are usually held on the basis of a two-year secondment from the departments (see Wilson 1976:94).

Roosevelt himself contributed significantly to the cynical attitude of the press towards Brownlow's staffing proposal. Luther Gulick noted that when the sentence describing the attributes of the staff was first read to the president, "he burst out chuckling and laughing and read the phrase out loud a second time" (Brownlow 1958:381). And, when Roosevelt presented the report to a press conference on 11 January 1937, he told the journalists "to sharpen your pencils and take this down. This is a purple patch, one you will never forget." Brownlow commented later: "The President got a laugh, as he had expected, but he also got a chorus of various audible expressions of cynical disbelief. In fact one man spoke up and said 'There ain't no such animal' " (Brownlow 1958:397). The press had a field day with "passion for anonymity" and there was even a contest amongst journalists for a poem lampooning the proposal (Polenberg 1966:222). The staffing proposal was tainted from the start.

THE ADMINISTRATIVE-MANAGEMENT FRAMEWORK

The staff system that Brownlow proposed was neither radical nor the most important of the recommendations contained in the report. It was but one part of a new structure of centralized administrative management that represented the clearest expression of the ideas and ideals of the management movement in American public administration. Brownlow, Merriam and Gulick were squarely located in that movement; indeed Gulick was one of its foremost intellectual leaders. To them sound government meant sound management and that, in turn, implied rational organization, professionalism, specialization, accountability, a clear hierarchy of authority and, above all, a single directing executive leader at the top. The Brownlow report is steeped in the language of management. "Its language is too managerial," wrote Richard Neustadt, and suggested, as others have done, that its obsession with principles of rational management ignored politics (Neustadt 1963:855). In trying to defend himself from this charge, Brownlow only succeeded in providing his critics with more ammunition. In a letter written to Neustadt just two weeks before his death, Brownlow said: "On the contrary it (i.e., management) seems to me to be a definition of politics in the higher sense" (Brownlow 1963:864).

The presidential staff quickly broke loose from the tight constraints of Brownlow's administrative-managerial framework. By 1949 Clinton Rossiter was able to claim that "the Executive Office is no longer simply a staff that aids the President directly in the discharge of the most exacting of his major responsibilities, that of chief administrator . . . From a purely staff service it is fast developing into an agency that also formulates and co-ordinates policies at the highest level" (Rossiter 1949: 1214). Today, the presidential staff regularly does what Brownlow said it should not do. Senior staffers do make decisions and issue instructions. They do interpose themselves between the president and heads of departments. They do exercise power on their own account and tend not to discharge their functions with restraint. In recent years few have demonstrated the high competence which Brownlow said they should possess, and even fewer display any passion for anonymity. Brownlow's purple patch has long been of no consequence to the reality of life in the White House.

For much the same reason, political scientists have discarded Brownlow's model of staffing, even though the report as a whole has influenced generations of political scientists. Its notions about political management and the managerial presidency have been carried over into virtually all the presidential reform commissions since, and the most recent, the Price-Siciliano report, serves as an excellent example of the continuing impact of the Brownlow approach (see National Academy of Public Administration 1980). The staffing proposal, however, is seen to be rooted in the unrealistic assumptions of the politics-administration dichotomy and therefore serves no useful analytical purpose. Political scientists tend to share, along with Roosevelt's journalist, the view that "there ain't no such animal" and assume that no staff assistant working at the level of presidential politics could be confined to the rigid administrative role that Brownlow had envisaged.

Evidence supports that view, but that is no reason to ignore what Brownlow had to say about staffing. He may certainly have been unrealistic in his assumptions about how executive assistants would behave in office and he seems to have assumed a morality of public administration that was either short-lived or never existed in the United States. Yet his administrative-managerial model of staffing still has its uses for it delineates the precise requirements and conditions necessary for non-political staff assistance to the president. Brownlow's message to the present-day observer of the Executive Office of the President is that organizational and structural constraints are not sufficient to prevent presidential assistants moving from a confined administrative role to a flexible political one. The constraints can only be self-constraint on the part of the president and the staff itself. Nothing but their own attitudes, characters and perception of their role would prevent those inside the White House assuming the political prominence that has characterized the Executive Office of the President and, more particularly, the White House Office, for the last two decades.

In some ways Brownlow stands as the only serious contribution to the problem of controlling presidential staff in the American system of government. Implicit in his model is the notion that the presidential staff has the potential to upset established power relationships within the executive branch and, to prevent it doing so, requires a tightly constrained role along the lines that he has prescribed. To do otherwise would result in a new political force within the executive branch. Brownlow would lead us to believe there is no half-way house. A president has the choice of either a purely administrative staff or a political one.

THE MANAGEMENT-POLITICS FRAMEWORK

In the post-Watergate era, the literature on the American presidency has placed considerable emphasis on the need to curb and control the role of the White House staff. But, unlike Brownlow, most reformists seem to have found some half-way house. They have settled on a "managerial" role for the staff. The difference, however, is that, whereas Brownlow devised the White House staff to service the management structure in the Executive branch, the post-Watergate reformers tend to see the staff as management itself. They envisage the staff as managers of the political process, or "facilitators" or "honest-brokers" to use the terms adopted in the Price-Siciliano report (National Academy of Public Administration 1980:16). "Process management" is the latest key phrase for students of the presidency (see, for example, Heclo and Salamon 1981:83).

What the post-Watergate reformists have created is an alternative model of presidential staff functions. If Brownlow's proposals can be seen as a constrained administrative-management model, then the post-Watergate schemes might best be described as a constrained management-politics model. Brownlow thought that the proper functions of the White House staff had to be defined rigidly and checked by the self-constraint of the staff and the President. The post-Watergate reformists reject that notion. They are, quite rightly, unwilling to accept the idea that administration at presidential level can be divorced from politics, or that presidential staff can be relied upon to curb their worst excesses. In its place, they have constructed a model which recognises that White House aides are political animals and will, inevitably, perform political functions, but must be constrained by external forces.

The constraint, in this case, is the return to a more traditional system of what is sometimes labelled "collegial leadership." This can take many forms, but, in essence, most proposals involve restoring some measure of authority and power to heads of departments individually or the cabinet collectively. Stephen Hess, perhaps the best-known proponent of this view, believes that "Cabinet officers collectively define what is double in the executive branch" (1976:207) and thinks that cabinet members should be the primary spokesmen for the administration, with the cabinet as the focal point of the White House system (1976: 214). Graham Allison has advanced the idea of an executive committee of the cabinet (he calls it "Ex-Cab") as the chief forum for decisions on all major policy issues (1980:45). The multiple advocacy theorists also emphasize that their new advisory system must operate at the cabinet level (see, for example,

Porter 1980:214). The Price-Siciliano report shies away from the notion of the cabinet as a collective decision making body, but does argue a case for a much closer and confidential relationship between the president and the heads of executive departments (National Academy of Public Administration 1980:37).

The cabinet is such a crucial element in the constrained management-politics model of presidential staffing that one might justifiably argue that the model has been designed primarily to reflect the desire of the post-Watergate reformists to revive cabinet government, or some variation of it, rather than to make sense of how the White House staff actually fits into the American system of government. This current revival of the cabinet is a reflection of the post-Watergate concern with the problem of presidential accountability, but, in trying to devise suitable methods of making the presidency accountable, political scientists have operated firmly within the existing constitutional framework in order not to weaken the president permanently and irreparably (see Hart 1977: 49–53). Thus there is not much left for them to play with but the Cabinet.

There is nothing remarkable about reviving ideas of cabinet government. American political scientists have done so each time the U.S. experiences a "crisis of government" and the response to Watergate is no exception. Recent presidents have also indulged themselves in constitutional illiteracy and made election campaign promises about cabinet government, although the reality of power always takes them in the opposite direction (see, for example, Bonafede 1978). Nor is this the first occasion that reform of the cabinet has been tied to the operation of the presidential staff system (see Fenno 1959:263–66). What is different about the post-Watergate re-

vival of the cabinet is that the cabinet is now envisaged as a constraint mechanism on the presidential staff.

Fenno's classic study, written at the end of the 1950s, has long been the conventional wisdom on the political weakness of the American cabinet (see Fenno 1959) and that alone should be enough to cast doubt upon the ability of the cabinet and its members to check the presidential staff. However, since the Eisenhower presidency, a number of developments which have adversely affected the position and status of the cabinet need to be noted. These developments can only be summarized here but, together, they make the idealistic vision of many of the post-Watergate reformists appear that much further removed from reality.

To begin with, there was a decline in the use of the cabinet after Eisenhower left the White House. He averaged 28.75 meetings per year during his term of office (Porter 1981:210) and no president since has matched that. Instead, his successors have shown a propensity to use what might be called specific issue cabinets, such as the National Security Council, the Domestic Council (under Nixon), the Economic Policy Board (under Ford) and the six cabinet councils set up by Reagan. In specific issue cabinets, the presidential staff are more or less in control. They attend in significant numbers, they can, like Kissinger and Ehrlichman, dominate to the exclusion of heads of departments, or they can simply play the role of process managers which does go a long way towards undercutting the departmental representatives. The specific issue cabinets have acted as a great leveller of status between the presidential staff and the members of cabinet.

Furthermore, when the cabinet does meet, it is now accepted practice for presidential aides to attend, and some attend as full members in their own right. Until Reagan, the practice of conferring cabinet rank on presidential staff was confined to a few senior positions in the Executive Office of the President, such as the director of the Office of Management and Budget, but the appointment of Edwin Meese was the first occasion that an assistant from within the White House Office itself had been elevated to the cabinet.

Neither can one overlook the permanent damage done to the status of the cabinet collectively, and heads of departments individually, during the Nixon presidency. Nixon established a system of White House staff acting as policy overlords to whom department heads were explicitly subordinate (see Hart 1974) and although the plan was foiled by Nixon's Watergate problems and broke down completely when Haldeman and Ehrlichman were forced to resign in April 1973, its significance cannot be overestimated. Whereas other presidents have ignored their cabinet while maintaining a pretence, Nixon managed to destroy any symbolic meaning that the cabinet may have had.

Another indication of the pre-eminence of the White House staff is the number of occasions that department heads have lost their battles with the president's men. The fate of Walter Hickel, William Rogers, Joseph Califano and Cyrus Vance provide ample evidence of just how ineffective department heads are likely to be as a check on the White House staff.

The so-called "reformed" presidential nomination process and changes in campaign finance law have also had a profound effect on White House-cabinet relations. Those changes have weakened the ties between President and party and made it less likely that cabinet recruitment will be based on rewards to important power-brokers. There are no power-

brokers in presidential nomination contests today. Thus, as a result of candidate-centered election campaigns, the political base of individual cabinet members can only be even weaker than it has been in the past.

But even more important is that the reformed nomination process has made the White House staff more politically significant and visible than ever before. It has also been, I would suggest, a major contributory factor to the expansion of the White House staff during the last decade. In essence, the new nomination and election arrangements have made it imperative for presidents to keep a larger, more complex and more professional campaign team intact throughout their terms of office. Incumbent presidents can no longer rely on automatic renomination after four years. The process is far too open for that. The re-election campaign must begin not long after the president initially enters the White House and, as a result, the White House Office in particular has become a dumping ground for election campaign specialists. One doubts, for example, that the jobs and titles President Carter bestowed upon White House staffers Peter Bourne (special assistant for Health issues), Joseph Aragon (Ombudsman?) and Greg Schneiders (special assistant for Special Projects) had much to do with the day-to-day work of the White House Office. All three had played a prominent part in Carter's campaign successes. To borrow David Mayhew's term and apply it to the presidency, the "electoral connection" looms large in the work of the White House staff (Mayhew 1974:6), and as electoral, rather than governing, considerations become more relevant, so the cabinet collectively and department heads individually will become even more remote.

Finally, contrary to Brownlow's blueprint, senior White House staff have, during the last decade, become policy advocates in their own right. Policy advocacy is now expected from them and this function is too well-entrenched in the White House Office to reverse. The Price-Siciliano report goes as far as to urge an increased policy advocacy role for presidential staff, even though it admits that this is not entirely compatible with the constrained management-politics model it proposes (National Academy of Public Administration 1980:38). Yet, as long as the White House staff persists in policy advocacy, tension between it and the line departments and agencies is inevitable. In this conflict the White House staff appears to have the upper hand; indeed its power has been strengthened by the very fact of its importance in the policy making process. Much of that power has been gained at the expense of the cabinet, which makes the idea of the cabinet as a check on the staff much less credible than ever before.

A POLITICAL APPROACH TO PRESIDENTIAL STAFFING

For all these reasons, it is unrealistic to build the cabinet and department secretaries into a model of White House staff functions, as many of the post-Watergate reformists have done. To do so is to establish one structure as a constraint on another without any delineation of the functions those structures are meant to perform, and therein lies an important difference between Brownlow and contemporary critics of the presidency. Brownlow did, at least, attempt to delineate functions. The crucial question the post-Watergate reformists fail to come to terms with is where does the political power of the White House staff stop. Presumably, that is intended to be at the discretion of the Cabinet, but such an arrangement could hardly

apply to a political force that already has power and pre-eminence over the cabinet.

It is even more irrelevant when one considers the reason why the White House staff has grown in power and status at the expense of the cabinet. It is simply because presidents have wanted it that way and, whatever the short-comings of the presidential staff system, postwar presidents have believed that it has served their purpose better than the cabinet system. Ultimately, the president's purpose will prevail and post-Watergate reformists seem to ignore the obvious truth spelt out by Fenno that:

> It cannot be emphasized too often that the governing factor in reorganizing the Presidency must be the President himself. He can hardly blink the need for co-ordination, but it is difficult to see how he can be forced to be assisted in any particular way by the general will of political scientists if he does not so wish. Assuming his preeminent leadership position, he is free to find help in co-ordination wherever and from whomever he wishes. The most elaborate scheme is no stronger than the base of presidential acquiescence on which it must rest (1959:268).

Why then do political scientists show such a determination to stick with notions of cabinet government and particularly to invoke it as a check on the White House staff? Two reasons have already been suggested in this paper. Firstly, the tradition of this type of reformism in the literature is a long-established one going back to Woodrow Wilson (although many commentators seem to forget how quickly he disposed of the idea) and, secondly, because the American system of government offers little else to build upon. The alternative to the many variations on cabinet government would be reform involving substantial constitutional change and that is always a non-starter.

A third reason might be offered in terms of the reluctance on the part of political scientists to accept how the White House staff has been able to dislodge the cabinet. The cabinet was an historical accident in the American scheme of things. The Founding Fathers clearly intended the Senate to be the body that should perform cabinet-type functions as a dispenser of collective advice and support to the president (see Corwin 1957:82 and Wilson 1908:138). However, as Corwin notes, the Senate was unwilling to perform this function and the Founding Fathers' conception "broke down the first time it was put to the test" (1957:209). The president then turned to the cabinet to fill the vacuum. Of course, the cabinet has no constitutional basis and little independent political power. Cabinet-type functions may well be rooted in the American political system, but certainly not the institution or structure to perform those functions. The cabinet survived for as long as it did only because it had never encountered any challenge or opposition to its authority, but that challenge has now been mounted successfully by a powerful White House staff performing a political role that was originally assigned to the Senate.

If the constrained management-politics model is unrealistic, so too is a return to Brownlow. But Brownlow's importance is that he makes the alternative to his constrained administrative model clear. One must surely recognize that the presidential staff now constitutes a political force that competes for power in the pluralistic and fragmented system of American government. As such its activities and power will only be constrained by political forces competing against it and a more realistic approach to reform must search for a political rather than an institutional response. The post-Watergate reformists have simply not come to terms with Brownlow's purple patch.

NOTES

1. On the differences between the Brookings and Brownlow proposals see Schaffer 1962.
2. All quotations are from chapter one of the Report.
3. Roosevelt rejected this recommendation prior to the publication of the Report because he was strongly opposed to the idea of a chief-of-staff in the White House. See Brownlow 1949:106 and Polenberg 1966:20.

REFERENCES

Allison, Graham (1980), "An Executive Cabinet," *Society*, 17, 5:41–47.

Bailey, Stephen K. (1956), "The President and His Political Executives," *Annals of the American Academy of Political and Social Science*, 307:24–36.

Bonafede, Dom (1978), "Carter Sounds Retreat from Cabinet Government," *The National Journal*, 10, 46:1852–57.

Brownlow, Louis (1949), *The President and the Presidency*, Public Administration Service, Chicago.

⸻ (1958), *A Passion for Anonymity*, University of Chicago Press, Chicago.

⸻ (1963), Letter from Louis Brownlow to Richard Neustadt, *American Political Science Review*, LVII, 4:863–64.

Corwin, Edward S. (1957), *The President: Office and Powers*, Fourth Revised Edition, New York University Press, New York.

Cronin, Thomas E. (1975), *The State of the Presidency*, Little Brown, Boston.

Emmerich, Herbert (1950), *Essays on Federal Reorganization*, University of Alabama Press, Alabama.

Fenno, Richard (1959), *The President's Cabinet*, Harvard University Press, Cambridge.

Hart, John (1974), "Executive Reorganization in the USA and the Growth of Presidential Power," *Public Administration*, 52:179–91.

⸻ (1977, "Presidential Power Revisited," *Political Studies*, XXV, 1:48–61.

Heclo, Hugh (1981), "The Changing Presidential Office," in Meltsner, Arnold J. (ed.), *Politics and the Oval Office*, Institute for Contemporary Studies, San Francisco.

Heclo, Hugh and Salamon, Lester M. (1981), *The Illusion of Presidential Government*, Westview Press, Boulder.

Heineman, Ben W. and Hessler, Curtis A. (1980), *Memorandum for the President: A Strategic*

Approach to Domestic Affairs in the 1980s, Random House, New York.

Hess, Stephen (1976), *Organizing the Presidency*, The Brookings Institution, Washington, D.C.

Karl, Barry D. (1963), *Executive Reorganization and Reform in the New Deal*, Harvard University Press, Cambridge.

Mayhew, David P. (1974), *Congress: The Electoral Connection*, Yale University Press, New Haven, CT.

Nash, Bradley D. *et al* (1980), *Organizing and Staffing the Presidency*, Center for the Study of the Presidency, New York.

National Academy of Public Administration (1980), *A Presidency for the 1980s*, National Academy of Public Administration, Washington, D.C.

Neustadt, Richard E. (1963), "Approaches to Staffing the Presidency: Notes on FDR and JFK," *American Political Science Review*, LVII, 4:855–63.

Polenberg, Richard (1966), *Reorganizing Roosevelt's Government*, Harvard University Press, Cambridge.

Porter, Roger B. (1980), *Presidential Decision Making: The Economic Policy Board*, Cambridge University Press, Cambridge.

Porter, Roger B. (1981), "The President and Economic Policy: Problems, Patterns and Alternatives," in Heclo, H. and Salamon, L. M. (eds), *The Illusion of Presidential Government*, Westview Press, Boulder.

President's Committee on Administrative Management (1937), *Administrative Management in the Government of the United States*, Government Printing Office, Washington, D.C.

Reedy, George E. (1970), *The Twilight of the Presidency*, World, New York.

Roosevelt, James (1982), "Staffing My Father's Presidency: A Personal Reminiscence," *Presidential Studies Quarterly*, XII, 1:48–49.

Rose, Richard (1980), "Government Against Sub-Governments: A European Perspective on Washington," in Rose, Richard and Suleiman, Ezra N. (eds), *Presidents and Prime Ministers*, American Enterprise Institute, Washington, D.C.

Rossiter, Clinton (1949), "The Constitutional Significance of the Executive Office of the President," *American Political Science Review*, XLIII, 6:1206–17.

Schaffer, B. B. (1962), "Brownlow or Brookings: Approaches to the Improvement of the Machinery of Government," *New Zealand Journal of Public Administration*, 24, 2:37–63.

Seligman, Lester (1956), "Presidential Leadership: The Inner Circle and Institutionalization," *Journal of Politics*, 18, 3:410–26.

Szanton, Peter L. (1981), "Reconstructing the Presidency," in Meltsner, Arnold J. (ed.), *Politics and the Oval Office*, Institute for Contemporary Studies, San Francisco.

Wilson, Harold (1976), *The Governance of Britain*, Weidenfeld & Nicolson and Michael Joseph, London.

Wilson, Woodrow (1908), *Constitutional Government in the United States*, Columbia University Press, New York.

13
Presidential Cabinet Making: Lessons for the Political System

Nelson W. Polsby

When a new president picks his cabinet, he gives observers the first set of solid clues about the kind of president he intends to be. Like the campaign rhetoric that preceded the election, a cabinet can be read in a variety of ways. And it affords only fragmentary evidence about how the president plans to run the government. But fragmentary though it is, it is hard to ignore, for

Source: Political Science Quarterly 93, no. 1 (Spring 1978).

TABLE 1 · DECLINE IN PRIOR POLITICAL EXPERIENCE OF NIXON CABINET

	President Nixon's First Cabinet	President Nixon's Last Cabinet
Prior political experience extensive (includes office-holding)	William Rogers, State Melvin Laird, Defense Walter Hickel, Interior Maurice Stans, Commerce Robert Finch, HEW George Romney, HUD John Volpe, DOT	Rogers C. B. Morton, Interior Earl Butz, Agriculture
Prior political experience moderate (active in state party, etc.)	Winton Blount, Post Office	Frederick Dent, Commerce Peter Brennan, Labor Caspar Weinberger, HEW
Prior political experience slight	David Kennedy, Treasury John Mitchell, Attorney General Clifford Hardin, Agriculture George Shultz, Labor	Henry Kissinger, State William Simon, Treasury James Schlesinger, Defense Robert Bork, Acting Attorney General James Lynn, HUD Claude Brinegar, DOT

unlike campaign promises, cabinet members do not disappear into thin air. Rather they take office, and, to a greater or lesser extent, actually administer the affairs of the nation. President Eisenhower's appointment of "nine millionaires and a plumber" gave quite a good forecast of the sort of presidency General Eisenhower wanted to have. When John Kennedy became president he struck a dominant theme of self-consciously moving beyond his own range of personal acquaintance to form a governing coalition. Likewise, his appointment of his brother as attorney general telegraphed a strong desire to keep close control of the civil rights issue.

It is possible to see in Richard Nixon's cabinet appointments a mirror of his emerging view of the role of the president vis-à-vis the rest of the government (Table 1).[1] After beginning with a politically diverse and reasonably visible group of cabinet appointees, Nixon increasingly appointed people of no independent public standing, and with no constituencies of their own. In this shift we can read a distinctive change in the fundamental political goals and strategies of the Nixon administration, from

[1] For much of my discussion of President Nixon I draw on Nelson W. Polsby, *Congress and the Presidency*, 3rd ed. (Englewood Cliffs, N.J.: Prentice-Hall, 1976), pp. 48–61. An account of President Nixon's administrative goals and activities early in his presidency is contained in Rowland Evans and Robert Novak, *Nixon in the White House: The Frustration of Power* (New York: Random House, 1971). It is useful to contrast Richard Nathan's *The Plot That Failed: Nixon and the Administrative Presidency* (New York: John Wiley & Sons, 1975), written from the perspective of later events.

early concerns with constituency-building to a later preoccupation, once Mr. Nixon's reelection was assured, with centralizing power in the White House.

His first Secretary of Labor, George Shultz, though unknown to begin with, became an early star of the Nixon cabinet owing to his intelligence and quick grasp of problems. The first major reorganization of the Nixon presidency shuffled Mr. Shultz into the White House. He was replaced by an efficient but unprepossessing figure, who in turn gave way to a maverick union official who was not even on speaking terms with the head of the AFL-CIO. This was not the only example of a movement away from clientele concerns in cabinet-building, and toward the accretion of managerial capacity within the White House. Seemingly by design the access of large and significant interest groups to the president was greatly hampered. Labor, education, the scientific community, conservationists, and others felt not merely that Richard Nixon was a president whose goals differed from their own, but also that their voices were being choked off, that they were shut out from the White House, and that their case was being rejected before it was heard.

If Mr. Nixon's administrative appointments were designed to be increasingly weak in their capacity to carry messages from interest groups to policy makers, they were far stronger in executing orders, in providing a conduit from the various arms of the White House executive apparatus—the Domestic Council, the Office of Management and Budget, the National Security Advisor—to the levels of policy execution.

Centralization of policy making was only half of the latter-day Nixon administrative program. The other half consisted in systematic attempts to place functionaries who can only be described

as political commissars in the bureaus and departments, agents whose job it was to report to the White House on the political fidelity of the executive branch.[2]

Presidents and their political appointees have frequently puzzled over the problem of making the enormous apparatus of the executive branch responsive to their will. The legitimacy of this claim is based upon the results of the last election; presumably a president is elected and makes appointments, at least in part, to carry out his promises with respect to the future conduct of public policy, and the necessary instruments of that conduct reside in the unelected agencies of the executive branch.

Executive agencies, however, are seldom merely passive receptacles awaiting the expression of a president's preferences. Rather, they embody a number of persistent characteristics that from time to time may serve as bases for conflict with presidential directives. Expertise, for example, a body of doctrine about the right way to do things, may well thwart responsiveness to presidential demands. So may alliances between agency executives and the congressional committees that have program and budgetary oversight over them. So may strong ties between agencies and the client groups they serve.

The case of a conservative president facing an executive agency doing what he believes is liberal work is especially poignant. The very existence of a bureaucratic apparatus attests to the

[2] Additional discussion of the Nixon administration's public administration problems, together with documentation, is contained in Subcommittee on Manpower and Civil Service, *Final Report on Violations and Abuses of Merit Principles in Federal Employment* (Washington, D.C.: U.S. House of Representatives Committee on Post Office and Civil Service, December 30, 1976).

lization, at some time in the past, of a majority of sufficient strength to pass a law and put an agency to work. So long as the law is on the books, and Congress appropriates funds for it, the agency presumably has some sort of legitimate standing. Yet it was precisely the existence of all too many of these federal activities, all staffed with people devoted to the execution of their programs, that Mr. Nixon wished to question. In one famous instance—the case of the Office of Economic Opportunity—President Nixon attempted prematurely to put an agency out of business altogether.

In each of Mr. Nixon's attempts to organize and reorganize the executive branch an observer can note efforts to cope with a hostile administrative environment. Revenue sharing, of course, had the effect of removing responsibilities altogether from federal agencies. Nixon vastly strengthened the White House National Security Office and invented a domestic counterpart in the Domestic Council, politicized and reincarnated the Bureau of the Budget as the Office of Management and Budget, and drastically increased the number of employees in the Executive Office of the President. Just as the storm of Watergate was breaking over his head he proposed a reorganization plan that would have officially denied cabinet officers direct access to the president by shifting supervisory power to four "supercabinet" officers who were supposed to act as special presidential assistants.

It would be wrong to suggest that these devices for limiting the power of government departments, agencies, and bureaus were in some sense illicit. For the most part they were not, yet they reflect a distinctive view of executive branch legitimacy, and its monopoly in the presidential office. Mr. Nixon's view, it became clear, was that his re-

election by a landslide not only provided him with a special entitlement to pursue his vision of public policy, but it had, in addition, delegitimized all other possible actors in the system.[3]

The last pre-Watergate months of the Nixon presidency saw neither the first, nor necessarily the last manifestation of the view that the president is the source of all the legitimacy on which the entire government runs. Indeed, even today the theory is widely held that because the president is the only elected official in the executive branch, political choice by the executive branch is legitimized only insofar as it can be plausibly seen to have been radiated down from a presidential choice or order or preference.

Sustenance for this view comes from a conception of the American political system in which legitimacy arises chiefly, if not exclusively, from the electoral process. If the direct results of elections are the only source of political legitimacy, then it follows that the legitimacy of the entire executive branch rests, like a gigantic inverted pyramid, on the quadrennial election of the single member of that branch who is elected, the president. Given this view of the situation, there can be no grounds upon which hierarchical subordinates of the president might legitimately act to thwart, undermine, modify or attenuate the will of the president in public policy, once it is expressed.

This is not, to be sure, the only view of political legitimacy in the executive branch. Another view is that while the

---

[3] This evidently included even the Congress that had been elected at the same time, as contemporary accounts suggest. See, e.g., Elizabeth Drew, *Washington Journal* (New York: Random House, 1975). A more thorough elaboration of this theme is contained in Nelson W. Polsby, *Political Promises* (New York: Oxford University Press, 1974), pp. 6–14.

electoral process does provide a very significant measure of legitimacy for the acts of government, this process by itself is neither adequate to the task of providing accountability, nor the only process actually provided for in the constitutional design and in the pattern of American politics that has since evolved in harmony with the spirit of the constitution. In contrast with this hierarchical, pyramidal, or plebiscitary view of legitimacy there is the check-and-balance, or multiprocess view favored, for example, by the authors of *The Federalist*, in which the rightful power to govern is spread about in the government, and even, in a more modern version, extended to interest groups and other mobilizers and organizers of popular desires, needs, and sentiments.

PATTERNS OF CABINET BUILDING

It is interesting to contemplate the extent to which a presidency-centered view of the proper relations between the presidency and the bureaucracy has survived intact through Watergate, and indeed through the fashionable disparagement of the Imperial Presidency. This is reflected in President Carter's address to the problem of cabinet building and what appears, consequently, to be his initial perspective on the permanent government.

There are at least three alternative ways to build a cabinet. First alternative: Each of the great departments of government serves clientele in the population at large. Each has custody over a range of policies that tend to affect some Americans more sharply than others. Thus one strategy for building a cabinet is to enter into a coalition with the client groups of departments by finding appointees who already have extensive rela-

tionships or political alliances with relevant client groups. A cabinet in which this alternative is dominant is one heavy with former political office holders. Characteristic pathologies of this mode of cabinet building are those associated with complaints from interest groups whose competitors have succeeded where they have not. So, for example, conservationist groups may feel exceedingly well served by the appointment of one sort of secretary of interior. Grazers, miners, and loggers may feel quite differently about the matter. The impossibility of accommodating all the groups into which Americans may legally divide themselves for the purpose of pursuing a common interest is, no doubt, one of the facts of life that give vitality to a competitive two-party system at the presidential level. The fact that ungratified client groups can form alliances with the out-party helps to legitimize the inevitable choices that presidents must make among contending interests, since a mechanism is thereby provided for limiting the extent to which any incumbent may ignore the strongly held preferences of large numbers of citizens, without suffering electoral defeat.

Second alternative: A president may choose a cabinet of substantive specialists. Specialists possess technical mastery, knowledge of programmatic alternatives, and understanding of particular governmental agencies and their impact on the world. Where the client-oriented cabinet member seeks to do his job to the satisfaction of the customers, the specialist cabinet member's internal definition of success depends on satisfying the norms of performance that the agency itself (and its associated professions) generate. The characteristic pathology of this sort of leadership is given constant publicity in the folklore of government: domination by arbitrary, insensitive, "faceless" bureaucrats, the proliferation of meaningless paperwork, the manufacture of red tape, the triumph of custodial convenience over sensitivity to clientele or to political realities.

The basis for the political legitimacy of specialist leadership is far less thoroughly understood. It is, I think, fundamentally historical. At some point in the past, after all, someone had to pass a valid law for a bureaucracy to exist at all. Presumably, government agencies are administering programs because once upon a time a law-making majority, a winning coalition of president and Congress, produced a mandate for them to do so. In the absence of some equally valid set of more recent instructions, government agencies have a right to presume that what they are doing is proper and legitimate. Specialist leadership rests its legitimacy heavily upon the notion that effective, knowledgeable pursuit of an agency's mission constitutes a continuing renewal of its historic mandate.

Those cabinet members who are connected neither to clientele nor to agencies suggest a third alternative: the generalist executive. The generalist may be responsive primarily to the siren song of his own career and thus be connected to, and ultimately reachable by, nothing at all. Or he may respond with particular alertness to presidential priorities, plans and orders, to be, in fact, the president's ambassador both to the agency and to its client groups. I have already given the familiar rationale for a cabinet dominated by executives of this stripe. In such executives the presumption is strongest that the president, being the most recently elected chief executive, is entitled by his electoral mandate to command the resources of the executive branch, and to shape its programs according to his desires. The careers of generalist executives are tied not to in-terest groups or to agencies but to the president personally or, alternatively, to law firms, public relations firms, universities, or other organizations that provide technical skills and services to a variety of clients not closely clustered around some narrow set of policies.

Until the beginnings of President Nixon's second term, I think it is fair to say that observers were not excessively attentive to the possibility of pathology in the execution of this alternative. Yet presidents, it now appears, can ask members of the executive branch to do illegal and immoral acts, acts not contemplated and in some cases prohibited by the charters of the agencies involved. A president or his agent can seek to close down activities provided for by law, or can repudiate political alliances with devastating future effects for himself, his party and/or his successors. Generalist executives, without expertise or independent standing with interest groups, are presumably best situated to further, and least well situated to resist, these tendencies when they appear.

THE CARTER STRATEGY

No president, to my knowledge, has in modern times pursued a pure strategy of cabinet building. In all cases of which I am aware the strategy has been mixed. Yet the character of the mixture at any given time has been instructive about the claims to legitimacy made by each incumbent administration. So it is, also, with President Carter, as a consideration of the seventeen cabinet-level appointments of his administration will illustrate (Table 2).

In matters of foreign and defense policy, with the very important exception of Ambassador Andrew Young, Mr. Carter has sought subject-matter experts. Cyrus Vance, Zbigniew Brzezinski, Michael Blumenthal, and Harold Brown have all put in substantial time

TABLE 2 · PRESIDENT CARTER'S CABINET, 1977

	Specialists	Client-Oriented	Generalists
State	Vance[a]		
Treasury	Blumenthal[b]		
Defense	Brown[b]		
Justice			Bell[a]
Interior		Andrus	
Agriculture		Bergland	
Commerce			Kreps[b]
Labor	Marshall?	Marshall (?)[b]	
HEW			Califano[a]
HUD			Harris[a]
Transportation			Adams[a]
Energy			Schlesinger (?)[b]
CIA			Turner
Nat'l Sec. Council	Brzezinski[b]		
OMB			Lance
Council Econ. Ad.	Schultze[b]		
UN Ambassador			Young

[a] Lawyers.
[b] Ph.D.s.

working for the government on problems associated with the departments they now head.

In two, arguably three, instances, Mr. Carter has picked cabinet members who can be considered ambassadors from interest group constituencies. One, Bob Bergland, supervises the interest group constituency closest to Mr. Carter's own in private life, agriculture. The second is Cecil Andrus, who brings to the Interior Department close ties with environmentalist groups. I am less certain that Ray Marshall of the Labor Department belongs to this category, rather than to that of the specialists.

Nine of the remaining ten appointees are, I believe, best understood as generalists. An academic labor economist serves as the chief link between the business community and the administration.

Three lawyers—all Washington D.C. careerists in one way or another who might well have been interchanged—head the main urban departments. There are, as many people have observed, three Georgians, presumably presidential ambassadors par excellence, among the top seventeen, seven Ph.D.'s, five in economics, one each in physics and political science, and five lawyers.

It is not their high level of education, however, that observers have fastened upon in noting the odd resemblance between this Democratic cabinet and the Republican cabinets that immediately preceded it. Rather it is the curious neutrality of the Carter cabinet toward the vast stew of interest groups, both within and outside the government, that make up the traditional Democratic coalition.

Of Carter's top seventeen appointees, how many reach into the constituencies suggested by the old New Deal voting coalition? Where are the representatives of the Irish, the Polish, the Jews, the Italians? The cities? The labor unions? Where, indeed, are the long-time active members of the Democratic party? Not wholly absent, to be sure. But hard to find.

CAUSES OF THE CARTER STRATEGY

I have observed that in his second term Richard Nixon chose generalists for his cabinet because of his abiding hostility to the central purposes of the permanent government, as he saw them. Although he ran as an outsider to Washington politics, there is no reason to suppose that Mr. Carter shares Mr. Nixon's deep and clear-cut doctrinal disagreement with so many of the routine purposes of government. And so rather than seek the key to Mr. Carter's leadership of the government in programmatic antagonism, I believe we must look elsewhere for clues.

A first, and extremely interesting, examination of the problem has been made by Jack Knott and Aaron Wildavsky in a close analysis of President Carter as a theorist of public administration.[4] They observe, quite correctly, that President Carter has repeatedly expressed strong views about the proper procedures for making public policy. Very much in a tradition of political engineering that stretches back through Herbert Hoover to Woodrow Wilson, Mr. Carter has emphasized the importance of design considerations in the making and the presentation of public policy, and has deemphasized the content of those policies.

The goals President Carter has stressed are essentially administrative in character: simplification, reduction of duplication, and the establishment of uniformity, predictability and long-range goals. He is a believer in comprehensive reform, in finding once-and-for-all solutions to problems.

Theoretical commitment on the part of President Carter to general and far-reaching purposes, and a desire to separate himself from the piecemeal accommodations of bureaucrats and the narrowly focused desires of interest groups is thus surely part of the answer. But this answer poses a still more fundamental problem: how is it that President Carter finds it possible to gratify this theoretical preference in the harsh arena of national politics?

The answer to this, I believe, can be found in the political conditions which made Jimmy Carter's nomination and election possible. Mr. Carter is the latest in a lengthening line of political leaders—of which Mr. Nixon was also an example—who have made the claim that their electoral victories conferred on them a legitimacy direct from the people, unmediated by special interest groups, or by parochial considerations.

For a Democratic politician, the basis of this claim must rest in large measure on the transformation of the rules for nominating presidents that has occurred over the past decade.[5] Finance through mass mailings and through the public purse has replaced the mobilization of well-heeled backers and the seeking of alliances with interest groups. The stim-

---

[4] Jack Knott and Aaron Wildavsky, "Jimmy Carter's Theory of Governing," *The Wilson Quarterly* I (Winter, 1977): 49–67.

[5] A review of some of these in the context of electoral strategies rather than, as here, in relation to their consequences for public administration, can be found in Nelson W. Polsby and Aaron Wildavsky, *Presidential Elections*, 4th ed. (New York: Scribner's, 1976).

ulation of coverage by the mass media and the building of a state-by-state personal organization have replaced the cultivation of party regulars and state and local leaders. Primary elections, not party wheelhorses, select the vast preponderance of convention delegates.

So the idea of a party as a coalition of interests bound together by the hope of electing a president is becoming an anachronism. Party is increasingly a label for masses of individual voters who pick among alternate candidates as they would among any alternatives marketed by the mass media.

The mass news media in America, though highly professional and in many respects unideological, are nevertheless far from random in their behavior. Thus while interest groups that are mobilized in traditional ways, around the economic interests or the communal ties of their members, have diminished in their political influence, the fortunes of other interest groups have been greatly enhanced because the managers of the mass media have decided to smile upon them. Prominent among these are groups embodying what the media recognize as disinterested rectitude, such as Common Cause and the Ralph Nader organizations, and those speaking for interests widely perceived as disadvantaged, such as black, Hispanic-American, and militant women's groups.

This is not the place to argue about the realities behind the palpable gains and losses that have befallen these groups in national politics. Black leaders, like labor leaders, surely mobilize large numbers of Democratic voters, and so might have fared equally as well under the old dispensation as under the new, whereas militant women are far less successful in demonstrating that they deliver the votes even of most voting women. What is significant for our purposes is the fact that in a straight fight

between leaders of militant women's groups and black groups on the one hand and, on the other, the leadership of the dominant faction of the U.S. labor movement over who was to become secretary of labor, as we all know it was labor that lost.[6] This, it seems to me, is as emblematic as anything could possibly be of the disestablishment of one sort of interest group in the Democratic party and the establishment of another.

CONSEQUENCES FOR PUBLIC ADMINISTRATION

The consequences of this change in the actual workings of government are difficult to fathom. Two, at least, are worth considering, and both suggest an increase in certain sorts of stress in the political system.

The forces that have revolutionized the presidential nominating process have been far slower to affect the thousand-odd nominating processes that supply us with candidates for Congress and the Senate. Congress is a greatly changed place from the way it was even a decade ago. The previously moribund Democratic caucus is now available as an instrument of majority will, when that will exists. But the mobilization of that will is by no means the unchallenged prerogative of the president. If anything, Congress is today better equipped than ever to find its own way into the intricacies of policy and to arrive at its own balancing of forces and priorities.

So long as elections in America are of the staggered, prescheduled, nonreferendum type, and so long as nominations to Congress are decentralized,

---

[6] See, e.g. Robert G. Kaiser, "Women Lobby for Role in Carter Camp," *Washington Post*, December 5, 1976; "Dunlop Backers Call Him Victim of Unfair Action," *New York Times*, January 26, 1977.

it will be difficult if not impossible for presidents to attempt to persuade Congress by going over its head to the people. This is no substitute for the hard, frustrating, and frequently unavailing work of doing business directly with Congress. Because of the divergence that currently exists in the ways in which presidents and Congress mobilize their electorates and arrive in office, we may be entering an era in which tensions and misunderstandings between president and Congress increase—even when both are controlled by what is labeled the same party.

Another possible consequence of the modern trend in cabinet building is a decrease in the reliance of political executives on the accumulated expertise of the permanent government. When the top of the government was dominated by client-oriented political executives, bureaucrats supplied technical information, policy analysis, know-how and knowledge of programs. Some specialist cabinet officers are going to ignore the agencies they head altogether; others, specialist and generalist alike, will undertake policy evaluation and analysis in competition with their own agencies. Much of this activity, no doubt, will result in vastly improved understanding of policy alternatives at the top of government. Moreover, it can create over the long term a corps of people outside the government who can contribute to the analysis and understanding of policy.

But as the comparative advantage of being inside a bureaucracy begins to diminish, the caliber of the agency begins to slip. As agencies begin to view their nominal superiors as competitors in the supply of what they supply best, expertise, the incentives to firm up other sorts of alliances—with clientele, with Congress—increase. Thus over the long run, without strenuous effort and much good will on both sides, the cure can aggravate symptoms of the disease.

TWO MODELS OF LEGITIMACY

I have suggested that there are currently two models available through which the claims of the executive branch to be properly vested with power can be validated. One model, the presidential model, sees the conferring of legitimacy in our political system as having the following four features. It is episodic, in that it relies heavily upon the results of the last presidential election, which for present purposes is treated as conferring a sweeping mandate. It is concentrated, in that only the winner of the last election receives the endorsement that is claimed to be at the root of the government's entitlement to act. It is direct, in that it is claimed that permission to act is conferred by voters not on the basis of their interest group or other affiliations but through their individual, atomized responses to a particular candidate and his presentation of self during the campaign. Finally, it reflects the present or the recent past, in that only the results of the most recent presidential election are taken into account in determining the right of an official to claim the acquiescence of citizens in public policy.

A view of legitimacy in our political system alternative to the presidential model is contained in what readers will recognize as a Federalist model since it draws upon the thoughts of the earliest expositors of the logic underlying the original design of the U.S. Constitution. In this view, legitimacy is conferred not episodically, as in elections, but continuously. It is conferred both through elections and through continuous interaction among decision makers. Legitimacy is not concentrated, but dispersed, to elected officials, to appointed officials, to career bureaucrats. It is based not on election alone but on organizational norms such as seniority, or selection by congressional caucus, or neutral competence or expertise. In the Federalist view, legitimacy is conferred not just directly, but also indirectly; for example, by the workings of the congressional committee system. Finally, not the present alone, but the more distant past as well is invoked by the Federalist model, which explicitly recognizes the legitimacy of law-making majorities of the earlier eras that produced programs that persist to this day and are embodied in the agencies of government.

The ascendancy of the presidential model has evidently survived the discredited presidency of Richard Nixon, who militantly espoused it. This has come about because of sweeping changes in the politics of presidential nomination that have fundamentally affected the ways in which interest groups must be mobilized and attended to by a Democratic presidential nominee, although it is less certain that the same vector of forces applies to a Democratic president. Nevertheless, the record of this new approach can be read in President Carter's cabinet choices.

CHAPTER V

Executive-Bureaucratic Relations

Edie Goldenberg has written that "neither the Constitution itself nor other documents of the period provide a cogent description of the place of the bureaucracy in our system; instead, the role of the civil servant was left to evolve without explicit guidance." According to Goldenberg, "most of the democratic theories see some form of political control as essential, but . . . one of the many questions left unanswered in the Constitution is how much control over the civil service should be exerted by whom. . . . Since the early days of the Republic, opinions have diverged on whether . . . the executive departments should be wholly subordinate to the president."[1] But for good or ill, the structural design of the American national government makes complete subordination a virtual impossibility.

Despite the fact that the president is the chief executive, his control over the bureaucracy is less than complete because legislated authority from the Congress flows to cabinet officers and agency heads and not to the president for his further delegation.[2] The idea that the president should manage the bureaucracy has been favored by public administration experts and by every president since the turn of the century, but especially since the creation of the Brownlow Committee.[3] Francis E. Rourke writes that there are three directions a president can take to control or manage the bureaucracy.[4] First, a president can fill the top echelons of executive departments and agencies with political appointees who will advocate presidential interests in agency decisions. This strategy was utilized by President Eisenhower. Second, the president can assign White House staff to monitor the work of executive departments and agencies. This strategy has been utilized increasingly by all the presidents since the New Deal. Finally, the president can create structures in the White House that will take the lead in areas of policy important to him. Rourke adds that the utilization of this last strategy reflects maximum presidential dissatisfaction with the performance of various bureaucratic agencies. This tactic was utilized by Presidents Lyndon Johnson and Richard Nixon.[5]

The articles that follow address the president's ability to manage the bureaucracy. Both spell out the opportunities and limitations of the appointments strategy.

Richard Cole and David Caputo assess the extent of President Nixon's success in gaining some degree of managerial control over the executive bureaucracy through the manipulation of the civil service personnel system. The authors point out that to maximize White House managerial control over the bureaucracy, the Nixon presidency set as its goal the placement of trusted appointees in positions to directly manage key elements of the bureaucracy.

The Nixon administration called on Frederick Malek to prepare a comprehensive plan to guide executives in the hiring and placement of personnel.[6] The net result of the Malek proposals, codified in the "Malek Manual," was to develop the process by which vacancies were identified or by which senior officials would be encouraged to vacate positions. Then candidates supportive of the administration's positions would be referred to appropriate political contacts in the departments and agencies.

Based on survey data, Cole and Caputo found that Republicans were more likely to be selected to top career positions during the Nixon administration and that career executives calling themselves "independents" were more likely to side with the Republicans to support Nixon's policies and goals. Cole and Caputo conclude that because a large number of career executives identify themselves as independents, independent career executives may provide a president with considerable bureaucratic support. Their analysis, "Presidential Control of the Senior Service: Assessing the Strategies of the Nixon Years," is reprinted here.

President Reagan is the most recent in the line of presidents from the New Deal to the present who have sought to manage the bureaucracy in the pursuit of their administrations' goals. Reagan, however, went further than his predecessors in the use of the appointments strategy to gain leverage over the bureaucracy. The primary qualification of a Reagan appointee to the government was that he or she shared the president's values and would vigorously pursue them.

Laurence E. Lynn, Jr., is concerned with how effective Reagan's appointments strategy has been. To evaluate this question, Lynn analyzes the accomplishments of five Reagan appointees to subcabinet positions according to the changes in the activities of each agency that appeared to be associated with the management actions of the appointees, the facts that appeared to account for each appointee's performance, and the consequences for agency performance of the change brought about by each appointee.

Preliminary to his assessment, Lynn spelled out what he saw to be the core activities of an organization, that is, those directly related to fulfilling an organization's purposes, to include promulgating standards, awarding grants and contracts, and making benefits payments. Each appointee's influence was defined in terms of his success in making lasting changes in the core activity consistent with President Reagan's policy preferences.

Lynn went on to postulate that the effectiveness of an appointee in changing an organization's core activity depended on four factors: the appointed executive's managerial skills and experience, the executive's personality, the nature of the opportunity he or she had to accomplish change, and the appointee's design, that is, the expressed goals for the behavior or performance of the agency and the means for accomplishing those goals.

After selecting the agencies and determining the appointees to be interviewed, Lynn found that some change attributable to these five Reagan appointees occurred in each of their respective agencies; however, the extent and character of change varied widely among them. Lynn argues that the Reagan administration is changing the government, but not nearly so much as it might have had these officials been more capable: The appointment of like-minded subordinates is a plus, but insufficient for maximum policy achievement if separated from an emphasis on managerial ability. Lynn's analysis, "The Reagan Administration and the Renitent Bureaucracy," is reprinted here.

NOTES

1. Edie N. Goldenberg, "The Permanent Government in an Era of Retrenchment and Redirection," in *The Reagan Presidency and the Governing of America,* ed. Lester M. Salamon and Michael S. Lund (Washington, D.C.: Urban Institute Press, 1985), p. 383.

2. See Charles Bingham, "To Be or Not to Be," *The Bureaucrats* 13, no. 4 (Winter 1984–85), p. 18.

3. For an excellent study of the efforts to augment the managerial capacity of the presidency before Brownlow, see Peri E. Arnold, "Executive Reorganization and the Origins of the Managerial Presidency," *Polity* 13, no. 4 (1981), pp. 568–99. For the most recent presidential commission study citing a need for the president as manager, see the *Report of the President's Private Sector Survey on Cost Control,* delivered to the President on January 12, 1984, by J. Peter Grace, Chairman and Chief Executive Officer of W. R. Grace and Co. Parenthetically, the Watergate abuses did stem the enthusiasm of public administration experts at least temporarily for the managerial presidency; on this point, see Richard P. Nathan, "The Administrative Presidency," *Public Interest* 44 (Summer 1976), p. 52.

4. Francis E. Rourke, "The Presidency and the Bureaucracy: Strategic Alternatives," in *The Presidency and the Political System,* ed. Michael Nelson (Washington, D.C.: C.Q. Press, 1984), pp. 340–41.

5. For another view of the strategies President Johnson utilized to manage the bureaucracy, see James E. Anderson, "Presidential Management of the Bureaucracy and the Johnson Presidency: A Preliminary Exploration," *Congress and the Presidency* 11, no. 4 (1984), pp. 137–64.

6. White House Personnel Manual, Subcommittee on Manpower and Civil Service, 1976, pp. 573–686. For "Malek Manual" excerpts, see Frank J. Thompson, *Classics of Public Personnel Policy* (Oak Park, Ill.: Moore Publishing, 1979), pp. 159–87.

14
Presidential Control of the Senior Civil Service: Assessing the Strategies of the Nixon Years

Richard L. Cole & David A. Caputo

Contemporary American presidents have often expressed suspicion, frustration, and dismay in dealing with a bureaucracy which may seem aloof, unconcerned, and at times even hostile to them and their policies. President Franklin D. Roosevelt, in commenting on bureaucratic recalcitrance, once said, "The Treasury and the State Departments put together are nothing compared with the Navy. To change anything in the Navy is like punching a feather bed. You punch it with your right and you punch it with your left until you are finally exhausted, and then you find the damn bed just as it was before you started punching" (Neustadt, 1960, p. 42). President Kennedy once described the State Department as a "bowl of jelly. It's got all those people over there who are constantly smiling. I think we need to smile less and be tougher" (Schlesinger, 1965, p. 406).

Of course, the contemporary president, in attempting to shape and direct public policy, cannot ignore the bureaucracy. The classic model of a neutral bureaucracy responsible only for deciding the best means for implementing policy whose goals and objectives have been established by elected political officials has long been replaced by one recognizing, as Hugh Heclo says (1977, p. 21), the role of the civil servant as "an

unexpected and insecurely placed [full] participant to the original grand design of American government." Francis Rourke (1969) has impressively documented the impact the bureaucracy can have on public policy because of its ability to mobilize political support and to apply or deny bureaucratic expertise. Rourke (1969, pp. 50–51) finds that "no aspect of the growth of bureaucratic power in this country has been more important than the steady expansion in the scope of administrative discretion. . . . Today all bureaucratic decisions [have] some implications for policy."

Modern presidents, then, must be attentive to bureaucratic influences on policy directions and it is clear that all recent presidents have attempted some measure of bureaucratic control and direction. The literature on this aspect of the presidency (Koenig, 1968; Rourke, 1969; Thomas, 1970) usually distinguishes between the more formal and hierarchical approach utilized by President Eisenhower with the less structured, more open and competitive approach used by a Roosevelt or a Kennedy.

As the literature on the Nixon presidency grows in volume, it is becoming evident that Nixon's struggle with the bureaucracy was more intense, more calculated, and far more political in design

Source: American Political Science Review 73 (June 1979). Reprinted with the permission of the authors and the American Political Science Association.

than that of any previous president. Heclo (1977, p. 75) has concluded that "old-time government officials might have thought that they knew that management meant business-like administration, but [under Nixon] they were in for an awakening." Richard Nathan, himself an early member of Nixon's staff, states (1975, pp. 7–8) that with the full deployment of the Nixon strategy, "no longer would the Cabinet be composed of men with national standing in their own right. . . . The President's men—trusted lieutenants, tied closely to Richard Nixon and without national reputations of their own—were to be placed in direct charge of the major program bureaucracies of domestic government. . . ."

This article examines one of the means by which the Nixon White House attempted to gain such a high degree of management control over the bureaucracy—the manipulation of the civil service personnel system. This article's *principal goal is to document the extent to which the administration actually succeeded in its design.*[1] How did the Nixon White House propose to assume, in the words of Nathan (1975), "control of the machinery of domestic government" and to what degree was the Nixon administration able to change the partisan nature and issue positions of the seniormost levels of the career civil service through its personnel policies? These are important questions for an understanding of domestic policy making and im-

plementation in the Nixon years (and by implication, for future presidents).

PRESIDENT NIXON AND THE FEDERAL BUREAUCRACY

The Nixon White House held conflicting views of the federal bureaucracy. On the one hand, the bureaucracy was seen as a major (often hostile) impediment; on the other hand, it was seen as a potentially powerful political resource. As an impediment, the bureaucracy was believed by the Nixon White House to be staffed at the senior-most levels with personnel remaining loyal and dedicated to the programs and goals of the previous Democratic presidents. Nixon assumed the presidency at a time when the federal bureaucracy was experiencing substantial growth. In the early 1960s, the number of federal employees was 2.4 million; by 1970 the number had increased to about 3 million. Furthermore, the departments and agencies concerned with domestic social issues recorded the most rapid staff and budgetary growth rates during this period. The Department of Housing and Urban Development (including its pre-cabinet status) grew by 37 percent and Health, Education and Welfare expanded by 75 percent. In addition, the federal budget grew from approximately $92 billion in 1960 to nearly $200 billion by 1970. While the proportion of the federal budget allocated to defense decreased during the sixties, the proportion (*Statistical Abstract*, pp. 236, 306, 221) allocated in such areas as health and education continued to rise. Thus, the Democratic administrations preceding the Nixon years were characterized by growth in the federal bureaucracy and expansion in budgetary outlays, and this growth was most noticeable in domestic social service programs.

Possibly influenced by these develop-

---

[1] Of course, personnel management is but one tactic a president may employ in attempting to gain some measure of bureaucratic control. Nixon, himself, also attempted to impose extensive reorganization programs which also would have brought greater presidential management. We focus here, however, on personnel management—the dominant theme of Nixon's management efforts.

ments, one Nixon aide indicated in 1969 (Nathan, p. 82) that "the White House was surrounded" by powerful bureaucratic interests opposed to the president's program. President Nixon himself (1971a, p. 167) referred to his opponents in the bureaucracy as "dug-in establishmentarians fighting for the status quo," and stated further that, "I think it is repugnant to the American system that only the bureaucratic elite at the top of the heap in Washington [believes it] knows what is best for the people. . . ." (Nixon, 1971b, p. 463).

These tensions between the White House and the bureaucracy were intensified as many of Nixon's new federalism proposals called for a reduction in the number of categorical grants, the consolidation of various departments and agencies, and the elimination of federal bureaucratic discretion in various grant-in-aid programs. Not only was the bureaucracy viewed as consisting largely of personnel selected during and remaining loyal to previous administrations, but also many of Nixon's domestic programs could be interpreted as posing direct threats to the careers of many federal executives. It is not surprising that the White House anticipated negative reactions from the senior bureaucracy and, indeed, Joel Aberbach and Bert Rockman (1976) have shown that in 1970 a sizeable proportion of the senior bureaucratic corps was ideologically and politically opposed to the Republican White House.

The Nixon White House, on the other hand, also viewed the bureaucracy as a potential source of power and influence. In his first term, Nixon had been largely unsuccessful in generating much support within Congress for his domestic program—a program he equated to a "New American Revolution." In Nixon's first term his general revenue sharing program had died in Congress (although, of course, the program did eventually pass), the Congress refused to consider his massive departmental reorganization scheme, none of his special revenue sharing programs appeared close to passage, and his major welfare reform proposal had not been reported out of the Congress. Frustrated by Congress' early reluctance to act swiftly and positively on his major domestic legislative programs, Nixon sought to maximize managerial control over the bureaucracy and both isolate it from Congress and make it more responsive to the White House. Thus began a concerted strategy of placing top aides and loyalists in key civil service positions. Richard Nathan (1969, pp. 8, 61–62) best describes the process when he says that following Nixon's first term the "traditional legislative strategy" of governing was abandoned and a "fundamentally different approach" was adopted. The new strategy, according to Nathan, would be designed "to *take over* the bureaucracy and *take on* Congress." This would be accomplished, says Nathan, by placing Nixon's "own trusted appointees in positions to manage directly key elements of the bureaucracy. . . . The new appointees would be the President's men. The bureaucracy would report to them; they would be held accountable."

Nathan (1969, pp. 59–95) labeled these bureaucratic strategies the "administrative presidency"; Heclo (1977, p. 75) calls it "management control." Regardless of labels, the design was to achieve such control over the top policy-making positions in the bureaucracy that policy and program objectives denied the White House by the legislative process could be achieved through bureaucratic decision making.

These two views of the bureaucracy, often confusing and contradictory, were paramount in shaping Nixon's strategy of dealing with the bureaucracy. On the one hand the Nixon White House viewed senior career executives as, on the whole, disloyal. On the other hand, the bureaucracy was seen as a possible alternative for achieving at least some of the domestic objectives which Congress appeared unwilling to approve. Redirecting the basic values and the partisan orientations of the senior levels of the bureaucracy became a major focus of the Nixon White House and the major political strategy used to pursue the administration's domestic policies. This, indeed, did represent a fundamental shift in bureaucratic-presidential relations and requires careful examination both in terms of its impact on the federal bureaucracy and on domestic policy making in general.

DATA AND METHODOLOGY

Data for this analysis are drawn from several sources, but primarily from a larger survey of top federal officials conducted by the authors in 1976. Since we are concerned with assessing the role of the bureaucracy in domestic policy making—most specifically, "new federalism"—our sample is drawn from the federal departments and agencies most concerned with domestic affairs, thus excluding administrators from the Defense and State Departments.[2] To be eligible for the sample, officials in these domestic agencies had to occupy positions with full-time policy and program responsibility (eliminating those concerned only with internal duties such as personnel, employee safety, information matters, and the like). From a list

supplied by the U.S. Civil Service Commission indicating the names, titles, and positions of every supergrade official, we identified the top political and career executives within each agency. These were those specified as political executives or career civil servants holding "supergrade" status (GS 16–18, or the equivalent). Of the 524 so identified, 195 completed and returned our survey. Table 1 presents the agency by agency response rate—ranging from a high of 50 percent from HUD to a low of 24 percent from Treasury—and also examines the representativeness of the sample. As Table 1 indicates, Agriculture and HUD are slightly over-represented and Treasury is slightly under-represented but, overall, the response sample is quite representative of the totality. Additional measures of sample representativeness are discussed below.

Much of the following analysis will compare political appointees with career executives at the supergrade level. However, the distinction between political and career executives is not precise and experts often disagree as to the boundaries defining each. According to Heclo (1977, pp. 36–55), the proportion of top executives classified as political appointees can range from 9 to 25 percent depending on how various positions are defined and classified.

Following Aberbach and Rockman, we classified all positions as either career executives or political appointees. Schedule A, B, and C positions are considered political appointees for purposes of this study as are all Noncareer Executive Assignments (NEAs). This classification follows the usually accepted nature of these appointments. Since we are specifically interested in the extent to which the attitudes and characteristics of those federal bureaucrats selected during the Nixon administration differ from those selected during prior adminis-

---

[2] We received replies from each of the following departments and agencies included in our study: Agriculture, Commerce, HEW, HUD, Interior, Justice, Labor, Transportation, Treasury, GSA, FCC, FEA, FPC, FTC, ICC, SEC, SBA, VA, EPA.

TABLE 1 • SAMPLE AND RESPONSE RATE

Department	Percent of Universe	Response Rate	Percent of Sample
Agriculture	8%	46%	10%
Commerce	8	40	9
HEW	13	33	12
HUD	8	50	12
Interior	13	34	12
Justice	7	31	6
Labor	4	41	5
Transportation	4	27	3
Treasury	6	24	4
All others	28	33	27
Totals	99%		100%

Note: Here and throughout this study percentages may not total 100% because of rounding.
Source: Data compiled from authors' survey of senior federal officials conducted in 1976.

trations, the following analysis often will divide the sample accordingly.

The Aberbach and Rockman study (1976) conducted shortly after Nixon's first term began provides an important comparative perspective for this study. Students of the federal bureaucracy will recognize our sample as closely paralleling theirs. In fact, our pool of departments and agencies is identical to theirs except that OEO had been disbanded by 1976 and the Federal Energy Administration and the Environmental Protection Agency had recently been established. These changes, of course, are reflected in our sample.[3]

[3] The Aberbach and Rockman study is also useful in assessing the representativeness of our sample. Aberbach and Rockman limited their sample to 144 possible respondents and interviewed 126. Our universe was larger since we attempted to include everyone meeting the above described sample requirements. Our return rate was lower than their rate of completed interviews; however, our response samples are similar in many respects. For example, Aberbach and Rockman found that 17 percent of the career executives in their sample identified with the Republican party; 16 percent in our sample identified with the Republicans.

Aberbach and Rockman were concerned with questions of general political and issue orientations (such as attitudes toward more or less government service), while our survey probed the attitudes of those senior officials to a number of specific domestic programs proposed and supported by President Nixon. Still, the two surveys provide an excellent opportunity to make "before and after" inferences about the

Sixty-six percent of the political appointees in the Aberbach and Rockman sample identified with the Republican party, as opposed to 61 percent in our sample. Twenty-nine percent of all those in the Aberbach and Rockman study were associated with a social service agency (HEW, HUD, OEO), while 23 percent of our sample were associated with either HEW or HUD. Since our studies are separated by six years, some variance is expected; yet in those areas where comparisons are possible, the response samples are quite similar. Another indication of the representativeness of our sample is that 29 percent of our respondents are classified as political appointees, a figure which deviates from the population by only 4 percent according to Heclo when he employed the classification scheme used in this study.

Nixon bureaucracy. The Aberbach and Rockman study indicated the general orientations of the top bureaucrats during the first two years of the Nixon administration, while our data permit an examination of attitudes toward a number of specific issues at the conclusion of the Nixon years. If the Heclo/Nathan thesis is correct—that Nixon was determined to achieve a degree of bureaucratic politicization—this should be reflected in these comparisons.

We are not suggesting that Aberbach's and Rockman's measure of general orientations toward the provision of government services is equivalent to our measures of attitudes toward specific policies and programs, but we do believe that useful comparisons are possible. To the extent that philosophical differences exist between a president and the bureaucracy, these differences become politically important when considered in the context of specific programs and policies. A president has little to fear from a bureaucracy ideologically opposed to the president's philosophy yet willing to accommodate without reservation policy directives in pursuit of that philosophy. If we demonstrate that such accommodation has taken place either within the population of supergrade officials as a whole or some subpopulation of that group, we believe this has political significance. Still, we readily acknowledge that we cannot demonstrate in this study whether changes have taken place in the general attitudes of senior executives toward government provision of services.

RESHAPING THE BUREAUCRACY

Seeking out and placing in key leadership positions individuals philosophically compatible with and loyal to Nixon became the stated objectives of the White House personnel organiza-

tion. A management study prepared by the White House (Subcommittee on Manpower and Civil Service, 1976, p. 411) stated that "management control could be achieved by attracting the best qualified individuals who are philosophically compatible and loyal to the President, placing them in leadership positions, motivating them by recognizing and promoting outstanding performance, and removing any whose performance is poor. At the same time, personnel decisions should be made and announced to maximize political benefit and minimize political loss." The question arises as to how was it that the White House hoped to successfully influence the selection of top officials—a process supposedly protected from such incursions by a host of civil service rules and regulations. Obviously, the president was expected to name his own appointees to important political positions. However, the essence of the administrative presidency argument is that White House influence was to extend to the career civil service as well. How was this to be accomplished?

Shortly after Nixon's first term began, the White House Personnel Operation (WHPO), headed by Harry Flemming, was established to identify and place individuals in presidential appointment positions. Following initial White House dissatisfaction with Flemming's direction of the personnel operation, Frederick Malek (then HEW Deputy Under-Secretary) was asked to study the Flemming operation and to prepare a comprehensive plan. Ultimately the White House Personnel Manual (Subcommittee on Manpower and Civil Service, 1976, pp. 573–686) was produced and distributed in November, 1972 as a guide to executives in the hiring and placement of personnel.

The first step, according to the manual (Subcommittee on Manpower, 1976, p. 163), was to identify vacancies.

When no vacancies existed, some would have to be created and the manual provided specific guidelines for this activity:

> There are several techniques which can be designed, carefully, to skirt around the [difficult problem of firing established career executives]. You simply call an individual in and tell him he is no longer wanted . . . you expect him to immediately relinquish his duties. There should be no witnesses in the room at the time.

If this "frontal assault" (the manual's own terminology) were not successful, the manual went on to suggest transferring unwanted personnel to regional offices, described by the manual as "dumping grounds." "If you have an employee," the manual advised, "who was born and raised in New England and is currently serving in your Boston regional office, and his record shows reluctance to move far from that location, a transfer accompanied by a promotion to an existing or newly created position in Dallas might just fill the bill." If the transfer technique failed, the manual recommended other "special assignments" as well as other techniques. But the point was clear: where no positions at the senior career levels were open, political executives were instructed in the art of creating such openings by encouraging the firing or transferring of personnel.

In addition, once an open position was identified, the White House wanted to ensure that "its" personnel were appointed to that position. Malek (Subcommittee on Manpower, 1976, p. 166) described this process in Senate testimony as follows:

> What we are doing in the case of a career position is we would be submitting the name of a person to a department and asking them to determine where this person would be qualified and competitive, to serve in that position, to try to get them into it.

So, what we were really doing is facilitating the personnel process in getting somebody in that door, where, without the political push, they may not have been getting into the door.

Thus, through the process of first identifying vacancies (or "encouraging" senior personnel to vacate) and secondly by ensuring that candidates supportive of the administration's position were referred to appropriate political personnel contacts in the departments and agencies, the White House expected to maximize the placement of "its people" in senior career positions. In this manner, the Nixon administration hoped to circumvent the "normal" civil service process and to achieve a high degree of managerial control over the federal bureaucracy. The following sections measure the extent to which the White House succeeded in achieving these goals.

THE FEDERAL BUREAUCRACY: THE CHANGING NATURE OF PARTY IDENTIFICATION

As Richard Nixon began his first term, he faced a bureaucracy whose personnel and character had largely been shaped in the Kennedy/Johnson years. Nathan (1975, p. 49) argues that Nixon's staff *initially* recommended personnel for top civil service and appointive positions on the basis of "ability first, loyalty second." This began to change in earnest in the fall of 1970 when Nixon's aides began their concerted attempts to alter the bureaucracy. As recounted by Heclo, the Civil Service Commission found itself increasingly subject to White House pressure during this period. Quoting from an Executive Order of July 1, 1970, Heclo (1977, p. 27) finds that the Bureau of the Budget (later changed to the Office of Management and Budget) was "charged with advising the President on the development of new programs to recruit, train, motivate, deploy and evaluate the men and women who make up the top ranks of the civil service."

An important empirical question, then, is the extent to which the Nixon White House was able to affect the partisan affiliation of the top levels of the federal bureaucracy. In order to answer this, of course, we need data for both the early and late Nixon years. Here, as elsewhere in this article, we compare the 1970 Aberbach and Rockman survey with our 1976 data. Table 2 presents this comparison for partisan affiliation.

As Aberbach and Rockman have concluded, few Republicans (17 percent) were found among those holding top career executive positions in the early Nixon years (see Table 2). The 1970 differences are even more striking when one recalls that the "Independents" in the Aberbach and Rockman survey were more likely to resemble Democrats than Republicans. Typically, about two-thirds of these Independents were found by Aberbach and Rockman to side with Democrats when answering questions of general policy orientations. If these Independents had been forced to select one party (Aberbach and Rockman did not attempt this), a generous assessment of the proportion of top career executives who in 1970 identified with the Republican Party would be only about one-third (assigning half of the Independents to each party).[4]

[4] Caution must be exercised when interpreting the Aberbach and Rockman data in this fashion. Aberbach and Rockman recorded their respondents' voting behavior rather than their actual party identification, as we asked. Further, noting that Independents are more likely to resemble Democrats in general policy orientations (as do Aberbach and Rockman) is not necessarily the same as finding Independents more likely to vote Democratic at the ballot box. Still, we believe that these items are similar enough to ours to suggest *possible* inferences of partisan choice. At the same time, we realize that when dealing with slightly different questions, one incurs certain unavoidable risks. Perhaps future research may clarify these distinctions.

Considering the 1976 data presented in Table 2, the most noticeable change one finds over this period is in the decline of top executives (both political and career) identifying with the Democratic Party and the increase in the proportion calling themselves Independents. The proportion of Republican executives remained about the same. At the very least, one might conclude that after eight years of a Republican administration, Democratic identifiers were less likely to reveal their partisan choice.

In order to determine the partisan leanings of the Independents, this study forced a party selection by asking Independents to indicate for which party they usually voted. We then found significant distinctions, as noted in Table 2. Slightly more than 50 percent of both political and career executives who indicated that they were Independents stated a preference for the Republican Party at the ballot box. The proportion of Independents who by 1976 sided with the Republican perspective was clearly greater than that found by Aberbach and Rockman in 1970. Examining the "forced choice" partisan distribution one can see that in 1976, 75 percent of the political appointees and 40 percent of the career executives either were Republicans or voted Republican.

This represents a significant increase over 1970 and indicates that although the White House's strategy may not have succeeded in markedly increasing the number of Republican Party members at the most senior levels of the civil service, it did result in the selection of a high proportion of Independents who voted Republican or, perhaps, in influencing some Independent identifiers to lean in a Republican direction.

By dividing the sample into time frames representing the date of an executive's appointment, we can gain greater insight into the effects of the administrative presidency. Table 3 divides, by job status, the 1976 sample into those se-

TABLE 2 · PARTY AFFILIATION AND JOB STATUS, 1970–1976

Party Affiliation

Job Description	1970				1976				1976[b]		
	Dem.	Ind.	Rep.	(N)	Dem.	Ind.	Rep.	(N)	Dem.	Rep.	(N)
Political appointees[a]	24%	10%	66%	57	19%	19%	61%	57	25%	75%	55
Supergrade career[a]	47	36	17	58	38	46	16	111	60	40	100
Totals:				115				168			155
Gammas:		−.58				−.59				−.63	

[a] Percentages add row-wise.
[b] Data represent "forced" party choice. Independents were asked to indicate for which party they usually voted.
Source: Joel Aberbach and Bert Rockman, "Clashing Beliefs within the Executive Branch," American Political Science Review 70:459, and authors' survey of senior federal officials conducted in 1976.

TABLE 3 · THE CHANGING NATURE OF PARTY AFFILIATION BY JOB STATUS

Party Identification	Political Appointees		Career Executives	
	Pre-Nixon	Post 1968	Pre-Nixon	Post 1968
Democrat	26%	13%	40%	24%
Independent	22	17	45	53
Republican	52	70	15	24
Total:	100%	100%	100%	101%
N:	27	30	94	17
Gamma:	.34		.31	

Source: Data compiled from authors' survey of senior federal officials conducted in 1976.

lected prior to the Nixon administration and those selected during the Nixon years.[5]

Table 3 reveals two points of interest. First, Democrats were considerably less likely and Republicans and Independents considerably more likely to be se-

[5] A methodological problem particularly relevant to this study is the problem of inferring longitudinal representativeness of cohort samples based on data collected at one point in time. Even though our sample fairly accurately represents the 1976 population of senior bureaucrats, there is no way of determining whether time cohorts generated from this sample necessarily represent the attitudes and characteristics of all those in office during the particular time intervals selected for analysis. Employees come and go, and it might be argued that those who were most favorable to the goals and objectives of new federalism and Nixon's domestic policies were more likely to remain with their particular agencies throughout the years. While we realize the seriousness of this problem, two factors mitigate its impact on this study. First, our study will show that the cohorts generated do differ significantly in the attitudes and characteristics to be examined. To the extent that self-selection has taken place and that some officials critical of new federalism issues resigned in protest, *our arguments actually are strengthened.* More important, the Aberbach and Rockman study provides an essentially identical sample frame drawn from an earlier period. These data do allow for "before and after" comparisons and we make use of their sample whenever possible.

lected for senior political and career executive positions in the Nixon years than before. The proportional decline in Democrats selected for career positions (from 40 to 24 percent) seems particularly significant. Obviously, affiliation with the Republican party was a greater asset and affiliation with the Democrats a greater liability to job aspirants during the Nixon era than before.

Second, Table 3 demonstrates the limits of a strategy designed to effect major change at the top levels of the federal bureaucracy in a short period. Of the total 1976 sample of top executives, almost 70 percent assumed their positions before the Nixon administration began. Considering only career executives (to which the strategies described above were really directed), almost 85 percent had assumed their positions in the pre-Nixon years. Thus, in the short time span of a single presidency the proportion of appointments available compared with the total number of top federal bureaucrats is relatively small. Even if every career vacancy had been filled during the Nixon years by a Republican, the numerical impact would have been marginal.[6] This would

[6] We are grateful to Hugh Heclo for this important observation.

suggest that truly effective presidential management of the bureaucracy must combine elements of control over the selection process with influence over bureaucrats already holding top policy positions.

PARTY AFFILIATION BY AGENCY

A question of additional interest concerns the actual placement of personnel. As demonstrated above, those agencies experiencing greatest expansion in the decade of the 1960s were those usually defined as social service-oriented, i.e., HEW, HUD, and OEO. It is no secret that the clientele of these agencies were not viewed as particularly central to the Nixon base of political power. The conflicts resulting in Nixon's attempt to dismantle OEO attest to the mutual bitterness and disdain between the White House and some agency officials. Thus, the administrative presidency was designed also to correct what was considered to be an imbalance in the partisan leanings of top officials in the social service agencies. Table 4 examines the extent to which the partisan affiliation of

senior officials in social service and non-social service agencies was affected during the Nixon years.

Table 4 reveals a noticeable shift in the partisan composition of these domestic agencies between 1970 and 1976. Relying once again on the Aberbach and Rockman 1970 survey, we can see that Republicans comprised only 24 percent of the top bureaucratic positions in the social service agencies (HEW, HUD, OEO) as the Nixon administration began. Aberbach and Rockman found that 46 percent of these top social service positions were staffed by Democrats, 30 percent by Independents. Since Aberbach and Rockman found Independents to resemble Democrats more frequently, a safe estimation of the actual proportion of executives supporting or leaning toward the Republican party would have been around one-third.

By 1976 we observe a pattern somewhat similar to that identified above when we examined the changing partisanship of political and career executives of this period (Table 2). That is, a lower proportion of Democrats was found among the top service positions in 1976 (from 46 to 33 percent) and the ranks

TABLE 4 • PARTISAN AFFILIATION BY AGENCY, 1970–1976

	Agency					
	1970		1976		1976[a]	
Party Identification	Social Service	Other	Social Service	Other	Social Service	Other
Democrat	46%	33%	33%	32%	56%	46%
Independent	30	21	37	38		
Republican	24	46	30	30	44	54
Totals:	100%	100%	100%	100%	100%	100%
N:	33	82	43	141	36	132
Gammas:	.32		.002		.19	

[a] Data represent "forced" party choice. See text for explanation.
Source: Joel Aberbach and Bert Rockman, "Clashing Beliefs within the Executive Branch," *American Political Science Review* 70:459, and authors' survey of senior federal officials conducted in 1976.

of Republicans had increased somewhat (24 to 30 percent). As was the case when we examined job status, an important shift also is evident in the proportionate number of executives calling themselves Independents. Thirty-seven percent of those top executives in the social service agencies considered themselves Independents in 1976 (compared with 30 percent in 1970) and 38 percent of those executives in non-social service agencies considered themselves Independents (compared with 21 percent in 1970). Also, as we found when considering job status, the most interesting relationship over this period is revealed when we asked questions forcing these Independents to make a partisan choice. What appeared to be a slight Republican increase in social service executives (from 24 to 30 percent) was, in reality, rather large (from 24 to 44 percent) and what appeared to be a drop in Republican executives in non-social service agencies (from 46 to 30 percent) actually is an increase (from 46 to 54 percent). Forcing such a selection obviously increases the proportion of Democrats in these various agencies as well, but Republicans still maintained their advantage over Democrats in non-social service agencies, as noted by Aberbach and Rockman in 1970, and their proportion serving in the social service agencies noticeably increased.

It has been shown that proportionally more Republicans were selected for senior political and career positions during the Nixon years than before (Table 3) and that social service personnel were more likely in 1976 than in 1970 to identify with the Republican Party (Table 4). It remains to be discovered whether the increasing Republican composition of the social service agencies is reflective only of the president's political appointments, or whether significant partisan change among career executives is also evident. In other words, is the

apparent shift in Republican identifiers among social service personnel accounted for by political appointees only; or were those trends indicative of more basic partisan changes among the career service personnel as well? Table 5 examines this important question.

As indicated in Table 5, the sample sizes, in refining the analysis in this manner, sometimes become quite small. Only four political appointees selected prior to 1968 serving in the social service agencies were represented in this survey (and only one of these was a Democrat). This information, then, must be considered with some degree of caution; still, interesting trends are evident.

It can be seen that for all categories of agency affiliation and appointment status, Democrats were proportionally *less* likely to be selected in the Nixon era than before. This is especially true (as would be expected) of political appointees, but we also found that *career executives* identifying with the Democratic party selected to social service agencies and all other departments were proportionally fewer during the Nixon administration. The decline in Democratic identifiers corresponds with a proportionate increase in both Independents and Republicans. While small sample sizes here dictate extreme caution, the data indicate that Republican career executives were about 3 times as likely to be promoted to senior positions in the social service agencies during the Nixon years and more than 1.5 times as likely to be promoted to senior positions in all other departments and agencies. Table 5 demonstrates that it is also true that Democrats were not totally excluded from these senior-level positions during the Nixon years. While their proportionate numbers clearly declined, some Democrats succeeded in achieving high political and career positions during the Nixon years. Thus, while partisanship was not an exclusive factor in the

TABLE 5 · PARTISAN AFFILIATION BY APPOINTMENT AUTHORITY, AGENCY, AND APPOINTMENT DATE

Party Identification	Pre-Nixon				Post 1968			
	Agency				Agency			
	Social Service		Other		Social Service		Other	
	Political	Career	Political	Career	Political	Career	Political	Career
Democrat	25%	52%	26%	39%	8%	33%	17%	18%
Independent	25	41	22	45	25	50	11	55
Republican	50	6	52	16	67	16	72	27
Totals:	100%	99%	100%	100%	100%	99%	100%	100%
N:	4	17	23	75	12	6	18	11

Source: Data compiled from authors' survey of senior federal officials conducted in 1976.

selection of senior level positions during the Nixon years, it obviously was one important consideration. Republicans were more likely to be selected for all these categories of appointed and career social service and "other" positions during the Nixon years than before.

In support of Heclo and Nathan, then, we have found that the "administrative presidency" was having a noticeable impact in strengthening the proportionate number of Republicans selected not only for political positions (as would be expected) but also for high-level career senior civil service positions. Proportionately more Republicans were selected for more career executive positions during the Nixon years than before and, through this process, the White House was beginning to achieve partisan equality in the key social service agencies. Additionally, by the selection of Independents who voted Republican or by influencing some Independents to lean in a Republican direction (or through some combination of these), the administrative presidency was to achieve among Independent bureaucrats a level of support for the Republican party much greater than before.

Partisan affiliation is one key barometer of the changes taking place during the administrative presidency. Just as important are the actual attitudes of those selected for political and career positions. To what extent did those selected during the Nixon years differ in their attitudes toward key Nixon proposals from those selected before the Nixon presidency? This question is considered in the following section.

THE FEDERAL BUREAUCRACY: ATTITUDES TOWARD NEW FEDERALISM

Aberbach and Rockman (1976, p. 461) examined bureaucratic attitudes toward government provision of social services. After constructing a five-point continuum ranging from favoring much more to favoring much less government provision of social services, Aberbach and Rockman found that 44 percent of their sample favored such provision and 26 percent opposed. This finding, they argued, at least partially confirms suspicions by the Nixon White House that the orientation of senior career officials was biased against a more conservative approach.

By 1976, of course, the domestic policies and goals of the Nixon administration had been clearly articulated and, for the present study, it is appropriate to consider questions dealing with bureaucratic attitudes toward these specific programs. Whereas Aberbach and Rockman focused on general orientations, these 1976 respondents were asked to indicate their attitudes concerning a number of specific program and policy goals of Nixon's domestic proposals. Each of these questions dealt with some aspect of Nixon's new federalism program—a program designed to consolidate a number of categorical grants and return decision making to state and local officials. As in the Aberbach and Rockman study, officials were asked to record their responses along a five-point continuum. Thus, we are able to examine more directly bureaucratic attitudes toward the president's specific policy program and objectives.[7] Table 6 (pp. 120–21),

[7] We acknowledge the problems of measuring attitudes about a president's program after the president has left office. By 1976 Nixon's domestic programs were gaining wider acceptance in the Congress, among state and local officials, and among the public as a whole. It is not surprising that the bureaucracy, too, would be more positive in its evaluation. However, it is not so much the absolute level of acceptance or rejection of the president's program which concerns us here. We are more concerned with the *relative* level of acceptance among the various subpopulations examined. To the extent that differences in subgroups are found, the central issue posed by this study—the attitudinal differences between those senior executives selected prior to and during the Nixon years—can be explored.

examines the marginal distribution of responses to the four new federalism programs which actually were enacted by the Congress and to four key policy objectives of the new federalism philosophy.

The most obvious conclusion to be drawn from Table 6 is that by 1976 considerable support for Nixon's new federalism programs and objectives existed among top political and career federal executives. For each program examined, over 60 percent of those surveyed expressed positive support. Very little variance in overall response is noted except that a slightly higher proportion expressed negative attitudes toward the general revenue sharing program than to the programs of special revenue sharing.

When we examine party identification, agency affiliation, and job status, we notice additional variances which generally are in the direction predicted by the Aberbach and Rockman study. With the exception of ease of the grant application procedures, strongly endorsed by all groups, Republican bureaucrats were consistently more favorable to both the programs and policy goals of new federalism than were Democrats. Again, it is very important to note that Independents generally were more likely to resemble Republicans in their responses to these questions—especially those questions dealing with specific programs. This is a significant change from 1970 when, it will be recalled, Aberbach and Rockman found Independents generally siding with Democrats.

Agency affiliation made surprisingly little difference in response patterns, but we found job status to have a considerable effect on attitudes toward new federalism programs and goals. Political appointees indicated quite favorable attitudes; career executives were more mixed.

Perhaps the most important conclusion to be reached from these data is

that by 1976 top political and career executives were on the whole quite supportive of Nixon's new federalism programs and goals. Over a majority of all executives, regardless of party identification, agency affiliation, or job status supported every program and policy we examined.

THE CHANGING NATURE OF BUREAUCRATIC ATTITUDES

The central theme of proponents of the administrative presidency is that the Nixon White House was able to influence placement of people sympathetic to Nixon's domestic policy proposals in important civil service positions. It has already been shown that a higher proportion of Republicans were selected for these positions in the Nixon years and that Republican executives in general were more sympathetic to the policies and goals of new federalism. This section focuses on the question of *changing* bureaucratic attitudes over time. If, as Nathan and Heclo have argued, the Nixon White House extended the politicization of the bureaucracy further than any previous administration, it would be expected that the attitudes of bureaucrats placed during the Nixon years would deviate from those receiving their appointments earlier.[8] Table 7 summarizes these findings.

Table 7 generally confirms these expectations. Considering first the entire sample of senior officials (political appointees as well as career executives), in all cases those selected during the

---

[8] It might be argued that those selected in later years to these top positions would be more favorable to new federalism goals and objectives simply because they lacked the working knowledge of and commitment to previous policy alternatives. This might be the case with some political appointees; however, most officials promoted to top career positions have had years of experience with the federal government. We are primarily interested in this study in assessing the attitudes and characteristics of those career executives.

TABLE 6 · ATTITUDES TOWARD NEW FEDERALISM PROGRAMS AND POLICIES

	Party Identification				Agency Affiliation		Job Status	
	All 195	Dem. 59	Ind. 71	Rep. 56	Social Service 47	Others 145	Political 57	Career 116
A. Attitude toward program of:								
1. General revenue sharing								
Positive	62%	54%	65%	71%	61%	63%	77%	56%
Neutral	14	10	16	15	10	15	9	15
Negative	24	36	19	15	29	22	14	29
2. Housing & community development (CDBG)								
Positive	63	55	65	66	69	61	68	61
Neutral	18	16	23	14	16	21	18	18
Negative	19	29	12	20	16	19	14	21
3. Law enforcement (LEAA)								
Positive	67	54	70	76	57	70	71	66
Neutral	14	16	15	13	19	13	13	14
Negative	19	30	15	11	24	17	16	20
4. Manpower (CETA)								
Positive	61	53	61	68	61	61	74	55
Neutral	18	14	26	14	21	18	16	19
Negative	21	33	13	18	18	21	11	27

B. Attitude toward policy of:

1. Formula distribution								
Positive	79	71	79	88	85	78	97	73
Neutral	6	5	9	5	2	7	2	7
Negative	14	23	12	7	13	15	2	20
2. Return of decision making to states and localities								
Positive	78	68	77	89	76	79	90	74
Neutral	4	5	4	2	4	4	4	4
Negative	18	26	19	9	20	18	7	23
3. Ease of application								
Positive	94	97	91	93	94	92	95	93
Neutral	4	3	4	5	4	4	5	4
Negative	2	0	4	1	2	3	0	4
4. New federalism philosophy as an improvement over categorical grants								
Positive	65	54	64	75	71	61	76	60
Neutral	14	14	16	11	2	17	12	13
Negative	21	33	20	15	27	22	12	27

Note: In responding to these items, the executives were presented the list of program and policy goals and asked to indicate their feelings about each along a five-point continuum ranging from "very positive" to "very negative." For the final question, respondents were asked to indicate along a continuum of "strongly agree" to "strongly disagree" their feelings as to whether or not the philosophies reflected in Nixon's new federalism proposals represented improvements over the categorical grant system. In this table the two positive and the two negative responses for all items are collapsed into a single "positive" or "negative" response for clarification and ease of presentation. Because of missing data, subcategory totals vary and are somewhat lower than the total N. Of course LEAA was first established before the Nixon administration; however, the program grew substantially during the Nixon years and often was called by Nixon his "model" for his own special revenue-sharing proposals.

Source: Data compiled from authors' survey of senior federal officials conducted in 1976.

TABLE 7 · MEAN DIFFERENCES BETWEEN PRE- AND POST-
NIXON APPOINTEES

Attitudes toward:	Entire Sample			Career Executives Only		
	Pre-Nixon	Post-Nixon	Sig.	Pre-Nixon	Post-Nixon	Sig.
Programs						
General revenue sharing	2.6	2.1	0.1	2.7	2.2	.05
Housing and community development (CDBG)	2.4	2.2	NS	2.5	1.8	.01
Law enforcement (LEAA)	2.5	2.2	.05	2.5	2.1	NS
Manpower (CETA)	2.5	2.4	NS	2.6	2.6	NS
Policies						
Formula distribution	2.2	1.6	.01	2.2	1.6	.01
Return of decision making to states and localities	2.2	1.8	.01	2.3	1.7	.05
Ease of application process	1.5	1.3	.05	1.5	1.3	NS
New federalism philosophy as an improvement over categorical grants	2.6	2.2	.01	2.7	2,4	NS

Note: In this table a *lower* mean score reflects a more *positive* attitude.
Source: Data compiled from authors' survey of senior federal officials conducted in 1976.

Nixon years are more positive toward those programs and policy issues of Nixon's new federalism than those selected in previous years. Nathan (1975) argues that in the later Nixon years loyalty really became the dominant factor in promotions and appointments. While it is not shown in Table 7, we found later Nixon appointees to be more positive even than those selected early in the administration.

It also is true, as shown in Table 7, that these differences were found among *both* political and career executives. While political appointees are expected to reflect the philosophy of the current administration, the essence of the Heclo/Nathan argument is that the Nixon White House extended this to include career executives as well. While the data

may not be overwhelming (in four instances the differences are not found to be statistically significant), it is true that in all instances, with the exception of the CETA program, career executives selected during the Nixon years were more sympathetic to the president's program than those selected during previous years. Sometimes, these differences were rather large. For example, of those career executives selected during the Nixon years, 71 percent and 75 percent expressed positive attitudes toward the General Revenue Sharing and Community Development Block Grant programs, respectively. By contrast, only about half of those career officials selected prior to the Nixon years indicated positive attitudes toward these programs (not shown in Table 7). Indeed, those advanced to top career civil service positions in the Nixon years were on a whole more positive toward Nixon's own programs and philosophies than were those selected in previous years.

SUMMARY AND CONCLUSIONS

This article has attempted to assess the impact which a president can have, even in a short period of time, on the senior personnel of the federal bureaucracy. Of course the Nixon presidency was in many ways unique: a Republican president committed to eliminating or consolidating many social service programs and reducing many areas of federal bureaucratic discretion facing a bureaucracy accustomed to the considerable growth and social service orientation experienced during the Great Society days. Still, the Nixon presidency can be seen as representing a more general problem common to all presidents: the difficulty of gaining some degree of management control over the federal bureaucracy. The very fact that Nixon's struggles were more intense and more calculated than those of most presidents makes his a most fascinating and instructive case study. If the Nixon strategies were successful, future presidents might consider adopting similar tactics, however alien these may be to the concept of an independent career service. If the Nixon strategies failed, one might question whether any president could ever achieve control over the bureaucracy.

We may first conclude that the strategy of the Nixon White House was beginning to have a measurable effect. Those selected to the top bureaucratic positions during the Nixon years were more likely to be Republican and to favor Nixon's own goals and objectives than those selected earlier. Of course, this would be expected of political appointees, but we found this also to be true of career executives. These differences were not absolutes (many Democrats were promoted to the senior levels during the Nixon years and some were appointed by Nixon to the top positions), yet the data leave no doubt that Republicans and those supporting Nixon's policies were favored during the Nixon years. This is true of appointments to social service as well as all other agencies and departments.

Secondly, while marginal changes were found, the strategy pursued by the Nixon White House was doomed to insignificance from the outset. So few top officials are selected during any single presidency compared with the total number of senior level executives that any numerical impact which those selected can have must be slight. Of course, the White House hoped to overcome this problem by "encouraging" resignations, retirements, and transfers. Also, it might be argued that those few career officials selected by the White House were in "key" positions. Despite these tactics, even if every career executive selected during the Nixon years had been a Republican and totally dedicated to Nixon's programs and policies, they would have comprised only about 15 percent of all career officials. If future bureaucratic development moves toward further consolidation, waste-reduction, and personnel stability, a president cannot overlook the fact that far fewer positions will become vacant than will remain filled.

Thirdly, the data show that bureaucrats not strongly identifying with one partisan philosophy or the other nonetheless favor the president's program. This is especially interesting when compared with the Aberbach and Rockman data collected at the very beginning of the Nixon years which showed

Independents to disproportionately resemble Democrats (and, combined, to reject the philosophies of a Republican administration). By the conclusion of the Republican era, we find Independents to resemble Republicans disproportionately (and, combined, to largely accept Nixon-era specific programs and philosophies). This is significant to presidential control because of the large numbers of bureaucrats calling themselves Independents. Aberbach and Rockman found 36 percent of the career officials in their sample to indicate an Independent status; we found 44 percent in our sample so responding. Using either figure, the number of Independents is far greater than the total number of career executives selected during any particular presidency.

We cannot conclude with certainty why Independents appeared more supportive of Nixon's programs in 1976 than in 1970. Certainly we do not believe that large numbers of senior career executives, many with years of experience and devotion to government service and many of whom had served under several presidencies, would suddenly and capriciously change their partisan leanings. We would not even argue that wholesale changes occurred in basic philosophic attitudes toward the general provision of social services (as measured by Aberbach and Rockman). Yet, the proportion of Independents who supported Nixon's *specific* programs and goals in 1976 clearly is higher than one would expect from the 1970 data.

Some of this accommodation is accounted for by White House influence over the selection process which, as we have documented, during the Nixon years placed those Independents in top career positions who were more likely to support the Republican party than were those selected before 1968. Some bureaucratic accommodation may reflect the growing support reached by 1976 for Nixon's domestic policy in the Congress and among state and local officials.[9] Perhaps these accommodations were also to some extent "self-motivated"— Independent executives may be more volatile than strong partisans and more likely to accept as their own the goals of the current administration. Whatever the answer (no doubt some combination of the above), by 1976 Independent career executives closely resembled Republicans in their support of the president's program. It is very likely that the large body of Independent bureaucrats may represent a considerable reservoir of potential presidential support.

The issues raised here have important implications in the broader context of national policy making and relate, as well, to long-standing debates about the appropriate role of the bureaucracy in a democratic society. Rational and consistent policy making and execution, it sometimes is argued, are best achieved by greater hierarchical control. Further, if such control over the federal bureaucracy can be enhanced by the selection of senior officials sympathetic to the president's policies, then it might seem desirable to extend the president's influence to senior career executives as well. From this perspective, the actions of the Nixon presidency may appear to represent simply a logical and even desirable extension of practices carried out by previous presidents. A Republican president facing both a Democratic Congress and a bureaucracy perceived to be unsympathetic to the president's policy directives might appear to be totally stymied without such influence. Aberbach and Rockman (1976, p. 467) have cautioned that the misdeeds of the Nixon administration should not be allowed

[9] We are grateful to an anonymous reader for this insight.

to obscure the very real political problems the president faced, and Richard Nathan (1975, pp. 85–95) seems to suggest that were it not for Watergate, Nixon's bureaucratic tactics would have been judged successful and perhaps even desirable.[10]

Of course, the counter-argument—that the bureaucracy best serves democratic objectives by retaining its independence even in the face of strong presidential pressures—remains persuasive as well. From this perspective, policy making is more seriously threatened when control from the top inhibits the free exchange of ideas at the lower levels. The bureaucracy may be the best (perhaps the only) source of representation for some interests ignored by the elected branches of the government (one need only consider the attachment of social service organizations to HEW during the Nixon years). Indeed, Rourke (1969, p. 153) argues that bureaucratic politics has replaced party politics as the dominant decision-making arena in modern societies; unless the bureaucracy is free to generate innovative policy alternatives—occasionally even in conflict with elected representatives—the goals of democracy are ill served. According to Rourke (1969, p. 150), "A decision-making system subject to [rigid hierarchical control] is incapable of meeting all the requirements of a democratic society committed—in theory at least—to full and frank exploration of all options as a prerequisite to rational decisions."

Our data cannot resolve these debates over the "proper" role of the bureaucracy

in a modern society. However, we believe the data presented here do demonstrate the near-impossibility of achieving presidential control through manipulation of the personnel system. In the span of one presidency, the total number of vacant positions at senior levels simply is too small for a president to have more than a marginal impact. The conclusion that absolute presidential control is unlikely should be particularly satisfying to advocates of a free and independent bureaucracy.

On the other hand, we find the "pull" of the presidency to be strong, indeed. Like Aberbach and Rockman, we find Democratic bureaucratic identifiers consistently less favorable to a Republican president than Republican identifiers. Yet, by 1976 we find substantial proportions of *all* party identifiers (Democrats, Republicans, Independents) sympathetic to Nixon's proposals. In fact, Independents as a group were found to be almost indistinguishable from Republicans in their support of Nixon's policies and programs. Independents and party identifiers combined assure either a Republican or a Democratic president substantial support at the senior career levels of the federal bureaucracy. The important point is that, if these trends are reflective of typical bureaucratic accommodation to a president's specific programs and goals, presidents can achieve a measure of bureaucratic support in spite of the relatively few vacancies to be filled during any given administration.

Thus, Aberbach and Rockman's perceptive observation is correct: "The framers of the Constitution, having given us little guidance [in the area of bureaucratic control and responsibility], have left these problems as part of their enduring legacy" (1976, p. 468). Yet, lacking constitutional directives we find that political realities provide

---

[10] Nathan, actually, equivocates on this point, judiciously pointing out both sides of the issue. However, a fair interpretation of Nathan's arguments seems to imply sympathy for the goals, if not always the tactics, of the administrative presidency.

considerable relief. The influence of the president is so strong as to sway even protected career service personnel. While maintaining its formal independence (and perhaps even basic philosophic differences), the bureaucracy still responds to specific presidential initiatives. To this extent a certain degree of presidential control is accomplished even in the absence of clear constitutional direction.

REFERENCES

Aberbach, Joel D. and Bert A. Rockman (1976). "Clashing Beliefs Within the Executive Branch." *American Political Science Review* 70:456–68.

Heclo, Hugh (1977). *A Government of Strangers.* Washington: Brookings.

Koenig, Louis W. (1968). *The Chief Executive.* New York: Harcourt, Brace.

Nathan, Richard P. (1975). *The Plot That Failed.* New York: John Wiley.

Neustadt, Richard (1960). *Presidential Power.* New York: John Wiley.

Nixon, Richard M. (1971a). News Conference, February 17, 1971. *Public Papers of the Presidents, 1971.* Washington: Government Printing Office, 158–69.

_____ (1971b). Interview with Howard K. Smith, March 22, 1971. *Public Papers of the Presidents, 1971.* Washington: Government Printing Office, 448–65.

Rourke, Francis E. (1969). *Bureaucracy, Politics, and Public Policy.* Boston: Little, Brown.

Schlesinger, Arthur M., Jr. (1965). *A Thousand Days.* New York: Fawcett.

Statistical Abstract of the United States (1974). Washington: Government Printing Office.

Subcommittee on Manpower and Civil Service of the Committee on Post Office and Civil Service (1976). *Final Report on Violations and Abuses of Merit Principles in Federal Employment.* Washington: Government Printing Office.

Thomas, Norman C. (1970). "Presidential Advice and Information: Policy and Program Formulation." *Law and Contemporary Problems* 35:540–72.

15
The Reagan Administration and the Renitent Bureaucracy
Laurence E. Lynn, Jr.

Although every president wishes to gain the upper hand over the federal bureaucracy, Ronald Reagan has made perhaps the most determined effort of any recent president to bend the permanent government to his will. His methods have included mobilizing broad public support for his policies, making aggressive use of the budget to reshape policy priorities, and imposing hiring freezes and reductions in force to shrink the size of government. His most notable departure from the leadership methods of his predecessors, however, has been in the deliberate

All field interviews were conducted by Paul Starobin of Harvard University's John F. Kennedy School of Government. Starobin's skills in eliciting useful information and producing summaries of what he learned were indispensable to completion of this study.
Source: Reprinted from Lester M. Salamon and Michael S. Lund, eds., *The Reagan Presidency and the Governing of America* (Washington, D.C.: Urban Institute, 1981), pp. 339–70. Copyright by The Urban Institute.

way he has used his power of appointment to fill senior executive positions in federal departments and agencies with loyal advocates of his policies.

Typically, incoming administrations have professed to seek strong, well-qualified people for top executive positions. Actual appointments, however, depart from a strict criterion of merit to allow for the variety of political pressures affecting the appointment process: the need to reward specific constituencies and contributors, the success of some cabinet appointees in negotiating the right to control the appointment of subordinates, and the wish to have appointees who will be dedicated to the president and to his political philosophy. The usual result is cadres of appointees who exhibit divided loyalties and uncertain reliability. Anticipating this result, presidents are reluctant to delegate or decentralize control over policy to political appointees or even to view the use of their appointment power as more than peripheral to the achievement of their policy goals.

Departing from this view, the Reagan administration appeared from the outset to embrace the notion that faithful supporters in key executive positions could be a potent tool of administrative leadership. The primary qualification for appointment—overshadowing managerial competence and experience or familiarity with issues—appeared to be the extent to which an appointee shared the president's values and would be reliable and persistent both in transfusing these values into agency practices and in executing central directives bound to be unpopular in his or her agency. The right appointees could, it was believed, significantly advance the president's cause in the face of opposition expected from a government long in moderate or liberal hands.

Reagan's emphasis on the role of his appointees in the administrative management of the federal bureaucracy raises several interesting questions. Has Reagan effectively used the power of appointment to advance his cause? How have the efforts of his appointees affected the activities of their departments or agencies? Have the changes brought about by these appointees been consistent with Reagan's goals? Consistency aside, how have these changes influenced the effectiveness, efficiency, and overall capabilities of these agencies? What factors explain differences in the performance of Reagan appointees? What are the lessons of the Reagan experience for future administrations?

These questions are addressed in this paper by analyzing the accomplishments of five Reagan appointees to subcabinet positions. The emphasis here is on identifying (1) the changes in the activities of each agency that appear to be associated with the management actions of the appointees, (2) the factors that appear to account for each appointee's performance, and (3) the consequences for agency performance of the changes brought about by each appointee. Evidence from these five cases is used to draw conclusions about Reagan's success in using his appointment authority and about the implications of the Reagan experience for future administrations. First, however, it is important to discuss the concept of core activities and the factors contributing to executive performance.

POLITICAL EXECUTIVES AND ORGANIZATIONAL CHANGE

Government organizations are created to carry out specific public purposes, which are spelled out with varying specificity both in the organization's authorizing statutes and in appropriations acts and are further amplified or delimited in executive orders, in regulations, and in the internal routines and practices of the agency. To make these purposes a reality, bureaucratic structures and routines are established to allocate authority and responsibility within the agency and to set the standards for specific tasks that are to be performed.

Those activities relating directly to fulfilling the organization's purposes may be termed the organization's *core activities*, consisting of actions or practices such as promulgating standards, conducting inspections, awarding grants and contracts, making benefit payments, and administering or protecting a natural resource or geographical area such as a park or military base. Organizational interests and the organization's "culture" gradually materialize around these core activities. Operational routines and standards are created to support them. The way core activity is carried out defines the purposes or mission of the organization as its employees see it.

The concept of core activity provides a useful basis for measuring the performance of Reagan appointees in altering the behavior of their agencies. The nature of appointees' influence may be defined in terms of their success in making lasting changes in the character of core activity that are consistent with Reagan's policy preferences. Evaluating executive performance in terms of core activity permits a comparison of the executives' conceptions of their goals and of their approaches to achieving them. It becomes possible to ask: How well have these executives identified the main business of their agencies, and how well are their ideas formulated to bring about change in their agencies' basic operations? Among those executives who focus on core activities—many may focus on peripheral issues—it may be further asked: What factors seem to account

for a pattern of success and failure? If the executives had fundamental change in core activity in mind, for example, did they also have the skills and resources to carry it out?

Questions such as these can be framed in terms of a model that links change in governmental behavior to the political appointee's role in bringing it about. The effectiveness of a political appointee in changing the behavior of his or her agency (behavior is defined here as core activity) can be postulated as depending on four distinct factors. First is the appointed executive's *managerial skills and experience*. A public executive's performance might be expected to depend in part on his or her facility in carrying out the ordinary tasks of public management. Potentially valuable skills include the traditional managerial tasks—planning, organizing, communicating, motivating subordinates, and the like; skill in relating to the agency's political environment—such as building legislative support, negotiating, and sensitivity to varied and changing interests; and, finally, technical competence with respect to the problems and issues facing the agency—that is, the extent to which the executive understands and can intelligently intervene in the substance of the agency's activities. Experience in government, moreover, especially in positions of executive responsibility at the federal or state level, might be expected to be an asset to an appointee confronting the ambiguities, pressures, and uncertainties of a federal executive post. Knowing what to anticipate and how to act can greatly shorten the time needed to master the specific demands of the job.

The second factor affecting the appointee's effectiveness in carrying out core activity is the executive's *personality*. As used here, personality encompasses the appointee's habitual responses to the job situation, including his or her styles of thinking, of identifying and solving problems, and of relating to people and to tasks. The underlying proposition here is that, all other things being equal, appointees with a high level of cognitive and emotional development—in other words, with high tolerance for and an ability to be creative in the face of ambiguity and uncertainty, with sensitivity to the needs and motivations of subordinates and employees, and with a liking for open and candid relationships—will be more effective than those who lack these characteristics and who alienate subordinates, disrupt agency routines, and misconstrue issues.

High levels of managerial skill and desirable personality traits may substitute for one another. An inexperienced and unskilled manager may nonetheless succeed if he or she has a personality that stimulates trust and cooperation or a charismatic personality that inspires effort. Similarly, less adaptable, more aloof individuals may still succeed if they are skilled administrators able to earn respect for their expertise and technical skill.

The third factor is the nature of the *opportunity to accomplish change* that is inherent in the situation. Circumstances internal or external to the agency may favor or oppose changes in core activity. Cataloguing the possibilities is difficult because an agency's readiness and ability to incorporate changes in its basic operations is likely to depend on numerous variables: Employee attitudes and values may be more or less accommodating to new ideas; organizational structures and processes may be more or less malleable, as may the issue networks that support or monitor agency activity; and authorizing statutes may be difficult or impossible to amend, or they may permit little discretion in interpretation. Thus, depending on the setting and the problems to be confronted, accomplishing change may be harder in some agencies than in others.

Fourth is the appointee's *design*, in other words, his or her expressed goals or intentions with respect to the behavior or performance of the agency, together with the specific means chosen to implement them. Some executives will quickly identify core activities and the organizational structures and processes that support them and design a strategy for change aimed directly at these activities. Other executives, however, may measure their influence in terms of specific decisions rather than in terms of agency routines or practices. The objective of the head of the National Highway Traffic and Safety Administration, for example, might be the rescission of the regulations prescribing air bags in automobiles rather than changing the philosophy and process of setting vehicle safety standards. Or a political executive might have as an objective the installation of zero-base budgeting or some other management reform rather than changes in core activity, under the theory that management is properly process- rather than task-oriented.

Conventional management theory might suggest that design is a joint product of several facets: personality, primarily determining which phenomena in the agency setting are classified as "problems" or are otherwise selected for managerial attention; opportunity, primarily determining the general approach to problems; and skills, determining the precise tactics to implement the approach. But there are other possibilities. Of special interest to this study, for instance, is the possibility that appointees' designs are products of a general ideological orientation—either that of the appointee, of the president, or of both. That is, no matter what the particular circumstances, an appointee's design may feature, for example, less regulation, more reliance on market mechanisms, stricter eligibility requirements, or less bureaucratic discretion.

One might expect some correlation—or a minimum of variation—among these factors for a given group of appointees, provided that the appointments reflected a careful matching of personalities, skills, and opportunities and that appointees were given latitude to choose their own designs. The appointments process seldom approaches this degree of rationality, however, and certainly has not appeared to do so in the Reagan administration. Thus among Reagan appointees we expect considerable independent variation among these four contributors to executive performance.

DESIGN OF THE STUDY

The data for this study consist primarily of information obtained from interviews with five executives appointed to their positions in 1981 and other individuals associated with five federal agencies: the Employment and Training Administration (ETA) of the Department of Labor; the Forest Service in the Department of Agriculture (FSDA); the Mine Health and Safety Administration (MHSA) of the Department of Labor; the Federal Communications Commission (FCC); and the National Highway Traffic and Safety Administration (NHTSA) of the Department of Transportation. Five agencies constituted the maximum number of which sufficiently detailed information could be obtained within available time and resources.

These agencies and their selected appointees were chosen to be interviewed for four reasons: (1) Each appointee has appeared to reflect Reagan's philosophy and intentions in making appointments to subcabinet positions. Moreover, in matters of program, each generally reflects Reagan's conservative ideology, has dutifully executed administration policies concerning budget and staff reductions, and has formulated specific goals consistent with Reagan's general policies; (2) Each agency is headed by or is within the administrative jurisdiction of a Reagan appointee who, once in office, has expressed definite ideas about changing the agency beyond merely carrying out Office of Management and Budget (OMB) and White House directives; (3) The appointee and a representative group of other appointed and career officials within the agency agreed to be interviewed; (4) Preliminary investigation suggested significant variation among the five appointees in the four factors discussed here as influencing their performances as well as their success. Thus, these five agencies and the appointed executives can be said to be representative of Reagan's apparent beliefs about the potential contributions of his appointees to the furtherance of his policies.

For each agency, interviews were conducted with the selected executive and with other appointed officials, career employees, former political appointees, members of legislative staffs, interest-group representatives, and other individuals—General Accounting Office (GAO) officials and agency consultants, for example—who are knowledgeable about the agency's activities.[1]

The interviewer sought the following types of information from each inter-

---

[1] The appointees agreed to be interviewed on the record; many others agreed only on the condition that their names not be revealed. Inevitably, interviewees betrayed biases; many of their assertions could not be adequately corroborated. Every effort was made, however, to check the veracity of sources and to verify appointees' views.

viewee: (1) the appointee's goals and objectives; (2) the methods chosen by the appointee to carry out his purposes; (3) opinions concerning the apparent effect of the appointee's managerial actions; (4) opinions concerning the consequences of changes in agency activity on agency performance; (5) any other information bearing on the appointee's style of leadership and management. Apart from this outline, the interviews were open ended.[2]

The resulting data were then searched for information concerning each appointee's managerial skills and experience, personality, opportunity, design, and accomplishments that seemed to directly relate to the appointee's managerial efforts. The resulting assessments were necessarily doubly subjective. They reflect, first, the opinions of observers rather than objectively drawn indicators or measures. Second, they reflect the author's judgments concerning the proper interpretation and value of these opinions. The pictures of these appointees and agencies that emerged from the interviews were quite robust, however. While other interpreters of the data would doubtless differ concerning nuances, it is unlikely that they would arrive at altogether different views.

FIVE EXECUTIVES AND THEIR STORIES

As background for the analysis to follow, this section summarizes the stories of

the five executives included in the study.[3]

Albert Angrisani and the Employment and Training Administration

Thirty-five-year-old Albert Angrisani was appointed to the position of assistant secretary of labor for employment and training. A vice-president of Chase Manhattan Bank, he had a bachelor's degree in political science, a master of arts degree in finance, and a certificate in accounting. He would be responsible for managing the department's Employment and Training Administration. By all accounts, his political contacts, not his business acumen or his experience with staffing programs (he had none of the latter), led to his appointment. He had helped Secretary of Labor Raymond Donovan manage Ronald Reagan's presidential campaign in New Jersey, and he was to become Donovan's chief assistant at the Department of Labor.

ETA awards some $30 billion annually in grants and contracts to private firms, nonprofit groups, and state and local governments for operating employment and training programs. It is a highly politicized agency, "corrupt" and "wasteful" in the view of many agency observers. Over the years, control over contracting had shifted both between Washington, D.C., and the field and between program officers and financial officers. The agency had been the subject of numerous GAO audits, reorganizations, and management evaluations, and there had been little stability and a minimal sense of professionalism except in the Job Corps, which had a strong mission orientation. Angrisani would be under continuing pressure from the White

---

[2] In most instances permission was received to record the interviews on tape, even when the interviewee requested anonymity. Where appropriate, the interviewer supplemented his information with documentary evidence, such as speeches, testimony, and other interview transcripts. Comprehensive assessment of all activities in every agency proved impossible. Emphasis was placed on activities in which appointees expressed considerable personal interest and initiative.

[3] Unless otherwise cited, quotations in this section of the paper may be assumed to be from interviews with the author. Officials not identified in the text requested anonymity.

House and from OMB to end the fraud and waste that were frequently cited in the media.

Short, heavy-set, and youthful, Angrisani projected self-confidence, ambition, and a distrust of bureaucrats. This distrust was reflected in his comment, "We have people who have tenure in their jobs. They're totally inefficient." He viewed himself as a tough-minded businessperson. "The difference between me and my predecessor is, I'm a manager, not a manpower specialist," he said. He saw ETA's Comprehensive Employment and Training Program as "just another big welfare program,"[4] and conservatives expected him to clean up the mess. He expressed great faith in business management systems: "You can have the best person in the world in charge of a system, and if that system is incapable of functioning right, that person's going to fail." Critics described him as a "bully" who was terrible at relating to people.

Of necessity, one of Angrisani's primary goals was to phase out or redesign programs that were not in accord with the president's philosophy. For example, he carried out Reagan's decision to terminate the Public Service Employment Program, and he assisted the White House and Senate Republicans in replacing the Comprehensive Employment and Training Act (CETA) with legislation providing for block grants for job training dispensed through private industry councils. He also directed an OMB-dictated 20 percent reduction in force, and he was prepared to cut the staff even further.

In addition, Angrisani set about making the procurement process more "efficient" and less susceptible to corruption. "The first thing a manager has to have

is control," he said. He thus required that all contracts, including those modifying existing contracts, be approved by a staff created in his office. (A computer in his office gave him access to the status of each of the thousands of ETA contracts, and for a while he looked at everything himself.) He created a special task force to reduce the backlog of audits, and he shifted responsibility for contract administration from program officials to financial officials. (He commented that "financial people are basically the same everywhere; there is something in their nature . . . that you can count on.") Furthermore, he established a model procurement process that encouraged competition and limited the discretionary judgments of contracting officials. Contracting officers in ETA program offices in headquarters ("political hacks," Angrisani called them) were stripped of their authority, and contracting authority was shifted to the Financial Control and Systems Management Division. Contracting officers in the regional offices were placed under the surveillance of headquarters.

Reactions to these moves were predictably mixed. ETA veterans referred to Angrisani's hand-picked staff as "Snow White and the Seven Dwarfs." Some seasoned procurement officials expressed outrage at what they saw as Angrisani's ham-handed approach, even suspecting him of deliberately sabotaging the agency's procurement activities—"strangling them," said one, "then letting them breathe a little." In the field offices there was considerable confusion, fear, and resentment; in one regional office, the Job Corps director had to answer his own phone, and his staff, depleted to 12 persons, worked in one large room with torn-up carpets and empty desks scattered about. Yet even critics conceded that Angrisani deserved credit for eliminating the audit backlog.

[4] Quoted by Mark Huber, "Angry AC," *Conservative Digest*, November 1982, p. 42.

A GAO official called him "one of the good guys" for "tightening things up" and making the agency more management conscious. In 1983, Angrisani resigned his ETA post and left government service.

John Crowell and the Forest Service

A lawyer and an outdoors enthusiast, John Crowell was appointed assistant secretary for natural resources and the environment at the Department of Agriculture—the official responsible for overseeing the Forest Service. Crowell, who at this writing still remains at the Forest Service, has been one of the most controversial of Reagan's appointees. In his previous career with the timber products industry, he had been charged with shady dealings in an antitrust case involving timber companies. His Forest Service confirmation was opposed by twenty-five senators. He bristled at the opposition: "I am not a lawyer who was just plucked out of some law firm because I had worked on a Reagan campaign. And I'm not an ideologue. . . ." Yet his conservative philosophy of deemphasizing the concept of wilderness in favor of economic values was clearly in line with Reagan's own philosophy.

Headed by a nonpolitical chief forester, the Forest Service is a highly decentralized, quasi-military organization dedicated to administering the national forests. Foresters comprise most of the agency's 28,000 employees, they typically have a college degree in forestry, and the agency espouses the dictum that "the (person) on the ground knows best what to do." Said one forester, "We're close to the ground. We can feel things. We have a certain amount of righteousness about us, too. The cost shouldn't dictate how you treat the land. You take care of the land, in a physical sense, a practical sense."

Although an exploiter of resources and active in the National Forest Products Association, Crowell quickly earned the respect of the Forest Service. Observers of the agency saw him as a leader by example, a straight arrow, not cocky, and a good listener. Unlike Angrisani, he had no wish to shake up his agency. "I'm not going to be a dictator," he said. Crowell thought it important to give managers "clear ideas about his philosophy" and to "develop credibility and respect" among people in the agency. During the period under study he exhibited a lawyerly, case-by-case, detail-by-detail way of thinking, based on the attitude that persuasion is a matter of marshaling facts. He was not known as a conceptualizer, a strategic thinker, or a poker player. And he appeared to look at politics as a necessary but burdensome chore.

Crowell had two primary and related goals: to increase the timber harvest from national forest lands and to incorporate "economics" into the national forest planning process and into other agency activities. "It is inevitable," he said, "that we have to get more of our wood from the national forests. It's just bad management for us to get into a situation where we've got a housing boom coming along and don't have enough wood coming out of the forest to supply it."

He saw no need to amend the National Forest Management Act, believing that the act's legislative history made it clear that departures from the act's timber harvest policy should be undertaken wherever necessary in the interest of good management. His strategy was to increase the budget for timber sales at the expense of both the research and the state and private forestry budget. Yet, although supported in his views by the secretary and undersecretary of agriculture, he was unable to offer a convincing rationale to OMB for seeking increased timber sales during a severe construction recession (all he could come up with was that old growth forests needed to be cut), and Congress was unresponsive to a budgetary tradeoff that appeared to favor the Northwest at the expense of the Southeast (which benefited from the state and private forestry account). Crowell obviously failed in this initiative, a failure that he readily concedes.

Crowell was somewhat more successful in promoting economic values in the planning process. He promoted this objective not by creating a team of economists, planners, and policy analysts in his office or by dictating that people with these qualifications be hired in the Forest Service. Crowell and his aides were reluctant to interfere with the Forest Service's personnel system in such a way as to risk charges of politicization. Rather they moved the service in this direction indirectly by requiring the service to perform more economic analysis.

Vice-President George Bush's Task Force on Regulatory Relief, created in 1981, had identified as a "high priority for review" the Carter administration's rule guiding the planning process (the Reagan White House viewed the rule as too broad and vague and as affording wilderness advocates too much scope for influencing the process). With White House support (and its acquiescence to Crowell's compromises with environmental groups) the Department of Agriculture revised the guidelines for the national forest planning process to increase emphasis on economic analysis. Crowell also issued specific guidance to the Forest Service as to what he expected. "He meant business," said an observer. "There are a lot of memos that go out to the Forest Service that get lost. This one did not get lost."

One career official in the field observed,

> We find him a very fine and capable leader. But I would not say the Forest Service has fundamentally changed as an institution as a result of John Crowell. Our duties have not changed. I think that the forest supervisor is very conscious of Crowell—the supervisor is in the meetings a lot, travels to Washington, and reads a lot of paper. And yes, the supervisor does direct the ranger. But the ranger lives in the forest . . . is a relatively independent person and is a doer, and his allegiance is to the natural resources, not to some political philosophy.

Ford B. Ford and the Mine Health and Safety Administration

Ford B. Ford, who was appointed assistant secretary of labor responsible for the Mine Health and Safety Administration, came to the job with a reputation as having "White House connections." With a degree in production management and control from the University of California, he spent over twenty years in California state government. Five of those years were spent as Governor Reagan's chairperson of the Occupational Safety and Health Appeals Board and as the employer advocate on the board. When he was not reappointed by Reagan's successor, Ford lobbied the board on behalf of businesses as vice-president of the California Institute of Industrial and Government Relations. He was a believer in Reagan's mission.

The Mine Health and Safety Administration is responsible for enforcing the Federal Mine Safety and Health Act of 1977, as amended, a classic piece of command and control legislation. The agency was built around coal and metal/nonmetal mine inspection and the detection, correction, and punishment of violations. Its corps of inspectors consists primarily of former miners, organized into sixteen relatively autonomous districts, who have been described as "physical people" who "know how to mine coal and inspect mines." The inspectorate is clearly the power center of the agency. Although heterogeneous in their loyalties to labor or management, inspectors and their supervisors form a relatively close-knit culture, loyal to each other and to the agency's mission.

Variously termed "a nice guy," "inoffensive," "low key," "unaggressive," and "bland," Ford was viewed by critics as a "yes man" to Reagan and to Vice-President Bush's Task Force on Regulatory Relief. Nonpartisan observers of the agency, however, saw in him a great determination and a healthy instinct for doing the intelligent thing, and called him a "driven" man who knows where he wants to go. He was given high marks for respecting and listening to the career staff and for relying on them, rather than bringing in outsiders (for instance, he chose his deputy from the career ranks).

Before taking the federal position, Ford studied the agency closely and carefully formulated a strategy. "Clearly," he said,

> MHSA's effectiveness should not be measured in the number of inspections conducted, citations issued, or penalties collected, but in the reduction of injuries and illnesses. And a broadly focused, co-ordinated approach that encourages an active partnership between managers, workers, and the government is the best way of achieving those reductions.

The existing statute seemed to require the confrontational approach Ford abhorred. The American Mining Congress was urging the vice-president's Task Force on Regulatory Relief to seek changes in the 1977 Federal Mine Safety and Health Act to foster cooperation among industry, labor, and government

to improve workplace safety. Ford detected no consensus to change the act, however, and he decided to interpret it as broadly as possible.

Ford thus decided to consolidate inspections, civil penalty assessments, and education and training under the district managers, thereby increasing their authority and, incidentally, creating a potential base of support for the reorganization. This reorganization stimulated some temporary internal conflict. The administrator for the coal area, for example, liked the idea of having education and training under his wing, whereas Ford's deputy feared that the education and training function might be decimated in the process. Reorganization also coincided with a number of other actions, including administration-imposed budget cuts that were perceived as adverse by the inspectors, who accused the administration of "going soft" on safety. Then came a series of mine disasters, which galvanized the agency's critics, who charged that Ford's reorganization "results in less inspections, more responsibility, less violations written, lower assessments, and a more relaxed attitude toward mine health and safety." Though slowed down somewhat, the reorganization generally was put into effect with the overall support of the mining industry.

Ford encountered fewer difficulties with another internal change, that of requiring a conference between mine and MHSA officials before citations were issued. His move, however, to change the system of appraising inspectors' performances by, among other things, replacing reports on the number of inspections with reports of accident and injury reductions as a performance criterion stimulated the greatest opposition. Some administrators worried that inspectors would bribe operators not to report accidents. Inspectors also were uneasy about the new and less precise role they were being asked to play, and opposition to reductions in the staffing of the inspectorate intensified. Said one expert:

> The inspectors don't like the new system one bit. They've got to do all kinds of new things that they're not trained to do (such as holding conferences with mine operators). In particular, they are not interpersonal types, they are not managerial types, they are not trained to sit nose to nose with the operator and talk with him.

A different view, however, came from a district manager, who thought inspectors should learn to act like "gentlemen" and behave themselves at the mine site. Ford, he believed, is not going to let the inspectors get away with pushing the operator around; inspectors, he said, will have to learn how to "handle authority."

Ford's actions therefore sparked controversy and discontent. Inspectors appeared to be unhappy and angry. A nonpartisan agency observer commented, however, that Ford "turned that agency around without any major disturbance." Ford himself believes that "we've gone just about as far as we can [with] policy without infringing on the law." In the summer of 1983, Ford was promoted to the position of under secretary of labor.

Mark Fowler and the Federal Communications Commission

Mark Fowler came to the post of chairperson of the Federal Communications Commission from a career in the broadcasting industry. A former lawyer for a Washington, D.C., firm representing mostly small-size radio stations, he adopted the outlook of a small businessperson. He was also communications counsel for the Reagan presidential cam-

paigns of 1976 and 1980 and was sponsored for a federal appointment by Reagan intimate Charles Z. Wick. His belief in the virtues of the marketplace as a protector of freedom of the press was qualification enough for the FCC appointment.

The FCC has become one of the most visible agencies of government. Organized into four largely autonomous operating bureaus—for broadcasting, cable television, common carrier, and private radio—the agency is formally independent of the executive branch and is headed by a five-person commission. Rapid advances in telecommunications technology transformed the agency from a preoccupation with awarding licenses to very high frequency (VHF) television and to amplitude modulation (AM) and frequency modulation (FM) radio applicants to a concern with access to the entire spectrum of new services. Fast change made the agency staff apprehensive, all the more so as it became obvious that the proliferation of new services made the rationale for restrictive regulation of the old services much less persuasive. In addition, the fact that every major or controversial FCC action is publicized in some part of the communications field, if not in other fields, makes lawsuits likely.

As a fervent believer in the free market and an ideologue, Fowler views the FCC as Big Brother and a dinosaur, an inefficient, lackadaisical agency. His inflexible commitment to principle becomes palatable to friend and foe alike, however, because of his folksy, outgoing, and buoyant personality. He is a preacher but is not pontifical, and he is good natured and willing to hear criticism. Rather than confronting the bureaucracy, he believed in establishing clear expectations, in rewarding people for fine performance and in providing constructive criticism when warranted.

However, even his defenders see him as a babe in the woods.

Fowler had several specific goals. First, to make the FCC more responsive, he wanted to articulate its mission so clearly that even the smallest division could see where its activities fit into the big picture. He approached this task by creating a management-by-objective (MBO) system. Second, he wanted to extend "freedom of the press" to the electronic media by securing repeal of Section 315 of the Communications Act of 1934, as amended, which required the commission to enforce the "fairness doctrine" and the "equal time" clause. Third, he wanted to streamline licensing procedures so as to increase access to the communications media. Each of these goals was related to Fowler's larger purpose: reducing FCC interference in the free-market process.

Fowler moved swiftly to install his MBO system in 1981, successfully establishing in the minds of FCC watchers that the agency was now management conscious. A lengthy GAO report issued the year before had condemned FCC management and lent impetus to this initiative. FCC bureaus were required to produce action plans and were expected to adhere to them. The aide who was responsible for holding bureaus to their action plans was installed in an office next to Fowler's and had virtually unlimited access to him.

Unlike Ford, Fowler acted quickly to name loyal Reaganites to key FCC jobs; ten to thirteen offices and bureaus received new chiefs who were "free-market advocates actively working toward unregulation." At the same time Fowler took steps to "reach out to the employees" of FCC through incentive awards, pay increases, and other recognitions. According to one observer "even if people disagree with him, they like him," although his perceived opposition to af-

firmative action has antagonized some women and minorities.

Fowler's proposal to repeal Section 315 encountered a brick wall in Congress. Although the broadcasting content rules had respectable critics, the move was portrayed by opponents as a great boon to the three networks. Fowler's insistence on the amendment was irritating to many in Congress, and his handling of this and other issues earned him a reputation as being politically naive. "Some people just know how this town works," a Senate aide said. "Mark wasn't one of them." As a result, administrative critics were made more suspicious of the FCC's enforcement of the Communications Act, despite the fact that operating results do not reveal any differences between complaint rulings under Fowler and rulings under previous commissioners.

In a continuation of practices begun under his predecessor and facilitated by congressional amendments to the Communications Act, Fowler placed great emphasis on simplifying applications procedures. Extensive review by lawyers, engineers, and other specialists was replaced by "machinelike" processing by paraprofessional broadcast analysts. Morale among agency professionals suffered because of this deregulation emphasis. Said one: "We feel it. We see it. We hear it. Lawyers are doing very routine work. . . . if you're going to be a grade-13 attorney, then you need to be doing certain kinds of complex work." Yet there is a greater volume of work to be done—for example, in AM and FM licenses—because the number of applicants had increased markedly.

Under Fowler, who as of this writing still remains at the FCC, the commission's basic functions have not changed; the agency's resources continue to be devoted chiefly to processing applications and responding to complaints.

Many FCC watchers are convinced, however, that the agency is "more responsive" under Fowler. Many of the changes are subtle. Said one agency veteran:

> You can't put out of your mind that they want to abolish the content rules. We all know it. We're cognizant of the commissioner's desires. We will try to do that within the limit of the law. How? I don't know. Our procedures are based on precedent.

Raymond Peck and the National Highway Traffic and Safety Administration

Raymond Peck was appointed director of the National Highway Traffic and Safety Administration from the position of director of regulatory affairs for the National Coal Association. A lawyer who had practiced for several years in New York, he came to Washington, D.C., in 1971 and served successively as environmental counsel at the Department of Commerce, director of the Office of Energy Regulation and Legislative Policy in the Treasury Department, and deputy assistant secretary for energy and minerals in the Department of Interior. He was an unknown in the automobile safety community. However, his reputation for fearlessly confronting environmentalists in opposing strip-mining regulations appealed to Reagan, who placed his high priority on the NHTSA's providing regulatory relief for the automobile industry in the face of opposition from Ralph Nader and his staff of zealous watchdogs of the agency.

Though the agency is divided into components emphasizing vehicle safety and driver safety, the Ralph Nader-slated orientation of NHTSA is toward regulating motor vehicle design, not promoting safe behavior by drivers. Ninety percent of the agency's employ-ees, a diverse group of engineers, scientists, and lawyers, work in Washington, D.C. Many are bright, independent, and outspoken, much quicker to challenge political leadership than the top staff of other agencies. Said one, "we are the agency with the highest ideological content . . . within DOT [Department of Transportation]. The rest of the department builds stuff."

The first thing Peck told his staff, said this employee, was that he was "very bright" and a "very quick study." To most observers Peck appeared combative, self-assured, suspicious, and hard to pin down. He saw no need for a personnel shakeup at NHTSA, but he claimed not to be "blindfolded as to the possibility of duplicity on the part of the staff." "He is an extremely bright guy," said one, "but he is his own worst enemy." By instinct neither an ideologue nor a manager, Peck thought he possessed the qualities the White House wanted—a "litigator," not "gun shy," and someone who could see the job as challenging, tough, fun.

Peck's primary goal was to shift emphasis away from standards, such as that requiring the installation of airbags by car manufacturers, and toward promoting safety awareness, such as the voluntary wearing of seat belts; in other words, "to restore balance to the agency" by creating a proper mix of technical safety standards and behavior modification. Neither Peck nor the White House viewed NHTSA's statutory mandate to establish vehicle safety standards that are reasonable, practical, and appropriate as an obstacle, as it appeared to allow wide latitude in designing regulations. Another of Peck's goals was to achieve better cooperation between the agency and industry. By all appearances, however, he had no specific plan to achieve these goals. When he became interested in an activity, he tended to become personally involved regardless of agency routines, and he exhibited a lawyerly, argumentative, wits-matching style. When uninterested, he remained uninvolved. Thus his personal style, rather than his ideas, his strategy, or his accomplishments, became the basis for his reputation.

Among Peck's personal interests was promoting the use of seat belts, in part, associates believe, to challenge the preeminence of Joan Claybrook, Peck's highly visible predecessor. When NHTSA staff expressed skepticism, he planned his own seat belt campaign. Ignoring traditional traffic safety advocates and other potential allies, he hired a private consultant to create a Traffic Safety Foundation to raise funds for safety awareness programs. However, the vehicle safety community and its congressional allies pounced on Peck in hearings to investigate the foundation, and the enterprise was abandoned. Even Republicans were dismayed by Peck's "filibustering" and irritating personality. Peck was able to gain President Reagan's participation in his campaign to encourage seat belt use and to discourage drunk driving, and seat belt advocates in NHTSA cooperated, but Peck never gave the campaign either a goal or a solid political base.

To promote changes in agency priorities, Peck convened a weekend conference to discuss the possibilities. A memorandum recording decisions reached at the conference was not published until he was leaving office in May of 1983, and Peck never showed serious interest in it. A similar fate was met by a proposal for joint industry-agency research on side-impact protection and steering column design; following a law suit brought by Joan Claybrook, the project was canceled.

Said an automobile industry spokesperson,

The only difference between the Claybrook era and the Ray Peck era is that under Peck we got a fair hearing. . . . but I don't think the changes were fundamental. The changes were all reversible. If Joan Claybrook and the Democrats came in in 1984, I think we would go right back to the adversary position we were in before.

The industry did not have to wait that long. Following Peck's resignation in the summer of 1983, and the promotion of his deputy to replace him, NHTSA watchers immediately detected a revival of enthusiasm for safety regulations (as well as a decline of enthusiasm for deregulation in the White House). Peck and his goals were gone and forgotten.

REAGAN'S MANAGERS AS CHANGE AGENTS

The extent and character of change promulgated by these five officials varied widely from agency to agency, as Table 1 makes clear. Some change attributable to these appointees occurred in each of the five agencies, however. Each appointee made a deliberate, sustained effort to bring about change, and each found some kind of leverage over agency activity through which his personal influence could be and ultimately was felt.

However, the particular reinforcements employed by the Executive Office of the President (EOP) had significant consequences for these managers' influences on their agencies and on their agencies' constituencies. President Reagan, by creating ties that bound his appointees to his philosophy of government—for example, enlisting them in budget and staff reduction and deregulation—appeared to attenuate the influence on agency performance of each appointee's skills, ambition, and personality. Each appointee was acting

TABLE 1 • FIVE FEDERAL MANAGERS AND THE RESULTS
THEY ACHIEVED

Agency Official/ Core Activity	Skills/ Experience	Personality	Opportunity
Employment and Training Administration			
Albert Angrisani (*awarding grants and contracts*)	Inexperience in congressional politics; good bureaucratic instincts; few managerial skills; good grasp of grant and contract administration	Strongly adversarial; action-oriented, impulsive; oriented toward progress rather than people	Authority centralized; weak sense of mission; little professionalism (except for Job Corps); history of flux in character of agency operations—thus little cohesion or cultural identity
Forest Service			
John Crowell (*administering national forests*)	Politically naive; highly competent manager; no government experience; highly competent in resource administration; long associated with timber industry	Organization-builder; product-oriented; a "traditionalist" in attitude toward manager's responsibilities; determined, decisive, yet flexible; respectful of staff	Authority decentralized to field organization; strong sense of mission; professionalism; distinctive organizational cultures; well-organized constituencies; considerable stability
Mine Health and Safety Administration			
Ford B. Ford (*inspecting mines*)	Good political instincts; capable manager; state government, but no federal government experience; little knowledge of mining industry	Organization-builder; a "traditionalist" in attitude toward manager's responsibilities; open, a listener, low key	Authority decentralized to field organization; close-knit protective organizational culture; low level of professionalism

TABLE 1 · *(continued)*

Design	Results
Increase control over procurement by centralizing approval of requests for proposals (RFPs), sole-source justifications, contract awards, contracting modifications; shift control over contracting from program officials to financial managers; promulgate standard procurement model to reduce scope of contract officer discretion; expedite audit resolution	Shift of control over procurement to central office and from program to financial officials Evidence of lengthening of procurement cycle; increase in paperwork Significant disruption of agency routines and sharp decline in career staff morale; apparent increase in staff workloads and reduction of contract monitoring because of personnel cutbacks
Seek immediate increase in timber harvest by increasing timber sales budget, reducing state and private foresty and research budgets; change of policy of multiple-use, even-flow management; increase emphasis on economic values in planning forest uses by revising the planning process, insisting on economic analysis from field staff	No increase in planned timber sales or change in forest management policy Increased emphasis on econimic analysis in planning; increased appreciation of economic issues by career foresters
Reduce command and control emphasis in enforcement by enhancing authority, discretion of district manager to issue citations; take steps to increase health and safety by changing role of inspector through performance appraisal, institution of conferences with company officials	Significant change in inspection/enforcement process; shift of bureaucratic power toward district supervisors; some attitudinal change in field: many no longer see themselves as "just cops"

TABLE 1 • *(continued)*

Agency Official/ Core Activity	Skills/ Experience	Personality	Opportunity
Federal Communications Commission			
Mark Fowler *(awarding spectrum)*	Poor political instincts; adequate management skills; Washington, D.C., lawyer; well-developed appreciation of communications issues	True believer; outgoing and good natured; process-oriented	Authority decentralized to four functional bureaus; conservative, parochial agency culture; plural executive-rule by majority
National Highway Traffic and Safety Administration			
Raymond Peck *(establishing vehicle safety standards)*	Politically maladroit; ineffective as a manager; several years of federal government experience; no particular technical competence	Egoistic, wary; lawyerly rather than conceptual or ideological	Authority highly centralized; organizational culture infused with ideology, high sense of professionalism; strong sense of mission

as an agent for the president's policy preferences, and none showed much inclination to go into business for himself.

Thus the president and his EOP advisers were able to project their influence deeply into the bureaucracy, thereby occupying a substantial amount of executive "space" and leaving much less to chance or to the whims of appointees. In analyzing the interview data, one senses that Reagan's practices of appointing like-minded subordinates and reinforcing their belief that, although assigned to remote provinces, they are united in a common cause have helped to further his policies. Far from limiting

his appointees' persuasion to bringing the bureaucracy into line with his policies, the president used them as agents provocateurs, enforcers, and proconsuls in the agencies. Intimidation and the threat of reductions in force (RIFs) and budget cuts undeniably caught the attention of career bureaucrats.

For example, with the exception of Mark Fowler, whose agency's budget was beyond the purview of OMB, each appointee became an agent of an effort led by OMB Director David Stockman to force retrenchment on the federal bureaucracy, and all but Angrisani were associated with implementing deregulation in line with guidance from Bush's

TABLE 1 • (concluded)

Design	Results
Seek statutory repeal of "fairness" and "equal time" doctrines; install and use management by objectives to establish direction and accountability; require bureaus to prepare action plans; increase access to communications media by making licensing process less judgmental and by reducing discretion of bureaucrats; appoint Reagan loyalists to key posts	Bureau autonomy somewhat reduced: increased sense of accountability and of awareness of performance and responsiveness to outside inquiries; morale of career staff improved; continued trend toward streamlined procedures; less reliance on lawyers; increased applications—thus some increases in backlogs
	No repeal of section 315, though some congressional moves toward deregulation; deemphasis on "fairness doctrine"; heightened suspicion of administration in Congress and among consumer groups
Reduce emphasis on vehicle safety standards by suspending, moderating, or delaying vehicle standards; institute cooperative research to increase cooperation between government and industry; use motivational research, safety-awareness research to achieve behavior modification—for example, seat-belt use; reallocate priorities between vehicle standards and highway safety by planning "retreats"; broaden quarterly agenda of meetings between industry representatives and agency to include policy issues	Some standards modified; passive-restraint decision overruled
	Little change in agency emphasis on safety standards, though slightly increased appreciation of behavioral modifications among career staff; some new thinking
	Planned increases in cooperative research canceled

Task Force on Regulatory Relief. Managerial moves associated with implementation of Reagan budgetary or regulatory policies thus generated more controversy and opposition than might otherwise have been the case. Ford B. Ford's patient efforts to alter the character of mine inspections, for instance, which could be justified on their own merits, were criticized all the more severely because they were viewed as part of the president's crusade to disembowel enforcement of health and safety statutes. By the same token, many of these managers' moves were taken seriously and supported, both inside their agencies and in Congress, because they were seen as associated with a popular and determined president's policies.

Loyalty to the president's goals, however, was not inconsistent with open, trusting, and participative approaches to agency management by those presidential appointees. Only Angrisani confronted his agency's employees, openly distrusted them, and kept his distance from them. By contrast, Ford, Fowler, Crowell, and, to a lesser extent, Peck, sought to make full use of the human resources in their agencies, and they went out of their way to motivate subordinates to be cooperative. Promoting change in government, far from requiring confrontation and conflict, is doubtless inhibited by adoption of a "we-they" attitude.

Although some kind of externally provoked change was the rule rather than the exception in these agencies, their experiences also demonstrate convincingly that change is a slow, costly process attended by controversy and exceedingly demanding of executive effort. Though one can imagine a group of public executives who might exhibit greater economy, facility, and acumen in approaching their tasks than these five, it is hard to imagine any public executive succeeding by moving more boldly, ambitiously, or dramatically against the resistances he or she faced. That policy change under most circumstances comes about through incremental change is nowhere better illustrated than in these five agencies.

These generalizations notwithstanding, there was still considerable room for individual influence. The executives in this study differed in skills and personality, in the kinds of opportunities they faced, and in the quality of the designs they chose to exploit these opportunities. These differences, summarized in Table 1, help explain the pattern of changes occurring in these agencies, although the interactions among the changes are complex.

FACTORS IN MANAGERIAL SUCCESS

The most extensive changes in core activity appear to have occurred in the Mine Health and Safety Administration. By shifting power from mine inspectors to district supervisors through reorganization, and by redefining the role of the mine inspector, Ford succeeded in fundamentally altering his agency's approach to and attitudes toward its primary mission, that of inspecting mines. At the opposite extreme, Raymond Peck appears to have had relatively little effect on his agency's emphasis on and approach to establishing motor vehicle safety standards. Accomplishments of the other three executives appear to lie somewhere in between those of Ford and Peck. Significant, though not necessarily far-reaching, changes occurred both in the core activity of the Employment and Training Administration, where Angrisani succeeded, through a design similar to Ford's, in modifying the agency's approach to contracting, as well as in the core activity of the FCC, where Fowler has apparently increased his agency's sense of accountability, has changed its licensing process, and has reduced its emphasis on command and control regulation. Crowell, at the Forest Service, has reinforced already growing awareness among foresters of economic values in planning, although as yet without tangible results. However, during the period covered by this study, Crowell failed to achieve his primary objective, that of increasing timber sales (an objective, incidentally, not directly related to the agency's primary mission).

How to account for this pattern of success and failure? At first glance, managerial skills, including political sophistication and an open and respectful attitude toward one's organization, seem to be decisive. Ford had many of the skills and the personality of one who would be commonly called a "good manager." Though low key, he appreciated and used his organization to good effect. Among the five appointees, moreover, he was the only one with exceptionally good political instincts. Peck, in sharp contrast, would not be widely regarded as a "good manager" because he lacked skill both in the tasks of management and in political maneuvering. Moreover, his personality made him unpopular with many persons inside and outside the agency. His success was limited to actions—such as refusing to sign regulations—in which he could directly exercise his authority. Ford and Peck, one could argue, earned their just desserts: a good manager got good results, a poor one failed.

In terms of the other three appointees, although neither Angrisani nor Fowler could be fairly labeled as altogether lacking in managerial qualifications, neither their skills nor their personality notably qualified them for managerial roles in the public sector. Angrisani accumulated a substantial roster of critics outside of his inner circle, and Fowler, although well liked, was not viewed as a strong or authoritative figure. Yet each achieved notable results. As compared to Fowler and Angrisani, Crowell seemed to have the potential to be an effective manager, despite his lack of political acumen. Among the five, for example, Crowell earned the highest regard among his career subordinates. Despite his potential, however, Crowell's achievements were clearly inferior to all except Peck. If these results are any indication, possession of managerial skills and a good managerial personality may not be powerful predictors of success in public management.

The picture of factors in success or failure becomes somewhat clearer when comparing the opportunities these appointees faced, in other words, the relative ease or difficulty of accomplishing change in core activity in these five agencies. Agencies in which authority over core activity is decentralized to dispersed sites in the field, in which career personnel have strong professional identities, and in which career personnel participate in tightly woven issue networks of well-organized constituencies probably constitute the most difficult challenges to a political appointee. On the other hand, an agency executive who has significant authority over core activity and confronts relatively weak organizational cultures and disorganized, powerless constituencies has a greater opportunity to bring about change.

If opportunity is so conceived, Crowell probably had the least promising opportunity. Core activity was highly decentralized, and the status quo was reinforced by a strong organizational culture. Crowell's relatively homogeneous group of college-educated foresters could be expected to offer considerable resistance to externally imposed changes that threatened their sense of how their jobs ought to be done and their control over field activities. Crowell also had to contend with well-organized interest groups—environmental groups and the wood products industry—who had substantial economic and ideological stakes in agency activity. The dispersal of agency activity meant substantial congressional interest in agency affairs.

The Mine Health and Safety Administration also had highly decentralized core activity and a strong, though more heterogeneous, agency culture. The principal difference between the Forest Service and the MHSA was the latter agency's obscurity. Unlike the Forest Service, MHSA activities were centered in relatively few congressional districts, and the economic interests were less powerful. Barring a mine disaster, Ford labored on a bureaucratic back street, and for that reason faced a less confining situation than Crowell.

In the other three agencies, authority over activity was centered for the most part in Washington, D.C., physically and bureaucratically closer to the offices of the political appointees. Fowler nonetheless faced problems. He was only one of five commissioners, though supported by a Republican majority, and his four bureaus possessed considerable autonomy. Rapid technological and economic

changes in the communications industry, and their attendant uncertainties,
increased the problem of pursuing a
proactive policy. Change at the FCC
was far from certain.

Angrisani and Peck both had more
favorable situations. Angrisani had considerable leverage over his agency's core
activity. Though numerous procurement decisions were made in the Labor
Department's regional offices, he captured control over his agency's procurement process relatively easily. As mentioned earlier, the ETA was widely
regarded as a problem agency ripe for
leadership, reform, and good management. The National Highway Traffic
and Safety Administration was a somewhat tougher nut. Zealously guarded
by Ralph Nader-inspired advocates of
strong federal regulation of car and
highway safety, the agency was staffed
with a disparate group of well-educated
professionals who identified strongly
with the agency's objectives and established means for achieving them. Nonetheless the agency's core activity, that
of setting standards, was relatively accessible to an appointed executive; standards could not be issued without Peck's
approval. Thus Peck had the necessary
authority over the issuance of standards
to exert substantial influence on how
and why and, to a lesser extent, when
they were prepared.

Taking opportunity into account
brings a little more coherence to the
search for explanations for managerial
success and failure, and, in particular,
to the importance of the appointee's personal strengths and weaknesses. Ford's
skills and political acumen seem well
suited to his moderately difficult assignment. In the same vein, Angrisani faced
a significantly more promising situation,
and his modest managerial endowment,
especially his financial management orientation, was sufficient to enable him

to make headway in restructuring the
procurement process. He confronted
something of a power vacuum, and his
authoritarian, process-oriented personality led him to coerce his relatively
helpless subordinates into submission.
Fowler, too, was equal to the challenge
posed by his situation. He was liked better than his predecessor, and his persis-
tence, consistency and facility with bureaucratic routines were successful in
deflecting the FCC toward different policy orientations. In contrast, Crowell's
managerial capacity was insufficient for
a challenge of much greater magnitude
than any of the others faced. His efforts
earned him respect but not results. It
is not far fetched to imagine that a manager with Crowell's endowments might
have done well in Peck's agency. Angrisani, on the other hand, might have
been sunk by the turbulence he would
have generated in more renitent agencies such as those of Ford or Crowell.

A comparison of these executives' designs—that is, the particular goals they
chose to pursue and the means by which
they pursued them—sheds more definitive light on their achievements. Considering these managers' varying accomplishments, it is not surprising that their
designs also differed substantially in
quality. Ford and Angrisani quickly
achieved a pronounced effect on their
agencies' core activities—mine inspections and procurement, respectively.
Ford adopted a creative, complex strategy for changing his agency. By increasing the authority and the discretion of
district supervisors in overseeing the inspection process, he sought to reduce
the command and control emphasis in
enforcement of the laws governing mine
safety and health. At the same time,
he redefined the role of the mine inspector—making him an agent for safety
rather than an enforcer of rules—and
reinforced this role by focusing heavily

on the process of appraising the inspector's performance. Although capitalizing on pressures already present to deregulate mine safety enforcement, Ford was skilled in translating these pressures into a program for change.

Angrisani's goal was to make contracting more "efficient" and less subject to favoritism and other abuses by imposing more stringent criteria over contract awards and by standardizing the procurement process. He pursued these objectives by increasing the role of his office in approving procurement actions, by shifting authority over contracting from program officers to financial officers, and by promulgating a standard procurement model to reduce contract officer discretion in making awards. The flaw in this design is that it is internally inconsistent; procedural changes aimed at reducing fraud, waste, and abuse conflict with the objective of streamlining the process and of making it less arbitrary and uncertain. His failure to notice this inconsistency was responsible for considerable confusion and resentment in his agency.

Crowell and Fowler both had clear goals; Crowell's was to increase timber sales from the national forests and Fowler's was to reduce the federal role in regulating broadcast content and to increase access to communications media. Both appointees, however, chose ill-advised strategies to achieve these goals. Crowell attempted to increase budgetary allocations for timber sales at a time when there was little apparent rationale for such a policy. And Fowler sought congressional repeal of the "fairness" and "equal time" doctrines despite advice that pursuit of this goal, for which there were better strategies, would be jeopardized by the ensuing controversies. Crowell's design included little else than the attempt to increase timber sales and when it collapsed he had nothing of real consequence left to emphasize.

He failed to recognize that to achieve his goals, he would have to change the duties of the forest ranger. Fowler's strategy, which included internal changes, was more diverse, and he was less vulnerable to the failure of any particular aspect of it. For example, he sought to increase the sense of direction and accountability within the FCC by relying on a management-by-objectives process and by requiring each bureau to prepare action plans. He endeavored also to increase access to the communications media by making the licensing process less judgmental. In these pursuits, which were concerned with the core activity of licensing, he was much more successful.

Peck had a reasonable goal: shifting the emphasis of his agency away from issuance of stringent vehicle safety standards toward stimulating increased public awareness of safety through behavior modification. His plan for achieving this goal was vague and diffuse, however, and he did not appear to devote sustained attention to it. Some vehicle standards are different than they would otherwise have been because of his interventions, but his efforts to increase cooperative research between government and industry and to reeducate his career subordinates through a planning process came to nothing. Of the five designs, Peck's was the least precise and coherent.

Design, or, to use a more familiar term, strategy, thus emerges as an important factor in managerial success. Of the three most successful managers, Ford alone had a relatively well-conceived design, and the designs of Fowler and Angrisani had strengths sufficient to counterbalance their weaknesses. The two least effective managers, Crowell and Peck, had relatively poor designs. Indeed, an inadequate managerial strategy led to failure for a relatively good

TABLE 2 • FIVE FEDERAL MANAGERS AND THE RESULTS THEY
ACHIEVED: A SUMMARY ASSESSMENT

Agency Official	Skill	Personality	Opportunity	Design	Accomplishments
Albert Angrisani	Fair	Poor	Good	Good	Fair
John Crowell	Good	Excellent	Poor	Poor	Poor
Ford B. Ford	Good	Good	Fair	Excellent	Excellent
Mark Fowler	Fair	Fair	Good	Good	Good
Raymond Peck	Poor	Poor	Excellent	Fair	Poor

manager, Crowell, facing a difficult situation.

What conclusions can be drawn about determinants of managerial success or failure? Table 2 summarizes the foregoing discussion by rating each appointee as excellent, good, fair, or poor for each variable considered important in an appointee's success. The information in the table suggests the following conjectures: good to excellent accomplishments are associated primarily with good to excellent designs and not directly with good to excellent skills or personality. Creating good designs may be difficult, however, and the degree of difficulty may be associated, in turn, with the difficulty of the opportunity. Both Ford and Crowell needed a sophisticated design to accomplish their goals in a decentralized agency. The problem of design for Angrisani and Fowler was less difficult. The experiences of these four suggest the importance of skills and personality—perhaps especially political skills and qualities of imagination and flexibility. *The greater the challenge—that is, the more difficult the opportunity and thus the more sophisticated the design needed to exploit it—the greater the premium on managerial skills and personality.* Although he had much going for him in terms of outside support, Ford's success can nonetheless be attributed to his personality and skills as a manager. Neither Angrisani nor Fowler needed managerial qualities equal to Ford's in order to suc-

ceed in relatively less challenging circumstances. Inspired and supported by a strong, ideologically consistent administration, these appointees were sufficient to their tasks. By contrast, Crowell, as capable as he was, lacked the political skill and the flexibility to give him a real chance to alter the practices of his venerable agency.

POLICY CHANGE AND AGENCY PERFORMANCE

The suggestion that an executive has been successful in changing his agency's core activity should not be taken to imply that the overall performance of the agency has therefore improved. Ford B. Ford's administration of the Mine Health and Safety Administration drew sustained criticism from organized labor and from some internal critics who suggested that safety has been jeopardized by Reagan's and Ford's policies.[5] All five Reagan appointees have been criticized for failures to enforce existing statutes and for sacrificing the public interest in favor of more parochial, selfish, or ideological interests. Fundamental change is bound to be controversial, especially when there is a polarization in relations between political parties or be-

[5] Ford B. Ford, "An Update on MSHA: Reorganization and Regulatory Reform," *American Mining Congress Journal,* April 1982, p. 24.

tween the president and Congress, and change agents are almost certain to be surrounded by conflict. The question is whether there are any objective, or less relative, criteria by which to appraise the changes brought about by the appointees. What has been their impact on the quality of governance?

Available information is unfortunately insufficient to permit any comprehensive judgments, or even very good guesses, as to how these five appointees have affected the quantity, quality, or unit cost of their agencies' services, apart from the effects on these variables brought about by centrally imposed budget and staff reductions. It is not possible, for example, to determine whether Angrisani's policies affected the number of trainees, job placements, or trainee earnings or whether Ford has affected the safety of mines. And judgments as to whether Fowler's success in dampening his agency's enthusiasm for the "fairness" and "equal time" doctrines or on whether Crowell's success in increasing his agency's sensitivity to economic values has enhanced or retarded his agency's performance depend on one's views as to the wisdom of the policies being changed.

Nevertheless, the study interviews provide scattered information, largely of an impressionistic nature, bearing indirectly on changes in agency performance. The morale of career employees, and by implication their productivity, declined sharply in the ETA, the MHSA, and the NHTSA. Ford appeared to be building a base of support for his policies at the MHSA, however, and Peck was viewed more in sorrow than in anger and appeared to do no lasting harm at the NHSTA. Angrisani's rough treatment of the ETA seemed to have some damaging effects on performance. By centralizing and constricting the procurement process, Angrisani appeared to create a number of perverse effects, including heightened delays, increased resort to sole source awards and contract extensions, and meaningless paperwork. Impartial observers believed, however, that these disruptions were a small price to pay for what they saw as greatly heightened agency concern for management. In contrast, Fowler's actions at the FCC appeared to be working. Though processing delays increased, the cause appeared to be the greatly increased volume of applications for licenses. FCC watchers reported an improved agency responsiveness to various inquiries, and employee morale, which had been low under Fowler's predecessor, rose under Fowler.

Of interest, however, is that each appointee had to confront the issue of whether or not his agency's authorizing statute would constrain his freedom to act. Angrisani and Fowler both sought changes in authorizing legislation, though Fowler was unsuccessful. The other three appointees (Fowler, too, after he saw the futility of obtaining legislative changes) made conscious decisions to stretch interpretations of authorizing language as far as necessary to accommodate their policy views, even if commonly accepted interpretations of intent were breached in the process. And all were at least partially successful in this regard.

Did Reagan's electoral mandate justify a sustained assault on previously accepted versions of legislative intent? Should a presidential appointee ask, "What does the law, as interpreted by a clever general counsel, permit?" rather than "What did the legislature intend?"—making due allowance for the vague and inconsistent nature of most statutes? Reagan's is not the only administration, of course, to seek relief from the chafing of legislative intent—nor should our Constitution and system of laws be regarded as narrowly binding—but the extent of the Reagan administration's efforts to evade the law instead of confronting the legislature makes it doubtful that its approach to administrative management can be unequivocally branded "good governance."

The evidence, then, does not support claims either that Reagan's appointees, as opposed to Reagan's budgetary or personnel policies, have caused widespread deterioration in agency performance or that they have made federal management generally more efficient and more businesslike. If anything, they have demonstrated the extent to which federal statutes can be reinterpreted to permit significant organizational change.

IMPROVING MANAGERIAL PERFORMANCE: THE PRESIDENT'S ROLE

These five appointees do not, of course, an administration make. A significant number of Reagan appointees have made spectacular exits from public service or have fallen from grace for real or perceived transgressions. While most Reagan appointees were part of the effort to cut back and deregulate, some, especially in the area of defense, were engaged in expanding governmental activity. Expansion makes different demands on executives than does contraction, and an appraisal of the success of such executives engaged in expansionist change might identify different variables. The five appointees in this study may be taken to broadly represent Reagan's domestic appointees, however, and lessons derived from their performance can be instructive for future administrations.

Reagan's practice of appointing like-minded subordinates and of expecting loyal service from them has served him reasonably well. Although his appoin-

tees' performances were uneven, on balance all moved the government in directions consistent with his policies. How their particular contributions rank in terms of changes attributable to RIFs and budget cuts depends on the administration's overall purposes, but a good case can be made that an administration committed to reshaping governmental roles and performance will place substantial emphasis on its cabinet and subcabinet appointees and their potential roles in bringing about fundamental change.

The record of Reagan's five appointees, however, supports the impression that the power of appointment is an uncertain instrument of presidential influence. Presidential advisers might well have hoped for greater achievements from this group of officials. The Reagan administration is changing the government, but not nearly to the extent that it might have if these officials as a group had been more capable. Opportunities were missed in as least four of the five agencies.

It is likely, moreover, that actual performances departed from expectations in unpredictable ways, given the administration's insufficient prior knowledge of these appointees. Presidential recruiters seldom assess skills, personality, and opportunity in the depth that this study suggests is relevant. Nor is a candidate's likely design ordinarily ascertained. The cost of undertaking such assessments would be significant. The question is whether the benefits in terms of appointee contributions to presidential goals would be worth it.

The results of this study can only suggest the answer to this question. The attributes of these appointees are sufficiently pronounced that careful investigation of references would probably have revealed most of them. Assessing the precise nature of the opportunities for which appointees are to be sought might be more difficult and costly, but the insights gained thereby could be valuable; skilled and patient managers could be placed where these qualities are particularly necessary in accomplishing presidential purposes. Advance insight into a candidate's competence at designing a strategy may be the most difficult capability of all to obtain. Evidence that a candidate has created good designs in other responsible positions is an imperfect but useful indicator of how he or she will perform in government. Unlike skills and personality, however, appointees' strategies are not altogether beyond presidential control once they are in office, and continuing oversight by OMB and the president's policy staffs can aid appointees' performances.

President Reagan helped his cause by choosing appointees who shared his vision and by communicating and implicitly enforcing his sense of purpose among subordinate political executives. If Reagan and his recruiters had had a more explicit understanding of how lasting change in governmental activity is achieved, they might have used the power of appointment to even greater effect. Investing in an effort to match skills, personality, and opportunity, and assisting appointees in designing managerial strategies, could yield significant benefits to the president's program.

CHAPTER VI

Executive-Legislative Relations

Article II, Section 3 of the Constitution is notable for its spartan treatment of the president's participation in legislative activity. It reads:

> He shall from time to time give the Congress Information of the State of the Union, and recommend to their Consideration such Measures as he shall judge necessary and expedient; he may on extraordinary occasions, convene both Houses, or either of them, and in Case of Disagreement between them, with respect to the Time of Adjournment, he may adjourn them to such Time as he shall think proper . . . he shall take Care that the Laws be faithfully executed.

While early State of the Union messages seldom recommended specific legislation to Congress, the president's role as legislative leader has nevertheless become one of his foremost responsibilities. Since the presidency of William Howard Taft, presidents have regularly utilized the State of the Union message to pursue their legislative agendas.[1]

Between 1801 and 1913, presidents submitted their State of the Union messages in writing. Since 1913, however, Woodrow Wilson and subsequent presidents have addressed Congress in person. The president now appears before a joint session of Congress and reads the State of the Union address live to Congress and the nation's television audience. Indeed, the address is carried by satellite to most of the television audiences of the world. The address of a president who has just arrived in office states the coming administration's priorities and appeals to Congress and the public at large for support. A president who is in the second year of a term or beyond will typically review the administration's successes and shortcomings and restate its goals and priorities for Congress. In any event, a few days later, the president sends the written address to Congress with detailed proposals of the legislation he or she would like to see enacted. To be considered seriously, a president's legislative proposals require both leadership and effective liaison from the president's office in the Congress.[2] As Barbara Hinkley points out: to provide leadership, presidents must make their priorities clear to Congress and define what they seek by way of legislation.[3] As for liaison, presidents must work with their White House and liaison staffs who have the job of shepherding and prodding the president's bills through the legislative process.

The priorities established, friendly members of Congress from the various committees are consulted by the White House liaison[4] and asked to introduce, in their respective houses, bills prepared by the various executive agencies, which have passed through the Office of Management and Budget's central clearance process and received approval.[5] OMB clearance is usually tantamount to presidential clearance.

These bills are almost automatically then referred to the appropriate committees for study. Once in committee, the bills are no longer automatically processed.[6] From this point onward, the president, the legislative liaison, and congressional supporters must carefully nurture the bills through committee hearings and floor debate or they will never reach the president's desk for consideration.

In this process, we may expect that considerable conflict and/or cooperation may occur between the executive and legislative branches. Roger Davidson points out some of the sources of conflict. Among them are: the separation of powers which spreads authority across the two branches; different constituencies, resulting from the president being elected nationally while the senators and representatives are elected by citizens of individual states and congressional districts, respectively; and different time perspectives resulting from the president working in a four-year time frame while senators work in six-year time frames and representatives in two-year time frames.

Davidson also discusses the sources of cooperation between the two branches. These emanate from the sheer necessity for accommodation between the two to make government work because they share powers.[7] Davidson subsequently reviews the kinds of agendas incoming administrations may have as well as the patterns of interbranch control: the party government model, the truncated majority model, and the divided government model. Each of these models can have considerable impact, either positive or negative, on a president's agenda. Of particular note is the observation that presidential support in Congress is heavily influenced by its partisan makeup. Davidson's insightful analysis of executive-legislative relations is presented in his essay, "The President and Congress," which is reprinted here.

Once a bill is agreed upon in conference committee and is passed in identical form by both houses, it goes to the president for a signature.[8] If the president signs the bill it becomes law. If the president fails to sign the bill within ten days of receiving it (Sundays do not count toward the ten-day period), the bill becomes law. However, if Congress has adjourned before the ten-day period expires and the president has not signed the bill, the president has, in fact, pocket vetoed the bill, and it fails of enactment. In effect, the president "pockets" the bill and denies Congress the opportunity to override the veto.

Interestingly enough, the pocket-veto strategy may seem only a minor irritation to Congress. It is more than that. In fact, Congress passes a great deal of legislation near the end of a session, thus making it possible for a president to exercise the pocket veto on numerous bills. Indeed, presidents often take advantage of this opportunity to reject, without formal veto message, legislation they do not like.

Considerable controversy surrounds the question whether a president may pocket a bill when Congress adjourns between sessions of the same Congress. President

Reagan, for example, exercised the pocket veto between the first and second sessions of the 97th Congress and again during the intercession of the 98th Congress. In 1984, the U.S. Circuit Court ruled that a president may not pocket veto legislation between sessions of Congress. The Reagan administration has appealed and the Supreme Court has agreed to determine whether a president can prevent a bill from becoming law during recesses between sessions of the same Congress.[9]

Considerably more important than the pocket veto is the veto, itself. This is so because a determined Congress could prevent a pocket veto by simply not waiting until the last minute to pass legislation; Congress cannot, however, blame the president when it fails to override vetoes of bills passed in the regular legislative time frame. Under Article I, Section 7 of the Constitution, the president may return a bill, with his objections, to the house in which it originated. The bill may then be reconsidered and if both houses pass the bill in identical form by a two-thirds vote, it becomes law. This extraordinary majority needed in both houses to override a veto makes the president's veto power a formidable weapon. Parenthetically, the U.S. Supreme Court has ruled that two-thirds of a quorum present in each house, rather than two-thirds of the total membership, is sufficient to override a president's veto.[10]

The tremendous power of the president's veto, the categories of vetoes, and a president's own motivations for vetoing legislation are the subjects of the next selection. Albert Ringelstein reviews the major findings of previous studies of the president's veto, reporting that virtually all of them concerned the number, form, strategy, or constitutional power of presidential vetoes. The one exception was Gary Copeland's study that deals with the effect of *external* factors on a president's vetoes.[11]

Ringelstein's findings were as follows:

1. Republican presidents tend to veto a higher number of *public* bills than do Democrats.
2. Few vetoes occur in the area of foreign policy.
3. In the category of domestic legislation, resources and government management bills received two thirds of the total presidential vetoes, while social services bills were vetoed relatively few times.
4. Republican presidents vetoed more legislation in the social service category than did Democrats.
5. More bills were vetoed by presidents because they were "too costly" than for any other single reason; Republicans show a slight tendency to use this reason more than Democrats.
6. Few bills were vetoed by presidents because they were felt to be unconstitutional.
7. When controlling for party, each of the presidents has about the same veto rate as the others.

8. Republican presidents led in vetoing legislation because it was "too expensive" and "not a federal responsibility."

9. Democratic presidents led in vetoing legislation in the "restricts executive action" category.

Overall, Ringelstein found the categories of and reasons for presidential vetoes remarkably similar from president to president, independent of party. He noted that, frequently, presidents have just as much in common with each other in their struggles with Congress, as they differ as Republicans or Democrats fighting for different ideological programs and considerations. Ringelstein's provocative essay, "Presidential Vetoes: Motivation and Classification," is reprinted here.

NOTES

1. On this point see Louis Fisher, *The Politics of Shared Power: Congress and the Executive* (Washington, D.C.: C.Q. Press, 1981), p. 23.

2. See Barbara Hinkley, *Problems of the Presidency: A Text with Readings* (Glenview, Ill.: Scott, Foresman, 1985), p. 163.

3. Ibid.

4. For recent studies of the presidential-congressional liaison relations see Eric L. Davis, "Legislative Liaison in the Carter Administration," *Political Science Quarterly* 9 (Summer 1979), pp. 287–301; Stephen J. Wayne, "Congressional Liaison in the Reagan White House: A Preliminary Assessment of the First Year" in *President and Congress: Assessing Reagan's First Year*, ed. Norman J. Ornstein (Washington, D.C.: American Enterprise Institute, 1982), pp. 44–45.

5. On the central clearance role in proposed legislation see Richard E. Neustadt, "Presidency and Legislation: The Growth of Central Clearance," *American Political Science Review* 48 (1954), pp. 641–57; the current policy for central clearance is spelled out in OMB Circular No. A–19, revised September 20, 1979.

6. See Nelson M. Polsby, *Congress and the Presidency*, 4th ed. (Englewood Cliffs, N.J.: Prentice-Hall, 1986), p. 141.

7. Hinckley, *Problems of the Presidency*, p. 148, writes that "Although political commentators stress the executive dominance of twentieth century government, it is appropriate to reaffirm the shared nature of the governing mandate."

8. Interestingly, while a bill is in enrolled form, that is, it has been passed by both houses but awaits the signatures of the officers of each house, a facsimile of the bill is forwarded to the OMB, which, in turn, will forward it to the line department or agency that prepared it initially for review and recommendations. The department or agency may recommend approval or veto. If it recommends veto, it prepares the veto message for the president. The OMB and the president will, however, make the final decision whether to sign or veto a bill. See Stephen J. Wayne, Richard L. Cole, and James F. C. Hyde, Jr., "Advising the President on Enrolled Legislation: Patterns of Executive Influence," *Political Science Quarterly* 94, no. 2 (Summer 1979), pp. 303–17; see also OMB Circular No. A–19, revised September 20, 1979, which outlines the OMB's rules for legislative coordination and clearance, including enrolled bills.

9. Reported in Larry Berman, *The New American Presidency* (Boston: Little, Brown, 1986), p. 32.

10. *Missouri Pacific Railroad Co. v. Kansas,* 248 U.S. 177 (1919).

11. See Gary Copeland, "When Congress and the President Collide: Why Presidents Veto Legislation," *Journal of Politics* 45 (August 1983), pp. 696–710.

16
The President and Congress
Roger H. Davidson

After the Democrats captured both houses of Congress in the wake of the 1986 elections, the chairman of the House Democratic Caucus proclaimed that "the Reagan era is ending." Said Missouri's Richard A. Gephardt, himself a presidential hopeful: "This is our time to lead. The long days of playing defense are over." At the same time, the newly chosen speaker, Jim Wright of Texas, announced that his first order of business would be to pass a bill the president had vetoed just a few weeks before, and to name a committee to inquire into the administration's controversial Iranian arms deal.[1]

The return of divided government in the nation's capital was only the latest chapter in the sometimes stormy, sometimes benign relations between the White House and Capitol Hill. The Constitution offers no simple or direct formula for working out this relationship, despite the fact that its success is undoubtedly the leading institutional question posed by the document. Throughout history the relationship has proven delicate, multifaceted, and constantly changing.

Like a pair of wrestlers in a ring, presidents and Congresses are locked in a contest for advantage. Some of their moves lead to real body contact; other moves are evasive or for dramatic effect. Both must seize their political opportunities; yet each finds it convenient to cede ground to the other. Confrontation is built into the relationship. Legislators are suspicious of White House occupants (not only presidents but their advisors as well) and the attention they get; they fear that presidents would rather operate without so much as a nod in Congress's direction. All the so-called strong presidents have in fact been accused of "usurpation" at one time or another. Presidents and their advisors, by the same token, sometimes regard Congress as a nuisance or an anachronism. At least some of them come to believe that a

[1] Janet Hook, "House Leadership Elections: Wright Era Begins," *Congressional Quarterly Weekly Report* (December 13, 1986), 3067–70.

Source: This is a revision of an article that originally appeared in *The Presidency and the Political System,* pp. 363–91, edited by Michael Nelson, 1984, Washington, D.C.: CQ Press. Copyright © 1984 Congressional Quarterly, Inc. The views expressed in this article are those of the author alone and do not represent the views or positions of the Congressional Research Service.

little usurpation is required to make the system work.

SOURCES OF CONFLICT

The designer of the Nation's Capital, Major Pierre L'Enfant, followed logic and advice when he placed the president and Congress on opposite sides of the city. Congress would occupy a single large building on Jenkins Hill, the highest promontory. On a plain a mile or so to the northwest would be the executive mansion. A broad avenue was to link them for ceremonial exchanges of communications; but a bridge linking them by spanning Tiber Creek was not built until the third decade of the nineteenth century. Characteristically, the Capitol faced eastward and the Executive Mansion northward, their backs turned on each other.[2]

Constitutional Conflicts

"An invitation to struggle" is the way one constitutional scholar describes the Constitution's delineation of powers between the two elected branches. Article I invests Congress with "all legislative powers," which embrace nearly all the governmental functions known to eighteenth-century thinkers. Reflecting the founders' Whig heritage, the powers include the historic parliamentary power of the purse, in addition to broad economic powers and even a hand in foreign and defense policies—traditionally royal prerogatives. Finally, Congress was granted in Section 8 an elastic power to make all laws "necessary and proper" to carry out its enumerated powers.

In working out these policies, however, the Constitution spreads authority across the two branches. Although Congress possesses "all legislative powers," the president can veto legislation passed by the two houses. The president concludes treaties with foreign nations, but these must be ratified with the "advice and consent" of the Senate. The Constitution does not say how the Senate is to render its advice and consent. At first George Washington tried to consult the Senate personally about a treaty with the southern Indians; but the encounter was so uncomfortable that Washington left in a huff, and neither he nor any of his successors ever again attempted to seek direct advice.[3] It took the Senate thirty-seven years to approve the genocide convention, first signed in 1949. Senate opposition killed ratification of the Treaty of Versailles in 1919 and 1920. Interest in the 1978 Panama Canal Treaties was so keen that nearly half the Senators visited Panama to talk personally with its government leaders, and several senators rewrote the treaties by authoring crucial amendments.

In short, the Constitution blends executive and legislative authority and assigns each branch special duties. The resulting arrangement is usually called "separation of powers," and the Supreme Court has occasionally come down on the side of strict partitioning of responsibilities.[4] However, theory and practice of the arrangement point to someting quite different: separate institutions sharing the same powers. The relationship was designed, as James

[2] James S. Young, *The Washington Community, 1800–1828* (New York: Columbia University Press, 1966), pp. 75–76.

[3] William Maclay, *Journal of William Maclay*, ed. Edgar S. Maclay (New York: D. Appleton, 1890), pp. 128–33.

[4] *Federalist 48*, Alexander Hamilton, James Madison, and John Jay, *The Federalist Papers* (New York: New American Library 1961), p. 308. See also Richard E. Neustadt, *Presidential Power: The Politics of Leadership from FDR to Carter* (New York: John Wiley & Sons, 1980), pp. 26–28.

Madison put it, so that "these departments be so far connected and blended as to give each a constitutional control over the others."[5] From the very beginning, practical considerations have dictated a blurry blending, not a neat division of functions.

Differing Constituencies

Presidents and their running mates are, as some of them are fond of pointing out, the only nationally elected public officials. To gain election they must construct electoral coalitions that are national in scope. Practically speaking, this means criss-crossing the nation in search of votes and support—in the process brushing against a host of local concerns. Although local commitments may be made, presidential candidates must shape successful appeals that transcend local politics and appeals on a more general level. Members of Congress, acting singly, represent these same local concerns and thus have a somewhat different perspective on them.

As transplanted locals, senators and representatives tend to see the nation's problems through their constituents' eyes. Even if they concede that a certain local benefit is bad public policy, they may not oppose it. Especially on economic issues—for example, public works, farm programs, import restrictions—members usually give unqualified support to their district's needs because, as they see it, no one else is likely to do so.[6] A president or cabinet member who is pursuing, for example, macroeco-

nomic policy mandates or more efficient distribution of military installations will find the welfare of auto workers or a given area's Camp Swampy standing in the way.

From the president's point of view, the key to winning victories on Capitol Hill is to build coalitions of members whose constituencies benefit or at least are indifferent to the consequences of given policies. In an institution in which stopping policies is easier than enacting them, the objective often is to avoid singling out sizable numbers of constituencies for adverse policy effects. This is not an easy assignment, especially if economic output and productivity fail to provide a cushion of growth to sweeten the pot. Distributing hardships, in other words, is more hazardous politically than distributing benefits.

Disparities in constituencies are underscored by a disparity in the way that voters judge presidents and members of Congress. Studies of presidential popularity ratings since Franklin D. Roosevelt's administration show that presidents tend to be judged on the basis of general criteria—economic boom or bust, the presence or absence of wars or other types of crises, the effects of policies on given groups.[7] Legislators, by contrast, tend to be assessed on the basis of their personalities, their communication with the district, and their service to the district in material ways. Relatively few voters, it seems, mention policy issues in rating their representatives.[8] Not only do presidents and legis-

---

[5] See, for example, the pronouncement of Chief Justice Warren Burger in *Immigration and Naturalization Service* v. *Chadha* (1983) and *Bowsher* v. *Synar* (1986).

[6] Thomas E. Cavanagh, "Role Orientations of House Members: The Process of Representation" (Paper delivered at the annual meeting of the American Political Science Association, 1979), p. 20.

[7] See, for example, Stephen J. Wayne, "Great Expectations: What People Want from Presidents," in Thomas E. Cronin (ed.), *Rethinking the Presidency* (Boston: Little, Brown, 1982), pp. 185–199.

[8] Glenn R. Parker and Roger H. Davidson, "Why Do Americans Love Their Congressmen So Much More Than Their Congress?" *Legislative Studies Quarterly* 7 (February 1979), pp. 53–61.

lators serve differing constituencies; they labor under divergent incentives.

Different Time Perspectives

The president and members of Congress also operate under different timetables. It is commonly claimed that while legislators look only to the next election—every two years, in the case of House members—presidents can take a longer historical perspective. The opposite is more nearly the truth. Presidents work under a four-year time frame. Once they have been reelected, presidents are lame-ducks who have nothing to run for except the historical record books: "running for the Nobel Peace Prize," as Thomas E. Cronin puts it. Among modern presidents, only Dwight Eisenhower and Ronald Reagan have enjoyed that luxury. Even at that, a one-term president is an old-timer compared with other political appointees in the Executive branch, whose average tenure has been only eighteen months.[9]

A president's political timetable in practice is briefer than the four-year term. Presidents and their advisors face the harsh fact that their honeymoon with Congress usually is short-lived. They are aware of the need to strike quickly and preempt the nation's agenda. Formerly presidents accomplished this by submitting packages of legislative proposals, sometimes with catchy labels like "New Deal," "Fair Deal," or "New Frontier." President Reagan, whose goals lay less in enacting new laws than in curtailing old ones, relied instead upon the budget process to carry his proposals for drastically shifting national priorities.

While the two-year electoral cycle affects the pace of Capitol Hill business,

it does not dominate the policymaking timetable of members or their committees. After all, the average senator's or representative's tenure exceeds that of presidents and their appointed executives. Today's typical House member has been in Congress for about five terms (ten years); the typical senator for nearly two terms (eleven years). Committee and subcommittee leaders boast even greater longevity. Most of them have witnessed the evolution of issues over a number of years, perhaps even a generation. They have watched administrations and their policies come and go. Most legislators, then, will be in office longer than the presidents they deal with, and many of them have more stable policy perspectives.

SOURCES OF COOPERATION

Despite the built-in tensions between the two branches of government, cooperation is at least as common as conflict. Day in and day out, Congress and the president work together. Bills get passed and signed into law: the ninety-four volumes of *United States Statutes at Large,* in which all enactments are compiled, testify to the cooperative impulses of the two branches. Presidential appointments are confirmed by the Senate; budgets are approved and the government is kept afloat—though sometimes just barely. Cooperation is evident even when the White House and capitol are in the hands of opposing parties.

Constitutional Blending of Powers

As we have seen, the Constitution separated the instruments of governmental powers rather than the powers themselves. Quite obviously, accommodation between the branches is essential to make the intricate mechanism work. As Justice Joseph Story once wrote, the framers sought to "prove that rigid

[9] Hugh Heclo, *A Government of Strangers* (Washington: Brookings Institution, 1977), pp. 103–5.

herence to [separation of powers] in all cases would be subversive of the efficiency of government and result in the destruction of the public liberties."[10] And Justice Robert Jackson wrote in 1952, "While the Constitution diffuses power the better to secure liberty, it also contemplates that practice will integrate the dispersed powers into a workable government."[11]

Cooperation—or at least civilized give and take—is more the rule than the exception. White House personnel screening and selection, when it functions effectively, takes congressional preferences into account. Within the president's party, various Capitol Hill factions sponsor and lobby for sympathetic candidates; floor and committee leaders must be informed, if not always catered to, during the selection process. Most cabinets include a sprinkling of former members of Congress, chosen not only to appeal to Capitol Hill but to bring political savvy to the administration's councils. Unusually sensitive appointments—for example, in the wake of forced resignations, scandals, or acute policy conflicts—will be made with an eye to pacifying congressional factions.

Once sent to Capitol Hill, the president's appointments are traditionally accorded great respect. Not since the Eisenhower administration has a cabinet designee been turned down: Lewis L. Strauss was rejected as secretary of commerce by a 46–49 vote on the Senate floor in 1959. A combination of policy differences and questions of integrity led to the defeat. Subcabinet nominees are almost always approved.

Certain types of appointees demand special congressional scrutiny. Regula-

tory commissioners are, after all, located in the nether world between the legislative and executive branches. While nominated by the president, these appointees are not strictly members of the president's administration. Supreme Court appointees also lie outside the executive branch and are subject to serious Senate review. During the Nixon administration, two appointments to the Supreme Court—Clement Haynsworth and G. Harold Carswell—were rejected by the Senate after questions were raised about their competence and dedication to civil rights. President Nixon sent a controversial letter to Senator William Saxbe (R-Ohio) arguing that senators should defer to presidential judgment in judicial choices. Neither the Constitution nor senatorial traditions lend any support to that viewpoint. Only a couple of years earlier, President Lyndon B. Johnson failed in two Supreme Court nominations—one of them withdrawn, the other not acted upon.

In general, though, few nominees are turned down outright. Of the 106,616 nominations submitted in 1981 by Ronald Reagan (the great bulk of them military officers), 105,282 were confirmed. None was rejected. But 33 were withdrawn (the most notable being Ernest Lefever, nominated as Assistant Secretary of State for Human Rights). Going unconfirmed were 1,299. Some of these were eventually approved; others were later withdrawn, and still others were simply left vacant—a White House tactic for holding firm while avoiding direct clash with Congress.

In exercising other constitutionally blended powers, deference is paid at both ends of Pennsylvania Avenue. Presidents are expected to take strong initiatives; if they do not, Congress will voice equally strong complaints. When presidential initiatives are presented and pushed, Congress can be expected to follow suit in a majority of instances.

---

[10] Joseph Story, *Commentaries on the Constitution of the United States*, 5th ed. vol. 1 (Boston: Little, Brown, 1905), p. 396.

[11] *Youngstown Sheet & Tube Co.* v. *Sawyer*, 343 US 579, 635 (1952).

Yet congressional committees and subcommittees remain jealous of their prerogatives and jurisdictions: their viewpoints must be checked out before new executive initiatives are launched and their wishes accommodated in negotiations.

Coinciding Interests

Partisan or ideological ties often bind the two branches. Presidents and congressional leaders have consulted informally on issues ever since the first Congress, when George Washington sought out the advice of Representative James Madison. Regular meetings between the chief executive and House and Senate leaders have occurred since Theodore Roosevelt's time. Today, congressional leaders of the president's party are two-way conduits, communicating legislative views to the president and, conversely, informing lawmakers of executive preferences and intentions. As Senate Majority Leader Howard H. Baker, Jr., described the relationship during the Reagan administration,

> [T]he majority leadership of this body has a special obligation to see to it that the President's initiatives are accorded full and fair hearing on Capitol Hill. By the same token, we have a special duty to advise the President and his counselors concerning parliamentary strategy and tactics.[12]

Ideological or factional affinities sometimes enable presidents to forge Capitol Hill coalitions outside their own party lines. Reagan was by no means the first conservative president to capitalize on the presence of "Boll Weevil" Democrats in Congress. Eisenhower and Nixon (during his first administration) also bargained with southern Democrats to pass compromise White House mea-

sures and thwart more liberal alternatives. (Senate Majority Leader Lyndon B. Johnson used to carry a laminated scorecard showing how much legislation he had helped pass for President Eisenhower.)

These same Dixie conservatives were the bane of more liberal presidents such as Franklin D. Roosevelt, Harry S. Truman, and John F. Kennedy. Yet these chief executives could enlist help from moderate or liberal Republicans. Passage of Truman's internationalist foreign policy initiatives would have been far more difficult without the bipartisan imprint of Senator Arthur Vandenberg. Senate passage of the 1964 Civil Rights Act hinged on support from Republican Minority Leader Everett McKinley Dirksen who, though no liberal, became convinced that civil rights was "an idea whose time has come."

Thus the White House must seek out votes from a wide range of lawmakers on both sides of the aisle. There is plainly no other way to get legislative results. As FDR declared in his second State of the Union address, the "impulse of common purpose," remains a potent cause of cooperation between the two branches.[13]

Public Expectations

Regardless of the policy commitments of the two branches, the basic necessity of sustaining the federal government stimulates cooperation. Legislators and presidents have at least several common interests: winning elections, maximizing policy objectives, and keeping the government running. Sometimes there is little more to compel cooperation than the need to keep the government solvent. In 1981, Republican senators faced, many of them for the first time, the question of supporting their

---

[12] *Congressional Record* 128 (97th Congress, 2nd session), S 16115. (December 23, 1982, daily edition).

[13] *Congressional Record* 78 (73rd Congress, 2nd session), 7 (January 3, 1934).

president's call for a hike in the national debt ceiling in order to fund government operations. Most of them opposed debt hikes on philosophical grounds; many had never voted for them. During a heated meeting on the issue, Strom Thurmond, the senior Republican and the Senate's president pro tempore, rose and addressed his colleagues:

> Gentlemen, I understand you are concerned that you always opposed an increase in the debt limit. Some of you served in the House, and you never voted to increase it. Well, neither have I. But I never had Ronald Reagan for President before, so I'm going to vote for it, and I believe you should too.[14]

Thurmond's appeal helped sway his wavering colleagues. The debt limit hike passed by a 64–34 margin, with Democrats holding back until a majority of Republicans went on record to support their chief executive.

THE PRESIDENT AS LEGISLATOR

Political scientists have long called the president "the chief legislator" because of his crucial role in the legislative process. This is a metaphor. Presidents do not directly introduce legislation; nor do they appear as witnesses or participate in floor debate. But the president can propose legislation, deputize allies and agents in Congress, and use or threaten to use the veto power.

The President's Legislative Powers

The president's legislative role springs from Article II, Section 3, of the constitution: "He [the president] shall from time to time give to the Congress infor-

mation on the state of the Union, and recommend to their consideration such measures as he shall judge necessary and expedient." Since Woodrow Wilson, these addresses have been delivered in person, recently in prime TV time. Presidents help shape the congressional agenda. They focus attention, publicize priorities, and mobilize public opinion. By so doing they supply Congress with something that its scattered and decentralized structure prevents it from providing itself—an agenda.

Setting the Agenda. Framing agendas is what the presidency is all about. Within the White House, priorities are established for using the president's precious commodities of time, energy, and influence. Setting the national agenda poses the same problem written large: how to control other actors rather than be dominated by their initiatives. That is the essence of leadership for all presidents with extensive program goals— Wilson, the two Roosevelts, Jackson, and others at certain moments. Ronald Reagan's early days in the White House dramatically exemplified leadership through agenda control. It is easy enough to say after the fact that "Reaganomics" was an unworkable mixture of incompatible and wrong-headed decisions. (White House advisors like David Stockman, director of the Office of Management and Budget, apparently understood these inconsistencies from the start.[15]) The Reagan program swept through the nation's capital not because it was a "better idea," but because it was the only game in town. Acting swiftly and communicating skillfully, the new president had imposed his agenda at both ends of Pennsylvania Avenue.

Agenda setting assumes that other ac-

---

[14] Quoted in John H. Averill, "Thurmond Joins Insiders at Last," *Los Angeles Times* (April 25, 1982), Part I, p. 12.

[15] See David A. Stockman, *The Triumph of Politics* (New York: Harper & Row, 1986).

tors welcome presidential leadership. For Congress, such leadership fulfills a need it has rarely been able to fulfill on its own. The First Congress lost no time turning to Treasury Secretary Alexander Hamilton for guidance on weighty economic matters. As time passed, Congress more and more equipped itself to respond to presidential initiatives, through the standing committee system and later through expert staffs. But central leadership from within is Congress's notoriously weak suit, especially in the contemporary "reformed" Congress with its panoply of committees, subcommittees, informal caucuses, and party bodies. Thus Congress is vulnerable to manipulation by presidents who understand its traits.

Presidents communicate their agenda in a variety of ways—not only in State of the Union addresses, but in special messages, reports, and required documents such as annual budgets. Through them presidents highlight priorities, provoke public debate, stimulate congressional deliberation, and exhort for attention and support. Modern Congresses also expect the president to translate executive proposals into draft bills, or to give explicit guidance on legislation that does not originate in the White House. When such guidance is not forthcoming, complaints are heard. Thus in 1982 a Reagan employment and training bill to replace the tainted CETA program was slow to appear. Senator Dan Quayle and other Labor and Human Resources Committee Republicans threatened to proceed with hearings whether the administration produced a bill or not. At the last moment the threat worked and the White House sent up its own proposal.

How do presidents arrive at their legislative priorities? Many arise from long-held beliefs or convictions, like those held by Wilson or Reagan. Others are byproducts of a style or frame of mind; the New Deal emerged from Franklin Roosevelt's pragmatic optimism. Other elements may stem from campaign promises, platform planks, or demands of influential backers or powerful lobbies. Needless to say, there are far more claimants for White House support than can ever be satisfied.

From the perspective of presidents and their supporters, some priorities are decidedly more pressing than others. Charles Bingman, a federal career executive, describes three agenda levels for incoming administrations: a priority agenda, an uncertainty agenda, and an unformed agenda.[16] The *priority agenda* is what an administration knows it wants to do in given areas and what its campaign supporters expect it to accomplish. For better or worse, this agenda is part of the baggage a new president brings to the White House. In its *uncertainty* agenda, the new crowd knows it wants to move in a particular direction but is unsure exactly what steps to take. The administration therefore looks around for formulas that fit its ideological and programmatic goals. Finally, there is an *unformed agenda* that consists of a host of problems that the incoming political leaders did not anticipate or did not understand. It is a special challenge for presidents and their advisors to move into these second and third agenda levels, adapting their known goal to unfamiliar or emerging problems. Outsiders, including the permanent bureaucracy, can help the White House identify and clarify its stance at these agenda levels.

The formal mechanisms for sifting and choosing the "president's program" from the thousands of possible proposals are budgeting and central clearance. These functions are performed by key

[16] In *Management* 3 (1982), p. 6.

White House staff aides and by OMB, the president's management arm.

The annual budget season, when the president reaches final decisions on the budget submitted for the following fiscal year, is a high point of agenda setting. Options are outlined, major decisions are posed, and at some point the president must say yes or no. A great part of federal spending (about three quarters) is relatively "uncontrollable" because it has been mandated by prior actions of president and Congress and cannot be changed without revising the legislation. But within the budget's discretionary portion, presidents can indicate clearly the directions they wish to take. Indeed, the budget is such a powerful instrument of priority setting and agenda control that President Reagan chose it, rather than a list of new proposals, as the vehicle for his initial program. In addition to budget requests, federal departments and agencies submit to the White House their reaction to proposals in the pipeline. Along with White House staffers, OMB selects the approaches that fit best with the president's objectives. The final say, of course, rests with the president, though not all decisions reach his desk.

The Veto Power. The president's other direct window on the legislative process is the veto power. The Constitution (Article I, Section 7) requires the president to approve or disapprove bills passed by Congress. If the president disapproves, a two thirds vote in both houses is needed to override the veto. Because presidents can usually muster one third plus one of their own supporters, their vetoes are rarely overturned. Of approximately 2,500 vetoes from George Washington through Ronald Reagan, fewer than 4 percent were overridden by Congress.

If agenda setting is the carrot, vetoing is the stick in the president's array of powers. However, the veto is not merely a negative power; the most potent vetoes are those that are never used but are merely posed as threats. "Make my day!" shot back a feisty Reagan when lawmakers talked of raising taxes to reduce the deficit. Indeed, it was Reagan's implacable opposition to tax hikes that kept budget-minded senators and representatives at bay throughout much of his administration.

At each stage of the legislative process, lawmakers, lobbyists, and staff members are asking, in one way or another, "What is the White House willing to live with?" Supporters of a bill normally would rather have it passed than not, even if they must yield points to the president to gain his signature. During times of conflict, however, lawmakers who oppose the president are not above passing a bill they know will be vetoed. Then they can take the issue to the country, portraying the president as heartless or unresponsive. Of course, presidents play the same game, portraying their detractors as irresponsible spendthrifts.

Most vetoes represent a collective White House judgment. Presidents receive advice from their aides, OMB staff members, agency officials, legislators, and interest group representatives. Veto decisions usually are rationalized by one or more of the following considerations. (1) The bill may be regarded as unconstitutional by the president—the most common rationale prior to Jackson and a reason that is still occasionally given. (2) The measure encroaches upon the president's independence. Sometimes legislators load so many limitations onto a bill that presidents conclude their role will be compromised. (3) The bill is unwise public policy. (4) The bill as written is impossible to administer. (5) The bill will cost too much—a favorite theme of modern presidents.

Coalition Building

"Merely placing a program before Congress is not enough," President Johnson once declared. "Without constant attention from the administration, most legislation moves through the congressional process at the speed of a glacier."[17] No task is more central to presidential leadership, and no task is more difficult or more misunderstood. As Cronin puts it:

> The office does not guarantee political leadership; it merely offers incumbents an invitation to lead politically. It is in this sense that those best suited to the job are those who can creatively shape their political environment and savor the rough-and-tumble give-and-take of political life.[18]

Perhaps the rarest of all executive talents is the ability to build support among legislators. Franklin Roosevelt and Johnson had this talent in abundance; they truly enjoyed lobbying members of Congress and were uncommonly successful in recruiting allies. Wilson and Reagan had their periods of success, though both faced increased resistance as their administrations matured. Other presidents have had tougher sledding on Capitol Hill. Some, such as Nixon or Carter, displayed real distaste or lack of talent in dealing with Congress. Indeed, their inability to build coalitions was in a very real sense the measure of the shortcomings of their administrations.

In applying persuasive and bargaining powers, presidents must deal with Congress, as a complex and decentralized institution, on at least four fronts: the congressional leaders, especially those of the president's own party; the scattered committee and subcommittee work groups of Capitol Hill; the individual members of Congress; and Congress as a whole, as the object of media attention and grass-roots pressure.

Congressional Leaders. Presidents meet periodically with House and Senate leaders from their own party and occasionally from the opposing party as well. From these meetings party leaders gain valuable information on the president's plans and programs that can be turned into the coin of influence in dealing with their colleagues. Needless to say, face-to-face meetings with the president are only the tip of the iceberg. Leaders who are responsible for shepherding the administration's program through the Capitol Hill labyrinth may confer with White House staff as well.

Two Reagan administration examples illustrate how White House actions can help or hinder legislative leaders in advancing the president's cause. During the June 1981 struggle to approve the Gramm-Latta budget package backed by President Reagan, House Republican leaders were conspicuously aided by the president. A steady stream of legislators was called off the floor to take personal calls from Reagan. "I just wanted to tell you the president's on the phone," John H. Rousselot announced gleefully to his House colleagues.[19] Needless to say, leaders are buoyed by the knowledge that "the president's on the phone" backing up their actions. In contrast, Senate Majority Leader Howard Baker's effort late in 1982 to take up a controversial arms control agency nomination opposed by North Carolina Senator Jesse Helms was undercut by the president. Baker had assured the White House he had the votes to confirm the

---

[17] Lyndon B. Johnson, *The Vantage Point* (New York: Holt, Rinehart and Winston, 1971), p. 448.

[18] Thomas E. Cronin, *The State of the Presidency*, 2nd ed. (Boston: Little, Brown, 1980), p. 168.

[19] *Congressional Record* 127 (97th Congress, 1st session), H 3365 (June 25, 1981 daily edition).

nomination, but when he moved to take up the nomination, Helms rose to announce that the president would soon withdraw the name. Although Baker hastily dropped the matter, he was not amused at the White House reversal.[20] Failing to inform leaders on the Hill of current strategy is an unforgivable sin: legislative leaders would rather go down to defeat on a clearly defined issue than have the rug pulled out from under them by quixotic White House maneuvering.

What do presidents get out of their contacts with congressional leaders? At best they gain loyalty and support. Accurate information about Congress's mood as well as advice about where to look in seeking votes are other benefits. Sometimes the message is not what the president wants to hear. Late in 1986, Republican leaders assumed the task of informing the president that bold steps had to be taken to quell the runaway "Iran-gate" scandal. Thus, congressional allies not only sustain and support but also inform or even warn.

Capitol Hill Work Groups. Bargaining with a few influential leaders no longer ensures passage of the president's program. Today Congress embraces a large number of work groups—committees, subcommittees, task forces, informal caucuses. Indeed, the proliferation of these groups is perhaps the distinguishing characteristic of the modern Congress. In the 99th Congress (1985–1986), there were 106 *standing* work groups (committees and subcommittees) in the Senate and more than 150 in the House. The average senator held nearly 10 seats on standing work groups, while the average representative held between five and six assignments. Leadership posts are nearly as numerous: every senator, regardless of party, is eligi-

ble to serve as chairman or ranking minority member on at least one standing committee or subcommittee. Even in the larger House of Representatives, well over half of all members hold such leadership posts.[21]

Informal voting-bloc groups outside the standing committee system also allow members to involve themselves in policies of interest to them. Before 1970 there were only a handful of informal caucuses; today there are more than 100 of them. The Northeast-Midwest Coalition, known as the "Frost Belt Caucus," looks after regional interests; so do the Rural Caucus and the High Altitude Coalition. Industry concerns are voiced by such groups as the Textile Caucus, the Senate Steel Caucus, or the Mushroom Caucus. Other groups include the Black Caucus, Hispanic Caucus, Arts Caucus, and the Environmental Study Group. Informal groups have grown and prospered because they perform useful functions for individual members, in particular assistance with legislative, political, and electoral goals. For many members, such groups offer alternative channels of information and voting cues that are tailored to the legislators' own values as members of regional, ethnic, issue, or ideological blocs.

On any given subject, therefore, not one but many work groups may be involved. This confronts executive agencies with a bewildering array of access points in Congress. Formerly, a White House aide or agency lobbyist could forge alliances with the handful of legislators who served on the relevant committee. Those members could be counted upon to carry the word to their colleagues. Today, liaison officers from

[20] Mary McGrory, "Sen. Baker, Ever Decorous, Yanks at His Middleman's Strings," *Washington Post* (January 13, 1983), p. A.3.

[21] See Roger H. Davidson, "Subcommittee Government: New Channels of Policy Making," in Thomas E. Mann and Norman J. Ornstein (eds.), *The New Congress* (Washington, D.C.: American Enterprise Institute, 1981), pp. 109–11.

executive agencies must work with voting-bloc groups and frequently canvass large numbers of members, not excluding the most junior ones. As one State Department liaison officer observed, "It used to be that all one had to do was to contact the chairman and a few ranking members of a committee; now all 435 members and 100 senators have to be contacted."[22]

Individual Lawmakers. Much has been made of the autonomy of today's senators and representatives. Yet they are not free of outside influences; quite the contrary. Indeed, given the multiplicity of interested citizens and groups, and their unprecedented invasion into electoral politics, "special interests" are as powerful and pervasive today as they have ever been. One effect is that it is hard to pigeonhole legislators by referring to their party loyalties; rather, today's elected politicians are encouraged by circumstances to construct their own political parties out of bits and pieces of appeals tailored to attract their constituencies. As a result, members march not only to different drummers, but to *many* different drummers—first one, then the other. A different but equally evocative metaphor was used by John B. Breaux, who with colleagues from Louisiana and Florida went along with Reagan's 1981 budget package in exchange for reconsideration of sugar price supports, which it had opposed as inflationary. Asked if his vote could be bought, Breaux replied: "No, but it can be rented."[23] Sooner or later, presidents and their aides must "retail" their appeals, going individually to members of Congress to sell the White House position, ask for votes, and provide incentives for support.

Presidents have always had to make these personal, informal overtures. Washington dispatched Treasury Secretary Hamilton to consult with members; Jefferson socialized at the White House with congressional allies. The modern presidency, with its stress on legislative programs, led to the assignment of White House staffers to conduct day-to-day relations with Capitol Hill. Roosevelt and Truman dispatched close aides to contact members and help build support for legislation. Eisenhower set up the first separate congressional liaison office, under Wilton B. "Jerry" Persons and then Bryce Harlow.[24] Eisenhower's legislative goals were modest, and the style of his liaison staff was low-key and mainly bipartisan.

In 1961 President Kennedy expanded legislative liaison to advance his New Frontier legislation, appointing Lawrence F. O'Brien to head the renamed Office of Congressional Relations. O'Brien, the father of modern legislative liaison, dispatched staff aides to Congress to familiarize themselves with members from each geographical area, learn their interests, and plan how to win their votes for the president's program. Departmental and agency liaison activities were coordinated to complement White House efforts.

Presidents since Kennedy have added their individual touches, but all have continued the liaison apparatus. Nixon elevated his first liaison head, Bryce Harlow, to cabinet status; Ford enlarged the staff; Carter added computers to analyze congressional votes and target members for persuasion. In other respects, Carter's liaison operation drew less than rave reviews. Speaker O'Neill reportedly was

---

[22] Daniel P. Mulhollan and Arthur G. Stevens, "Congressional Liaison and the Rise of Informal Groups in Congress" (Paper presented at the 1979 annual meeting of the Western Political Science Association), p. 5.

[23] *Congressional Quarterly Weekly Report* 39 (July 4, 1981), p. 1169.

[24] Stephen J. Wayne, *The Legislative Presidency* (New York: Harper & Row, 1978), pp. 142 ff.

miffed when he was denied extra tickets to Carter's inaugural; he claimed to have met with top Carter aide Hamilton Jordan (whom he dubbed "Hannibal Jerkin") only three times in four years. While the inexperience of Carter's liaison people may have contributed to the appearance of ineptitude, Carter's own indifference to Congress was probably more to blame. When a president gives only sporadic attention to a function, staff productivity is bound to suffer.

Effective congressional liaison embraces a wide variety of services that aid legislators in their careers and induce them to go along with the president's initiatives. Being able to announce government contracts or projects in one's state or district is a valuable privilege, and liaison officers make an effort to relay this information so members can make such announcements. Special White House tours are a popular item. So are invitations to White House dinners and social events. President Reagan was known for dispensing gift cuff links and theater tickets along with brief homilies on the legislation at hand, aided by index cards. Campaign appearances with the president, including opportunities for press photos, are valued for the favorable impression they convey that the lawmaker "has the ear" of the chief executive. By the same token, astute presidents avoid personal appearances that might harm incumbents' reelection chances.

Conversely, lawmakers who defy the White House can be made to pay a price for their independence. Legislators who belittle the president may expect a cool reception or tough phonecalls from the president's advisors or even the president himself. After he began attacking the Vietnam War, Senator J. William Fulbright (D-Ark.) was banished from White House state dinners, even though as chairman of the Senate Foreign Relations Committee he would normally

have been invited. More recently, Senator Robert Packwood's criticisms of Reagan led the White House to remove his name from a party fundraising letter and, later, to aid efforts to oust him as chairman of the Republican Senatorial Campaign Committee. There were even reports that the White House had compiled a "hit list" of Republicans slated for disciplining.[25] Withholding favors, it seems, is almost as important as conferring them. However, vendettas or "hit lists" may be counterproductive because they place the president in the unseemly posture of appearing to squash honest disagreement.

Presidents and their staffs, then, devote large amounts of time to granting or withholding resources in order to cultivate support on Capitol Hill. This includes not only patronage—executive and judicial posts—but also construction projects, government installations, offers of campaign support, access to strategic information, plane rides on Air Force One, White House meetings, signed photographs, and countless other favors both large and small that can be traded for needed votes. Some of these services may seem petty or even tawdry; but it is out of a patchwork of such appeals that legislative majorities are often constructed.

The Public Fever-Chart. Washington decision makers are endlessly fascinated by what "the people" are thinking; and, as Richard Neustadt has noted, their response to the president depends in part on their reading of public sentiment.[26] Put another way, to lead Congress, a president must first convince the public. With public support, Congress can be

---

[25] Jack Nelson, "President's 'Bad-Boy' List Aims for Republican Unity," *Los Angeles Times* (May 23, 1982), Part I, p. 1.

[26] Richard E. Neustadt, *Presidential Power: The Politics of Leadership from FDR to Carter* (New York: John Wiley & Sons, 1980), p. 64.

coaxed, goaded, or intimidated into following the president's initiatives; without that support, members have added incentives to act independently.[27]

Presidents and their advisors realize they must act quickly to win support for their programs. Every modern president, no matter how popular, faces the fading of the "honeymoon period" when public hopes and approval run high. Popularity usually slips as the administration remains in office. For some presidents, such as Eisenhower and Reagan, the decline was minimal. For others, such as Truman, Johnson, Nixon, or Carter, the decline was precipitous. For all presidents, it means a brief-lived "window of opportunity" early in the term when bold initiatives are expected and most apt to receive favorable reaction. As time goes by, the likelihood of success fades.

The brevity of the honeymoon period was a major factor which led Reagan and his advisors to act quickly to imprint the president's priorities upon public policy. Rather than choose the lengthy, laborious path of pushing proposals through the authorizing committees of Congress, the administration shrewdly concentrated its efforts on the budget process as a short-cut way of shifting spending patterns. The honeymoon would be brief, they reasoned, and committees would be unwilling to curtail programs they had developed and nurtured. By passing budget targets, committees were given spending ceilings and told to conform. When the painful process yielded results somewhat short of the administration's goals, a second budget resolution was prepared and pushed through. The administration's strategy paid off: Reagan's popularity, and his plans for solving the nation's economic ills, persuaded the public to give unstinting support to "Reaganomics" during the early months of 1981. Members of Congress faced an unprecedented volume of mail, much of it voicing the same simple message: support the president. Enough lawmakers followed those instructions that Reagan enjoyed stunning victories early in his administration.

The downfall of presidents, as measured by survey results, can constrict presidential leadership just as surely as honeymoon support can enhance it. Thus, as Nixon's popularity slipped in the wake of the Watergate scandal, the Democratically controlled Congress grew bolder in defying the White House and insisting on its own programs. The same thing happened in other administrations. During the Reagan administration the contrasts were dramatic. The president's mastery over Congress seemed complete throughout his first year; by the second year, Republican leaders on Capitol Hill were forcing Reagan to accept new taxes which he had pledged to avoid; by the third year, Congress was in open revolt against the Reagan program—a revolt that extended to both chambers and all shades of the political spectrum and continued more or less for the balance of his administration.

Events or trends can boost or depress a president's popularity. Some think the downward pull on presidential popularity is caused by a "coalition of minorities" phenomenon: every time a president decides or acts on an issue, he alienates those people who feel intensely on the opposite side. As the president reaches more and more decisions over time, the number of alienated people grows.[28] Others hold that downturns are caused by the "fickle" segment of the

---

[27] George C. Edwards III, *Presidential Influence in Congress* (San Francisco: W. H. Freeman, 1980), pp. 86–115.

[28] John E. Mueller, *War, Presidents, and Public Opinion* (New York: John Wiley, 1973), pp. 205–8.

public, those who are least knowledgeable, involved, or committed. They uncritically accept a new president's proposals; but when things go wrong, they quickly turn against him.[29] Neither of these views is totally persuasive. Public opinion fluctuations indicate that shifts flow not just from the coalition of minorities and the quirks of the least-informed people, but from wars, economic cycles, scandals, and the like.

As the most visible and understandable part of the government, the president tends to be praised or blamed for whatever happens in the public arena.[30] In today's competitive and hostile environment, it seems easier for presidents to fall short than to live up to expectations. If presidents are the unwitting recipients of windfall support, they are also the undeserved objects of criticism when things go wrong.

To neutralize or reverse erosions of public support, presidents are often tempted to "take their case to the people." The assumption is that Congress, the press, and other Washington power centers are excessively negative and cynical and that a vast reservoir of support exists "beyond the beltway" if only the president can unleash and exploit it. Thus, a "fireside chat," a nationally televised address, a carefully planned event, or a nationwide tour may be able to reverse the president's fortunes. In an all-out White House campaign on an issue, the support of state and local officials will be mobilized. Members of interest groups will be brought to Washington and briefed by the White House public liaison office. Media exposure will be orchestrated to highlight White House policy objectives.

"Going public" on an issue is not without its risks. The president may raise expectations that cannot be fulfilled, make inept presentations, lose control over the issue, anger legislators whose support is needed, or put forward hastily conceived proposals. "Going to the country" is a potent weapon, but if the president already has overall support on Capitol Hill, such concerted efforts are not necessary.

PATTERNS OF INTER-BRANCH CONTROL

Shifts in power between Congress and the president are a recurring feature of American politics. The power balance is in a constant state of flux. It is certainly affected by partisan control of the two chambers and by issues, circumstances, and personalities. Legislative-executive relationships are not zero-sum games, however. If one branch is up, the other is not necessarily down. Internal power fluctuations—within the executive branch or within the two legislative chambers—complicate the ebb and flow of power.

Of all the factors that affect interbranch relationships, partisan control is the most obvious. Three patterns have occurred historically. Both executive and legislative branches may be controlled by the same single party—a situation we might term, albeit euphemistically, *party government.* Or a president's party may control one but not both houses of Congress, a *truncated majority.* Finally, there may be *divided government,* placing Congress and the White House in the hands of opposing partisans.

Party Government

In about two thirds of the Congresses in this century, the same party has controlled the White House and both

[29] James A. Stimson, "Public Support for American Presidents: A Cyclical Model," *Public Opinion Quarterly* 40 (Spring 1976), pp. 1–21.

[30] James David Barber, *Presidential Character*, 2d ed. (Englewood Cliffs, N.J.: Prentice-Hall, 1977), p. 5.

TABLE 1 · PARTISAN CONTROL OF PRESIDENCY AND CONGRESS,
1901–1989

	Congresses since 1901	Since 1947
Party government	29	9
Truncated majority	5	3
Divided government	10	9
Total Congresses	44	21

houses of Congress. But this orderly state of affairs is less common than it once was, as Table 1 indicates. Divided control has marked the majority of Congresses that have convened since 1947. During much of this period, tensions between White House and Capitol Hill were high.

The rarity of party government in the modern era flows from the overall decline in party identification and the rise of ticket-splitting by voters. Party labels are worn lightly these days, and voters split their loyalties as freely as they do their ballots. Thus, politicians at all levels are tempted to fashion their own candidacies, bypassing partisan appeals and relying on personal factors or campaign technology. The Democrats remain the choice of a plurality of voters, and Democratic candidates normally capture a majority of the votes cast in congressional elections. In the House of Representatives this has translated into something approaching permanent control, inasmuch as House members have methods of constituency outreach that allow them to build personal reelection coalitions and insulate themselves from nationwide swings in attitudes.[31]

At the presidential and senatorial levels, however, party disaggregation has produced more competitive contests: national tides matter, and candidates can win by minimizing partisan appeals.[32] Whichever party benefits or loses, the decline of party support betokens continued division of party control of the branches of government.

Eras of true legislative harmony—party government in the parliamentary sense of the term—are in this country few and far between: Wilson's first administration (1913–1917); Roosevelt's celebrated "New Deal" (1933–1936); and the balmiest days of Johnson's "Great Society" (1963–1965). For good or ill, these were periods of frantic lawmaking, which produced landmark legislation and innovative governmental programs.

Wilson's "New Freedom." Wilson's first term must have seemed a textbook fulfillment for a man who idolized the British Constitution and saw himself as a kind of prime minister shepherding his party's program into law. The president's leadership was timely because in 1910 insurgents had stripped the House Speaker of important prerogatives, leaving a power vacuum that was temporarily filled by party caucuses. "Ever mindful of the unique powers of the British prime

[31] Robert S. Erikson, "Malapportionment, Gerrymandering, and Party Fortunes in Congressional Elections," *American Political Science Review* 66 (December 1972), 1295–1300; Thomas E. Mann and Raymond E. Wolfinger, "Candidates and Parties in Congressional Elections," *American Political Science Review* 74 (September 1980), pp. 617–32.

[32] Barbara Hinckley, "Incumbency and Presidential Vote in Senate Elections," *American Political Science Review* 64 (September 1970), pp. 836–42.

minister," notes one historian, "Wilson sought to establish as never before the position of the President as leader of both his party and the nation."[33] Wilson conferred repeatedly with the Democratic majority leaders—Senator John Worth Kern of Indiana and Representative Oscar Underwood of Alabama—not only at the White House but also in the little-used president's room at the Capitol. He had a special telephone line installed to reach party leaders quickly and directly. He stressed the importance of party loyalty: Democrats could freely differ and debate an issue in their caucus, but they should close ranks once the majority had decided the party's course.

Calling upon Democratic majorities in the two chambers, Wilson and Congress in two years' time made fundamental changes in the nation's tariffs, business laws, banking system, and agricultural education and research. Further key pieces of legislation flowed from the ensuing 64th Congress (1915–1917). But the advent of World War I clouded Wilson's party government; in the last two years of his administration Congress was in Republican hands and his postwar peace plan in ruins.

"The Roosevelt Revolution." Franklin Roosevelt's first term, especially the celebrated first "hundred days," was another era of party government. A few days after taking office, Roosevelt called a special session of Congress to consider emergency banking legislation. By unanimous consent Democratic leaders introduced the act to conform to Roosevelt's wishes and grant him new powers over banking and currency. The bill was completed by the president and his advisors at two o'clock one morning. When it went to Capitol Hill, it was still in

rough form, but before the forty minutes allocated for House debate had expired, shouts of "Vote! Vote!" were heard on the House floor. As there were no copies of the bill in the House, the Speaker recited the text from a penciled draft bearing last-minute corrections. After only thirty-eight minutes, the House passed the bill, sight unseen, with a unanimous shout.[34]

The Roosevelt "hundred days" was perhaps the most remarkable period of legislative innovation in the nation's history. After the Emergency Banking Act, there were laws relating to the budget, taxation, unemployment relief, federal grants to the states, agricultural subsidies, federal supervision of investment securities, public ownership of public utilities, refinancing of home mortgages, federal bank deposit insurance, financial reorganization of the railroads, industrial self-regulation, public works, and an industrial recovery program. More acts followed in the 74th Congress (1935–1937).

Momentous as Roosevelt's initial achievements were, they did not ensure a smooth course with Congress after 1936. The second Roosevelt administration confronted such explosive issues as anti-lynching, tax reform, farm policies, and the president's disastrous Court-packing scheme. "Deadlock on the Potomac" was the way one historian described relations between the White House and Congress in the late 1930s.[35]

Johnson's "Great Society." The Great Society legislative outpouring of the mid-1960s, like Wilson's New Freedom a half-century before, grew from a germi-

---

[33] E. David Cronon (ed.), *The Political Thought of Woodrow Wilson* (Indianapolis: Bobbs-Merrill, 1965), p. iii.

[34] William Leuchtenburg, *Franklin D. Roosevelt and the New Deal, 1932–1940* (New York: Harper & Row, 1963), pp. 43–44.

[35] James MacGregor Burns, *Roosevelt: The Lion and the Fox* (New York: Harcourt, Brace, 1956), especially pp. 337–42.

nating process that had extended over a decade or more. During the Eisenhower administration of the 1950s, Capitol Hill Democrats developed and refined in hearings and reports a lengthy agenda of proposed programs—most notably Medicare, aid to education, employment programs, civil rights, and environmental preservation. When Democrat John F. Kennedy came to office in 1961, this agenda was ready for action. Although initially stalled in Congress, Kennedy's program had begun to gain momentum when he was assassinated in November 1963.[36] Seizing upon the wave of feeling which followed the tragedy, Lyndon B. Johnson, a master legislative tactician, pushed through the remainder of the Kennedy agenda and added other programs including the war on poverty and the food stamp program.

The unpopularity of the Republican party's 1964 presidential candidate, Senator Barry Goldwater, brought a tide of new Democrats to Washington— more than two-to-one majorities in both chambers to help build Johnson's Great Society. "The obstacles to that [Democratic] program had simply been washed away by the Goldwater debacle," James L. Sundquist writes.[37]

The legislative record of the 89th Congress (1965–1967) reads like a roll call of contemporary government programs: Medicare/Medicaid, Voting Rights Act of 1965, Older Americans Act, Freedom of Information Act, National Foundation on the Arts and the Humanities, highway beautification, urban mass transit, clean water, and the Departments of Transportation and Housing and Urban Development,

among others. The legislative output rivalled Roosevelt's "hundred days" and might justifiably be called a second New Deal. Yet, as before, the legislative honeymoon was short-lived: Johnson's consensus began to fall apart even before the 89th Congress adjourned, a casualty of escalating involvement in the Vietnam War.

Periods of "party government" as productive as these three are not problem free. The pace of lawmaking is sometimes so rapid that political institutions require years to absorb the new programs. Succeeding generations may retrench or even reverse ill-considered or ineffective programs. Some New Deal enactments, like the first Agricultural Adjustment Act and the National Industrial Recovery Act, were of this type. Important portions of Johnson's Great Society proved expensive or ineffectual and were dismantled (like the War on Poverty) or cut back (like food stamps) in the 1980s. One generation's achievements can turn into another's stumbling blocks.

Few eras of party control produce so much legislation. More than control of the two branches is needed for legislative productivity. High turnover on Capitol Hill, a landslide presidential election, a sense of national urgency—these are among the forces that turn party control into party government.

Truncated Majorities

Truncated majorities are relative rarities in national politics. Only five Congresses in the twentieth century have been so divided: the 62nd Congress (1911–1913), the 72nd (1931–1933), and the 97th–99th (1981–1986). In every case, Republican presidents—William Howard Taft, Herbert Hoover, Ronald Reagan—faced a Republican Senate and a Democratic House. In the first two instances, the president's party

[36] James L. Sundquist, *Politics and Policy: The Eisenhower, Kennedy, and Johnson Years* (Washington, D.C.: Brookings Institution, 1968), p. 481.

[37] Ibid.

had controlled both houses at the start of his term, but swings toward the Democratic Party captured the House in midterm elections. In both those cases, Democrats went on to capture both branches of government two years later. Thus, the truncated majorities were the side products of momentous social or economic events or a political realignment.

The truncated Republican majorities of the 1980s flowed from factors less dramatic than social upheaval or political realignment. First, the Republicans captured nearly all the closely contested seats, including those of several vulnerable Democrats. A second reason was the Republicans' strength in the sparsely populated states of the Upper Plains and the Mountain West which are "overrepresented" in the Senate. In raw votes, Democratic senatorial candidates outpolled their opponents by a margin of about 51–48 in 1980, 55–45 in 1982, and 51–49 in 1984.

Whether it was luck, skillful Republicans campaigning, the electorate's desire for change, or some other combination of circumstances, there is no denying that split chamber control significantly shaped Reagan's first six years. The media spotlighted the president's initial successes in winning votes in the Democratic-controlled House; but it was Republican control of the Senate that provided the motor power for the administration's economic program. The fate of Reagan's 1981 budget and tax proposals probably hinged on Senate control by his party. In succeeding years, when the president's budget and tax leadership was challenged, it was Republican Senate leaders who grasped the initiative and moved in to fill the void.

Truncated majorities, then, do not always produce legislative stalemate. Before he left office in 1913, President Taft signed bills to create the territory of Alaska, establish the Department of Labor, and regulate interstate traffic in liquor. Under Hoover, the 72nd Congress passed the Glass-Steagall Banking Act, the Federal Home Loan Bank Act, the Reconstruction Finance Corporation Act, and the Twentieth and Twenty-first amendments. President Reagan's first year yielded a legislative outburst of a magnitude that recalled the early days of the New Deal nearly fifty years before.

Like legislative outbursts in the past, the Reagan juggernaut soon ran out of steam. As constitutents felt the effects of budget cuts, grass-roots support for "Reaganomics" sagged. Members, too, harbored misgivings about the way the budget process had roughed up the authorizing committees. By 1982 the president's budget and tax leadership was challenged. The Republican Senate grasped the initiative, drafting a corrective tax measure that eventually passed in modified form. When the 1982 midterm elections boosted Democratic ranks in the House, Reagan's extraordinary legislative leadership was undermined even farther.

Divided Government

Government divided between the two parties has become commonplace in modern times: nine of the twenty-one Congresses between 1947 and 1989 have been in the hands of the party opposed to the president. This includes two years of the Truman presidency, all but two years of Eisenhower's and Reagan's, and all of Nixon's and Ford's.

Under divided government, interbranch relationships range from lukewarm to hostile. During the Eisenhower administration, Democratic Congresses refrained from attacking the popular president, developing instead modest legislative alternatives and pushing them in election years. Hostility marked the relations between President Truman and the Republican Congress of 1947–1948, which he called the "awful, 80th Congress" during his 1948 reelection campaign. The same hostility marked relations between Nixon and Democratic Congresses (1969–1974).

Stalemate is a constant danger in divided government. Sometimes the two branches wage a pitched battle over policies and prerogatives; at other times, a quiet distance is more the order of the day. Whatever the outcome, divided government seems to be sanctioned by the general public: public opinion surveys indicate that people condone or even prefer having dividing government so that the two branches can check each other.[38]

Today, as a result of shifting and indistinct party lines, politicians at both ends of Pennsylvania Avenue are in business for themselves. Like others in the "Me Generation," they are putting their career interests first. For legislators, this usually means picking their way carefully among issues, keeping some daylight between themselves and the president. For White House occupants, it means constructing coalitions for each new issue and reaching beyond party leaders to shape public opinion and bargain with individual lawmakers.

The psychology of divided government wears upon presidents and their advisors. No doubt it has something to do with the swift cycles of presidential popularity, not to mention the frequency of one-term presidencies. It also explains why some ex-White House aides are beguiled by the parliamentary system as a way to ensure working majorities for the chief executive's plans and programs.[39]

ASSESSING THE PRESIDENT'S SUCCESS

Shifts of influence between the White House and Capitol Hill are a recurrent feature of American politics. Scholars are tempted to designate certain eras as times of "congressional government" or "presidential government." Certainly there is an ebb and flow of power between the two branches, but one must be cautious in making such generalizations.

For one thing, influence in legislation is difficult to measure with certainty. Who really initiates legislation? A president can draw publicity by articulating a proposal and giving it currency, but the real origins may be embedded in years of political agitation, congressional hearings, or academic discussion. What exactly is "the president's program"? Major proposals are publicized by the president; but what of minor proposals? Lyndon Johnson used to announce support for measures already assured of passage to boost his record of success. Thus, not all measures endorsed by a president ought to be given equal weight. And who actually wields the decisive influence in passing a piece of legislation? Presidential lobbying may be persuasive, but no legislation passes Congress without help from many quarters. For these and other reasons, measuring White House influence over legislation is hazardous.

The ups and downs of Congress and the presidency should be interpreted

[38] See Roger H. Davidson, David M. Kovenock, and Michael K. O'Leary, *Congress in Crisis* (Belmont, Calif.: Wadsworth Publishing Company, 1966), pp. 62–63.

[39] Lloyd C. Cutler, "To Form a Government," *Harper's* 59 (Fall 1980), pp. 126–43.

with care. The balance of power is in constant flux. The structure of either branch can be influenced by issues, circumstances, or personalities. Even during periods when one branch is in eclipse, it may exert potent influence. Nor are legislative-executive struggles zero-sum games. If one branch gains power, it does not mean that the other branch necessarily loses it. Generally speaking, expanding governmental authority since World War II has augmented the authority of both branches. Their growth rates may differ and their temporary fortunes diverge, but the lesson thus far has been that there is enough work for both the branches. Finally, power shifts may affect some issues but

not others. In foreign relations, cycles of isolationism and internationalism, noninterventionism and interventionism, have followed each other at fairly regular intervals.

Our constitutional system demands mutual accommodation on the part of the two political branches. Neither the presidency nor Congress is monolithic, and neither dominates all facets of policy. Nonetheless, the two branches are fated to confront each other; they can be adversaries even when controlled by the same political party. The relationship between president and Congress, then, yields temporary winners and losers but is unlikely to produce a long-term victor or vanquished.

17
Presidential Vetoes: Motivations and Classification

Albert C. Ringelstein

The president in using the veto power, "acts not as the executive but as a third branch of the legislature. . . . [He] is no greater than his prerogative of veto makes him; he is, in other words, powerful rather as a branch of the legislature than as the titular head of the Executive" (quoted by Oleszek, 1984: 218 and 224).

Since Woodrow Wilson articulated these ideas nearly 100 years ago, the relationship between Congress and the executive has undergone a number of changes, but the veto remains a powerful, if somewhat blunt, weapon. It is an impressive resource for all presidents, but it is a particularly important source of influence for a President who is op-

posed by an opposition majority in Congress (Jones, 1982: 346). For all its importance, comparatively few studies have centered on the veto, and virtually none have sought to classify vetoes by policy area or presidential motivation. This article seeks to correct these deficiencies through an analysis of vetoes from Eisenhower to Reagan.

BACKGROUND

The prime purpose for the inclusion of the veto in the Constitution (Article I, Section 7) was to give the President a means of protecting his office from

Source: Congress and the Presidency 12, no. 1 (Spring 1985).

congressional encroachment. The framers also anticipated that it might be used to vindicate the President's own constitutional views by being utilized against legislation he considered unconstitutional. Accordingly, they believed it should be used sparingly. This indeed turned out to be the case in the early years. The first six presidents vetoed a combined total of nine bills. John Tyler was the first President to veto freely. The reaction to his vetoes was the first move in U.S. history to impeach a President. He was accused of strangling legislation through misuse of the veto power (Black, 1976: 89–91). From that time on, presidents have varied in their use of the veto, ranging from lows of zero for Taylor, Filmore, and Garfield, three for Polk, and six for Harding, to highs of 635 for Franklin Roosevelt and 584 for Grover Cleveland (Fisher, 1981: 26).

The power of the veto in contemporary politics is fundamentally different from its original design. Both branches have forced changes in the system (Fisher, 1981: 24). With Franklin Roosevelt, the veto became an important means by which the President sought to influence the legislative process (Jones, 1982: 347). The decision to sign or veto a bill depends upon substantive and strategic considerations. Substantive concerns include the extent to which a bill satisfies the original request, the feasibility or suitability of a program not requested, the relationship of the legislative action to existing law, and the constitutionality of the legislation. Strategic considerations include timing (a bill vetoed early in a session has time to be passed again in a form more acceptable to the President—a threat of a veto late in the session can force congressional concessions), and whether or not the members of Congress are open to compromise or are adamantly against the President and are prepared to attempt

an override. Most times a President does not want his vetoes overridden; however, if he thinks a veto would be popular outside of Congress, he may risk the veto even though an override is likely (Jones, 1982: 344–345).

Congress, conversely, had developed the practice of sending bills to the President that have many elements, often unrelated, thus not allowing him to consider a single, discrete measure. This practice can become even more coercive with the attachment of irrelevant amendments (riders) to appropriations bills with the assumption that presidents cannot afford to veto money bills late in the fiscal year. In response, presidents have appropriated for themselves an informal type of item veto to counter this practice wherein they consider parts of legislation mere "recommendations," but the constitutionality of this type of veto has yet to be tested in the courts (Fisher, 1981: 24–25). All in all, the role and practice of the veto has become important and complicated in the modern American political scene. Identification of patterns associated with the use of the veto will advance our understanding of the presidency and its relationship to the Congress.

Previous studies have uncovered a number of tendencies concerning presidential vetoes. For instance, Lee (1975), using all presidential vetoes from Washington to Nixon, found that the presidential propensity to veto increases when the President is a Democrat; when Congress is controlled by the opposition party; is inversely proportional to the number of years the President has spent in Congress; and is directly proportional to the percentage of electoral votes the President received in previous elections (1975: 546). Wayne, Cole, and Hyde (1979) studied how recommendations of the Office of Management and Budget affected the vetoes of Nixon and Ford, finding that OMB had more influence in this area than any other executive agency (1979: 314). Levin (1983) examined the constraints the President is under when he tries to persuade Congress to sustain his veto, and argued that he is more restricted than is commonly believed. Among the constraints are: having to take into account that he cannot be too firm in his announced intention to veto a bill without precluding other options; lobbying only the initiating chamber of Congress or risk appearing weak; and being the victim of his own success when Congress decides it must assert its own independence (1983: 649–650). Copeland (1983), in studying a number of external factors that explain the use of a presidential veto, finds that the expanding scope of government, opposition control of Congress, and previous congressional overrides are positively correlated with veto use (1983: 696).

Virtually all the studies through the 1970s, as Wayne, Cole, and Hyde (1979: 303) point out, concerned the number, form, strategy, or the constitutional power of presidential vetoes. Although Copeland's study deals with the effect of external factors on vetoing, the substance and motivation of presidential vetoes remain largely ignored.

What can the study of these facets of the veto reveal about the workings of the presidency? Lowi (1964), in his oft-cited article contended that political relationships are "determined by the type of policy at stake, so that for every type of policy there is likely to be a distinctive type of political relationship . . . [individual] issues . . . are too ephemeral; it is on the basis of established expectations and a history of earlier government decisions *of the same type* that single issues are fought out. The study of single issues provides a good test of hypotheses about structure, but

the hypotheses must be arrived at in some other, independent way" (pp. 688–689). Clausen (1973) elaborates upon this theme by formulating the "law of categorization," by which he means the attempts in all areas of life "to group a large number of individuals, organizations, and actions into a much smaller number of categories." Categorizing tendencies in past behavior helps in the attempt "to anticipate tendencies in future behavior." Therefore, one of the tasks of the scholar . . . is to create ever more useful categories . . . [t]he observer's success in analyzing human behavior is dependent upon his ability to abstract the ordinary principle. . . ." (pp. 6–7).

Policy areas have been categorized in many other studies. Wildavsky (1966) introduced the concept of the "two presidencies" based on the differences in presidential activities towards foreign and domestic policies. Sigelman (1979), Zeidenstein (1981), and Cohen (1982) have refined his work. A number of researchers have sought to demonstrate that the President and Congress dominate different policy areas. Shull (1979) argues that the domestic sphere has become more the province of Congress and numerous subgovernments, while the President has become preeminent in foreign policy (p. 302). Closely related to this argument, Shull and LeLoup (1979) suggest that foreign and defense policy tends to be the highest priority for Republican presidents while social welfare is the highest priority for Democrats.

Another dimension of policy classification that has been utilized by scholars has focused on differences by party. Shull, for instance, contends that congressional policy initiative tends to be greater under Republican presidents (1979: 69). Clausen finds that Republicans in Congress tend to have low support for government management, social welfare, and agricultural assistance programs, compared to Democrats (1973: 107). Do these party patterns hold for presidents also? An examination of the policy areas of vetoes should shed some light on this question.

Consistent with previous studies, some hypotheses can be proposed. It is likely that presidents, being dominant in the area of foreign policy, will have a low percentage of their vetoes in this area (Congress will defer more to the President). Conversely, because of the dominance of Congress in domestic areas, the President will challenge it more often and thus tend to have a higher percentage of vetoes in domestic areas. Also, within the domestic policy areas, Republican presidents should have a higher percentage of vetoes in government management, social services, and resources policy areas than Democrats. Democratic presidents will therefore have higher percentages in one of the remaining policy areas, i.e., foreign policy.

The stated rationale for vetoes should be of assistance in revealing the Presidents' conception of their role. Madison and Hamilton believed that the veto would be used only for limited purposes, namely the protection of the integrity of the presidential office and the rejection of flagrantly unconstitutional or poorly drafted legislation (Fisher, 1978: 84). However, the framers of the Constitution did not foresee the emergence of party politics, and along with this the development of competing ideologies. It would appear then, that the modern President would veto legislation for any single or combination of the above reasons. While it is undoubtedly true that there is overlap and some degree of interdependence among the three large categories of veto rationales (protection of office, unconstitutional or poorly drafted legislation, and ideology), there are distinctions; and it is not unreasonable to suggest that different presidents would emphasize different motives in their veto messages based on their perceptions of and concerns about the office.

While difficult to hypothesize what the overall percentages of veto motivations by category would be for all presidents, hypotheses about presidents of different parties are comparatively easy to formulate. Thus it is suggested that Republican presidents, consistent with their general view of limited government and fiscal and ideological conservatism, will tend to veto bills more for reasons of unconstitutionality and on ideological grounds of economy, non-federal responsibility, and violation of free trade; while Democratic presidents, tending more toward activism and extension of the President's powers, will be more likely to veto bills that contain legislative vetoes and restrictions on executive action (both confine presidential action) and also those that have provisions for special relief (it seems likely that this last category would contain many wealthy or privileged interests whose natural protector would be the Republican party).

DATA AND METHODOLOGY

The administrations included in this study are Eisenhower's through Reagan's first term (83rd through 98th Congresses). Earlier administrations were not included because of the difficulty in obtaining information on veto rationale, which is not readily available before Eisenhower's administration. The first task in rendering the data into the desired form involved eliminating private bill vetoes from the data. Private bills name a particular individual or entity who is to receive relief, such as payment on a pension claim, granting of citizenship, or waiving of immigration requirements. There is usually more interest in vetoes of public bills, which have much broader consequences for society than do private bills (Edwards, 1980: 23). Curiously enough, most studies and lists do not make this distinction, opting instead to study all vetoes in toto. Part of the reason is that the government source book for vetoes (U.S. Senate Library, 1978) makes no distinction between public and private bills, choosing only to break them down by the type of veto, i.e., regular or pocket. And even in the few studies where public bills are calculated separately, there are sometimes discrepancies between sources.[1]

In any case, the basic data for this study were obtained from *Congressional Quarterly Almanac*, 1953–1964, and *Congress and the Nation*, Volumes II–V (1965–1980). Additionally, the Reagan data were obtained from various *Congressional Quarterly Weekly Reports*. These sources were used because they provide brief explanations of why each bill was vetoed and/or excerpts from the veto message.

Table 1 presents the basic data on vetoes by administration and Congress, the purpose of which is to give an overview of the frequency and circumstances of presidential vetoes. Also included are the number of overrides for each president. However, since there are so few overrides (25 in 32 years—9 percent of the total number of vetoes), no attempt will be made to include them in the analysis. All that will be noted is that almost all of them came about when

TABLE 1 · VETOES OF PUBLIC BILLS

President		Congress	Party Control[*]	Vetoes	Sub-totals	Average per Year	Over-rides	Sub-totals
Eisenhower (R)		83rd (1953–54)	S	21	—	—	0	—
		84th (1955–56)	O	21	—	—	0	—
		85th (1957–58)	O	16	—	—	0	—
		86th (1959–60)	O	24	82	10.25	2	2
Kennedy (D)		87th (1961–62)	S	9	—	—	0	—
	part	88th (1963)	S	0	9	3.18	0	0
Johnson (D)	part	88th (1963–64)	S	1	—	—	0	—
		89th (1965–66)	S⅔	8	—	—	0	—
		90th (1967–68)	S	4	13	2.51	0	0
Nixon (R)		91st (1969–70)	O	9	—	—	2	—
		92nd (1971–72)	O	19	—	—	2	—
	part	93rd (1973–74)	O	12	40	7.17	1	5
Ford (R)	part	93rd (1974)	O	24	—	—	4	—
		94th (1975–76)	O	37	61	25.21	8	12
Carter (D)		95th (1977–78)	S	19	—	—	0	—
		96th (1979–80)	S	10	29	7.25	2	2
Reagan (R)		97th (1981–82)	Split	14	—	—	2	—
		98th (1983–84)	Split	20	34	8.50	2	4
Total					268	8.38		25

S   = control by same party.
O   = control by opposite party.
⅔   = that margin of control by majority party.
Split = each party controls one house.

Congress was controlled by the opposition party. Gerald Ford's administration alone, in less than 2½ years in office, accounts for almost half of all overrides during the 32-year span of the study. Among other factors, such as OMB offering many negative recommendations, a growing domestic policy staff, and the natural aging of the Republican presidency, perhaps the greatest reason for Ford's more frequent use of the veto and its subsequently high percentage of overrides was his decision to use the veto more as a strategy to obtain enrolled legislation (Wayne, 1978: 85).

Table 1 reveals a number of interesting facts. Richard Nixon and Jimmy Carter have almost precisely the same number of average vetoes per year, yet one had the opposition party in control of Congress, and the other had his own party in control. In the only instance where party control changed hands during one president's administration, Dwight Eisenhower had his party in control of the 83rd Congress, and the Democrats in control of the 84th, yet he vetoed 21 bills in each two-year period. Richard Nixon had 12 vetoes in the 93rd Congress, while Gerald Ford, dealing with the same Congress, had twice as many vetoes in only slightly more than one-quarter of the time. The point to be made is that vetoing a bill appears to vary regardless of the opposition status of Congress.

The variable nature of presidents' vetoes will be considered in aggregate comparison by party, and in 26 of the 32 years this coincides with the Republican opposition/Democratic support dimension (the 83rd, 97th and 98th Congresses being the only ones in which Republicans had at least one-house support in Congress—Democrats in all instances had majority support Congresses). A two-thirds control of Congress variable will not be used because it only occurs once (89th Congress) among the 16 Congresses studied. It is

interesting to note, however, that Johnson vetoed twice as many bills when he had two-thirds support in Congress than when he had just a simple majority. Perhaps Congress becomes more independent on some policies when one party obtains a veto-proof majority, independent of which party controls the White House.

The veto categories utilized in this study were adapted from Clausen's five policy dimensions, which were developed from his study of Congress. His dimensions are international involvement, agricultural assistance, government management, social welfare, and civil liberties.[2] The government management and international involvement (called in this article "foreign policy") dimensions are utilized without change. Civil liberties had to be dropped since not one veto in 32 years could be found which fit that category. Agricultural assistance was expanded into "resources," and social welfare expanded into "social services." A new category of "cross-departmental appropriations" was added to contain those vetoed bills which cut across more than one policy dimension.

The categories of stated reasons for presidential vetoes were developed from the data directly, key words being used to determine placement. The number of categories (10) is a bit unwieldy, but important distinctions would be lost if they were collapsed any further.[3] It is important to note that these are publicly stated reasons and thus do not capture the enormous range of backstage calculations that are part of presidential "motivation."

FINDINGS

Table 1 reveals that Gerald Ford utilized the veto much more than any other White House occupant during the period studied. His average of over 25 vetoes per year is more than twice as high as the second highest, Eisenhower, who averaged 10.25 vetoes per year. The general trend is for Republicans to veto a higher number of public bills than Democrats. Johnson and Kennedy have quite low averages, while Nixon, Carter, and Reagan all have about the same average. Eisenhower averaged only about three vetoes more per year than the latter group. The Republican average number of vetoes for the period is 10.85, while the Democratic average is 4.25, which is a substantial difference. The gap is narrowed if Ford is removed from consideration (the Republican average falls to 8.87), but it is still twice as high as the Democratic average.

Categorizing vetoes by policy area reveals a number of interesting facts (see Table 2). It should be noted, however, that due to a small number of Ns for some of the Presidents (notably Kennedy and Johnson) these percentages, although accurate, should be used as general indicators of tendencies and not as hard and fast percentages that can be used with other percentages to obtain a definite ranking and/or relationship.

With the above caution in mind, some general tendencies are evident. Looking at all the vetoes, as would be expected, few occur in the area of foreign policy, indicating perhaps that indeed presidents do tend to have their own way there and are not challenged as much by Congress as in the domestic areas. In the latter categories, where relative congressional power is generally acknowledged, resources and government management bills receive two-thirds of the total vetoes, while social services bills were vetoed relatively few times. What this appears to indicate is that the first two categories are the domestic areas in which presidents are most likely to challenge Congress, while in social services, the President is more likely to let Congress have its own way.

More research needs to be done to determine the accuracy of this speculation.

Looking at individual presidents and party differences, Carter and Johnson have the highest percentages in foreign policy, while Nixon, Eisenhower, and Reagan all have low percentages of vetoes. In resources, all the presidents except Kennedy and Johnson have relatively high percentages, ranging from 17.6 percent to 31.1 percent. Government management finds Eisenhower, Kennedy, Johnson and Reagan with high percentages, and Ford with the lowest at 23 percent. In the social services category, one finds, as might be expected, that the presidents with the highest percentages are Republicans Nixon, Ford, and Reagan. In the category of cross-departmental appropriation vetoes, Nixon, Ford, and Reagan have garnered 13 of the 15 vetoes. The trend of vetoing large and multipurpose appropriation bills seems to be a recent phenomenon starting with Nixon. Underscoring the earlier discussion that many of these vetoes are undertaken because of unacceptable riders, four of these recent vetoes were executed for that reason: Nixon's veto of a supplemental appropriation bill that also prohibited his using funds to bomb in Cambodia; Ford's two vetoes of appropriation bills that prohibited funds going to Turkey; and Carter's veto of an appropriation bill for the State, Justice, and Commerce Departments because it contained an anti-busing rider.

The reasons given by presidents for their vetoes (Table 3) sheds more light on the differences between Republicans and Democrats in their approach to the office. First, more bills were vetoed for the reason that they were "too costly" than any other reason, and there is a slight tendency for Republicans to use this reason more than Democrats. Con-

TABLE 2 · CATEGORIES OF VETOES

President	Foreign Policy		Resources		Government Management		Social Services		Cross-Departmental Appropriations		Total Ns
	%	N	%	N	%	N	%	N	%	N	
Eisenhower (R)	6.1	(5)	26.8	(22)	57.3	(47)	8.5	(7)	1.2	(1)	82
Kennedy (D)	11.1	(1)	11.1	(1)	66.7	(6)	11.1	(1)	—	—	9
Johnson (D)	23.1	(3)	7.7	(1)	61.5	(8)	7.7	(1)	—	—	13
Nixon (R)	5.0	(2)	22.5	(9)	30.0	(12)	27.5	(11)	15.0	(6)	40
Ford (R)	18.0	(11)	31.1	(19)	23.0	(14)	21.3	(13)	6.6	(4)	61
Carter (D)	24.1	(7)	27.6	(8)	37.9	(11)	6.9	(2)	3.4	(1)	29
Reagan (R)	5.9	(2)	17.6	(6)	50.0	(17)	17.6	(6)	8.8	(3)	34
Grand total	11.6	(31)	24.6	(66)	42.9	(115)	15.3	(41)	5.6	(15)	268
Republican total	9.2	(20)	25.8	(56)	41.5	(90)	17.1	(37)	6.5	(14)	217
Democratic total	21.6	(11)	19.6	(10)	49.0	(25)	7.8	(4)	2.0	(1)	51

Note: Percentages are calculated across rows.

TABLE 3 · REASON FOR VETOES

President	Ideological							
	Too Expensive/Money Not Appropriated/ Government Purchase Unnecessary/ Inflationary		Non-Federal Responsibility		Special/Unfair Relief, Benefit, or Penalty		Violates Free Trade	
	%	N	%	N	%	N	%	N
Eisenhower (R)	25.6	(21)	13.4	(11)	6.1	(5)	4.9	(4)
Kennedy (D)	11.1	(1)	—	—	22.2	(2)	11.1	(1)
Johnson (D)	23.1	(3)	7.7	(1)	7.7	(1)	7.7	(1)
Nixon (R)	50.0	(20)	12.5	(5)	5.0	(2)	—	—
Ford (R)	39.3	(24)	8.2	(5)	9.8	(6)	1.6	(1)
Carter (D)	34.5	(10)	3.4	(1)	3.4	(1)	6.9	(2)
Reagan (R)	41.2	(14)	23.5	(8)	14.7	(5)	2.9	(1)
Grand total	34.7	(93)	11.6	(31)	8.2	(22)	3.7	(10)
Republican total	36.4	(79)	13.4	(29)	8.3	(18)	2.8	(6)
Democratic total	27.5	(14)	3.9	(2)	7.8	(4)	7.8	(4)

Protect Office   Defective

President	Restricts Executive Action		Unconstitutional				Not Necessary/ Already Incorporated		Miscellaneous		No Reason Given	
			Legislative Veto		Other							
	%	N	%	N	%	N	%	N	%	N	%	N
Eisenhower (R)	1.2	(1)	2.4	(2)	1.2	(1)	7.3	(6)	36.6	(30)	9.8	(8)
Kennedy (D)	—	—	—	—	11.1	(1)	11.1	(1)	22.2	(2)	11.1	(1)
Johnson (D)	15.4	(2)	7.7	(1)	—	—	—	—	30.8	(4)	—	—
Nixon (R)	7.5	(3)	5.0	(2)	5.0	(2)	20.0	(8)	2.5	(1)	—	—
Ford (R)	13.1	(8)	4.9	(3)	4.9	(3)	11.5	(7)	14.8	(9)	4.9	(3)
Carter (D)	24.1	(7)	6.9	(2)	—	—	13.8	(4)	13.8	(4)	3.4	(1)
Reagan (R)	11.8	(4)	5.9	(2)	8.8	(3)	20.6	(7)	—	—	—	—
Grand total	9.3	(25)	4.5	(12)	3.7	(10)	12.3	(33)	18.7	(50)	4.9	(13)
Republican total	7.4	(16)	4.1	(9)	4.1	(9)	12.9	(28)	18.4	(40)	5.1	(11)
Democratic total	17.6	(9)	5.9	(3)	2.0	(1)	9.8	(5)	19.6	(10)	3.9	(2)

Note: Percentages in some rows add to more than 100 percent because some vetoes have more than one stated veto reason and have been assigned to more than one category.

versely, few bills were vetoed because they were felt to be unconstitutional, although bills containing legislative vetoes met that criterion and there is a slight trend for increased usage toward the end of the study, indicating more active resistance to presidential definitions of congressional encroachment. Republicans, as might be expected, vetoed more bills because they felt they were infringing on areas of state, local, or private domain. Carter and Ford felt that a number of bills would have restricted executive action, and they accounted for 15 of the 25 vetoes in that category.

Looking at the categories by party, most have approximately the same veto rate as each other. The only three categories with noteworthy differences are the ideological categories of "too expensive" and "non-federal responsibility," with Republicans having 8.9 and 9.5 higher percentages respectively. In the office-protecting "restricts executive action" category, Democrats were 10.2 higher in their proportion than Republicans. Much of the difference in the last category can, however, be attributed to Carter's comparatively high percentage—he alone accounted for seven of the 25 bills vetoed by all the presidents for this reason.

DISCUSSION AND CONCLUSIONS

What observations and conclusions can be drawn from this study? The first is obvious: Republicans, almost always having opposition Congresses, tended to veto more often than Democrats.

Turning to the hypotheses concerning categories of vetoes, general confirmation is found. Among all presidents, the relative number of vetoes in the area of foreign policy is low (11.6), and conversely, higher in domestic areas. This finding reinforces the notion of Congress and the President contesting for dominance in domestic policy while, excepting a few high profile foreign policy disputes, finding ways to cooperate in international affairs. Controlling by party, Republicans have higher percentages in the categories of resources and social services, while, counter to my hypothesis, Democrats have a higher percentage in the area of government management. This difference, attributable to Johnson and Kennedy, probably reflects the struggle between liberal presidents and a more conservative Congress. Why this veto pattern is not evident in the closely allied social services category is not discernible from the data in this paper but is in all likelihood closely related to the individual priorities, strategies, and strengths of Kennedy and Johnson and those of the leadership of Congress. Democrats also, as the hypothesis suggests, have a higher percentage of foreign policy vetoes than do Republicans.

In the realm of publicly-stated rationales for using a veto, it was found that Republicans do indeed justify decisions on the basis of ideological reasons of economy and non-federal responsibility, and Democrats veto a higher percentage of bills because of asserted restrictions on executive action. Counter to the hypotheses, Democrats have a slight tendency to veto more bills in the name of free trade, while there is little difference between the parties in vetoing on the grounds of unconstitutionality, a legislative veto, or because it provides special relief. This suggests that presidents of both parties may have a similar conception of their office when it comes to protecting its prerogatives from Congress, and when dealing with defective legislation, and that their differences, which are not large, emerge primarily on ideological grounds.

Overall, this study suggests one important caveat to past assumptions and findings about presidential vetoes: *the categories of and reasons for presidential* vetoes are remarkably similar from president to president; frequently, they seem to have just as much in common as presidents doing battle with Congress as Republicans and Democrats fighting for differing ideological programs and considerations. Kennedy and Johnson vetoed bills because they were too expensive, and Reagan and Eisenhower vetoed bills because they encroached upon the power of the executive. If one were examining these vetoes, using conventional assumptions about party and ideology, this strong office-specific motivation would be lost.

It is very likely that the enlarged scope of government in recent years, which Copeland's (1983) study clearly shows is positively related to increased veto use, is largely responsible for this. It would be useful to extend the scope of my study to administrations previous to Eisenhower's (if the data on rationale and classifications could be obtained) to determine if the relationships reflected in the past 30 years were evident then. Knowledge of this would help in chronicling the changes that have occurred in the relationship both between the President and Congress, and between presidents of different parties.

APPENDIX
ISSUES INCLUDED IN EACH VETO CATEGORY

Foreign Policy	Resources	Government Management	Social Services
Military aid	National parks	Federal tax changes	Handicapped
Foreign affairs	Rural electricity	Regulatory power	Rehabilitation
National defense	Flood/water projects	Economic regulation	Urban renewal
Tariffs	Energy/natural gas controls	Labor-management relations	Veterans benefits
Trade	Stripmining/mineral leases	Power rates	Social welfare
Military installations	Transportation	Court jurisdiction	Jobs
Ship construction	Public works	Federal benefits/pay raises	Housing
U.S. Information Agency	Agriculture	Payment/assistance to state/local government	Area redevelopment
Foreign lawsuits	Natural resources	Public broadcasting	Federal appropriations for disasters
Protection for diplomatic missions	Price supports/ subsidies/surplus	Minimum wage	Health care
	Energy development	Government reorganization/new agencies	Education
	Fire prevention	Compensation/payment to private groups	Elderly
	EPA	Currency	Migrant workers
		Meeting of Congress	Disaster relief
		Food/drug law	
		Criminal code	
		District of Columbia	

NOTES

This is a revised version of a paper presented at the 1984 Annual Meeting of the Louisiana Political Science Association. I especially want to thank Steven A. Shull for the time, effort, and advice he contributed assisting in the preparation of this article.

1. For instance, totaling the number of Eisenhower's public bill vetoes listed in the *Congressional Quarterly Almanacs*, one obtains a figure of 82, while Edwards (1980: 25), citing the government source book, comes up with a figure of 81.

2. Kessel (1974), searching for patterns of presidential behavior based on a content analysis of State of the Union addresses, came up with virtually identical categories, with the exception of using an economic management dimension and a natural resources dimension rather than a government management category. In any case, these two studies are considered basic, and using either of them as a source for policy dimension categorizations makes for ready comparison with numerous other like-based studies.

3. It should be noted that the "miscellaneous" category is quite large (18.7 percent of all vetoes). This is unfortunate but necessary because a large number of bills were vetoed for unclassifiable reasons. Examples of this are: Eisenhower's veto of bills authorizing commemorative 50¢ pieces because the public would be confused and they would detract from the basic function of coins, prohibiting publication of apple price predictions because field workers and farmers need the ability to counteract price rumors, and setting the date of the meeting of the 85th Congress—Congress requested the veto because not enough time was allowed to count electoral votes; Kennedy's veto of a bill to amend the Life Insurance Act of D.C. because it didn't give some purchasers adequate voice in the control of the company; Johnson's veto of a bill setting boundaries on the Colorado River because he felt the courts were the proper forum for this particular dispute; Ford's veto of a bill naming a courthouse and federal building after him because it violated the precedent of naming buildings after a sitting president; and Carter's veto of a bill authorizing payments to citizens of Guam and the Virgin Islands for lost revenues because it didn't address their underlying long-range economic problems. These and the other miscellaneous vetoes lacked the key words and motivations in their message which would allow them to be placed in one of the other categories.

REFERENCES

Black, C. L., Jr. 1976. "Some Thoughts on the Veto," *Law and Contemporary Problems* 40:2 (Spring): 87–101.

Clausen, A. R. 1973. *How Congressmen Decide: A Policy Focus*. New York: St. Martin's Press.

Cohen, J. E. 1982. "A Historical Reassessment of Wildavsky's 'Two Presidencies' Thesis," *Social Science Quarterly* 63:3 (September): 549–555.

Congressional Quarterly. *Congress and the Nation*, vol. II–IV (1964–1980).

_____ . *Congressional Quarterly Almanac*, vols. 1953–1964.

_____ . *Congressional Quarterly Weekly Report*, 1981–1983 (various).

Copeland, G. W. 1983. "When Congress and the President Collide: Why Presidents Veto Legislation," *Journal of Politics* 45:3 (August): 696–710.

Edwards, G. C., III. 1980. *Presidential Influence in Congress*. San Francisco: W. H. Freeman and Company.

Fisher, L. 1981. *The Politics of Shared Power: Congress and the Executive*. Washington, D.C.: Congressional Quarterly Press.

_____ . 1978. *The Constitution Between Friends*. New York: St. Martin's Press.

Jones, C. O. 1982. *The United States Congress: People, Place and Policy*. Homewood, Ill.: The Dorsey Press.

Kessel, J. H. 1974. "The Parameters of Presidential Politics," *Social Science Quarterly* 55:1 (June): 8–24.

Lee, J. R. 1975. "Presidential Vetoes from Washington to Nixon," *Journal of Politics* 37:2 (May): 522–546.

Levine, M. A. 1983. "Tactical Constraints and Presidential Influence on Veto Overrides." *Presidential Studies Quarterly* 13:4 (Fall): 646–650.

Lowi, T. J. 1964. "American Business, Public Policy, Case-Studies, and Political Theory," *World Politics* 16:4 (July): 677–715.

Oleszek, W. J. 1984. *Congressional Procedures and the Policy Process*, 2nd ed. Washington, D.C.: Congressional Quarterly Press.

Shull, S. A. 1979. *Presidential Policy Making: An Analysis*. Brunswick, Ohio: King's Court Communications, Inc.

_____ and L. T. LeLoup. 1979. "Dimensions of Presidential Policy Making," in S. A. Shull and L. T. LeLoup, *The Presidency: Studies in Policy Making*. Brunswick, Ohio: King's Court Communications, Inc.

Sigelman, L. 1979. "A Reassessment of the Two Presidencies Thesis," *Journal of Politics* 41:4 (November): 1195–1205.

U.S. Senate Library. 1978. *Presidential Vetoes, 1789–1976*. Washington, D.C.: Government Printing Office.

Wayne, S. J. 1978. *The Legislative Presidency*. New York: Harper & Row.

_____ , R. Cole, and J. Hyde. 1979. "Advising the President on Enrolled Legislation: Patterns of Executive Influence," *Political Science Quarterly* 94:2 (Summer): 303–317.

Wildavsky, A. 1966. "The Two Presidencies," *Trans-Action* 4:2 (December): 7–14.

Zeidenstein, H. G. 1981. "The Two Presidencies Thesis Is Alive and Well and Has Been Living in the U.S. Senate," *Presidential Studies Quarterly* 11:4 (Fall): 511–525.

CHAPTER VII

The Domestic Policy Presidency

The term *domestic policy presidency* refers to presidential efforts to gain programmatic packages from the bureaucracy consistent with the president's goals and interests and to securing from Congress a reasonable record of approvals of such packages in nearly the same shape as when they were sent to the Hill. This was not always so. Presidents have a far greater role in initiating domestic policy today than they did at the turn of the century. Previously the province of Congress, agenda formulation and initiation is now, preeminently, the responsibility of the presidency.[1]

The framers of the Constitution did not foresee the president becoming the chief domestic policymaker. The Constitution simply assigned him the duty of giving Congress, from time to time, information on the State of the Union and recommending such measures as he thought necessary and expedient. During the first 100 plus years of the Republic, presidents recommended various measures to Congress and occasionally drafted bills on given measures; however, the drafting of bills and the formulation of comprehensive domestic policy was not done on a sustained basis.[2] This involvement remained ad hoc, sporadic, and largely unorganized.[3] Indeed, on the budget, in particular, Percival Brundage wrote: "From 1780 to 1921, the different departments and branches of the federal government prepared their financial requests separately, each setting forth its own needs. These requests were assembled in the Treasury Department and presented to Congress without comment or revision."[4]

Significant presidential involvement in the domestic policymaking process began with Theodore Roosevelt who worked closely with House Speaker Joseph Cannon in developing major policy initiatives.[5] Woodrow Wilson enlarged the president's domestic policy role even more. He used the State of the Union address to spell out his goals and objectives directly to Congress and then cajoled his Cabinet and members of Congress to support his policies and programs.[6]

As matters now stand, the preparation of strategies, policies, and programs for the domestic policy presidency lies essentially in four offices: the Bureau of the Budget (BOB) now the Office of Management and Budget (OMB), the White House Office (WHO), the Council of Economic Advisers (CEA) and the Domestic Policy Council now the Domestic Policy Staff. Each of these will be discussed.

Even though Theodore Roosevelt and Woodrow Wilson participated extensively in domestic policymaking, it was not until the Budget and Accounting Act of 1921, which created the Bureau of the Budget in the Department of the Treasury, that a routinized system of presidential review of agency legislative proposals became possible.[7] Importantly, with advance notice of the departments' and agencies' proposals, the president could forestall initiatives that conflicted with his own priorities.

In 1934, the central clearance process was extended by Franklin Roosevelt to include all executive branch requests for legislation whether fiscal or nonfiscal. Moreover, by 1938, the Bureau of the Budget began receiving multiple copies of enrolled bills from the Public Printer thus making it possible for the bureau and the pertinent departments and agencies to review proposed legislation and to prepare approval or veto messages for the president before it arrived at the president's desk.[8]

Subsequently, the capacity of the presidency, as opposed to the line departments, in the arena of domestic policy became more institutionalized with the creation of the Executive Office of the President (EOP), the creation of the White House Office, and the transfer of the BOB from Treasury to the EOP under the Reorganization Act of 1939. By 1980, for example, the White House Office included an Assistant to the President for Domestic Affairs and Policy whose job it is to supervise the Domestic Policy Staff within the EOP.

Since the Reorganization Act of 1939, Congress has passed additional laws requiring the president or the departments and agencies to submit a domestic program or report. Among these is the Employment Act of 1946 requiring the president to submit annual reports on the economy and creating a Council of Economic Advisers (CEA) in the Executive Office of the President to assist him in this effort.[9] The CEA, in addition to preparing the president's Annual Economic Report to Congress, advises the president on economic policy matters, analyzes economic information, and makes economic forecasts. The CEA consists of three economists, one of whom the president designates chairman. The CEA is itself staffed by a small number, twelve at last count, of professional economists. Essentially, it has not changed in size or structure since its creation in 1946. What has changed from administration to administration is the degree of importance given the CEA and the way in which each successive president has utilized it.

Roger Porter reports that "presidents have sought the advice of the CEA with varying frequency over the post–World War II period. While the principal function of the CEA has been expert analysis, it has, from time to time, served as a coordinator of views for the president."[10] President Eisenhower made extensive use of the economic advice of the CEA as well as that of his Treasury Secretary.

Some presidents have tended to rely much more heavily on a combination of agencies than on a single one for economic advice.[11] Presidents Kennedy and Johnson looked to a "troika" consisting of the CEA Chairman, the OMB Director, and the Treasury Secretary. From time to time a fourth party, outside the realm of presidential direction, would meet with the troika to make it a "quadriad."

This individual was the Chairman of the Federal Reserve Board. More recently, President Reagan has utilized a Cabinet Council on Economic Affairs (CCEA) which includes the secretaries of the Treasury, State, Commerce, Labor, Transportation, the Director of the OMB, the Chairman of the CEA, and the U.S. Trade Representative. Notable also is the fact that the CCEA is not the only cabinet council that considers economic issues in the Reagan administration.[12] When the subjects on the agendas of the other cabinet councils have substantial economic content, the president uses their advice as well.

With the Bureau of the Budget, the Council of Economic Advisers, and other extant agencies now available to the president, Congress has come to expect the president to submit a full-fledged domestic policy program for it to consider. When, for example, Dwight Eisenhower failed to present a legislative program during his first year in office, he was roundly criticized by members of both his party and the Democrats.[13]

Larry Berman reports that the Bureau of the Budget was quite successful as a legislative clearance agency, but that it "was institutionally incapable of positive policy formation."[14] As a result of the very difficult time the BOB had responding to the activist presidents of the 1960s, domestic policy initiatives shifted from the bureau to the White House Office.

George Edwards and Stephen Wayne write that the first domestic policy office was actually organized by the White House Office in 1965 to coordinate President Johnson's Great Society program.[15] The office did, essentially, three things: it staffed the outside task forces, reviewed their recommendations, and developed policy initiatives for President Johnson in the form of proposed bills for Congress to consider; prepared executive orders for the president to sign; and developed departmental regulations for the direction of departmental policy and behavior.

President Nixon expanded the White House domestic policy operation. Acting on the advice of his Advisory Council on Executive Organization chaired by Roy Ash of Litton Industries, Nixon created a Domestic Council to work ostensibly in the same way as the National Security Council.[16] The upper tier of the Domestic Council would consist of the president's cabinet secretaries; the lower tier would be a separate domestic council staff under the direction of an assistant to the president.[17]

In theory, the Domestic Council's responsibility was to wed new ideas to the institutional and administrative insights of the line departments; in practice, the council became the principal locus of domestic policy decision-making.[18]

Although the Nixon Domestic Council excluded the cabinet from much of its decision-making, the EOP had a domestic policy mechanism which worked. As Raymond Waldmann points out:

> It succeeded to a degree never before attempted in gaining centralized political control over the executive branch for the president. The Council and its staff produced a massive number of legislative proposals involving the environment, drug abuse, programs for the elderly, land use planning, District of Columbia Affairs, revenue sharing for transportation, community development, education, and general government support.[19]

With the advent of Watergate and the struggle of the Nixon administration simply to save itself, the Domestic Council collapsed with disuse.

President Ford determined to revive the Domestic Council and named Vice President Rockefeller to be its vice chairman with responsibility for overseeing domestic policy formulation and supervising domestic programs.[20] While the Domestic Council staff expanded under Rockefeller's leadership,[21] Ford's reliance on a series of interagency policy task forces chaired by department or agency heads and monitored by the White House policy staff resulted in the Domestic Council being of less significance than it was during the Nixon administration.

President Carter abolished the cabinet level tier of the Domestic Council begun under President Nixon, but retained a domestic policy staff for the purpose of presenting a range of policy options to the president and for advising the president on proposals that were developed in the departments. In addition, Carter continued the interagency policy task forces begun under President Ford.

President Reagan redesignated Carter's Domestic Policy Staff as the Office of Policy Development (OPD). To recommend domestic policy, however, Reagan created five cabinet councils each chaired by a cabinet member, but staffed by professionals from the OPD. While the OPD has had some policymaking clout under Reagan due to its capacity to moderate cabinet council recommendations with its own analyses, it is considerably weaker than might be expected because of Reagan's propensity to rely on a small legislative strategy group consisting of several of his top White House staffers.[22]

Thus, a president has several central mechanisms through which to take the initiative in domestic policymaking. A president will sometimes rely on a single one of these resources, on part of them, on all of them, or on some special arrangement suitable for specific purposes. Any of these arrangements in combination with an individual president's values and power situation, and the demands of the people will determine what policies receive presidential support.

We will now look at two specific domestic policies: civil rights and fiscal or economic policy. By doing so, we can see what part presidents play in the policymaking process and how their actions fit into broader presidential goals and objectives. A president usually chooses a domestic policy issue (or several) to give the highest priority to among all the possible policy issues. Lyndon Johnson chose poverty and civil rights; Ronald Reagan chose the economy.[23]

Bruce Miroff looks at the civil rights movement as a good example of a social movement and analyzes the president's relationship to it. Miroff defines a social movement as a group seeking structural and ideological changes in the society and argues that, as such, it poses problems for a president because of its preference for mass mobilization over elite negotiations and its propensity to rely on public rather than private discourse for the achievement of its goals.

Miroff found that while President Johnson had committed himself fully to civil rights for black Americans, when black emancipation was defined in terms that could tie the administration to dangerous militancy in the eyes of some, and timidity in the eyes of others, Johnson was obliged to manage his relations with this social movement through legislative proposals. These proposals would dramatize his own commitment to civil rights through (a) rhetorical gestures which sought to delimit the movement's objectives and (b) exerting leverage over the movement by supporting moderate over extreme leaders without undermining the former. The overarching White House objective became that of shifting the channels of black action from movement politics to party politics.

Miroff discusses the considerable array of strategies and maneuvers available to the presidency as well as some of the limits of presidential power to exercise leverage over a social movement.[24] The insights Miroff provides should contribute to a more complete understanding of the president's domestic policy role, especially where the president must grapple with the demands of emerging social groups. Miroff's analysis, "Presidential Leverage over Social Movements," is reprinted here.

The president has been held accountable for the health of the American economy ever since the Great Depression, but especially since Congress passed the Employment Act of 1946 committing the government to maintaining maximum employment, production, and purchasing power. In an economic downturn or crisis, the American people turn to the White House for policies which they hope will revitalize the economy. And so they did in electing Ronald Reagan to the presidency at the time of the record high inflation rates.

Hugh Heclo and Rudolph Penner write that President Reagan came into office with a detailed and comprehensive economic strategy which he believed would stabilize the economy. Reagan's solution: persuade the Federal Reserve System to gradually reduce the rate at which money was created, reduce government spending, and reduce taxes (one of the major goals of the supply siders who represented a sizable component of President Reagan's political supporters).

Heclo and Penner point out that Reagan's economic strategy was founded on a political, not an economic theory. Reducing taxes to cut inflation was clearly at variance with orthodox economic theory. Heclo and Penner write that Reagan was able to get his budget through Congress, albeit it was thought to be politically unacceptable, because Congress had great difficulty in formulating a package of its own. The moral of this experience: Congress cannot lead.

Soon after the Reagan strategy was put into practice, flaws began to emerge: military spending went up, nondefense spending did not go down as much as anticipated, tax cuts were massive, and the deficit increased.

Nevertheless, Heclo and Penner point to the Reagan White House as an excellent example of strategic management of their major domestic policy concern: Reagan was able to respond to the growing deficit by moving toward a new tax policy without ever denying the merits of his original economic program; he kept the economy as his top priority; he also reduced nonmilitary spending, eliminated government regulation in many sectors of the economy, and permitted the private sector to revive itself. This strategic management of the economy as a domestic policy issue was carried out by a small group of policy managers on the White House Office staff. Heclo and Penner's essay, "Fiscal and Political Strategy in the Reagan Administration" which details the policy and its management, is reprinted here.

NOTES

1. See Steven A. Shull, "The President and Congress: Researching Their Interaction in Domestic Policy Formation," *Presidential Studies Quarterly* 12, no. 4 (Fall 1982), p. 535.

2. On this point, see George C. Edwards III and Stephen J. Wayne, *Presidential Leadership: Politics and Policymaking* (New York: St. Martin's Press, 1985), p. 236.

3. See Lester M. Salamon, "The Presidency and Domestic Policy Formulation," in *Analyzing the Presidency*, ed. Robert E. DiClerico (Guilford, Conn.: Dushkin Publishing Group, 1985), p. 210.

4. Percival Flack Brundage, *The Bureau of the Budget* (New York: Praeger Publishers, 1970), p. 3.

5. Edwards and Wayne, *Presidential Leadership*.

6. Ibid.

7. See Richard E. Neustadt, "Presidency and Legislation: The Growth of Central Clearance," in *Classics of the American Presidency*, ed. Harry A. Bailey, Jr. (Oak Park, Ill.: Moore Publishing, 1980), p. 238; and Salamon, *Presidency and Domestic Policy*, p. 210.

8. Larry Berman, *The Office of Management and Budget and the Presidency, 1921–1979* (Princeton, N.J.: Princeton University Press, 1979), p. 10.

9. See Richard M. Pious, *The American Presidency* (New York: Basic Books, 1979), p. 148.

10. Roger B. Porter, "Economic Advice to the President: From Eisenhower to Reagan," *Political Science Quarterly* 98, no. 3 (Fall 1983), p. 405.

11. Ibid., p. 406.

12. See Murray L. Wiedenbaum, "Economic Policymaking in the Reagan Administration," *Presidential Studies Quarterly* 12, no. 1 (Winter 1982), pp. 96, 98.

13. See Berman, *OMB and the Presidency*, p. 50; and Edwards and Wayne, *Presidential Leadership*, p. 237.

14. Berman, *OMB and the Presidency*, p. 103.

15. See Edwards and Wayne, *Presidential Leadership*, p. 246; see also Bradley D. Nash et al., *Organizing and Staffing the Presidency* (New York: Center for the Study of the Presidency, Proceedings, vol. III, no. 1, 1980), p. 37.

16. See Roger G. Noll, *Reforming Regulation: An Evaluation of the Ash Council Proposals* (Washington, D.C.: Brookings Institution, 1971); see also Ronald C. Moe, "The Domestic Council in Perspective," *The Bureaucrat* 5 (October 1976), pp. 251–72.

17. See Margaret Jane Wyszomirski, "A Domestic Policy Office: A Presidential Agency in Search of a Role," *Policy Studies Journal* 12, no. 4 (June 1984), p. 707.

18. Raymond J. Waldmann, "The Domestic Council: Innovation in Presidential Government," *Public Administration Review* 36, no. 3 (May/June 1976), p. 263.

19. Ibid., p. 266.

20. Moe, *Domestic Council in Perspective*, p. 263.

21. Ibid., p. 266.

22. Erwin C. Hargrove and Michael Nelson, *Presidents, Politics and Policy* (New York: Knopf, 1984), p. 184.

23. For the evidence see Paul Light, *The President's Agenda* (Baltimore, Md.: Johns Hopkins University Press, 1982), p. 70; see also Larry Berman, *The New American Presidency* (Boston: Little, Brown, 1986), pp. 248 and 324.

24. For the limits of presidential leadership in domestic policy generally, see Michael Mumper, "The Presidency and Domestic Policy Making," *Congress and the Presidency* 12, no. 1 (Spring 1985), p. 79.

18
Presidential Leverage over Social Movements

Bruce Miroff

For the contemporary Presidency, social movements can pose an unsettling prospect. Social movements raise divisive issues, drawing attention to controversies more likely to polarize than to unify a president's supporters. They call into question a president's commmitments, contrasting their extensive objectives to an administration's modest proposals. They threaten electoral punishment, tying an administration to dangerous militancy in the eyes of some, to timidity and ineffectiveness in the eyes of others.

In the face of these worries, the White House will ordinarily devote some measure of attention to managing its relations with social movements. Legislative proposals and rhetorical gestures are the most obvious, public form its response will take. Less visible, but equally significant, are White House attempts to exercise leverage over social movements. The White House thus may try to modify the character of a social movement; it may seek to influence its leadership, to

delimit its objectives, or to slow the tempo of its actions. It may attempt to forestall movement projects that conflict with its own projects, thereby averting the explosion into public notice of embarrassing clashes. It may hope, ultimately, to transform social movements from political liabilities into political advantages.

Despite their significance, the difficulties that social movements present for the White House have received scant attention in the literature on presidential politics. Following the lead of Richard E. Neustadt in *Presidential Power*, most political scientists have concentrated their efforts on studying the president's dealings with other members of the "Washington Community": "the men who share in governing this country."[1] As a result of this emphasis, we possess a rapidly growing body of works

[1] *Presidential Power* (New York: John Wiley & Sons, 1976), 126.

Source: Journal of Politics 43 (February 1981). Reprinted with permission.

on presidential transactions with Congress, the bureaucracy, the White House staff. But we know little about presidential relationships with social and economic groups whose roots lie outside the "Washington Community." White House strategies and tactics for handling these groups have seldom been examined.

In this article I analyze presidential responses to social movements. The historical case upon which I focus is the relationship between the Johnson White House and the civil rights movement. A single case study cannot, of course, produce definitive generalizations. Its findings must be tested in analogous cases before generalized relationships can be confidently asserted. Nonetheless, a case study may be important both in generating new hypotheses and in revealing the limitations or inadequacies of prevailing theoretical formulations.

The challenges posed by social movements have not been restricted to the Johnson presidency. In the Carter Administration, for example, troublesome political controversies have repeatedly marked White House relationships with the women's movement and with environmentalist and antinuclear activists. President Carter's efforts to identify his Administration with a moderate feminism have come under increasing fire from the women's movement. Angered by his dismissal of Bella Abzug as head of a presidential commission on women, and by his allegedly halfhearted gestures on behalf of the Equal Rights Amendment, women's groups have bestowed few plaudits on Carter; the largest feminist organization, the National Organization for Women, pointedly refused to support him for re-election. Carter's relations with environmentalists and antinuclear activists have similarly soured. Initially pleased by his record and campaign promises, these movements have subsequently accused the Carter Admin-

istration of downgrading environmental and safety concerns in light of pressures for rapid energy development.

While little documentary material is available yet on such recent cases, the relationship between the Johnson White House and the civil rights movement affords a ripe topic for research. The relationship is, moreover, an especially suggestive one. Confronted with burgeoning black militancy and white backlash, the Johnson Administration knew that much of its political future was at stake in its moves to manage civil rights activity. As the most extreme and dramatic case in recent years of an administration troubled by a social movement, the story of the Johnson White House and civil rights groups exhibits the array of maneuvers available to the presidency—but also some limits of its power —to exercise leverage over a social movement.[2]

Unfortunately, standard accounts of the Johnson Presidency disclose little of this story. In books such as Eric Goldman's *The Tragedy of Lyndon Johnson*[3] and Doris Kearns's *Lyndon Johnson and the American Dream*,[4] President John-

[2] The attempts by the Johnson White House to exercise leverage over the civil rights struggle were, in one sense, a continuation of efforts begun in the Kennedy Administration. But the tensions and risks of that struggle reached greater heights during Johnson's years as President. On the Kennedy Administration and the civil rights movement, see the following: Howard Zinn, *SNCC: The New Abolitionists* (Boston: Beacon Press, 1965); Victor S. Navasky, *Kennedy Justice* (New York: Atheneum, 1971); Bruce Miroff, *Pragmatic Illusions: The Presidential Politics of John F. Kennedy* (New York: David McKay Co., 1976); Carl Brauer, *John F. Kennedy and the Second Reconstruction* (New York: Columbia University Press, 1977).

[3] *The Tragedy of Lyndon Johnson* (New York: Dell Books, 1974).

[4] *Lyndon Johnson and the American Dream* (New York: New American Library, 1977). The one full-length study of Johnson and civil rights— James C. Harvey, *Black Civil Rights During the*

son's involvement with civil rights is portrayed largely as a dramatic political transformation, in which a southern politician transcends a regional bias and assumes a bold moral stance. Information on the less visible side of Johnson's actions in the civil rights field is available, however, at the Lyndon Baines Johnson Library in Austin, Texas. While I have consulted contemporary accounts, secondary sources, and oral history interviews, most of the data in this article is drawn from the memoranda of White House aides and advisers on file at the Johnson Library. The recommendations contained in these memos were not always put into practice; sometimes they were rejected by the President, or rendered infeasible by the flow of events. Nonetheless, these memos offer valuable, direct evidence (and, in numerous instances, the only evidence available) of the terms in which the Johnson White House evaluated the problems posed by the civil rights movement, as well as the maneuvers through which it sought to exercise leverage over that movement.

SOCIAL MOVEMENTS AND THE STUDY OF THE PRESIDENCY

Sociologists have defined social movements as groups seeking structural and ideological changes in the society.[5] The emphasis of social movements on collective action, social change, and unconventional political expression distinguishes them from interest groups. The boundaries, however, are not always distinct. The civil rights movement included elements such as the NAACP, whose involvement in lobbying was a characteristic usually associated with interest groups.

From the standpoint of presidential politics, what is distinctive—and troublesome—about social movements is their preference for mass mobilization over elite negotiations, their propensity to confront issues directly rather than exerting pressure through Washington lobbying, and their desire for public attention and controversy rather than quiet coalition-building. While interest group politics poses its own set of problems for the White House, it generally takes place in a delimited and predictable sphere. Because its relationship with social movements is less easily controlled, the White House is less certain of the impact on presidential power, policy-making, and popularity.

Richard Neustadt's treatment of the president as bargainer in *Presidential Power* highlights elements of mutual need between presidents and movement leaders that sometimes allow profitable exchanges. But Neustadt's model depends upon a symmetry of interest calculations between bargaining partners that cannot be assumed in the case of social movements. Bargaining between elites is precisely the kind of politics that a social movement generally repudiates. To its members, with their sense of urgency and commitment to major social change, the gains to be anticipated from striking a bargain with the White House are likely to be viewed not only as inadequate but also as co-optative, aimed at diverting the movement from its just objectives. Given a constituency so mistrustful of bargaining, Neustadt's widely employed framework for analyzing presidential behavior appears to be of limited usefulness.[6]

Johnson Administration (Jackson: The University and College Press of Mississippi, 1973)—is more critical of Johnson's efforts, but it too contains little information on White House attempts to influence the black movement.

[5] Roberta Ash, *Social Movements in America* (Chicago: Markham Publishing Co., 1972), 1.

[6] Neustadt, *Presidential Power*, especially 101–125.

Since social movements create dramatic public challenges to presidential power and commitment, Thomas E. Cronin's concept of the "theatrical presidency" provides a basis for understanding why White House responses seek to maintain the president's dominant presence in the public eye. Analysis can focus on how the White House attempts to dramatize its own commitments to the "noble" objectives of a social movement while blocking or playing down movement dramas that might prove embarrassing. Yet, while Cronin views the "theatrical presidency" as a cover for inaction and as the "subordination of policy substance to presidential style," in the case of social movements White House capacity to convey effective appearances may be crucial for its ability to define issues and shape policies. "Theater" may not always be separable from, or alternative to, the central policy-making or political tasks of the presidency.[7]

Since the publication of Aaron Wildavsky's "The Two Presidencies" in 1966, most scholars have accepted the thesis that the president is relatively weak in domestic affairs.[8] Many writers have elaborated upon the executive weakness in domestic policy-making, particularly in the areas of policy formulation, congressional relations, and implementation. But the literature's preoccupation with how Washington institutions constrain the president limits its value for an understanding of how forces outside Washington serve as constraints. Its measures for presidential effectiveness or ineffectiveness (e.g., legislative scorecards) do not tap the more

subtle lines of influence that obtain between the White House and a social movement.

A more inclusive conceptualization of the presidential role in domestic politics seems necessary for an understanding of the White House response to social movements. The president wants to dominate the definition of issues. Policy formulation, bargaining, theater, and other modes of action are interrelated aspects of presidential strategy to achieve this domination. Despite their limitations as domestic leaders, presidents attempt to retain control over the content and tempo of domestic issues. If they are successful, they gain legislative victories and an enhanced reputation for political mastery. But if they appear to have lost control over an issue—especially a controversial one such as race—their losses can be considerable. The public's perception of weakness, as well as the backlash from major constituencies, are dangerous weapons in the hands of rival leaders. With so much at stake, the shaping and defining of issues to White House advantage becomes an imperative of presidential politics.

The present study examines the Johnson Administration's strategy for dominating the definition of an extremely explosive social issue. Further theoretical and empirical elaboration are required in order to determine the utility of a strategic perspective for understanding other areas of presidential politics. Because the civil rights movement posed so direct a challenge to President Johnson's ability to define issues, however, an analysis of their relationship offers an apt starting point for developing this perspective. In the maneuvers of the Johnson White House to keep on top of the racial issue by exercising leverage over the civil rights movement, several important elements of

[7] *The State of the Presidency* (Boston: Little, Brown & Co., 1975), 140–151.

[8] "The Two Presidencies," in *The Presidency*, ed. Aaron Wildavsky (Boston: Little, Brown & Co., 1969).

White House strategy can be identified.

THE SOCIAL MOVEMENT AS WHITE HOUSE PROBLEM

The objectives, tactics, and constituency of a social movement, as well as the broader political context within which it operates, define its salience for an administration. The case of Johnson and civil rights indicates some of the conditions under which a social movement becomes especially problematical for the White House:

1. when the movement's activists and sympathizers are drawn from constituencies that are vital to a President's present or potential electoral base;
2. when the movement and the administration claim similar broad objectives, but increasingly diverge on how to attain those objectives;
3. when the demands of the movement point toward clear-cut presidential commitments likely to alienate other important constituencies;
4. when the issue in question is central to the public image a president has projected—and to the self-image he privately cherishes.

For the Johnson White House, the importance—and the explosive potential—of civil rights politics were apparent at the outset. When Lyndon Johnson assumed the presidency, he had substantial reasons for taking a strong civil rights stand. Black voters, a key element of the Democratic party's presidential electorate, were suspicious of a southern President. So, too, were many northern liberals who had become emotionally committed to the black cause

after the Birmingham demonstrations and the March on Washington in 1963. President Johnson wanted to prove himself to blacks and liberals by carrying out the uncompleted civil rights program of the Kennedy Administration. Even more, numerous observers have suggested, Johnson wanted to surpass Kennedy's program, and to make his own historic mark as the President ". . . who really accomplished something in civil rights for blacks."[9]

Johnson's first year in office, however, indicated some of the risks involved in identifying his Administration with the black cause. Governor George Wallace of Alabama, the symbol of segregationist resistance, ran surprisingly well in northern Democratic primaries in 1964. Senator Barry Goldwater, voting against the Civil Rights Act of 1964, captured the electoral votes of the deep South. "White backlash"—the new phrase for white resentment of black gains through political action—thus loomed as a glaring threat to the solidity of the Democratic coalition.

Nor were Johnson's problems restricted to whites. Several civil rights organizations were becoming militant in ways that disturbed and embarrassed the Johnson Administration. The challenge by the black Mississippi Freedom Democratic Party to the regular Mississippi delegation at the Democratic convention, for example, punctured the celebration of President Johnson's renomination. Even worse was the specter of black riots; 1964 witnessed the first of the "long, hot summers" that revealed the previously unsuspected depths of black discontent. Black advancement was central to Lyndon Johnson's call for a consensus politics. Black militancy

[9] James Farmer, Oral History Interview, July 20, 1971, Lyndon Baines Johnson Library, 25.

and rioting fundamentally called into question the feasibility of consensus.

These developments did not shake Johnson's determination to obtain civil rights progress through legislation and executive action. They did, however, intensify his desire to control the expanding energies of the black struggle. It was clear to his aides that the President wanted the course of civil rights politics to be shaped, as much as possible, from the White House.

RATIONALES FOR WHITE HOUSE MANAGEMENT

The White House is likely to seek leverage over any social movement that presents it with substantial political difficulties. However, since the development of influence over supposedly autonomous social forces is not one of the recognized or official tasks of the presidency, rationales for White House managerial efforts must be elaborated. The President and his aides engage in a process of mutual persuasion, demonstrating to one another that such efforts are legitimate, worthy of considerable effort, and practicable. Since the President must count on his aides to engage in most of the actual managerial efforts, he must convey to them his concern about this subject. Those aides to whom the task is delegated must, in turn, keep its importance before his eyes through their sensitivity to his political instincts and personal preoccupations.

The files at the Johnson Library do not contain any full expression of Lyndon Johnson's own perspective on the civil rights movement; presidents do not generally write memos. But Johnson's position on mass political action was well-known to his staff. The essence of that position is conveyed in a statement he made to Doris Kearns: "The biggest danger to American stability . . . is the politics of principle, which brings out the masses in irrational fights for unlimited goals, for once the masses begin to move, then the whole thing begins to explode. Thus, it is for the sake of nothing less than stability that I consider myself a consensus man."[10]

Johnson's aides spoke to these preoccupations when they addressed issues raised by the black struggle. In their memos three distinct rationales for White House leverage over the civil rights movement were advanced: (1) historic responsibility, (2) expertise, and (3) political advantage. Douglass Cater, in a memo to the President on May 4, 1964, characterized the existing situation in terms of an analogy with the period preceding the Civil War. In that unhappy period, he stated, the politicians had failed to act, and had permitted abolitionists and defenders of slavery to push matters out of control. In a manner well-designed to appeal both to Johnson's fear of mass politics and his dream of great achievements, Cater concluded: "There are moments in history when politics must act or the forces of anarchy take charge. America does not want another civil war even if it is confined to the streets of Birmingham or the expressways of New York. It takes the skill and dedication of those who have been elected by the people to build the great society toward which we must be constantly moving."[11]

Another line of reasoning pursued by Johnson's aides emphasized the superior political expertise and persuasive skills of the presidency. Since most black leaders seemed unable to accept political realities, the White House would have to instill the civil rights movement with

[10] Kearns, *Lyndon Johnson*, 161.

[11] Douglass Cater, Memorandum to the President, May 4, 1964, Files of Douglass Cater, Box 13, Johnson Library.

good political sense. Hobart Taylor, Jr., a black presidential assistant, sketched out this argument in a memo to Johnson on July 17, 1964:

> I am disturbed about the continued demonstrations and what I see on radio and TV. I am convinced that a great deal of the Negro leadership simply does not understand the political facts of life, and think that they are advancing their cause by uttering threats in the newspapers and on TV. They are not sophisticated enough to understand the theory of the backlash unless they are told about it by someone whom they believe. We have not done with the Negro leaders what we did with the business community and with southern public officials—i.e., make a major and organized effort to direct their thinking along a proper course, but I believe this is possible and that demonstrations and picketing can be avoided through personal contact and explanations of the seriousness of the problem. [12]

Political calculations were never far from the surface in these arguments. This was especially true in 1964, as the Wallace and Goldwater candidacies and the summer's riots made the racial issue central to election-year politics. Since he had linked his Administration with the black cause, Johnson was deeply concerned about the reverberations the mushrooming black struggle might have on his re-election. Recommendations from his aides frequently spoke to this concern. In a memo to the President on May 4, 1964, for example, Richard Goodwin suggested a strategy through which the White House might hold down the number of incidents of racial upheaval while avoiding blame for those that did occur. The stakes in such a strategy were largely political: "I believe that this is worth an awful lot of energy

and foresight, since it is an issue which could dominate the campaign." [13]

Johnson's aides believed that the White House occupied a superior "vantage point" for understanding and guiding the campaign for racial progress. It was, therefore, their special function to adjust black aspirations to the realities of white sentiment. It was their function, too, to forestall violence and to foster consensual change. The primary difficulty that they faced was to devise effective techniques for the exercise of White House leverage. This task was complicated, because the black movement was in the process of exploding the usual categories of American group politics. The familiar, "responsible" black leadership, for example, was losing its grip over the movement. And while White House support was still solicited by all the black groups in 1964 and 1965, any appearance that the White House was calling the shots for established civil rights leaders only fed the mistrust of younger militants and contributed to the further weakening of the leadership.

In this setting, White House managerial efforts had to be subtle and indirect. Those efforts involved three interrelated objectives: (1) moderating the actions of the civil rights movement; (2) managing the appearances of black politics; and (3) shifting the channels of black action from movement toward party politics.

MODERATING MOVEMENT ACTIONS

Even when a social movement claims objectives akin to those of an administration, its timetable for progress toward

---

[12] Hobart Taylor, Jr., Memorandum to the President, July 17, 1964, White House Central Files, EX HU 2, Box 2, Johnson Library.

[13] Richard Goodwin, Memorandum to the President, May 4, 1964, White House Central Files, EX HU 2, Box 2, Johnson Library.

those objectives is likely to differ radically. At the core of a social movement are a passion and a sense of urgency about the social good that the movement pursues. To adherents of the movement, its goals are more pressing than the panoply of issues with which it shares the existing political agenda. Fired by their passionate sense of urgency, members of social movements generally regard political elites with suspicion, as purveyors of dilatory action and bland compromise. They are not easily contented with following official political channels, since such channels have rarely been productive for their goals in the past.

The White House has a different political timetable. While it may be working for progress toward the goals it shares with a social movement, it is concerned with a mix of issues and a diversity of constituencies. To White House political strategists, the danger is that a social movement may force the pace of change too rapidly, leaving the administration with the unpleasant choice of appearing laggard in its commitments or else venturing out onto a shaky political limb. Equally dangerous is a movement's employment of militant tactics, which can embarrass an administration connected to it in the public mind. Given such unattractive possibilities, the White House can be expected to utilize whatever leverage it possesses to slow down a social movement, and to contain its action within moderate limits.

One of the Johnson Administration's principal worries was the potential escalation of civil rights demonstrations. As Eric Goldman has observed, Lyndon Johnson "was no enthusiast of mass demonstrations."[14] His enthusiasm grew even fainter during the election year of 1964, when demonstrations threatened to turn white voters against a President

identified with the black cause. Despite these feelings, Johnson did not take a public stand against demonstrations, as had President Kennedy in the summer of 1963.[15] As Lee White, a presidential assistant whose chief responsibility was the field of civil rights, observed in a memo to Johnson on August 19, 1964, "The Administration has never publicly urged discontinuance of demonstrations or intimated that there was anything improper [about them]. . . ."[16]

In private conferences, however, President Johnson made clear his desire to see demonstrations held to a minimum. After signing the 1964 Civil Rights Act on July 2, for example, he met with civil rights leaders and told them that the rights of blacks were now secured by law, ". . . making demonstrations unnecessary and possibly even self-defeating."[17] Johnson avoided such expressions in public, where they might alienate or even activate black militants; privately he urged the established black leadership to keep matters under control.

On July 29, several weeks after their meeting with the President, and shortly after the eruption of rioting in New York and Rochester, the six principal black leaders met in New York. Their conference produced a statement accusing Senator Goldwater of injecting racism into the campaign and jeopardizing civil rights progress. The situation, this statement proclaimed, was so grave that

---

[14] Goldman, *Tragedy*, 369.

[15] *Public Papers of the President: 1963* (Washington, D.C.: Government Printing Office, 1964), 493, 572–573.

[16] Lee White, Notes [for the President] for Meeting with Negro Leaders, August 19, 1964, White House Central Files, EX HU 2, Box 3, Johnson Library.

[17] Lee White, Memorandum for the White House Files, July 6, 1964, White House Central Files, EX HU 2, Box 2, Johnson Library.

members of civil rights organizations were requested to observe "a broad curtailment, if not total moratorium, of all mass marches, mass picketing, and mass demonstrations until after Election Day," and to concentrate their energies on voter registration drives.[18] Four of the black leaders present (Roy Wilkins of the NAACP, Whitney Young of the Urban League, Martin Luther King, Jr. of the Southern Christian Leadership Conference, and A. Philip Randolph of the Negro American Labor Council) endorsed the statement. The leaders of the two most militant civil rights groups (James Farmer of CORE and John Lewis of SNCC) refused to sign it.

Did the Johnson Administration have a hand in creating a statement that meshed so neatly with its objectives? Later testimony from participants is conflicting. Roy Wilkins, who had called the meeting, denied that the White House had been involved: "I don't think Mr. Johnson ever directly requested . . . any such moratorium."[19] James Farmer, on the other hand, interpreted the statement differently: "The implication was very clear . . . that it was at the President's request."[20]

While direct evidence is lacking, two pieces of circumstantial evidence suggest White House involvement. Hobart Taylor's memo of July 17, calling for a major White House effort to direct the thinking of civil rights leaders away from demonstrations, has already been quoted. It is also notable that President Johnson was in close contact with Roy Wilkins in the days immediately preceding the New York meeting. Johnson's Daily Diary indicates that he made a lengthy

call to Wilkins on July 27 and another brief call to Wilkins on July 28.[21]

If the role of the Johnson White House in this affair was veiled, its subsequent ire at Farmer and Lewis for refusing to endorse the "moratorium" was quite visible. Prior to the New York meeting, Farmer had been on good terms with the President; Johnson had told him to call any time he had a problem. After the meeting the head of CORE was repeatedly given the cold shoulder by the White House. Presidential retribution extended to petty details. During the signing ceremony for the 1965 Voting Rights Act, Farmer recalled, "As we went to another place from the White House, where the President was passing out pens to everyone, he passed over me several times."[22]

MANAGING THE APPEARANCES

In its relationship with social movements the White House is concerned with appearances as well as actions. The White House naturally shies away from too close a symbolic link with a controversial social movement, lest it alienate other supporters. Yet it also desires the appearance of moving in the forefront of progressive change, and of serving the same high ideals (e.g., racial justice, equal treatment for women, a healthy environment) that a social movement professes. Its aim, therefore, is to find a symbolic balance point, where it appears to cooperate with a social movement for noble purposes while retaining its special commitment to law, order, and the general good.

Compounding this task is the necessity of protecting not only the administration's own image, but also that of

[18] *New York Times*, July 30, 1964, 1.

[19] Roy Wilkins, Oral History Interview, April 1, 1969, Johnson Library, 12–13.

[20] Farmer, Oral History Interview, 2.

[21] President Lyndon Baines Johnson, Daily Diary, July 1964, Johnson Library.

[22] Farmer, Oral History Interview, 5.

movement leaders whose position most nearly resembles the president's stance. An administration will want to cast in a favorable light those leaders—usually moderates—who sympathize with the concerns of the White House and work comfortably with it. In power struggles between moderates and militants in a social movement, the White House may use its resources to boost the moderates' attractiveness. Yet it will also try to avoid open clashes with the militants, who might launch bitter attacks embarrassing both to moderate leaders and to the administration.

In the Johnson Presidency one area of concern was the public statements of black leaders. When black leaders met with Johnson, for example, their comments to the press upon leaving the Oval Office received special attention. Sometimes the White House sought to preclude unfavorable comments and to enhance its image by spelling out in the meetings what the black leaders ought to tell the press. When Martin Luther King met with President Johnson during the early phase of the Selma, Alabama voting rights drive, the White House knew exactly what King should say to reporters. Lee White's memo to the President of February 8, 1965, ended with the heading, "Points for King to Make":

> The President has had a long record [of] support for securing the right to vote and his commitment expressed in the State of the Union message has been most reassuring. The meetings with Administration leaders have given King an opportunity to explain what he has seen in Alabama and he is confident that any legislative proposals will be well thought out and that he appreciates how deep the Administration's concern is that the right to register and vote be universal in this country. The President was obviously interested and although his time did not permit him to go into great detail he was obviously conversant with

the problem and his determination was clear.[23]

King's subsequent statement to the press incorporated several of White's points. But the civil rights leader also used the occasion to publicize his own guidelines for voting rights legislation.[24]

In his meetings with black leaders Johnson had to avoid the image of co-opting the moderates and excluding the militants. The President felt more comfortable with Roy Wilkins or Whitney Young, who possessed a similar set of political beliefs and sense of political decorum, than he did with Martin Luther King and especially with the increasingly militant leaders of CORE and SNCC. But his aides were cognizant of the pitfalls in meetings restricted on the basis of Johnson's comfort. Presidential assistant Harry C. McPherson, Jr. noted in a memo of September 20, 1966: "Bringing Wilkins and Young in alone does clearly give them problems. Bringing in King . . . and others would take the curse of 'President's boy' off Whitney and Roy."[25] This concern to balance White House meetings for the sake of appearances was perceived by black leaders. Andrew Young, King's aide in those years, recalled that King ". . . felt as though whenever he went to the White House with Roy Wilkins and Whitney Young and Bayard [Rustin] that they were using his presence."[26]

[23] Lee White, Memorandum for the President, February 8, 1965, White House Central Files, EX HU 2, Box 3, Johnson Library.

[24] *New York Times*, February 10, 1965, 1.

[25] Harry C. McPherson, Jr., Memorandum to Attorney General Nicholas Katzenbach, September 20, 1966, Files of Harry C. McPherson, Jr., Box 5, Johnson Library.

[26] Andrew Young, Oral History Interview, June 18, 1971, Johnson Library, 17. White House interest in the public image of black leaders took a special form in the case of King. As J. Edgar

The Johnson Administration's concern for the public status of moderate black leaders intensified in 1965 and 1966, as militant younger leaders began to seize the spotlight. Not only were these younger leaders regarded as dangerous zealots; they were particularly worrisome because of their capacity to embarrass the Administration. The White House thus became anxious late in 1965 that militants might dominate or disrupt the President's Conference on Civil Rights, scheduled for the spring of 1966. As Harry McPherson related in his memoir, *A Political Education*, "After the planning session [for the conference], the danger was that this movement, with all its potential for resentment, would be controlled by a small army of abrasive men whose language alienated the moderate center. . . . If we were to move on to the next stage, the leadership would have to be returned to the centrists, to the sensitive establishment—to business, labor, Wilkins and Young."[27]

Johnson's aides thus revised the organizational leadership for the conference. Ben Heineman, President of the Chicago and Northwestern Railroad, was appointed as chairman. A. Philip Randolph, once a militant black leader, but now a fervent admirer of President Johnson, was made honorary chairman. The format and agenda for the conference were reshaped as well, to ensure that

its final report would buttress the Administration's own position. Black leaders considered unsympathetic to the White House (a category that by now included King because of his publicly-expressed doubts about the Vietnam War) were kept safely out on the periphery of the conference.[28]

SHIFTING THE CHANNELS OF ACTION

From the perspective of the White House, the most effective way for adherents to a social cause to promote their goals is to operate through "normal" political channels such as legislative lobbying and administration-sponsored projects. Ideally, a concern for effectiveness would also lead movement activists and sympathizers to become involved in the President's party and electoral operations. Shifting the channels of political action from movement toward party politics is thus a major goal of presidential relationships with social movements. If this shift can be initiated, White House influence over the issue in question is markedly expanded. The definition of this issue, and the methods by which it is addressed, are now more susceptible to administration control. The supporters of a cause are more subject to White House restraints. And the possibilities for extracting political gain from the issue are greatly improved. It is not surprising that, beset by the strains of movement politics, the White House looks for strategies that can restore "normal" politics.

President Johnson's political aides periodically devoted attention to such strategies. Particularly after the useful-

---

Hoover mounted a vitriolic campaign against the civil rights leader, the White House lent a measure of support by circulating the FBI's abusive anti-King monograph to several executive agencies. U.S. Congress, Senate Select Committee to Study Governmental Operations with Respect to Intelligence Activities, *Supplementary Detailed Staff Reports on Intelligence Activities and the Rights of Americans* (Washington, D.C.: Government Printing Office, 1976), 143.

[27] *A Political Education* (Boston: Atlantic-Little, Brown & Co., 1972), 345.

[28] David L. Lewis, *King: A Critical Biography* (Baltimore: Penguin Books, 1970), 308–312; McPherson, *Political Education*, 345–352; Farmer, Oral History Interview, 16–19.

ness of Johnson's connection with the movement seemed exhausted, aides began to envision a welcome shift in black politics from civil rights to elections and officeholding. Shortly after the 1964 campaign, Hobart Taylor outlined to Johnson a rationale for this shift. He predicted that the Republicans would soon move toward the center and begin to compete with the Democrats for black voters. In that case, continuing White House preoccupation with the civil rights groups would "downgrade regular political leadership" and leave the Democrats at a competitive disadvantage. Consequently, Taylor recommended that Johnson increase his distance from the civil rights leadership, while ". . . placing more emphasis on Negro participation in the management of the Party and Negro candidates for state and local office. . . ."[29]

Development of a new black elite, rooted in the Democratic party, was regarded as valuable in areas apart from electoral politics as well. Some Johnson aides entertained hopes that such an elite could put a damper on black urban upheavals. Established civil rights leaders, the White House recognized, carried little weight in the black ghettoes of the North; their public comments were ineffectual in riot situations. Indeed, given President Johnson's symbolic link to these leaders, a White House concern by 1965 was to put distance between rioters and the civil rights movement. George Reedy wrote to the President shortly after the Watts uprising, "It is to be hoped that national civil rights leaders will stay as far from the riots as they can. . . . Unless they are extraordinarily careful, the civil rights leaders run the risk of identifying their move-

ments with ordinary hooliganism and savagery."[30]

A network of local black leaders responsive to the Administration and the Democratic party, however, might wield more influence in explosive urban situations. The White House made use of an existing but inchoate network in the late summer of 1964. Following the President's directions, Hobart Taylor and Lee White dispatched black federal officials to their hometowns to meet with the local black leadership and establish lines of contact. As Taylor reported to Johnson, the establishment of this network had improved the political atmosphere in the ghettoes. "There is less belligerence and more constructive activity aimed at getting out the vote. There has been no more rioting and all of the activist leaders I talk to agree that no more is anticipated."[31]

THE LIMITS OF WHITE HOUSE LEVERAGE

Although the White House can exercise some degree of leverage over most social movements, its influence may ultimately fall considerably short of its desires. The case of the Johnson Administration and the civil rights movement suggests some of the conditions that operate to circumscribe White House leverage. A social movement will welcome a White House connection so long as its objectives parallel those of the administration; to the

[29] Hobart Taylor, Jr., Memorandum to the President, November 27, 1964, White House Central Files, EX HU 2, Box 3, Johnson Library.

[30] George Reedy, Memorandum to the President, August 22, 1965, Files of Harry C. McPherson, Jr., Box 5, Johnson Library.

[31] Hobart Taylor, Jr., Memorandum to the President, October 13, 1964. White House Central Files, EX HU 2, Box 3, Johnson Library. Some of the black activists involved in the War on Poverty (a subject beyond the scope of this article) aided the Johnson Administration in a similar fashion, though with less satisfactory results.

extent that objectives begin to diverge, the movement will become more resistant to presidential efforts. White House influence is especially scorned if a movement develops a radical vision that doubts the benevolence of federal action and looks to the kind of fundamental changes in socioeconomic structures and cultural values that no administration will support.

White House leverage is also dependent upon continuing presidential involvement. Limited resources and the press of other business may divert the administration from managing its relations with a social movement. Escalating controversy, and calculations of attendant political backlash, may spur the White House to lengthen its distance from movement activities. Presidential preoccupations and piques may rupture channels of communication and hinder continuing cooperation.

That the Johnson White House was losing control over black politics was evident as early as the summer of 1966. The Administration found itself increasingly beleaguered on the racial front, with "white backlash" menacing it from the right and "black power" assailing it from the left. President Johnson, however, was deeply absorbed in the Vietnam War by this time, and loathe to give his full attention to other subjects. In addition, his anger at civil rights groups had mounted after SNCC, CORE, and Martin Luther King had come out against the war. Conditions scarcely seemed propitious for the White House to recapture its leverage over the black struggle.

Nevertheless, two events at the end of that summer catalyzed a debate in the White House over the possibility of a new Administration strategy. The Administration's string of brilliant legislative triumphs in civil rights was snapped; its 1966 Civil Rights Bill (whose chief provision attempted to se-

cure "fair housing") fell to a Senate filibuster. At the same moment as this white political backlash threatened the Administration's achievements, the emergence of a "black power" movement jeopardized its peace and security. A black Johnson aide reported chilling news of a "black power" planning conference in Washington; white reporters had been compelled to leave the premises, after which black leaders unknown to the Administration had delivered fiery, "visionary" speeches.[32]

In light of these developments, Harry McPherson recommended a new strategy for presidential intervention. He suggested to President Johnson that he call an immediate meeting of civil rights leaders. With the civil rights movement flying apart, and white resentment building, the President's political stakes were high; identified as the leader of the black cause in triumph in 1964 and 1965, Johnson was, McPherson argued, "stuck with it, in sickness as in health." The purpose of the proposed meeting would be to determine the future direction of the civil rights movement. That direction, McPherson suggested, should involve a repudiation of rioting and an emphasis upon peaceful change. It would necessitate the grooming of new black leadership: "*Young* leaders must also be brought along—those who believe in the American system. . . ." (emphasis in original).

McPherson recommended inviting the established black leaders and a smattering of younger blacks. He emphasized that representatives from CORE and SNCC were no longer wanted. The conclusion of the memo was optimistic: "There is a stirring in the Negro commu-

---

[32] Harry C. McPherson, Jr., Memorandum to the President, September 7, 1966, Files of Harry C. McPherson, Jr., Box 5, Johnson Library. McPherson was relaying a report by Louis Martin, a black Johnson aide at the Democratic National Committee.

nity now for moderation. Many, many Negroes—and not just the Uncle Toms—know that [Stokely] Carmichael and [Floyd] McKissick and their people are jeopardizing the Negroes' future. I believe you can strengthen the resolve of these responsible people, and reassert what is undeniable, as well as inescapable—your leadership of the civil rights movement."[33]

President Johnson referred these recommendations to Attorney General Nicholas Katzenbach. Katzenbach agreed with McPherson that the racial situation had taken a disturbing turn, but in a memo to McPherson he opposed the notion of an immediate presidential meeting with the civil rights leadership. His argument suggested that previous methods of managing White House relations with the movement were no longer productive. "The President does not strengthen the leadership of Roy Wilkins or Martin Luther King when they are made to appear to be his lieutenants or apologists. Indeed, whatever appeal the extreme groups have is based upon arguments that the older leaders are the pacific captives of the administration-establishment and are thus not sufficiently militant." The Attorney General also expressed doubts about McPherson's call for Administration sponsorship of a young black leadership cadre. "The fact is that the younger leaders who now exist are precisely those who you say should not be included and who have consistently chosen an 'outside course. . . .' "[34]

The President sided with Katzenbach, and the meeting was not held. Linked

with older leaders whose hold over black activism had declined, unable (and unwilling) to make contact with a more militant generation of leaders, the Johnson White House watched uncomfortably as its influence over black politics slipped away. As black objectives became couched in a militant vocabulary that the Administration could not possibly accept, and as racial conflict became more dispersed throughout the country, the White House discovered that it had few effective means left for imposing its stamp upon the black movement.

Since Johnson's preoccupation with the Vietnam War continued to mount, his involvement in the travails of racial politics diminished even further after 1966. The Administration did continue to propose civil rights legislation to Congress, and in the aftermath of the King assassination an open-housing bill was finally enacted. But the confident sense of leverage over black political activity was undeniably gone. In its final years the Johnson White House trailed uncertainly behind the dynamic of black politics.

SUMMARY AND CONCLUSIONS

Both the possibilities and the pitfalls of White House relationships with social movements are illustrated in the case of the Johnson Administration and civil rights. Fearful of mass activism and desirous of defining the racial issue in the terms of consensus politics, Lyndon Johnson wanted to exercise maximum leverage over the civil rights movement. Responding to his concerns, his aides developed rationales for White House efforts directed at the movement. They stressed the President's historic responsibility, expertise, and political advantage as justifications for discreet managerial approaches.

In accordance with these rationales, behind-the-scenes moves by the

[33] Harry C. McPherson, Jr., Memorandum for the President, September 12, 1966, Files of Harry C. McPherson, Jr., Box 5, Johnson Library.

[34] Nicholas Katzenbach, Memorandum for Harry C. McPherson, Jr., September 17, 1966, Files of Harry C. McPherson, Jr., Box 5, Johnson Library.

Johnson White House operated to moderate movement actions, especially during the 1964 campaign. Appearances were carefully managed: the White House sought to influence statements by black spokesmen, protected the image of the most moderate black leaders, and took steps to ensure that a presidential conference on civil rights would reflect favorably on Johnson. Periodic attention was given to shifting black activity from civil rights to party politics, and to developing a black Democratic network useful for riot prevention as well as electoral gain.

Yet, the ability of the White House to influence the civil rights movement remained tenuous, contingent upon the movement's continuing moderation and the President's continuing involvement. As the movement turned militant, and as President Johnson became preoccupied with Vietnam, White House leverage declined. By mid-1966, it had lost control over the racial issue. Discussions of how to recapture its control foundered, as the gulf between the White House and black activism came to appear unbridgeable.

The story of the Johnson White House and the civil rights movement suggests a presidential concern to dominate the definition of domestic political issues. By exercising leverage over the civil rights movement, President Johnson hoped that he would remain the real leader of the civil rights campaign, and be able to define the timetable for racial progress with minimal disturbance to the existing social order. Johnson and his aides envisioned an expanding consensus that would incorporate blacks in much the same manner as the New Deal had incorporated organized workers. But as black political and economic aspirations began to outdistance the consensus philosophy of the Administration, a presidential definition of the racial issue

could not be sustained. Once black emancipation came to be depicted by activists in terms alien to the Administration's definition of reform, as well as to its political interests, the confident exercise of presidential leverage gave way to a frustrated recognition of its limits.

Presidential attempts to influence and constrain a social movement do not imply a lack of serious commitment or solid accomplishment on the part of an administration. No other administration has achieved as much as the Johnson Administration in the field of civil rights legislation, or has undertaken as bold a rhetorical commitment to racial justice. Nor does the desire to exercise leverage over a movement suggest an idiosyncratic presidential obsession with control. James Farmer, who opposed Johnson's move to halt civil rights demonstrations in 1964, points out that such attempts at control are an imperative of the modern presidency: "This wasn't just Johnson. Every administration, 'just try to keep it cool.' And one could understand it. If we were the administration, we'd want to keep it cool."[35]

"Keeping it cool" is, as Farmer suggests, the aim of every administration. But to understand the White House perspective on social movements is not to endorse it. For the exercise of presidential power in this area may exact certain costs that are worth considering. Social movements introduce controversy into American political life; while they disrupt political tranquility, they also extend the boundaries of political thought and action. Past movements (e.g., the abolitionists, the Populists, the women's suffrage movement, the labor movement, the civil rights movement) have been a vital source of new ideas and an indispensable stimulus to political

[35] Farmer, Oral History Interview, 19.

change. To the extent that the White House succeeds in circumscribing a social movement, it may thereby be circumscribing the agenda of American politics.

White House objectives also need to be weighed against the possibilities for popular participation. Social movements have produced some of the most important experiments in grass roots democracy in American history. Presidential attempts to constrain their actions threaten to impair their autonomy and to diminish their democratic potential. When the White House does "keep it cool," problems may be handled with less disruptiveness; but the sense of urgency and importance crucial for drawing ordinary citizens into public affairs is lost. The employment of presidential power in these cases may be at the expense not so much of Congress or the courts as of mass participation in American political life.

19
Fiscal and Political Strategy in the Reagan Administration
Hugh Heclo & Rudolph G. Penner

The Reagan administration came into office possessing a detailed comprehensive economic strategy that was to represent a radical departure from the economic policies of the previous fifteen years. Contrary to the views of most traditional economists, administration officials believed strongly that inflation could be conquered without imposing major short-run economic costs in the form of slow economic growth and rising unemployment. To them, inflation was a purely monetary phenomenon caused by an excessive growth in the money supply. Inflation could therefore be eliminated gradually by persuading the Federal Reserve System gradually to reduce the rate at which money was created. In an unusual intrusion into the business of an "independent" Federal Reserve System, a detailed monetary plan, including prescribed rates of growth for the money supply through 1986, was outlined in the administration's first budget document.

Although it was conceded that a shift to a more restrictive monetary policy might create a minor recession at the end of 1981, more severe costs were to be avoided by following a radically new fiscal policy. The administration believed that the unusually slow rates of productivity growth experienced during the 1970s were caused by excessive growth in government spending and in tax burdens. By reversing these trends, it was thought that the economy could be made so productive that the negative effects of a tight monetary policy would be overwhelmed and that the United States would enter a prolonged period of healthy economic growth. Despite major tax cuts, the growth was assumed to be adequate, when combined with spending cuts, to bring in sufficient revenues to balance the budget by 1984.

It seems fair to say that no incoming administration had ever before staked so much on a specific, comprehensive economic program. In contrast, the administration of Franklin Roosevelt, with which Ronald Reagan and his supporters liked to compare themselves, was a hodgepodge of political expediency and unresolved economic theorizing.[1] Observing the more recent experience of economic policy in the Nixon, Ford, and Carter presidencies, one might well have been justified in advising any new administration to avoid raising expectations about how far a president could control, much less improve, the functioning of the U.S. economy. External supply shocks, productivity slowdowns, and recurring combinations of both high unemployment and high inflation led many observers by 1980 to question whether anyone understood the rules of economic management. And yet the Reagan presidency committed its fortunes to an unambiguous promise and program for economic recovery. In this paper we seek to interlace economic and political analyses to understand how this programmatic commitment came about, how it worked in practice, and what it might portend. Of course, all of the results are not yet in, but enough evidence has accumulated to provide the basis for at least a tentative midterm assessment.

CREATING "THE NEW BEGINNING"

In strictly economic terms there were strong reasons to favor the main components of the Reagan strategy for economic policy. Accelerating money growth had clearly fueled accelerating inflation. The money supply (M-1), which had grown at an annual rate of

less than 4 percent during the 1960s, grew at about 6 percent in the 1969–74 period and at about 7 percent between 1974 and 1979, partly as a response to the cost pressures resulting from world oil price increases. Federal outlays had grown from 18.2 percent of GNP in the 1955–59 period to 23.4 percent by 1980–81 (fiscal years) despite the fact that absolute defense spending remained roughly constant in real terms over the entire period. Since there was substantial agreement that the strength of the American military establishment was no longer adequate to carry out America's foreign policy by the end of the 1970s, strong upward pressures on total spending were likely to persist.

Total federal tax receipts had grown from 17.7 percent of GNP in 1955–59 to 20.6 percent by 1980–81. Over the same period the total deficit was also on a strong upward trend, rising from 0.5 percent of GNP in 1955–59 to 2.9 percent in 1980–81.

At the same time as average tax burdens were rising rapidly, the structure of the tax system was creating greater and greater impediments to productivity growth, particularly in the period after the Kennedy-Johnson tax cuts of 1964–65. After inflation began to accelerate during the Vietnam War, Congress passed periodic tax cuts to offset "bracket creep" in the personal income tax. However, the legislated tax cuts took a very different form from those that would occur in a tax system perfectly indexed for inflation. The legislature's cuts overcompensated the lower half of the income distribution for the effects of inflation, while those above the middle drifted into higher and higher tax brackets. By the early 1980s it was not uncommon for ordinary upper-middle-income families of four to face marginal income tax rates of about 40 percent—a level conceived of only for the very rich at the time of the Kennedy-Johnson reforms of the middle 1960s. The use of tax shelters was proliferating, and antagonism toward rising tax burdens grew at the federal, state, and local levels of government. Undoubtedly, this so-called tax revolt was an important factor in President Reagan's decisive electoral victory in 1980.

While the personal tax structure was clearly becoming less efficient as a result of inflation and legislative action, the effects of inflation on business taxation may have been even more destructive. Although the generosity of depreciation allowances had been increased in the early 1960s and again in the early 1970s, depreciation was still based on the original cost of an investment. As a result, inflation eroded the real value of the depreciation deduction. As recently as 1973 the U.S. Department of Commerce estimated that the depreciation deduction used by corporations for tax purposes had exceeded economic depreciation by $2.6 billion, but by 1980 it was insufficient by $14.4 billion, an amount equal to almost 8 percent of before-tax profits. In addition, corporations paid taxes on $45.7 billion of inflation-induced inventory profits in 1980 and investors were forced to pay capital gains taxes on equity holdings whose money value was inflated even if real values remained constant. Bond holders were also penalized because regular income tax rates were applied to the inflation premium embodied in interest rates. Borrowers could deduct those same inflation premiums from taxable income, but nevertheless, the effective tax rate on real corporate income rose significantly above statutory rates. Perhaps more important, the effective tax rate varied greatly from investment to investment depending on the nature of the investment and the characteristics of the investor's balance sheet. Not only was in-

vestment discouraged on average, but the allocation of that investment which did occur must have been badly distorted.

In short, the problems of the late 1970s provided strong justification for the major elements of what was later to become known as the Reagan economic strategy. Indeed, a number of policy shifts had already occurred in the Carter administration with a Democratic-controlled Congress. The Revenue Act passed by Congress and signed by President Carter in 1978 turned away from the approach of earlier tax cut legislation by skewing tax reductions more toward higher income brackets and by seeking to spur investment through major reductions in business and capital gains taxation. By the same token, in early 1980 the Carter administration, alarmed at mounting inflation and the negative reaction of financial circles to its initial budget proposal, collaborated with Congress to produce a much more austere spending program for fiscal year 1981. Perhaps the shift of greatest long-term importance occurred in the winter of 1979–80 when the Federal Reserve Board introduced a regime of strict restraint in the supply of money and credit. All of these changes indicated an important transformation in priorities, but the strategy of the incoming Reagan administration moved in more radical directions. In particular, the difficulties that eventually developed arose from the administration's extreme faith in the power of tax cuts to enhance the efficiency of the economy and to eliminate the pain usually associated with a shift from a proinflationary to an anti-inflationary monetary policy. The main reasons for the distinctive, self-confident optimism of the Reagan economic strategy had more to do with domestic politics than with the economics of policy-making in contemporary America.

We should begin by recognizing that Ronald Reagan was the first modern president to arise from what might be loosely termed a popular political movement. Dwight Eisenhower had already clearly emerged as a national figure before taking over leadership of the Republican party. John Kennedy pushed himself into the Democratic nomination in a few brief years through media exposure and primary victories while never challenging the ultimate authority of party organizations. Johnson, Nixon, and Ford were in this sense all creatures of the established Washington community. Like Jimmy Carter, Ronald Reagan enjoyed a strong regional political base as a former governor and compiled a string of successes in presidential primaries. But unlike Carter's, Reagan's candidacy represented the culmination of almost fifteen years of grass-roots political agitation and organization across the nation.[2] Following the Republican defeat of 1964, a multifaceted populism of the Right gradually evolved at the local level of American politics. It was a stream of political persuasions with many currents—of unabashed patriotism in a time of self-doubt about American power; of social conservatism alarmed at permissive "lifestyles"; of resentment against high taxes and high-handed bureaucrats. As the 1970s unfolded, it was a set of inclinations mobilized and sharpened by new direct-mail techniques and heavy investments in conservative media outlets and think tanks. Ronald Reagan certainly was not its sole leader, but he was one of the principal attendants and cultivators of this movement of opinion.

The fact that the Reagan presidency grew out of such a political agglomeration, and not simply from the virtuoso performance of a political entrepreneur (as with Kennedy and Carter) or from a long Washington apprenticeship (as with Johnson, Nixon, and Ford), had important implications for the incoming administration's economic approach. Economic policy positions were more than policy positions; they tended to become articles of faith during the long march to the White House. The validity of these positions depended on their ability, not to convince intellectuals and experts, but to resonate with the deepest yearnings and dissatisfactions of ordinary people. Thus, when compared with all other postwar contenders for the presidency, Ronald Reagan ended his long, drawn-out candidacy and entered the Oval Office with two unique predispositions: first, an explicit set of deeply held beliefs about the American economic order; and second, a willingness to be less than normally deferential to elite opinion, particularly that of the established economic profession.

At the same time, the community of economic scholars and financial advisers, which had largely dominated serious economic discussion and advice since World War II, was itself in considerable disarray. Chastened by the experiences of the past decade, liberal economists spoke with less confidence about the capacity to achieve rapid growth with price stability, and many accepted the inevitability of a recession that would result from the Carter administration's anti-inflation measures of 1979 and 1980. Mainstream conservative economists differed mainly by arguing for much more severe and sustained fiscal restraint to combat inflation. Adding to the confusion of this traditional cleavage in the profession was a self-consciously distinct monetarist school that had grown in strength in the 1970s. It gave little credence to any of the customary tools of fiscal policy.

The administration's faith that tax cuts would restore healthy economic growth was based on the work of yet another group of economists and economic commentators who eventually became known as "supply-siders." Supply-side economics was a peculiar addition to the economic scene of the 1970s in that it grew up outside mainstream economics and its propositions were debated in the popular press rather than in academic journals. The relevant theoretical work was done by economists such as Arthur Laffer, Craig Roberts, Robert Mundell, and Norman Ture, who eventually became an undersecretary of the Treasury. The work was popularized by Jude Wanniski, an editorial writer for the *Wall Street Journal,* and by Congressman Jack Kemp, who became an important adviser to Ronald Reagan during the election campaign.[3]

Supply-siders, who engaged in a quite conscious and effective campaign to mold public opinion, blamed almost all of the problems of the 1970s on rising marginal tax rates and argued that massive tax cuts would put the nation on the road to economic growth. Academic research provided a bit of support as scholars found the supply of labor and savings responded to tax cuts,[4] but the supply-siders greatly exaggerated the response. Some extremists even believed that general tax cuts would bring forth so much additional work, savings, and investment that tax receipts would actually rise rather than fall as a result of cutting tax rates. This proposition could not be disproved theoretically, but it had absolutely no empirical support in scholarly studies.[5] Nevertheless, the supply-siders managed to convince President Reagan of the validity of their views.

Considerably greater empirical support lay behind another strand of economic analysis devoted to the microeconomic effects of public policy. Beginning with R. H. Coase's paper, "The Problem of Social Costs," a host of economic

analyses had accumulated to establish a strong case that much government regulation imposed excessive costs on the economy and promoted inefficiencies.[6] By the end of the 1970s the conservative movement had adopted these findings and generalized them into the policy principle that overregulation was a major cause of poor performance in the U.S. economy.

Since presidential campaigns are synthesizing processes it is not surprising that these various strands of economic thinking were woven together in the course of 1980. They were given expression in Ronald Reagan's September 9 speech in Chicago, which laid down the guidelines followed later in framing the new president's economic recovery program. For mainstream conservative economists there was the traditional stress on reduced government spending and balanced budgets. For monetarists there was a commitment to slower, more strictly controlled growth in the money supply. For deregulators there was the pledge to cut back government controls and regulations that could not be economically justified. Above all, Reagan enthusiastically endorsed the tax-cutting strategy of supply-side fiscal theory as the centerpiece of his economic program. The political attractiveness of this supply-side vision of growth is not difficult to understand. It seemed to allow the Reagan candidacy to escape the dismal prospect offered both by traditional Republican economics and by monetarism, a prospect of austerity and distributional conflict in the name of long-term solvency. Tax-induced "growthmanship" meant that there could be economic success without pain, as monetary policy held back inflation and faster growth in a private sector relieved of high taxes benefited everyone. As far as treating an ailing economy was concerned, supply-side theory was the equivalent of laughing gas when compared to the monetarists' and orthodox conservatives' devotion to chemotherapy. It is not difficult to convince people that the world would be a better place if their taxes were cut.

None of this, however, fully explains the incoming administration's remarkable confidence that in the initial economic recovery program announced in February 1981, it had discovered the guiding principles of successful economic management for the ensuing four to six years. After one month in office the new president's fortunes were publicly staked to a number of high-risk promises predicting lower unemployment and inflation rates, faster economic growth, and balanced budgets.

There was, of course, the euphoria and confidence initially created during the transition period by the unexpectedly large Reagan victory.[7] Added to this was a passive consensus that could be created among the different economic schools of thought contributing to the economic strategy, each of which tended to regard the others as tolerable because fundamentally irrelevant.[8] Monetarists dismissed supply-side theory and downgraded the balanced-budget goals of fiscal conservatives as cures for inflation. Fiscal conservatives worried about the irresponsibility of supply-side tax cuts, but also saw the advantage of reducing revenues as a permanent constraint on government spending. Hard-charging supply-siders were simply disdainful of everyone else's nostrums. The Reagan administration's disinclination to satisfy intellectuals by integrating the different strands of thought allowed each school to believe that its remedy was the one effective part of the Reagan package that would assure success. In effect, the array of offsetting advice from the economics profession created a kind of vacuum providing an opportunity for the political

ideology of the Reagan administration to predominate. The economic course set by the White House in 1981 promised that all good things were compatible.

The ultimate reason for the Reagan presidency's confidence in its multiyear economic strategy lay in the fact that it was founded on a political, not economic, theory. Economic analysis alone was tentative and incomplete, changing as economic conditions changed. Not so the political analysis behind this economic strategy. Within the conservative movement two concerns, each identifying something real, had become inextricably linked: the problem of a malfunctioning economy and the problem of a malfunctioning big government. It was an act of political theory to link the latter as the chief cause of the former. Under this overriding concept, which lay at the heart of the movement and of Reagan's fifteen-year campaign, all strands of the Reagan economic program were fully compatible and mutually reinforcing. All were means of hemming in government so as to release the inherent forces of the market economy and thus create sustained economic growth. Hemming in government meant spending cuts to balance the budget, monetary restrictions to rein in the creation of money, deregulation to remove non-market controls, and, perhaps most important of all, a tax-cut tourniquet to restrict the flow of private productive resources into the maw of big government. Given this underlying rationale, any doubts expressed by economic experts, whose own ideological disarray often occasioned public ridicule, could be discounted. It was perhaps this feeling that prompted a quip by the president-elect questioning why he even needed a Council of Economic Advisers.

For all these reasons, therefore, it is unlikely that the Reagan administration's economic strategy would have been very different with or without what was perceived as a major electoral mandate. The idea of such a mandate did, however, help ensure that the new administration was rather quickly given the chance to put its strategy into practice. At that point, things began to go wrong for the new beginning.

THE STRATEGY IN PRACTICE

Flaws in the Reagan economic strategy began to emerge when that strategy was translated into detailed legislative proposals.

The tax cuts advocated by the administration were massive. The initial proposal was for a 30 percent cut in personal marginal tax rates, to be implemented in three yearly installments of 10 percent each, beginning retroactively January 1, 1981. This was combined with an extraordinarily generous accelerated depreciation proposal, which, when fully implemented, would imply a negative tax rate on most equipment investment given the inflation- and interest-rate forecasts of the administration. The personal tax cut proposal was later modified to imply a 23 percent total cut implemented in three steps—a 5 percent cut in tax-withholding on October 1, 1981; a further 10 percent cut effective July 1, 1982; and a further 10 percent cut on July 1, 1983. The three reductions— 5, 10, and 10 percent—add up to a total of only 23 percent because the last two reductions are cuts from a lower base. While the total marginal rate cut and the consequent revenue loss from this source were reduced, the administration agreed to various new congressional initiatives to provide additional savings incentives, increase incentives for charitable donations, and bring tax relief for married couples. The total revenue cost of the final package through 1984 was roughly equal to the cost of Reagan's original 30 percent marginal rate cut.

At the same time, the administration advocated nondefense spending cuts of $40 billion in fiscal 1982, growing to $100 billion in 1986. These were not cuts relative to 1981 spending levels. They were, instead, cuts relative to the levels to which spending was projected to rise under 1981 laws, if all programs were increased both to cover the growth in the number of those receiving entitlements and to compensate for inflation. Nevertheless, total spending, which had been growing faster than GNP, was now to grow at only about one-half the rate of GNP, while defense alone was to grow at an 8.6 percent real rate over the period. Total outlays were to fall from over 23 percent of GNP to 19 percent.

However, the administration did not project a falling ratio of outlays to GNP because they were advocating massive cuts in spending programs. In fact they wanted a huge increase in defense spending that largely offset desired cuts in nondefense programs. The projected ratio of outlays to GNP fell mainly because the administration projected a very high growth rate for GNP. Real economic growth was supposed to proceed at an average annual rate of 4.5 percent between 1981 and 1986 while inflation was expected to average 6 percent per year. Putting the two together meant that the growth in the money value of GNP would have to be almost 11 percent per year. This was not unreasonable relative to GNP growth rates during some recent recoveries. But earlier high growth rates had been fueled by a very rapid rate of growth in the money supply. The projected GNP growth rates were totally unreasonable given the monetary policy advocated by the administration, unless the amount of economic activity that could be financed by a given money supply grew at a rate far higher than anything experienced in past history.

It was possible to make the projections more consistent by assuming that inflation would come down much faster than the administration promised, but then taxable income would not grow as fast, taxpayers would not be pushed into higher tax brackets as rapidly, and receipts would be lower than expected. It would then become impossible for the administration to promise a balanced budget by 1984. Indeed it was clear that administration economists had chosen to project a high inflation rate so that projected deficits would be lower. More reasonable inflation assumptions led to deficits close to $100 billion for 1984 and 1985.

Of course, the current deficit outlook is much worse than that, and we shall later describe what went wrong. But before doing that, it is useful to step back and reflect on the merits of the Reagan plan as it existed in March 1981. Despite the fact that it implied very large deficits from the beginning, it could be rationalized as an appropriate strategy even if one believed that its merits were greatly exaggerated by the administration.

There was a broad consensus that the United States had to reduce inflation and to devote additional resources to defense and business capital formation. There was also a consensus that the tax system had become extremely inefficient. While the combination of tight money and large deficits would inevitably lead to high real interest rates, it was not unreasonable to believe that the latter's effect on business capital formation would be offset by the increased generosity of depreciation allowances. The negative impact of high interest rates would then be focused on housing and interest-sensitive consumer durables, and most American economists believed that we had been devoting too high a portion of the nation's resources

to such goods in the past. Simultaneously, cuts in nondefense government spending would make room for a greatly enhanced American defense effort while allowing tax relief to overburdened taxpayers. Thus, despite large deficits, the program could be rationalized. Unfortunately, the strategy got out of hand for reasons to be explained in the next section.

What Went Wrong?

The Reagan administration clearly erred in thinking that spending and tax cuts would make it possible to conquer inflation while suffering only trivial costs. While a major recession was not inevitable, it was hard to believe that inflation could be reduced while the economy grew robustly. At a minimum, a period of slow and erratic growth seemed almost certain. However, it must be noted that the administration got far more of a monetary shock than it wanted. It had advocated a gradual reduction in the rate of growth of the money supply. Monetary growth turned out to be significantly lower than that recommended in the administration's plan. Moreover, for complicated technical reasons that will not be described here, the regulatory changes that allowed the invention of NOW accounts probably made the monetary growth that occurred less stimulative than it would have been otherwise. While a significant recession might have occurred even if the administration had obtained its preferred monetary policy, the greater-than-expected shock clearly intensified the problem.

The serious recession that emerged significantly increased the 1982 deficit, adding permanently to the interest costs, and also made it more difficult to cut social programs during the debate on the 1983 budget. Moreover, the recession implied that a rapid recovery was necessary to approach the administration's original targets, and it is not clear that this was possible without monetary accommodation. Such accommodation had occurred in all other postwar recoveries, but the Federal Reserve could not allow it this time if it hoped to achieve credibility against inflation in the long run.

The 1981–82 recession had an unexpectedly large impact on inflation, and it is now possible to project much lower price increases than were projected in the administration's original budget documents (see Table 1). This should be regarded as a large success for the administration, and it is odd to include a description of falling inflation in a section that asks "what went wrong?" In fact, it is something that went right, but it has had a negative impact on the budget deficit because, as already explained,

lower inflation rates depress total receipts. The legislated cuts in marginal tax rates were not offset by bracket creep to the degree expected, and the tax cut was, in fact, significantly larger than expected. Similarly, the depreciation reform has proved more generous than expected because the real value of the new depreciation deduction is being eroded less by inflation than was projected.

On the spending side, decelerating inflation tends to raise real outlays. The indexing of social benefits works with a time lag, with the adjustments in the current year dependent on last year's inflation rate. Real spending on indexed programs therefore rose more rapidly than expected as inflation decelerated in 1982. The real value of nonindexed programs was also higher than expected because past money appropriations as-

TABLE 1 · CHANGES IN THE ADMINISTRATION'S BUDGET PROJECTIONS MARCH 1981 TO JULY 1982 (BILLIONS OF DOLLARS)

	Projections for Fiscal Year				
	1982	1983	1984	1985	1986
Outlay projections					
As of 3/81	695.3	732.0	770.2	884.0	912.0
As of 7/82	731.0	761.5	812.5	874.7	932.7
Difference	35.7	29.5	42.3	30.7	20.7
Receipts projections					
As of 3/81	650.3	709.1	770.7	849.9	940.2
As of 7/82	622.1	646.5	719.9	801.1	867.1
Difference	28.2	62.6	50.8	48.8	73.1
Deficit projections					
As of 3/81	−45.0	−22.8	0.5	5.8	28.2
As of 7/82	−108.9	−115.0	−92.6	−73.6	−65.6
Difference	63.9	92.2	93.1	79.4	93.8

Sources: Office of Management and Budget, *Fiscal Year 1982 Budget Revisions* (Washington, D.C.: Office of Management and Budget, March 1982): 15, table 7; and Office of Management and Budget, *Mid-Session Review of the 1983 Budget* (Washington, D.C.: Office of Management and Budget, July 1982): 57, table 8.

sumed too high an inflation rate. Under the American system of budgeting it is hard to take money back from agencies once it has been appropriated.

Real spending will also be higher than the administration originally projected because Congress did not accept all of the nondefense cuts requested by the administration. The president asked for slightly more than $40 billion in cuts for fiscal 1982. Congress claims to have cut somewhat more than $30 billion. But this claim has to be examined critically. The policy changes in the summer of 1981 were so complex that it is difficult to get a proper accounting of all their effects. However, Congress made optimistic assumptions regarding savings resulting from program design changes and probably did not take proper account of the fact that cuts in one income-maintenance program often increase spending in some other program. For example, a cut in unemployment benefits may raise the demand for food stamps and AFDC (Aid to Families with Dependent Children). It is, in fact, quite possible that cuts were less than half the amount claimed.[9]

Another serious spending problem is related to interest on the public debt. A year ago one would have thought that if the economy were weaker than expected and if inflation lower than expected, there would be some reduction in projected interest because with that combination of events nominal interest rates would surely be lower than expected. Alas, the world has not worked the way it should, and the interest rate on ninety-day Treasury bills, projected in the original budget to average 8.9 percent in 1982, will actually average about 10.5 percent. This, combined with a higher-than-expected deficit, has caused interest costs to explode. The rise will exceed a reasonable estimate of all the budget cuts legislated in the

summer of 1981. Interest has become a driving force in the budget.

While Congress did not accept all of the president's nondefense cuts, it did, much to the surprise of many observers, accept his defense program with only minor modifications. There may be cuts in the future, but the program enacted in 1981 initiated a number of expensive weapons programs that cannot easily be turned off.

Thus, America was put on a path of higher spending and a bigger real tax cut than the administration originally projected. With the policies in effect at the beginning of 1982, the implications for the deficit were frightening. Even if one assumed a significant economic recovery from the current recession, projected deficits would continue to rise in the long run if policies were held constant. With the president's defense program and other tax and spending laws as they existed at the beginning of 1982, the Congressional Budget Office estimated the 1985 deficit at $245 billion, or 5.9 percent of GNP.

A Midcourse Correction

Despite economic adversity, the president remained firmly committed to his economic strategy during the first half of 1982. He refused to contemplate any significant change on the tax side of the budget and attempted to close the deficit gap by constantly urging further cuts in nondefense spending. Those proposed cuts were highly concentrated because the president protected the elderly and disabled from any cuts in their social security benefits.

In February 1982 Reagan proposed total fiscal 1983 spending of $757.6 billion, of which $221.1 billion was for defense. Of the remaining $536.5 billion, $173.5 billion, or about one-third, represented the "untouchable" social security program and $96.4 billion, or about 13 percent, represented the net interest bill. Outlays, excluding defense, social security, and net interest, were to be $266.6 billion, but this amount could be obtained only by cutting more than $40 billion from other programs, an amount far higher than the cuts Reagan obtained in the summer of 1981 when he was at the height of his political power.

The proposed budget was generally thought to be politically unacceptable when it was first presented. But initially Congress had great difficulty formulating a viable alternative. Our decision-making processes were in considerable disarray.

However, things began to come together late in the spring. After intense bargaining between the administration and congressional leaders, and after several false starts once the bargaining failed to produce a bipartisan compromise, Congress finally passed a budget on June 23. That budget called for tax increases that were much more significant with respect to existing law than the relatively minor changes requested by the president. Spending cuts were also much less extensive. But, overall, the congressional budget turned out to be much closer to the president's initial February recommendations than anyone earlier thought possible.

After the budget finally passed, Congress faced the more difficult task of translating its recommended spending cuts and higher revenue projections into detailed legislation. Given that it was an election year and unemployment was at a post-World War II record, it was hard to be optimistic about implementation of the congressional budget.

However, Senator Dole, chairman of the Senate Finance Committee, exhibited extraordinary legislative skill and, with White House support, crafted a tax and spending-reduction bill that

went a long way toward satisfying the requirements of the congressional budget passed earlier. Moreover, the bill was quite reasonably substantive, although not bearing much similarity to one that would be drafted by economists working in a world remote from political pressures. The bill had many provisions, but, in its most appealing sections, it corrected the depreciation reforms of 1981 to account for inflation being far less than expected when the original reforms were enacted.

Nevertheless, the bill was controversial. It would not have passed the House of Representatives were it not for the fact that the president gave it vigorous support. In doing so, he showed himself to be much more flexible regarding tax policy than he had been earlier in the year. While some accuse him of doing a policy flip-flop, this is an exaggeration. The tax bill is too important to be called a fine tuning of his overall fiscal policy, but it only offsets a relatively small portion of the 1981 tax cut and leaves in place more than a 5 percent cut in overall tax burdens relative to GNP between fiscal 1982 and fiscal 1983.

The tax and spending policy changes that occurred during the summer of 1982 are crucially important, for they take us off a path where deficits explode relative to GNP. They instead put us on one where the deficits stabilize, albeit at uncomfortably high levels, during the 1983–85 period. Absent a recession and assuming that the Federal Reserve Board continues its anti-inflationary strategy, it is probable that the deficit will average considerably more than 5 percent of GNP in 1983, 1984, and 1985, given the policies in effect at the end of fiscal 1982. This is far higher than official congressional and administration estimates, but the official estimates are based on extremely optimistic assumptions regarding the timing and strength of the recovery and on exogenous factors such as crop yields that determine spending on agricultural price-support payments.

What Went Right in Political Strategy?

Despite its economic difficulties, the Reagan administration has been strikingly successful in maintaining a united political front around its changing economic predictions and in retaining the initiative in the debate on national economic policy. This was true in passing the original spending and tax reduction program, and in returning subsequently to Congress for yet more cuts in domestic spending. It remained true as President Reagan was forced to embrace government deficits as the lesser of other evils, and as he reluctantly endorsed a 1982 program of raising federal tax revenues. While the president's policy change with regard to deficits and taxes was only a little more than fine tuning in economic terms, his earlier refusal to consider any change at all in the basic thrust of his 1981 policy made his vigorous support of the 1982 legislation seem like a political sea change. To those who hoped for a "Reagan revolution," the idea that accepting higher deficits and higher taxes did no violence to Ronald Reagan's original economic strategy seemed to require the sort of reasoning that would allow one to say, as Arthur Okun once put it, "the ship is fine except for two holes where the torpedoes hit." Whatever the rhetoric, policy did have to change to accommodate changing political and economic realities, and one of the most noteworthy achievements of the Reagan presidency in its first two years was its capacity to manage these changes without losing the political offensive or appearing indecisive.

Many reasons for this success in political management could be given. Ultimately they would all come back to one important fact: The Reagan presidency developed a capacity to deal with its economic ideology in a strategic rather than ideological manner. It would be difficult to exaggerate the significance of this factor. Without a capability for strategic management in this most ideological of administrations, the Reagan presidency would probably have quickly dissolved into a series of internal struggles reflecting the disarray in economic thought in the outside world. It probably would have gratuitously antagonized broad segments of public opinion and would almost certainly have fought with Congress in a self-defeating manner, as did the Nixon administration. Strategic management meant that the Reagan presidency self-consciously maneuvered to meet its opponents under favorable conditions, to thrust and parry depending on circumstances, and still to maintain an overall appearance of consistent commitment to its goals. Strategic management also meant that the basic political theory behind the Reagan economic policy—that of reviving the economy through retrenchment in government—was itself never open to question and debate. A typical script found the president enunciating some simple principle, followed by reports of the president resisting counterpressures with great stubbornness, then an eventual compromise sufficient for the president's proposal to win passage without the president himself appearing to engage in political bargaining, and finally a White House claim of victory.

The problem of the federal deficit as it emerged during 1981 and 1982 provides an excellent example of strategic management in the Reagan White House. As originally envisioned in the president's economic recovery program, there simply was no deficit problem; spending cuts in domestic programs would rein in budget outlays, tax cuts would revive growth and revenues, and monetary policy would reduce inflation. By 1984 or 1985 the budget would be in balance. But in August 1981, even as the administration was celebrating congressional passage of its budget and tax reduction program, some senior presidential advisers were worrying that the deficit projections were not unfolding as planned. It would be misleading to overschematize the policy discussions that occurred within the White House. What actually seems to have taken place was a continuous series of conversations and arguments spread over many months, occupying a handful of senior staff with occasional participation by the president. As one account aptly put it, the December 1981 *Atlantic Monthly* article on David Stockman "did not provoke a debate within the administration; it reflected it."[10] Then, as later, administration leaders were engaged in an endless effort to reconcile the major elements of the Reagan program as it had been broadcast in the first months of assuming office. Plans for the disappearing deficit were caught between constrictions in the scope for budget-cutting (given major defense increases and a political commitment to deal gently with "safety-net" programs) and a shortfall in revenues (produced initially by a failure of the economy to respond as expected to anticipated tax cuts and by the economic effects of highly restrictive monetary policies, and projected over the longer term by a three-year program of tax cuts and revenue indexing).

In essence the White House responded to the emerging deficit problem by carefully and gradually repositioning itself, without ever explicitly denying the merits of its original economic program.

One early device was to argue that doubts and criticisms were premature: the president's program had not yet taken effect. Even though the original selling of the program had made a considerable point of the expectations that would quickly change in advance of implementation, the appeal to patience could answer many critics during the latter part of 1981. Another tack was for the administration to make use of the deficit problem to serve its own purposes. Key administration strategists quietly welcomed the congressional and media alarums that greeted the periodically leaked projections of federal budget deficits.[11] This climate allowed the Reagan presidency to meet its opponents on quite favorable political terrain. To be alarmed at the projected deficits meant one had to either take the politically difficult step of supporting higher taxes and/or lower defense spending, or move toward the preferred Reagan approach of making still further cuts in federal civilian programs.

Notwithstanding these calculations, the real problem of a massive projected budget deficit persisted and grew even larger. The appeal to patience could not be counted on for long, and dissatisfaction with deficits had real and depressing effects in financial markets, the wellspring of the hoped-for Reagan recovery. Thus, during late 1981 the White House policy-makers seriously debated "revenue enhancement," launching the first trial balloons in a tentative manner always well distanced from the president's own public positions. At the same time the president also rejected the other logical possibility identified by the strategists, a scaled-back program of defense increases. The fact is that Ronald Reagan as well as his opponents were caught up in the logic of a situation characterized by major tax cuts, a sluggish economy, and the restricted scope for further spending cuts. One approach to the deficit problem continually tried by the president and senior staff in 1981 and the first half of 1982 was almost instinctive: to deny the value of economists' projections. This view could suffice for Reagan-the-candidate, but it could not survive presidential staff work in the Office of Management and Budget and Council of Economic Advisers. Something had to be done. At the beginning of 1982, the next step was grudgingly taken in the president's budget proposal and State of the Union message. Despite a lifelong commitment to balanced budgets, the president was led to argue that his projected deficits were less undesirable than raising taxes or cutting back on national security. More cuts in domestic programs would, of course, be required, but here, too, the administration turned its lamented deficit problem into a strategic advantage. It did so by using its dilemma as an offensive weapon and challenging those dissatisfied in Congress and elsewhere to come up with a better formula. Given the fragmented nature of legislative decision-making, it was a fairly safe bet that no one else could produce a comprehensive package without White House involvement. Hence, during 1982 the White House managed to shift a good deal of responsibility for its economic problems to Capitol Hill, while still setting the general terms of debate (i.e., how to solve the deficit problem, or, as a practical matter, how to come in with a fiscal 1983 deficit projection of around $100 billion) and without losing its chance to help shape the detailed outcomes on taxing and spending.

Ronald Reagan was constrained as well as helped by strategic management of his economic policy. Shifting the focus to Congress, with active participation by White House aides in framing spending and tax-increase proposals, meant that some of his own freedom of action and initiative was being lost.

It became more difficult for Reagan to assume a stance of opposition to the Washington establishment.

By the summer of 1982 Ronald Reagan had taken the next grudging step in dealing with the deficit problem and accepted a tax increase package worked out by Republican congressional leaders with the active cooperation of senior White House aides. It was an idea the president had rejected the previous winter when it was advanced by his staff without the leverage of congressional backing. Passage of this tax program signaled the first major break in Republican ranks behind President Reagan's leadership, dividing antideficit fiscal conservatives from antitax supply-siders—among other cleavages. It is noteworthy, however, that the president himself was—until the very last moment when a public appeal was deemed necessary—not directly identified with the tax proposals and indeed reverted to his familiar antitax themes immediately following their passage.[12] There followed a number of highly dramatized presidential vetoes of congressional spending bills. Since these appropriation bills, which the White House labeled "budget busters," were generally within the president's agreed total spending target (but with different priorities), it seems safe to say that the chief motivation behind the presidential vetoes was to reassert the image of an antideficit, antitaxation presidency.

The deficit problem was only one of many examples of skillful policy management during the first two years of Reagan's term. There was, of course, no escaping economic realities, but the administration's capacity for strategic management allowed it to take advantage of its opportunities in the first year and to make the best of some difficult circumstances in the second. At least three factors help account for what appears—especially when compared with recent predecessors in the White House—to be a remarkable ability.

In the first place, Ronald Reagan and his immediate staff were willing to limit drastically the number of presidential priorities. There was, inevitably, a familiar need to deal with crises, usually of a foreign policy nature (e.g., Libya, the Falklands, the AWACS sale, the PLO in Beirut). But in terms of commitments of presidential time and effort, these were ad hoc and sporadic affairs. Likewise, defense policy issues, once the initial go-ahead for more spending was given, seemed to require little detailed presidential involvement. The economy was Reagan's first, second, and third priority. It was here that Ronald Reagan engaged in sustained struggles with Congress, launched his major public appeals, and put his personal reputation on the line. Nor was the president's commitment to all areas of economic policy broadly understood. The narrow compass of presidential priorities had little to say about industrial policies for particular economic sectors, about regional development, about industrial relations and wage bargaining (apart from air traffic controllers), or about international economic relations. The presidential priority in economic affairs was to reduce the role of government—its taxes, spending, and regulations—and then stand aside for an economic revival in the private sector.

All of this had a vastly simplifying effect on strategic calculations made in the White House. By drastically narrowing his priorities, the president appeared to rise above the prevailing complexities, most of which were obscure to the general public. The message to Washington contained in this presidential agenda was to the effect that there was a vast amount of government activity that was just not of any presidential interest, except as it might be cut back. Departmental bureaucracies found it difficult, if not impossible, to gain White House attention for their roles and missions. Any major national debate on social policy was sidestepped by subordinating social spending issues to the requirements of economic policy. In place of talk about policy trade-offs and arcane complexities there could be the appearance of simplicity and decision.

In short, the president's leadership was comprehensible even if, or rather because, it was narrowly focused.

In the second place, the president allowed his immediate staff broad scope to engage in strategic planning and coalition building. If that sounds a rather commonplace feature of the modern presidency, it is not. Recent presidents have been too hyperactive (as with Johnson), too suspicious (Nixon), or too bogged down in detailed decision-making (Carter) to create a White House atmosphere conducive to strategic thinking. Within the guidelines of an overarching economic ideology, Ronald Reagan expected his staff to think through possible contingencies and operational practicalities in producing a rolling game-plan for the administration's economic policy. It was this tolerance and expectation that allowed the continuing internal conversation on the deficit problem to occur and that produced a sequence of adaptations to control its political damage.

Finally, strategic management was made possible by the development of a small, rather close-knit group of policy managers in the White House. Future political scientists, and possibly psychologists specializing in small-group dynamics, will undoubtedly devote considerable attention to the internal groupings of the Reagan White House—the

Deaver Luncheon Group, the Legislative Strategy Group, and the like.[13] The formal names are unimportant, and, indeed, overformalizing the description would obscure the very important informal qualities of what came to exist. In essence what evolved in the first two years of the Reagan administration was a working committee of the presidency, composed exclusively of senior staff, meeting on a continuous, daily basis, and responsible for meshing day-to-day tactics with longer-term goals. To put it most baldly, their loyalty was to the idea of a successful Reagan presidency rather than to any particular economic theory. This was a stance that infuriated true believers of the supply-side school, several of the most prominent of whom resigned in the second year of the administration. Well-known monetarists, as well as supply-siders, were absent from these inner councils, although their views were certainly taken into account. The more dogmatically oriented the presidential adviser, the less likely he was to gain entry into the ongoing circle of conversation that revolved around Deaver, Meese, and Baker.[14] Economic views from the Council of Economic Advisers were registered and deemed important, but the chairman of the CEA could resign in the summer of 1982 with little discernible impact on the process of top-level economic decision-making in the Reagan White House. By contrast, David Stockman probably survived the extremely embarrassing quotations in the December 1981 *Atlantic Monthly* because participants in this inner circle saw his strategic ability as essential to their efforts.

The existence of a relatively cohesive, strategy-conscious group in the Reagan White House meant that everyday decisions tended to be seen in reference to an evolving "game-plan," as it was known. At times this required that the president move into the forefront of confrontation with Congress; at other times events were allowed to run their course with the White House deliberately fading into the background. It meant that decisions were approached not only on the basis of immediate tactical advantage, but also with regard to calculations of longer-run consistency and/or the appearance thereof. None of this guaranteed success in dealing with economic policy in the first two years of the Reagan presidency. It did, however, vastly improve the odds for managing policy contradictions and disappointments in a politically productive manner.

NOTES

1. See, for example, Ellis W. Hawley, *The New Deal and the Problem of Monopoly* (Princeton: Princeton University Press, 1966), ch. 2; Arthur M. Schlesinger, Jr., *The Coming of the New Deal* (Boston: Houghton Mifflin, 1959), pp. 179–83; and *The Politics of Upheaval* (Boston: Houghton Mifflin, 1960), pp. 386–407.

2. Lou Cannon, *Reagan* (New York: G. P. Putnam's Sons, 1982); Sidney Blumenthal, "The Ideology Makers," *Boston Globe,* August 8, 1982, p. 88; Kevin Phillips, "Post-Conservative America," *New York Review of Books,* May 13, 1982.

3. A fuller description of the theory and the relevant cast of characters can be found in Jack Brooks, "The Annals of Finance (Supply-Side Economics)," *New Yorker,* April 19, 1982, pp. 96–150.

4. For an example, see Jerry A. Hausman, "Labor Supply," in *How Taxes Affect Economic Behavior,* Henry J. Aaron and Joseph A. Pechman, eds. (Washington, D.C.: Brookings Institution, 1981), pp. 27–83.

5. Don Fullerton, "On the Possibility of an Inverse Relationship between Tax Rates and Government Revenues," National Bureau of Economic Research, Working Paper no. 467, April 1980.

6. R. H. Coase, "The Problem of Social Cost," *Journal of Law and Economics* 3 (October 1960):1.

7. Dick Kirschten, "The Reagan Team Comes to Washington," *National Journal*, November 15, 1980, pp. 1924–26.

8. Gail Gregg and Dale Tate, "Reagan Economic Officials Put Differences Behind Them," *Congressional Quarterly Weekly Reports*, February 7, 1981, pp. 259–61.

9. John William Ellwood, ed., *Reductions in U.S. Domestic Spending: How They Affect State and Local Governments* (New Brunswick, N.J.: Transaction Books, 1982).

10. Sidney Blumenthal, "The Crisis of Reagonomics," *Boston Globe*, May 2, 1982, p. 11. See also the results of an investigation by Steven R. Weisman, in *New York Times Magazine*, October 24, 1982.

11. "Stockman on the Budget Outlook," *National Journal*, September 19, 1981, pp. 1665–67.

12. Thus the president's Saturday radio broadcast (of September 4, 1982) following his congressional victory on the tax bill was devoted to the theme of how current unemployment was due to the long record of high taxation.

13. Dick Kirschten, "Decision Making in the White House," *National Journal*, April 3, 1982, pp. 584–89; "Reagan's Legislative Strategy Team," *National Journal*, June 26, 1982, pp. 1127–30.

14. David Hoffman, "Reagan's Crusaders Fail to Find the Grail," *Washington Post*, July 4, 1982, p. 1.

CHAPTER VIII

The Foreign Policy Presidency

The foreign policy of the United States defines this nation's relationships with the other countries of the world: recognition or nonrecognition, trade or trade embargo, foreign aid or no aid, peace or war, are all part of the fabric of foreign policy and of foreign relations.

The Constitution in Article I, Section 10, makes clear that foreign policy is exclusively a federal matter. But in which branch that authority ultimately lies is not entirely clear, even though the main outlines of foreign policy authority appear to rest in Article II—the executive branch article. Article II, Sections 2 and 3, provide the president with much critical foreign policy power. Section 2 reads in part: "The President shall be Commander in Chief of the Army and Navy of the United States." While Congress holds the power to declare war, presidential control of the military is a powerful foreign policy tool, especially where national security is often an important foreign policy consideration.

Section 2 also provides that "He shall have Power, by and with the Advice and Consent of the Senate, to make Treaties, provided two thirds of the Senators present concur."[1] By this authority, the president becomes chief diplomat bringing the Senate into the process usually only at the final point of ratification.

Thirdly, Section 2 provides that "he [the president] shall nominate, and by and with the consent of the Senate, shall appoint Ambassadors." Here again the Senate must give its advice and consent or its disapproval. Yet, once confirmed, each ambassador becomes the president's major representative in the country in which he or she is stationed.

Finally, Article II, Section 3, provides that "he shall receive Ambassadors and other public ministers." Thus the president is given the sole power to receive another country's representative and accordingly to recognize that country or, by refusing, make that country persona non grata in American foreign relations. While some observers place little significance on the president's recognition power,[2] President Roosevelt's recognition of the Soviet Union in 1933, President Truman's recognition of Israel in 1948 and President Carter's recognition of the People's Republic of China in 1979 were all momentous decisions which had important policy consequences for both the recognized nations and for the United States.

Over the years the foreign policy authority of the national government has come by precedent, the federal courts, and by statutes enacted by Congress itself, to rest mainly with the president.

President George Washington established several precedents early on. First he asserted "executive privilege" by not giving the House of Representatives documents relating to the Jay Treaty—he was firmly convinced that the House really wanted to establish the precedent that its concurrence (in addition to the Senate's) was necessary in treaty-making.[3] Second, Washington refused to allow the Senate to participate in negotiating treaties; thus restricting it to consent and very little advice. Finally, Washington issued the Proclamation of Neutrality in 1793 while Congress was in recess thus keeping the United States from allying with France against Great Britain. While James Madison unsuccessfully argued that the president, acting without Congress, could not use his powers of diplomacy and military command, Washington by this action established the president as the sole organ of diplomacy in the executive branch.

The Supreme Court has usually ruled on the side of the president in foreign policy matters. The precedent Washington established by his Proclamation of Neutrality was affirmed by the Court over 100 years later in *United States* v. *Curtiss Wright Corporation*.[4] In this case, Justice Sutherland speaking for the court delivered the most expansive statement ever of doctrine of the president as diplomatic chief. He wrote:

> It results that the investment of the federal government with the powers of eternal sovereignty did not depend upon the affirmative grants of the Constitution. The powers to declare and wage war, to conclude peace, to make treaties, to maintain diplomatic relations with other sovereignties, if they had never been mentioned in the Constitution, would have been vested in the federal government as necessary concomitants of nationality. . . .
>
> In this vast external realm, with its important, complicated, delicate and manifold problems, the President alone has the power to speak or listen as a representative of the nation.
>
> It is important to bear in mind that we are here dealing not alone with an authority vested in the President by an exertion of legislative power, but with such an authority plus the very delicate, plenary and exclusive power of the President as the sole organ of the federal government in the field of international relations—a power which does not require as a basis for its exercise an act of Congress, but which, of course, like every other governmental power, must be exercised in subordination to the applicable provisions of the Constitution.

The expansive foreign policy power to the president enumerated in *United States* v. *Curtiss Wright Corporation* inevitably led to the president securing his capacity to legitimately conclude executive agreements. In *United States* v. *Belmont* decided in 1937,[5] the Supreme Court sustained Franklin Roosevelt's executive agreement with the USSR in which he recognized the Soviet Union without consulting the U.S. Senate. Mr. Justice Sutherland, speaking for the Court said, in part:

In respect of what was done here, the Executive had authority to speak as the sole organ of that government. The assignment and the agreements on connection therewith did not, as in the case of treaties, as that term is used in the treaty making clause of the Constitution (Art. II, Section 2), require the advice and consent of the Senate. A treaty signifies a compact made between two or more independent nations with a view to the public welfare. . . . But an international compact, as this was, is not always a treaty which requires the participation of the Senate.

Parenthetically, the State Department has now spelled out the differences between the treaty and the executive agreement.[6] Those differences, Richard Pious writes, may be summed up in this way: a treaty expresses a continuing obligation between nations, while an executive agreement facilitates a particular arrangement during a limited period of time between governments.[7] However, the Supreme Court has not spelled out any distinctions, and, in fact, none have been observed.

Another in the arsenal of the president's foreign policy powers, established first by precedent and now by the Supreme Court is that of executive privilege— the claim that the president's communications with his aides and department officers may be kept from Congress and the judiciary. Historically, executive privilege was applied to national security and foreign policy matters; more recently, it has been applied to all kinds of interagency communications and to communications between a president and his staff.[8]

In *United States v. Nixon,* decided in 1973,[9] the Supreme Court upheld the president's executive privilege. While the Court held "that the legitimate needs of the judicial process may outweigh presidential privilege . . . and must yield to the demonstrated specific need for evidence in a pending trial . . . ," it also ruled that "a president and those who assist him must be free to explore alternatives in the process of shaping policies and making decisions and to do so in a way many would be unwilling to express except privately. These are the considerations justifying a presumptive privilege for presidential communications."[10]

The U.S. Constitution outlines how treaties are to be made; it is silent, however, about how treaties are to be terminated. This issue arose when President Carter recognized the People's Republic of China effective January 1, 1979, and withdrew recognition from Taiwan effective the same date. Commensurate with this action, Carter announced that the 1955 National Defense Treaty with the Nationalist Chinese would terminate on January 1, 1980, in accordance with the treaty's proviso permitting termination by either party with one year's notice.

President Carter obviously assumed that presidential authority existed to abrogate the treaty. Senator Barry Goldwater disagreed and filed an appeal with the federal district court, which granted Goldwater and his colleagues from the Senate and House standing to sue. The court then ruled President Carter's abrogation of the treaty unconstitutional.[11]

On appeal, the circuit court for the District of Columbia held improper the district court's finding that the necessary authority in this instance for terminating a treaty may be granted by a majority of each house.[12] The district court's argument was: the treaty being a part of the supreme law of the land, can only be terminated by a subsequent federal statute.

The circuit court went on to say "the constitutional institution of advice and consent of Senate, provided two-thirds of the Senators concur, is a special and extraordinary condition of the exercise by the president of certain specified powers under Article II. It is not lightly to be extended in instances not set forth in the Constitution. Such an extension by implication is not proper unless that implication is unmistakably clear." And on appeal, the Supreme Court ordered, without hearing arguments, that the complaint be dismissed. The president's power to terminate treaties has been affirmed.[13]

The president's authority over foreign policy has been enhanced also by statutory delegation.[14] From the fifth Congress's passage of the Logan Act in 1799 providing fines and imprisonment for Americans who carry on unauthorized correspondence or intercourse with foreign governments for the purpose of influencing American foreign policy to the 99th Congress's enactment of legislation awarding the Nicaraguan contras $100 million in aid (despite Congress's lack of enthusiasm for the venture) a steady stream of legislation has given over to the president greater responsibilities in foreign affairs. This is so despite congressional passage of numerous pieces of legislation that include clauses permitting congressional review, deferral, or approval of executive action.

The Constitution, the precedents, the Supreme Court decisions, and legislative enactments all have led the president to assume a dominant role in foreign policy matters. This led Aaron Wildavsky to conclude that there are two presidencies—a foreign policy presidency and a domestic policy presidency—and that since World War II, presidents have been more successful in foreign than in domestic policy.

The logic behind Wildavsky's hypothesis was his assumption that a number of events and conditions emanating from the development of the modern presidency, which rested in considerable part on the rise of internationalism over isolationism since 1941, paved the way for increasing presidential leadership in foreign policy.

To test his hypothesis Wildavsky examined congressional action on presidential proposals from 1948 to 1964. For this period Congress approved 58.5 percent of foreign policy bills, including 73.3 percent of defense policy bills, and 70.8 percent of the treaties, general foreign relations, State Department, and foreign aid bills. During this same period Congress approved only 40.2 percent of the president's domestic policy proposals. Thus, the two presidencies thesis was confirmed.

Wildavsky's work has spawned a bevy of research articles, none of which has materially diminished his original thesis.[15] While some of this research does not reflect Wildavsky's neatly differentiated two presidencies, due mainly to most of it being conducted in the 1970s and thus reflecting an insurgent Congress's challenges of the president for control of foreign policy in the aftermath of Vietnam and Watergate,[16] the president remains preeminent in foreign policy matters. Wildavsky's seminal essay, "The Two Presidencies," is reprinted here.

Some of the struggle over who makes foreign policy is not seen as a matter of the president versus Congress, but as a question of whether primacy over foreign policy belongs in the State Department or in the National Security Council, with the Secretary of State as opposed to the Secretary of Defense, or with the Secretary of State as opposed to the National Security Adviser.[17] In short, the president's problems in foreign policy may be viewed as managerial.[18] Such managerial questions seem to have confronted most recent presidents.

Perhaps the most unique notion of how foreign policy is developed, who codifies it, and who manages it has been postulated by Harlan Cleveland. He argues that American foreign policy is reactive, that it is seldom initiated by a president of the United States. People, not their leaders, Cleveland writes, make the policy.[19] Foreign policy thus develops as popular consensus, is codified by experts, and is announced by leaders, including the president.

Cleveland then spells out "The People's Policy" in the form of propositions to which he believes the American people would subscribe. Some of these are as follows:

1. We are for the rights of human beings so we will continue to work for freedom for all.

2. We want to be in step with the world, thus we prefer not to be cast with two-bit dictators.

3. We are prepared to deploy our armed forces in quick and decisive operations in limited areas, but we are not prepared to hang around for long as we did in Vietnam.

4. We are determined to remain the world's strongest power and support a strong military.

5. We are glad to be getting along with China—they are a different breed of Communists—moreover, they represent a quarter of the world's population.

6. In the Middle East, Israel's survival is a must and we hope the Arabs and Israelis can find a lasting peace—the United States will help with the process, but basically it's up to them.

7. In South Africa we want majority rule, but we want a peaceful changeover— we are uncertain, however, of the means to accomplish this.

8. We want fair and free trade, but we worry that we can't sell enough of our products to foreigners to pay for the products we buy from them.

These and other propositions spelled out by Cleveland make up "The People's Policy." The president, who is responsible for external relations, bears the main responsibility to "sniff out" the people's policy and to make it a coherent whole. Beyond this, Cleveland views the management of foreign policy as an exercise in the politics of consent. The job of the president in eliciting consent, then, is to consult with the large number of nationally sovereign political actors. Coherence plus consultation, Cleveland concludes, will make for a viable American foreign policy. His fascinating and intellectually stimulating essay, "Coherence and Consultation: The President as Manager of American Foreign Policy," is reprinted here.

Harland Cleveland's view that American foreign policy is reactive and seldom initiated by a president of the United States, while attractive because of its remarkably democratic assumptions, may not always be the case. Presidents have been known to make and initiate foreign policy without a popular consensus to support that policy. Nowhere is the evidence of this clearer than in the behavior of the Reagan White House in the Iran-Contra Affair. This controversy first arose in the fall of 1986 when it was revealed that the Reagan administration had secretly sold arms to the government of Iran (so that Iran would use its "good offices" to gain the release of American hostages in Lebanon) at higher than normal prices and used the "profits" to fund the Contras (the counterrevolutionaries) in Nicaragua. This grew into a scandal because it was contrary to American policy to sell arms to Iran or to fund the Contras beyond limits set by Congress. It was also the expressed policy of the United States not to negotiate for, let alone trade arms for, the release of hostages. Because the Iran-Contra operation was undertaken primarily by the National Security Council without the formal approval of the Departments of Defense and State, the affair suggested that Reagan was making foreign policy unilaterally.

Soon after the scandal broke President Ronald Reagan created the President's Special Review Board to investigate the entire Iran-Contra affair as well as the operations of the National Security Council. The commission, known as the Tower Commission after its chairman John G. Tower, former Senator from Texas, had two other members: Edmund S. Muskie, former Senator and former Secretary of States; and Brent Scowcroft, former National Security Adviser to President Gerald Ford.

Its February 1987 report found that the National Security Council had indeed arranged to trade arms for hostages with Iran and sought to use funds from the arms sale to illegally aid the Contras in Nicaragua, and that certain members of the White House staff sought to cover up these facts as the Iran-Contra affair evolved. The most immediate effect of the report was the resignation of Donald Regan, the president's chief of staff; and his replacement by Howard Baker, former Senator from Tennessee. The first two parts of the report, its introduction and description of the role of the National Security Council (the principal forum for consideration of national security policy issues requiring Presidential decision), is reprinted here.

NOTES

1. On the tremendous significance of the treaty power in the hands of the president and the Senate see *Missouri v. Holland*, 252 U.S. 416 (1920).

2. For one view that recognition or nonrecognition has diminished in importance in foreign affairs see L. Thomas Galloway, *Recognizing Foreign Governments: The Practice of the United States* (Washington, D.C.: American Enterprise Institute, 1978), passim.

3. On the role of the House in treaty matters see Louis Fisher, *The Constitution between*

Friends: Congress, the President and the Law (New York: St. Martin's Press, 1978), pp. 197–204.

4. 299 U.S. 304 (1936).

5. 301 U.S. 324 (1937).

6. See Christopher H. Pyle and Richard M. Pious (eds.), *The President, Congress and the Constitution: Power and Legitimacy in American Politics* (New York: Free Press, 1984), p. 273.

7. Richard M. Pious, *The American Presidency* (New York: Basic Books, 1979), p. 340.

8. See Raymond Tatalovich and Byron W. Daynes, *Presidential Power in the United States* (Monterey, Calif.: Brooks/Cole Publishing, 1984), p. 301.

9. 418 U.S. 683 (1974); see also Harry A. Bailey, Jr. (ed.), *Classics of the American Presidency* (Oak Park, Ill.: Moore Publishing, 1980), pp. 308, 347–57.

10. For the view, however, that the president's claim of constitutional authority to withhold information from Congress is a myth, see Raoul Berger, *Executive Privilege: A Constitutional Myth* (Cambridge, Mass.: Harvard University Press, 1974), passim.

11. 481 F. Supp. 949 (1979); for Senator Barry Goldwater's view that "Treaty Termination Is a Shared Power," see Pyle and Pious, *The President, Congress, and the Constitution,* pp. 252–55. For a second view that the president's constitutional authority does not extend to the termination of treaties see L. Peter Schultz, "Goldwater v. Carter: The Separation of Powers and the Problem of Executive Prerogative," *Presidential Studies Quarterly* 12, no. 1 (Winter 1982), pp. 34–41.

12. 617 F. 2d 697 (1979); Senator Edward Kennedy holds strong views favoring the president's right of treaty termination. See his "Treaty Termination Is Not a Shared Power" in Pyle and Pious, *The President, Congress and the Constitution,* pp. 255–57. For additional support for the president's right to terminate treaties, see R. Gordon Hoxie, "Presidential Leadership and American Foreign Policy: Some Reflections on the Taiwan Issue, with Particular Considerations on Alexander Hamilton, Dwight Eisenhower, and Jimmy Carter," *Presidential Studies Quarterly* 9, no. 2 (Spring 1979), pp. 131–43.

13. 444 U.S. 996 (1979).

14. For a compilation of the foreign policy laws enacted between 1932 and 1975 see Clark S. Norton, *Congressional Review, Deferral, and Disapproval of Executive Actions: A Summary and an Inventory of Statutory Authority* (Washington, D.C.: Congressional Research Service, Library of Congress, April 30, 1976), pp. 120–21. An additional comprehensive source of foreign policy legislation through 1970 is Aspen Systems Corporation, *The Powers and Responsibilities of the President of the United States,* prepared for the President's Advisory Council on Executive Organization (Pittsburgh, Penn.: Aspen Systems Corporation, 1970), especially pp. 213–14.

15. For the evidence, see Donald A. Peppers, " 'The Two Presidencies': Eight Years Later," in *Perspectives on the Presidency* ed. Aaron Wildavsky (Little, Brown, 1975), pp. 448–51; Lance T. LeLoup and Steven A. Shull, "Congress versus the Executive: The 'Two Presidencies' Reconsidered," *Social Sciences Quarterly* 59, no. 4 (March 1979), pp. 704–19; Lee Sigelman, "Reassessment of the Two Presidencies Thesis," *Journal of Politics* 41, no. 4 (November 1979), pp. 1195–1205; Frederick Paul Lee, " 'The Two Presidencies' Revisited," *Presidential Studies Quarterly* 10, no. 4 (Fall 1980), pp. 620–28; Harvey G. Zeidenstein, "The Two Presidencies Thesis Is Alive and Well and Has Been Living in the U.S. Senate Since 1973," *Presidential Studies Quarterly* 11,

no. 4 (Fall 1981), pp. 511–25; Jeffrey E. Cohen, "A Historical Reassessment of Wildavsky's 'Two Presidencies,'" *Social Science Quarterly* 63, no. 3 (September 1982), pp. 549–55; Frederick Paul Lee, "The Two Presidencies: Political Elite Perspectives through Time, 1976–1980," *Presidential Studies Quarterly* 13, no. 1 (Winter 1983), pp. 26–36; and George C. Edwards III, "The Two Presidencies: A Reevaluation," *American Political Science Quarterly* 14, no. 3 (July 1986), pp. 247–63.

16. Much of the presidency-curbing legislation in the foreign policy area and the debate over the president's proper role vis-à-vis Congress came on the heels of Watergate and Vietnam. For two reports of congressional activity and the debate see John G. Tower, "Congress versus the President: The Formulation and Implementation of American Foreign Policy," *Foreign Affairs* 60 (Winter 1981/82), pp. 229–46; and Hrach Gregorian, "Assessing Congressional Involvement in Foreign Policy: Lessons of the Post-Vietnam Period," *Review of Politics* 46 (January 1984), pp. 91–112.

17. On this issue, see Zbigniew Brzezinski "Deciding Who Makes Foreign Policy," in *Analyzing the Presidency*, ed. Robert E. DiClerico (Guilford, Conn.: Dushkin Publishing Group, 1985), pp. 250–55.

18. On the difficulty of controlling one part of the foreign policy bureaucracy, see Laurence H. Silberman, "Toward Presidential Control of the State Department," *Foreign Affairs* 54, no. 4 (Spring/Summer 1979), pp. 872–93; on the presidential problem as managerial see also Richard Pious, *American Presidency*, p. 332.

19. Some observers have serious doubts about a considerable role for public opinion in foreign policy matters. See, for example, James N. Rosenau, *Public Opinion and Foreign Policy* (New York: Random House, 1961), pp. 35–37; and Warren E. Miller and Donald E. Stokes, "Constituency Influence in Congress," *American Political Science Review* 57, no. 1 (March 1963), pp. 45–56. Other observers are not so sanguine that public opinion in foreign affairs is insignificant or can be ignored. See Benjamin I. Page and Mark P. Petracca, *The American Presidency* (New York: McGraw-Hill 1983), p. 362; Erwin C. Hargrove, *The Power of the Modern Presidency* (New York: Alfred A. Knopf, 1974), pp. 114–18; and Milton Rosenberg, "Attitude Change and Foreign Policy in the Cold War Era," in *Domestic Sources of Foreign Policy*, ed. James N. Rosenau (New York: Free Press, 1967), p. 116.

20
The Two Presidencies
Aaron Wildavsky

The United States has one President, but it has two presidencies; one presidency is for domestic affairs, and the other is concerned with defense and foreign policy. Since World War II, Presidents have had much greater success in controlling the nation's defense and foreign policies than in dominating its domestic policies. Even Lyndon Johnson has seen his early record of victories in

Source: Transaction 4, no. 2 (December 1966).

domestic legislation diminish as his concern with foreign affairs grows.

What powers does the President have to control defense and foreign policies and so completely overwhelm those who might wish to thwart him?

The President's normal problem with domestic policy is to get congressional support for the programs he prefers. In foreign affairs, in contrast, he can almost always get support for policies that he believes will protect the nation—but his problem is to find a viable policy.

Whoever they are, whether they begin by caring about foreign policy like Eisenhower and Kennedy or about domestic policies like Truman and Johnson, Presidents soon discover they have more policy preferences in domestic matters than in foreign policy. The Republican and Democratic parties possess a traditional roster of policies, which can easily be adopted by a new President—for example, he can be either for or against Medicare and aid to education. Since existing domestic policy usually changes in only small steps, Presidents find it relatively simple to make minor adjustments. However, although any President knows he supports foreign aid and NATO, the world outside changes much more rapidly than the nation inside—Presidents and their parties have no prior policies on Argentina and the Congo. The world has become a highly intractable place with a whirl of forces we cannot or do not know how to alter.

THE RECORD OF PRESIDENTIAL CONTROL

It takes great crises, such as Roosevelt's hundred days in the midst of the depression, or the extraordinary majorities that Barry Goldwater's candidacy willed to Lyndon Johnson, for Presidents to succeed in controlling domestic policy. From the end of the 1930s to the present (what may roughly be called the modern era), Presidents have often been frustrated in their domestic programs. From 1938, when conservatives regrouped their forces, to the time of his death, Franklin Roosevelt did not get a single piece of significant domestic legislation passed. Truman lost out on most of his intense domestic preferences, except perhaps for housing. Since Eisenhower did not ask for much domestic legislation, he did not meet consistent defeat, yet he failed in his general policy of curtailing governmental commitments. Kennedy, of course, faced great difficulties with domestic legislation.

In the realm of foreign policy there has not been a single major issue on which Presidents, when they were serious and determined, have failed. The list of their victories is impressive: entry into the United Nations, the Marshall Plan, NATO, the Truman Doctrine, the decisions to stay out of Indochina in 1954 and to intervene in Vietnam in the 1960s, aid to Poland and Yugoslavia, the test-ban treaty, and many more. Serious setbacks to the President in controlling foreign policy are extraordinary and unusual.

Table I, compiled from the Congressional Quarterly Service tabulation of presidential initiative and congressional response from 1948 through 1964, shows that Presidents have significantly better records in foreign and defense matters than in domestic policies. When refugees and immigration—which Congress considers primarily a domestic concern—are removed from the general foreign policy area, it is clear that Presidents prevail about 70 percent of the time in defense and foreign policy, compared with 40 percent in the domestic sphere.

TABLE I · CONGRESSIONAL ACTION ON PRESIDENTIAL PROPOSALS
FROM 1948 TO 1964

Policy Area	Congressional Action		Number of Proposals
	% Pass	% Fail	
Domestic policy (natural resources, labor, agriculture, taxes, etc.)	40.2	59.8	2,499
Defense policy (defense, disarmament, manpower, misc.)	73.3	26.7	90
Foreign policy	58.5	41.5	655
Immigration, refugees	13.2	86.0	129
Treaties, general foreign relations, State Department, foreign aid	70.8	29.2	445

Source: Congressional Quarterly Service, *Congress and the Nation,* 1945–1964 (Washington, 1965).

WORLD EVENTS AND PRESIDENTIAL RESOURCES

Power in politics is control over governmental decisions. How does the President manage his control of foreign and defense policy? The answer does not reside in the greater constitutional power in foreign affairs that Presidents have possessed since the founding of the Republic. The answer lies in the changes that have taken place since 1945.

The number of nations with which the United States has diplomatic relations has increased from 53 in 1939 to 113 in 1966. But sheer numbers do not tell enough; the world has also become a much more dangerous place. However remote it may seem at times, our government must always be aware of the possibility of nuclear war.

Yet the mere existence of great powers with effective thermonuclear weapons would not, in and of itself, vastly increase our rate of interaction with most other nations. We see events in Assam or Burundi as important because they are also part of a larger worldwide contest, called the cold war, in which great powers are rivals for the control or support of other nations. Moreover, the reaction against the blatant isolationism of the 1930s has led to a concern with foreign policy that is worldwide in scope. We are interested in what happens everywhere because we see these events as connected with larger interests involving, at the worst, the possibility of ultimate destruction.

Given the overriding fact that the world is dangerous and that small causes are perceived to have potentially great effects in an unstable world, it follows that Presidents must be interested in relatively "small" matters. So they give Azerbaijan or Lebanon or Vietnam huge amounts of their time. Arthur Schlesinger, Jr., wrote of Kennedy that "in the first two months of his administration he probably spent more time on Laos than on anything else." Few failures in domestic policy, Presidents soon realize, could have as disastrous consequences as any one of dozens of mistakes in the international arena.

The result is that foreign policy concerns tend to drive out domestic policy. Except for occasional questions of domestic prosperity and for civil rights, foreign affairs have consistently higher priority for Presidents. Once, when trying to talk to President Kennedy about natural resources, Secretary of the Interior Stewart Udall remarked, "He's imprisoned by Berlin."

The importance of foreign affairs to Presidents is intensified by the increasing speed of events in the international arena. The event and its consequences follow closely on top of one another. The blunder at the Bay of Pigs is swiftly followed by the near catastrophe of the Cuban missile crisis. Presidents can no longer count on passing along their most difficult problems to their successors. They must expect to face the consequences of their actions—or failure to act—while still in office.

Domestic policy-making is usually based on experimental adjustments to an existing situation. Only a few decisions, such as those involving large dams, irretrievably commit future generations. Decisions in foreign affairs, however, are often perceived to be irreversible. This is expressed, for example, in the fear of escalation or the various "spiral" or "domino" theories of international conflict.

If decisions are perceived to be both important and irreversible, there is every reason for Presidents to devote a great deal of resources to them. Presidents have to be oriented toward the future in the use of their resources. They serve a fixed term in office, and they cannot automatically count on support from the populace, Congress, or the administrative apparatus. They have to be careful, therefore, to husband their resources for pressing future needs. But because the consequences of events in foreign affairs are potentially more grave, faster to manifest themselves, and less easily re-

versible than in domestic affairs, Presidents are more willing to use up their resources.

THE POWER TO ACT

Their formal powers to commit resources in foreign affairs and defense are vast. Particularly important is their power as Commander-in-Chief to move troops. Faced with situations like the invasion of South Korea or the emplacement of missiles in Cuba, fast action is required. Presidents possess both the formal power to act and the knowledge that elites and the general public expect them to act. Once they have committed American forces, it is difficult for Congress or anyone else to alter the course of events. The Dominican venture is a recent case in point.

Presidential discretion in foreign affairs also makes it difficult (though not impossible) for Congress to restrict their actions. Presidents can use executive agreements instead of treaties, enter into tacit agreements instead of written ones, and otherwise help create *de facto* situations not easily reversed. Presidents also have far greater ability than anyone else to obtain information on developments abroad through the Departments of State and Defense. The need for secrecy in some aspects of foreign and defense policy further restricts the ability of others to compete with Presidents. These things are all well known. What is not so generally appreciated is the growing presidential ability to *use* information to achieve goals.

In the past Presidents were amateurs in military strategy. They could not even get much useful advice outside of the military. As late as the 1930s the number of people outside the military establishment who were professionally engaged in the study of defense policy could be numbered on the fingers. Today there are hundreds of such men. The rise of the defense intellectuals has given the President of the United States enhanced ability to control defense policy. He is no longer dependent on the military for advice. He can choose among defense intellectuals from the research corporations and the academies for alternative sources of advice. He can install these men in his own office. He can play them off against each other or use them to extend spheres of coordination.

Even with these advisers, however, Presidents and Secretaries of Defense might still be too bewildered by the complexity of nuclear situations to take action—unless they had an understanding of the doctrine and concepts of deterrence. But knowledge of the doctrine about deterrence has been widely diffused; it can be picked up by any intelligent person who will read books or listen to enough hours of conversation. Whether or not the doctrine is good is a separate question; the point is that civilians can feel they understand what is going on in defense policy. Perhaps the most extraordinary feature of presidential action during the Cuban missile crisis was the degree to which the Commander-in-Chief of the Armed Forces insisted on controlling even the smallest moves. From the positioning of ships to the methods of boarding, to the precise words and actions to be taken by individual soldiers and sailors, the President and his civilian advisers were in control.

Although Presidents have rivals for power in foreign affairs, the rivals do not usually succeed. Presidents prevail not only because they may have superior resources but because their potential opponents are weak, divided, or believe that they should not control foreign policy. Let us consider the potential rivals—the general citizenry, special interest groups, the Congress, the military, the so-called military-industrial complex, and the State Department.

Competitors for Control of Policy

The Public. The general public is much more dependent on Presidents in foreign affairs than in domestic matters. While many people know about the impact of social security and Medicare, few know about politics in Malawi. So it is not surprising that people expect the President to act in foreign affairs and reward him with their confidence. Gallup Polls consistently show that presidential popularity rises after he takes action in a crisis—whether the action is disastrous as in the Bay of Pigs or successful as in the Cuban missile crisis. Decisive action, such as the bombing of oil fields near Haiphong, resulted in a sharp (though temporary) increase in Johnson's popularity.

The Vietnam situation illustrates another problem of public opinion in foreign affairs: it is extremely difficult to get operational policy directions from the general public. It took a long time before any sizable public interest in the subject developed. Nothing short of the large scale involvement of American troops under fire probably could have brought about the current high level of concern. Yet this relatively well developed popular opinion is difficult to interpret. While a majority appear to support President Johnson's policy, it appears that they could easily be persuaded to withdraw from Vietnam if the administration changed its line. Although a sizable majority would support various initiatives to end the war, they would seemingly be appalled if this action led to

Communist encroachments elsewhere in Southeast Asia. (See "The President, the Polls, and Vietnam" by Seymour Martin Lipset, *Trans-action*, Sept/Oct 1966.)

Although Presidents lead opinion in foreign affairs, they know they will be held accountable for the consequences of their actions. President Johnson has maintained a large commitment in Vietnam. His popularity shoots up now and again in the midst of some imposing action. But the fact that a body of citizens do not like the war comes back to damage his overall popularity. We will support your initiatives, the people seem to say, but we will reserve the right to punish you (or your party) if we do not like the results.

Special Interest Groups. Opinions are easier to gauge in domestic affairs because, for one thing, there is a stable structure of interest groups that covers virtually all matters of concern. The farm, labor, business, conservation, veteran, civil rights, and other interest groups provide cues when a proposed policy affects them. Thus people who identify with these groups may adopt their views. But in foreign policy matters the interest group structure is weak, unstable, and thin rather than dense. In many matters affecting Africa and Asia, for example, it is hard to think of well-known interest groups. While ephemeral groups arise from time to time to support or protest particular policies, they usually disappear when the immediate problem is resolved. In contrast, longer-lasting elite groups like the Foreign Policy Association and Council on Foreign Relations are composed of people of diverse views; refusal to take strong positions on controversial matters is a condition of their continued viability.

The strongest interest groups are probably the ethnic associations whose members have strong ties with a homeland, as in Poland or Cuba, so they are rarely activated simultaneously on any specific issue. They are most effective when most narrowly and intensely focused—as in the fierce pressure from Jews to recognize the state of Israel. But their relatively small numbers limits their significance to Presidents in the vastly more important general foreign policy picture—as continued aid to the Arab countries shows. Moreover, some ethnic groups may conflict on significant issues such as American acceptance of the Oder-Neisse line separating Poland from what is now East Germany.

The Congress. Congressmen also exercise power in foreign affairs. Yet they are ordinarily not serious competitors with the President because they follow a self-denying ordinance. They do not think it is their job to determine the nation's defense policies. Lewis A. Dexter's extensive interviews with members of the Senate Armed Services Committee, who might be expected to want a voice in defense policy, reveal that they do not desire for men like themselves to run the nation's defense establishment. Aside from a few specific conflicts among the armed services which allow both the possibility and desirability of direct intervention, the Armed Services Committee constitutes a sort of real estate committee dealing with the regional economic consequences of the location of military facilities.

The congressional appropriations power is potentially a significant resource, but circumstances since the end of World War II have tended to reduce its effectiveness. The appropriations committees and Congress itself might make their will felt by refusing to allot funds unless basic policies were altered. But this has not happened. While Congress makes its traditional small cuts in the military budget, Presidents have mostly found themselves warding off congressional attempts to increase specific items still further.

Most of the time, the administration's refusal to spend has not been seriously challenged. However, there have been occasions when individual legislators or committees have been influential. Senator Henry Jackson in his campaign (with the aid of colleagues on the Joint Committee on Atomic Energy) was able to gain acceptance for the Polaris weapons system and Senator Arthur H. Vandenberg played a part in determining the shape of the Marshall Plan and so on. The few congressmen who are expert in defense policy act, as Samuel P. Huntington says, largely as lobbyists with the executive branch. It is apparently more fruitful for these congressional experts to use their resources in order to get a hearing from the executive than to work on other congressmen.

When an issue involves the actual use or threat of violence, it takes a great deal to convince congressmen not to follow the President's lead. James Robinson's tabulation of foreign and defense policy issues from the late 1930s to 1961 (Table II) shows dominant influence by Congress in only one case out of seven—the 1954 decision not to intervene with armed force in Indochina. In that instance President Eisenhower deliberately sounded out congressional opinion and, finding it negative, decided not to intervene—against the advice of Admiral Radford, chairman of the Joint Chiefs of Staff. This attempt to abandon responsibility did not succeed, as the years of American involvement demonstrate.

The Military. The outstanding feature of the military's participation in making defense policy is their amazing weakness. Whether the policy decisions involve the size of the armed forces, the choice of weapons systems, the total defense budget, or its division into components,

the military have not prevailed. Let us take budgetary decisions as representative of the key choices to be made in defense policy. Since the end of World War II the military has not been able to achieve significant (billion dollar) increases in appropriations by their own efforts. Under Truman and Eisenhower defense budgets were determined by what Huntington calls the remainder method: the two Presidents estimated revenues, decided what they could spend on domestic matters, and the remainder was assigned to defense. The usual controversy was between some military and congressional groups supporting much larger expenditures while the President and his executive allies refused. A typical case, involving the desire of the Air Force to increase the number of groups of planes is described by Huntington in *The Common Defense:*

> The FY [fiscal year] 1949 budget provided 48 groups. After the Czech coup, the Administration yielded and backed an Air Force of 55 groups in its spring rearmament program. Congress added additional funds to aid Air Force expansion to 70 groups. The Administration refused to utilize them, however, and in the gathering economy wave of the summer and fall of 1948, the Air Force goal was cut back again to 48 groups. In 1949 the House of Representatives picked up the challenge and appropriated funds for 58 groups. The President impounded the money. In June, 1950, the Air Force had 48 groups.

The great increases in the defense budget were due far more to Stalin and modern technology than to the military. The Korean War resulted in an increase from 12 to 44 billions and much of the rest followed Sputnik and the huge costs of missile programs. Thus modern technology and international conflict put an end to the one major effort to subordinate foreign affairs to domestic policies through the budget.

TABLE II · CONGRESSIONAL INVOLVEMENT IN FOREIGN AND DEFENSE POLICY DECISIONS

Issue	Congressional Involvement (High, Low, None)	Initiator (Congress or Executive)	Predominant Influence (Congress or Executive)	Legislation or Resolution (Yes or No)	Violence at Stake (Yes or No)	Decision Time (Long or Short)
Neutrality legislation, the 1930s	High	Exec	Cong	Yes	No	Long
Lend-lease, 1941	High	Exec	Exec	Yes	Yes	Long
Aid to Russia, 1941	Low	Exec	Exec	No	No	Long
Repeal of Chinese exclusion, 1943	High	Cong	Cong	Yes	No	Long
Fulbright Resolution, 1943	High	Cong	Cong	Yes	No	Long
Building the atomic bomb, 1944	Low	Exec	Exec	Yes	Yes	Long
Foreign Services Act of 1946	High	Exec	Exec	Yes	No	Long
Truman Doctrine, 1947	High	Exec	Exec	Yes	No	Long
The Marshall Plan, 1947–48	High	Exec	Exec	Yes	No	Long
Berlin airlift, 1948	None	Exec	Exec	No	Yes	Long
Vandenberg Resolution, 1948	High	Exec	Cong	Yes	No	Long
North Atlantic Treaty, 1947–49	High	Exec	Exec	Yes	No	Long
Korean decision, 1950	None	Exec	Exec	No	Yes	Short
Japanese peace treaty, 1952	High	Exec	Exec	Yes	No	Long
Bohlen nomination, 1953	High	Exec	Exec	Yes	No	Long
Indo-China, 1954	High	Exec	Cong	No	Yes	Short
Formosan Resolution, 1955	High	Exec	Exec	Yes	Yes	Long
International Finance Corporation, 1956	Low	Exec	Exec	Yes	No	Long
Foreign aid, 1957	High	Exec	Exec	Yes	No	Long
Reciprocal trade agreements, 1958	High	Exec	Exec	Yes	No	Long
Monroney Resolution, 1958	High	Cong	Cong	Yes	No	Long
Cuban decision, 1961	Low	Exec	Exec	No	Yes	Long

Source: James A. Robinson, *Congress and Foreign Policy-Making* (Homewood, Ill.: Dorsey Press, 1962).

It could be argued that the President merely ratifies the decisions made by the military and their allies. If the military and/or Congress were united and insistent on defense policy, it would certainly be difficult for Presidents to resist these forces. But it is precisely the disunity of the military that has characterized the entire postwar period. Indeed, the military have not been united on any major matter of defense policy. The apparent unity of the Joint Chiefs of Staff turns out to be illusory. The vast majority of their recommendations appear to be unanimous and are accepted by the Secretary of Defense and the President. But this facade of unity can only be achieved by methods that vitiate the impact of the recommendations. Genuine disagreements are hidden by vague language that commits no one to anything. Mutually contradictory plans are strung together so everyone appears to get something, but nothing is decided. Since it is impossible to agree on really important matters, all sorts of trivia are brought in to make a record of agreement. While it may be true, as Admiral Denfield, a former Chief of Naval Operations, said, that "On nine-tenths of the matters that come before them the Joint Chiefs of Staff reach agreement themselves," the vastly more important truth is that "normally the *only* disputes are on strategic concepts, the size and composition of forces, and budget matters."

Military-Industrial. But what about the fabled military-industrial complex? If the military alone is divided and weak, perhaps the giant industrial firms that are so dependent on defense contracts play a large part in making policy.

First, there is an important distinction between the questions "Who will get a given contract?" and "What will our defense policy be?" It is apparent that different answers may be given to these quite different questions. There are literally tens of thousands of defense contractors. They may compete vigorously for business. In the course of this competition, they may wine and dine military officers, use retired generals, seek intervention by their congressmen, place ads in trade journals, and even contribute to political campaigns. The famous TFX controversy—should General Dynamics or Boeing get the expensive contract?—is a larger than life example of the pressure brought to bear in search of lucrative contracts.

But neither the TFX case nor the usual vigorous competition for contracts is involved with the making of substantive defense policy. Vital questions like the size of the defense budget, the choice of strategic programs, massive retaliation vs. a counter-city strategy, and the like were far beyond the policy aims of any company. Industrial firms, then, do not control such decisions, nor is there much evidence that they actually try. No doubt a precipitous and drastic rush to disarmament would meet with opposition from industrial firms among other interests. However, there has never been a time when any significant element in the government considered a disarmament policy to be feasible.

It may appear that industrial firms had no special reason to concern themselves with the government's stance on defense because they agree with the national consensus on resisting communism, maintaining a large defense establishment, and rejecting isolationism. However, this hypothesis about the climate of opinion explains everything and nothing. For every policy that is adopted or rejected can be explained away on the grounds that the cold war climate of opinion dictated what happened. Did the United States fail to intervene with armed force in Vietnam in 1954? That must be because the climate of opinion was against it. Did the United States send troops to Vietnam in the 1960s? That must be because the cold war climate demanded it. If the United States builds more missiles, negotiates a test-ban treaty, intervenes in the Dominican Republic, fails to intervene in a dozen other situations, all these actions fit the hypothesis by definition. The argument is reminiscent of those who defined the Soviet Union as permanently hostile and therefore interpreted increases of Soviet troops as menacing and decreases of troop strength as equally sinister.

If the growth of the military establishment is not directly equated with increasing military control of defense policy, the extraordinary weakness of the professional soldier still requires explanation. Huntington has written about how major military leaders were seduced in the Truman and Eisenhower years into believing that they should bow to the judgment of civilians that the economy could not stand much larger military expenditures. Once the size of the military pie was accepted as a fixed constraint, the military services were compelled to put their major energies into quarreling with one another over who should get the larger share. Given the natural rivalries of the military and their traditional acceptance of civilian rule, the President and his advisers—who could claim responsibility for the broader picture of reconciling defense and domestic policies—had the upper hand. There are, however, additional explanations to be considered.

The dominant role of the congressional appropriations committee is to be guardian of the treasury. This is manifested in the pride of its members in cutting the President's budget. Thus it was difficult to get this crucial committee to recommend even a few hundred million increase in defense; it was practi-

cally impossible to get them to consider the several billion jump that might really have made a difference. A related budgetary matter concerned the planning, programming, and budgeting system introduced by Secretary of Defense McNamara. For if the defense budget contained major categories that crisscrossed the services, only the Secretary of Defense could put it together. Whatever the other debatable consequences of program budgeting, its major consequence was to grant power to the secretary and his civilian advisers.

The subordination of the military through program budgeting is just one symptom of a more general weakness of the military. In the past decade the military has suffered a lack of intellectual skills appropriate to the nuclear age. For no one has (and no one wants) direct experience with nuclear war. So the usual military talk about being the only people to have combat experience is not very impressive. Instead, the imaginative creation of possible future wars— in order to avoid them—requires people with a high capacity for abstract thought combined with the ability to manipulate symbols using quantitative methods. West Point has not produced many such men.

The State Department. Modern Presidents expect the State Department to carry out their policies. John F. Kennedy felt that State was "in some particular sense 'his' department." If a Secretary of State forgets this, as was apparently the case with James Byrnes under Truman, a President may find another man. But the State Department, especially the Foreign Service, is also a highly professional organization with a life and momentum of its own. If a President does not push hard, he may find his preferences somehow dissipated in time. Arthur Schlesinger fills his book on

Kennedy with laments about the bureaucratic inertia and recalcitrance of the State Department.

Yet Schlesinger's own account suggests that State could not ordinarily resist the President. At one point, he writes of "the President, himself, increasingly the day-to-day director of American foreign policy." On the next page, we learn that "Kennedy dealt personally with almost every aspect of policy around the globe. He knew more about certain areas than the senior officials at State and probably called as many issues to their attention as they did to his." The President insisted on his way in Laos. He pushed through his policy on the Congo against strong opposition with the State Department. Had Kennedy wanted to get a great deal more initiative out of the State Department, as Schlesinger insists, he could have replaced the Secretary of State, a man who did not command special support in the Democratic party or in Congress. It may be that Kennedy wanted too strongly to run his own foreign policy. Dean Rusk may have known far better than Schlesinger that the one thing Kennedy did not want was a man who might rival him in the field of foreign affairs.

Schlesinger comes closest to the truth when he writes that "the White House could always win any battle it chose over the [Foreign] Service; but the prestige and proficiency of the Service limited the number of battles any White House would find it profitable to fight." When the President knew what he wanted, he got it. When he was doubtful and perplexed, he sought good advice and frequently did not get that. But there is no evidence that the people on his staff came up with better ideas. The real problem may have been a lack of good ideas anywhere. Kennedy undoubtedly encouraged his staff to prod the State Department. But the President was sufficiently cautious not to push so hard that he got his way when he was not certain what that way should be. In this context Kennedy appears to have played his staff off against elements in the State Department.

The growth of a special White House staff to help Presidents in foreign affairs expresses their need for assistance, their refusal to rely completely on the regular executive agencies, and their ability to find competent men. The deployment of this staff must remain a presidential prerogative, however, if its members are to serve Presidents and not their opponents. Whenever critics do not like existing foreign and defense policies, they are likely to complain that the White House staff is screening out divergent views from the President's attention. Naturally, the critics recommend introducing many more different viewpoints. If the critics could maneuver the President into counting hands all day ("on the one hand and on the other"), they would make it impossible for him to act. Such a viewpoint is also congenial to those who believe that action rather than inaction is the greatest present danger in foreign policy. But Presidents resolutely refuse to become prisoners of their advisers by using them as other people would like. Presidents remain in control of their staff as well as of major foreign policy decisions.

HOW COMPLETE IS THE CONTROL?

Some analysts say that the success of Presidents in controlling foreign policy decisions is largely illusory. It is achieved, they say, by anticipating the reactions of others, and eliminating proposals that would run into severe opposition. There is some truth in this objection. In politics, where transactions are based on a high degree of mutual interdependence, what others may do has to be taken into account. But basing presidential success in foreign and defense policy on anticipated reactions suggests a static situation which does not exist. For if Presidents propose only those policies that would get support in Congress, and Congress opposes them only when it knows that it can muster overwhelming strength, there would never be any conflict. Indeed, there might never be any action.

How can "anticipated reaction" explain the conflict over policies like the Marshall Plan and the test-ban treaty in which severe opposition was overcome only by strenuous efforts? Furthermore, why doesn't "anticipated reaction" work in domestic affairs? One would have to argue that for some reason presidential perception of what would be successful is consistently confused on domestic issues and most always accurate on major foreign policy issues. But the role of "anticipated reactions" should be greater in the more familiar domestic situations, which provide a backlog of experience for forecasting, than in foreign policy with many novel situations such as the Suez crisis or the Rhodesian affair.

Are there significant historical examples which might refute the thesis of presidential control of foreign policy? Foreign aid may be a case in point. For many years, Presidents have struggled to get foreign aid appropriations because of hostility from public and congressional opinion. Yet several billion dollars a year are appropriated regularly despite the evident unpopularity of the program. In the aid programs to Communist countries like Poland and Yugoslavia, the Congress attaches all sorts of restrictions to the aid, but Presidents find ways of getting around them.

What about the example of recognition of Communist China? The sentiment of the country always has been against recognizing Red China or admitting it to the United Nations. But have Presidents wanted to recognize Red China and been hamstrung by opposition? The answer, I suggest, is a qualified "no." By the time recognition of Red China might have become a serious issue for the Truman administration, the war in Korea effectively precluded its consideration. There is no evidence that President Eisenhower or Secretary Dulles ever thought it wise to recognize Red China or help admit her to the United Nations. The Kennedy administration viewed the matter as not of major importance and, considering the opposition, moved cautiously in suggesting change. Then came the war in Vietnam. If the advantages for foreign policy had been perceived to be much higher, then Kennedy or Johnson might have proposed changing American policy toward recognition of Red China.

One possible exception, in the case of Red China, however, does not seem sufficient to invalidate the general thesis that Presidents do considerably better in getting their way in foreign and defense policy than in domestic policies.

THE WORLD INFLUENCE

The forces impelling Presidents to be concerned with the widest range of foreign and defense policies also affect the ways in which they calculate their power stakes. As Kennedy used to say, "Domestic policy . . . can only defeat us; foreign policy can kill us."

It no longer makes sense for Presidents to "play politics" with foreign and defense policies. In the past, Presidents might have thought that they could gain by prolonged delay or by not acting at all. The problem might disappear or be passed on to their successors. Presidents must now expect to pay the high costs themselves if the world situation deteriorates. The advantages of pursuing a policy that is viable in the world, that will not blow up on Presidents or their fellow citizens, far outweigh any temporary political disadvantages accrued in supporting an initially unpopular policy. Compared with domestic affairs, Presidents engaged in world politics are immensely more concerned with meeting problems on their own terms. Who supports and opposes a policy, though a matter of considerable interest, does not assume the crucial importance that it does in domestic affairs. The best policy Presidents can find is also the best politics.

The fact that there are numerous foreign and defense policy situations competing for a President's attention means that it is worthwhile to organize political activity in order to effect his agenda. For if a President pays more attention to certain problems he may develop different preferences; he may seek and receive different advice; his new calculations may lead him to devote greater resources to seeking a solution. Interested congressmen may exert influence not by directly determining a presidential decision, but indirectly by making it costly for a President to avoid reconsidering the basis for his action. For example, citizen groups, such as those concerned with a change in China policy, may have an impact simply by keeping their proposals on the public agenda. A President may be compelled to reconsider a problem even though he could not overtly be forced to alter the prevailing policy.

In foreign affairs we may be approaching the stage where knowledge is power. There is a tremendous receptivity to good ideas in Washington. Most anyone who can present a convincing rationale for dealing with a hard world finds a ready audience. The best way to convince Presidents to follow a desired policy is to show that it might work. A man like McNamara thrives because he performs; he comes up with answers he can defend. It is, to be sure, extremely difficult to devise good policies or to predict their consequences accurately. Nor is it easy to convince others that a given policy is superior to other alternatives. But it is the way to influence with Presidents. For if they are convinced that the current policy is best, the likelihood of gaining sufficient force to compel a change is quite small. The man who can build better foreign policies will find Presidents beating a path to his door.

FURTHER READING SUGGESTED BY THE AUTHOR

The Common Defense, by Samuel P. Huntington. New York: Columbia University Press, 1963. The best study of presidential participation in the making of defense policy.

Congress and the Presidency, by Nelson W. Polsby. Englewood Cliffs, New Jersey: Prentice-Hall, 1965. A fine short study of executive-legislative relationships.

21
Coherence and Consultation: The President as Manager of American Foreign Policy
Harlan Cleveland

I. AN INCHOATE CONSENSUS

"American foreign policy" is not an abstraction. It is what the governed and their government do from day to day about world security and international relations. "Policy" is driven by what happens. What happens is seldom initiated by the President of the United States. So U.S. policy is mostly and necessarily reactive. But in reacting, the President and his advisers are guided by some general ideas, articulated or not, about where they want to go, what they are trying to do. And this frame of reference is heavily influenced in turn by the leaders' perceptions of what actions will elicit "the consent of the governed" (on TV tonight, in Congress next month, at the polls next year).

The leaders' problem is that they often get left behind. Public opinion may move both faster and farther than the perceptions "of policy makers." My colleague, Royce Hanson, speaks of "the tendency of officials (. . . especially policy professionals) to use Higher Idiocy rather than common sense in arriving at policy pronouncements."

Back when he was running for President in 1976, Jimmy Carter wisely didn't say he wanted to be the architect of U.S. foreign policy. "No one can make our foreign policy for us as well as we can make it ourselves," he told a Chicago audience, speaking as a private citizen. He did volunteer to manage it for us, though.

The division of labor implied in this campaign rhetoric is sound. People, not leaders, really do make the policy. At any given moment in time, therefore, most of the elements of American foreign policy are already lying around, in an inchoate consensus not yet fully codified by the foreign policy establishment and the professionals and amateurs temporarily residing in Washington, D.C. Despite what one reads in the newspapers, sees in television debates, and hears from partisan podiums (the three forms of organized communication most dedicated to highlighting differences of opinion), the mandatory mode of American foreign policy is essentially bipartisan, even nonpartisan. The people's policy is their commonsense reaction to the changing facts of international life.

II. THE PEOPLE'S POLICY

What are the elements of this "people's policy"? Each analyst is entitled to an opinion, of course; but I believe that the American people by sizable majorities would sign onto the following propositions.

- We are for the rights of human beings, a fair chance of life, liberty, and the pur-

Source: Public Administration Review 46 (March/April 1986), pp. 97–104. Reprinted with permission from Public Administration Review © 1986 by The American Society for Public Administration, 1120 G Street, N.W., Suite 500, Washington, D.C. All rights reserved.

suit of happiness for all, just as it says in the Declaration of Independence, the Preamble to the Constitution, and the early United Nations documents we helped write. We can't accomplish this for everyone just yet, even in our own country, and anyway each people must ultimately organize its own destiny, just as we have had to do these past two centuries. But we'll continue to work at freedom for all, because it's our nation's very reason for being.

- It bugs us that we are so often out of step with the rest of the world—or they with us. It ought to be possible for us more often to be leading the self-reliant, pro-prosperity, pro-enterprise, pro-development—and, yes, pro-U.S.—tendencies in other countries. We're frustrated by finding ourselves cast, again and again, as the fall guy for every two-bit dictator—Makarios, Castro, Somoza, Khomeini, Marcos, etc., etc.—who learns how to manipulate the power of weakness.

- We're willing to use our armed forces for quick and decisive operations in limited arenas (Grenada in living memory, the shores of Tripoli in song and story), but don't ask us to hang in there by ourselves beyond all reason the way we did in Vietnam.

- We're determined to remain the world's strongest power overall. That doesn't have to be done entirely with military strength; we have all sorts of other assets to work with—our money, our food, our freedom, and the fact that most of the world's people who have to move want to come here. (Jack Paar, no foreign policy expert, said it: "Immigration is the sincerest form of flattery.") But we'll support a strong military defense too, just to make sure.

- We have a hunch that nuclear weapons are unusable except to keep the other side from using theirs: after all, we were willing to stalemate a war in Korea and lose a war in Vietnam without using them ourselves. But we want to prevent their spread just in case. We'll also maintain a "rough equivalence" with the Soviets on all this fancy weaponry and make sure of that in the future through a strong research and development effort, too—and we'll pay whatever that policy costs.

- We know by instinct that *détente* translates not as relaxation but as something more like "the continuation of tension by other means"—and that the Soviets are out there to play hardball. But we also know that there's no point in both of us having far more unusable weapons than would be needed even for all-out retaliation against each other. So we want to make this nuclear balance of power less expensive and also safer, more stable; those are two good reasons for getting on with arms control. By very large majorities, we think it would be sensible, by agreement with the Soviets, at least to freeze the production and deployment of nuclear weapons.

- We think we've got the world's best Allies and want to keep it that way. Some of them are handling their economic management better than we are, and maybe we have something to learn from them. But when it comes to the defense of NATO and the Pacific, the Europeans and the Japanese are just going to have to assume more of the responsibility. It's simply unfair for the Japanese to be spending one percent of their national product on defense and the Europeans three percent while we spend six or seven percent of ours, partly to defend them. Why should we be in the position of having to decide how much risk it's all right for them to take?

- We keep hearing experts talk about the twenty-first century as the "Pacific century," and we think there is something in that. Certainly the peoples to the west of us have made a better try at development, with help from us that was mostly *not* wasted, than other countries have.

- We're glad that it seems to be possible to get along with China these days. They're a different breed of Communists from the Soviets. They do after all have a quarter of the world's population, and they're obviously on the move, so we have to take them very seriously. We thought it was silly not to "recognize" China for so long, but we don't think it's up to us to figure out the future relationship between Taiwan and the Chinese mainland. They can work that out, or fail to work it out, between themselves.

- We are coming to realize that turbulence and resentments in the developing world, the product of rising expectations and rising frustrations, are now driving those older, more settled relationships in world politics—the U.S.-Soviet standoff and our Atlantic-Pacific alliances. We know we can't escape the task of helping keep change peaceful worldwide.

- In the Middle East, Israel's survival is a must. In the long-running fight between Israel and its Arab neighbors, we want whatever outcome the Arabs and Israelis can agree on ("Let's you and him make peace"). We'll even help the deal along, whatever it turns out to be, with aid and security guarantees.

- In Southern Africa we want the majority to rule but we also want the changeover to be peaceful. We're not about to plunge in with a solution of our own, but the situation is too dangerous for us not to be willing to mediate if necessary—and meanwhile to help educate South Africa's coming black leadership.

- Fidel Castro is a thorn in our side, but neither the Cubans nor their Russian guests are really a mortal threat to the United States of America. Much more important in this hemisphere is developing a viable relationship, in a spirit of bargaining among equals, with Canada, with Mexico, with Argentina and with Brazil, which could soon be one of the world's great economic powers. As far as the smaller countries are concerned, we want to prevent Communist inroads but we shouldn't get drawn in too deeply the way we did in Vietnam.

- We want fair trade—*free* trade seems to cost us too many jobs, so we think markets work better when they are rigged (uh, regulated by agreement). That's what most of the rest of the world seems to think, too, so we ought to get on with the bargaining. We can't seem to sell enough to foreigners to pay for their oil

and steel and small cars and microchips and color television sets, so we're obviously going to have to do something about our capacity to produce more efficiently, and cut back on the oil we get from the Arabs and others whose dependability as suppliers is uncertain. Most important, while protecting what we used to do well we're going to have to crank up what made America great: doing what nobody's ever done before, and doing it first.

- We don't even pretend to understand the international money system. But we have a hunch things would work better, without these wild ups and downs in the value of our money and the interest rates we have to pay, if the world's major trading countries, who also happen to be mostly democracies and our allies, could coordinate their economies better and relieve us of some of the trouble that comes from everybody using the U.S. dollar as *their* means of exchange and measure of value.

- We would like to see a fair shake for the world's poor and especially for the world's hungry, but we're sick and tired of foreign aid as it's presently administered. We might even go for an international campaign to get rid of the worst aspects of world poverty, or at least bring an end to hunger, by the end of this century— if our leaders can convince us that it can be done and that others will do their share. Meanwhile we will insist that the benefits of trade and aid get to the people who need them most—not just enrich the monarchs and colonels and politicians and corporations that still seem to get most of the gravy.

- We're justly proud of producing big food and feed surpluses with less than three percent of our work force—by putting modern science and American ingenuity to work on the farm. We don't think food should be used as a weapon, exactly, but it *is* a prime source of our national strength in world affairs, and we should make sure that serving as the world's residual supplier is made profitable for the American farmer.

- We're also proud of the science and technology that has learned to use outer space not only to land men on the Moon, but for worldwide human benefits—satellite communications, arms control inspection, weather forecasting, remote sensing, and keeping track of environmental risks. Global systems will have to be organized in the '80s and '90s to secure the benefits such new technologies make both possible and necessary; plenty of international cooperation will evidently be required, and U.S. leadership is going to be indispensable. (It's hard to understand why—after President Kennedy's leadership on the Apollo mission, satellite communications, and the World Weather Watch—no national political leader seized this quintessentially American torch, the exploration and human use of outer space, until President Reagan espoused the manned space station in January 1984, then followed up with the Strategic Defense Initiative ["Star Wars"] later that year.)

• Above all, we're beginning to believe in ourselves again. We picked ourselves up off the floor after Vietnam, Watergate, and a global recession and found we were still the only nation with a truly global reach. Our destiny may no longer be so manifest, but it still looks better than anyone else's. It's the job of the leaders we have elected, and will elect, to keep it that way.

III. THE CAPACITY TO COHERE

Sniffing out the "people's policy" is the crucial task of political leadership. The trouble is, the people don't tell their leaders what to *do*, exactly. The instructions are like those of the Delphic oracle, who spoke with great conviction but in riddles.

It is the task of political leadership, and in our system especially of the President, to mold this latent consensus into U.S. popular and legislative support for coherent actions that *work*—that is, actions which help make the world safe for diversity and therefore for the American people. They have to be coherent

because one of the President's key functions is to build a constitutency for the situation as a whole—as an offset to all the single-issue organizations and one-note themes (Madison called them "factions") that are so characteristic of American politics.

The U.S. Presidency is well placed to be, at one and the same time, the "coherence factor" both in U.S. policy and in international politics. The President is constitutionally responsible for conducting the nation's external relations; he is expected to initiate policies and programs, including spending programs; he can consult through dozens of channels with other national governments; and he has a modernized "bully pulpit" for timely electronic communication with masses of people at home and abroad.

There is danger in such exposure: if he acts in an *ad hoc* fashion, it will look *ad hoc*. The "people's policy" does not come with its own doctrinal glue. It must be continuously clarified, codified, programmed, budgeted, and above all articulated so that it fits together as a coherent and understandable whole—not only in the minds of speechwriters and other professional rationalizers but in the commonsense reaction of the people.

The need for coherence is not just the need to explain discrete policies in their relations to one another. It arises from the main boundary condition in international affairs: everything really is connected to everything else. It is not good enough for leaders to do good things on purpose, if they are not effectively related to each other. Examples of ad hockery abound in the several decades of history during which I have been an active participant and observer of U.S. international relations. Those I shall cite come from one Democratic administration, not because it was uniquely unstrategic in its international actions but to counter any impression that this writing by a lifelong Democrat is provoked by more recent ad hockery under Republican auspices.

Suppose a group of American political strategists had been asked to meet with President Carter in January 1977, the week after his inauguration. Suppose each member of the group had been asked what overriding foreign-policy issue should preempt most of the President's time, preoccupy the White House staff, immobilize the United States Senate, and test the prestige of the President during the first year of his term of office. Would any of them have put the Panama Canal Treaty at the top of the batting order?

How did the Canal treaties vault over SALT, China, the Middle East, unemployment, energy, health insurance, the trade deficit, the budget deficit, and the dollar's weakness to get to the head of the policy parade? I asked that question of a number of friends in Washington that season and concluded from their replies that it was not the product of strategic thinking. It was an accident.

The composite answer I derived from those interviews at the time, according to my 1978 notes, went something like this: "There was this Panama negotiation, see, and it was almost completed by the Ford Administration. We're activists, so we added a dynamic negotiator and got the treaties finished in jig time." (Six months is jig time in diplomacy.) "So what do you do with a couple of treaties that are agreed upon? You have to sign them, don't you? And once you've signed them, you can't just let them wriggle there on the President's desk. You have to send them up to the Senate for ratification, don't you?"

The Carter staff was very good at sniffing the political winds when it was traveling the campaign trail in 1975 and 1976. In 1977, immured in the White House, the same staff (that may have been part of the problem) seems not to have realized that for millions of citizens the Canal was emotionally a piece of the American flag—and that the President's political opponents would make the most of it.

The President, and our Latin American relations, were fortunate that the opposition to the treaties peaked before Christmas, so that after a pompous and boring debate the treaties squeaked through the United States Senate in March and April 1978. But wouldn't the time, the chips, and the clout that were spent so early and so lavishly on this project have been better used to get Senate action on a national energy policy and a strategic arms control agreement?

Instead, in March 1977, President Carter sent his Secretary of State to Moscow preceded by a barrage of leaks and explanations about the fundamentally new proposals for strategic arms reduction which Secretary Vance, over his own objections, was carrying in his briefcase. The Soviets predictably thought the first step should be to confirm by treaty the higher ceilings on land-based nuclear warheads and delivery systems that had been agreed upon in principle at Vladivostok in November 1974 by President Ford and Chairman Brezhnev. ("In principle" is diplomatese for "We haven't yet agreed, really, but we both have to announce *something*.") The popular consensus favoring progress in arms control had been overridden by a partisan reluctance to start by finishing an achievement on which the previous administration was deemed to hold the political copyright.

The Soviets promptly rejected the new bargaining ploy. Two years later our negotiators produced a modestly improved version of the Vladivostok deal. When this treaty, SALT II, came to the Senate for advice and consent, it was hardly surprising that some Republican opponents, relieved by White House tactics and timing of the obligation to support a Republican president's bargain, charged the U.S. negotiators with retreating from President Carter's own March 1977 bargaining position. The Soviet invasion of Afghanistan in 1980 then made it impossible to fight for ratification of SALT II—which made it all the more regrettable that something like the same deal hadn't been struck when it could have been struck, in 1977.

During the same period, it seemed to be necessary to learn by trial and error that SALT and human rights and the World Bank and the Horn of Africa are all linked together—not only out there in the real world but back here in commonsense American opinion. President Carter inherited his own campaign rhetoric, which chided Henry Kissinger for "linkage." Later, in a revealing press conference reply, he commented that he was surprised by the effect his human rights campaign had on the achievement of arms control objectives.

The international human rights theme struck so deep a chord in the American political psyche, and (when bracketed by President Carter with doing something about poverty) had such widespread appeal around the world, that it survived its clumsy launching. The speed and direction of a great wave are not much affected by the skill of the surfer who tries to ride it. But at the outset, the advocacy of human rights was all heart and no strategy. As it impacted the real world, it became a textbook example of the principle, in politics or in ethics, that there are no overriding principles. Answering a letter from Academician Sakharov produced an embarrassing flow of similar requests from less famous Soviet dissidents for reassurances on White House stationery. Insisting that American representatives use their voice and vote to restrain U.N. agencies from helping governments that torture political prisoners helped politicize international agencies which the United States had been saying should *not* be treated as political footballs.

Denying "linkage" at first, then tying Soviet African policy to the SALT negotiations, the Carter administration managed to get the worst of both worlds: It first looked naive to its domestic critics, then later looked as if it were finding an excuse to stall the SALT talks—whether because the Senate was still busy with the Canal or because we wanted to get on with cruise missile development was not clear to our would-be friends overseas.

Lacking a strategic view, the administration was often taken by surprise. When Egyptian President Anwar Sadat announced that "I will go to Jerusalem," paving the way for a separate peace between Egypt and Israel, it took the White House a couple of days to catch up with the fast break. The reaction in Iran to the hospitalization of the Shah in New York was merely the most dramatic—and, in the outcome, politically fatal—example of a tactical mistake that generated an excruciating and unnecessary crisis.

IV. THE ROLE OF RETHINKING

In the interdependent world economy it is especially evident that everything is related to everything else. With the U.S. dollar still the world's key currency, Washington's relaxed attitude during much of 1977 toward the weakening of the dollar against other currencies was hard for U.S. business people to understand, but it was easily exploited by foreign speculators. Later the administration became genuinely alarmed, but the government's bipartisan immobilism on energy policy kept the dollar hemorrhage flowing to pay for more and more oil. The belated efforts to control the money supply were the product less of

U.S. leadership than of pressure on the Federal Reserve Board from our allies, notably from those (such as Japan and the Federal Republic of Germany) which were containing their own inflation better than we were. Today, eight years later, the situation is reversed. The complaints from overseas (and from U.S. exporters) are about an unhealthily strong dollar; but the United States is still not acting effectively to harmonize economic and financial policy with its political partners around the globe.

The complexities of the world political economy—for the management of which the United States is clearly chairman of the executive committee—are such that rigid master plans and eloquent grand strategies do not prove very useful. But the support of the American people, necessary for actions by their government, does require a clear and understandable general sense of direction. The initiatives of others, rational or irrational, must be reacted to. Crises must be managed. But U.S. purposes, U.S. intentions, and U.S. limits of tolerance have to show clearly through the underbrush of tactical diplomacy.

Coherence is hard for political leaders to achieve at any time: the processes of government are fashioned for action and inhospitable to thinking, planning, and especially to asking "Why?" In consequence most of the general policy ideas, assumptions, and initiatives on which a President acts in office are developed *before* he is elected, or *outside* the precedent-bound official conformity, or both.

I have heard Henry Kissinger say that there hasn't been a new idea on arms control since the early 1960s (the Kennedy administration) or on military strategy since the late 1950s (when Kissinger was helping Nelson Rockefeller develop ideas about U.S. national security policy). The third time I heard him

say this I had an opportunity to ask whether he really meant that, in the eight years he served, in effect, as Assistant President for military strategy and arms control, no new ideas on these subjects were hatched. He cheerfully agreed: You come into public office well stocked with intellectual capital, he explained; you spend it freely, but you certainly don't add to it.

If the government must therefore depend on a flow of facts and ideas from nongovernmental thinkers, it has to be said that the flow is far from uninhibited. On national security policy especially, funds for external research are allotted mostly for studies by consultants (among them the so-called "beltway bandits") who are so dependent on government contracts that they cannot be expected to question basic assumptions. Those academic strategic analysts who don't depend on government consulting form a very thin community by comparison.

Even if the flow of independent research, fresh ideas, and discomfiting questions were without impediment, there is a more fundamental problem for policy makers in the 1980s. We have quite suddenly run out of applicable general theory on several fronts at once. Over the past decade or less, a whole range of underlying assumptions which have guided U.S. foreign policy for half a century, have turned out to be undependable as a basis for relevant action.

In economics the legacy of Lord Keynes no longer explains a business cycle in which inflation and recession are glued together in ways that public policies seem powerless to control. Conservatives to whom deficit financing used to be anathema now are willing to live with an enormous and continuing federal budget deficit which holds interest rates up, hampers U.S. exports, and impedes business recovery.

In public administration and social

policy, the New Deal era of federal initiative seems to have ended with no new sense of direction to put in its place; "more governance with less government" is the Delphic instruction from the American electorate.

Information is now the dominant resource in the economy of "advanced" countries, but this expandable, leaky, shareable resource cannot be managed with the theories and calculations that served so well in the managing of depletive resources. We do not even know how to refer to the era we live in: we call it by names that describe what went before—post-Keynesian, post-New Deal, post-industrial—which do not help explain what is and will be.

Similarly in national security policy, the military unusability of nuclear explosions and the fact that so much of the initiative in world politics now comes from turbulence and ambition in developing countries, requires a rethinking of strategic theory and national security policy. (Are we also entering the post-nuclear and post-Atlantic phases of world history?)

The puzzle for a President, and for those who would succeed him, is not merely how to tie their tactical actions and advocacies to a widely-shared conventional wisdom. It is to rethink, reformulate, and persuasively project a strategic vision for a world changing so fast that existing assumptions are almost bound to be wrong—while preserving durable values: fairness, progress, freedom, and peace.

V. THE POLITICS OF CONSENT

Whatever their differences in teaching and temperament, most Republicans and most Democrats—and most independents, too—yearn in parallel (with carefully differentiated wording) for common, if paradoxical, outcomes: better weapons and a safer world, prosperity and fairness for all (but a lion's share for Americans), peaceful settlements everywhere without involving us unduly anywhere.

But most of the levers of power to reach these goals and resolve these contradictions are not connected to the Oval Office, and the one form of power clearly reserved to the President personally to exercise—command and control of nuclear weapons—doesn't seem to be much help. Suasion and consultation and patience and unremitting diplomatic effort are the mandatory style of leadership in a leaderless world.

The perilous luxury of sudden and secret operations such as Israel's hostage snatch at the Entebbe airport in 1976 is not available to big powers except in rare and comparatively easy cases (the peacekeeping mission in the Dominican Republic, the rescue of the Mayaguez, the invasion of Grenada, the interception of the Achille Lauro hijackers). Larger or more protracted operations (the Bay of Pigs, the training of Nicaraguan *contras*) collide with the people's aversion to secrecy and revulsion at heavy-handedness that isn't successful right away.

This is one reason why U.S. presidents of whatever political hue are attracted to multilateral operations. Our defense of Europe since 1949, our response (as the main element of a United Nations Force) in Korea in 1950, our support for U.N. peacekeeping in Greece, Palestine, Kashmir, Suez and the Sinai, Lebanon, the Congo, West New Guinea, and Cyprus, all featured a multilateral framework and the involvement of contingents from several nations.

Five-thousand men, drawn from seven countries, kept watch over the Gaza Strip and the Israeli-Egyptian frontier; 20,000 men, drawn from 21 countries, patrolled and periodically fought for four years in the Congo; 6,000 men, drawn from six countries, sat on the lid in Cyprus. Each of these missions was backed by a U.S. Air Force airlift. The Congo lift in the early 1960s was (at the time) the longest and largest such operation in the history of military aviation, moving 76,000 soldiers and 14,000 tons of military cargo with high professional skill and no serious accident.

Even in Vietnam, which tragically became a made-in-America war, President Lyndon Johnson kept insisting on "many flags"—and achieved in the late '60s a presence of more non-American troops helping the South Vietnamese than we ever had in the United Nations-sponsored defense of South Korea during the early '50s. It never looked that way, because in Korea we had the enormous advantage of international legitimacy (the U.N. Security Council had blessed the operation at the very outset), whereas in Vietnam the gradual Washington-managed escalation made the war American no matter how many others joined in.

In planning the U.S. Marines' 1983–84 "peacekeeping" mission in Lebanon, the Reagan administration also wanted plenty of company. But its timid diplomacy produced a military grotesquerie: the "multinational," not *multilateral,* force turned out to be four separate contingents (from the U.K., France, Italy, and the U.S.) each responsible to its own political authorities, with no common theatre commander on the ground. When the lack of political foresight was compounded by military sloppiness (a juicy terrorist target protected by a lightly defended perimeter), the massacre of the Marines and the consequent decision to withdraw the survivors were foreordained.

In the real world, the management of peace is an exercise not in shouting or declaiming or bullying but in the politics of consent. Even in regional or narrowly functional issues, the sheer numbers of notionally sovereign actors is often quite large. In global operations (the World Weather Watch, the eradication of small pox, the tracking of epidemics, the allocation of the electro-magnetic frequency spectrum, the assignment of "parking spaces" at geostationary orbit, the development of agricultural research, the protection of data flows, the inspection of nuclear power plants, etc., etc.) there is no escaping the need for wide participation and tedious consent-building.

The multilateral imperative comes both from troubles and technologies that physically span the globe—atmospheric pollution, migrations of people (with their infectious diseases and ideas), orbiting satellites, weather balloons, information-bearing radio waves—and from the sheer number of actors in international relations.

As the number of countries rises one by one, the relationships among them grow by logarithmic leaps. It is usually a matter of simple efficiency to deal with a group of nations on whatever affects all members of the group. The 16 nations that sit around the table at the North Atlantic Council, NATO's political board of directors, would require 120 bilateral discussions to reach the consensus that can be reached in one multilateral negotiation (which, of course, may involve a good many one-on-one sessions outside the conference room or back home in capitals). A diplomacy built on bilateral relations would be like mathematics without the zero.

It is true that an enormous amount of bilateral conversation takes place between pairs of countries all over the world, and that the President conducts bilateral relations, in one form or another, with every nation in the world today: the 159 members of the United Nations and a dozen more small sovereignties which are not U.N. members. (Those we do not "recognize," such as Cuba, Albania, Outer Mongolia, Vietnam, and North Korea, our government deals with in various ways anyhow.)

But an analysis of the content of these bilateral relations reveals that most of the subjects being discussed are scheduled for decision, not between the two countries conducting the bilateral conversation, but in some multilateral forum (a U.N. agency, the North Atlantic Treaty Organization, the General Agreement on Tariffs and Trade, the Organization for Economic Cooperation and Development, the Organization of American States, the European Economic Community, the International Atomic Energy Agency, several arms-control and disarmament negotiations, the European Security Conference), in international conferences and consultations on environment, population, food, women, deserts, water, science and technology for development, the law of the sea, in the World Bank and the International Monetary Fund, and through international agreements on fishing rights, weather forecasting, Antarctica, and outer space—to mention only a few.

In the late 1960s when I had occasion to visit each U.S. mission in NATO Europe, I made a point of asking what proportion of the business on each U.S. ambassador's desk was strictly bilateral business, and what proportion was essentially bilateral conversation about business done multilaterally. My estimate at the time was that the multilateral content of bilateral diplomacy ranged between 60 and 75 percent; a British Foreign Office study at the time showed a similar result. Now, a decade and a half later, the average would likely be at the high end of that range. The United States government is represented by an official delegation at seven- or eight-hundred conferences a year—and that doesn't count the several thousand professional and private international meetings that impinge in some way on "the management of peace."

VI. THE ART OF CONSULTATION

The art of international consultation is thus central to the American presidency. If there is a general rule about consultation, it is the Golden Rule. When about to take an action affecting others, the President or other officials need to ask: how would we react if one of our friends or one of our adversaries behaved as we are about to behave without consulting us about it?

Something like this is, or has mostly been in recent history, the declaratory policy of the United States. It was expressed, for example, by Vice President Hubert Humphrey when he spoke to the North Atlantic Council on April 7, 1967:

> To put it bluntly, how do you make sure that our negotiations with the Soviets—as on disarmament, on nonproliferation, or anti-ballistic missiles—do not do violence to your vital interests?
>
> And conversely, how do we make sure that the initiatives and negotiations of our allies do not adversely affect our own vital interests and responsibilities?
>
> We have a way of safeguarding and harmonizing our interests as traffic quickens through the "open door." It is by consultation through this Council. . . .
>
> And if we follow the Golden Rule—that each of us consult as soon, as often, and as frankly as he would wish the others to consult—the Alliance will prove to be the midwife of more hopeful times.

The purpose of international consultation is not just to buy support for what we have already decided to do. The history so far of managed multilateralism suggests a more heretical notion: that by consulting with others before we have finished thinking ourselves, we force ourselves to think harder about what we are doing and why. It is comparatively easy for a President of the United States to be deluded, especially if he consults mostly with staff members and political friends most likely to agree with his (often unstated) basic premises. It is always much harder to delude friends and allies abroad: they have their own interests to look after and are not so reluctant as a President's advisers to ask the fundamental questions.

The notion that consulting with foreigners improves the quality of our own decisions is not easy to sell to Americans whose feel for foreign policy is limited to bureaucratic bargains and legislative tactics in the District of Columbia. I know because I have tried. But by finding out what others are likely to say and do, before the "domestic" bargains have been struck and our own policy has been frozen, the President secures a valuable input into his own thinking. Simply imagining what various kinds of foreigners are likely to say and do (for example by having the State Department's desk officers for the affected countries in the room) is too pale a substitute for the real thing.

Once NATO at U.S. initiative had created in the Nuclear Planning Group a forum which required that the use of tactical nuclear weapons be professionally discussed among responsible and increasingly knowledgeable Defense Ministers of allied governments, we had to think much harder ourselves about the rationale for the presence and potentials for use of tactical nuclear weapons in Europe. The original top-secret justification, in the late '50s, for placing the equivalent of 7,000 Hiroshima bombs

in Europe had been almost unbelievably thin. The result of having to explain it to skeptical peers in the '60s was dramatic: some brilliant analytical work was done in Washington, better than anything produced on the subject prior to the self-created requirement for international consultation.

"Consultation" covers a wide spectrum of activity. It includes the exchange of information, briefings, analysis, and expertise. Briefing is about all we did with our allies on the Vietnam war, and our allies in consequence felt no responsibility for the quagmire into which we had wandered. It can mean advance notification as a matter of general interest (where U.S. naval units will be visiting next), consent-building notification just before a public announcement (President Kennedy telling key European leaders about the missiles in Cuba and what we had decided to do about them), or advance discussion on national intentions (talks with friends and allies around the world before a Presidential meeting with Soviet leaders).

Toward the "harder" end of the spectrum, there is "before and during" consultation with a view to developing parallel national actions and attitudes—as was done extensively in promoting the Nuclear Non-Proliferation Treaty, and is regularly (if not always skillfully) done on peace-and-security crises and fiscal and monetary policy. And in the most serious cases, "before and during" consultation can take place with a view to genuinely collective action—the appointment of a United Nations or NATO Secretary General, the mobilization of an international peacekeeping force, the rescue of a debt-ridden developing country.

Whether to consult early or late is not subject to rule-making; the answer depends so much on what the topic is.

In general, if the consultation is "real"—in the sense that the nation starting the conversation is prepared to modify its views on the basis of the discussion it starts—the conversation should be opened as early as possible. Where something more like notification is intended, but consent is needed for a decision taken, the best practice seems to be to tell those affected about the decision before they read about it in the newspapers, but not so long before as to create the opportunity to object. (President Charles de Gaulle of France was clear about this distinction. When Dean Acheson flew to Paris in October 1962 to tell him what President Kennedy had decided to do about the Soviet missiles in Cuba, de Gaulle's first question was, "Are you informing me or consulting me?")

Most international arguments about consultation stem from a sense of surprise; and timely consultation can at least obviate the use of procedural complaints as a surrogate for substantive objections. Surprise can normally be avoided by continuously informing and consulting. But no government can assume that in early discussions of a vital issue it is ascertaining the dependable and responsible reactions of other governments. Governments, like people, seldom address policy questions until they are unavoidable.

Once in office, then, a very large part of the job description for a President of the United States is *to cohere and to consult*—to glue together in an understandable strategy the many things the U.S. government is trying to do at once to make the world safe for diversity and to decide with whom, how early, how often, and how candidly to consult about carrying it into action.

Every President in living memory has been astonished, once he has moved into the White House, to discover how much of his job is "foreign policy" (and how much of foreign policy is also "domestic" politics). Asked in a January 1984 interview with *The Washington Post* what he had learned in the White House, President Reagan replied: "I think I was surprised at how much a part of the job, that is how much . . . percentage of your time and effort and thinking is devoted to the international situation." He can say that again—and so can his successors in 1989 and beyond.

NOTES

Most of this writing was originally prepared as part of a longer paper entitled *Foreign Policy and Presidential Selection* for "The Presidential Selection Process," a 1984 Sloan Foundation Project at Vanderbilt University, Alexander Heard, Director.

* * *

22
Tower Commission Report
John Tower, Edmund Muskie, & Brent Scowcroft

PART I: INTRODUCTION

In November, 1986, it was disclosed that the United States had, in August, 1985, and subsequently, participated in secret dealings with Iran involving the sale of military equipment. There appeared to be a linkage between these dealings and efforts to obtain the release of U.S. citizens held hostage in Lebanon by terrorists believed to be closely associated with the Iranian regime. After the initial story broke, the Attorney General announced that proceeds from the arms transfers may have been diverted to assist U.S.-backed rebel forces in Nicaragua, known as Contras. This possibility enlarged the controversy and added questions not only of policy and propriety but also violations of law.

These disclosures became the focus of substantial public attention. The secret arms transfers appeared to run directly counter to declared U.S. policies. The United States had announced a policy of neutrality in the six-year-old Iran/Iraq war and had proclaimed an embargo on arms sales to Iran. It had worked actively to isolate Iran and other regimes known to give aid and comfort to terrorists. It had declared that it would not pay ransom to hostage-takers.

Public concern was not limited to the issues of policy, however. Questions arose as to the propriety of certain actions taken by the National Security Council staff and the manner in which the decision to transfer arms to Iran had

been made. Congress was never informed. A variety of intermediaries, both private and governmental, some with motives open to question, had central roles. The NSC staff rather than the CIA seemed to be running the operation. The President appeared to be unaware of key elements of the operation. The controversy threatened a crisis of confidence in the manner in which national security decisions are made and the role played by the NSC staff.

It was this latter set of concerns that prompted the President to establish this Special Review Board on December 1, 1986. The President directed the Board to examine the proper role of the National Security Council staff in national security operations, including the arms transfers to Iran. The President made clear that he wanted "all the facts to come out."

The Board was not, however, called upon to assess individual culpability or be the final arbiter of the facts. These tasks have been properly left to others. Indeed, the short deadline set by the President for completion of the Board's work and its limited resources precluded a separate and thorough field investigation. Instead, the Board has examined the events surrounding the transfer of arms to Iran as a principal case study in evaluating the operations of the National Security Council in general and the role of the NSC staff in particular.

The President gave the Board a broad

Source: Excerpted from *Report of the President's Special Review Board* (Washington, D.C.: U.S. Government Printing Office, 1987).

charter. It was directed to conduct "a comprehensive study of the future role and procedures of the National Security Council (NSC) staff in the development, coordination, oversight, and conduct of foreign and national security policy.

It has been forty years since the enactment of the National Security Act of 1947 and the creation of the National Security Council. Since that time the NSC staff has grown in importance and the Assistant to the President for National Security Affairs has emerged as a key player in national security decision-making. This is the first Presidential Commission to have as its sole responsibility a comprehensive review of how these institutions have performed. We believe that, quite aside from the circumstances which brought about the Board's creation, such a review was overdue.

The Board divided its work into three major inquiries: the circumstances surrounding the Iran/Contra matter, other case studies that might reveal strengths and weaknesses in the operation of the National Security Council system under stress, and the manner in which that system has served eight different Presidents since its inception in 1947.

During the Board's work, it received evidence concerning the role of the NSC staff in support of the Contras during the period that such support was either barred or restricted by Congress. The Board had neither the time nor the resources to make a systematic inquiry into this area. Notwithstanding, substantial evidence came before the Board.

The Board found that the issues raised by the Iran/Contra matter are in most instances not new. Every Administration has faced similar issues, although arising in different factual contexts. The Board examined in some detail the performance of the National Security Council system in 12 different crises dating back to the Truman Administration. Former government officials participating in many of these crises were interviewed. This learning provided a broad historical perspective to the issues before the Board.

Those who expect from us a radical prescription for wholesale change may be disappointed. Not all major problems—and Iran/Contra has been a major one—can be solved simply by rearranging organizational blocks or passing new laws.

In addition, it is important to emphasize that the President is responsible for the national security policy of the United States. In the development and execution of that policy, the President is the decision-maker. He is not obliged to consult with or seek approval from anyone in the Executive Branch. The structure and procedures of the National Security Council system should be designed to give the President every assistance in discharging these heavy responsibilities. It is not possible to make a system immune from error without paralyzing its capacity to act.

At its senior levels, the National Security Council is primarily the interaction of people. We have examined with care its operation in the Iran/Contra matter and have set out in considerable detail mistakes of omission, commission, judgment, and perspective. We believe that this record and analysis can warn future Presidents, members of the National Security Council, and National Security Advisors of the potential pitfalls they face even when they are operating with what they consider the best of motives. We would hope that this record would be carefully read and its lessons fully absorbed by all aspirants to senior positions in the National Security Council system.

This report will serve another

purpose. In preparing it, we contacted every living past President, three former Vice Presidents, and every living Secretary of State, Secretary of Defense, National Security Advisor, most Directors of Central Intelligence, and several Chairmen of the Joint Chiefs of Staff to solicit their views. We sought to learn how well, in their experience, the system had operated or, in the case of past Presidents, how well it served them. We asked all former participants how they would change the system to make it more useful to the President.

Our review validates the current National Security Council system. That system has been utilized by different Presidents in very different ways, in accordance with their individual work habits and philosophical predilections. On occasion over the years it has functioned with real brilliance; at other times serious mistakes have been made. The problems we examined in the case of Iran/Contra caused us deep concern. But their solution does not lie in revamping the National Security Council system.

That system is properly the President's creature. It must be left flexible to be molded by the President into the form most useful to him. Otherwise it will become either an obstacle to the President, and a source of frustration; or an institutional irrelevance, as the President fashions informal structures more to his liking.

Having said that, there are certain functions which need to be performed in some way for any President. What we have tried to do is to distill from the wisdom of those who have participated in the National Security Council system over the past forty years the essence of these functions and the manner in which that system can be operated so as to minimize the likelihood of major error without destroying the creative impulses of the President.

PART II: ORGANIZING FOR NATIONAL SECURITY

Ours is a government of checks and balances, of shared power and responsibility. The Constitution places the President and the Congress in dynamic tension. They both cooperate and compete in the making of national policy.

National security is no exception. The Constitution gives both the President and the Congress an important role. The Congress is critical in formulating national policies and in marshalling the resources to carry them out. But those resources—the nation's military personnel, its diplomats, its intelligence capability—are lodged in the Executive Branch. As Chief Executive and Commander-in-Chief, and with broad authority in the area of foreign affairs, it is the President who is empowered to act for the nation and protect its interests.

A. The National Security Council

The present organization of the Executive Branch for national security matters was established by the National Security Act of 1947. That Act created the National Security Council. As now constituted, its statutory members are the President, Vice President, Secretary of State, and Secretary of Defense. The President is the head of the National Security Council.

Presidents have from time to time invited the heads of other departments or agencies to attend National Security Council meetings or to participate as de facto members. These have included the Director of Central Intelligence (the "DCI") and the Chairman of the Joint Chiefs of Staff (the "CJCS"). The President (or, in his absence, his designee) presides.

The National Security Council deals with the most vital issues in the nation's national security policy. It is this body that discusses recent developments in arms control and the Strategic Defense Initiative; that discussed whether or not to bomb the Cambodia mainland after the *Mayaguez* was captured; that debated the timetable for the U.S. withdrawal from Vietnam; and that considered the risky and daring attempt to rescue U.S. hostages in Iran in 1980. The National Security Council deals with issues that are difficult, complex, and often secret. Decisions are often required in hours rather than weeks. Advice must be given under great stress and with imperfect information.

The National Security Council is not a decision-making body. Although its other members hold official positions in the Government, when meeting as the National Security Council they sit as advisors to the President. This is clear from the language of the 1947 Act:

> The function of the Council shall be to advise the President with respect to the integration of domestic, foreign, and military policies relating to the national security so as to enable the military services and the other departments and agencies of the Government to cooperate more effectively in matters involving the national security.

The National Security Council has from its inception been a highly personal instrument. Every President has turned for advice to those individuals and institutions whose judgment he has valued and trusted. For some Presidents, such as President Eisenhower, the National Security Council served as a primary forum for obtaining advice on national security matters. Other Presidents, such as President Kennedy, relied on more informal groupings of advisors, often including some but not all of the Council members.

One official summarized the way the system has been adjusted by different Presidents:

The NSC is going to be pretty well what a President wants it to be and what he determines it should be. Kennedy—and these are some exaggerations and generalities of course—with an anti-organizational bias, disestablished all [the Eisenhower created] committees and put a tight group in the White House totally attuned to his philosophic approach . . . Johnson didn't change that very much, except certain difficulties began to develop in the informality which was [otherwise] characterized by speed, unity of purpose, precision. So it had great efficiency and responsiveness. The difficulties began to develop in the informality of the thing.

The Nixon Administration saw a return to the use of the National Security Council as a principal forum for national security advice. This pattern was continued by President Ford and President Carter, and in large measure by President Reagan.

Regardless of the frequency of its use, the NSC has remained a strictly advisory body. Each President has kept the burden of decision for himself, in accordance with his Constitutional responsibilities.

B. The Assistant to the President for National Security Affairs

Although closely associated with the National Security Council in the public mind, the Assistant to the President for National Security Affairs is not one of its members. Indeed, no mention of this position is made in the National Security Act of 1947.

The position was created by President Eisenhower in 1953. Although its precise title has varied, the position has come to be known (somewhat misleadingly) as the National Security Advisor.

Under President Eisenhower, the holder of this position served as the principal executive officer of the Council, setting the agenda, briefing the President on Council matters, and supervising the staff. He was not a policy advocate.

It was not until President Kennedy, with McGeorge Bundy in the role, that the position took on its current form. Bundy emerged as an important personal advisor to the President on national security affairs. This introduced an element of direct competition into Bundy's relationship with the members of the National Security Council. Although President Johnson changed the title of the position to simply "Special Assistant," in the hands of Walt Rostow it continued to play an important role.

President Nixon relied heavily on his National Security Advisor, maintaining and even enhancing its prominence. In that position, Henry Kissinger became a key spokesman for the President's national security policies both to the U.S. press and to foreign governments. President Nixon used him to negotiate on behalf of the United States with Vietnam, China, the Soviet Union, and other countries. The roles of spokesman and negotiator had traditionally been the province of the Secretary of State, not of the National Security Advisor. The emerging tension between the two positions was only resolved when Kissinger assumed them both.

Under President Ford, Lt. Gen. Brent Scowcroft became National Security Advisor, with Henry Kissinger remaining as Secretary of State. The National Security Advisor exercised major responsibility for coordinating for the President the advice of his NSC principals and overseeing the process of policy development and implementation within the Executive Branch.

President Carter returned in large part to the early Kissinger model, with a resulting increase in tensions with the Secretary of State. President Carter wanted to take the lead in matters of foreign policy, and used his National Security Advisor as a source of information, ideas, and new initiatives.

The role of the National Security Advisor, like the role of the NSC itself, has in large measure been a function of the operating style of the President. Notwithstanding, the National Security Advisor has come to perform, to a greater or lesser extent, certain functions which appear essential to the effective discharge of the President's responsibilities in national security affairs.

- He is an "honest broker" for the NSC process. He assures that issues are clearly presented to the President; that all reasonable options, together with an analysis of their disadvantages and risks, are brought to his attention; and that the views of the President's other principal advisors are accurately conveyed.

- He provides advice from the President's vantage point, unalloyed by institutional responsibilities and biases. Unlike the Secretaries of State or Defense, who have substantial organizations for which they are responsible, the President is the National Security Advisor's only constituency.

- He monitors the actions taken by the executive departments in implementing the President's national security policies. He asks the question whether these actions are consistent with Presidential decisions and whether, over time, the underlying policies continue to serve U.S. interests.

- He has a special role in crisis management. This has resulted from the need for prompt and coordinated action under Presidential control, often with secrecy being essential.

- He reaches out for new ideas and initiatives that will give substance to broad Presidential objectives for national security.

- He keeps the President informed about international developments and developments in the Congress and the Executive Branch that affect the President's policies and priorities.

But the National Security Advisor remains the creature of the President. The position will be largely what he wants it to be. This presents any President with a series of dilemmas.

• The President must surround himself with people he trusts and to whom he can speak in confidence. To this end, the National Security Advisor, unlike the Secretaries of State and Defense, is not subject to confirmation by the Senate and does not testify before Congress. But the more the President relies on the National Security Advisor for advice, especially to the exclusion of his Cabinet officials, the greater will be the unease with this arrangement.

• As the "honest broker" of the NSC process, the National Security Advisor must ensure that the different and often conflicting views of the NSC principals are presented fairly to the President. But as an independent advisor to the President, he must provide his own judgment. To the extent that the National Security Advisor becomes a strong advocate for a particular point of view, his role as "honest broker" may be compromised and the President's access to the unedited views of the NSC principals may be impaired.

• The Secretaries of State and Defense, and the Director of Central Intelligence, head agencies of government that have specific statutory responsibilities and are subject to Congressional oversight for the implementation of U.S. national security policy. To the extent that the National Security Advisor assumes operational responsibilities, whether by negotiating with foreign governments or becoming heavily involved in military or intelligence operations, the legitimacy of that role and his authority to perform it may be challenged.

• The more the National Security Advisor becomes an "operator" in implementing policy, the less will he be able objectively to review that implementation—and whether the underlying policy continues to serve the interests of the President and the nation.

• The Secretary of State has traditionally been the President's spokesman on matters of national security and foreign affairs. To the extent that the National Security Advisor speaks publicly on these matters or meets with representatives of foreign governments, the result may be confusion as to what is the President's policy.

C. The NSC Staff

At the time it established the National Security Council, Congress authorized a staff headed by an Executive Secretary appointed by the President. Initially quite small, the NSC staff expanded substantially under President Eisenhower.

During the Eisenhower Administration, the NSC staff assumed two important functions: coordinating the executive departments in the development of national policy (through the NSC Planning Board) and overseeing the implementation of that policy (through the Operations Coordination Board). A systematic effort was made to coordinate policy development and its implementation by the various agencies through an elaborate set of committees. The system worked fairly well in bringing together for the President the views of the other NSC principals. But it has been criticized as biased toward reaching consensus among these principals rather than developing options for Presidential decision. By the end of his second term, President Eisenhower himself had reached the conclusion that a highly competent individual and a small staff could perform the needed functions in a better way. Such a change was made by President Kennedy.

Under President Kennedy, a number of the functions of the NSC staff were eliminated and its size was sharply reduced. The Planning and Operations Coordinating Boards were abolished. Policy development and policy implementation were assigned to individual Cabinet officers, responsible directly to the President. By late 1962 the staff was only 12 professionals, serving largely as an independent source of ideas and information to the President. The system was lean and responsive, but frequently suffered from a lack of coordination. The Johnson Administration followed much the same pattern.

The Nixon Administration returned to a model more like Eisenhower's but with something of the informality of the Kennedy/Johnson staffs. The Eisenhower system had emphasized coordination; the Kennedy-Johnson system tilted to innovation and the generation of new ideas. The Nixon system emphasized both. The objective was not interdepartmental consensus but the generation of policy options for Presidential decision, and then ensuring that those decisions were carried out. The staff grew to 50 professionals in 1970 and became a major factor in the national security decision-making process. This approach was largely continued under President Ford.

The NSC staff retained an important role under President Carter. While continuing to have responsibility for coordinating policy among the various executive agencies, President Carter particularly looked to the NSC staff as a personal source of independent advice. President Carter felt the need to have a group loyal only to him from which to launch his own initiatives and to move a vast and lethargic government. During his time in office, President Carter reduced the size of the professional staff to 35, feeling that a smaller group could do the job and would have a closer relationship to him.

What emerges from this history is an NSC staff used by each President in a way that reflected his individual preferences and working style. Over time, it has developed an important role within the Executive Branch of coordinating

policy review, preparing issues for Presidential decision, and monitoring implementation. But it has remained the President's creature, molded as he sees fit, to serve as his personal staff for national security affairs. For this reason, it has generally operated out of the public view and has not been subject to direct oversight by the Congress.

D. The Interagency Committee System

The National Security Council has frequently been supported by committees made up of representatives of the relevant national security departments and agencies. These committees analyze issues prior to consideration by the Council. There are generally several levels of committees. At the top level, officials from each agency (at the Deputy Secretary or Under Secretary level) meet to provide a senior level policy review. These senior-level committees are in turn supported by more junior interagency groups (usually at the Assistant Secretary level). These in turn may oversee staff level working groups that prepare detailed analyses of important issues.

Administrations have differed in the extent to which they have used these interagency committees. President Kennedy placed little stock in them. The Nixon and Carter Administrations, by contrast, made much use of them.

E. The Reagan Model

President Reagan entered office with a strong commitment to cabinet government. His principal advisors on national security affairs were to be the Secretaries of State and Defense, and to a lesser extent the Director of Central Intelligence. The position of the National Security Advisor was initially downgraded in both status and access to the President. Over the next six years, five different people held that position.

The Administration's first National Security Advisor, Richard Allen, reported to the President through the senior White House staff. Consequently, the NSC staff assumed a reduced role. Mr. Allen believed that the Secretary of State had primacy in the field of foreign policy. He viewed the job of the National Security Advisor as that of a policy coordinator.

President Reagan initially declared that the National Security Council would be the principal forum for consideration of national security issues. To support the work of the Council, President Reagan established an interagency committee system headed by three Senior Interagency Groups (or "SIGs"), one each for foreign policy, defense policy, and intelligence. They were chaired by the Secretary of State, the Secretary of Defense, and the Director of Central Intelligence, respectively.

Over time, the Administration's original conception of the role of the National Security Advisor changed. William Clark, who succeeded Richard Allen in 1982, was a longtime associate of the President and dealt directly with him. Robert McFarlane, who replaced Judge Clark in 1983, although personally less close to the President, continued to have direct access to him. The same was true for VADM John Poindexter, who was appointed to the position in December, 1985.

President Reagan appointed several additional members to his National Security Council and allowed staff attendance at meetings. The resultant size of the meetings led the President to turn increasingly to a smaller group (called the National Security Planning Group or "NSPG"). Attendance at its meetings was more restricted but included the statutory principals of the NSC. The

NSPG was supported by the SIGs, and new SIGs were occasionally created to deal with particular issues. These were frequently chaired by the National Security Advisor. But generally the SIGs and many of their subsidiary groups (called Interagency Groups or "IGs") fell into disuse.

As a supplement to the normal NSC process, the Reagan Administration adopted comprehensive procedures for covert actions. These are contained in a classified document, NSDD-159, establishing the process for deciding, implementing, monitoring, and reviewing covert activities.

F. The Problem of Covert Operations

Covert activities place a great strain on the process of decision in a free society. Disclosure of even the existence of the operation could threaten its effectiveness and risk embarrassment to the Government. As a result, there is strong pressure to withhold information, to limit knowledge of the operation to a minimum number of people.

These pressures come into play with great force when covert activities are undertaken in an effort to obtain the release of U.S. citizens held hostage abroad. Because of the legitimate human concern all Presidents have felt over the fate of such hostages, our national pride as a powerful country with a tradition of protecting its citizens abroad, and the great attention paid by the news media to hostage situations, the pressures on any President to take action to free hostages are enormous. Frequently to be effective, this action must necessarily be covert. Disclosure would directly threaten the lives of the hostages as well as those willing to contemplate their release.

Since covert arms sales to Iran played such a central role in the creation of this Board, it has focused its attention in large measure on the role of the NSC staff where covert activity is involved. This is not to denigrate, however, the importance of other decisions taken by the government. In those areas as well the National Security Council and its staff play a critical role. But in many respects the best test of a system is its performance under stress. The conditions of greatest stress are often found in the crucible of covert activities.

CHAPTER IX

The President as Party Leader

There is no provision in the American Constitution for political parties. Indeed, the founders felt that parties were not only unnecessary, but undesirable. They were disdainful of political parties as divisive forces which would undermine national unity and would subvert republican government. Importantly, the founders felt that the president should be apartisan and avoid association with any factions or parties that might develop in the nation.[1]

George Washington, one of the delegates at the Constitutional Convention and the first president, was opposed to parties. In his Farewell Address of September 17, 1796, he said, in part:

> Let me . . . warn you in the most solemn manner against the baneful effects of the spirit of party, generally. The alternate domination of one faction over another, sharpened by the spirit of revenge natural to party dissension, which in different ages and countries has perpetrated the most horrid enormities, is itself a frightful despotism. But . . . sooner or later the chief of some prevailing faction, more able or more fortunate than his competitors, turns this disposition to the purposes of his own elevation, on the ruins of public liberty . . . the common and continual mischiefs of the spirit of party are sufficient to make it the interest and duty of a wise people to discourage and restrain it.[2]

George Washington thus lived up to the apartisan presidential role envisioned by the founders.[3]

Not only did the founders envision an apartisan president, they constructed a Constitution with arrangements that made exceedingly difficult presidential leadership of, and cooperation with, a political party. Separation of powers dividing the three national branches of government and federalism making for a persistent localism have inhibited the development of strong national parties. Indeed, the two major parties often look as if they were each a hundred and two parties (two for each of the states and the District of Columbia).[4] In short, the existing structures and linkages of the national and state parties are "antipresidential."[5]

Despite the constitutional arrangements, and the occupation of the presidency first by an antiparty president, the party system has become thoroughly established as a political institution, despite continuing debates over its usefulness.[6] It was President Thomas Jefferson who built the first national political party and used it to secure his election to the presidency in 1800. More than any of the early presidents, Jefferson saw the party as the essential ingredient of majority rule and he governed through it.[7] Under Jefferson, party and party leadership flourished.

In the early 1800s presidential nominations were made by congressional parties. After 1828 presidential nominations were made by national conventions. However, delegates to these national conventions were selected in local, district, and state caucuses where party leaders had a good deal of clout to determine who would represent the party at the national convention. Thus, would-be presidents had to build an electoral coalition with governors, state chairmen, mayors, and other state and local party leaders who could appoint delegates to the national convention. The building of an effective electoral coalition was tantamount to building an effective governing coalition.

By the end of the century, corruption in state and local politics led reformers to push for measures which would put an end to party bosses and the politics of "smoke-filled rooms." Their major strategy for eliminating boss control was the direct primary. The adoption of the direct primary for state and local offices led to the adoption of a primary for presidential races.[8] Many of these primaries were, until the 1960s, merely beauty contests (nonbinding preference polls) which gave the voters in each state a chance to express their preference for a candidate for the presidency. Party leaders, while under increasing pressure to heed the preference polls, could still determine, in the main, who would serve as delegates to a national convention.

The party reforms of the 1970s, especially in the Democratic party but to some extent in the Republican party as well, and fundamental changes in mass electoral behavior altered all this. Among the party reforms which resulted in less presidential reliance on the parties were:

a. the new campaign financing laws for both parties[9]

b. the requirement that 75 percent of the Democratic delegates be selected in primaries

c. the requirement that delegates be bound or pledged to the candidate who won in the primary

d. the abolition of the winner-take-all primary, making it possible for even the lowest vote getters to win some delegates and

e. the increased use of direct primaries for both parties.

The fundamental changes in mass electoral behavior that reduced presidents' reliance on the parties include:[10]

a. the decline in party identification by large numbers of voters in the electorate

b. the large increase in the numbers of persons calling themselves independents and

c. the increase in split-ticket voting.

Finally, presidential candidates and elected presidents have access to resources not afforded premodern candidates and presidents. These include:

a. ready access to the electronic media permitting them to speak directly to the people and

b. the availability of large personal staffs that can and do perform for the candidates functions which previously were the responsibility of national party committees.[11]

But, if the president does not rely on the party, neither does the party rely on the president. In this regard, Richard Pious has written that presidents, when it comes to congressional campaigns, cannot control nominations, campaign financing, advertising, polling, and local party organizations—all important elements in a successful congressional career.[12] Also Bert Rockman has concluded that "members of Congress can emphasize constituency tending at the price of undermining support for a president of their own party."[13]

If party identification has little significance and a presidential candidate or elected president is in reality on his own in the political arena, does he rise above party or rely upon it, however weak and tenuous his relationship to it may be? Does having his own independent constituency, as Theodore J. Lowi says the data confirm, require him to be apartisan?[14]

Austin Ranney thinks that the gap between the president and the Congress requires him to adopt a nonpartisan stance. Ranney considers those factors that constrain as well as facilitate a president's ability to function as the leader of the party in Congress, with emphasis on the former.

The president is constrained and must be nonpartisan because the presidential and congressional parties are separate, because the president has no significant role to play in the selection of the party's congressional candidates, because the president's coattails are usually not long enough for members of Congress to ride to reelection, and because on almost any issue the president needs support from the opposition party, as well.[15]

Importantly, Ranney notes, presidential leadership of his party in Congress is further constrained by the way in which candidates win nomination: no longer do they make deals with state and local party leaders, including members of Congress, for delegate votes; they win these votes through party primaries based on personal appeal to the voters.[16] Having developed no electoral coalition with quid pro quos that would facilitate a governing coalition, the president owes the party leaders in Congress nothing and they, in turn, owe him nothing.

Ranney finds that twentieth-century presidents, on a partisan scale with zero at one end for the least partisan presidents and 100 at the other for the most partisan presidents, earned an average partisan score of 33.3. Presidents, he concludes, are not very partisan and should not be:[17] their roles as party chiefs simply do not overcome the chasm between the president and Congress created by the separation of powers. Ranney's complete analysis, "The President and His Party," is reprinted here.

Roger Brown and David Welborn are not so sanguine that a president should be nonpartisan. They examine the party-related activities of presidents since 1961 and find that despite the well-known reasons for a weak presidency in the party leadership role, presidents have been successful in doing some noteworthy party chores. They cite presidential activity in fencemending among warring party factions, presidential fundraising for the party, presidential campaigning for fellow party members and presidential appointments to office of persons from the president's party, as examples of presidential attention to party affairs. Using a bidimensional concept of party activity with party leadership constituting one dimension and partisanship constituting the second dimension, the authors determine that John Kennedy and Gerald Ford were strong in both dimensions, that Lyndon Johnson and Jimmy Carter were weak in both dimensions, and that Richard Nixon was weak in leading his party, but was, nonetheless, strongly partisan.

Brown and Welborn conclude that this continuing variability in a president's party relationship suggests that many traditional linkages persist between president and party and that in a more problematic and uncertain political environment, greater presidential attention to party affairs may be the appropriate path to take. Their essay, "Presidents and Their Parties: Performance and Prospects," is reprinted here.

NOTES

1. See Joseph Parker and Edward N. Kearny, "The President and Political Parties," in *Dimensions of the Modern Presidency*, ed. Edward N. Kearny (St. Louis, Mo.: Forum Press, 1981), p. 81.

2. John Mabry Mathews and Clarence Arthur Berdahl, *Documents and Readings in American Government: National and State* (New York: Macmillan, 1940), p. 133.

3. See Louis W. Koenig, *The Chief Executive*, 4th ed. (New York: Harcourt Brace Jovanovich, 1981), p. 124.

4. See Bert Rockman, *The Leadership Question: The Presidency and the Political System* (New York: Praeger Publishers, 1984), pp. 60, 64.

5. Richard M. Pious, *The American Presidency* (New York: Basic Books, 1979), p. 121.

6. Everett Carll Ladd, Jr., for example, argues that since recent presidents have been elected as a result of personal rather than party appeal, political parties are unnecessary for the election process. See his *Transformations of the American Party System* (New York: W. W. Norton, 1975), pp. 14–19.

7. See James MacGregor Burns, *Presidential Government: The Crucible of Leadership* (Boston: Houghton Mifflin, 1965), pp. 28–29; 110–12 for his Jeffersonian model of the presidency.

8. For a history of the development of presidential primaries, see James W. Davis, *Presidential Primaries: Road to the White House* (New York: Thomas Y. Crowell, 1967), pp. 24–41.

9. Joshua Sandman argues that the party organization, *not* the political action committee or independent spending on the part of the individuals or candidates, should finance essential services to the candidate running under the party's banner. See his "The Reemerging Role of the Political Party: Campaign '84 and Beyond," *Presidential Studies Quarterly* 14, no. 4 (Fall 1984), p. 516.

10. Theodore Lowi's four dimensions of the president's personal, mass constituency, which he asserts have contributed to the decline of party, overlap the arguments made here.

See his *The Personal Presidency: Power Invested, Promise Unfulfilled* (Ithaca, N.Y.: Cornell University Press, 1985), p. 79.

11. On this point see Roger G. Brown, "Party and Bureaucracy: From Kennedy to Reagan," *Political Science Quarterly* 97, no. 2 (Summer 1982), pp. 280, 287, 290, 291.

12. Richard M. Pious, *American Politics and Government* (New York: McGraw-Hill, 1986), p. 333.

13. Rockman, *Leadership Question*, p. 62.

14. Lowi, *Personal Presidency*, p. 85.

15. For a concurring view on this point, see Koenig, *Chief Executive*, p. 125.

16. Jeane Kirkpatrick writes on a confirming note that the single most important fact about the presidency is the inability of either major party to control the nomination for that office. See her *Dismantling the Parties: Reflections on Party Reform and Party Decomposition* (Washington, D.C.: American Enterprise Institute, 1979), p. 2.

17. Interestingly, Lowi, *Personal Presidency*, p. 85 finds that partisanship remains a significant force in many local elections, but the farther upward toward the governorship and presidency, the less stable and consistent partisanship tends to be. Parker and Kearny, *President and Parties*, p. 82 note that partisanship is a function of phases in the life cycle of a candidate-cum-president. Partisanship is highest, they argue, in the nomination or renomination phase, declines some during the election phase when one needs the support of independent voters, and declines even further after the election when the task of governing begins.

23
The President and His Party
Austin Ranney

The basic problem of American government is finding and perfecting institutions that will enable the president to lead Congress with maximum effectiveness.

In the opinion of many analysts over the years, one of the most promising devices stems from the fact that every president since George Washington has been a member of the political party to which many members of Congress— ideally majorities in both chambers— also belong. Moreover, the president is not just an ordinary member of his party.

He is its leader, and he can and should use his party leadership as a way—perhaps the most effective way—of inducing Congress to adopt his programs.

The most forceful presentation of those ideas was made by Woodrow Wilson in his *Constitutional Government in the United States*, published in 1908 when he was still an academic political scientist. As Wilson summed it up:

[The president] is the party nominee and the only party nominee for whom the whole nation votes. . . . He can dominate his party by being spokesman for

Source: Both Ends of the Avenue, edited by Anthony King (Washington, D.C.: American Enterprise Institute, 1985). Excerpted material reprinted with permission of the American Enterprise Institute.

the real sentiment and purpose of the country, by giving direction to opinion, by giving the country at once the information and the statements of policy which will enable it to form its judgments alike of parties and of men. . . . He may be both the leader of his party and the leader of the nation, or he may be one or the other. If he can lead the nation, his party can hardly resist him.[1]

In this article I consider how well Woodrow Wilson's description fits the presidencies of Ronald Reagan and his immediate predecessors. I then outline the extent to which recent presidents' copartisans in Congress have been faithful followers of presidential leadership. I conclude by trying to estimate how important the president's role as head of his party is in his efforts to lead the government.

THE PRESIDENT AS THE LEADER OF HIS PARTY

Senses in Which He Is the Leader

According to the *Oxford English Dictionary*, a leader is "one who guides others in action and opinion; one who takes the lead in any business, enterprise, or movement; one who is followed by disciples or adherents. The foremost or most eminent member."[2] Clearly, the president's party leadership has some of these qualities more than others. Let us briefly examine each.

The Party's Most Eminent Member. The president of the United States is clearly the country's most eminent citizen. He holds its highest public office, which combines the symbolic and ceremonial functions of chief of state and the political and administrative powers of head of government. He is the first political object that children perceive as they begin to learn about government; for a while he is just about

the only part of government they perceive clearly, and most adults know more about him and what he does than they know about any congressman or Supreme Court justice.

The president is also a partisan, even if, like Dwight Eisenhower, he has had little previous public association with his party. He has fought through the state primaries, caucuses, and conventions of the party; he has been nominated for the office by its national convention; he has appeared before the convention to accept the nomination; and he participates often in a variety of party affairs—speaking at fundraising dinners, campaigning on behalf of party candidates for other offices, meeting with the party's national chairman and committee, and so on.

Accordingly, since the president is clearly the country's most eminent citizen and equally clearly a member of a political party, he is, by definition, that party's most eminent member. If he is widely regarded as an especially good president, he adds luster to the party's name as well, as Franklin Roosevelt did in the 1930s. By the same token, if he is seen to be an especially corrupt president, as Richard Nixon was in the early 1970s, or an especially weak one, as Jimmy Carter was in the late 1970s, some of the tarnish on him can rub off on his party. For this reason, if for no other, all his fellow partisans hope that their president's reputation will prosper.

Leader of the National Committee. The president has no formal role in his party's national committee. Yet his informal control over its leaders and activities is nearly total. At any time from the moment he wins his party's nomination to the day he leaves office he need only pass the word about whom he wants as national chairman to the national committee, and the committee will promptly elect his choice, usually without dissent. Moreover, presidents typically want the chairman to be the president's man rather than the committee's man with a constituency of his own.

Two recent examples illustrate the point. In 1975 Robert Strauss, one of the most successful and popular Democratic national chairmen of recent times, appointed the Commission on the Role and Future of the Presidential Primaries, a small group chaired by Morley Winograd, Democratic state chairman of Michigan, and charged it with studying the causes and consequences of the proliferation of presidential primaries since 1968. On January 6, 1977, Jimmy Carter "recommended" that Kenneth W. Curtis, the former governor of Maine, replace Strauss, and the Democratic National Committee duly ratified the president's choice on January 21. The committee also renamed the Winograd Commission the Commission on Presidential Nomination and Party Structure, nearly doubled its membership, and appointed faithful Carter supporters, including Rick Hutcheson, a White House aide, and Pat Caddell, Carter's pollster, to the new slots. The whole point was to make sure that the commission did not exercise its enlarged mandate to review the party's national convention delegate selection rules in any way that might make Carter's renomination more difficult in 1980, and the commission's report, published in 1978, showed that the administration's strategy had worked splendidly. Nevertheless, rumors persisted that the White House felt that Curtis's leadership could have been a good deal more vigorous, and on December 7 Curtis announced his intention to resign from what he described as "this lousy job." On December 28 Carter "recommended" John C. White, his deputy secretary of agricul-

ture, for the job, and on January 27, 1978, the national committee ratified the choice.

In many respects the Republican case is even more striking. On January 14, 1977, with Gerald Ford about to leave the White House, the Republican National Committee conducted one of the most open and hotly contested elections for a national chairman in its history. The two leading contenders (there were five in all) were Bill Brock, the former senator from Tennessee who had lost his seat in the 1976 election, and Richard Richards, the Republican state chairman of Utah. Brock had supported Ford in the close and sometimes bitter contest for the party's 1976 presidential nomination, and Richards had supported Ronald Reagan. Hence Ford's supporters now backed Brock for the chairmanship, and Reagan's supporters backed Richards. After three ballots Brock won a close victory.

In the next three years Brock became one of the most active, successful, and respected national chairmen in history. This is not the place to recount his achievements in detail, but they included the active recruitment of promising candidates for Congress and state legislatures, the conduct of "schools" on campaign organization and techniques for those candidates, the support of their campaigns in 1978 and 1980 with money and materials, national party provision of and financial support for directors of organizational development in the state parties, the development of REPNET (a national program of computer services, including mailing lists of potential donors, political targeting, survey processing, and the like, all made available to state parties at a minimum charge), a Local Elections Campaign Division devoted to winning more state legislative seats, and a lively new journal of ideas called *Common Sense.* Most observers gave Brock's leadership a great deal of the credit for the party's gains in the 1978 and 1980 elections for Congress and for the state legislatures.[3]

Despite Brock's achievements, however, many of Ronald Reagan's inner circle of advisers still considered that his 1976 opposition to Reagan and his moderate policy views showed that he was not a true Reagan man. In June 1980, a month before the Republican convention but well after Reagan had the nomination locked up, these advisers urged Reagan to ask Brock to step down immediately. Reagan finally decided against this move, but the convention adopted a new rule providing that "the chairman, co-chairman and all other officers except the chairman should be elected immediately following the National Convention 1980, and *in January of each odd numbered year thereafter.*"[4] Brock was duly reelected in July—though Drew Lewis, Reagan's campaign chairman in Pennsylvania and later secretary of transportation, was also elected as deputy chairman and "chief operating officer." And in January 1981 Reagan gave his backing to Richard Richards, who was duly elected by the national committee. (As a reward for his past services, Brock was named to a post formerly held by Robert Strauss— U.S. trade representative, with the rank of ambassador.) There could hardly be a clearer example of the president's dominance over his party's national committee and the choice of the national chairman. He takes the lead. He calls the tune.

Initiation of the Party's Policies. American political parties have two kinds of party policies, and the president or the presidential candidate takes the lead in initiating both kinds. One kind consists of the policies advocated by an incumbent president. By simple virtue of the fact that they are his policies, they are generally referred to in the news media and in political conversation as his party's policies. This does not mean, of course, that all his party's members in Congress—or, for that matter, in the national committee and in the state and local party organizations—support the president's policies. It only means that there is no other party official or agency that claims to have a voice in setting the party's policies that is equal or superior to the president's. The party out of power, as we shall observe below, is in quite a different position.

The other kind of policies that American parties are said to have are those set forth in the platforms they adopt at their quadrennial conventions. Some commentators dismiss the platforms as collections of ritual endorsements of policies on which nearly everyone agrees and paperings-over of issues on which there is widespread and bitter dispute. The fact is, however, that most convention delegates and party leaders—including presidents running for reelection—take the platforms quite seriously, for they perform two significant functions. The first is the external function of appealing to as many voters, and offending as few, as possible. The second—and, in recent years, more important—is the internal function of helping to unite the party's various factions behind the ticket so that they will support it enthusiastically.

Any incumbent president who, like Richard Nixon in 1972 or Jimmy Carter in 1980, has the nomination clearly in hand also has to control what goes into and what is excluded from the party platform. In both parties the platform-writing process is administered by the national committee, and in 1980 most members of the Democratic platform committee held their first hearings in March, five months before the national convention assembled. They finished the first draft of the platform in mid-June, two months before the convention. Since the president dominates the national committee, he is bound to dominate the writing of the platform. But if he faces a disgruntled minority whose support he badly needs to win reelection, as Jimmy Carter did with the Edward Kennedy faction in 1980, then he is well advised to do what Carter did: let them have their way over almost anything in the platform about which they feel strongly, barring only direct and explicit repudiations of policies his administration has pursued or the endorsement of policies (in this case wage and price controls) to which he is unalterably opposed. In 1980 the Democratic convention adopted a new rule, backed by the Kennedy forces, to the effect that, after the platform has been adopted, all the presidential candidates must state in writing what differences they have with it and must pledge to carry it out despite those differences. But Carter finessed the matter by issuing a statement that neither flatly rejected nor explicitly embraced the Kennedy amendments that had been added to the Carter-dominated platform. The upshot is that a Republican president's control over his party's platform is as strong as ever and, although a Democratic president's control may not be quite as strong, he retains most of the initiative in its drafting and a substantial if not absolute veto over its contents.

It is arguable, of course, that American political parties do not have party policies in the sense that parties in most other democratic countries do—that is, a series of proposals for government action that are (1) developed by party agencies, (2) set forth in official party pronouncements, and (3) supported by nearly all of the party's elected public officials nearly all of the time. Both the president's policies and the presidential-candidate-dominated party platforms satisfy the first two conditions, but the third condition raises the most serious questions about what it means to say that the president is the leader of his party.

Senses in Which He Is Not the Leader

The Separation of Party Organizations. When we speak of Jimmy Carter as leader of the Democratic party or Ronald Reagan as leader of the Republican party, we speak as though each party were, like most parties in other democratic countries, a single organizational entity with a hierarchical structure headed by the president. American parties, however, are not like that. Organizationally speaking, the "presidential parties" are quite separate from the "congressional parties," a separation which stems from and fully reflects the constitutional separation of powers between the two branches of government. The core of each party's presidential party is its national committee and national convention, and the Democratic party charter adopted in 1974 adds a few auxiliary agencies, such as a midterm delegate conference, a judicial council, a national finance council, and a national education and training council. As we have seen, the president certainly leads his party's presidential party.

Each party also has a full party organization in each house of Congress, the principal agencies being a party conference or caucus, a policy or steering committee, a research organization or committee, a campaign committee, a whip, a floor leader, and, in the majority party only, a Speaker of the House and a president pro tempore of the Senate.

The congressional parties play a number of important roles, especially in the appointment of committee and subcommittee chairmen and members and in the organization and allocation of the two chambers' time. But the president of the United States certainly does not take the lead in their affairs, and in many important respects he stands entirely outside them.

Most important, the president plays no role in the selection of his party's candidates for either house of Congress. They are all chosen in their districts or states by direct primary elections. The president may on rare occasions encourage someone to run in a particular primary, but he cannot prevent anyone else from running; he rarely supports one candidate over another; and, even when presidents have done so, presidentially supported candidates have lost more often than they have won.[5] Unlike the leaders of most democratic parties, then, the president has no power to ensure the nomination of a particularly desirable candidate for the House or Senate or to veto the nomination of a particularly undesirable candidate.

It works the other way as well. Congressmen and senators in both parties from 1972 to 1980 had almost no influence on the presidential nominating process. About 74 percent of the delegates to the national conventions were chosen in state presidential primaries. Congressional endorsements had little or no effect on the outcome of those primaries, and no presidential nominee bothered much to seek such endorsements. Congressmen and senators had lost the automatic delegate slots that used to be reserved for many of them at the national convention, and only very small fractions of the congressional parties even bothered to attend the conventions.

After 1980 the Democratic party made some effort to alter this situation. The new national chairman, Charles Manatt, appointed a commission, chaired by Governor James B. Hunt, Jr. of North Carolina, to recommend changes in the rules for selecting national convention delegates. In 1982 the Hunt commission recommended, among other things, that up to two-thirds of the party's senators and representatives, chosen by their respective congressional caucuses, be made delegates to the 1984 convention without being required to pledge in advance their support for a particular presidential aspirant.

This may restore some congressional voice in the selection of Democratic presidential candidates, but it will not materially improve congressmen's chances of winning the nomination. The special requirements of the presidential nominating process will still demand full-time campaigning for two years or more before the election year, especially in preparation for the early and crucial Iowa caucuses and New Hampshire primary; no prominent or conscientious senator or representative can afford so much time, and the failure of Representative Morris Udall and Senator Henry Jackson in 1976 and of Senator Howard Baker and Senator Edward Kennedy in 1980 suggests that Congress is no longer a desirable—or perhaps even a viable—base from which to run for president.[6] In short, members of Congress have about as little power over whom their party nominates for the presidency as the president has over whom his party nominates for the House and Senate. The consequences that Richard Neustadt pointed out in 1960 are even stronger and clearer in the 1980s:

> What the Constitution separates our political parties do not combine. The parties are themselves composed of separated organizations sharing public authority. The authority consists of nominating powers.

Our national parties are confederations of state and local party institutions, with a headquarters that represents the White House, more or less, if the party has a President in office. These confederacies manage presidential nominations. All other public offices depend upon electorates confined within the states. All other nominations are controlled within the states. The President and congressmen who bear one party's label are divided by dependence upon different sets of voters. The differences are sharpest at the stage of nomination. The White House has too small a share in nominating congressmen, and Congress has too little weight in nominating Presidents for party to erase their constitutional separation. Party links are stronger than is frequently supposed, but nominating processes assure the separation.[7]

After a president is elected, he has little to say about, and even less influence on, the selection of his party's leaders in Congress. I am unable to find any verified instance in which a president has tried to get a Speaker or floor leader or whip removed. Occasionally a president or a president-elect has expressed support for a congressional party leader whose position is in some jeopardy, but even that is rare, and congressmen strongly resent such outside interference in their affairs. Shortly after his election in 1980, Ronald Reagan announced that he endorsed the reelection of Howard Baker (Republican, Tennessee), who was under some fire for being too moderate, as Republican leader in the Senate, but also announced that his old friend and campaign chairman Senator Paul Laxalt (Republican, Nevada) would be the only member of Congress to be included in his "super-cabinet"— his inner circle of advisers. That promised to make for a novel and instructive set of relations among the three men.

The Threadbare Coattails. There was a time when observers believed that many of the presidential party's representatives and senators would follow the president's lead because they hoped to "ride his coattails" to reelection. They knew, so the argument ran, that most voters voted straight party tickets, with the result that congressmen's electoral destinies depended largely on the popularity of the man at the head of the ticket. It was therefore very much in the congressmen's interests to help the president make the kind of record in office that would sweep the whole ticket to victory. A smart president could convert this feeling into a powerful weapon in several ways. For one, he could threaten to withhold his endorsement from any fellow partisan in Congress who failed to support his programs. For another, he could make the argument that he and his fellow party members were all in the same electoral boat and would sink or sail together, so it behooved Democrats (or Republicans) at both ends of Pennsylvania Avenue to build a party legislative record that would carry them all to victory.

A number of political scientists have studied this presumed "coattail effect," some by using sample survey techniques and others by analyzing comparative election returns. They have generally concluded that, whether or not presidential coattails were ever important in reelecting congressmen, they had little or no significance in the 1970s and are likely to have even less in the 1980s. There appear to be many reasons for the unraveling of the coattails, but those mentioned most often are the decreasing number of competitive districts and the increasing campaigning resources and electoral security of incumbent representatives (senators appear to be a different matter). In short, a president running for reelection these days leads his party's ticket only in the sense that he is its best-known candidate, not in the sense that the electoral fate of his party's congressional candidates depends heavily on how well or how badly he does.[8]

Moreover, presidents in the 1980s control almost no party resources that congressmen count on in their campaigns for reelection. Because of the low ceilings imposed upon the expenditures of presidential campaign organizations by the Federal Campaign Finance Act amendments of 1974, most presidents are now reluctant to campaign jointly with their party's congressional candidates lest some of the latters' activities and expenditures be charged against the presidential campaign's limits. The national committees' limited campaign funds are spent mainly on the presidential campaigns, although in 1980 the Republican committee spent a lot on a general campaign for the party's presidential *and* congressional candidates. "Vote Republican—for a Change!" Indeed, the national committees' historical focus on presidential campaigns was the main reason for the creation of the two parties' congressional and senatorial campaign committees in 1866, and it has continued to sustain their independence from the national committees ever since.

The fact that the president now controls so few of the resources needed by congressmen leads one to ask, Does it really matter to most congressmen whether the president is of their party? The answer appears to be, Yes, but not as much as it used to. For one thing, most congressmen still have some sense of belonging to one of two teams engaged in a continuing series of contests, and their team loyalties generally make them prefer their man to win over the other team's. For another thing, their party's candidate is likely to have more policy positions similar to their own than the

other party's candidate. For still another, senatorial courtesy—the de facto power of a state's senior senator to have a controlling voice in the selection of federal judges and other federal appointees to serve in his state—operates only with a president of one's own party, not with an opposition president. But most congressmen now feel, as they did not a generation ago, that their own electoral fortunes depend little or not at all on how well or how badly their party's presidential candidate does at the polls.

Building Presidential Coalitions

He becomes the leader of his party only when he wins its presidential nomination, and he continues only if he wins the election. As president he can try to cobble together a different coalition for each issue that comes along, and even the most ineffective presidents can manage a few such coalitions. But things are likely to go much better on many more issues if he can somehow build a relatively strong and enduring coalition that will provide him with ideas and support for most of the problems he must face.

Before the 1970s many presidents of both parties began to build their governing coalitions in the course of winning their party's nomination. They and their lieutenants met with a number of congressmen, governors, mayors, state chairmen, and other state and local party leaders who had the power to appoint significant numbers of delegates to the national conventions and therefore the power to "deliver" their votes to whichever presidential aspirant they chose. In "cutting deals" with these leaders for their support, presidential aspirants had to make promises—cabinet appointments and lesser patronage appointments to persons named by the party leaders, pledges to press for certain policies and oppose others, even commitment to a particular person as the vice-presidential nominee. The main object of these negotiations was to win delegate votes, but they also had a side benefit; the president-to-be got to know well many of the people who would be important to him when he took office, and consequently the process of building his nominating coalition was an important foundation for the subsequent process by which he built his governing coalition.

That is no longer the case. The "reforms" of the presidential nominating process since 1968 were intended mainly to strip party "bosses" and "power brokers" of their power to name delegates, and they succeeded brilliantly. By 1980 about 74 percent of the delegates to the conventions were chosen by presidential primaries, not by party leaders. Moreover, almost all of those delegates were chosen because they supported a presidential candidate who had done well in their state's primary, not because of their personal service to or eminence in the party and certainly not because they had been hand-picked by some state or local party leader. In addition, each party's elected public officials have been largely cut out of the presidential nominating process, and few of them now even attend the national conventions or serve as delegates (the proposals of the Hunt commission, noted above, may change this for the Democrats).

The net effect of these changes has been to separate completely the process of building the coalition needed for nomination from the process of building the coalition needed for governing. In the 1980s presidential nominations are not won by making a series of deals with powerful state and local party leaders and congressmen; indeed, an aspirant is actually handicapped by being known as the bosses' candidate, even though the bosses no longer have power to ad-

vance the cause of any candidate. Presidential nominations are instead won by tireless personal campaigning by the candidate in the smaller caucus/convention and primary states and by elaborate television campaigns in the larger primary states. The winner has little or no contact with his party's leaders in Congress and owes them nothing for his victory. By the same token, they owe him nothing. Accordingly, when a president takes office in the 1980s, he has to build his governing coalition from scratch, for nothing in the way he has won either the nomination or the election has created a network of mutual obligations with his party's leaders and organizations in Congress and in the states on which he can base his new coalition. Hence his effectiveness as a leader of his fellow party members in Congress depends on their willingness to follow—and that is quite a different matter.

CONGRESSIONAL FOLLOWING OF THE PRESIDENT'S LEAD

Presidential Support Scores

Since the early 1950s the *Congressional Quarterly* has been keeping track of "presidential support" scores expressing the extent to which the various members of Congress have supported the president on those roll-call votes in which he has indicated a clear preference for a particular vote. The average scores from 1953 to 1978 are summarized in Table 1. They show clearly that each party's members in each house of Congress have supported presidents of their own party about two-thirds of the time and presidents of the opposing party less than half the time.

These data, however, are not conclusive evidence that members of Congress follow their president's lead most of the

TABLE 1 · AVERAGE PRESIDENTIAL SUPPORT SCORES BY PARTY,
1953–1978

	Percentage of Roll-Call Votes Supporting the President's Position	
Chamber	**Democrats**	**Republicans**
With Democratic presidents in office		
House	69	40
Senate	62	45
With Republican presidents in office		
House	46	64
Senate	44	66

Source: Edwards, *Presidential Influence*, pp. 61–62.

time, for they might merely indicate that the congressmen are voting their own convictions, which often happen to agree with those of their parties' presidents. Several studies have attempted to overcome this difficulty by seeing whether congressmen's policy stands change noticeably when a president of the opposite party is replaced by one of their own party. They have found that to some degree such changes do take place. For example, about one-fifth of the Republicans in both chambers who had been voting consistently against foreign-aid bills proposed by Democratic presidents shifted to support similar bills when they were proposed by Republican presidents—and about the same proportion of the Democrats in both chambers shifted their votes in the opposite direction. Another study found that Republican congressmen support activist federal domestic policies more often when they are proposed by Republican presidents than when they are proposed by Democratic presidents, while Democratic congressmen's support of such policies remains about the same regardless of whether the president is a Democrat or a Republican.[9]

Presidential Party Leadership in Competition with Other Factors in Congressional Voting

Students of Congress generally agree that a number of factors influence congressional voting. One is the congressman's own convictions. Another is his perceptions of the needs of his constituency and the views of his constituents. And a third, often overlooked but still of considerable importance, is his identification with his party and his desire to support it whenever he can. As Randall Ripley says of members of the House:

Most members . . . think of party before they think of anything else, particularly at the stage of voting on the floor. Even if a member often votes against his party, he is still concerned with retaining the good will of the leaders and members. His friends are likely to be in his own party, and he knows that he can jeopardize his standing with some of them unless he is willing to stretch a point and occasionally help the party, even though he may feel somewhat differently about the issue. Only a handful act almost independently of party. Their friends are few—usually other mavericks. . . . What the leaders do, in a variety of ways, is to appeal both to the sense of solidarity that the member is likely to feel with his party and to the fear of possible ostracism, which means the immediate loss of psychological preferment and a possible future loss of tangible preferment.[10]

Ripley is speaking here of the party leaders in the House—the Speaker, the floor leader, and the whip. Where does the president come in? The answer is that by far the most effective way for the president to appeal to his fellow partisans in Congress is to enlist the help of his party's leaders in each chamber to appeal to their followers. A direct presidential appeal to members over their leaders' heads is not only likely to fail; it is likely to stir up resentment in both the leaders and the rank and file, which will make it more difficult for the president to get what he wants next time. In short, while a presidential candidate may find it useful, even necessary, to campaign for his own nomination and election with frequent attacks on "the Washington establishment," he cannot make much use of his "party leadership" in Congress unless he works with and through his party's congressional establishment.

It is not difficult to do, especially in the House. As Ripley points out:

> Since the beginning of Franklin Roosevelt's administration, the House leaders of the President's party have, in effect, acted as lieutenants of the President, accepting virtually his whole legislative package and working for its adoption. . . . It is now assumed that if the President proposes a bill, they will support it.[11]

This is considerably less true for some committee and subcommittee chairmen in the House than for the floor leaders and whips and somewhat less true for the Senate than for the House, but in both chambers the leaders of the president's party start from a strong desire to work with him.

There are several reasons for that desire. We have already noted that, despite the often-mentioned weakness of their party ties, most congressmen still have a lively sense of belonging to one or the other of two great competing teams, and their team loyalty impels most of them to vote as a president of their party asks, except where such a vote would clearly go against what they perceive to be their constituents' interests or wishes. The leaders of the president's party in Congress not only have these same team loyalties but, as leaders of the congressional part of the team, also have a considerable stake in moving the president's program along as swiftly and smoothly as possible. Professionally speaking, his legislative success is their success, and poor relations and meager results may harm their reputations as much as they harm the president's or more.

The main instruments for cooperation between the two branches of the president's party are communication and consultation. Since the late 1950s every president has held regular meetings with his party's congressional leaders (and less regular but frequent meetings with the leaders of the opposing party). The meetings usually take place once a week over breakfast at the White House,[12] and the agenda usually has several items: the president tells the congressional leaders what new pieces of legislation he plans to send to the Hill and when and how he feels about the progress of the legislation he has already sent. Sometimes he even asks their advice about legislation he is considering for the future.[13] The congressional leaders, in turn, tell the president what is happening to his legislation, why, and how he might help it along.

Like any institutional arrangement conducted by human beings, these meetings depend for their success to a great degree upon the meshing of the experience, skills, and personalities of the people involved. Most observers believe that Lyndon Johnson and Gerald Ford, for example, had excellent relations with the congressional leaders of their parties, in part because they themselves had been such leaders before they became president (Johnson as Senate majority leader and Ford as House minority leader); both of them understood the ways of Congress, enjoyed the company of congressmen, and got on well with the leaders of Congress after they became president. In contrast, John Kennedy and Richard Nixon, although they had been congressmen and senators, had never held leadership positions in Congress. Moreover, neither had particularly enjoyed the congressional life, and neither was a particularly prominent member of his congressional party. As presidents, their relations with their parties' congressional leaders were markedly less warm and successful than those of Johnson and Ford. Franklin Roosevelt had never served in Congress, but he understood and liked congressmen; his relations with the Democratic congressional leaders were excellent. Dwight Eisenhower was much more of a stranger to the ways of Congress, and his relations with congressional Republican leaders, especially Senator William Knowland, were never better than correct.[14] Jimmy Carter came to the presidency with no previous congressional experience—indeed, with no Washington experience of any kind. Moreover, according to one of his chief speech writers,

> his skin crawled at the thought of the time-consuming consultations and persuasion that might be required to bring a legislator around. He did not know how congressmen talked, worked, and thought, how to pressure them without being a bully or flatter them without seeming a fool. He needed help from someone

who knew all those things, who had spent time absorbing that culture. But for his congressional liaison he chose a Georgian named Frank Moore, a man whose general aptitude was difficult for anyone outside the first circle to detect, and who had barely laid eyes upon the Capitol before Inauguration Day.[15]

Ronald Reagan and Jimmy Carter are the only two presidents in the twentieth century to take office with no previous Washington experience whatever. But Reagan, unlike Carter, began with a special effort to cultivate good relations with congressmen in general and Republican congressional leaders in particular. He visited the Hill right after his election and several times in his first months in office. He resisted all efforts of his more conservative advisers to persuade him to oppose the reelection of the moderate Howard Baker as Senate Republican leader; indeed, he persuaded his closest friend on the Hill, Senator Paul Laxalt (Republican, Nevada), to nominate Baker for reelection. He appointed as head of his congressional liaison office Max Friedersdorf, who had served on the Nixon and Ford liaison staffs and was well known and liked by congressmen of both parties in both houses. As a result, there was general agreement that in the early days of his administration Reagan's relations with the Republican leaders in Congress were much better than Carter's had been with the Democratic leaders during his term of office.[16]

No matter how well or how badly one or another has managed it, however, every president since Franklin Roosevelt has used regular meetings with—and occasional advice from—his party's congressional leaders as one of his more important instruments for persuading Congress to enact his legislative program.

HOW PARTISAN ARE AMERICAN PRESIDENTS?

Some Rankings

Let us imagine a presidential partisanship scale. At one extreme (let us set it, as it should be set in all good scales, at 100) is the most partisan president we can imagine: one who has been active in party affairs at all levels for many years; who both says and believes that all wisdom and most patriotism reside in his party; who believes that any candidate of his party for any office should be elected over any candidate of the opposition party, and who regularly and intensively campaigns for his party's ticket from top to bottom; who takes a strong and active interest in his national committee's activities, insists that it be well led, well staffed, and well financed; who makes past party service and party loyalty prime criteria in making all his major and minor appointments; who works closely with his party's leaders in Congress in developing his programs and considers the party one of his most important instruments of leadership; and who places high priority on leaving his party in the best possible condition to win elections after he has left the White House.

At the other extreme (let us score it 0) is the least partisan president we can imagine: one whose acceptance of a party's nomination is his first official association with it; who campaigns strictly for himself and his policies and never mentions his party or its other candidates; who has no interest in his party's national committee or other organizational affairs except when they threaten to cause him embarrassment; who treats with the leaders and members of Congress entirely on a nonpartisan basis and never makes any special appeals to his nominal fellow partisans or

does special favors for them; who pays no attention whatever to partisan affiliation in making his appointments; and who has no concern whatever for the state of his party after he has left office.

In my highly subjective judgment, the only presidents in the twentieth century who would score close to 50 on such a scale would be Woodrow Wilson and Franklin D. Roosevelt, with Wilson ranking a notch above Roosevelt. (A few early signs suggest that Ronald Reagan may rank among the high-partisanship presidents, but at the present writing it is too early to say so with confidence.) Ranking the lowest would probably be Warren Harding, Calvin Coolidge, Herbert Hoover, and Jimmy Carter. And the average score for all fifteen twentieth-century presidents would be, say, 33.3.[17]

Why Are American Presidents So Unpartisan?

Such an average score would surely be far lower than any we would assign to the head of government in any other modern democratic country. Why is it so low for American presidents? No doubt there are too many reasons to be covered in detail here, but let me briefly outline a few of the most important.

Weak Congressional Parties. Most of the time, especially in the twentieth century, American political parties have been too weak and uncohesive to constitute an agency capable of providing a president with the votes he needs to get his programs adopted. He can and often does work closely with his party leaders in both chambers, as we have seen; but their powers over their rank and file are those of scheduling the business and trying to persuade the members to support the president. They certainly do not include any power to order the members to get behind the president or to expel them if they oppose him. Given the parties' weakness, what is remarkable about the fact that the president usually gets the support of about two-thirds of his congressional party is that he gets so much, not that he gets so little.

The Need for Support from the Opposition Party. Given that on almost any issue before Congress a president will lose from a quarter to more than half of his own party, there are very few issues on which he will not need at least some support from members of the opposition party, and not infrequently he will need quite substantial support from them. Such support has, of course, been crucial for all Republican presidents since Herbert Hoover; for in the total of twenty years in which they held office from 1929 to 1977, in only four years (1929–1931 and 1953–1955) did any of them enjoy a Congress with Republican majorities in both houses. (Ronald Reagan, dealing with a Republican senate and a Democratic house, was better off than most Republican presidents.) Democratic presidents have been much better situated in this regard; even so, in order to get most of the important parts of their programs through Congress, most of them have needed at least some Republican votes to make up for defecting Democrats. Hence no president has felt that he could afford to be so completely partisan in word and deed that he would offend all the members of the opposition party so much that they would never support him on anything.

The Increasing Irrelevance of Party to Presidential Politics. We noted earlier that party organizations and leaders at all levels have been largely stripped of their once-considerable power to select national convention delegates and deliver them to one candidate or another. Hence no presidential aspirant today bothers much with the party organizations in his drive for the nomination; indeed it may be most effective, as it certainly was for Jimmy Carter in 1974–1976, to run for the nomination as the candidate who is not in any way involved with or supported by the "party bosses."

The Increasing Antiparty Tone of American Political Culture. I have argued elsewhere that from the nation's beginnings most ordinary Americans have had a poor opinion of political parties in general, as institutions—though most of them have most of the time "identified" with one party over the other.[18] Since the mid-1960s, however, even these party identifications have weakened substantially; there are more independents now than there have been for a long time, and party has a worse name than ever.[19] Most Americans evidently want to weaken parties still further, not strengthen them.[20]

The Antipolitician Bias of Network Television. These traditionally strong antiparty strains in American political culture have been considerably reinforced in recent years by the manner in which the television networks have portrayed American politics. In America, as in all other modern democratic countries, most people get most of their information about politics from television; but, unlike many other democracies, America has no party-controlled broadcasts, except for a few thirty-second "commercials" shown in election years. Hence most broadcasting about politics emanates from the local stations' news programs, the three national commercial networks' news programs, and an occasional longer documentary on a particular issue or person. For a variety of reasons—including the nonparty backgrounds and attitudes of most correspondents and producers and the antiestablishment, adversary posture of the broadcasting profession—political parties do not fare well in these broadcasts. Being collectivities, they are much harder to portray in dramatic pictures than personalities. Being such ancient features of the political landscape (the Republicans go back to 1854 and the Democrats to 1792), they are not novel or exciting in the way that a new issue or a new personality is. Worst of all, they are composed entirely of politicians, and everyone—certainly every network correspondent—is sure that politicians are by nature tricky, deceitful, and often dishonest characters who do what they do entirely because they want to be reelected, not because they have any sincere concern for the public interest.[21]

The President's Objectives

For all these reasons, any president is likely to pay a considerable price for appearing to be a strong party man. If he acts—or is portrayed—too much as Mr. Democrat or Mr. Republican, he is almost certain to lose some of the support from the opposition party that he needs in Congress. He will also present a very large target for the networks' tireless snipers. Worst of all, he will deeply offend a good many ordinary people who believe he should be "president of all the people," not an all-out leader of some gang of self-seeking politicians.

If the president were to set as one of his prime objectives strengthening his party organizationally, financially, and in public esteem so that it would go on to even greater success after he had left office, then these prices might be well worth paying. But most presidents give the highest priority to making a presidential record that will secure them a high position in history; and being a strong partisan and strong leader of a party has struck most presidents in this century as a poor way of winning good notices from contemporary or future historians.

There is no reason to suppose that Ronald Reagan and his successors will see things differently.

NOTES

1. *Constitutional Government in the United States* (New York: Columbia University Press, 1908), pp. 67–69.

2. *Oxford English Dictionary*, vol. 1, compact ed. (London: Oxford University Press, 1971), p. 1589.

3. Cf. Cornelius P. Cotter and John F. Bibby, "Institutional Development of Parties and the Thesis of Party Decline," *Political Science Quarterly*, vol. 95 (Spring 1980), pp. 1–27.

4. Rule 25, paragraph (b), *Rules Adopted by the 1980 Republican National Convention* (Washington, D.C.: Republican National Committee, 1980), p. 10, italics added.

5. For a brief account of the few efforts by presidents to support or oppose the nomination of particular candidates in 1910, 1918, 1930, 1946, and 1980—and especially for Franklin Roosevelt's failure to "purge" anti-New Deal Democratic congressmen in the 1938 primaries—see Austin Ranney and Willmoore Kendall, *Democracy and the American Party System* (Westport, Conn.: Greenwood Press, Publishers, 1956, reprinted in 1974), pp. 286–98.

6. For a more complete discussion of how the new presidential nominating process has substantially reduced the role of congressmen, see Jeane J. Kirkpatrick, Michael J. Malbin, Thomas E. Mann, Howard R. Penniman, and Austin Ranney, *The Presidential Nominating Process: Can It Be Improved?* (Washington, D.C.: American Enterprise Institute, 1980).

7. Richard E. Neustadt, *Presidential Power* (New York: John Wiley & Sons, 1960), pp. 33–34.

8. For a useful summary of the studies on and current skepticism about the "coattail effect," see George C. Edwards III, *Presidential Influence in Congress* (San Francisco: W. H. Freeman and Company, 1980), pp. 70–78.

9. The findings of the various studies are summarized in more detail in Edwards, *Presidential Influence*, pp. 61–66.

10. Randall B. Ripley, *Party Leaders in the House of Representatives* (Washington, D.C.: Brookings Institution, 1967), pp. 158–59. John Kingdon is probably correct in arguing that the party tie is less important to congressmen today than it was when Ripley wrote his book in the 1960s: *Congressmen's Voting Decisions* (New York: Harper and Row, 1973). Nevertheless, it remains one of the most important forces affecting most congressmen's votes.

11. Ripley, *Party Leaders*, p. 3.

12. This can have its problems. At the very first meeting between Jimmy Carter and the Democratic congressional leaders in 1977, for example, only coffee and rolls were served. Speaker Thomas "Tip" O'Neill complained about the poor treatment, and at the next meeting a full breakfast was served—but each congressman was billed for the full cost of his breakfast. That touched off another round of complaints, and finally the White House decided that good congressional relations justified paying for a few breakfasts. Some of the people involved, however, still mention the episode as a typical example of Carter's ineptness in dealing with Congress.

13. If the president consistently fails to ask for congressional advice on legislation in its formative stage, his relations with the congressional leaders will soon sour. Just three months after he had taken office in 1977, for example, Jimmy Carter presented to Congress his mammoth and complex energy program. Right from the start many congressional Democrats strongly objected to the fact that the program had been prepared in secret by presidential adviser James Schlesinger (later secretary of energy) and other White House aides without asking any advice from congressional leaders or giving them any information. It took over two years for Congress to enact the full program (much of it in substantially altered form), and many observers felt that Carter's failure to keep congressional leaders informed while the program was being developed had a good deal to do with its subsequent tortuous passage through Congress.

14. Cf. the evaluations of various presidents' congressional relations in Randall B. Ripley, *Congress: Process and Policy*, 2d ed. (New York: W. W. Norton and Company, 1978), pp. 297–98.

15. James Fallows, "The Passionless Presidency," *Atlantic* (May 1979), pp. 33–46, at p. 41.

16. Cf. Dick Kirschten, "The Pennsylvania Avenue Connection—Making Peace on Capitol Hill," *National Journal*, March 7, 1981, pp. 384–87.

17. For somewhat similar rankings using somewhat similar criteria, see Ripley, *Congress*, pp. 308–23.

18. Cf. Austin Ranney, *Curing the Mischiefs of Faction: Party Reform in America* (Berkeley: University of California Press, 1975), chap. 2.

19. In 1964, for example, a Gallup poll reported that 49 percent of the people called themselves Democrats, 27 percent Republicans, and 24 percent independents. In 1980 Gallup reported 47 percent Democrats, 32 percent independents, and 21 percent Republicans.

20. In 1980 a Gallup poll reported 66 percent of the people in favor of abolishing the national party conventions entirely and replacing them with a one-day national primary; 24 percent opposed the idea, and 10 percent were undecided.

21. The most careful and convincing analysis of network television's antipolitican bias is Edward Jay Epstein, *News from Nowhere* (New York: Random House, Vintage Books, 1974).

24

Presidents and Their Parties: Performance and Prospects

Roger G. Brown & David M. Welborn

One of the fundamental characteristics of the American political system is the dynamic and problematic relationships among its various parts. Among the murkiest are those linking Presidents and the political parties which they represent and ostensibly lead. Ill-defined and troublesome relationships between the two are properly sources of serious concern, given their implications for the vitality of democratic processes. The hallmark of the presidency, the nation's premier political position, is great power in government and in relation to other elements of the political system. Serious dilemmas are presented regarding responsibility and accountability in the uses of that power. Parties can be a major means for reflecting popular impulses in ways that inform and channel uses of presidential power. Thus, they are potentially one means of holding the presidency within appropriate bounds.

Historically, the relationship has not been a comfortable one. But many contemporary observers report a further estrangement of Presidents and parties, even to the point of suggesting the emergence of a non-partisan, if not an anti-party presidency, in concert with parties which incorporate anti-presidential impulses. The striking element of the conventional trend of analysis is that it goes beyond the failure to find evidence of strong and effective party leadership on the part of contemporary Presidents. Many writers go further and ascribe di-

rectly to the President the burden of blame for divorcing the office from traditional party ties and accountability. Burnham worried that Jimmy Carter's extraparty campaign in 1976 signaled "the final liberation of the presidency from all organized coalitions or other external constraints."[1] Bass argues that the current President-party relationship consists of "recurring and systematic presidential efforts to undermine the establishment and maintenance of a strong national party apparatus."[2] The implications of such a development are serious indeed for presidential leadership, capacity in government, and the weight of political restraints playing upon presidential incumbents and their associates.

The purpose of this paper is to examine the factors most frequently cited as contributing to a "post-party" presidency and to present an alternative interpretation of the evolving President-party relationship. The view presented here is that given the lengthy list of disincentives which operate to discourage overt party leadership on the part of contemporary Presidents, incumbents since 1960 still have committed a significant amount of personal and staff resources to just such activities. To illustrate this point, the party-related activities of the five most recent Presidents, John F. Kennedy to James E. Carter, will be examined in some detail. Further, it will be argued that the potential exists for stronger party organizations and a closer

Source: Presidential Studies Quarterly 12, no. 3 (Summer 1982).

interdependence between those organizations and future Presidents.

A NONPARTISAN PRESIDENCY?

Party leadership, taken to be a major presidential role, usually is the focal point for commentary on the relationship between Presidents and their parties. The dominant view is that the role most often is poorly and reluctantly played.[3] Koenig asserts that few Presidents have had the necessary tastes and skills to be successful in it.[4] Pious concludes that "no president is an effective party leader."[5]

Many reasons are adduced in explanation of historically weak presidential performance in this sphere. Among the more important ones are the decentralized and fragmented character of party structures; the existence of congressional, state and local electoral systems apart from the presidential; endemic weakness in feelings of party loyalty within the population; the lack of central presidential control measures able to counter centrifugal tendencies within parties; intra-party tension and suspicion left from nomination struggles; incongruities between presidential electoral majorities and party membership; the necessity for Presidents to reach for alliances beyond the perimeters of party in support of their objectives; and, in general, a prevalent tension between partisan claims and presidential responsibilities.

Perceptions of a transition from simply a difficult relationship toward estrangement are shaped by several recent changes in the party system, in the presidency, and in the fundamental political circumstances of the time. In essence, the current view is that the possibilities for the constructive uses of party structures by Presidents have lessened and the liabilities of close association and vigorous party leadership have in-creased. Among the contributing factors most often cited are the decline in partisan identification and voting in the electorate, the effects of "reforms" in party procedures for the selection of presidential nominees, and the dispersion of power within Congress. It is further noted that the access of Presidents to electronic media, to independent sources of campaign finances and expertise, and the large staffs at their command enable them if they wish to follow a course somewhat apart from party in their political endeavors.[6]

Despite this apparently hostile environment for active party leadership, as will be shown, recent Presidents in instance after instance have used their position as nominal party head to attempt fence-mending among warring party factions, both on the national and state levels; have invested time and the prestige of their office for party fund-raising purposes and in the election campaigns of fellow partisans; and have, with varying degrees of success, sought a measure of party cohesion in Congress. The point is not that Presidents have been spectacularly successful in these party-related endeavors. The point is that all have made room on hopelessly overcrowded agendas for the duties associated with party leadership, despite the low probability of positive results.

The case of Republican candidates and Presidents is especially interesting in this regard. Since the number of registered Democrats remains nearly twice the number of registered Republicans, GOP candidates and incumbents would seem likely to profit from a nonpartisan, coalition-building strategy, both in campaigning and in governing. However, the evidence runs quite to the contrary. The list of Republican candidates and Presidents since Eisenhower is overwhelmingly one of vigorous partisans. One could hardly accuse such candidates as Richard Nixon, Barry Goldwater,

Nelson Rockefeller, Gerald Ford, Ronald Reagan, Philip Crane or Robert Dole of attempting to conceal or even downplay their party affiliations. This list alone is enough to suggest that the claims of a separation of presidential politics from organized parties have been overstated.

Although his administration is not included in this study, President Eisenhower's experience provides further illustration for this point. Widely regarded as the quintessential non-partisan, Eisenhower apparently felt compelled nonetheless to respond to the demands of the party leader role. Archival evidence indicates that he met a number of times with leading Republicans for the purpose of planning political strategy and fund-raising endeavors. According to Greenstein, these "activities were part of Eisenhower's continued efforts to broaden, unify, strengthen, and modify the Republican party, notwithstanding his simultaneous efforts to convey the impression of nonpartisanship."[7]

Eisenhower's case suggests several reasons that Presidents may choose to behave as "closet" party leaders. For one thing, legislative leadership often requires at least the appearance of broad bipartisanship on the part of the President, especially when one or both houses of Congress is controlled by the opposition party. Further, as Greenstein argues, open presidential support for a party-related initiative may cost support from disparate factions even within the President's party.[8] And, of course, the President must always take care to be seen as the leader of the entire nation, not just of one political party.

A MATTER OF DEGREE

Given the fact that recent Presidents appear not to have related to their parties in precisely the same way, the question arises, what major differences and similarities are manifest and what accounts for them? The bulk of the analysis to follow addresses the key distinction between two related but separable dimensions of the President-party relationship. The first is *party leadership,* upon which commentary usually concentrates and the avoidance of which gives rise to suggestions of an emergent nonpartisanship in the presidential office. It refers, of course, to the encouragement and development of party organization and to the active solicitation of public support for a party's objectives and candidates. The second dimension is *partisanship,* or a President's attitudinal dispositions toward his party in the affective and symbolic sense.

In his studies of political power and influence. Harold Lasswell suggested that such instrumental behavior as party leadership is largely shaped by the affective domain of beliefs and attitudes, as in partisanship.[9] In most discussions of the President-party relationship, the linkages between partisanship and party leadership are not clearly delineated. Indeed, structural factors and considerations of presidential *realpolitik* independent of affective elements ordinarily are taken to be of greatest salience. The relationship between the two dimensions proves useful to explore as a means for further illuminating presidential behavior in this important area.

Consequently, the records of the five presidents serving since 1960 are assessed to ascertain their degree of partisanship and the strength of their party leadership. Measurement is not an easy task, especially in the affective domain of partisanship. Qualitative judgments are derived mainly from commentaries, presidential memoirs, papers, and the reports of close associates. Three indicators are employed to assess the strengths of party leadership: the amount and nature of contact between a President and party organizations, principally the national chairman and committee; the extent of involvement in midterm congressional campaigns; and the percentage of presidential appointments to office selected from the President's party.[10]

This analysis attempts to separate the party leader role from the broader collection of presidential activities known as legislative leadership. Naturally, the President's relations with congressional leaders of both parties are of vital importance in the political process, and those relations are themselves the focus of recent studies.[11] But of primary concern here are the relationships which have existed between contemporary Presidents and the party organizations outside Congress.

Admittedly, the distinction between party leadership and legislative leadership becomes blurred in practice. For example, the activities of mid-term campaigning and patronage appointments are often undertaken with the goal of furthering the President's influence with members of Congress. Also, a President's party affiliation in and of itself can become an important source of legislative influence with fellow partisans.[12] But a full exposition of presidential-congressional relations via party organizations is beyond the scope of this study.

In view of the bi-demensional concept of party activity described above, it is reasonable to suspect that a strongly partisan President will be more likely to exercise strong party leadership, while one with less commitment and loyalty will be concerned less with party leadership. When recent Presidents are typed, based upon partisanship and party leadership this relationship holds for four of the five cases as shown by Figure 1. Strong partisanship and party leadership are joined in the presidencies of Kennedy and Ford. In contrast, both Johnson and Carter emerge as relatively weak partisans and party leaders. Nixon is the exception to congruence in the two dimensions. For most of his career and part of his presidency he demonstrated strong partisanship, but as President he stood somewhat at a distance from the affairs of the Republican Party.

EMBRACING PARTY

Partisanship. It is striking and perhaps significant that Kennedy and Ford, ranked high in both partisanship and party leadership, served abbreviated terms of office. Longer tenures might have produced different results. The fact remains, however, that in their public life, including time as President, neither made a secret of his partisanship.

FIGURE 1 · PARTISANSHIP AND PARTY LEADERSHIP IN RECENT PRESIDENCIES

		Partisanship	
		Strong	Weak
Party Leadership	Strong	John F. Kennedy Gerald R. Ford	
	Weak	Richard M. Nixon	Lyndon B. Johnson James E. Carter

Theodore Sorensen, a Kennedy intimate for many years, noted that even in campaign rhetoric where emphasis ordinarily is placed on nonpartisan appeals, Kennedy introduced partisan themes.[13] Throughout his Presidency, he consistently voiced commitment and loyalty to the Democratic Party and to the idea of partisanship. In remarks to the Democratic National Committee one day after his inaugural he said:

> I believe in strong political organizations in our country. . . . The party is the means by which programs can be put into action—the means by which people of talent can come to the service of the country. And in this great free society of ours, both of our parties . . . serve the interests of the people.[14]

In a speech prepared for delivery on the day of his assassination, Kennedy planned to tell Texas Democrats:

> The Democratic Party is not a collection of diverse interests brought together only to win elections. We are united instead by a common history and heritage. . . . It was the policies and programs of the Democratic Party which helped bring income to your farmers, industries to your cities, employment to your workers, and the promotion and preservation of your natural resources.[15]

Not all observers of Kennedy view him as a strong partisan. One historian, for example, argues that he made a major contribution to the creation of "the personalized and plebiscitic Presidency" and to the diminution of party through his use of personal staff and the media.[16] Another intepretation is more persuasive, however. Heavy reliance on a personal organization for campaigns and presidential activities did not indicate partisan reservations, but was an attempt to bring new emphases and principles to the party which he led. According to David S. Broder, Kennedy was "a partisan Democrat," but not a blind one.

He was not enamored of many of the " 'professional' party leaders, 'pols' hacks and hangers on" such as he had known in Massachusetts.[17] One of the major objectives, according to Sorensen, was to envigorate and make more progressive the Democratic Party by shifting party activity from "smoke-filled hotel rooms" into "vote-filled pool-rooms."[18]

Ford's partisanship was demonstrated clearly during his long and successful career in the House of Representatives, in both leadership positions and in his tireless promotion of the Republican Party and its candidates across the country. Indeed, Jules Witcover argues that it was precisely his reputation as a partisan that put Ford at the top of Nixon's list for the Vice Presidency following Spiro Agnew's resignation.[19]

As President, Ford's strong sense of affiliation with the Republican party was not diminished. During fund raising and candidate endorsement efforts in 1975 he made this clear. He also spelled out what the role of party leader meant to him. Explaining that in dozens of appearances at Republican rallies and dinners he had raised over $2 million for the party at both state and national levels, he added:

> As President and as a member of the Republican Party and the leader of the Republican Party, I have an obligation to try and strengthen and rebuild the Republican Party organization in many, many states.[20]

In spirit, if not in precise content, there are commonalities here with earlier avowals of President Kennedy. During a 1961 speech, for example, Kennedy referred to an exhibit in President Truman's library built around the various responsibilities of the presidency.

> But one of these responsibilities—and I think all of our Presidents, our great Presidents, in both our political parties have

recognized it—is also to be head of a political party. . . . I have come here tonight as the leader of the Democratic Party.[21]

Relations with the Party Organization. Despite similarities in views regarding the party leadership role, Kennedy's pointed intervention in party affairs was perhaps more extensive than Ford's. He used the Democratic National Committee as a vehicle to influence the affairs of state and local parties in New York, Illinois, Pennsylvania, Texas, Ohio, Florida and Michigan. For the most part, the purpose was to solve factional problems in these key areas and thus to make the Democratic Party a more effective organization nationally.[22]

In addition to maneuvering of this type, Kennedy provided visible party leadership in appearances at numerous fund raising affairs in behalf of the national party. He spoke at eight such gatherings in his first presidential year alone. Furthermore, "he achieved a degree of success, despite the protest of many congressional Democrats, in centralizing the party's fund raising in the Democratic National Committee and using those . . . funds as a tool of executive leadership in behalf of candidates committed to the party program."[23]

Kennedy's efforts at more than nominal party leadership turned toward reform of national party convention procedures shortly before his death. Sorensen explains that the President supported a reapportionment of delegates which would have liberalized the convention and more accurately reflected Democratic strength in the various states.[24]

His relations with the national party organization were not always harmonious, however. Chairman John Bailey, while enjoying more access and communication with the President than many of his predecessors, was still disappointed

in some aspects of the relationship.[25] Most of the political liaison work with Congress was handled through White House, not party channels. And at times, Bailey was overly partisan from the presidential perspective. He once was repudiated publicly by the President for a statement assigning racist tendencies to Governor Nelson Rockefeller of New York, a prospective candidate for the 1964 Republican presidential nomination.[26]

As President, Ford continued the promotion of his party's interests in various ways, especially in fund raising. But he did not become as engaged in organizational questions as Kennedy. When announcing the appointment of Mary Louise Smith to chair the committee in 1974, Ford expressed a desire for a close partnership. In particular, he indicated that he wanted the 1976 presidential campaign to be run by the national committee. But the ways of his most recent predecessors were not so easily changed.[27] As it turned out, in mid-1975 the Ford campaign was given to an independent group. By August, 1976, Ford was being criticized in the press for relegating the committee and Mrs. Smith to the dark corners of the policy process and relying instead on a "select circle of personal advisers."[28]

Mid-Term Campaigning. Both Kennedy and Ford were vigorous participants in the single mid-term congressional campaign of their presidencies. In 1962, the White House announcement of campaign plans boasted of a schedule more active than that of "any President or Vice-President . . . in the last century."[29] From late July to November, 1962, Kennedy and Vice President Johnson campaigned in over a dozen states each in an all-out effort to limit congressional losses. During the lively contest, in which former Presidents Truman and Eisenhower took part, Kennedy did not shy away from an open stand as leader of the Democrats.

> I do not intend to conceal the differences between our two parties. . . . If the Democratic Party is charged with disturbing the status quo, with stirring up the great interests of this country, with daring to try something new, I plead "guilty," and if the Republican Party is charged with wanting to return to the past, with opposing nearly every constructive measure we have put forward, then they must plead "guilty" and the American people will make their judgment.[30]

The results of the campaign were as impressive as the President's energetic participation. Instead of expected losses of up to 39 House and five Senate seats,[31] the net results were a reduction of two House seats and a gain of four Senate seats, and the same number of governorships were retained. The showing was the best mid-term result for any administration since 1934 and demonstrated the potential benefits of open party leadership as a presidential activity.

Ford's partisanship was translated into action during the 1974 elections, just months after he had taken the reins of a government in shambles. He campaigned in 20 states and "warned repeatedly . . . that election of too many Democrats would result in a runaway, 'veto-proof' Congress."[32] But his efforts did not overcome the devastating effects of Watergate and the Nixon resignation, as the Democrats made substantial gains across the country.

Presidential Appointments. Traditionally the power of appointment has been a major intersection point for presidential activity and party interests. Although patronage positions are reduced in number and political considerations have lost ground to merit considerations in filling political and judicial posi-

tions,[33] the comparative performance of Presidents in this area remains indicative. On this measure, Kennedy scored somewhat higher than Ford, no doubt in part because of changes in the institutional processes of appointment developed in intervening administrations. Overall, Kennedy made 583 appointments to office. Seventy percent of these went to Democrats, 21 percent to independents or persons whose party affiliation was undesignated, and nine percent to Republicans. In the process, Heclo reports regular use was made of the Democratic National Committee and its extensive patronage files. In contrast, during Ford's time the Republican National Committee apparently was not an important factor. And of his 361 appointments, 61 percent went to Republicans, 25 percent to independents or undesignated party affiliates, and 14 percent to Democrats.

Although differences are to be noted between Ford and Kennedy, less so in their expressed partisanship than in performance of certain facets of their party leadership role, the reasonableness of placing them together becomes clear when their opposites, Johnson and Carter, are examined.

STANDING THEIR DISTANCE

Partisanship. For Kennedy and Ford, party considerations occupied prominent, if not central places in their presidencies. But for their respective successors, Lyndon Johnson and Jimmy Carter, party seemed of relatively less concern.

Johnson indicated his basic disposition in his memoirs when commenting on his feelings at taking office that the principal need of the times was "consensus throughout the country." The idea of consensus became the dominating theme of his administration. It meant, "first, deciding what needed to be done regardless of the political implications and, second, convincing a majority of the Congress and the American people of the necessity for doing those things." Johnson went on to say, ". . . I never questioned the capacity or the sincerity, or the ability of a man because he belonged to a different political party."[34]

This comparatively nonpartisan attitude appears repeatedly in speeches Johnson delivered as President. Even during one of his numerous outpourings of congratulations to the Democrats of the 89th Congress for its prolific passage of Great Society programs, Johnson chose to temper the partisan atmosphere with these remarks.

> For it is not as Democrats, and it is not as partisans, and it is not as members of factions that we shall prove ourselves worthy of the public's trust, but it is only as free men and only as Americans first.[35]

Whereas the Johnson view might be described in terms of the irrelevancy of party, the Carter view is tinged with distrust of party as an entrenched political structure. Nothwithstanding leadership of the Georgia Young Democrats, state office as a Democrat, and head of 1974 congressional campaign efforts for the Democratic National Committee, during most of his political career he adopted the stance of the outsider. He finally secured a place in the Georgia Senate over the opposition of the local Democratic Party organization, despite its employment of a host of devices to deny him what was won. He commented, "I really learned a lot from this first experience with politics."[36] Later, as candidate and then as governor, these lessons were manifest in his behavior. And he followed a similar course in his quest for the presidency. To an extent, Carter's avoidance of party and the debts which party support entails contributed

to his electoral victory. He justified his independence in campaigning, saying, "That's my nature and that's part of my political strength."[37]

Relations with the Party Organizations. The performance of both Presidents Johnson and Carter in the party leadership role clearly corresponded to their limited zeal for partisanship. Johnson avoided a close relationship with the national party organization because he saw it as a useless and extraneous expense and believed the excessive partisanship it elicited to be "the enemy, not the servant, of responsible government."[38] But in spite of this attitude, he responded to the duties of party leadership by making fund raising appearances and attending three Democratic dinners in 1965 as compared to Kennedy's eight in 1961.

Even with his relatively low level of partisanship and attention to the duties of party leadership, however, Johnson maintained a full-time liaison with the Democratic National Committee from early 1964 until August, 1966, in the person of Clifton C. Carter.[39] A longtime Johnson associate from his home congressional district in Texas, Carter served as executive director of the DNC. Besides his involvement in the omnipresent fund-raising activities, Carter helped direct an orientation program for forty-six new Democratic members of Congress elected in the 1964 election. In a series of follow-up contacts with the freshmen legislators, the Committee assisted them with letters to constituents, news releases for hometown media, and provided access to DNC mailing lists.[40]

President Carter's relations with the national party organization, like his initial experiences in other areas of the presidency, were tentative and slow to develop, a major reason given for the resignation of Democratic National

Chairman Kenneth Curtis late in 1977. When the President and his staff did turn their attention to the party and the further alteration of nomination procedures, it was interpreted as a self-serving move in preparation for Carter's re-election bid. According to press reports:

> Any Democrat thinking of challenging President Carter . . . two years from now can find little to cheer about in the work of the party's special panel on delegate selection. . . . White House staff and friends dominated important votes by the commission.[41]

John C. White followed Curtis as national chairman and immediately made an effort to correct the deficient Carter image in party leadership by outlining major presidential plans for fund raising and participation in the 1978 elections. Included were the following promises: "Mr. Carter will see to it that his national chairman sits frequently at his elbow, providing counsel on political issues"; a special effort will be made to bring together the President and state party leaders; and "the President will be on call to campaign or help out wherever the party needs him."[42]

By mid-1978, however, the relationship between Carter and his party was still an uneasy one. Broder pointed out that "17 months after Carter took office, the White House finally got around to the basic courtesy of having the Democratic state chairmen and national committee members in for a drink and a chat."[43] An important factor affecting the relationship was the independence of party elements which had been nurtured over the years by the absence of presidential leadership and the occupancy of the White House by Republicans between 1969 and 1977. Another factor was Carter's low popularity, which for many made his presidency a political liability. As Carter's public standing began to rebound in the aftermath of the

Camp David accords, however, receptivity to his involvement in party affairs increased dramatically. Concurrently, with an eye to enlarging public and congressional support and to 1980, presidential fund raising and other inititatives suggested a new mood of cooperation and mutual support between the President and the national party. As one observer noted later in 1978, "Carter has been much more willing recently to play the party game."[44]

Mid-Term Campaigning. After saying it might be possible to visit all 50 states on behalf of Democratic members of that "wonderful 89th Congress,"[45] Johnson made a good start, with 28 campaign stops between July 23 and October 13. But in an abrupt change of plans, he set fall visits with foreign leaders both in Washington and as part of a 16-day Asian tour. Rather than resume campaigning in the week between his return and the elections, Johnson decided to undergo minor throat surgery. In the meantime, "Johnson made no endorsement of any Democratic candidate," even when prompted by journalists.[46] Whether the President was to blame, or whether it was projected results that dampened his campaign ardor, the Republicans scored major gains in Congress. Johnson's seeming indifference, plus the election results, damaged further his relations with Democratic leaders in Congress and elsewhere.

Carter's plans for mid-term campaigning were put into action early in 1978 as the President began a snowy February swing through New England. One report stated:

> Carter's politicking was partly the result of some urgent advice from Vice President Walter Mondale and other White House strategists: mend your fences with the Democratic Party and Congress—quickly. . . . Anxious party pros at the Democratic National Committee and dissident

Democrats in Congress also complain that Carter has little understanding or sympathy for their constituencies or political vulnerability.[47]

The President promised 15 to 20 days of campaign traveling by November, in addition to numerous trips by Mondale, members of his cabinet, and family. But plans were impeded for a time by the reluctance of many Democratic candidates to be associated with the President. As the electoral season neared its conclusion, however "Democrats decided *en masse . . .* that they wanted Carter to visit them."[48] The obvious reason for this change of heart on the part of such Democratic candidates as senatorial hopeful Bill Bradley of New Jersey was the popularity boost enjoyed by President Carter following the Camp David summit. The final result of the 1978 elections, a loss for the Democrats of three Senate seats and 12 House seats, was considerably less serious than that suffered by the Democrats in 1966. And while Carter received little credit for his party's showing, he would have risked bearing much of the blame had he failed to campaign vigorously for his fellow Democrats.

Presidential Appointments. The basic approach of both Johnson and Carter to making presidential appointments was similar in several respects. Central White House staffing operations were employed which emphasized the systematic search for persons meeting various criteria. Partisan service, regularity, and enhancement of the party's organizational interests were not important among them. It is difficult in either case to describe concisely the various criteria and their application. For Johnson, however, it is clear that a dominant concern was loyalty to the President and his Administration to the extent he was not constrained to maintain continuity with the Kennedy Administration. For

Carter, it seems that in many instances it was diversification of the upper levels of government through the inclusion of persons reflecting presidential points of view in key issue areas and persons representing groups—women, minorities, and others—up to now "outsiders" as was the President himself.

Johnson scores lowest among the five Presidents in the uses of appointments as a means of party leadership. He filled 702 positions during his time as President. Just over half the appointments, 56 percent, went to Democrats. Quite a high number, 34 percent, went to independents or persons whose party affiliation was undesignated, and ten percent went to Republicans. Despite the nature of the distribution, Johnson was not subject to partisan criticism, perhaps because of his adept handling of the process.

Not so with Carter. The staffing process and its results were so unsatisfactory to campaign loyalists, Democratic congressmen, and state party organizations that the Democratic National Committee in 1977 drafted a resolution criticizing the President's performance.[49] Even so, the proportion of his own party members included in Carter's first year appointments was greater than in the presidencies of Johnson or of Ford, albeit less than in those of Kennedy and Nixon. During 1977, Carter filled 361 positions. Sixty-one percent went to Democrats, 25 percent to independents or persons of undesignated affiliation, and 14 percent to Republicans.

As with Kennedy and Ford, examination of the Johnson and Carter Presidencies seems to show a relationship between the strengths of basic partisan affiliation and performance in the party leadership role. That explanation may not always be quite so simple as is suggested by the deviant case, that of Richard M. Nixon.

AMBIVALENCE

The enigmatic character of Nixon as politician and President carries over into his relationships with the Republican Party. On the one hand, few men in public life have earned as strong a reputation for unbridled partisanship. On the other hand, as President a certain reserve appeared to mark his performance of the party leadership role. Reserve is not to be equated with weakness or absolute disinterest, however, making his classification a close call. He is described as a weak party leader, despite his strong record of partisanship, because in his reserve there appeared to be irresolution and near rejection of his party in its existing form.

The record is clear that as a member of Congress and as Vice President, Nixon was openly and sometimes bitterly partisan. A sympathetic biography published for the 1960 presidential campaign includes these remarks by the candidate:

> In an election campaign, party unity is essential. If I were asked how I can go out and support all Republican candidates for Congress if, in some instances, individual Democrats are better qualified, I would be very frank to answer that ours is not a government of individuals.[50]

Such instances of unquestioning party loyalty won Nixon the support of the national party leadership and the contempt of his political opposition. He advocated fierce partisanship and total subordination of individual viewpoints to party decisions. In an ironically prophetic warning to those who would not follow party discipline, Nixon said, "Anyone who attacks his own party will get publicity at the moment. But in the end, if his party or his administration goes down, he will go down with it."[51]

Nixon's autobiographical account of *Six Crises* in his life explains the difficulty

he had in rising above his partisan image enough to attract "five to six million Democrats to leave their own candidate and vote Republican" in his presidential bid against John Kennedy. He received a strong warning from Eisenhower to keep his speeches nonpartisan and to avoid sharing the campaign platform with other Republican candidates in traditionally Democratic districts. Nixon wrote:

> But I saw the candidate for President as leader of the party, with an obligation to do everything possible to build up his party. Consequently, in all my stops throughout the country, I appeared on the platform with each local Republican candidate who desired it, and I endorsed all the major candidates by name.[52]

Nixon's toil in the party vineyards continued following his defeat by Kennedy. It was he who received the lion's share of credit for the large Republican gains in the 1966 Congressional elections. While President Johnson was touring Asia and ignoring his party leadership, Nixon "campaigned tirelessly"[53] for Republican candidates and regained the popular leadership of the GOP, exhibiting again the extent of his party loyalty. But as President, Nixon saw the need to play down his membership in the minority party in favor of his role as national and legislative leader. Surprisingly few references were made to the Republican Party in his speeches. More typical of his public stance was the statement made on the eve of the 1970 congressional elections: "It is customary as we get close to an election to speak of voting Republican or voting Democratic. But the issues this year are too important to speak in partisan terms."[54] While unable to be openly partisan in his dealings with a Democratic Congress and an electorate whose predominant affiliation was with the opposition party, Nixon chose instead to be "superpartisan—that is, aggressively majoritarian. . . , as he sought to bring together the Silent Majority."[55]

In pursuit of superpartisanship, Nixon built one of the most insulated and personalized administrations ever seen in this country. The national party organization was increasingly by-passed and ignored by the White House. After the controversial appointment of his friend Rogers Morton to replace Ray Bliss as national committee chairman, Nixon proceeded to ignore the party machinery entirely.

> Approximately one month after Morton became chairman, Bob Haldeman told fellow Presidential aides that the National Committee was not going to amount to anything, ever. . . . The fears of state party leaders that Richard Nixon, party man par excellence, was about to ignore the party . . . were now confirmed.[56]

Further confirmation of Haldeman's prediction came in the 1972 campaign. The regular party organization was made irrelevant by use of the now infamous Committee to Re-elect the President. Morton's successor as national chairman, Senator Robert Dole, was unable even to reach Nixon during the campaign, and his status was made clear when an anonymous White House caller told him he could see the President by turning on the television set.[57]

In spite of this evidence of weak party leadership, Nixon did not ignore other aspects of the role. He engaged in an intensive effort on behalf of Republican candidates in the 1970 elections. He traveled to 23 states during October and sent Vice President Agnew on a two-month crusade against "radical-liberals." The results were not as satisfying as those of 1966, but neither were they disastrous. The Democrats picked up nine House seats and 11 governorships, but the Republicans gained two Senate seats.

On the surface, the Nixon record in appointments seems to indicate relatively strong party leadership. Of 976 appointments, 70 percent went to Republicans, 22 percent to independents and those without partisan designation, and only 8 percent to Democrats. Two qualifications need to be entered, however. First, Nixon more than other recent Presidents removed himself from the selection process, so the figures reflect the outputs of a staff-directed system. Second, there are indications that the Republicanism of many appointees was nominal, in the sense that although the affiliation might be worn, the sense of party and partisan commitments was often weak.[58]

THE PRESIDENT-PARTY RELATIONSHIP IN PERSPECTIVE

Several key points about the President-party relationship are suggested by the foregoing discussion. It is true that no recent President has been an ambitious and effective party leader in the Jeffersonian sense. But neither have the last five Presidents been wholly inattentive to party affairs. The behavior of Kennedy and Ford in particular suggest caution in announcing the partisan cleansing of the presidential office. At the same time, ambiguity toward party is clear in some recent Presidents. On the whole, the examination of five recent presidencies underscores a continuing variability in the relationship.

Thus the question is raised, what shapes the character of the relationship that Presidents seek with their parties? An answer is desirable for explaining past behavior and for considering future prospects. Given the room allowed by the presidential office for the play of personalities and exogenous forces, attempts to theorize precisely about any aspect of presidential behavior are hazardous and likely to be misleading. But the analysis does provide a basis for some observations which may be of general utility.

Most discussions of the President-party relationship appear to see presidential behavior in reactive terms. That is, the circumstances enveloping Presidents—such as public expectations, requirements of national leadership, the conditions of parties and their place in presidentially-relevant political processes—force strategic judgment on Presidents about partisan stances and activities. For some contemporary commentators, systemic impediments make vigorous leadership strategically unwise, in turn enlarging the gulf between Presidents and their parties. Undoubtedly one elemental factor in the relationship is the strategic calculations of Presidents and their aides about the utility of overt party leadership in meeting the diverse requirements of the office and in the attainment of presidential objectives. But it may be that a perspective which centers exclusively on instrumental considerations is incomplete. There is basis in this analysis for asserting that a second elemental factor is also at work: the partisan dispositions of Presidents, dispositions grounded in pre-presidential experiences and which become a component of presidential "style."[59]

Partisan dispositions may coincide with strategic considerations, or they may conflict with them. The principal clue to the relationship, then, is in the connection between partisanship and party leadership in the presidencies of Kennedy, Ford, Johnson and Carter. Kennedy and Ford came out of family and political environments in which partisan awareness and concern were prominent.[60] Indeed, their political advancement was closely associated with party. Kennedy's nomination in 1960

was due in large part to the support of the Democratic organizations in many of the larger cities and states. Ford's ladder to prominence was a partisan, not a legislative one. In contrast, Johnson and Carter came out of political environments dominated by a single party. Their political experiences and courses were selected. Johnson in the Congress, especially in the Senate, and Carter in Georgia state politics, did not sharpen partisan dispositions. Given the circumstances, it was sensible for Johnson as Senate Democratic minority and majority leader and Carter as governor to minimize partisanship. The circumstances of their advance to the presidency did nothing to call established dispositions into question, and in fact probably strengthened them.[61]

The independent effect of affective, partisan dispositions on presidential behavior is suggested by the possibility that they may override strategic considerations and create negative consequences. Would Ford perhaps have been more successful with Congress and in the 1976 election—the challenge from Reagan for the nomination notwithstanding—if he had been less a partisan? Might Johnson have limited the damages to his presidency by being somewhat more of a partisan, or at least attending to the Democratic Party and exploiting its potential for the development of public support for his policies? And could Carter's presidency have proceeded more smoothly if he had played the party leadership role more energetically?

Whereas these cases suggest, to a degree, that affective dispositions toward both partisanship and nonpartisanship, ingrained in style, may offset "objective" strategic considerations, the Nixon case suggests the possibility of the reverse of such a relationship, i.e., that strategic considerations may compromise partisanship. That is to say, during his presidency Nixon saw his larger interests best served by becoming less the Republican partisan and more the leader of a national majority which departed from established party alignments. Strategic adaptation may have been facilitated in this instance by a partisanship which, while not weak, was less firmly in place than that, say, of Kennedy and Ford. It should be recalled that Nixon's origins were in California during a period of nonpartisan politics. Until he became a candidate for Congress in 1946, he was not associated with the Republican Party. It is possible that the strong partisanship evidenced as a member of Congress, as Vice-President, and as presidential candidate was to a substantial extent instrumental, not affective in its origins, thus allowing for adaptability in its employment during the presidential period.

These observations, and some of their logical derivatives, may be stated in summary form as follows.

1. Presidential behavior in relation to party is the product of the interaction of established partisan dispositions and strategic assessment about the utility of party-related activity in the attainment of presidential purposes.

2. The behavior of a particular President will result from the subtle interaction of these two factors in ways that are difficult to foresee and even describe in retrospect, but which make a number of results theoretically possible.

3. Strong affective dispositions, or partisanship, may lead Presidents to give substantial emphasis to party, even in the face of strategic disadvantage.

4. This need not always be the case, however. Strategic considerations may moderate the effects of strong partisan dispositions.

5. Similarly, the possibility of strategic advantage may lead weak partisans to energetic party leadership.

PARTY LEADERSHIP: PROSPECTS FOR A REJUVENATION

Conventional assessments of recent President-party relations go far toward announcing the emergence of a nonpartisan Presidency devoid of the ties and interdependencies between Presidents and the parties of which they are nominal chiefs. To be sure, many factors do militate against a close and mutually satisfactory relationship. But again it is apparent from the evidence of the past two decades that many of the traditional linkages persist.

It is important to recognize that despite recent trends that unquestionably aggravate the relationship, there remain forces pulling in the other direction. Despite the widely-reported changes in party affiliation among the electorate and in the organization and function of political parties, partisanship and party are still forces with which Presidents must contend. Party identification remains the single most important variable in explanations of voter behavior.[62] Thus, Presidents continue to use party affiliation as a cue to prospective voters. Further, there are still strong expectations from other actors in the political process that Presidents will perform as party leaders. All recent incumbents have participated, to a greater or lesser degree, in party organizational determinations, fund-raising, candidate endorsements, and appointment of fellow partisans to administration positions. The nomination struggles of 1980 also showed that Presidents and presidential contenders place themselves above party even now at their peril. They showed in Edward Kennedy and Ronald Reagan, in particular, candidates whose partisanship appeared strong and real. It is not likely that a strong partisan, once in the presidential office, would turn his back on his party and fail to be sensitive to its interests.

But perhaps the most important factor bearing on the future President-party relationship is the degree to which expressed partisanship and active party leadership may be in the strategic interests of Presidents, no matter their dispositions. In other words, in contrast to prior periods, Presidents may find that they have more to gain than to lose through associations with party. Whereas in the past, party affairs and partisanship in the office may have been impediments to the conduct of presidential business and the exercise of core presidential responsibilities, in the future the situation may be altered to a significant degree.

There are several reasons why this conceivably can prove to be the case. The factionalization of American politics and the divisiveness which attends issues of public policy make presidential leadership difficult and impair presidential effectiveness. Many of the resources which Presidents have traditionally exploited have been eroded or have been lessened in effect by such growing political querulousness. For example, the apparent intractability of many contemporary public policy problems, the new interest group politics, congressional independence, and a critical watchdog media, among other phenomena, make garnering support for presidential efforts an onerous task.

What the presidency now lacks is an accumulation of substantial generic support for presidential efforts. One source that remains, though diminished to some degree, is party. Parties, despite the diversity they reflect, present opportunities for the attraction of generic support which may in part offset the particularistic pulls of other forces and contribute to presidential capacity. Furthermore, because of their modernization in the organizational and technological sense, party structures may provide Presidents improved means for forging and articulating generic support.[63] For reasons such as these Presidents with strong partisan disposition may not feel impelled to mute them, and Presidents with weak partisan disposition may feel it in their interest to direct some of their energies toward party affairs.

For those inclined to believe that an effective party system and a workable relationship between the parties and the President is a sign of health in the society, this assessment is a cautiously optimistic one. Presidents are far from a total break from the ties and constraints of political parties. And as Carter and Bibby have demonstrated, the parties may well be embarked on a period of rebuilding and internal strengthening which will enable them both to assist the President in governing the nation and to impose a measure of popular control on the most powerful of our modern institutions.

NOTES

1. Walter Dean Burnham, "Jimmy Carter and the Democratic Crisis," *New Republic* (July 3 and 10, 1976), pp. 17–19.

2. Harold F. Bass, Jr., "Presidential Responsibility for National Party Atrophy," Paper delivered at the 1977 Annual Meeting of the American Political Science Association, August, 1977, p. 1.

3. This section draws upon a number of works on the presidency and political parties, including: Hugh A. Bone, *Party Committees and National Politics* (Seattle: University of Washington Press, 1968); David S. Broder, *The Party's Over* (New York: Harper and Row, 1971); Stuart Gerry Brown, *The American Presidency: Leadership, Partisanship, and Popularity* (New York: Macmillan, 1966); James Mac Gregor Burns, *The Deadlock of Democracy: Four-Party Politics in America*

(Englewood Cliffs, N.J.: Prentice Hall, 1963) and *Presidential Government* (Boston: Houghton Mifflin, 1966); Edward S. Corwin, *The President: Office and Powers, 1787–1957* (New York: New York University Press, 1957); Cornelius P. Cotter and Bernard C. Hennessy, *Politics without Power: The National Party Committees* (New York: Atherton Press, 1964); Thomas E. Cronin, *The State of the Presidency*, 2nd ed. (Boston: Little Brown, 1979); William J. Crotty and Gary C. Jacobson, *American Parties in Decline*, (Boston: Little, Brown, 1980); Ralph M. Goldman, "Titular Leadership of the Presidential Parties," in Aaron Wildavsky, ed. *The Presidency* (Boston: Little, Brown, 1969); Erwin C. Hargrove, *The Power of the Modern Presidency* (New York: Knopf, 1974); Louis W. Koenig, *The Chief Executive*, 3rd ed. (New York: Harcourt Brace Jovanovich, 1975); Everett Carll Ladd, *Where Have All the Voters Gone* (New York: W. W. Norton, 1978); Peter H. Odegard, "Presidential Leadership and Party Responsibility," *The Annals*, vol. 307 (Sept. 1956); Richard M. Pious, *The American Presidency* (New York: Basic Books, 1979); Clinton Rossiter, *The American Presidency*, 2nd ed. (New York: Harcourt Brace and World, 1960); Lester G. Seligman, "The Presidential Office and the President as Party Leader," *Law and Contemporary Problems*, vol. 21 (Autumn, 1956); and Frank J. Sorauf, *Party Politics in America*, 3rd ed. (Boston: Little, Brown, 1976).

4. Koenig, p. 116.

5. Pious, p. 121.

6. Cf., Austin Ranney, "The Political Parties: Reform and Decline," in Anthony King, ed., *The New American Political System* (Washington, D.C.: American Enterprise Institute, 1978), pp. 213–247.

7. Fred I. Greenstein, "Eisenhower as an Activist President: A Look at New Evidence," *Political Science Quarterly*, vol. 94 (Winter 1979–80), p. 579.

8. Ibid.

9. Harold Lasswell, *Politics: Who Gets What, When, How* (New York: McGraw-Hill, 1936), and Lasswell and Abraham Kaplan, *Power and Society* (New Haven, Conn.: Yale University Press, 1950).

10. The three indicators for strength of party leadership were drawn from those facets of the role which presidential scholars traditionally have deemed to be of central importance. The indicators also reflect the availability of meaningful data on party leadership.

With respect to the percentage of appointments drawn from the President's party, the tabulations include: appointments to cabinet, sub-cabinet, and other policy-level positions in the Executive Branch, federal judgeships, and posts in other independent commissions and agencies. Data on party affiliation were taken from the annual summaries of confirmed presidential appointments in the *Congressional Quarterly Almanac* (Washington, D.C.: Congressional Quarterly, Inc.), vols. 17–33, 1961–1977.

It should be noted that in the case of some positions, particularly in the case of regulatory commissions, party ratios are specified. Therefore, an appointee publicly designated as "Independent" may actually be a party member whose affiliation is not announced to avoid violation of such ratios.

Finally, the consideration of presidential uses of patronage was taken to include, for purposes of this study, the distribution of financial benefits, commonly known as pork-barrel funding.

11. Stephen J. Wayne, *The Legislative Presidency* (New York: Harper & Row, 1978) and George C. Edwards III, *Presidential Influence in Congress* (San Francisco: W. H. Freeman and Co., 1980).

12. Edwards, p. 81.

13. Theodore C. Sorensen, *Kennedy* (New York: Bantam Books, 1966), p. 79.

14. John F. Kennedy, Remarks at a Meeting of the Democratic National Committee, Jan. 21, 1961, *Public Papers of the Presidents: John F. Kennedy, 1961* (Washington: U.S. Government Printing Office, 1962), p. 4.

15. Kennedy, *Public Papers*, 1963, p. 895.

16. William G. Carleton, "Kennedy in History: An Early Appraisal," *The Antioch Review*, vol. 24 (1964), pp. 277–299.

17. Broder, pp. 23, 29.

18. Sorensen, p. 79.

19. Jules Witcover, *Marathon: The Pursuit of The Presidency, 1972–1976*, (New York: Viking, 1977), pp. 37–38.

20. *Presidency 1975* (Washington: Congressional Quarterly, 1976), p. 87-A.

21. Kennedy, *Public Papers*, 1961, p. 695.

22. Broder, pp. 23–38, and Herbert S. Parmet, *The Democrats: The Years After FDR* (New York: Macmillan, 1976), p. 202.

23. Broder, p. 38.

24. Sorensen, p. 848.

25. *New York Times*, Oct. 16, 1961.

26. Cotter and Hennessy, p. 89.

27. Theodore H. White, *Breach of Faith: The Fall of Richard Nixon* (New York: Atheneum, 1975), p. 179.

28. *Washington Post*, August 16, 1976, and August 20, 1976.

29. *Congressional Quarterly Weekly Reports*, Oct. 19, 1962, p. 1969.

30. Ibid., 1973.

31. Ibid.

32. Ibid., Nov. 9, 1974, p. 3091.

33. Hugh Heclo, *A Government of Strangers* (Washington: Brookings Institution, 1977), pp. 63–68, 80–99.

34. Lyndon Baines Johnson, *The Vantage Point: Perspectives on the Presidency* (New York: Holt, Rinehart, and Winston, 1971), pp. 27–28.

35. Johnson, *Public Papers: 1965*, vol. 2, p. 330.

36. Jimmy Carter, *Why Not the Best?* (Nashville, Broadman Press, 1975), p. 85.

37. Witcover, p. 645.

38. Broder, p. 68.

39. Clifton C. Carter, Oral History Transcript, Lyndon B. Johnson Library, used with permission of Mrs. Clifton C. Carter.

40. Ibid., pp. 28–31.

41. *New York Times*, Jan. 23, 1978.

42. *Christian Science Monitor*, Jan. 4, 1978.

43. *Washington Post*, June 14, 1978.

44. *Newsweek*, Dec. 18, 1978.

45. *Congressional Quarterly Weekly Reports*, Oct. 21, 1966, p. 2608.

46. Koenig, p. 143.

47. *Newsweek*, Feb. 27, 1978.

48. *Congressional Quarterly Weekly Reports*, Nov. 4, 1978, p. 3171.

49. *Washington Post*, June 6, 1977.

50. Earl Mazo, *Richard Nixon: A Political and Personal Portrait* (New York: Harper and Brothers, 1959), p. 296.

51. Ibid.

52. Richard M. Nixon, *Six Crises* (New York: Doubleday, 1962), p. 304–322.

53. *Congressional Quarterly Weekly Reports*, Nov. 11, 1966, p. 2773.

54. Nixon, *Public Papers: 1970*, p. 1063.

55. William Safire, *Before the Fall: An Inside View of the Pre-Watergate White House* (New York: Doubleday, 1975), p. 309.

56. Rowland Evans and Robert Novak, *Nixon in the White House* (New York: Random House, 1971), p. 74.

57. Koenig, p. 145.

58. Richard P. Nathan, *The Plot that Failed: Nixon and the Administrative Presidency* (New York: John Wiley & Sons, 1975).

59. See James David Barber, *The Presidential Character: Predicting Performance in the White House*, 2nd ed. (Englewood Cliffs: Prentice Hall, 1977).

60. On Ford's partisan background, see Gerald F. ter Horst, *Gerald Ford and The Future of the Presidency* (New York: Third Press, 1974), p. 7.

61. There is an aspect of party leadership in the Johnson case that is not treated here but which suggests a dimension of the phenomenon that is of vital importance and deserves extensive attention: party leadership through policy-making. Johnson embodied it, pushing the enactment of a Democratic program and one responsive to partisan Democratic views and interests. See James L. Sundquist, *Politics and Policy: The Eisenhower, Kennedy, and Johnson Years* (Washington: Brookings Institution, 1968).

62. Philip Converse, "The Nature of Belief Systems in Mass Publics," in David Apter, ed., *Ideology and Discontent* (New York: Free Press, 1964), pp. 206–261 and Jeane J. Kirkpatrick, "Changing Patterns of Electoral Competition," in Anthony King, ed., *The New American Political System* (Washington, D.C.: American Enterprise Institute, 1978), pp. 249–285.

63. See Cornelius P. Cotter and John F. Bibby, "The Impact of Reform on the National Party Organizations: The Long-Term Determinants of Party Reform," paper delivered at the 1979 annual meeting of the American Political Science Association, Washington, D.C., September, 1979 and Cotter and Bibby, "Institutional Development of Parties and the Thesis of Party Decline," *Political Science Quarterly*, vol. 95 (Spring, 1980), pp. 1–27.

CHAPTER X

The Presidency and the Media

Robert Locander has written, "American presidents are not required to meet the press" and "the news media have no formal obligation to cover the chief executive."[1] Moreover, "the Constitution makes no provision for television networks nor does any act of Congress mandate their existence."[2] Yet the president does meet the news media and the media covers the president. After all, both sides have reciprocal needs: the news media depends upon the president and the White House in order to carry on their business; the president depends upon the news media to link him with the public.[3] Yet, "throughout the history of the republic," as Elmer Cornwell has said, "White House and the press have been living under at best, an armed truce."[4] Why do these two institutions experience so much hostility toward each other? Recall that the past is prologue.

George Washington, the first president of the United States, complained bitterly of the hostilities of the press toward his administration, especially the attacks of Philip Freneau, the editor of the Republican newspaper, the *National Gazette,* on what he (Freneau) considered Federalist domination of the political system.[5] The Federalists were so disturbed with the attacks of the press upon its policies during the administration of John Adams (the second president of the United States), that they enacted the Sedition Act of 1798, which made criminally libel any criticism or attempts to organize any criticism of the government or its leaders.[6] Adams himself had no direct responsibility for the Sedition Act and refused to enforce it in the manner that the Federalists wished. Thomas Jefferson, the third president and the leader of the Antifederalists (or Republicans as they were sometimes known) argued, although he believed strongly in a free press, that "our newspapers, for the most part, present only the caricatures of disaffected minds. Indeed, the abuses of the freedom of the press here have been carried to a length never before known or borne by any civilized nation."[7]

The American media experienced tremendous growth during the nearly three decades from Presidents Jefferson to Jackson.[8] To be sure, it was a period of blatant partisanship: there was no such thing as objective reporting. Importantly, this early era in mass media experience was one in which the press was heavily dependent upon government patronage, explaining, in part, the highly partisan nature of newspaper reporting.[9] This patronage usually came in the form of the party in power paying its favorite newspapers for printing and disseminating national legislation, but in other forms of printing contracts, as well.

By the time of the election of Andrew Jackson, the newspapers had made possible a new generation of political leaders: a breed of men willing to enlist the support of the common man to their cause.[10] From Jackson to the Civil War, the growth of the newspaper trade continued unabated. This growth enhanced popular democracy and served to expand the reach of the president by permitting him to mobilize relatively quiescent citizens into partisan voters and to gain a measure of hegemony over the national political system.[11] Except for the period of the Civil War, however, the Executive branch remained essentially equal if not subordinate to Congress. Moreover, the scale of the newspaper enterprise remained small in comparison with the present, a press really independent of a particular party, candidate, or faction had not yet emerged; and the line between government and the media continued to be blurred.[12]

A major leap forward toward the contemporary mass media occurred between 1870 and 1900. Together, advances in technology that made printing cheap and the advent of the telegraph made possible the truly mass-produced, mass-circulation daily newspaper. During this period, daily circulation went up 222 percent while the population increased by only 63 percent.[13] Significantly, a large number of independent newspapers emeged that could earn their own keep without becoming beholden to a particular party, interest, or individual. Richard Rubin writes that this

> combined departisanization of the press and loss of presidential influence over the flow of national political communications heightened the difficulties of presidential leadership. The independence of the press deprived the president and national leaders of an important tool for structuring and mobilizing public opinion and votes.[14]

The result was that presidents of this period became essentially passive objects of newspaper reports.[15] Indeed, relations between the presidents and the press from Reconstruction to 1900, as James Pollard writes, "were largely in the doldrums."[16]

The growing number of mass-circulation, independent newspapers devoted to a news rather than partisan function undoubtedly contributed to increasing public attention to the activities, policies, and programs of government and the rise of the Muckrakers and the Progressive Movement.

With Theodore Roosevelt's assumption of the presidency in 1901, relations between the president and the press changed.[17] No longer would presidents be objects of media reports; presidents would now influence much of that reporting. Douglass Cater writes that, as such, Theodore Roosevelt was the pioneer of modern press relations.[18]

Roosevelt understood the needs of the press. They needed news, and they needed to get it from the most authoritative source in the political system. More than anyone else at the national level, the president was that person. Roosevelt also understood that, as president, he needed the press to reach the public. Accordingly, he attempted to achieve a dynamic and profitable relationship with the media.[19]

Roosevelt originated the press conference when he began inviting small groups of reporters into the White House to whom he could convey information about his government and its policy goals.[20] Beyond the press conference, Roosevelt made important contributions to presidential-press relations in his practices of floating trial balloons designed to test in advance policies he had in mind and of encouraging the media to publish stories about programs in which he was interested. Parenthetically, Roosevelt's relations with the press were not entirely blissful. From time to time reporters would write stories that angered him. When he became extremely unhappy with a reporter, he would cut off all ties with him.[21]

William Howard Taft had little taste for publicity, did not enjoy meeting with reporters, was frequently annoyed by the press, and expressed his contempt for it.[22] As a consequence nothing new was added to White House media relations during his administration.

Wilson originated the first *formal* White House press conference.[23] Moreover, he held these conferences on a regular basis. Importantly, also, he invited all accredited news representatives to his meetings with reporters. All of this made for his easy and happy relationship with the press. Wilson's camaraderie with the media, however, soon cooled. From the very beginning of his administration, he could not understand why the glare of the press had to be so intense upon both his private life and his public policy efforts.[24] As the United States moved towards World War I, Wilson's negative view of the press became more pronounced. When the United States entered the war, Wilson ended the White House press conferences.[25]

After the war, Wilson did not keep the press informed of events while he was in attendance at the peace conference in Versailles, creating additional ill will with the media. Moreover, the treaty that emerged from Versailles, with the League of Nations proposal appended to it, suffered bad press. These circumstances combined with Wilson's collapse and illness after his swing around the country in behalf of the League of Nations, resulted in his allowing the press conferences to lapse completely.[26]

As a presidential candidate, Warren Harding made every effort toward good press relations. He met regularly with members of the press assigned to cover his campaign. In addition, he accommodated the press by erecting a small house near his home in Marion, Ohio, to give the media the opportunity to cover his much heralded "front porch" campaign.[27]

Harding was the first newspaper publisher to be elected president and, accordingly, sought to improve the interchange between the president and the press. He revived press conferences and held them twice a week. However, as a result of an indiscreet disclosure he made that was published, Harding revived the rule that all questions for the president must be submitted, in writing, in advance of a press conference.[28]

An additional contribution that Harding made to White House press relations was his issuance of White House identification cards to members of the White House News Photographers Association granting them access to all public, and occasionally private, events that he attended.[29] Harding thus elevated the status of White House press relations, improving the president's capacity to lead public opinion.

Calvin Coolidge continued the regular press conferences revived during Harding's administration. Coolidge, however, imposed his own style of president-press relations: he was never to be quoted directly without his express permission and much of what he said to the press was to be attributed to a "White House spokesman." Moreover, although Coolidge held press conferences frequently, most of them were considered dull and uneventful. A noted observer concluded: "If he [Coolidge] did not particularly advance the status of the relations between the White House and the press, neither did he harm them seriously."[30]

President Hoover's record of press relations was largely one of failure.[31] Hoover's problems began almost immediately after his election: he censored the dispatches of correspondents who accompanied him on a goodwill trip to South America between his election and his inauguration. Within three months after his inauguration, he ended regular press conferences. Long before the end of his administration Hoover was on worse terms with the press than any president had been since the turn of the century. Hoover had, as Secretary of Commerce in the Harding and Coolidge cabinets, enjoyed good press relations; as president, however, Hoover was aloof and kept the press at arm's length. Perhaps Hoover's biggest problem was that "he felt strongly that in the public interest there are some things the press had no right to print, at least until the White House gave the word."[32] Hoover thought it more discreet and consistent with the public interest for reporters to write only what was handed out officially.

Hoover's relationship with the press steadily declined, mainly because the press had difficulty getting news from him.[33] This tension was exacerbated by the press's perception that the president's veracity at his press conferences was doubtful. Hoover informed the press on several occasions that no questions had been submitted to him in advance as was his policy when, in fact, questions had been submitted to the president's secretary who often determined many of them too trivial for the president's consideration. Moreover, Hoover agitated the press by canceling press conferences when he chose with little or no notice. Toward the end of his administration, correspondents came to depend largely on their own resources to get the news on what initiatives were being taken and what policies were being supported by the executive branch.

Franklin Roosevelt must be given credit for revolutionizing presidential relations with the working press. He stuck faithfully to his schedule of holding two press conferences each week, he enlarged the scope of the conferences by furnishing reporters with educational information on the key issues of the day, and he provided correspondents with background information on the war in Europe that permitted them to write stories about international developments.[34]

For policy leadership purposes, FDR put himself into the homes of the public via radio, utilizing the strategies of the fireside chat, press conferences, and presidential addresses to the nation.[35] Richard Rubin writes that FDR "established a faster, more centralized and more direct circuitry between the mass public and the presidency than possible before him and used the unique personal qualities of radio to deeply penetrate into a vast new listening audience."[36]

Importantly for the press, FDR abolished the restrictive practice of requiring written questions in advance and permitted spontaneous questions from the floor. FDR's high standing with the media on this account was supplemented by his always providing the reporters with live and useful news. Later in his administration, FDR also ended the nonquotation rule which required that statements made by the president be attributed to White House spokesmen.[37] Even though FDR was often very critical of newspaper owners, and they of him, his relations with the working press were eminently superior to that of any of his predecessors. FDR capped his contributions to White House press relations by adding communications staff and thus institutionalizing press relations to an unprecedented degree.[38]

Harry Truman's tenure in the presidency marked the continued institutionalization of White House press relations. Truman moved the press conference from the Oval Office to the Indian Treaty Room, a much larger space, thus permitting a larger number of reporters and news representatives to be present at press conferences. Truman formalized press relations even more by requiring reporters to gather in the room before the president's entrance and to stand and identify themselves before putting a question to the president.[39] Truman prepared for his press conferences. His press secretary briefed him thoroughly on questions likely to arise in the conferences, and he usually began his conferences with carefully prepared statements.

While Dwight Eisenhower held fewer press conferences than his predecessors, the processes of institutionalization and formalization went forward. The staff assigned to communications and public relations work grew. Also, background information, provided to reporters by FDR himself in his administration, was provided by staffers, not the president, during the Eisenhower administration. Initially, Eisenhower was not comfortable with the press conference, but under Press Secretary James Hagerty's tutelage he learned to dominate it. By 1954 (two years into his first term), Eisenhower was at ease with the press conference, was better informed, and had learned to dodge questions for which he had no ready answers.[40]

Television aided Eisenhower's image. At the time of the first presidential television press conference on January 19, 1955, he was able to project himself very well. The image he projected was a man with a warm, easy smile, and an unpretentious manner. Nevertheless, Press Secretary Hagerty reserved the right to edit the press conference films that were usually recorded an hour before broadcast. In practice, there was very little need for Hagerty to edit the films, but because the conferences were not "live," they lacked immediacy. Contributing to this lack of immediacy was the tendency of the media to use only brief excerpts from the conferences.

John F. Kennedy continued the enlargement of White House press relations. He moved the news conferences from the Indian Treaty Room to the larger

State Department Auditorium thus accommodating even larger numbers of reporters and news representatives at White House press conferences.[41] "Enlargement" was also enhanced by Kennedy's practice of maintaining an open door policy for individual reporters.

Prior to Kennedy, press conferences had been taped for television presentation at a later hour. As such the media could and did usually cut and show only small segments of them. Kennedy, however, adopted the "live" television press conference format now making possible direct presidential communication to the public through this medium as FDR had done with radio twenty-seven years earlier. Kennedy's first live news conference from Washington occurred on January 25, 1961, just five days after he took his oath of office.[42] Charles Roberts, a career journalist, observes that the live press conference opened a new era in political communication: the live camera gave the president the upper hand in his verbal bouts with the press.[43] Kennedy's legacy to White House press relations was at least twofold: the groundbreaking live television press conference and an easy, comfortable relationship with the media.

Lyndon Johnson's style with the media differed from that of his predecessor. Johnson preferred small impromptu meetings with reporters over meetings with large groups. The large press conference was not a practice that he relished. In search for the happy medium, Johnson varied the meeting places of the television press conferences from the Oval Office, to the East Room, to the theater in the White House. Ray Scherer suggests that Johnson never found an ideal format.[44]

Johnson experienced his share of negative coverage by the press, mainly because of his Vietnam policy. Near the end of his life, he said:

> From my viewpoint how they twisted and imagined and built and magnified things that I didn't think were true at all. I never thought it was the President's credibility gap, I thought it was their credibility gap. But they owned the papers and networks; I didn't. And they come out every day. And they talk about my credibility, but there wasn't much I could do about their credibility.[45]

The recent history of the office of the president is, in considerable part, the history of the expansion of presidential resources in the White House to facilitate getting the president's message to the people. George Edwards and Stephen Wayne in their comprehensive essay, "The President and the Press," reprinted here, show how the president's relation to the media is an important aspect of his effort to lead public opinion. They review in detail the various strategies presidents use to influence the media. Edwards and Wayne discuss both sides of the public relations equation: the president and the White House press staff on the one side and the accredited members of the working press to the White House on the other. The authors argue persuasively that both sides, needing each other, usually find ways to cooperate, but that the inherently adversarial nature of the relationship results in a continuous low level tension between the two, which occasionally bursts out into open conflict.

Martha Kumar and Michael Grossman write that "the need for presidents to create an apparatus to organize and centralize their political communications . . . grew because of the increasing weakness in many of the traditional power centers in national politics."[46] And Theodore Wendt writes that "the Nixon administration was the first . . . to have a fully developed approach to presidential rhetoric, to the use of media to enhance presidential speeches, to the recognition of television as the central 'check' on presidential rhetorical power."[47] Accordingly, under President Nixon, the White House became a large, centralized communications apparatus with power to manipulate the president's image and to send highly dramatized messages to bureaucrats, Congress, interest groups, the public at large, and foreign governments. Institutionally, Nixon built up the size and responsibilities of the White House press and public relations staff. He separated major responsibilities between a press secretary who was to conduct relations with White House reporters, and a Director of Communications who was to conduct press relations for departments and agencies.

As a matter of personal style, Nixon made elaborate preparations for press conferences and thus was able to field questions from reporters without reference to notes. As a matter of political strategy, Nixon permitted long periods of time to lapse between press conferences and relied much more heavily on formal television addresses and the radio in order to bypass the Washington press corps and to speak directly to the public. Nixon was keenly aware that he had more control over radio and television addresses, while the media had the opportunity for more control over press conferences.

The Ford and especially the Carter and Reagan presidencies have continued the expansion and institutionalization of the White House communication and public relations capabilities. Both Carter and Reagan have themselves relied on a larger measure of rhetoric to support their policies and programs as well as their own personal and electoral ambitions.[48] President Reagan has been, without a doubt, the most successful rhetorician among the television age presidents. In recognition of this, media representatives often refer to him as "the great communicator."

With the dramatic increase in the number of presidential primaries in the 1970s, television began to loom larger as a link between the presidency and mass opinion. Some observers argue that television permits the president to dominate the public space.[49] Other observers say that television challenges the president's capacity to set political priorities.[50] Significantly, primaries and television have contributed to the separation of presidential candidates and presidents from their parties by requiring a candidate interested in election and a president interested in reelection to have their own personal campaign organizations. This separation of candidates and presidents from their parties has placed a premium on campaigning skills and on independent personal resources. Theodore Lowi argues that these and earlier trends have resulted in the personal or plebiscitary president who relies heavily on effective appearances and especially rhetoric for success.[51]

This heavy reliance on rhetoric as opposed to political parties and party organization for political success has resulted in what James Ceasar, Glen Thorow, Jeffrey Tulis, and Joseph Bessette call the rhetorical presidency. These authors argue that, historically, leadership through rhetoric was suspect, that presidents rarely spoke directly to the people, and that, in any event, presidents relied much more heavily on party and political leadership in Congress for their electoral and programmatic support.

Now presidents attempt to move mass opinion by speeches that exhort the public to support their policies and programs. Presidents are obliged to do this for three reasons: the modern doctrine of the presidency, which avers that the presidency is a place of moral leadership and should employ rhetoric to lead public opinion; the advent of the modern mass media, especially television, which facilitates the use of rhetoric; and the modern presidential campaign, which blurs campaigning and governing.[52] Ceasar, Thurow, Tulis, and Bessette fear some of the possible consequences of these new developments. Their analysis, "The rise of the Rhetorical Presidency," is reprinted here.

NOTES

1. Robert Locander, "The President and the News Media," in *Dimensions of the Modern Presidency*, ed. Edward N. Kearny (St. Louis, Mo.: Forum Press, 1981), p. 41.

2. Fred Smoller, "The Six O'Clock Presidency: Patterns of Network News Coverage of the President," *Presidential Studies Quarterly* 16, no. 1 (Winter 1986), p. 31.

3. See Barbara Hinckley, *Problems of the Presidency: A Text with Readings* (Glenview, Ill.: Scott, Foresman, 1985), pp. 47–48.

4. Elmer Cornwell, *The Presidency and the Press* (Morristown, N.J.: General Learning Press, 1974), p. 3.

5. See Richard L. Rubin, *Press, Party and Presidency* (New York: W. W. Norton, 1981), p. 13.

6. Ibid., p. 14.

7. Quoted in Cornwell, *Presidency and Press*, p. 2.

8. See Rubin, *Press, Party and Presidency*, p. 17.

9. For a comprehensive study of the press's dependence upon governmental patronage, see Culver H. Smith, *Press, Politics and Patronage: The American Government's Use of Newspaper, 1789–1875* (Athens, Ga.: University of Georgia Press, 1977), *passim*.

10. Rubin, *Press, Party and Presidency*, p. 44.

11. Ibid., p. 53.

12. See Elmer E. Cornwell, *Presidential Leadership of Public Opinion* (Bloomington, Ind.: Indiana University Press, 1965), p. 10.

13. Ibid., p. 11.

14. Rubin, *Press, Party and Presidency*, p. 65. See also p. 74.

15. Cornwell, *Presidential Leadership*, p. 12; also Rubin, pp. 68–69.

16. James E. Pollard, *The Presidents and the Press* (New York: Macmillan, 1947), p. vi.

17. Ibid.

18. Douglass Cater, "The President and the Press," *Annals of the American Academy of Political and Social Science* 307 (September 1956), p. 60.

19. Cornwell, *Presidential Leadership,* p. 14.

20. See Cornwell, *Presidency and Press,* p. 7.

21. Pollard, *Presidents and Press,* p. 574.

22. Ibid., pp. 601 and 608.

23. Ibid., p. 630.

24. Ibid., especially pp. 634, 635, 637, 639, and 640.

25. Ibid., p. 658.

26. See Cornwell, *Presidential Leadership,* p. 56.

27. Pollard, *Presidents and Press,* p. 699.

28. Ibid., p. 705.

29. Cornwell, *Presidential Leadership,* p. 68.

30. Pollard, *Presidents and Press,* p. 732.

31. Ibid., p. 769.

32. Ibid., p. 738.

33. Ibid., p. 744.

34. Rubin, *Press, Party and Presidency,* pp. 128–29.

35. Cornwell, *Presidency and Press,* p. 10.

36. Rubin, *Press, Party and Presidency,* p. 146.

37. Cater, *President and Press,* p. 61.

38. Cornwell, *Presidency and Press,* p. 11.

39. See Ray Scherer, "The Presidential Press Conference," in *The Media: The Credibility of Institutions, Policies and Leadership,* vol. 5, ed. Kenneth W. Thompson (Lanham, Md.: University Press of America, 1985), p. 69.

40. See Norman A. Graebner, "Eisenhower's Popular Leadership," in *Eisenhower as President,* ed. Dean Albertson (New York: Hill and Wang, 1963), p. 155; on the matter of Eisenhower's strategy for dodging questions he did not wish to answer, see Fred I. Greenstein, "Eisenhower as an Activist President," *Political Science Quarterly* 94, no. 4 (Winter 1979–80), pp. 587–88.

41. See Scherer, *Presidential Press Conference,* p. 70.

42. Charles Roberts, "John F. Kennedy and the Press," in *The Media,* ed. Thompson, p. 194.

43. Ibid., p. 195.

44. Scherer, *Presidential Press Conference,* p. 71.

45. Lyndon Johnson, interview with Walter Cronkite, December 27, 1969, cited in Doris A. Graber, ed., *The President and the Public* (Philadelphia: Institute for Study of Human Issues, 1982), p. 87.

46. Martha Joynt Kumar and Michael Baruch Grossman, "Political Communications from the White House: The Interest Group Connection," *Presidential Studies Quarterly* 16, no. 1 (Winter 1986), p. 93.

47. Theodore Otto Wendt, Jr., "Presidential Rhetoric: Definition of a Field of Study," *Presidential Studies Quarterly* 16, no. 1 (Winter 1986), p. 107.

48. For some of the evidence, see Robert Locander, "Carter and the Press: The First Two Years," *Presidential Studies Quarterly* 10, no. 1 (Winter 1980), pp. 106–20 and Helen Thomas, "Ronald Reagan," in *The Media*, ed. Thompson, pp. 209–38.

49. See Bruce Miroff, "Monopolizing the Public Space: The President as a Problem for Democratic Politics," in *Rethinking The Presidency*, ed. Thomas E. Cronin (Boston: Little, Brown, 1982), p. 221; and Alan P. Balutis, "The Presidency and the Press: the Expanding Presidential Image," *Presidential Studies Quarterly* 7, no. 4 (Fall 1977), pp. 244, 251.

50. On this point, see especially C. Don Livingston, "The Televised Presidency," *Presidential Studies Quarterly* 16, no. 1 (Winter 1986), pp. 25–26; and Herbert Schnertz, "The Media and the Presidency," *Presidential Studies Quarterly* 16, no. 1 (Winter 1986), p. 14.

51. See Theodore Lowi, *The Personal President: Power Invested, Promise Unfulfilled* (Ithaca, N.Y.: Cornell University Press, 1985), especially pp. 20, 62, and 151.

52. For a concurring view of the blurring of campaigning and governing, see Sidney Blumenthal, *The Permanent Campaign: Inside the World of Elite Political Operatives* (Boston: Beacon Press, 1980), especially pp. 7–10.

25

The President and the Press

George Edwards III & Stephen J. Wayne

Despite all their efforts to lead public opinion, presidents do not directly reach the American people on a day-to-day basis. It is the press that provides people with most of what they know about the chief executive, his policies, and the consequences of his policies. The media also interpret and analyze presidential activities, even the president's direct appeals to the public.

The press is thus the principal intermediary between the president and the public, and relations with the press are an important aspect of the president's efforts to lead public opinion. If the press portrays the president in a favorable light, he will face fewer obstacles in obtaining public support. If, on the other hand, the press is hostile toward his administration, the president's talk will be more difficult.

Because of the importance of the press to the president, the White House goes to great lengths to encourage the media to project a positive image of the president and his policies. These efforts include coordinating the news, holding press conferences, and providing a range of services such as formal briefings, interviews, photo opportunities, background sessions, travel accommodations, and daily handouts. On occasion it also

Source: Excerpted from *Presidential Leadership: Politics and Policymaking* by George Edwards III and Stephen J. Wayne. Copyright © 1985 by St. Martin's Press, Inc., and used with permission of the publisher. Notes have been renumbered.

resorts to attempts to punish the press for coverage the president perceives as unfair, unfavorable, or both.

In addition to the chief executive's efforts to influence the media, there is another side of this relationship we must examine: the content of the news. Ultimately, it is the written and spoken word that concerns the president. Leaks of confidential information and what is seen in the White House as superficial and biased reporting exacerbate the tensions inherent in presidential-press relations. Presidents commonly view the press as a major obstacle to their obtaining and maintaining public support. Criticism of media coverage as being trivial and distorted and as violating confidences is a standard feature of most administrations. The White House feels that this type of reporting hinders its efforts to develop public appreciation for the president and his policies.

We examine the nature and structure of presidential relationships with the press, emphasizing both the context of these relationships and the White House's attempts to obtain favorable coverage. We also discuss issues in presidential-press relations, especially the nature and consequences of media coverage of the presidency.

AN ADVERSARIAL RELATIONSHIP

The history of presidential-press relations has not involved unlimited goodwill. President George Washington complained that the "calumnies" against his administration were "outrages of common decency" motivated by the desire to destroy confidence in the new government.[1] John Adams was so upset at criticism in the press that he supported the Sedition Act and jailed some opposition journalists under its authority.

Thomas Jefferson, certainly one of our greatest defenders of freedom, became so exasperated with the press as president that he argued that "even the least informed of the people have learned that nothing in a newspaper is to be believed." He also felt that "newspapers, for the most part, present only the caricature of disaffected minds. Indeed, the abuses of freedom of the press have been carried to a length never before known or borne by any civilized nation." These observations, it should be noted, come from the man who earlier had written that "were it left to me to decide whether we should have a government without newspapers or newspapers without a government, I should not hesitate to prefer the latter."[2]

Almost two centuries later things have not changed very much. Although all presidents have supported the abstract right of the press to criticize them freely, most have not found this criticism very comfortable while in office. They have viewed some of the press as misrepresenting (perhaps maliciously) their views and actions, failing to perceive the correctness of their policies, and dedicated to impeding their goals.

No matter who is in the White House or who reports on him, presidents and the press tend to be in conflict. Presidents are inherently policy advocates. They will naturally assess the press in terms of its aiding or hindering their goals. The press, on the other hand, has the responsibility for presenting reality. While the press may fail in its efforts, it will assess itself on that criterion. The president wants to control the amount and timing of information about his administration, while the press wants all the information that exists without delay. As long as their goals are different, presidents and the press are likely to be adversaries.

THE WHITE HOUSE PRESS

Who are the reporters that regularly cover the White House? The regulars represent diverse media constituencies. These include daily newspapers like the *Washington Post* and the *New York Times;* weekly newsmagazines like *Time* and *Newsweek;* the wire services like the Associated Press (AP) and United Press International (UPI); newspaper chains like Hearst, Scripps-Howard, Newhouse, and Knight; the television and radio networks; the foreign press; and "opinion" magazines like the *New Republic* and the *National Review.* In addition, photographers, columnists, television commentators, and magazine writers are regularly involved in White House–press interactions. In 1981 about 1,700 persons had White House press credentials. Fortunately, not everyone shows up at once. About 60 reporters and 15 photographers regularly cover the White House, and the total of both increases to more than 100 when an important announcement is expected.

The great majority of daily newspapers in America have no Washington correspondents, much less someone assigned to cover the White House. The same can be said for almost all of the country's individual television and radio stations. These papers and stations rely heavily upon the AP and UPI wire services, each of which covers the White House continuously and in detail with three full-time reporters.

WHITE HOUSE PRESS OPERATION

The White House's relations with the media occupy a substantial portion of the time of a large number of aides. About one-third of the high-level White House staff are directly involved in media relations and policy of one type or another and most of the staff are involved at some time in influencing the media's portrayal of the president.

The person in the White House who most often deals directly with the press is the president's press secretary. Probably the central function of press secretaries is to serve as conduits of information from the White House to the press. They must be sure that clear statements of administration policies have been prepared on important policy matters. The press secretaries usually conduct the daily press briefings, giving prepared announcements and answering questions. In forming their answers they often do not have specific orders on what to say or not to say. They must be able to think on their feet to ensure that they accurately reflect the president's views. Sometimes these views may be unclear, however, or the president may not wish to articulate his views. Therefore, press secretaries may seem to be evasive or unimaginative in public settings. They also hold private meetings with individual reporters, where the information provided can be more candid and speculative.

To be effective in the conduit role the press secretary must maintain credibility with reporters. Credibility rests on at least two important pillars: (1) truth and (2) access to and respect of the president and senior White House officials. If a press secretary is viewed as not telling the truth or as not being close to top decision makers (and therefore not well informed), he will not be an effective presidential spokesman, because the press will give little credence to what he says. Credibility problems have arisen for several press secretaries, including Ron Ziegler (Nixon) and Ron Nessen (Ford), as a result of the first and second pillars, respectively.

Press secretaries also serve as conduits from the press to the president. They must sometimes explain the needs of the press to the president. For example, all of Johnson's press secretaries tried to persuade the president to issue advance information on his travel plans to the press. When he refused, they provided it anyway and then had it expunged from the briefing transcript so the president would not see it. Press secretaries also try to inform the White House staff of the press's needs and the rules of the game, and they help reporters gain access to staff members.

Press secretaries are typically not involved in substantive decisions, but they do give the president advice, usually on what information should be released, by whom, in what form, and to what audience. They also advise the president on rehearsals for press conferences and on how to project his image and use it to his political advantage.

Since the time of William Loeb, Theodore Roosevelt's press secretary, the White House has attempted to coordinate executive-branch news. Presidents have assigned aides to clear the appointments of departmental public affairs officials, to keep in touch with the officials to learn what news is forthcoming from the departments, and to meet with them to explain the president's policy views and try to prevent conflicting statements from emanating from the White House and other units of the executive branch. Specialists have had responsibility for coordinating national security news.

Of course, such tactics do not always work. President Ford wanted to announce the success of the *Mayaguez* operation from the White House, but he found to his disappointment that the Pentagon had already done so, making any presidential announcement anticlimactic. At the beginning of his second year in office, President Reagan issued an order that required advance White House approval of television appearances by cabinet members and other top officials, but it soon lapsed.

Coordinating the news from the White House itself has also been a presidential goal. Presidents have sometimes monitored and attempted to limit the press contacts of White House aides, who have annoyed their bosses by using the media for their own purposes. President Reagan, for example, instituted a policy midway through his administration that required his assistant for communications, David Gergen, to approve any interview requested by a member of the media for any White House official. All requests were monitored and entered on a computer so the White House could keep tabs on whom reporters wanted to see. Since even the White House press cannot wander through the East or West wings on their own, the only way to speak to aides without administration approval was to call them at home, a practice discouraged by presidential assistants and generally avoided by the media. Such efforts to limit press access are exceptional, however, and have proved to be largely fruitless.

Recent administrations have also made an effort to coordinate publicity functions within the White House, attempting to present the news in the most favorable light, such as preventing two major stories from breaking on the same day, smothering bad news with more positive news, and timing announcements for maximum effect.

All recent presidents, including Eisenhower, who had a reputation to the contrary, have read several newspapers each day, especially the *New York Times* and the *Washington Post*. Kennedy and Johnson were also very attentive to television news programs. Johnson had a television cabinet with three screens so he could watch all three networks at once. But even this was not enough to satisfy his thirst for news. He also had teletypes that carried the latest reports from the AP and UPI wire services installed in the Oval Office, and he monitored them regularly.

President Nixon rarely watched television news and did not peruse large numbers of newspapers or magazines, but he was extremely interested in press coverage of his administration. He had his staff prepare a daily news summary of newspapers, magazines, television news, and the AP and UPI news wires. Often this summary triggered ideas for the president, who gave orders to aides to follow up on something he read. The news summary also went to White House assistants. Subsequent presidents have continued the news summary, altering it to meet their individual needs, and have circulated it to top officials in their administrations. The Carter White House instituted a separate magazine survey and even a weekly summary of Jewish publications when it became concerned about a possible backlash within the American Jewish community against the administration's Middle East policy.

PRESS CONFERENCES

The best-known direct interaction between the president and the press is the presidential press conference. The frequency of press conferences has varied over time. Franklin Roosevelt held about seven a month; Truman cut this figure in half. Eisenhower further reduced their frequency, holding about two press conferences each month, a rate maintained by Kennedy, Johnson, and Carter, and somewhat bettered by Ford. The deviant case was Richard Nixon, who held only about one press conference every two months. Ronald Reagan has also averaged only about one

formal press conference every two months, despite his press secretary's promise at the beginning of his term that the president would hold formal televised press conferences "no less than once a month."[3] Such figures should not be accepted at face value, however. What presidents count as press conferences varies considerably, and the figures for average frequency of press conferences may conceal wide fluctuations in the time between conferences.

Naturally, the more time that has elapsed between press conferences, the more events and governmental actions that will have transpired since the last press conference. The more that has transpired, the more wide-ranging the questions asked of the president are likely to be. And the more wide-ranging the questions, the more superficial the coverage of any one topic is likely to be.

The notice presidents provide of their upcoming press conferences is no more uniform than their frequency of holding them. The short notice for many press conferences has advantages for presidents. If press conferences are not publicly scheduled until shortly before they take place, it is easier for presidents to cancel them if they find it convenient. In addition, short notice gives reporters less time to prepare probing questions. Moreover, many specialty reporters who cover all of Washington, who can ask detailed questions, and who can be less concerned with remaining on good terms with the president will miss impromptu press conferences.

Another factor that has perhaps reduced the utility of the press conferences for eliciting useful information about government has been their increasing size. Modern presidents have generally employed a large room (such as the State Department auditorium or the East Room in the White House) for press conferences, usually relying upon public address systems. The increased number of reporters covering press conferences and the setting in which they take place has inevitably made them more formal. More reporters mean more persons with different concerns and thus less likelihood of follow-up questions to cover a subject in depth. Spontaneity in questions and answers has largely been lost.

Presidents have taken other steps that have contributed to the formalization of press conferences. Beginning with Truman, they have undergone formal briefings and "dry runs" in preparation for questions that might be asked. Presidents have asked their aides and the departments and agencies to submit to them possible questions and suggested answers, and sometimes they call for further information. In 1982 President Reagan began holding full-scale mock news conferences. Guessing at questions is not too difficult. There are obvious areas of concern, and questions raised at White House and departmental briefings and other meetings with reporters provide useful cues. The president also can anticipate the interests of individual reporters, and he has discretion over whom to recognize. In Reagan's news conferences, reporters were assigned seats, and the president using a seating chart, called them by name. In one case Reagan called a reporter only to discover that he was not even attending the conference. The reporter, watching the news conference in his living room at home, asked a question anyway but only his family heard it. The next day the newspapers had a field day reporting the incident.

The change in the nature of the presidential press conferences from semiprivate to public events has diminished their utility in transmitting information from the president to the press. Since every word they say is transmitted verbatim to millions of people, presidents cannot speak as candidly as, say, Franklin D. Roosevelt could. Nor can they speculate freely about their potential actions or evaluations of persons, events, or circumstances. Instead, they must choose their words carefully, and their responses to questions are often not terribly enlightening.

Presidents like Truman have frequently begun their press conferences with carefully prepared opening statements. Examples include President Kennedy's 1962 blast at the steel companies for raising their prices (eventually leading to the increases being rescinded) and President Carter's five-minute monologue on his administration's accomplishments in a televised press conferences during the 1980 presidential election. Lyndon Johnson was especially likely to deliver an opening statement. These statements have given presidents an opportunity to reach the public on their own terms. Opening statements have also further reduced the opportunities for questions while at the same time focusing questions on issues of the president's choosing (contained in the statement).

Because the president is in control of his press conference, he can avoid the harder questions. Sometimes presidents state that they will not entertain questions on certain topics. They may also evade questions with clever rhetoric or simply answer with a "no comment." Or they can use a question as a vehicle to say something they planned ahead of time. If necessary they can reverse the attack and focus on the questioner, or conversely, they can call on a friendly reporter for a "soft" question. Eisenhower used a skilled evasiveness and impenetrable syntax to avoid direct answers to embarrassing or politically sensitive questions, something not unusual among presidents.

Presidents and their staffs have sometimes found it convenient to plant questions with the press. In other words, they end up asking themselves questions. This practice started at least as early as Franklin Roosevelt, and Eisenhower and Johnson often made use of it.

Many of the questions asked the president involve trivial topics. One reason for this is deference to the president. Reporters meet the president in his territory, not theirs, and dutifully rise when he enters the room. An adversarial relationship may exist outside the press conference, but it is rarely reflected during the sessions themselves. The author of a study of press conferences between 1961 and 1975 found only two occasions in fifteen years when the number of hostile quesions asked by reporters at any press conference exceeded three.[4]

The artificial nature of press conferences, especially on television, may lead to distortions. On the one hand, a truly spontaneous answer to a question may be candid, but it also may be foolish or expose the president's ignorance of an area. Generalizations based on such a reply may be inaccurate because the president may actually be well informed but require more than a few seconds to think about a complex problem. On the other hand, some presidents may be glib, charming, and attractive, and therefore perform well in a spontaneous press conference but really not be very competent. The advent of television has further increased the potential for distortion, since a president's physical attractiveness, delivery, and flair for the dramatic may leave more of an impression on the public's mind than the substance of his answers.

In sum, presidential press conferences are often not very informative. In the more formal and less spontaneous press conferences that characterize the more recent era, the president has a substantial opportunity to control the image he projects. He often begins with a prepared announcement, his answers to most questions are equally prepared, and he has leeway on when he will hold the conference and whom he will call upon. While the press conference does provide the president an opportunity to focus national attention upon himself, stimulate public opinion, and criticize or support various political actors, and while the preconference briefing may serve as a useful device for informing the president across a broad spectrum of issues, we cannot depend upon it for revealing the real president, and the nature of television may distort more than it reveals.

SERVICES FOR THE PRESS

In order to get their messages across to the American people and to influence the tone and content of the press's presentation of those messages, presidents have provided services for the press. One of the most important is the backgrounder. The president's comments to reporters may be "on the record" (remarks may be attributed to the speaker); "on background" (a specific source cannot be identified but the source's position and status can—such as a "White House source"); "deep background" (no attribution); or "off the record" (the information reporters receive may not be used in a story). For purposes of convenience we shall term all sessions between White House officials (including the president) and the press that are not "on the record" as "backgrounders." All recent presidents, especially Johnson and Ford, have engaged in background discussion with reporters, although President Nixon's involvement was rare. Some presidents, especially Eisenhower and Nixon, have relied heavily upon their principal foreign policy advisers to brief reporters on foreign affairs.

The most common type of presidential discussion with reporters on a background basis is a briefing. In these sessions the president typically explains a policy's development and what it is expected to accomplish. Interestingly, the president does not appear to stress the substance of policy. He seldom makes "hard" news statements in background briefings, because this would irritate absent members of the press. The reporters watch the president perform, and since the president controls the conditions of these briefings, the chances of making a favorable impression are good.

Reporters tend to view middle-level aides as the best information sources. They have in-depth knowledge about the substance of programs, and they are generally free from the constraints of high visibility, so they are in a good position to provide useful backgrounders. Backgrounders are particularly important for these officials because presidents are generally intolerant of staff members who seek publicity for themselves, and most interviews with White House staff are on this basis. Sometimes aides say more than their superiors would like in order to prod the president in a particular policy direction.

Backgrounders have a number of advantages for the White House. Avoiding direct quotation allows officials to speak on sensitive foreign policy and domestic policy matters candidly and in depth, something domestic politics and international diplomacy would not tolerate if speakers were held directly accountable for their words. The White House hopes such discussions will help it communicate its point of view more clearly and serve to educate journalists, perhaps preparing them for future policies, and make them more sympathetic to the president's position in their reporting.

An impressive performance in a background session can show the White House to be competent and perhaps elicit the benefit of the doubt in future stories. Moreover, background sessions can be used to scotch rumors and limit undesirable speculation about presidential plans and internal White House affairs.

On the other hand, backgrounders may be aimed at the public (in the form of trial balloons that the White House can disclaim if they meet with disapproval) or at policymakers in Washington. They may also be directed at other countries. To discourage the Soviet Union's support of India in its war with Pakistan, Henry Kissinger told reporters in a backgrounder that the Soviet policy might lead to the cancellation of President Nixon's trip to Moscow. Since the statement was not officially attributed to Kissinger, it constituted less of a public threat to the Soviet Union, while at the same time it communicated the president's message.[5]

Reporters have generally been happy to go along with protecting the identities of "spokesmen" and "sources" (although an experienced observer can identify most of them), because the system provides them more information than they would have without it. This increase of information available to reporters adds to the information available to the public, and it probably helps advance journalistic careers as well.

Backgrounders, of course, have also provided the White House opportunities to disseminate misleading or self-serving propaganda anonymously. Sometimes such propaganda concerns intramural warfare, an especially common theme in the Ford administration but also appearing in the Nixon and other administrations.

In addition to the more informal sessions, briefings are held each weekday for the White House press (they were held twice daily until the Nixon administration). In the daily briefings reporters are provided with information about appointments and resignations; decisions of the president to sign or not to sign routine bills and explanations for his actions; and the president's schedule (whom he will see that day, what meetings he has, what his future travel plans are, and when the press can see him). More significantly from the standpoint of the press, the briefing provides presidential reactions to events, the White House "line" on issues and whether it has changed, and a reading of the president's moods and ideas. This information is obtained through prepared statements or answers to reporters' queries. Responses to the latter are often prepared ahead of time by the White House staff. The daily briefings, of course, also provide the press with an opportunity to have the president's views placed on the public record, which eases the burdens of reporting.

Usually the president's press secretary or his deputy presides over these briefings, although sometimes the president participates. White House staff members and executive-branch officials with substantial expertise in specific policy areas such as the budget or foreign affairs sometimes brief the press and answer questions at the daily briefing or at special briefings, especially when the White House is launching a major publicity campaign.

Interviews with the president and top White House staff members are a valuable commodity to the press, and sometimes the White House uses them for its purposes. During the 1980 primaries, Jimmy Carter was angered by the *Boston Globe*'s pro-Kennedy slant. Thus, his staff arranged an exclusive presidential interview with the *Globe*'s rival, the Boston *Herald American*. [6]

In a less subtle move, President Nixon traded an exclusive interview to Hugh Sidey of *Time* for a cover story on him. In order to obtain an interview with President Ford, even the venerable Walter Cronkite agreed to use only questions the president could handle easily. At other times the White House may give exclusives to a paper like the *New York Times* in return for getting a story in which it is interested a prominent place in the paper. [7]

Providing the press exclusive information may be as ingratiating as an exclusive interview and may be used to distract reporters from more embarrassing stories. At other times the White House may trade advance notice of a story for information reporters possess about developments elsewhere in the government that are not clear to the president and his staff.

Recent presidents, with the exception of Richard Nixon, have regularly cultivated elite reporters and columnists, the editors and publishers of leading newspapers, and network news producers and executives with small favors, social flattery, and small background dinners at the White House. (Nixon turned these chores over to top aides). Indeed, since the 1960s the White House has had first a special person and then an office for media liaison to deal directly with the representatives of news organizations, such as editors, publishers, and producers, in addition to the press office that deals with reporters' routine needs.

There are many additional services that the White House provides for the press. It gives reporters transcripts of briefings and presidential speeches and daily handouts announcing a myriad of information about the president and his policies, including advance notice of travel plans and upcoming stories. Major announcements are timed to accommodate the deadlines of newspapers, magazines, and television networks.

Photographers covering the president are highly dependent on the White House press office, which provides facilities for photographers on presidential trips and arranges photo opportunities, making sure they will produce the most flattering shots of the president (such as Johnson's left profile). President Reagan even prohibited impromptu questions from reporters at photographing sessions. Moreover, the official White House photographers provide many of the photographs of the president that the media use. Naturally, these are screened so that the president is presented favorably.

When the president goes on trips, at home or abroad, extensive preparations are made for the press. These preparations include arranging transportation and lodging for the press, installing equipment for radio and television broadcasting, obtaining telephones for reporters, erecting platforms for photographers, preparing a detailed account of where and with whom the president will be at particular times, providing elaborate information about the countries the president is visiting, forming pools of press members to cover the president closely (as in a motorcade), and scheduling the press plane to arrive before the president's so the press can cover his arrival.

As many of these services suggest, the press is especially dependent upon the White House staff in covering presidential trips, particularly foreign trips. The number of sources of information is generally reduced, as is the access of the press to the principal figures they wish to cover. Thus the president's aides are in a good position to manipulate press coverage to their advantage. Coverage of foreign trips is generally favorable, although perhaps less so than in

the past now that reporters with expertise in foreign affairs accompany the president, and the press points out the relationship of the trip and its goals and accomplishments to the president's domestic political problems.

Even in Washington, however, reporters are very much in a controlled environment. They may not freely roam the halls of the White House, interviewing whomever they please. They are highly dependent upon the press officer for access to officials, and about half their interviews are with the press secretary and his staff. Much of their time is spent waiting for something to happen or watching the president at formal or ceremonial events. Since most news stories about such occurrences show the president in a favorable light, the press office does everything possible to help reporters record these activities. Similarly, the White House is happy to provide photographs featuring the president's "warm," "human," or "family" side. These please editors and the public alike.

Briefings, press releases, and the like can be used to divert the media's attention from embarrassing matters. The Reagan White House adopted a strategy of blitzing the media with information to divert its attention after the press raised questions about the president's sleeping through Libyan attacks on U.S. forces off the coast of Africa.[8] More frequently, the White House, by adopting an active approach to the press, gains an opportunity to shape the media's agenda for the day. Through announcements and press releases it attempts to focus attention on what will reflect positively on the president. Such information frequently generates questions from reporters and subsequent news stories. Representatives of the smaller papers, who have few resources, are more heavily dependent upon White House-provided news than are the larger news bureaus, including the major networks. They are the most likely to follow the White House's agenda. Moreover, since White House reporters, especially the wire services, are under pressure to file daily "hard news" reports, the White House is in a strong position to help by providing information, much of it trivial and all of it designed to reflect positively on the president. As a Ford official put it: "You can predict what the press is going to do with a story. It is almost by formula. Because of this they are usable."[9]

Many observers, including journalists, feel that the press tends to parrot the White House line, so conveniently provided at a briefing or in a press release, especially early in a president's term. The pressure among journalists to be first with a story increases the potential for White House manipulation inherent in this deferential approach, as concerns for accuracy give way to career interests.

Presidents have undoubtedly hoped that the handouts, briefings, and other services they and their staffs provide for reporters will gain them some goodwill. They may also hope that these services will keep the White House press from digging too deeply into presidential affairs. In addition, they want to keep reporters interested in the president's agenda, because bored journalists are more negative in their reporting and may base their stories on trivial incidents like the president's stumbling on a plane.

HARASSMENT OF THE PRESS

The White House can wield the stick as well as offer the carrot. While the Nixon administration did not ignore the latter, it emphasized the former—with a vengeance. The president and his aides were obsessed with the press and spent a disproportionate amount of time dealing with it, and they allowed the personalities and views of reporters to affect their working relationship with the press as a whole. The president regularly spoke of the press (to his staff) as the "enemy," as something to be hated and beaten.[10] At the end of direct American involvement in the Vietnam War he told reporters: "We finally have achieved a peace with honor. I know it gags some of you to write that phrase, but that is true."

Open hostility, however, was not the full story of the Nixon White House's relations with the press. This attitude led to harassment of the press and attempts to pressure it into quiescence. These attempts took many forms. One was a steady stream of criticism of the printed and electronic press by administration officials and by the president himself. They criticized the reporters for being prejudiced against the president and unrepresentative of the American people and for distorting the news and emphasizing negative instead of positive events. Complaints were made directly to the news organizations and reporters as well as to the public.

It is significant that the Nixon White House was not at all bothered by press treatment that was favorable to it. When it attacked the networks, it focused more on CBS and NBC than ABC, whose coverage was more favorable. When the Nixon White House criticized newspapers, it concentrated its wrath on the "Eastern" press, especially the *Washington Post* and *New York Times,* the two most prominent newspapers in the country. The editorial pages of both these papers are oriented toward a more liberal viewpoint. Most other papers, however, are not. Nixon was quite content to receive their support and was not concerned that the liberal point of view was not better represented in their coverage of the news.

The Nixon administration did not limit its efforts at harassing the press to mere criticism. Some reporters had their phones tapped or their taxes audited. One even was the focus of a full FBI field investigation aimed at discovering something negative in his past to discredit him. Others were excluded from White House press pools, briefings, and presidential and vice presidential trips or had their access to administration officials restricted. The White House also instituted antitrust suits against the networks and threatened them with the loss of the five highly profitable local television stations they each owned, and it inspired challenges to the license renewals of television stations owned by the *Washington Post*. Efforts were also made to have affiliates pressure their networks to provide more positive coverage of the administration and to force the Public Broadcasting Service to devote fewer resources to coverage and analysis of national news.

Despite the substantial time and energy the Nixon administration devoted to intimidating the press, the results were meager. Moreover, attempts to punish reporters and their organizations by cutting off their access to administration sources, for example, were undermined by White House aides who ignored orders to do so.

Other presidents have been angered by press coverage and have occasionally criticized and harassed reporters, of course. Nevertheless, such episodes have not been characteristic of past administrations. Nixon added an extra dimension to the adversarial relations between the president and the press. He preferred to bludgeon the press into submission. Failing that, he tried to discredit the press by creating doubt in the public's mind that the press was treating his administration fairly. He hoped that the public would pay less attention to the press criticism of him and his policies and also that he would have an acceptable excuse to avoid meeting the press directly.

INFORMATION LEAKS

In early 1982 President Reagan read the riot act to his cabinet, denouncing the release of confidential information to the press by anonymous sources as one of the major problems facing his administration. He was particularly concerned about leaks regarding his upcoming budget proposals for defense spending, a number of foreign policy matters, and the urban enterprise zones proposal that he wanted to save for his State of the Union message.[11] The president's frustration is evident in the quip with which he opened a press conference held at about the same time: "I was going to have an opening statement, but I decided that what I was going to say I wanted to get a lot of attention so I'm going to wait and leak it."

President Reagan was hardly the first president to be upset by leaks. Sometimes they can be potentially quite serious, as when the U.S. negotiating strategy in the first SALT talks was disclosed during the Nixon administration. When the *Pentagon Papers* were leaked to the public, President Nixon felt that there was a danger that other countries would lose confidence in our ability to keep secrets and that information on the delicate negotiations then in progress with China might also be leaked, endangering the possibility of rapprochement.[12] At other times they are just embarrassing, as when internal dissent in the administration is revealed to the public. President Johnson feared leaks would signal what he was thinking, and he would lose his freedom of action as a result.

Who leaks information? The best

answer is "everybody." Presidents themselves do so, sometimes inadvertently. As Lyndon Johnson once put it: "I have enough trouble with myself. I ought not to have to put up with everybody else too."[13] Top presidential aides may also reveal more than they intend. When a leak regarding President Reagan's willingness to compromise on his 1981 tax bill appeared in the *New York Times,* White House aides traced down the source of the story and found it was budget director David Stockman.[14] A year earlier a leak revealing secret CIA arms shipments to Afghan rebels was attributed to the office of the president's chief national security adviser.[15]

Most leaks, however, are deliberately planted. As one close presidential aide put it, "99 percent of all significant secrets are spilled by the principals or at their direction."[16] Presidents are included in those who purposefully leak. *Newsweek* used to hold space open for the items John Kennedy would phone in to his friend Benjamin Bradlee right before the magazine's deadline.[17] There are many reasons for leaks. They may be used as trial balloons to test public or congressional reaction to ideas and proposals or to stimulate public concern about an issue. Both the Ford and Carter White House used this technique to test reaction to a tax surcharge on gasoline. When the reaction turned out to be negative, they denied ever contemplating such a policy. At other times information is leaked to reporters who will use it to write favorable articles on a policy.

Diplomacy is an area in which delicate communications play an important role. Leaks are often used to send signals to other nations of our friendship, anger, or willingness to compromise. At the same time they provide the president with the opportunity to disavow publicly or to reinterpret what some might view as, for example, an overly "tough"

stance or an unexpected change in policy.

Leaks may also be used to influence personnel matters. The release of information letting a reluctant official know his superiors wish him to leave can force him to resign and thus save the problem of firing him. The release of information on an appointment before it is made places the president in a awkward position and can help ensure that he follows through on it or prematurely denies that he has such plans.

Some leaks are designed to force the president's hand on policy decisions. During the Indian-Pakistani War, President Nixon maintained a publicly neutral stance but was really favoring Pakistan. When this was leaked there was inevitably pressure to be neutral in action as well as in rhetoric. Conversely, in the case of Lyndon Johnson, a leak that he was thinking about a decision could ensure that he would take no such action.

Leaks may serve a number of other functions for individuals. They may make one feel important or help one gain favor with reporters. Leaks may also be used to criticize and intimidate personal or political adversaries in the White House itself or protect and enhance reputations. In the Ford administration, White House counsel Robert Hartmann and the chief of staff Richard Cheney often attacked each other anonymously in the press. Several members of the White House staff attacked Press Secretary Ron Nessen in an effort to persuade the president to replace him. When negotiations with North Vietnam broke down in late 1972, White House aides employed leaks to dissociate the president from his national security adviser.

Presidents sometimes leak information for their own political purposes. Lyndon Johnson leaked information on nuclear weapons to answer Barry Goldwater in the 1964 presidential election. A Nixon aide leaked a false story to *The Wall Street Journal* that the president was considering seeking legislation to reduce the independence of the Federal Reserve Board and that the board's chairman, Arthur Burns, was a hypocrite because he sought a personal salary increase while he was asking the rest of the country to dampen its demands. The UPI received a somewhat similar story. These leaks were attempts to make Burns more responsive to White House demands. The Nixon White House often employed leaks as a political tactic.

It is generally fruitless to try to discover the source of a leak. Nevertheless, some presidents have tried. The Reagan administration has added new sophistication to the effort to trace leakers. Reporters are required to make appointments when they visit top officials. These are logged into a computer. When the president's aides find an offending story based on an unidentified source, they can check the computer to learn which officials have been talking to the reporter. Such measures, of course, cannot stop an official who desires to leak information from doing so and hiding his identity from the White House.

BIAS IN PRESS COVERAGE

Bias is the most politically charged issue in presidential-press relations. Bias is also an elusive concept with many dimensions. Although we typically envision bias as news coverage favoring identifiable persons, parties, or points of view, there are more subtle and more pervasive forms of bias that are not motivated by the goal of furthering careers or policies.

A large number of studies covering topics such as presidential election campaigns, the war in Vietnam, and local news conclude that the news media are not biased *systematically* toward a particular person, party, or ideology, as measured in the amount or favorability of coverage. The bias found in such studies is inconsistent; the news is typically characterized by neutrality.[18]

Some people may equate objectivity with passivity and feel that the press should do no more than report what others present to it. This simple passing on of news is what occurs much of the time, and it is a fundamental reason for the superficiality of news coverage. Sometimes, however, reporters may feel the necessity of setting the story in a meaningful context. The construction of such a context may entail reporting what was *not* said as well as what was said, what had occurred before, and what political implications may be involved in a statement, policy, or event. If the press is passive, it can be more easily manipulated, even representing fiction as fact.

This discussion of the general neutrality of news coverage in the mass media pertains most directly to television, newspaper, and radio reporting. Columnists, commentators, and editorial writers usually cannot even pretend to be neutral. Newspaper endorsements for presidential candidates overwhelmingly favor Republicans. In 1972, 93 percent of the newspapers making endorsements supported Richard Nixon over George McGovern.[19] Newsmagazines are sometimes less neutral than newspapers or television. In the 1940s, 1950s, and 1960s Henry Luce used *Time* to criticize Harry Truman, to campaign for his view of a China policy, to help elect Dwight Eisenhower as president, and to support the war in Vietnam, and the magazine has continued to favor Republican presidents. Unfair but picturesque adjectives are often used in newsmagazines to liven up stories. So are cartoons and drawings, which are generally unflattering to the president.

A number of factors help to explain why most mass media news coverage is not biased systematically toward a particular person, party, or ideology. Reporters generally are not personally partisan or ideological; nor are they politically aligned or holders of strong political beliefs. Journalists are typically not intellectuals or deeply concerned with public policy. Moreover, they share journalism's professional norm of objectivity.

The organizational processes of story selection and editing provide opportunities for softening judgments of reporters. The rotation of assignments and rewards for objective newsgathering are further protections against bias. Local television station owners and newspaper publishers are in a position to apply pressure regarding the presentation of the news, and, although they rarely do so, their potential to act may restrain reporters.

Self-interest also plays a role in constraining bias. Individual reporters may earn a poor reputation if others view them as biased. The television networks, newspapers, newsmagazines, and the wire services, which provide most of the Washington news for newspapers, have a direct financial stake in attracting viewers and subscribers and do not want to lose their audience by appearing biased, especially when there are multiple versions of the same story available to major news outlets. Slander and libel laws; the Federal Communications Commission's "fairness doctrine," requiring electronic media news coverage of diverse points of view; and the "political attack" rule, providing those personally criticized on the electronic media with an opportunity to respond, are all formal limitations to bias.

To conclude that the news contains little explicit partisan or ideological bias is not to argue that the news does not distort reality in its coverage. It does. Even under the best of conditions, some distortion is inevitable due to simple error or such factors as lack of careful checking of facts, the efforts of the news source to deceive, and short deadlines.

In a very important sense, values are pervasive in the news, and it is difficult to imagine how it could be otherwise. As members of our society, journalists are imbued with such values as democracy, capitalism, and individualism, and these unconsciously receive positive treatment in the media. Similarly, journalists have concepts of what is "new," "abnormal," and "wrong" and notions of how the world works (e.g., how power is distributed) and how to draw inferences that guide them in their efforts to gather and present the news.

Journalism also contains a structural bias. Selecting, presenting, editing, and interpreting the news inevitably require judgments about what stories to cover and what to report about them, because there is simply not enough space for everything. Thus the news can never mirror reality. In addition, the particular ways in which news is gathered and presented have consequences for distortion in news coverage.

News coverage of the presidency often tends to emphasize the negative (although the negative stories are typically presented in a neutral manner). In the 1980 election campaign the press portrayed President Carter as mean and Ronald Reagan as imprecise rather than Carter as precise and Reagan as nice. The emphasis, in other words, was on the candidates' negative qualities. As the following excerpt from Jimmy Carter's diary regarding a visit to Panama in 1978 illustrates, "objective" reporting can be misleading:

> I told the Army troops that I was in the Navy for 11 years, and they booed. I told

them that we depended on the Army to keep the Canal open, and they cheered. Later, the news reporter said that there were boos and cheers during my speech. I reckon that was an accurate report![20]

On the other hand, one could argue that the press is biased *toward* the White House. Their general respect for the presidency is often transferred to individual presidents. Framed at a respectful distance by the television camera, the president is typically portrayed with an aura of dignity working in a context of rationality and coherence on activities benefiting the public. Word selection often reflects this orientation as well. In addition, journalists follow conventions that protect politicians and public officials from revelations of private misconduct.

The White House enjoys a consistent pattern of favorable coverage in newspapers, magazines, and network news. The most favorable coverage comes in the first year of a president's term, before he has a record to criticize and critics for reporters to interview. Coverage focuses on human interest stories of the president and his appointees and their personalities, goals, and plans. The president is pictured in a positive light as a policymaker dealing with problems. Controversies over solutions arise later. Newspaper headlines also favor the president, and news of foreign affairs provides basic support for the policies and personalities of the administration.[21]

MEDIA EFFECTS

The most significant question about the substance of media coverage, of course, is about the impact it has, if any, on public opinion. Unfortunately, we know very little about this subject. Most studies on media effects have focused on attitude changes, especially in voting for presidential candidates, and have

typically found little or no evidence of influence. Reinforcement of existing attitudes and opinions has been the strongest effect of the media.[22] There are other ways to look for media effects, however. The public appears to be a fairly passive audience and usually does not do a great deal of perceptual screening of the news. Repeated coverage of an issue or person by all the media, television's use of themes and simple story lines, and the vividness of live coverage of visually exciting events can buttress the media's effect on the public.

The media are more likely to influence perceptions than attitudes. The press can influence the perceptions of what public figures stand for and what their personalities are like, what issues are important, and what is at stake. By raising certain issues or personal characteristics to prominence, the salience of attitudes that people already hold may change and thus alter their evaluations of, say, presidential performance, without their attitudes themselves changing.

The public's information on and criteria for evaluating candidates parallel what is presented in the media: campaign performance, personality traits, mannerisms, and personal background rather than issue positions, ability to govern, and relevant experience. Moreover, what the press emphasizes about elections (the horse race) is what the people say is important about them, what they discuss about them in private conversations, and what they remember about them.[23]

While it cannot be conclusively proven that media coverage contributes to the public's de-emphasis of the professional capacities and policy plans of candidates, it is reasonable to speculate that the press's emphasis on the horse race and personality traits encourages the public to view campaigns in these terms. Thus, although the press may not directly influence voters to support a particular candidate, it probably amplifies the public's predispositions to view public affairs through personalities rather than more complex factors.

Earlier we saw that the press gave substantial coverage to President Ford's misstatement about Soviet domination of Eastern Europe. This coverage had an impact on the public. Polls show that most people did not realize the president made an error until they were told so by the press. After that, pro-Ford evaluations of the debate declined noticeably as voters' concerns for competence in foreign policy making became salient.[24]

The press probably has the greatest effect on public perceptions of individuals and issues between election campaigns, when people are less likely to activate their partisan defenses. The prominant coverage of Gerald Ford's alleged physical clumsiness was naturally translated into suggestions of mental ineptitude. In the president's own words:

> Every time I stumbled or bumped my head or fell in the snow, reporters zeroed in on that to the exclusion of almost everything else. The news coverage was harmful, but even more damaging was the fact that Johnny Carson and Chevy Chase used my "missteps" for their jokes. Their antics—and I'll admit that I laughed at them myself—helped create the public perception of me as a stumbler. And that wasn't funny.[25]

Once such an image is established in the mass media, it is very difficult to change, as reporters continue to emphasize behavior that is consistent with their previously established themes.

During the Iranian hostage crisis ABC originated a nightly program entitled "America Held Hostage," Walter Cronkite provided "countdown" on the number of days of the crisis at the end of each evening's news on CBS, many feature stories on the hostages and their families were reported in all the media, and the press gave complete coverage to "demonstrations" in front of the U.S. embassy in Tehran. The latter were often artificially created for consumption by Americans. This crisis gave President Carter's approval rating a tremendous boost, at least for a while. Conversely, when the *Pueblo* was captured by North Korea, there were many more American captives, but there were also no television cameras and few reporters to cover the situation. Thus the incident played a much smaller role in American politics.

Those with only marginal concern for politics may be especially susceptible to the impact of the media because they have few alternative sources of information and less-developed political allegiances. Thus, they have fewer strongly held attitudes to overcome. Similarly, coverage of new issues that are removed from the experiences of people and their political convictions is more likely to influence public opinion than coverage of continuing issues.

Almost all citizens are basically ignorant of such areas of the world as Central America, Afghanistan, and Poland. The press plays a pivotal role in shaping perceptions of the personalities and issues involved in conflicts abroad (generally only conflicts receive coverage) and the United States' stake in the outcomes of the disputes. In such situations we have seen that there is substantial potential for distortion. The public is heavily dependent on the media for information and has little basis for challenging what it reads and sees in the news. The illustrations of the conflict—scenes of combat or demonstrations, for example—may become the essence of the issue in the public's mind. The underlying problems, which the president must confront, may be largely ignored.

The president needs an understanding by the public of the difficulty of his job and the nature of the problems he faces. The role of the press here can be critical. Watching television news seems to do little to inform viewers about public affairs; reading the printed media is more useful. This may be because reading requires more active cognitive processing of information than watching television, and there is more information presented in newspapers.

CONCLUSION

The mass media play a prominent role in the public presidency, providing the public with most of its information about the White House and mediating the president's communications with his constituents. Presidents need the press in order to reach the public, and presidential-press relations are an important complement to the chief executive's efforts at leading public opinion. Through attempting to coordinate news, holding press conferences, and providing a wide range of services for the press, the White House tries to influence its portrayal in the news. On occasion, the inevitable adversarial nature of presidential-press relations leads to open warfare and various forms of harassment of the press.

Presidential-press relations pose many obstacles to the president's efforts to obtain and maintain public support. Although it is probably not true that press coverage of the White House is biased along partisan or ideological lines or toward or against a particular president, it frequently presents a distorted picture to the public and fails to impart an appropriate perspective from which to view complex events. Moreover, presidents are continuously harassed by leaks to the press and are faced with superficial, over-simplified coverage that devotes little attention to substantive discussion of policies and often focuses on trivial

matters. This type of reporting undoubtedly affects public perceptions of the president, usually in a negative way. It is no wonder that chief executives generally see the press as a hindrance to their efforts to develop appreciation for their performance and policies.

NOTES

1. Richard Harris, "The Presidency and the Press," *New Yorker*, October 1, 1973, p. 122; Dom Bonafede, "Powell and the Press—A New Mood in the White House," *National Journal*, June 25, 1977, p. 981.

2. Harris, "The Presidency and the Press," p. 122, Peter Forbath and Carey Winfrey, *The Adversaries: The President and the Press* (Cleveland: Regal Books, 1974), p. 5.

3. Dick Kirschten, "Life in the White House Fish Bowl—Brady Takes Charge as Press Chief," *National Journal*, January 31, 1981, p. 180.

4. Jarol B. Manheim, "The Honeymoon's Over: The News Conference and the Development of Presidential Style," *Journal of Politics* 41 (February 1979): 60–61.

5. Doris A. Graber, *Mass Media and American Politics* (Washington, D.C.: Congressional Quarterly Press, 1980), p. 207.

6. "Carter Gets Even with the *Boston Globe*," *Newsweek*, February 25, 1980, p. 21.

7. Michael Baruch Grossman and Martha Joynt Kumar, *Portraying the President: The White House and the Media* (Baltimore: Johns Hopkins University Press, 1981), pp. 59–60, 63–64, 280–81.

8. Dom Bonafede, "The Washington Press—It Magnifies the President's Flaws and Blemishes," *National Journal*, May 1, 1982, pp. 267–71.

9. David L. Paletz and Robert M. Entman, *Media—Power—Politics* (New York: Free Press, 1981), pp. 55–56.

10. See William Safire, *Before the Fall: An Inside View of the Pre-Watergate White House* (New York: Doubleday, 1975), especially pp. 75, 321–23, 341–65. See also John Ehrlichman, *Witness to Power: The Nixon Years* (New York: Simon and Schuster, 1982), p. 264.

11. "Reagan Outburst on Leaks," *Newsweek*, January 18, 1982, p. 23; Walter S. Mossberg,

"Reagan Prepares Curbs on U.S. Officials to Restrict News Leaks on Foreign Policy," *The Wall Street Journal*, January 13, 1982, p. 7.

12. Safire, *Before the Fall*, p. 373; Henry Kissinger, *Years of Upheaval* (Boston: Little, Brown, 1981), p. 116.

13. Lyndon Johnson, quoted in George Christian, *The President Steps Down: A Personal Memoir of the Transfer of Power* (New York: Macmillan, 1970), p. 203.

14. "The U.S. vs. William Colby," *Newsweek*, September 28, 1981, p. 30.

15. "The Tattletale White House," *Newsweek*, February 25, 1980, p. 21.

16. Robert T. Hartmann, *Palace Politics: An Inside Account of the Ford Years* (New York: McGraw-Hill, 1980), p. 38.

17. William J. Lanouette, "The Washington Press Corps—Is It All That Powerful?" *National Journal*, June 2, 1979, p. 898.

18. See Edwards, *The Public Presidency*, p. 156 and sources cited therein.

19. John P. Robinson, "The Press as King-Maker: What Surveys from Last Five Campaigns Show," *Journalism Quarterly* 51 (Winter 1974): 587–94, 606.

20. Jimmy Carter, *Keeping Faith: Memoirs of a President* (New York: Bantam, 1982), pp. 179–80.

21. On this topic see Edwards, *The Public Presidency*, p. 162 and sources cited therein.

22. For an overview, see Cliff Zukin, "Mass Communication and Public Opinion," in Dan D. Nimmo and Keith R. Sanders, eds., *Handbook of Political Communication* (Beverly Hills: Sage, 1981), pp. 359–90.

23. Thomas E. Patterson, *The Mass Media Election: How Americans Choose Their President* (New York: Praeger, 1980), pp. 84–86, 98–100, 105, chap. 12; Doris A. Graber, "Personal Qualities in Presidential Images: The Contribution of the Press," *Midwest Journal of Political Science* 16 (February 1972): 295; Graber, *Mass Media and American Politics*, pp. 184–85.

24. Frederick T. Steeper, "Public Response to Gerald Ford's Statements on Eastern Europe in the Second Debate," in George F. Bishop, Robert G. Meadow, and Marilyn Jackson-Beeck, eds., *The Presidential Debates: Media, Electoral, and Public Perspectives* (New York: Praeger, 1978), pp. 81–101.

25. Gerald R. Ford, *A Time to Heal: The Autobiography of Gerald R. Ford* (New York:

Harper and Row, 1979), p. 289; see also pp. 343–44.

SELECTED READINGS

Abel, Elie, ed. *What's News: The Media in American Society.* San Francisco: Institute for Contemporary Studies, 1981.

Braestrup, Peter. *Big Story.* Garden City, N.Y.: Anchor, 1978.

Christian, George. *The President Steps Down: A Personal Memoir of the Transfer of Power.* New York: Macmillan, 1970.

Edwards, George C., III. *The Public Presidency.* Chaps. 3 and 4. New York: St. Martin's, 1983.

Epstein, Edward Jay. *News from Nowhere: Television and the News.* New York: Vintage, 1973.

Gans, Herbert J. *Deciding What's News.* New York: Vintage, 1979.

Graber, Doris A. *Mass Media and American Politics.* Washington, D.C.: Congressional Quarterly Press, 1980.

Grossman, Michael Baruch, and Martha Joynt Kumar. *Portraying the President: The White House and the News Media.* Baltimore: Johns Hopkins University Press, 1981.

Hess, Stephen. *The Washington Reporters.* Washington, D.C.: Brookings Institution, 1981.

Hofstetter, Richard C. *Bias in the News: Network Television Coverage of the 1972 Election Campaign.* Columbus: Ohio State University Press, 1976.

Iyengar, Shanto; Mark D. Peters; and Donald R. Kinder. "Experimental Demonstrations of the 'Not-so-Minimal' Consequences of Television News Programs." *American Political Science Review* 76 (December 1982): 848–58.

Kaid, Lynda Lee; Donald L. Singleton; and Dwight Davis. "Instant Analysis of Televised Political Addresses: The Speaker versus the Commentator." In Brent D. Ruben, ed., *Communication Yearbook I.* New Brunswick, N.J.: Transaction Books, 1977.

Keogh, James. *President Nixon and the Press.* New York: Funk and Wagnalls, 1972.

Klein, Herbert G. *Making It Perfectly Clear.* Garden City, N.Y.: Doubleday, 1980.

Lammers, William W. "Presidential Press Conference Schedules: Who Hides and When?" *Political Science Quarterly* 96 (Summer 1981): 261–78.

Manheim, Jarol B. "The Honeymoon's Over: The News Conference and the Development of Presidential Style." *Journal of Politics* 41 (February 1979): 55–74.

Minow, Newton; John B. Martin; and Lee M. Mitchell. *Presidential Television.* New York: Basic Books, 1973.

Morgan, Edward R.; Max Ways; Clark Mollenhoff; Peter Lisagor; and Herbert G. Klein. *The Presidency and the Press Conference.* Washington, D.C.: American Enterprise Institute, 1971.

Nessen, Ron. *It Sure Looks Different from the Inside.* Chicago: Playboy Press, 1978.

Paletz, David L., and Robert M. Entman. *Media—Power—Politics.* New York: Free Press, 1981.

Patterson, Thomas E. *The Mass Media Election: How Americans Choose Their President.* New York: Praeger, 1980.

Porter, William E. *Assault on the Media: The Nixon Years.* Ann Arbor: University of Michigan Press, 1976.

Purvis, Hoyt, ed. *The Presidency and the Press.* Austin, Tex.: Lyndon B. Johnson School of Public Affairs, 1976.

Robinson, Michael Jay. "The Impact of Instant Analysis." *Journal of Communication* 27 (Spring 1977): 17–23.

Robinson, Michael Jay, and Margaret A. Sheehan. *Over the Wire and On TV: CBS and UPI in Campaign '80.* New York: Russell Sage Foundation, 1983.

Safire, William. *Before the Fall: An Inside View of the Pre-Watergate White House.* New York: Doubleday, 1975.

Steeper, Frederick T. "Public Response to Gerald Ford's Statements on Eastern Europe in the Second Debate." In George F. Bishop, Robert G. Meadow, and Marilyn Jackson-Beeck, eds., *The Presidential Debates: Media, Electoral, and Public Perspectives.* New York: Praeger, 1978.

Wise, David. *The Politics of Lying: Government Deception, Secrecy, and Power.* New York: Vintage, 1973.

26
The Rise of the Rhetorical Presidency

James W. Ceaser, Glen E. Thurow, Jeffrey Tulis, & Joseph M. Bessette

THE RISE OF THE RHETORICAL PRESIDENCY

One of the most revealing periods of President Carter's tenure in office—and perhaps of the modern presidency itself—occurred during the summer of 1979. Falling to a new low in the public's approval ratings and facing criticism from all quarters for his leadership, the President dramatically cancelled a scheduled televised speech on energy and gathered his advisors together for a so-called domestic summit. Discussions moved beyond energy and economics to a reappraisal of the nature of presidential leadership and to an analysis of what, for want of a better term, can only be called the state of the national consciousness. Having served already more than half of his term, the President came to the conclusion that he had been mistaken in his understanding of the presidential office; he had, as he told David Broder, fallen into the trap of being "head of the government" rather than "leader of the people." As for the state of the national consciousness, the President concluded that the nation was experiencing a crisis of spirit or "malaise" that went deeper and was

Source: Presidential Studies Quarterly 11 no. 2 (Spring 1981).

more ominous than the economic challenges at hand. Yet difficult as this problem of malaise was, the President believed it could be tackled—and by the very same means that would correct his own failures of leadership. By engaging in a rhetorical campaign to "wake up" the American people, the President hoped both to save his presidency and begin the long process of national moral revival. As a Washington Post front page headline proclaimed on the day preceding his newly scheduled national address: CARTER SEEKING ORATORY TO MOVE AN ENTIRE NATION.[1]

Looking back today at these unusual events, one must surely be surprised that all of this self-analysis and deep introspection was so quickly forgotten. True, the July 15th speech was no classic of American oratory; but it did receive an extraordinary amount of attention at the time and was commonly thought to mark a "turning point" in the Carter presidency, at least as measured by the President's own intentions. Yet just three months afterwards, no one in the administration was mentioning the crisis of malaise, and the President, after the Iranian hostage crisis, returned to the White House and began deliberately acting "presidential," which is to say more like "the head of the government" than the "leader of the people."

Were these events merely a peculiar "story" of the Carter presidency? Perhaps. On the other hand, it might be argued that they are revealing in an exaggerated form of a major institutional development in this century—the rise of the rhetorical presidency—and of some of the problems inherent in that development.

Popular or mass rhetoric, which Presidents once employed only rarely, now serves as one of their principal tools in attempting to govern the nation. What-

ever doubts Americans may now entertain about the limitations of presidential leadership, they do not consider it unfitting or inappropriate for presidents to attempt to "move" the public by programmatic speeches that exhort and set forth grand and ennobling views.

It was not always so. Prior to this century, popular leadership through rhetoric was suspect. Presidents rarely spoke directly to the people, preferring communications between the branches of the government. Washington seldom delivered more than one major speech per year of his administration, and that one—the Annual Address—was almost mandated by the Constitution and was addressed to Congress. Jefferson even ceased delivering the address in person, a precedent that continued until Woodrow Wilson's appearance before Congress in 1913. The spirit of these early presidents' examples was followed throughout the nineteenth century. The relatively few popular speeches that were made differed in character from today's addresses. Most were patriotic orations, some raised Constitutional issues, and several spoke to the conduct of war. Very few were domestic "policy speeches" of the sort so common today, and attempts to move the nation by means of an exalted picture of a perfect ideal were almost unknown. Indeed, in the conspicuous case where a president did "go to the people" in a "modern" sense—Andrew Johnson's speaking tour in the summer before the 1866 Congressional elections—the campaign not only failed, but was considered highly irregular.[2] It was not until well into the present century that presidential speeches addressed to the people became commonplace and presidents began to think that they were not effective leaders unless they constantly exhorted the public.[3]

Today, a president has an assembly-

line of speechwriters efficiently producing words that enable him to say something on every conceivable occasion.
Unless a president is deliberately "hiding" in the White House, a week
scarcely goes by without at least one
major news story devoted to coverage
of a radio or TV speech, an address to
Congress, a speech to a convention, a
press conference, a news release, or some
other presidential utterance. But more
important even than the quantity of
popular rhetoric is the fact that presidential speech and action increasingly reflect the opinion that speaking *is* governing. Speeches are written to become the
events to which people react no less
than "real" events themselves.

The use of rhetoric by some of our
recent presidents is revealing of this development. During his campaign and
throughout the first few months of his
presidency, President Kennedy spoke
continually of the existence of a national
crisis and of the need for sacrifice and
commitment, only to find it difficult at
times to explain just what the crisis was
and where the sacrifice and commitment
were actually needed. Today, seen in
perspective, much of Kennedy's talk
about our "hour of national peril" has
a nice ring but a hollow sound, as if it
were fashioned to meet the imperatives
of a certain rhetorical style and not those
of the concrete situation he faced.[4] It
seems to reflect the view expressed by
a former Kennedy White House aide:
"It will be less important in years to
come for presidents to work out programs
and serve as administrators than it will
be for presidents through the means of
television to serve as educational and
psychic leaders."[5]

President Johnson followed with a
steady stream of oratory that swelled
popular expectations of governmental
capacity to a level that even his apologists now concede far exceeded what
government could possibly achieve.

What Harry McPherson, one of Johnson's chief aides and speechwriters, said
of the goals of the Johnson administration characterizes perfectly the tone of
its rhetoric:

> People were [seen to be] suffering from
> a sense of alienation from one another,
> of anomie, of powerlessness. This affected
> the well-to-do as much as it did the poor.
> Middle-class women, bored and friendless
> in the suburban afternoons; fathers, work-
> ing at "meaningless" jobs, or slumped be-
> fore the television set; sons and daughters
> desperate for "relevance"—all were in
> need of community beauty, and purpose,
> all were guilty because so many others
> were deprived while they, rich beyond
> their ancestors' dreams, were depressed.
> What would change all this was a creative
> public effort.[6]

President Nixon sensed people's reaction to the feverish pitch of the mid-
sixties and countered with an anti-rheto-
ric rhetoric that soberly promised to
"lower our voices":

> In these difficult years, America has suf-
> fered from a fever of words; from inflated
> rhetoric that promises more than it can
> deliver; . . . from bombastic rhetoric
> that postures instead of persuading.[7]

But this calm and mature pose, typical
of Nixon's political superego, could not
contain his own desire to strike back
at his detractors, and together with
Vice-President Agnew, Nixon launched
his own rhetorical counteroffensive. If
they enjoyed, up to a point at least, a
great deal of success with their oratory,
it was because much of it had the self-
contained purpose of calling into question the rhetoric of their liberal opponents. With Agnew in particular, the
privilege of holding public office was less
important for what it could allow him
to do than for what it could allow him
to say.

President Carter, the outsider who
came to Washington promising to bring
a simple honesty and decency to govern-

ment, began his term speaking in a voice lowered to a point where many felt that it had become inaudible. By mid-term, falling in the polls and urged on by his media advisor, Gerald Rafshoon, the President began to look for more opportunities to display rhetorical forcefulness. And by the time of his July oratorical campaign he emerged with an assertive tone and vigorous body movement, his theme being the decline and revitalization of America:

> [We face] a crisis that strikes at the very heart and soul and spirit of our national will. We can see this crisis in the growing doubt about the meaning of our own lives and in the loss of unity of purpose for our nation. . . . The erosion of our confidence in the future is threatening to destroy the social and political fabric of America. . . . [What] we must do is to regenerate our sense of unity, joining hands with each other in a sense of commitment to a national purpose. . . . We must bring together the different elements in America—producers, consumers, labor, business—bring us all together from the battlefield of selfishness to a table of common purpose.[8]

In the face of no tangible crisis on the order of a war or domestic upheaval, Carter was seeking nevertheless to define a subtler crisis and, linking it to the pragmatic issues of energy politics, to lead a domestic cultural revival. As one of his aides claimed, "I think we have seen both the rebirth of the American spirit that he talks about and the rebirth of the Carter presidency as well."[9]

Much of this rhetoric is undoubtedly, as many say today, "mere rhetoric." The excess of speech has perhaps fed a cynicism about it that is the very opposite of the boundless faith in rhetoric that has been so far portrayed. Yet, despite this cynicism, it seems increasingly the case that for many who comment on and form opinions about the presidency, word rivals deed as the measure of presidential performance. The standard set for presidents has in large degree become an artifact of their own inflated rhetoric and one to which they frequently fall victim.[10] While part of this difficulty can be blamed on the ineptness of certain presidents' rhetorical strategies, it is also the case that presidents operate in a context that gives them much less discretion over their rhetoric than one might think. The problem is thus not one simply of individual rhetorics, but is rather an institutional dilemma for the modern presidency.

Beginning with the campaign, the candidates are obliged to demonstrate their leadership capacity through an ever growing number of rhetorical performances, with the potential impact of their words on future problems of governing often being the least of their concerns. The pressure to "say something" continues after the president has begun to govern. Presidents not only face the demand to explain what they have done and intend to do, but they also have come under increasing pressure to speak out on perceived crises and to minister to the moods and emotions of the populace. In the end, it may be the office of the presidency that is weakened by this form of leadership, puffed up by false expectations that bear little relationship to the practical tasks of governing and undermined by the resulting cynicism.[11]

How did the rhetorical presidency come into existence? What are its strengths and weaknesses? Can presidents escape its burdens, and to what extent should they try to do so? These are some of the important questions that need addressing.

I

The rise of the rhetorical presidency has been primarily the result of three factors: (1) a modern doctrine of presidential leadership, (2) the modern mass media, and (3) the modern presidential campaign. Of these three, doctrine is probably the most important.

As strange as it may seem to us today, the Framers of our Constitution looked with great suspicion on popular rhetoric. Their fear was that mass oratory, whether crudely demagogic or highly inspirational, would undermine the rational and enlightened self-interest of the citizenry which their system was designed to foster and on which it was thought to depend for its stability. The Framers' well-known mistrust of "pure" democracy by an assembly—and by extension, of the kind of representative government that looked only to public opinion as its guide—was not based, as is generally supposed, on a simple doubt about the people's capacity to govern, but on a more complex case concerning the evils that would result from the interplay between the public and popular orators.

In democracies, they reasoned, political success and fame are won by those orators who most skillfully give expression to transient, often inchoate, public opinion. [12] Governing by this means, if indeed it can be called governing, leads to constant instability as leaders compete with each other to tap the latest mood passing through the public. The paradox of government by mood is that it fosters neither democratic accountability nor statesmanly efficiency. Freed from the necessity to consult public opinion, understood as "the cool and deliberate sense of the community," popular orators would be so chained to public opinion, understood as "mood," that discretion and flexibility essential to statesmanship would be undermined. [13]

The Founders were not so impractical as to think that popular rhetoric could be entirely avoided in a republican system. But the government they designed was intended to minimize reliance on popular oratory and to establish institutions which could operate effectively without the immediate support of transient opinion. All of the powers of governing were to be given, not directly to the people, but to their representatives. These representatives would find themselves in a tri-partite government in which the various tasks of governing would be clearly discernable and assigned, and in which they would be forced to deal with knowledgeable and determined men not easily impressed by facile oratory. As part of their solution, the Founders were counting on the large size of the nation, which at the time erected a communication barrier that would mute the impact of national popular rhetoric, whether written or oral. Beyond this, the Founders instituted a presidential selection system that was designed to preclude active campaigning by the candidates. As for the presidency itself, the Founders discouraged any idea that the President should serve as a leader of the people who would stir mass opinion by rhetoric; their conception was rather that of a constitutional officer who would rely for his authority on the formal powers granted by the Constitution and on the informal authority that would flow from the office's strategic position.

These limitations on popular rhetoric did not mean, however, that presidents were expected to govern in silence. Ceremonial occasions presented a proper forum for reminding the public of the nation's basic principles; and communications to Congress, explicitly provided for by the Constitution, offered a mechanism by which the people also could be informed on matters of policy. Yet this intra-branch rhetoric, though public, was not meant to be popular. Addressed in the first instance to a body of informed representatives, it would possess a reasoned and deliberative character; and insofar as some in the public would read these speeches and state papers, they would implicitly be called on to raise their understanding to the level characteristic of deliberative speech.

Nineteenth century politics in America did not, of course, follow exactly the Founders' model of an essentially nonrhetorical regime. Campaigns quickly changed from their intended place as quiet affairs into spirited events replete with fanfare and highly charged popular rhetoric, though it is important to observe that the rhetoric was produced not by the candidates but by surrogates arranged for by the parties. Moreover, certain presidents—most notably Jackson and Lincoln—used their communications with Congress and some of their speeches and proclamations to address the people more or less directly. Yet the amount of nineteenth century presidential rhetoric that even loosely could be called popular is very little indeed, and the presidency remained, with some slight alterations, a Constitutional office rather than the seat of popular leadership.[14]

The Inaugural and the Annual Address (now called the State of the Union) were the principal speeches of a President given wide dissemination. The character of the Inaugural Address illustrates the general character of presidential popular speech during the period. Given on a formal occasion, it tended to follow a pattern which was set by Jefferson's First Inaugural Address in which he delivered an exposition of the principles of the union and its republican character. Although Jefferson's speech might in one sense be considered a partisan document, in fact he sought to be conciliatory towards his opponents. More important still, he presented his case not as an attempt to win support for the particular policies of a party but

rather as an effort to instruct the people in, and fortify their attachment to, true republican political principles. The form of inaugural address perfected by Jefferson proved a lasting model throughout the century. Although subsequent addresses did not often match the eloquence or understanding of Jefferson's—Lincoln's Second Inaugural, of course, being the most conspicuous exception—they consistently attempted to show how the actions of the new administrations would conform to Constitutional and republican principles.

Against this tradition Woodrow Wilson gave the Inaugural Address (and presidential speech generally) a new theme. Instead of showing how the policies of the incoming administration reflected the principles of our form of government, Wilson sought to articulate the unspoken desires of the people by holding out a vision of their fulfillment. Presidential speech, in Wilson's view, should articulate what is "in our hearts" and not necessarily what is in our Constitution.[15]

Theodore Roosevelt had presaged this change by his remarkable ability to capture the nation's attention through his understanding of the character of the new mass press and through his artful manipulation of the national press corps.[16] It was Wilson, however, who brought popular speech to the forefront of American politics by his dramatic appearances before Congress—breaking more than a century's precedent of presidential nonattendance—and by his famous speaking tour on behalf of the League of Nations. Most importantly, Wilson articulated the doctrinal foundation of the rhetorical presidency and thereby provided an alternative theoretical model to that of the Founders. In Wilson's view, the greatest power in modern democratic regimes lay potentially with the popular leader who could sway or—to use his word—"interpret" the wishes of the people. After some indecision Wilson finally concluded that the presidency was the institution best suited to assume this role: "There is but one national voice in the country and that is the voice of the President." And it is the "voice" that is most important for governing: "It is natural that orators should be the leaders of a self-governing people."[17]

The Wilsonian concept of the rhetorical presidency consists of two interfused elements. First, the President should employ oratory to create an active public opinion that, if necessary, will pressure the Congress into accepting his program: "He [the President] has no means of compelling Congress except through public opinion."[18] In advancing policy, deliberative, intrabranch rhetoric thus becomes secondary to popular rhetoric, and the President "speaks" to Congress not directly but through his popular addresses. Second, in order to reach and move the public, the character of the rhetoric must tap the public's feelings and articulate its wishes. Rhetoric does not instill old and established principles as much as it seeks to infuse a sense of vision into the President's particular legislative program.

> A nation is led by a man who . . . speaks, not the rumors of the street, but a new principle for a new age; a man in whose ears the voices of the nation do not sound like the accidental and discordant notes that come from the voice of a mob, but concurrent and concordant like the united voices of a chorus, whose many meanings, spoken by melodious tongues, unite in his understanding in a single meaning and reveal to him a single vision, so that he can speak what no man else knows, the common meaning of the common voice.[19]

Much the same idea, though stripped of some of its eloquence, was expressed by President Carter in his Convention acceptance speech when he promised to be a President "who is not isolated from the people, but who feels your pain and shares your dreams and takes his strength and his wisdom and his courage from you."[20] Presidents have not always found it easy to bring these two elements—policy and mood—together. Carter's "malaise" address of July 1979 again illustrates the point. The first half of the speech portrayed a national malaise of sweeping and profound proportions; the second half incongruously implied that we could secure our redemption by conserving energy and taxing the oil companies.

The Wilsonian concept of presidential leadership was echoed in FDR's claim that the presidency is "pre-eminently a place of moral leadership" and subsequently canonized in the scholarly literature by Clinton Rossiter's characterization of the presidency as the nation's "trumpet."[21] To be sure, not all presidents since Wilson have embraced this grandiloquent conception of their role, but as a doctrine the rhetorical presidency has become the predominant model. What these metaphorical terms like "voice of the nation," "moral leader" and "trumpet" all suggest is a form of presidential speech that soars above the realm of calm and deliberate discussion of reasons of state or appeals to enlightened self-interest. Rather, the picture of leadership that emerges under the influence of this doctrine is one that constantly exhorts in the name of a common purpose and a spirit of idealism.

If the doctrine of the rhetorical presidency leaves us today with the occasional feeling that it is hollow or outworn, it is not because of a decline in its influence but because of the inevitable consequences of its ascendancy. Presidents such as Wilson, Franklin Roosevelt and John Kennedy found in the doctrine a novelty which they could exploit to win attention—if not always success—for their program. Exercised against the prevailing expectation of moral leadership, however, presidents may find that the doctrine is sometimes more of a burden than an opportunity. Presidents can speak and exhort, but will anyone genuinely heed what they say?

The events leading up to President Carter's address of July 1979 are instructive. Late in June of that year the President received a memo from his chief domestic policy advisor, Stuart Eizenstat, recommending what has become by now the standard use of the rhetorical presidency:

> Every day you need to be dealing with— and publicly be seen as dealing with— the major energy problems now facing us. . . . You have a variety of speeches scheduled after your return. . . . Each of those occasions should be used to talk about energy. . . . The windfall tax campaign was successful because of your repeated discussion of it during a short time. With strong steps we can mobilize the nation around a real crisis and with a clear enemy.[22]

But on the day before his originally scheduled TV address, the President decided to cancel it because, in columnist David Broder's words, "He believed that neither the country nor the Congress would heed or respond to another energy speech—the fifth of his term—from him."[23] If a nationally televised presidential address, itself once a dramatic event, must be cancelled as a way of recapturing a sense of drama, one wonders what expedient presidents will turn to next.

II

The second factor that accounts for the rise of the rhetorical presidency is the modern mass media. The media did not create the rhetorical presidency—doctrine did—but it facilitated its development and has given to it some of its special characteristics. The mass media, meaning here primarily radio and television, must be understood first from the perspective of its technical capacities. It has given the President the means by which to communicate directly and instantaneously with a large national audience, thus tearing down the communications barrier on which the Founders had relied to insulate representative institutions from direct contact with the populace. Besides increasing the size of the President's audience, the mass media has changed the mode by which he communicates with the public, replacing the written with the spoken word delivered in a dramatic visible performance. The written word formerly provided a partial screen or check against the most simplistic argumentations, as it allowed more control of the text by the reader and limited the audience to those with the most interest in politics.

One might reply, of course, that presidents today produce more written documents than ever before and that all of their speeches are recorded and transcribed. But this matters little as few in the public ever bother to peruse, let alone read, the President's words. Significant messages are delivered today in speeches, and presidents understand that it is the visible performance, not the tangible text, that creates the public impression. Under the constant demand for new information that characterizes audiences of the media age, what is not seen or heard today does not exist. Presidents accordingly feel the pressure to speak more and to engage in what Eizenstat called "campaigns" to keep their message before the public. Words come to have an ephemeral quality to them, and the more the President speaks the less value can be put on any one speech he delivers. One of the great ironies of the modern presidency is that as the President relies more on rhetoric to govern, he finds it more difficult to deliver a truly important speech, one that will stand by itself and continue to shape events.

The influence of the mass media on presidential rhetoric is not limited to its technical capacities. The mass media has also created a new power center in American politics in the form of television news. If the technical aspect of the media has given the President an advantage or an opportunity, the existence of television news often serves as a rival or an impediment. Journalists are filters in the communication process, deciding what portions of the President's non-televised speeches they will show and how their arguments will be interpreted. When presidents speak in public today, their most important audience is not the one they are personally addressing, but rather the public as it is reached through the brief cuts aired on the news. Speeches accordingly tend to be written so that any segment can be taken to stand by itself—as a self-contained lead. Argument gives way to aphorism.

The direct impact of the news' interpretation of the President's words is perhaps less important for presidential rhetoric than the indirect influence that derives from the character of news itself. Television news not only carries the messages of governing officials to the people; it also selects the issues that are presented to the government for "action" of some sort. "Real" expressions of mass opinion, which in the past were sporadic, are replaced by the news' continuous "sophisticated" analyses that serve as a surrogate audience, speaking to the government and supposedly representing to it what the people are saying and thinking. Driven by its own inner dynamic to find and sustain exciting issues and to present them in dramatic terms, news creates—or gives the impression of creating—national moods and currents of opinion which appear to call for some form of action by the government and especially by the President.

The media and the modern presidency feed on each other. The media has found in the presidency a focal point on which to concentrate its peculiarly simplistic and dramatic interpretation of events; and the presidency has found a vehicle in the media that allows it to win public attention and with that attention the reality, but more often the pretense, of enhanced power.[24] What this two-sided relationship signifies is a change in the rhetorical context in which the President now operates, the implications of which extend beyond the question of how much power the President has to the issue of who he attempts to govern. Constitutional government, which was established in contradistinction to government by assembly, now has become a kind of government by assembly, with TV "speaking" to the President and the President responding to the demands and moods that it creates. The new government by assembly—operating without a genuine assembling of the people—makes it increasingly difficult for presidents to present an appearance of stability and to allow time for policies to mature and for events to respond to their measures. Instead, the President is under more pressure to act—or to appear to act—to respond to the moods generated by the news.

Partly as a result of these pressures from the media for more and more presidential speech, a major new staff capacity has been added to the White House to enable the President to produce the large number of speeches and messages that he speaks or writes. While not a major cause of the rhetorical presidency, like any staff capacity its existence becomes a reason for its continual use. Once known as "ghosts" and hidden in the presidential closet, rhetoric-makers today have come out into the full light of day and are openly employed under the title of speechwriters.[25] We have perhaps passed beyond the point of naïveté where we shudder at exposés which reveal that the personal convictions of the President are written by someone else, but it is worth noting the paradox that at a time when presidents are judged more by their rhetoric, they play less of a role in its actual formulation. If, as Francis Bacon once wrote, only writing makes a man exact, the incoherence of much presidential policymaking may owe something to the fact that presidents do so little of their own writing and sometimes schedule more speeches than they can possibly supervise closely.[26] Certain rapid shifts that occurred duing 1978 in President Carter's pronounced foreign policy, which Senator Kennedy attempted to make into an important campaign issue, are attributable to different viewpoints of the authors of his speeches, which the President either did not want or did not have the time to integrate.[27] An institutionalized speechwriting staff may bring to presidential speeches interests of its own that conflict with presidential policy or, to the extent that the staff becomes divorced from the President's chief political advisors, it may be incapable of resisting pressure from others for the inclusion of remarks in speeches at the expense of presidential coherence. Finally the speechwriting task has come more and more to be influenced by pollsters and admen whose understanding of rhetoric derives from the premises of modern advertising and its offshoot, political consulting. Such influence is even more visible in the modern presidential campaign.

III

The modern presidential campaign is the third factor that accounts for the rise of the rhetorical presidency. The roots of the modern campaign go back to Wilson and the Progressives and to many of the same ideas that helped to create the rhetorical presidency. Prior to 1912, the parties were largely responsible for conducting the campaigns, and the candidates, with few exceptions, restricted their communications to letters of acceptance of the nomination. Wilson was the first victorious presidential candidate to have engaged in a full-scale speaking tour during the campaign. In his view, it was essential that the candidates replace the parties as the main rhetorical instruments of the campaign. This change would serve not only to downgrade the influence of traditional parties but also to prepare the people for the new kind of presidency that he hoped to establish. Indeed, with Wilson the distinction between campaigning and governing is blurred, as both involve the same essential function of persuading through popular oratory.

Although Wilson himself did not campaign extensively in the pre-convention period, he supported the idea of a pre-convention campaign and pushed for nomination by national primaries. His ideal of a truly open presidential nomination campaign in which all candidates must take the "outside" route was not fully realized, however, until after the reforms that followed the 1968 election. Over the past two campaigns and in this one, we have seen the development of one of the most peculiarly irresponsible rhetorical processes ever devised. For a period of two years before the 1980 conventions, the various contenders had little else to offer except their rhetoric. Undisciplined by the responsiblity of matching word to deed, they sought to create events out of their speeches, all the while operating under the constant media-created pressure to say something new. As their goal was to win power, and as that goal, especially in the pre-convention period, was remote, candidates could easily afford to disregard the impact of their speech on the demands of governing and instead craft their rhetoric with a view merely to persuading.

Scholars of the electoral process, interested in such issues as accountability and democratic voting theory, have sought to determine just how much of the candidates' rhetoric goes into spelling out stands on issues as compared to other kinds of appeals, *e.g.* character or vaguely formed interpretation of events. If there is an operative normative theory to some of these inquiries, it is based on the premise that it would be desirable for the voters to know the candidate's stand on the full range of issues and to make up their minds on the basis of a rational calculation of their position as it compares to those of the candidates.[28] However, if one does not focus exclusively on campaigns but tries to see campaigns as part of the total process of governing, there is cause for wondering whether what is ideal from the standpoint of democratic voting theory is very helpful for promoting effective governing: too many specific commitments might, if taken seriously, undermine a necessary degree of discretion, or, if blatantly ignored, add to public cynicism. It is the empirical findings of such research that are, perhaps, of most interest, and here one discovers two contrasting tendencies.

Benjamin Page has shown that candidates devote very little time in their speeches to spelling out anything like concrete policy stands; instead most of their efforts goes into general interpretations of past records and highly ambiguous statements about future goals.[29] On the other hand, Jeff Fischel has found that the number of specific promises that candidates make over the course of a campaign has been increasing dramatically since 1952.[30] This paradox is easily explicable if one bears in mind that while candidates may discuss very little of substance in their speeches, they speak (and write) much more than they ever did in the past and thus accumulate more pledges. This research suggests, then, that we have the worst of both worlds—vague and uninstructive speeches on the one hand and more and more specific promises on the other. In this result one finds the perfect marriage of media and special interest politics.

It may also be that the distinctions scholars make in regard to "issue stands" and "image making" are increasingly irrelevant. For the candidates and their political consultants the campaign is often seen as a whole, with the most sophisticated campaigns today being run on the premise that the candidates must tap and express a popular mood. Issues and images are both fit into this general theme. As Jimmy Carter remarked in 1976, "Insofar as my political campaign has been successful, it is because I have learned from our people and have accurately reflected their concerns, their frustrations and their desires."[31] Reflecting but not necessarily educating the people's moods has in some instances been the order of the day. The old case against the political consultants and admen— that they build up an image of the candidate's person—largely underestimates their impact. Today, they are definitely in the "business" of dealing with "issues" no less than images, and both frequently are subordinated to mood.

Actually, the efforts that candidates

do make in some of their speeches to address the issues are often passed over and ignored in the media. Although it may take the public a long time to learn the candidates' basic themes—and many never learn them—the reporters covering the campaign often tire of repetitive stories and resist putting comments from formal speeches on the air. As Thomas Patterson has shown, the press, and especially television news coverage, looks for the "new" in the campaigns, and thus tends to cover those comments of candidates that are made in impromptu sessions. Indeed, journalists attempt to stimulate "campaign issues"—e.g., off the cuff responses to charges or to contemporary news events—rather than to cover what the candidates seek to communicate in their own rhetoric.[32] This form of news coverage may well help us learn something about the candidates' "character" or ability to think in public, but it hardly does very much to encourage among the people a respect for the formal rhetorical mode. That speeches might, if heard, be a helpful way of judging candidates, however, is suggested by the importance of the one main campaign speech that the public can view in its entirety—the campaign acceptance speech.

The presidential campaign is important for the kinds of inflated expectations it raises, but it is even more important for the effects it has on the process of governing. So formative has the campaign become of our tastes for oratory and of our conception of leadership that presidential speech and governing have come more and more to imitate the model of the campaign. In a dramatic reversal, campaigns set the tone for governing rather than governing for campaigns. This trend, which is becoming more embedded in public expectations, is furthered by another dynamic that works on the President and his staff.

Both may think of the campaign as their finest hour, to the extent that its techniques become internalized in their conception of governing. As pollster Pat Caddell advised Carter at the beginning of his term, "governing with public approval requires a continuing political campaign."[33] And in a memo that led up to the Camp David speech, Caddell suggested that "Carter should return to the style that had marked his campaign for the presidency, at least in its early stages: to address the nation's mood and to touch on the 'intangible' problems in our society."[34] Some of the President's political advisors, Vice President Mondale among them, opposed the whole idea of a campaign while holding office. But the political consultants stood together and won the day. As Gerald Rafshoon told Elizabeth Drew, "It was important for the President to be 'relevant,' which meant showing people he understood what was bothering them."[35]

The growing intrusion of the mentality of the campaign consultants into the governing process recalls the ancient philosophical battle between the original founders of the art of rhetoric—the sophists—and the political scientists. When rhetoric was first discovered as a teachable art in Ancient Greece, its masters emphasized its purely persuasive powers; and because rhetoric claimed to be able to instruct politicians on how to win power, it quickly began to pass itself off as the most important kind of political education. As Carnes Lord has stated, ". . . by encouraging the supposition that the exercise of political responsibility requires little substantive knowledge beyond rhetorical expertise itself, rhetoric as taught by the sophists tended to make men oblivious of the very need for a science of politics." The threat that the art of rhetoric so defined posed to political science, yet the evident necessity of politicians to use rhetoric, led Aristotle to write a rhetoric of his own. It was designed to recast the nature of the discipline so as to emphasize, within the realm of the potentially persuasive, the role of rational argumentation and to encourage politicians "to view rhetoric not as an instrument of personal aggrandizement in the sophistic manner, but rather as an instrument of responsible or prudent statesmanship."[36] This view, which came to constitute the rhetorical tradition of the West through its central place in a liberal arts education, exerted a powerful influence on our founding. Many of the Framers, as Gordon Wood has pointed out, were schooled in this tradition of rhetoric, and one of our presidents, John Quincy Adams, wrote a treatise on rhetoric that reflected many of its premises.[37] Clearly, however, under the impact of the modern campaign, this tradition has lost ground to a modern-day version of the sophistic tradition. Under the tutelage of political consultants and pollsters, the understanding of rhetoric as mere persuasion has come to be almost second nature to many of our politicians. The devolution of governing into campaigning is thus even more ominous than it first appeared, for it represents not just a change in the purpose of speeches but a decay in the standard of speech itself.

IV

President Carter's formulation of July, 1979, that a President should be "the leader of the people" rather than "the head of the government," was a perfect expression of his support for the doctrine of the rhetorical presidency. Acting explicitly on this doctrine, the President pledged to spend more time with the people and launched a campaign of speeches, largely inspirational in tone, that were designed to mobilize a popular

constituency which supposedly would translate into higher opinion ratings and more power in Washington. The evident failure of this campaign, however, should perhaps have given the President pause about the effectiveness of his newly discovered conception of his office. For all the momentary attention lavished on the President's words, they did not succeed—nor come close to succeeding—in creating "a rebirth of the American spirit." Nor is this surprising.

As the very name implies, the rhetorical presidency is based on words, not power. When connected in a practical way with the exercise of power, speech can be effective, but when used merely to generate public support it is apt to fail. However much attention and enthusiasm a President can momentarily garner, there is little assurance that the Congress will accede. As Henry Fairlie once observed, "There is in fact very little that the people can do to assist a President while he is in office; brought together at a general election, they are dispersed between elections; brought together in the evening by a television address, they are dispersed the next day."[38] Although a President may sometimes find that he can make the greatest public impression by attacking Congress for failing to pass his preferred programs, or by attributing such failures to archaic procedures or undue influence and power of special interests, such appeals are not likely to win friends in that body which still retains ultimate authority over legislation. Moreover, to the extent that Presidents *can* pressure Congress through popular appeals, such a strategy, like crying "wolf," is likely to work less well the more often it is used.

The inflated expectations engendered by the rhetorical presidency have by now become a matter of serious concern among those who study the presidency.

In response to this problem, a growing number of scholars have begun to argue that Presidents should remove themselves from much of the day-to-day management of government and reserve themselves for crisis management.[39] If this argument means only that Presidents should not immerse themselves in details or spread themselves too thinly, no one could quarrel with it. But if it means that the President should abandon the articulation of a broad legislative program or avoid general management of the bureaucracy at a time when the bureaucracy is becoming more and more unmanageable, then the argument is misguided. If the President does not give coherence to policy or enforce discipline on the executive branch, who will? Certainly not Congress. The President remains our only national officer who, as Jefferson once said, "commands a view of the whole ground."[40] A retrenched presidency that cedes much of its authority to others and merely reacts to crisis is hardly the answer to our difficulties. Nor is it the only possible response to the docrine of the rhetorical presidency. Advocates of the retrenched presidency contend that to reduce the expectations on the office, its authority must be diminished. But the high expectations for the office are not the result of its authority, but rather of the inflated conception of presidential leadership that governs our thinking. It is the publicly proclaimed pretensions of presidential power, not the power itself, that is the source of the problem.

The roots of the rhetorical presidency stretch so deeply into our political structure and national consciousness that talk of change may seem futile; and yet, the evident failures of the current doctrine, together with the growing scholarly debate about the crisis of the presidency, suggest that the moment has arrived for a discussion of alternatives. It should not be forgotten that the foundations of the rhetorical presidency were deliberately laid by Woodrow Wilson and that other presidents might establish new doctrines. If a sensible reform of the institution is ever possible, the key will be found in reversing the order of President Carter's formulation of July 1979—that is, in restoring the President to his natural place as the head of government, and subordinating his awkward role of an itinerant leader of the people. But how could such change take place, and what would the contours of the office look like?

First, since the modern campaign is the source of so many of the problems of the presidency, it is evident that no reform of the office can hope to succeed without a change in the selection process. The operative theoretical principle that must govern this change is that the selection process should be thought of not as an end in itself, but as a means of promoting, or at least not undermining, the character of the presidential office. Construed in practical terms this principle translates into a call for electoral reform that would reduce the duration of the campaign, especially in the pre-convention period. The elimination or dramatic reduction in the number of presidential primaries and the return of the power of selection to the parties would be helpful. This change would not eliminate the campaign, but it would reduce its public phase to a shorter period and thus focus public attention on the speechmaking that takes place after the nomination. Indeed, as Thomas Patterson has recently shown, the longer campaigns of recent years have *not* increased the level of public knowledge of the candidates' stands; and the psychology of mass attention may well be such that, after a certain point, there is an inverse relationship between information and learning.[41] Rhetorical performances may lose their drama as they become simply another in a long and expected series.

Second, Presidents should reduce the number of their speeches. As they speak less, there is at least the chance that their words will carry more weight; and if their words carry more weight, then perhaps more thought will be given to speech that can sensibly direct action. What applies to speeches applies equally to press conferences. Press conferences without cameras would probably allow for a more detailed exchange of information between the President and the press corps and avoid the pressures on the President (and the journalists) to make each news conference dramatic and newsworthy.[42] Written messages might replace many presently oral performances, and personal television appearances would be reserved for truly important issues of public concern.

Third, it is obvious that a reduction in the quantity of rhetoric itself is not enough; its character must also change. To avoid inspirational rhetoric does not mean that the President must abandon firm principles, practical ideals or even a political poetry that connects this generation with the moorings of our political system. Indeed, such a rhetoric is perfectly consistent with the dignity of a head of state and the character of our political order. In respect to policy, however, Presidents must recapture the capacity to address the nation's enlightened self-interest no less than its sense of idealism and the related capacity to approach Congress directly rather than through the people.

The gravest problem of the rhetorical presidency, however, goes deeper than any issue confined to presidential practice. It extends to the basic questions of how our nation can be governed. No one would deny that Presidents need to hold up America's basic principles and on occasion mobilize the public to meet genuine challenges. Indeed, in a liberal system of government that frees men's acquisitive instincts and allows them to devote their energies to individual material improvement, there is room on occasion for Presidents to lift up the public's vision to something beyond the clash of interests. But under the influence of the rhetorical presidency, we have seen an ever-increasing reliance on inspirational rhetoric to deal with the normal problems of politics. If there is a place for such rhetoric, it is necessary also to be aware of its danger and of the corresponding need to keep it within limits. By itself, rhetoric does not possess the power to make citizens devote themselves selflessly to the common weal, particularly where the basic principles of society protect and encourage men's independent and private activities. The Founders of our country created a complex representative government designed to foster a knowledgeable concern for the common good in the concrete circumstances of political life that would be difficult, if not impossible, to elicit directly from a people led by orators. What the continued use of inspirational rhetoric fosters is not a simple credibility problem, but a deep tension between the publicly articulated understanding of the nature of our politics and the actual springs that move the system. No wonder, then, that some politicians, deceived by their own rhetoric, find it difficult to come to terms with the job of governing a nation of complex multiple interests. Far from reinforcing our country's principles and protecting its institutions, the rhetorical presidency leads us to neglect our principles for our hopes and to ignore the benefits and needs of our institutions for a fleeting sense of oneness with our leaders.

NOTES

1. *The Washington Post,* July 14, 15, and 16, 1979.

2. For a discussion of Johnson's "swing around the circle," see Albert Castel, *The Presidency of Andrew Johnson* (Lawrence, Kan.: Regents Press, 1979).

3. Joseph Kallenbach, *The American Chief Executive* (New York: Harper & Row, 1966), pp. 333–40.

4. *Public Papers of the Presidents, John F. Kennedy 1961* (Washington: Government Printing Office, 1961), p. 19; see also Henry Fairlie, *The Kennedy Promise: The Politics of Expectation* (Garden City: Doubleday, 1973).

5. Cited in Thomas E. Cronin, *The State of the Presidency* (Boston: Little, Brown, 1975), p. 72. The identification of the aide is not revealed.

6. Harry McPherson, *A Political Education* (Boston: Little, Brown, 1972), pp. 301–2.

7. *The Public Papers of the Presidents, Richard Nixon 1969,* (Washington: Government Printing Office, 1969), p. 2.

8. President Carter, Speeches of July 15, 1979, (National Television Address) and July 16, 1979, (Detroit, Michigan). *Presidential Documents, Annual Index, 1979,* p. 1237 and 1248.

9. *The Washington Post,* July 17, 1979, p. A14.

10. See for example, Theodore Lowi, *The End of Liberalism* (New York: Norton, 1969), pp. 182–83.

11. In discussing matters which "force" Presidents to make decisions by specified dates, Richard Neustadt concludes: "It is hardly to be wondered at that during Truman's years such matters became focal points for policy development, especially in the domestic sphere." See Richard Neustadt, "Presidency and Legislation: Planning the President's Program" *American Political Science Review,* Dec. 1955, p. 1021. It is also interesting to note here that in reference to John Kennedy's decision to implement the moon shot program, Theodore Sorensen has implied that the decision was largely made "because we felt we were in need of some display of action." See Theodore Sorensen, Kennedy Library oral history.

12. Alexander Hamilton, James Madison and John Jay, *The Federalist Papers,* ed. Clinton

Rossiter (New York: New American Library, 1962), p. 360 (#58).

13. Ibid., p. 384 (#63).

14. See Marvin R. Weisbord, *Campaigning for President* (Washington: Public Affairs Press, 1964, pp. 1–55; Arthur Schlesinger, "Introduction" to Schlesinger and Israel, eds., *The State of the Union Messages of the President,* (New York: Chelsea House, 1966).

15. Woodrow Wilson, *Papers,* ed. Arthur S. Link, (Princeton, N.J.: Princeton University Press, 1978) vol. 27, p. 150.

16. Elmer Cornwell Jr., *Presidential Leadership and Public Opinion,* (Bloomington: Indiana University Press, 1965), pp. 1–30.

17. Woodrow Wilson, *Constitutional Government in the United States,* (New York: Columbia University Press, 1908), p. 67; Woodrow Wilson, *Congressional Government* (Cambridge: Riverside Press, 1885), p. 209.

18. Wilson, *Constitutional Government,* p. 65.

19. Wilson, *Papers,* Link ed., vol. 19, p. 42.

20. *Congressional Quarterly Almanac, 1976,* pp. 852–53.

21. Kallenbach, p. 253; and Clinton Rossiter, *The American Presidency* (New York: Harcourt Brace, 1960), p. 34.

22. *The Washington Post,* July 10, 1979.

23. *The Washington Post,* July 14, 1979, p. A1.

24. See Michael J. Robinson, "Television and American Politics, 1956–1976," *The Public Interest,* (Summer, 1972), pp. 3–39.

25. For a review of the transformation of speechwriters from secret aides to openly identified advisors, see Marie Hochmuth Nichols; *Rhetoric and Criticism,* (Baton Rouge: Louisiana State University Press, 1903), pp. 35–48.

26. Francis Bacon, *A Selection of His Works,* ed. Sidney Warhaft, (Indianapolis: Odyssey Press, 1965), p. 42.

27. James Fallows, Personal Interview, March 10, 1979. Also see James Fallows, "The Passionless Presidency" and "The Passionless Presidency, Part II," *Atlantic,* May & June, 1979.

28. Benjamin I. Page, *Choices and Echoes in Presidential Elections* (Chicago: University of Chicago Press, 1979), pp. 10–61.

29. Ibid., pp. 152–92.

30. Jeffrey Fischel, "From Campaign Promise to Presidential Performance," A paper prepared for a Colloquium at the Woodrow Wilson Center, June 20, 1979.

31. The Campaign of 1976: Jimmy Carter, (Washington: United States Government Printing Office, 1976), vol. 2: p. 274.

32. See Thomas Patterson, The Mass Media Election (New York: Praeger, 1980).

33. Patrick H. Caddell, "Initial Working Paper on Political Strategy," Mimeo. Dec. 10, 1976.

34. Elizabeth Drew, "Phase: In Search of a Definition" The New Yorker Magazine, Aug. 27, 1979, p. 49–73.

35. Ibid., p. 59.

36. Carnes Lord, "On Aristotle's Rhetoric" A conference paper delivered at the White Burkett Miller Center, July 1979.

37. John Quincy Adams, Lectures on Rhetoric and Oratory (Cambridge, Mass.: Hilliard and Metcalf, 1810).

38. Cited in Cronin, p. 73.

39. See David Broder's column, "Making the Presidency Man-sized," Washington Post, Dec. 5, 1979, p. A27. Broder summarizes the consensus of a conference on the Presidency held at the White Burkett Miller Center of Public Affairs at the University of Virginia.

40. Richardson, p. 3.

41. Patterson, pp. 67–75 and 173–181.

42. See Cornwell, op. cit., for the history of the press conference. In a series of forums on the press conference sponsored by the White Burkett Miller Center, most of the reporters present who have covered the president were of the opinion that, while television conferences were helpful on occasion, they often were superficial and did not allow for a genuine and in-depth exchange with the President. Most felt that greater use of the "reporters around the desk" format would improve the reading public's knowledge of the president.

CHAPTER XI

The Presidency and the Courts

Article II, Section 2 of the United States Constitution states that the president ". . . shall nominate, and by and with the advice and consent of the Senate, shall appoint . . . judges of the Supreme Court." Congress by law has provided for the same procedure for appointments to other federal courts.[1] Thus, the president is responsible for nominating all federal judges and their confirmation depends upon a simple majority vote in the Senate.

While the president nominates all federal judges, the selection process for federal district courts involves many others, as well. Usually, a nomination originates with one or both senators of the president's party from the state in which a vacancy exists. Since the judicial reforms of the Carter administration, United States senators have established district court panels for the purpose of soliciting and evaluating candidates for the courts and recommending names the senator(s) may send to the president.[2]

Even if a federal district court nomination does not originate with the home state senator or senators, their approval is very important. If a president nominates without that approval, senatorial courtesy will almost surely be invoked.[3]

Important, also, is the rating (exceptionally well qualified, well qualified, qualified, or unqualified) given a candidate by the Committee on the Federal Judiciary of the American Bar Association. Presidents rarely nominate someone that the committee finds unqualified. Numerous other people may make an input into the selection process but, ultimately, the Attorney General suggests candidates for federal district judgeships to the president, who, in turn, if he so decides, sends the nomination on to the Senate.

The president plays a much larger role and the senators a lesser role in nominations to the circuit courts of appeals. This is so because the geographical boundaries of courts of appeals include several states, thus reducing a senator's concern over the "area." Indeed, even if the senators from one state are committed to a candidate for a court of appeals post who is unsatisfactory to the president, he or she may solve the problem by finding a person in another state in the circuit whose confirmation will not be opposed by the nominee's home state senators.[4]

Presidential discretion is limited to some extent, however, by the unwritten rule that each state within a circuit will have at least one judge on that circuit's court of appeals. If a vacancy occurs on the court, for example, the president is under considerable pressure to select a person for the court from the state that is without representation.[5] In sum, circuit judgeships lie somewhere between Supreme Court appointments, which presidents tend to dominate, and district court judgeships, which senators regard as their prerogative.[6]

The nomination of Supreme Court justices belongs solely to the president. Unlike appointments to the federal district courts or the circuit courts of appeals, appointments to the Supreme Court are not limited by a tradition that would guarantee state or regional representation or deference to a particular state's senators. An appointment to the Supreme Court is not a local matter.

While senatorial courtesy is an insignificant factor at the Supreme Court level, not all of a president's nominations are confirmed. Through 1986, the Senate had rejected or not acted upon about 20 percent of presidential nominations for the Supreme Court.[7] In recent years, however, the Senate has rejected only two presidential nominees to the Supreme Court: Clement F. Haynesworth in 1969 and G. Harold Carswell in 1970. Earlier, in 1968, the Senate did not act upon the nomination of Associate Justice Abe Fortas for the position of chief justice; Fortas's resignation from the court forestalled any action.

How significant are a president's appointments to the federal courts? The answer is: quite significant. Long periods of American political life may be influenced immeasurably by the appointments the president makes to the lower federal courts as well as to the Supreme Court. Precisely because these are lifetime appointments, the decisions of the judges and the justices will go on long after a president has departed the political scene.

Studies show that the kind of appointments presidents make do make a difference. For example, one study found that federal district judges appointed by Democratic presidents were comparatively more liberal than those chosen by Republican chief executives.[8] Another study revealed that Democratic judges at the circuit court of appeals level were more likely to support the economic underdog than were their Republican colleagues in cases coming before them.[9]

A third study examined both district and circuit level federal court appointments and found that a Democratic president, Jimmy Carter, made the most conscious effort in the history of federal judicial selection to place women, black Americans, and Americans of Hispanic origin on the federal bench. By the end of the Carter administration, the proportion of women on the bench had increased from 1 percent to nearly 7 percent, and for blacks from 4 percent to nearly 9 percent.[10]

Presidential appointments of Supreme Court justices have also proven to be extremely significant. One study found that for the period 1801 to 1958, presidents were rather successful in appointing Supreme Court justices who would support the government in office, at least for the first four years.[11] Data in another study indicated that Supreme Court justices make policy and that the way to change policy is to appoint to the court a different brand of justice: President Nixon's appointments turned the court in a conservative direction.[12]

President Reagan also believes that to change policy one must change the justices. A fundamental ingredient of Reagan's New Federalism is the goal of curbing the federal courts and thus the role of the federal government in the lives of the American people. The appointment of strict constructionists is seen to be the means to achieve that end.

Sheldon Goldman tells us that to accomplish this new judiciary, Reagan created the President's Committee on Federal Judicial Selection. This nine-member body formalizes an active White House role in judicial selection that emphasizes ideology and policy-orientation at the expense of all else.

"All else" includes the Reagan administration's tactic of not utilizing and consulting the Standing Committee on the Federal Judiciary of the American Bar Association on potential judges, no pledge not to nominate any person rated "unqualified" by the American Bar Association Standing Committee, and repudiating the selection commission concept, which worked so effectively in the previous administration to expand the net of possible judicial candidates to include groups historically excluded from the federal judiciary.

Goldman finds that, in his first term, Ronald Reagan has been a smashing success. Every appointment made by President Reagan has during the first term demonstrated the desired judicial restraint. Goldman's research, "Reaganizing the Judiciary: The First Term Appointments," is reprinted here.

Glendon Schubert wrote that "in every major constitutional crisis between the executive and the judiciary, the President has emerged the victor."[13] A long line of presidential and court scholars have concurred with Schubert and it is now commonplace to argue that the president always has his way vis-à-vis the United States Supreme Court and, by virtue of the Supreme Court's preeminence, all of the lower federal courts as well.[14] A long line of presidency-regarding cases on a wide variety of domestic, military–national security, and foreign policy questions would appear to support that view.

Some of the presidency-regarding cases in the domestic policy area include: *Myers* v. *United States* (1926),[15] *Schick* v. *Reed* (1975),[16] and *Immigration and Naturalization Service* v. *Chadha* (1983).[17]

Presidency-regarding cases in the area of martial rule and preserving the peace of the United States include *Martin* v. *Mott* (1827),[18] *In re Neagle* (1890),[19] and *In re Debs* (1894).[20]

Foreign policy decisions that fall in the presidency-regarding category include *United States* v. *Curtiss Wright Corporation* (1936),[21] *United States* v. *Belmont* (1937),[22] *United States* v. *Pink* (1942),[23] and *Goldwater* v. *Carter* (1979).[24]

Outstanding presidency-regarding Supreme Court decisions in the arena of military policy include the *Prize Cases* (1863),[25] *Ex parte Quirin* (1942),[26] *Hirabayashi* v. *United States* (1943),[27] and *Korematsu* v. *United States* (1944).[28]

Despite the argument of many scholars that the president is deferred to by the Supreme Court in most of its encounters, and the cases listed above that illustrate some examples of that thesis, much evidence suggests that the Supreme Court will draw the line on presidential power under certain circumstances.

Some of the presidency-constraining decisions in the domestic-policy area include *Gilchrist v. Collector* (1808),[29] *Kendall v. United States* (1838),[30] *Schechter Poultry Co. v. United States* (1935),[31] *Humphrey's Executor v. United States* (1935),[32] *Wiener v. United States* (1958),[33] and *United States v. Nixon* (1974).[34]

Presidency-constraining decisions in the foreign policy arena include *Little et al. v. Barreme et al.* (1804),[35] *Gelston v. Hoyt* (1818),[36] and *Reid v. Covert* (1957).[37]

Military–national security policy decisions by the Supreme Court falling into the presidency-constraining area include *Ex parte Milligan* (1866),[38] *Duncan v. Kahanamoku* (1946),[39] *Youngstown Sheet and Tube v. Sawyer* (1952),[40] *New York Times v. United States* (1971)[41] and *United States v. U.S. District Court* (1972).[42]

The presidency-constraining cases indicate, then, that in some contexts judicial treatment of presidential actions will not always favor the president. Indeed, David Rosenbloom argues that the judiciary has emerged as an important check on the exercise of presidential power. This can be observed very clearly, Rosenbloom argues, when we distinguish the two main theories about executive power that have developed: the inherent and implied powers theory of presidential powers; and the specified powers theory of presidential power.

The judiciary will have the least to say, Rosenbloom argues, when presidents exercise their specified powers, but that the judiciary can and does determine and check how far a president may go in the use of inherent and implied powers.

Many of the presidency-regarding and presidency-constraining decisions, outlined earlier, are evaluated by Rosenbloom utilizing as a framework the differentiation between inherent and specified powers. He finds that the courts do permit the president inherent and implied powers, but that limits have been placed upon their use. His original essay, "Presidential Power and the Courts," is printed here.

NOTES

1. See 62 Stat. 895 (1948).
2. See W. Gary Fowler, "A Comparison of Initial Recommendation Procedures: Judicial Selection Under Reagan and Carter," *Yale Law and Policy Review* 1 (1983), pp. 308–10. To be sure, President Carter called for senators to create panels at the district court level, and himself issued Executive Order 11,972 establishing the U.S. Circuit Judge Nominating Commission with circuit court panelists from all states contained in each circuit for the purpose of making nominations directly to the Justice Department; President Reagan abolished these circuit panels by Executive Order 12,305 and placed less emphasis on the use of panels for district court positions.
3. For a detailed explanation of the role of senatorial courtesy in federal district court appointments, see Henry J. Abraham, *Justices and Presidents: A Political History of Appointments to the Supreme Court*, 2nd ed. (New York: Oxford University Press, 1985), pp. 26–27. To effect senatorial courtesy, the Judiciary Committee usually sends a "blue slip" of paper to each of the two senators in the state where the judgeship is vacant; the senators are given the opportunity to indicate disapproval of a nominee by not returning the blue slip.

4. On this point, see John R. Schmidhauser, *Judges and Justices: The Federal Appellate Judiciary* (Boston: Little, Brown, 1979), p. 20.

5. See Jerome R. Corsi, *Judicial Politics: An Introduction* (Englewood Cliffs, N.J.: Prentice-Hall, 1984), p. 120; see also Sheldon Goldman, "Judicial Appointments to the United States Courts of Appeals," *Wisconsin Law Review* 1967, no. 1 (Winter 1967), pp. 200–202 and 212.

6. See J. Woodford Howard, Jr., *Courts of Appeals in the Federal Judicial System: A Study of the Second, Fifth and District of Columbia Circuits* (Princeton, N.J.: Princeton University Press, 1981), p. 99.

7. See Robert Scigliano, *The Supreme Court and the Presidency* (New York: Free Press, 1971), pp. 96–97; see also Corsi, *Judicial Politics*, p. 145.

8. See Ronald Stidham, Robert A. Carp, and C. K. Rowland, "Patterns of Presidential Influence on the Federal District Courts: An Analysis of the Appointment Process," *Presidential Studies Quarterly* 14, no. 4 (Fall 1984), p. 588.

9. See Sheldon Goldman, "Voting Behavior on the United States Courts of Appeals Revisited," *American Political Science Review* 69 (June 1975), especially pp. 496, 501, 503, and 505.

10. Sheldon Goldman, "Carter's Judicial Appointments: A Lasting Legacy," *Judicature* 64, no. 8 (March 1981), p. 349; see also Judith H. Parris, "The President, the Senate, and the Judges: Innovation in the Federal Judicial Selection Process, 1977–1980," Paper prepared for delivery at the Annual Meeting of the Midwest Political Science Association, Chicago, April 23–26, 1980, p. 20.

11. Roger Handberg and Harold F. Hill, Jr., "Predicting the Judicial Performance of Presidential Appointments to the United States Supreme Court," *Presidential Studies Quarterly* 14, no. 4 (Fall 1984), pp. 542, 546. But, for the evidence that presidents do not always get what they want or expect from their appointments to the Supreme Court, see Scigliano, *Supreme Court and Presidency*, pp. 125–148. See also Edward V. Heck and Steven A. Shull, "Policy Preferences of Justices and Presidents: the Case of Civil Rights," Paper prepared for delivery at the Midwest Political Science Association Convention, Chicago, April 23–26, 1980.

12. S. Sidney Ulmer, "Supreme Court Justices as Strict and Not-So-Strict Constructionists: Some Implications," *Law and Society Review* (Fall 1973), especially pp. 13, 14, 21, 27, and 28.

13. Glendon A. Schubert, Jr., *The Presidency in the Courts* (Minneapolis: University of Minnesota Press, 1957), p. 4.

14. See, for examples, Robert Heineman, "The President and the Federal Courts," in *Dimensions of the Modern Presidency*, ed. Edward N. Kearny (St. Louis, Mo.: Forum Press, 1981), pp. 195, 197; Clinton Rossiter, *The American Presidency*, rev. ed. (New York: New American Library, 1960), pp. 52–53; Theodore C. Sorensen, *Watchmen in the Night: Presidential Accountability After Watergate* (Cambridge, Mass.: MIT Press, 1975), p. 122; and Dale Vinyard, *The Presidency* (New York: Charles Scribner's Sons, 1971), pp. 151–52.

15. 272 U.S. 52 (1926). *

* This and all the cases which follow with an asterisk are discussed in some detail by Professor Rosenbloom in his essay, "Presidential Power and the Courts."

16. 419 U.S. 236 (1975). In effect, this Supreme Court decision made the president's pardon power nearly absolute.

17. 51 USLW 4907, June 23, 1983. *

18. 12 Wheat 19 (1827). This case upheld the president's power to determine the existence of an emergency and the necessity for the use of troops.

19. 135 U.S. 1 (1890). *

20. 158 U.S. 564 (1895). *

21. 299 U.S. 304 (1936). *

22. 301 U.S. 324 (1937). *

23. 315 U.S. 203 (1942). *

24. 444 U.S. 996 (1979). The Court of Appeals for the District of Columbia (617 F.2d 697) held that neither a two thirds Senate consent or majority consent in both houses is necessary for a president to terminate a treaty. The Supreme Court, without hearing argument, ordered that the complaint be dismissed.

25. 2 Black 635 (1863). In these cases, the Supreme Court affirmed the right and duty of the president to effect a blockade and to exercise the war powers to defend the nation even in the absence of enabling legislation from Congress and albeit against a domestic belligerent.

26. 317 U.S. 1 (1942). In this case the Supreme Court ruled that President Franklin Roosevelt's military commission was lawfully constituted under his commander-in-chief powers and that saboteurs were subject to its jurisdiction.

27. 320 U.S. 81 (1943). *

28. 323 U.S. 214 (1944). *

29. 10 Fed. Cas. 355. Case No. 5,420 (1808). In this case the Supreme Court held that the president had no authority to limit the discretion vested by statute in customs collectors by specifically directing them to detain vessels seeking clearance for coastwide commerce.

30. 12 Peters 524 (1838). *

31. 295 U.S. 495 (1935). *

32. 295 U.S. 602 (1935). *

33. 357 U.S. 349 (1958). *

34. 418 U.S. 683 (1974). *

35. 2 Cranch 170 (1804). In this case the Supreme Court held invalid former President Adams's instructions to the captains of American ships directing seizure of vessels allegedly violating the non-intercourse act of Congress by trading with French ports. The court held that the president had directed a more vigorous enforcement of the statute than anticipated by Congress.

36. 2 Wheat 246 (1818). In this case the Supreme Court held invalid presidential orders directing civilian officials to seize a ship to prevent violation of the Neutrality Act. The court held the president's order void because he had delegated his statutory authority to civil rather than military officers as required by the law.

37. 351 U.S. 487 (1956); 354 U.S. 1 (1957). *

38. 4 Wallace 2 (1866). *

39. 327 U.S. 304 (1946). In this matter the Court ruled that the military governor of Hawaii, acting with the express approval of President Franklin Roosevelt, had exceeded his authority under the Hawaiian Organic Act by requiring military trials for civilians especially when the civilian courts were open and operating.
40. 343 U.S. 579 (1952).*
41. 403 U.S. 713 (1971).*
42. 407 U.S. 297 (1972).*

27
Reaganizing the Judiciary: The First Term Appointments

Sheldon Goldman

Ronald Reagan's reelection by a landslide victory in 1984 was hailed by some observers as a significant political event comparable to Franklin Roosevelt's reelection in 1936. Both presidents received overwhelming electoral approval, which was widely interpreted as a mandate to continue along the course set in the first term. Both were enormously popular with the large majority of the populace, although both stimulated considerable antipathy and even denigration from a vocal minority opposed to Administration philosophy and policy. Both elections could be seen as confirming a new electoral era in national politics and new voting patterns among young voters and other population groups.

In addition, both presidents had spent their first terms dealing with economic crises and both used Keynesian economics (without credit to Keynes in the latter instance) to nurse the economy back to health. Both presidents had a view of the role of government, including the courts, that was radically different from their immediate predecessors in office. Indeed, both sought to change the direction of government, saw the courts as frustrating their policy agendas, and self-consciously attempted to use the power of judicial appointment to place on the bench judges sharing their general philosophy. And with both, their presidential campaigns saw the courts and judicial appointments emerge as issues.

Franklin Roosevelt left a major legacy with his court appointments that fundamentally reshaped constitutional law and whose judges numerically dominated the lower federal courts for close to a decade after his presidency. Ronald Reagan has already begun the groundwork for his judicial legacy. With just two terms in office as compared to Roosevelt's three plus, Reagan will accomplish what only Roosevelt and Eisenhower accomplished during the last half century—naming a majority of the lower

Source: Judicature 68, nos. 9–10 (April-May 1985).

federal judiciary in active service.[1] This makes it all the more significant to inquire what has been the Reagan first term record in the realm of judicial selection. What changes have occurred in the selection process? What is the professional, demographic, and attribute profile of the Reagan appointees and how do they compare with appointees of previous administrations? Has the Administration been successful in placing on the bench those in harmony with Administration philosophy? What can we expect in the second term? These are the questions that this article confronts.

The data on the backgrounds and selection of the judges come from a variety of sources including personal interviews, examination of the questionnaires that all judicial nominees complete for the Senate Judiciary Committee,[2] various biographical directories, state legislative handbooks, newspapers from the appointees' home states, published and un-

published confirmation hearings by the Senate Judiciary Committee, the yearly *Congressional Quarterly Almanac*, and two recently available sources: the second edition of *Judges of the United States*[3] and the inaugural volume of what promises to be an annual series, *The Federal Judiciary Almanac*.[4]

The findings and analyses presented here concern all lifetime federal district and courts of appeals judges confirmed by the U.S. Senate of the 97th and 98th Congresses. The courts of appeals judges analyzed were only those appointed to the 11 numbered circuits and the Court of Appeals for the District of Columbia. Appointments to the Court of Appeals for the Federal Circuit, a court of specialized as opposed to general jurisdiction, were not included. The findings for the Reagan first term appointments[5] are compared to those for the Johnson, Nixon, Ford, and Carter lifetime appointments to courts of general jurisdiction. During his first term Reagan named 129 to the district courts and 31 to the appeals courts.

SELECTION UNDER REAGAN

A striking characteristic of the judicial selection process in the Reagan Administration has been the formalization of the process by institutionalizing interaction patterns and job tasks that in previ-

---

[1] The Administrative Office of U.S. Courts has calculated that Roosevelt appointed 81.4 percent of the judiciary, Truman 46.5 percent, Eisenhower 56.1 percent, Kennedy 32.8 percent, Johnson 37.9 percent, Nixon 45.7 percent, Ford 13.1 percent, and Carter 40.2 percent. During his first term, Reagan appointed 24.3 percent of the judiciary. The Administrative Office estimates that by the end of the second term Reagan will have appointed a majority of the judiciary. At the start of the second term there were 99 vacancies to be filled. In addition there were 52 judges eligible to retire. Furthermore, some 81 judges will become eligible to retire during the course of the second term. Although all these eligible to retire do not do so, a large proportion can be expected to assume senior status. Unexpected vacancies caused by death or resignation will undoubtedly occur and this too will add to the numbers and proportion of judges appointed. Administrative Office figures are cited in Ciolli, "Reagan Set for Judicial Record," *Newsday*, December 9, 1984, at p. 6.

[2] The author would like to thank Mark H. Gitenstein, Chip Reid, Christine Phillips, and other staff of the minority office, Senate Judiciary Committee, for their cooperation and assistance.

[3] (Washington, D.C.: Government Printing Office, 1983).

[4] Dornette and Cross, *Federal Judiciary Almanac* 1984 (New York: Wiley, 1984).

[5] Technically, Reagan's first term ended on January 20, 1985 after the 99th Congress already had been in session for several weeks. Therefore all nominations confirmed by the Senate up until then should be considered first term appointments. However, by January 20 no nominations had even been sent to the Senate of the 99th Congress, thus the analysis is confined to those confirmed during the 97th and 98th Congresses.

ous administrations were more informal and fluid. There have also been changes of more substantive import.

The center of judicial selection activity in previous administrations was the Deputy Attorney General's Office, with an assistant to the deputy responsible for the details, and at times negotiations, associated with the selection process.[6] During the Reagan Administration these responsibilities have shifted to the Office of Legal Policy. The Assistant Attorney General heading that office reports to the Deputy Attorney General but also has an independent role as a member of the President's Federal Judicial Selection Committee. Assisting the head of the Legal Policy division in matters concerning judicial selection is the Special Counsel for Judicial Selection, a post formally established in September of 1984. The Attorney General, Deputy Attorney General, the Assistant Attorney General for Legal Policy, the Special Counsel for Judicial Selection, and some of their assistants meet to make specific recommendations for judgeships to the President's Committee on Federal Judicial Selection.

The major substantive innovation in the selection process made by the Reagan Administration is the creation of the President's Committee on Federal Judicial Selection. This nine-member committee institutionalizes and formalizes an active White House role in judicial selection. Members of the Committee from the White House during the first term included presidential counselor Edwin Meese III, White House chief of staff James A. Baker III, John S. Herrington, assistant to the President for personnel, M. B. Oglesby, assistant to the President for legislative affairs, and

presidential counsel Fred Fielding, who serves as chair of the Committee. From the Justice Department are the Attorney General, Deputy Attorney General, Associate Attorney General, and the Assistant Attorney General for Legal Policy.

The highest levels of the White House staff have played a continuing active role in the selection of judges. Legislative, patronage, political, and policy considerations are considered to an extent never before so systematically taken into account. This has assured policy coordination between the White House and the Justice Department, as well as White House staff supervision of judicial appointments.

The Committee does not merely react to the Justice Department's recommendations; it is also a source of names of potential candidacies and a vehicle for the exchange of important and relevant information. Furthermore, the president's personnel office conducts an investigation of prospective nominees *independent of* the Justice Department's investigation.[7] It is perhaps not an overstatement to observe that the formal mechanism of the Committee has resulted in the most consistent ideological or policy-orientation screening of judicial candidates since the first term of Franklin Roosevelt.

It is also relevant to observe that this selection process innovation potentially contains an inherent source of tension as the perspective from the Justice Department can be quite different from that of the White House. The cooptation of judicial selection by the Reagan White House has now been completed with former presidential counsel Edwin Meese III now serving as Attorney General.

---

[6] See, for example, the discussion and citations in Goldman and Jahnige, *The Federal Courts as a Political System*, 3rd ed., 39–51 (New York: Harper & Row, 1985).

[7] Interview with Jane Swift, Special Counsel for Judicial Selection, Office of Legal Policy, Department of Justice, December 18, 1984.

Although the consequences of this shift are immediately apparent in terms of the screening of candidates, in the hands of a less ideologically oriented administration partisan patronage considerations could conceivably become the principal selection criterion. Professional credentials would then be minimized, resulting in a lower quality federal bench. This is not meant to fault the Reagan Administration for its innovations in the selection process. Indeed, from the standpoint of achieving Administration goals, those innovations are rational and functional. But there may be unintended consequences from these changes that should be watched by those who are concerned with the administration of justice.

Another change in the process worthy of note is that the Reagan Administration is the first Republican Administration in 30 years in which the American Bar Association Standing Committee on Federal Judiciary was not actively utilized and consulted in the prenomination stage. From the Eisenhower Administration through the Ford Administration, Justice Department officials sounded out the ABA Standing Committee for tentative preliminary ratings of the leading candidates for a specific judgeship. These informal reports could be used by Justice officials in negotiations with senators and other officials of the president's party. At times they influenced the Justice officials' final selection. During the Carter Administration, however, this close working relationship ended as the Administration established its own judicial selection commission for appeals court appointments and most Democratic senators established analogous commissions for district court positions.

The Reagan Administration abolished the selection commission but has, with few exceptions, maintained a more formal relationship with the ABA Standing Committee and has not sought preliminary ratings on anyone but the individual the Administration has already settled on to nominate.[8] This has also meant that unlike previous Republican Administrations which pledged not to nominate any person rated "Not Qualified" by the ABA Standing Committee,[9] this Administration has made no such pledge and is willing, if not persuaded by the Committee, to nominate the person of its choice even were the nominee rated "Not Qualified."[10]

This is not to suggest that relations were cool with the ABA Committee. Senate Judiciary Committee hearings on the nomination of J. Harvie Wilkinson to the Fourth Circuit revealed a close working relationship, but that relationship occurred *after* the Administration had decided on Wilkinson, not before.[11] Of course, the Administration has been concerned that its nominees receive high ABA ratings, but evidently it has not been willing to give the ABA Standing Committee an opportunity to influence the selection during the more fluid pre-nomination stage.

One further observation about the selection process is in order. The Reagan Administration repudiated the selection

[8] *Id.*

[9] But note on his last day in office President Richard M. Nixon broke that pledge. For details see Goldman and Jahnige, *supra* n. 6, at 44–45.

[10] In fact this happened with the nomination of Sherman E. Unger to the U.S. Court of Appeals for the Federal Circuit. Unger was rated Not Qualified. However, he died during Senate consideration of his nomination.

[11] In particular, see the hearings of the special session of the Senate Judiciary Committee held on August 7, 1984. *Hearings Before the Committee on the Judiciary, United States Senate, Ninety-Eighth Congress, Second Session, Part 3 Serial No. J–98–6*, 272–274, 280, 283 f f. (Washington, D.C.: U.S. Government Printing Office, 1985).

commission concept and in so doing abandoned the most potentially effective mechanism for expanding the net of possible judicial candidates to include women and racial minorities, groupings historically excluded from the judiciary. The Carter Administration's record in this regard was unprecedented, with Carter naming to the courts of appeals 11 women, nine black Americans (including one black woman), two Hispanics, and the first person of Asian ancestry (out of a total of 56 appointments). The Reagan record with regard to the appeals courts, as will be discussed shortly, falls markedly short of that.

DISTRICT COURT APPOINTMENTS

The findings for selected backgrounds and attributes of the 129 Reagan first term appointments to the federal district courts are presented in Table 1. Also presented in the table are comparable findings for the Carter, Ford, Nixon, and Johnson Administrations' appointees.

TABLE 1 · HOW THE REAGAN FIRST TERM APPOINTEES TO THE DISTRICT COURTS COMPARE TO THE APPOINTEES OF CARTER, FORD, NIXON, AND JOHNSON

	Reagan (first term) % N	Carter % N	Ford % N	Nixon % N	Johnson % N
Occupation:					
Politics/government	7.8%	4.4%	21.2%	10.6%	21.3%
	10	9	11	19	26
Judiciary	40.3%	44.6%	34.6%	28.5%	31.1%
	52	90	18	51	38
Large law firm					
100 + partners/associates	3.1%	2.0%	1.9%	0.6%	0.8%
	4	4	1	1	1
50–99	3.1%	6.0%	3.9%	0.6%	1.6%
	4	12	2	1	2
25–49	5.4%	6.0%	3.9%	10.1%	—
	7	12	2	18	—
Moderate size firm					
10–24 partners/associates	12.4%	9.4%	7.7%	8.9%	12.3%
	16	19	4	16	15
5–9	13.2%	10.4%	17.3%	19.0%	6.6%
	17	21	9	34	8
Small firm					
2–4 partners/associates	8.5%	11.4%	7.7%	14.5%	11.5%
	11	23	4	26	14
Solo practitioner	2.3%	2.5%	1.9%	4.5%	11.5%
	3	5	1	8	14

TABLE 1 (continued)

	Reagan (first term) % N	Carter % N	Ford % N	Nixon % N	Johnson % N
Professor of law	2.3%	3.0%	—	2.8%	3.3%
	3	6	—	5	4
Other	1.6%	0.5%	—	—	—
	2	1	—	—	—
Experience:					
Judicial	50.4%	54.5%	42.3%	35.2%	34.4%
	65	110	22	63	42
Prosecutorial	43.4%	38.6%	50.0%	41.9%	45.9%
	56	78	26	75	56
Neither one	28.7%	28.2%	30.8%	36.3%	33.6%
	37	57	16	65	41
Undergraduate education:					
Public-supported	34.1%	57.4%	48.1%	41.3%	38.5%
	44	116	25	74	47
Private (not Ivy)	49.6%	32.7%	34.6%	38.5%	31.1%
	64	66	18	69	38
Ivy League	16.3%	9.9%	17.3%	19.6%	16.4%
	21	20	9	35	20
None indicated	—	—	—	0.6%	13.9%
	—	—	—	1	17
Law school education:					
Public-supported	44.2%	50.5%	44.2%	41.9%	40.2%
	57	102	23	75	49
Private (not Ivy)	47.3%	32.2%	38.5%	36.9%	36.9%
	61	65	20	66	45
Ivy League	8.5%	17.3%	17.3%	21.2%	21.3%
	11	35	9	38	26
Gender:					
Male	90.7%	85.6%	98.1%	99.4%	98.4%
	117	173	51	178	120
Female	9.3%	14.4%	1.9%	0.6%	1.6%
	12	29	1	1	2
Ethnicity or race:					
White	93.0%	78.7%	88.5%	95.5%	93.4%
	120	159	46	171	114
Black	0.8%	13.9%	5.8%	3.4%	4.1%
	1	28	3	6	5
Hispanic	5.4%	6.9%	1.9%	1.1%	2.5%
	7	14	1	2	3

TABLE 1 *(concluded)*

	Reagan (first term) % N	Carter % N	Ford % N	Nixon % N	Johnson % N
Asian	0.8%	0.5%	3.9%	—	—
	1	1	2	—	—
A.B.A. ratings:					
Exceptionally well qualified	6.9%	4.0%	—	5.0%	7.4%
	9	8	—	9	9
Well qualified	43.4%	47.0%	46.1%	40.2%	40.9%
	56	95	24	72	50
Qualified	49.6%	47.5%	53.8%	54.8%	49.2%
	64	96	28	98	60
Not qualified	—	1.5%	—	—	2.5%
	—	3	—	—	3
Party:					
Democratic	3.1%	92.6%	21.2%	7.3%	94.3%
	4	187	11	13	115
Republican	96.9%	4.9%	78.8%	92.7%	5.7%
	125	10	41	166	7
Independent	—	2.5%	—	—	—
	—	5	—	—	—
Past party activism:	61.2%	60.9%	50.0%	48.6%	49.2%
	79	123	26	87	60
Religious origin or affiliation:					
Protestant	61.2%	60.4%	73.1%	73.2%	58.2%
	79	122	38	131	71
Catholic	31.8%	27.7%	17.3%	18.4%	31.1%
	41	56	9	33	38
Jewish	6.9%	11.9%	9.6%	8.4%	10.7%
	9	24	5	15	13
Total number of appointees	129	202	52	179	122
Average age at appointment	49.6	49.7	49.2	49.1	51.4

Occupation. If we look at the occupation at time of appointment we find that about 40 percent were members of the judiciary on the state bench or, in several instances, U.S. magistrates or bankruptcy judges. Only the Carter Administration of the past five administrations had a higher proportion of those who were serving as judges at the time they were chosen for the federal district bench. About eight percent of the Reagan district court appointees were in politics or governmental positions but few of these were U.S. Attorneys; this also had been true for the Carter appointees but not for the appointees of previous administrations. It would appear, for whatever the reason,[12] that the U.S. Attorney position is not the direct stepping-stone to a federal judgeship it once was, although both federal and state prosecutorial experience was prominent in the backgrounds of the judges. Also of note is that few law school professors were appointed, in contrast to the Reagan record for the courts of appeals. The Carter, Nixon, and Johnson Administrations appointed proportionately more law school professors than did Reagan in his first term.

Private law practice was the occupation at time of appointment for close to half the Reagan appointees. The range of the size of firm varied considerably, with close to 12 percent affiliated with large firms (with 25 or more partners and/or associates) and a slightly lower proportion at the other end of the spectrum practicing in firms with four or fewer members or associates. This is roughly comparable to the distribution of the Carter appointees. Since the Johnson Administration, proportionately fewer of those in a small practice have been chosen. Close to one out of four Johnson appointees, but only about one in seven Carter and one in ten Reagan first term appointees came from a small practice. Perhaps this is a reflection of the changing nature of the practice of law.[13]

Experience. Over 70 percent of the first term Reagan district court appointments had either judicial or prosecutorial experience, a proportion comparable to the appointees of the Carter Administration, and the second highest of all

five administrations' appointees. Of special interest and importance is that the proportion of those with judicial experience exceeded the proportion of those with prosecutorial experience—a trend begun only in the Carter Administration. Before Carter, prosecutorial experience was more frequent.

Why the shift toward a greater emphasis on judicial experience? The reasons may be twofold. First, to the extent that judicial selection commissions are involved in judicial selection, and as many as 18 Republican senators in 14 states have employed them during Reagan's first term,[14] judicial experience will be seen as a desirable and relevant credential. Commissions have been concerned with the professional quality of prospective nominees, and those with judicial experience have a professional track record that can be evaluated. Second, such track records can also be scrutinized by Justice Department officials to determine if the candidate shares the Administration's judicial philosophy and ideological outlook.[15] The result of this recent emphasis on judicial experience may be the growing professionalization of the American judiciary.

Education. The educational background of a majority of Reagan appointments to the district courts, as shown in Table 1, was private school including the highly prestigious Ivy League schools. Only about one-third of Reagan appointees attended a public university for undergraduate work, whereas over 57 percent of the Carter appointees attended public colleges—perhaps a reflection of poorer socioeconomic roots of a substantial segment of the Carter judges. Again, with law school

[12] See the discussion of possible reasons in Goldman, "Reagan's Judicial Appointments at Mid-Term: Shaping the Bench in His Own Image," 66 *Judicature* 334, at 337 (1983).

[13] Cf. Goldman and Jahnige, *supra* n. 6, at 56. In general, see, *The 1984 Lawyer Statistical Report: A Profile of the Legal Profession in the United States* (Chicago: American Bar Foundation, in press).

[14] Fowler, "A Comparison of Initial Recommendation Procedures: Judicial Selection under Reagan and Carter," 1 *Yale L. & Pol'Y Rev.* 299, 310–20, 347–49 (1983).

[15] Interview with Jane Swift, *supra* n. 7.

education, the majority of the Reagan appointees attended private law schools while a bare majority of the Carter appointees attended public-supported law schools.

Although there are some problems with equating being able to attend a private undergraduate college with socioeconomic status, the argument can be made that it is a rough indicator.[16] The findings for the Reagan appointees are consistent with earlier findings[17] and compatible with findings from other studies suggesting that the socioeconomic differences between the Republican and Democratic electorates are mirrored to some degree in the appointments of Republican and Democratic Administrations.[18] This has particular persuasiveness in light of the net worth findings presented in Table 2. In sum, we can observe that with relatively few exceptions, there is a tendency for the typical Republican appointee to be of a higher socioeconomic status than the typical Democratic appointee.

A word about the professional education of the appointees is in order. A study of the Reagan appointees at midterm tentatively concluded that as a group the Reagan appointees might have had a marginally less distinguished legal education than the appointees of the four previous presidents.[19] This was based on the relatively small proportion of appointees with an Ivy League law school education, the smallest proportion over the past five administrations. The proportion has remained constant for the entire first term appointments. However, the same caveat noted earlier

must be repeated here—that is, that a number of Reagan appointees as well as appointees of other presidents attended distinguished non-Ivy League schools including Michigan, Virginia, Berkeley, Stanford, and N.Y.U. Interestingly, a study conducted by Fowler found that a smaller proportion of the Reagan appointees than the Carter appointees attended "prestige" law schools,[20] which supports the earlier conclusion that the Reagan appointees' legal education, on the whole, was marginally less distinguished than the appointees of previous presidents.

Affirmative Action. The record of the Reagan first term district court appointments is a mixed one with regard to gender and race/ethnicity. The Reagan Administration was, of course, responsible for the historic appointment of the first woman to the Supreme Court. At the district court level, the record, as indicated by Table 1, shows that the Reagan Administration's appointment of women was second only to the Carter Administration. Over nine percent of the appointments went to women, and this suggests that the Administration, as well as some Republican senators, made an effort to recruit well qualified women. While it is true that the large majority of all appointees of all five administrations have been male, the Reagan Administration must be given credit for continuing the push for sexual equality in the recruitment of federal district judges. It is also significant to note that by the end of the first term two women held important Justice Department positions that are concerned with judicial selection: Carole Dinkins as Deputy Attorney General and Jane Swift as Special Counsel for Judicial Selection in the Office of Legal Policy. It is likely that women in key Justice Department positions will be sensitive to

---

[16] See the discussion in Goldman, *supra* n. 12, at 339.

[17] *Id.*

[18] See Goldman and Jahnige, *supra* n. 6, at 52–57.

[19] Goldman, *supra* n. 12, at 340.

[20] Fowler, *supra* n. 14, at 350.

TABLE 2 · NET WORTH OF REAGAN APPOINTEES COMPARED TO THE NET WORTH OF THE CARTER APPOINTEES

	Reagan (first term)		Carter (96th Congress)	
	District % N	Appeals % N	District % N	Appeals % N
Under $100,000	6.2% 8	3.3% 1	12.8% 19	5.1% 2
100,000–150,000	8.5% 11	3.3% 1	14.9% 22	12.8% 5
150,000–199,999	3.9% 5	3.3% 1	8.1% 12	15.4% 6
0–199,999 total	18.6% 24	10.0% 3	35.8% 53	33.3% 13
200,000–399,000	25.6% 33	23.3% 7	29.7% 44	28.2% 11
400,000–499,000	11.6% 15	13.3% 4	11.5% 17	10.3% 4
500,000–999,999	21.7% 28	30.0% 9	18.9% 28	17.9% 7
200,000–999,999 total	58.9% 76	66.7% 20	60.1% 89	56.4% 22
1 to 2 million	17.0% 22	20.0% 6	2.0% 3	7.7% 3
over 2 million	5.4% 7	3.3% 1	2.0% 3	2.6% 1
1 + million total	22.5% 29	23.3% 7	4.0% 6	10.3% 4
Total %	100.0%	100.0%	99.9%	100.0%
Total number of appointees	129	30[1]	148[2]	39[3]

[1] Net worth unavailable for one appointment. Source for all other Reagan appointees was the questionnaires submitted to the Senate Judiciary Committee and reviewed by the author.
[2] Professor Elliot Slotnick generously provided the net worth figures for all but six appointees for whom he had no data.
[3] There were five additional judges appointed by Carter for whom no information was listed in the source consulted, *Legal Times of Washington*, October 27, 1980, at 25.

sexual discrimination in the judicial selection process.

The record as to black appointments, however, is markedly different. The Reagan first term record is not only the worst of all five administrations, as suggested by Table 1, it is the worst since the Eisenhower Administration in which no blacks were appointed to lifetime district court positions. Justice Department officials are aware of this poor record and have said they would like it to improve, but feel that it is extraordinarily difficult to find well qualified blacks who share the President's philosophy and are also willing to serve.[21] Critics respond that the Administration has not made the recruitment of blacks a high priority in part because the black electorate votes overwhelmingly Democratic, and there is little political payoff in the appointment of blacks. In contrast, the proportion of Hispanics was second only to that of the Carter Administration. Some observers link that fact to the Republican Party effort to woo Hispanic voters in the 1984 election.

ABA Ratings and Other Factors. When we examine the ratings of the ABA Standing Committee on Federal Judiciary we find that about seven percent of the Reagan first term appointees to the district courts received the highest rating, that of Exceptionally Well Qualified. This is the best record since the Johnson Administration. The next highest rating, that of Well Qualified, was received by about 43 percent, which means that half the Reagan appointees were in the top two categories. The Carter appointees received proportionately more Well Qualified ratings than did the Reagan appointees but fewer Exceptionally Well Qualified ratings. However, when the top two ratings are combined, 51 percent of the Carter appointees fell into those categories—about the same as the Reagan appointees. If the ABA ratings are taken as a rough measure of "quality," the Reagan appointments may be seen as equaling the Carter appointees in quality and marginally surpassing the appointments of Ford, Nixon, and Johnson.

In terms of party affiliation of district court appointees, approximately 97 percent of the Reagan appointees were Republican, the highest partisanship level

of all five administrations and the highest proportion of a president choosing members of his own party since Woodrow Wilson.[22] The figures for previous prominent party activism suggest that the Reagan appointees had the highest proportion of all five administrations. However, there is no suggestion that the Reagan appointees with a record of party activism received their appointments solely because of their political activities. Instead, it must be recognized that a history of party activity is helpful to a judicial candidacy only when other factors are present such as distinguished legal credentials, and, particularly as far as the Reagan Administration is concerned, a judicial philosophy in harmony with that of the Administration. Suffice it to note that many of the Reagan appointees to both the district and appeals courts had impressive legal credentials as well as a background of partisan activism. Also observe that about four out of ten Reagan appointees did *not* have a record of prominent partisan activism, although they of course had to receive sufficient political backing or clearance in order to have been nominated.

The religious origins or religious affiliation of the Reagan first term district court appointees differed markedly from the appointees of previous Republican administrations; Reagan appointed more Catholics and fewer Protestants— proportions similar to those of Democratic administrations. In fact, as Table 1 shows, the Republican Reagan Administration appointed proportionately more Catholics than did the Democratic

[21] Interview with Jane Swift, *supra* n. 7.

[22] See Evans, "Political Influences in the Selection of Federal Judges," *Wis. L. Rev.* 330–51 (1948) reprinted in Scigliano, ed., *The Courts* 65–69 (Boston: Little, Brown, 1962). Also see, Burns, Peltason, and Cronin, *Government by the People*, 9th ed. 406 (Englewood Cliffs, New Jersey: Prentice-Hall, 1975).

Carter and Johnson Administrations. In the past, Republican administrations appointed more Protestants and fewer Catholics and Jews than did Democratic administrations; this could be attributed to the fact that the religious composition or mix of the parties was different and thus, to a large extent, so was the pool of potential judicial candidates from both parties. The finding for the Reagan appointees does not mean that the Administration gave greater preference to Catholics because of their religion than did previous Republican administrations, but rather that more Catholics have entered the potential pool from which Republican judicial nominees emerge thus increasing their proportion of appointees. This is consistent with the relatively heavy Catholic vote for Reagan in 1980 and especially 1984.

The average age of the Reagan appointees was about that of the Carter appointees and similar to that of the appointees of the previous three presidents.

The net worth of the Reagan appointees as compared to the Carter appointees is presented in Table 2. There are differences in degree at both ends of the financial spectrum. There were proportionately more millionaires among the Reagan district court appointees, over five times as many as the Carter appointees, and proportionately fewer Reagan appointees at the lower end of the economic spectrum. This suggests, along lines reported in the 1983 study of Reagan appointees,[23] that there is somewhat of a class difference between the Republican and Democratic appointees on the whole that is analogous to the socioeconomic differences among the electorates of the two parties. However, the findings also suggest that the Reagan

[23] Goldman, *supra* n. 12, at 345–46.

and Carter appointees were for the most part drawn from the middle to upper classes.

APPEALS COURT APPOINTMENTS

Traditionally, senators of the president's party have had considerably less influence in the selection of appeals court as distinct from district court judges. This has meant that administrations have had more of an opportunity to pursue their policy agendas (such as they may have them) by way of recruiting appeals judges who are thought to be philosophically sympathetic with such agendas. We can so view the 31 first term Reagan appointments to the courts of appeals with general jurisdiction as compared to the 56 Carter, 12 Ford, 45 Nixon and 40 Johnson appointees. Because there are fewer appeals judges than district judge appointments, differences in percentages, as reported in Table 3, must be treated with caution.

Occupation and Experience. A striking finding of Table 3 is that three out of five Reagan appeals court appointees and over half the Ford, Nixon, and Johnson appointees were already serving in the judiciary at the time of their appointment to the courts of appeals. Of the 19 Reagan appointees who were judges at the time of appointment, 16 were serving as federal district judges and the remaining three on the state bench. Just as with the selection of federal district judges, Justice Department officials felt more secure evaluating the candidacies of those with judicial track records. The Reagan Administration was particularly concerned not only with the professional quality of prospective nominees, but also with their judicial philosophy. As presidential counsel Fred F. Fielding

**TABLE 3 · HOW THE REAGAN FIRST TERM APPOINTEES
TO THE COURTS OF APPEALS COMPARE TO THE APPOINTEES
OF CARTER, FORD, NIXON, AND JOHNSON**

	Reagan (first term) % N	Carter % N	Ford % N	Nixon % N	Johnson % N
Occupation:					
Politics/government	3.2%	—	8.3%	4.4%	10.0%
	1	—	1	2	4
Judiciary	61.3%	46.4%	75.0%	53.3%	57.5%
	19	26	9	24	23
Large law firm					
100 + partners/associates	—	1.8%	—	—	—
	—	1	—	—	—
50–99	3.2%	5.4%	8.3%	2.2%	2.5%
	1	3	1	1	1
25–49	6.4%	3.6%	—	2.2%	2.5%
	2	2	—	1	1
Moderate size firm					
10–24 partners/associates	3.2%	14.3%	—	11.1%	7.5%
	1	8	—	5	3
5–9	6.4%	1.8%	8.3%	11.1%	10.0%
	2	1	1	5	4
Small firm					
2–4 partners/associates	—	3.6%	—	6.7%	2.5%
	—	2	—	3	1
Solo practitioner	—	1.8%	—	—	5.0%
	—	1	—	—	2
Professor of law	16.1%	14.3%	—	2.2%	2.5%
	5	8	—	1	1
Other	—	1.8%	—	6.7%	—
	—	1	—	3	—
Experience:					
Judicial	70.9%	53.6%	75.0%	57.8%	65.0%
	22	30	9	26	26
Prosecutorial	19.3%	32.1%	25.0%	46.7%	47.5%
	6	18	3	21	19
Neither one	25.8%	37.5%	25.0%	17.8%	20.0%
	8	21	3	8	8
Undergraduate education:					
Public-supported	29.0%	30.4%	50.0%	40.0%	32.5%
	9	17	6	18	13

TABLE 3 *(continued)*

	Reagan (first term) % N	Carter % N	Ford % N	Nixon % N	Johnson % N
Private (not Ivy)	45.2% 14	50.0% 28	41.7% 5	35.6% 16	40.0% 16
Ivy League	25.8% 8	19.6% 11	8.3% 1	20.0% 9	17.5% 7
None indicated	— —	— —	— —	4.4% 2	10.0% 4
Law school education:					
Public-supported	35.5% 11	39.3% 22	50.0% 6	37.8% 17	40.0% 16
Private (not Ivy)	48.4% 15	19.6% 11	25.0% 3	26.7% 12	32.5% 13
Ivy League	16.1% 5	41.1% 23	25.0% 3	35.6% 16	27.5% 11
Gender:					
Male	96.8% 30	80.4% 45	100.0% 12	100.0% 45	97.5% 39
Female	3.2% 1	19.6% 11	— —	— —	2.5% 1
Ethnicity or race:					
White	93.5% 29	78.6% 44	100.0% 12	97.8% 44	95.0% 38
Black	3.2% 1	16.1% 9	— —	— —	5.0% 2
Hispanic	3.2% 1	3.6% 2	— —	— —	— —
Asian	— —	1.8% 1	— —	2.2% 1	— —
A.B.A. ratings:					
Exceptionally well qualified	22.6% 7	16.1% 9	16.7% 2	15.6% 7	27.5% 11
Well qualified	41.9% 13	58.9% 33	41.7% 5	57.8% 26	47.5% 19
Qualified	35.5% 11	25.0% 14	33.3% 4	26.7% 12	20.0% 8
Not qualified	— —	— —	8.3% 1	— —	2.5% 1
No report requested	— —	— —	— —	— —	2.5% 1

TABLE 3 *(concluded)*

	Reagan (first term) % N	Carter % N	Ford % N	Nixon % N	Johnson % N
Party:					
Democratic	—	82.1%	8.3%	6.7%	95.0%
	—	46	1	1	38
Republican	100.0%	7.1%	91.7%	93.3%	5.0%
	31	4	11	42	2
Independent	—	10.7%	—	—	—
	—	6	—	—	—
Past party activism:	58.1%	73.2%	58.3%	60.0%	57.5%
	18	41	7	27	23
Religious origin or affiliation:					
Protestant	67.7%	60.7%	58.3%	75.6%	60.0%
	21	34	7	34	24
Catholic	22.6%	23.2%	33.3%	15.6%	25.0%
	7	13	4	7	10
Jewish	9.7%	16.1%	8.3%	8.9%	15.0%
	3	9	1	4	6
Total number of appointees	31	56	12	45	40
Average age at appointment	51.5	51.9	52.1	53.8	52.2

noted, "We have an opportunity to restore a philosophical balance that you don't have across the board right now."[24]

The promotion of a lower court judge to a higher court can also be seen as furthering the concept of a professional judiciary, although it does not appear that pure merit was the governing factor with the Reagan first term elevations.[25]

[24] Brownstein, "With or Without Supreme Court Changes, Reagan will Reshape the Federal Bench," 16 *National Journal* 2238 at 2340 (December 8, 1984).

[25] If the ABA ratings are taken as overall indicators of quality, only 4 of the 19 judicial promotions were rated Exceptionally Well Qualified, 12 received the Well Qualified designations, and 3 were given the lowest rating of Qualified.

The same undoubtedly holds true for the appointments of other administrations. Politically, the elevation of a federal district judge enables an administration to make two appointments: the elevation that fills the appeals court position; and the appointment to fill the vacancy thus created on the federal district bench.

Another striking finding of Table 3 is the proportion of Reagan appeals court appointees who were law school professors at the time of appointment. Because Robert Bork had left his professorship at Yale Law School some six months before and at the time of selection was a senior partner in the Washington, D.C. firm of Kirkland & Ellis, he was not counted in the professor of law category. Were he counted, the proportion of professors of law would be about one out of five Reagan appeals court appointees, a modern record.

Bork, as well as the five other law professors, were all known as conservative thinkers and advocates of judicial restraint with a tendency toward deference to government in matters of alleged civil liberties or civil rights violations. These appointees also had a track record of published works so that their candidacies could be evaluated as to their compatibility with the Administration's vision of the role of the courts. Further, the appointment of academics was expected to provide intellectual leadership on the circuits and a potential pool of candidates for vacancies that might occur on the Supreme Court. It will be of more than academic interest to see whether the second term appointments will draw as heavily from the law schools as did those from the first term. Over the last 20 years (and excluding the small number of Ford appointees), the Reagan Administration drew the least from the ranks of those in private practice.

In terms of experience, about three out of four Reagan appointees had judicial or prosecutorial experience in their backgrounds, with judicial experience being the most prominent. Indeed, over three times as many appeals court appointees had judicial experience as had prosecutorial experience, and the proportion with prosecutorial experience was the lowest of the five administrations. This also supports the suggestion that Justice officials were more concerned with judicial track records in evaluating ideological compatibility than with prosecutorial track records.

Education and Affirmative Action. The majority of the Reagan appointees as well as the Carter, Nixon, and Johnson appointees attended private schools for both their undergraduate and law school

training. About one out of four Reagan appointees had an Ivy League undergraduate education, the highest proportion of the appointees of the five administrations. However, the proportion of Reagan appointees with an Ivy League law school education was the *lowest* of all five administrations. Although some of the appointees attended prestigious non-Ivy League law schools both public and private, it may be that the quality of legal education of the Reagan appeals court appointees, like that of the district court appointees, was on the whole somewhat lower than the Carter appointees, a finding also reported by Fowler.[26]

In terms of appointments of women and minorities, the first term Reagan record for the appeals courts can be seen as a dramatic retreat from the Carter record. Of 31 appeals court appointees only one was a woman, only one was black, and only one was Hispanic. Whether the participation of Carole Dinkins (until her departure from the Justice Department in March 1985) and Jane Swift in the selection process will result in the active consideration and recruitment of women to the appeals courts will be something to watch for during the second term. It may be that the male dominated selection process is such that there is greater willingness to recruit women for the district bench than for the more important and prestigious appeals courts. The Administration may also want their women appointees to the district courts to prove themselves on the bench before being actively considered for promotion.

ABA Ratings and Other Factors. The proportion of Reagan appointees with the highest ABA rating, that of Exceptionally Well Qualified, was the highest since the Johnson Administration. However, the Reagan appointees also

---

[26] Fowler, *supra* n. 14, at 352.

had the highest proportion of all five administrations of those with the lowest Qualified rating. Interestingly, all five who were professors of law at the time of their nominations were only rated Qualified despite their distinguished legal scholarly achievements. This suggests that the ABA ratings are biased against legal academics who are not active practitioners. Had Robert Bork remained on the Yale Law School faculty rather than joining Kirkland & Ellis, it is a matter of conjecture whether he would have received the Exceptionally Well Qualified rating he in fact received as a senior partner of that prestigious District of Columbia firm.

None of the Reagan first term appointees to the appeals courts were Democrats. The absence of any appointees affiliated with the opposition political party last occurred in the Administration of Warren Harding.[27] As for prominent past partisan activism, however, the proportion is lower than that for the Carter appointees and comparable to that of the Ford, Nixon, and Johnson appointees.

As for religious origin or affiliation, the Reagan appeals court appointments were somewhat similar to his district court appointments with the proportion of Catholics akin to that of the previous Democratic Administrations of Carter and Johnson.

Given the importance of the appeals courts and the desire of the Reagan Administration to place on the bench those with a judicial philosophy compatible with that of the Administration, one might expect that there would be an active effort to recruit younger people

who could be expected to remain on the bench longer. There is a hint that this may have occurred. The average age of the Reagan appointees was 51.5, the lowest for all five administrations.

The net worth of the Reagan appointees compared to the Carter appointees is found in Table 2 and the differences between both groups of appointees are similar to those for the district court appointees. Over one in five Reagan appointees were millionaires as compared to one in ten Carter appointees. Two-thirds had a net worth between $200,000 and under $1 million, compared to 56 percent of the Carter appointees. At the lowest end of the net worth continuum, one in ten Reagan appointees had a net worth of under $200,000, compared to one in three of the Carter appointees.

The net worth findings for the appeals courts, as well as the district courts, underscore the importance of Chief Justice Warren Burger's urgent request that Congress dramatically increase the pay of the federal judiciary.[28] The Chief Justice observed that since he became Chief Justice 30 of the 43 resignations from the federal bench were due in part to financial reasons.[29] Although there are differences in degree between the Carter and Reagan appointees' wealth that may mirror to some extent different constituencies of the parties, there is a very real danger that the federal courts will soon become the preserve of the wealthy for only they will be able to afford the assumption of judicial office. If it is considered desirable that monetary considerations not affect judicial recruitment, then judicial salaries will have to be increased significantly.

[27] See, *Legislative History of the United States Circuit Courts of Appeals and the Judges who Served during the Period 1801 through May 1972,* U.S. Senate, Committee on the Judiciary, 92nd Cong., 2nd Sess. 2 (1972).

[28] See, Lauter, "Burger Lists 1985 Desires: More Pay, Another Justice," *National Law Journal,* January 14, 1985, at 5.

[29] *Id.*

IDEOLOGICAL SUCCESS?

We have thus far seen how the Reagan Administration has to some extent re-shaped the judicial selection process, and we have examined the demographic and attribute profiles of the Reagan district and appeals court appointees as compared to those of four previous presidents. The questions remain, have the Reagan appointees met the expectations of the Administration? Have the Reagan appointees begun to shift the ideological balance on the lower courts?

The answers to these questions must await systematic empirical analysis; there is fragmentary evidence that has begun to emerge, however, that suggests that the Reagan Administration on the whole is satisfied. For example, a study by the Center for Judicial Studies of every decision published by every Reagan appointee serving during the first two years of Reagan's first term concluded that the overwhelming majority of appointees demonstrated judicial restraint along the lines favored by the Administration.[30]

Students in a seminar at the University of Massachusetts-Amherst conducted a class project in which published decisions of selected appeals courts and Reagan appointees were analyzed.[31] Although these analyses were exploratory and their findings must be interpreted

with caution, here, too, it would appear that, with few exceptions, the Reagan appointees have joined the more conservative wings of their courts particularly on issues of alleged violations of civil liberties. Another finding that emerged was that the differences that occurred between the Reagan appointees and the Carter (and other Democratic) appointees were differences of degree and that it was rare for there to be the sort of dramatic cleavages on the appeals courts as is found on the Supreme Court. Nevertheless, the Reagan appointees appear to be making their imprint.

Other accounts of the Reagan appointees on the courts have also focused on the appeals courts. In one, Jonathan Rose, the former Assistant Attorney General for Legal Policy during the first three years of Reagan's first term, was quoted as being "tremendously pleased" with the records of the law professors chosen by the Administration for the appeals courts.[32] An extensive analysis of Robert Bork's record[33] and more anecdotal accounts[34] of other appointees also provide additional evidence on this point.

At the Supreme Court level there is reason for the Administration to be pleased with its appointee Justice Sandra Day O'Connor. O'Connor was either the second or third most conservative justice in matters of civil liberties, rejecting the civil liberties claim in 71 percent of the cases decided with full opinion in the 1981 term, and in the 1982 and 1983 terms rejecting 75 percent of such civil liberties arguments. Her opinions, whether for the majority, concurrences, or dissents on a variety of issues ranging

---

[30] Brownstein, *supra* n. 24, at 2341.

[31] The seminar was held in the Fall of 1984. The students involved were: Karen Ahlers, Julia L. Anderson, Leslie A. Brown, Nicole M. Caron, Michael J. Deltergo, Kathleen M. Moore, Matthew F. Moran, Paul M. Shepard, Barry J. Siegel, Valerie Singleton, David A. Smailes, and Paul W. Throne. Cases were generally classified using the methods described in Goldman, "Voting Behavior on the United States Courts of Appeals Revisited," 69 *Am. Pol. Sci. Rev.* 491 (1975). The circuits examined were the Second, Third, Fourth, Fifth, Sixth, Seventh, and the District of Columbia. Separate studies of Reagan appointees Robert Bork, Lawrence Pierce, Richard Posner, Antonin Scalia, and Ralph Winter were also conducted.

[32] *Legal Times of Washington*, October 22, 1984, at 15.

[33] *Id.* at 1, 10–15.

[34] See, for example, *New York Times*, August 23, 1984, at B-8 and *Boston Globe*, July 29, 1984, at A-28.

from abortion to criminal procedures were surely, with few exceptions, a source of satisfaction to the Administration.

Although political party platforms are notorious for being treated as merely campaign rhetoric, the 1984 Republican Party platform can be seen as containing a good summary of the Reaganizing philosophy for the judiciary that also points the way for the second term. The platform reads in part:

> Judicial power must be exercised with deference towards state and local officials. . . . It is not a judicial function to reorder the economic, political, and social priorities of our nation. . . . We commend the President for appointing federal judges committed to the rights of law-abiding citizens and traditional family values. . . . In his second term, President Reagan will continue to appoint Supreme Court and other federal judges who share our commitment to judicial restraint.[35]

FUTURE APPOINTMENTS

Although the above quote from the 1984 Republican Party platform does suggest the ideological or philosophical outlook of the people the Administration will be seeking for judgeships during the second term, we can also offer some projections as to the likely makeup of the demographic and attribute profiles of second term appointees. Central to this undertaking is the realization that just as there was no indication at the start of the second term that there would be sharp alterations in other areas of public policy, so with the judiciary there is no reason to anticipate a shift in the course already set during the first term. What this means is that second term appointees will continue to be predominantly white male Republicans, many of whom are at the upper end of the socioeconomic spectrum. Women will likely continue to receive appointments at a level comparable to that for the first term, which will place the Reagan Administration second only to the Carter Administration in terms of appointments to women. As for black Americans, there is no reason to believe that there will be a marked change from the poor record of the first term during the second term.

Judicial experience should continue to be important for the Administration and used to assess the track record of prospective appointees. For the courts of appeals, law school professors will likely continue to hold some attraction for the Administration, both because of the relative ease of identifying a judicial philosophy from published writings and the desire to place conservative intellectual leaders on these important collegial courts.

It will be of interest to see whether the Administration broadens its recruitment efforts, particularly at the appeals court level, to find Democrats who share the Administration's outlook or whether the extreme partisanship discussed previously will prevail during the second term.

Of major interest during the second term will be the filling of any Supreme Court vacancies that occur. There is frequent speculation along these lines in the media.[36] How a Supreme Court vacancy is filled will signal the seriousness of the Administration's ideological goals. If the Administration turns to a conservative personal friend of the President's not known for intellectual brilliance instead of one of the conservative intellectual leaders on the appeals

---

[35] See the text of the 1984 Republican Party platform and in particular the quoted material in 42 *Congressional Quarterly Weekly Report* 2110 (August 25, 1984).

[36] See, for example, Stark, "Will Court Bear Reagan Brand?" *Boston Globe*, July 29, 1984, at A-25, A-28.

courts, it may be interpreted as a failure to fully utilize the power of appointment to most effectively reshape judicial policy.

There has also been speculation about the Chief Justiceship. If the Chief Justiceship becomes vacant, it is possible that Justice O'Connor would be elevated to that position, thus enabling the Administration to make another historic appointment and at the same time have an associate justiceship to fill. But even if the President makes *no* Supreme Court appointments, the Reagan Administration will have left an indelible mark on the judiciary and the course of American law with its lower court appointments.

Ours is a historic political era that in the pendulum of American politics has come every 30 to 40 years.[37] The era of New Deal Democratic political domination of American politics ended with the election of 1968. In all likelihood, were it not for Watergate, the new conservative Republican era would then have been firmly established. It took Ronald Reagan and his Administration to seize the historic opportunity to reshape American politics. Barring economic or military catastrophies, the

[37] The argument that follows draws in part from the analysis presented in Goldman and Jahnige, *supra* n. 6, at 229–33.

cycle of conservative Republican domination may well last until the turn of the century. The Reagan Administration correctly sees the courts as having the power to further or hinder Administration goals; thus judicial appointments are of major importance for this Administration in its attempt to reshape public policy. How successful the Administration will ultimately be must await more extensive analysis of the judicial decisionmaking of the first and second term appointments.

The Roosevelt Administration was successful in its struggle with the federal judiciary and the federal courts abandoned or modified interpretations of the Constitution that, in the name of economic liberty, had prevented government from acting in certain areas of economic and social welfare policy. The crucial question now is will the Reagan Administration be successful in its struggle with the federal judiciary to have the federal courts abandon or modify interpretations of the Constitution that, in the name of civil liberty, place restraints on government when acting in certain areas concerning protection from criminals, public morality, and social policy? It is no surprise that students of the courts will be intently watching judicial appointments by a second term Reagan Administration.

28
Presidential Power and the Courts
David H. Rosenbloom

The United States presidency is often considered the most powerful elective office in the world. By contrast, the American judiciary has long been la-

Source: This essay by David H. Rosenbloom of Syracuse University was written specifically for this book.

belled the "least dangerous" branch of our constitutional government. In Alexander Hamilton's words, it ". . . has no influence over either the sword or the purse; no direction either of the strength or of the wealth of the society, and can take no active resolution whatever. It may truly be said to have neither *Force* nor *Will* but merely judgment; and must ultimately depend upon the aid of the executive arm even for the efficacy of its judgments."[1] Yet, the judiciary has emerged as an important check on the exercise of presidential power and, over the years, several specific court decisions have helped define the substance and limits of such power. Moreover, the courts have refined the analysis of and discourse about the proper scope of executive powers under the Constitution. Thus, the relationship between the presidency and the judiciary is somewhat paradoxical: the strong presidency may be effectively restrained by the weak judiciary. The main reasons for this lie in the peculiar nature of presidential power in constitutional theory and in political practice.

PRESIDENTIAL POWER UNDER THE CONSTITUTION: AN OVERVIEW

There is a great gap between the image of the president as an extremely powerful official and the reality of limited and ill-defined presidential power under the Constitution. It is necessary to explore this gap in some detail in order to grasp how the judiciary is able to play an important role in determining the scope of presidential power.

What has been called the "imaginary" presidency[2] holds that "the president is the strategic catalyst for progress in the American political system and the central figure in the international system as well."[3] According to this outlook,

"only the president can be the genuine architect of U.S. public policy, and only he, by attacking the problems frontally and aggressively and by interpreting his power expansively, can slay the dragons of crisis and be the engine of change to move this nation forward."[4] Indeed, the imaginary presidency has been thought to serve some deep-seated psychological function for the American people. James D. Barber claims that, "reassurance, action, legitimacy—at least a sense of those—encompass most of what Americans want to feel about their President. The people want those feelings so much that they will get projected onto a new President until he proves himself otherwise."[5]

Based on the imaginary vision of presidential power, one would expect to find a vast grant of constitutional power to the president. However, the *real* presidency as put forward in Article II of the Constitution is far from certain and specific in its establishment of presidential powers. This is in large part because the Framers of the Constitution were themselves divided and unsure about the entire issue of executive power. They took twelve votes on how to choose the president and five on the term of office. A number of important provisions concerning the presidency were not adopted until the final weeks of the Philadelphia Convention of 1787. Perhaps Alexander Hamilton described the Framer's frustration best in observing that "As to the Executive, it seemed to be admitted that no good one could be established on Republican principles."[6]

It is not surprising, therefore, that the Framers left matters somewhat vague. Article II, Section one, reads "The executive Power shall be vested in a President of the United States of America." These words have perplexed presidents, judges, and constitutional scholars ever since the founding. The central issues have been whether the clause is simply a statement that there is to be *one* chief executive—the Framers debated the merits of a plural executive—and that he will be called the "president" as opposed to some other title, such as "governor"; or whether the Framers had something more dramatic in mind. For instance, the clause can be read as conveying the "executive power" to the president, as though everyone knew what its content was. In that case, no further elaboration would be necessary since the scope of presidential power would have been known and accepted. It is also possible that the Framers were unable to reach agreement on the content of executive power and accordingly avoided deadlock, or at least further debate, by creating the broad outlines of the executive branch, while leaving the details of executive power to be worked out in practice by future generations.

Whatever the Framers' intention, two main theories about the executive power have been developed over the years. One is that the clause conveys *inherent* powers to the president. That is, it constitutes a grant of unspecified powers to act as the representative of the nation's best interests as unforeseen developments confront the polity. The other theory is that the executive power consists only of those powers specifically mentioned in the Constitution, such as the power to appoint certain officials, with the advice and consent of the Senate. Historically, some presidents have advanced the former view, while others have clung to the latter.

The belief that the Constitution conveys inherent powers to the president is often called the "stewardship" theory of the presidency. It was articulated by President Theodore Roosevelt as follows: "It was not only [the president's] right but his duty to do anything that the needs of the Nation demanded un-

less such action was forbidden by the Constitution or by the laws."[7] Examples of presidential actions that fit the stewardship theory have been the Louisiana Purchase and the invasion of foreign nations at presidential direction in the absence of a declaration of war or other prior approval by Congress. Some of President Abraham Lincoln's wartime measures also fit the stewardship approach. His dilemma was whether to adhere to the specific letter of the Constitution and perhaps lose the Union, or to preserve the Union and then restore the government to a stricter interpretation of constitutional requirements. Clearly, as Roosevelt suggested, there must be some presidential flexibility in the exercise of executive power if the nation is to be able to cope effectively with changing challenges and opportunities. Had President Thomas Jefferson shunned the notion of inherent powers in practice, the United States might have remained mostly east of the Mississippi River.

But there must also be some limits to presidential power if the constitutional scheme of checks and balances is to be meaningful. Presidents emphasizing a limited approach to executive power under the Constitution have espoused the "literalist" theory of the presidency. They have asserted that the chief executive can only do what the Constitution specifically allows, rather than what it does not specifically forbid. Presidents in this vein, such as William Howard Taft, Roosevelt's successor, have been more inclined to believe that challenges can be met and opportunities seized within the constitutional framework prescribing joint executive and legislative action.

Executive agreements are a good illustration of the difference between the stewardship and literalist approaches. These agreements are between heads of state. Originally, they were used for matters too minor to justify a treaty, such as postal conventions. Sometimes, however, they have been used where treaties would clearly be the process favored by the Constitution. Stewardship presidents are inclined to believe that since executive agreements are not prohibited by the Constitution, they can be used wherever politically desirable and feasible. A literalist president, by contrast, would avoid using executive agreements on important matters because they are not specifically authorized by the Constitution. Rather, they fall within the scope of inherent powers, as is discussed further on in this essay.

Closely allied to the issue of inherent powers is the matter of *implied* powers. Article II, Section three, states that the president "shall take Care that the Laws be faithfully executed." Was this clause intended to enable the president to exercise independent powers or establish administrative mechanisms necessary or desirable for the implementation of various laws? For instance, an early test of the existence of implied powers concerned the issue of whether the president could, in the absence of congressional authorization, supply federal protection against bodily attack to Supreme Court Justices. In the case of *In re Neagle* (1890)[8] the Supreme Court, not surprisingly, held that the president was entitled to do so as part of his power to see that the laws are faithfully executed. After all, it would be hard to enforce the law if members of the judiciary worked under constant threat of assassination and without any meaningful governmental protection. Common examples of the exercise of implied powers involve the issuance of executive orders providing federal bureaucrats with guidance as to how laws should be interpreted.

Not all exercises of inherent or implied powers are constitutional; nor are all unconstitutional. The constitution-

ality of presidential actions under Article II and other provisions has been the subject of much litigation. Presidents have sometimes won their cases; but other times they have lost. Either way, the vague quality of the Constitution's statements on these fundamental aspects of executive power have enabled the courts to play a very central role in determining the legitimacy of presidential actions. But that role is only part of the equation between president and judiciary. For judicial decisions to check the exercise of presidential power, the president must obey them.

At first thought the possibility that the president would ignore a judicial decision may seem alien to the constitutional system. Yet, historically, that threat has been a very real one. The Supreme Court's reasoning in the very fundamental case of *Marbury v. Madison* (1803)[9] is often thought to have taken into account the prospect that the executive branch might ignore a specific command from the judiciary. Allegedly, President Andrew Jackson once said, "[Chief Justice] John Marshall has made his decision, now let him enforce it."[10] Judicial decisions may be especially problematic from a president's perspective when they involve limitations on the powers or assumed prerogatives of the presidency, or the invalidation, on constitutional grounds, of laws that both the president and Congress consider constitutional *and* necessary to the immediate welfare of the nation. Presidential resistance to the courts in such cases varies. In response to decisions striking down fundamental New Deal legislation, President Franklin Roosevelt sought to expand the size of the Supreme Court so that he could "pack" it with his own appointees. More recently, President Richard Nixon averred that he would obey a "definitive" Supreme Court decision, thereby leaving open the possibility that he might ignore one if the Court were badly divided. Nevertheless, not just tradition, but the realities of contemporary presidential power make it highly likely that, today, presidents will obey the courts.

The imaginary presidency that has developed during the twentieth century is very different from the real one of the eighteenth century Constitution. The "most powerful" elected official in the world simply does not have enough power directly under that document to perform as he is now expected to; that is, to be the fundamental determinant of the working of the nation's government and politics.[11] In fact, a leading theory of contemporary presidential power finds that much of it consists of the power to "persuade."[12] This basis of presidential power was captured most graphically, if not most elegantly, by President Harry Truman. He said, "They talk about the power of the President, they talk about how I can push a button to get things done. Why, I spend most of my time kissing somebody's ass."[13] That may be one way to persuade, but Richard Neustadt's classic *Presidential Power* points to others.

Neustadt notes that much of the exercise of presidential leadership involves bargaining and that the president is in a better position to bargain when he enjoys the broad support of the American people, or at least of large or influential segments of it. But as noted above, Americans want, or perhaps even *need* to feel reassurance and legitimacy from their presidents. A president who violates the judiciary's view of his constitutional powers, especially if expressed by the Supreme Court, is not likely to appear either reassuring or legitimate. Consequently, such a president would be likely to lose popular support and, with it, much of the ability to bargain in a persuasive manner. Although he ultimately did obey the Supreme Court's

decision in *United States* v. *Nixon* (1974),[14] President Nixon's breach of fundamental political norms and his unsuccessful effort to hide these behind an assertion of constitutional "executive privilege" provide a dramatic example of what can occur when the political community loses its confidence in the president. On the other hand, though, when the courts uphold a questionable exercise of presidential power, they convey legitimacy to the president and help to defuse opposition to the action at issue. For instance, the Supreme Court's decisions in *United States* v. *Belmont* (1937)[15] and *United States* v. *Pink* (1942)[16] (both discussed below) helped to legitimize the use of executive agreements.

In sum, the vague quality of key constitutional clauses dealing with executive power and the realities of the contemporary presidency create a situation in which the courts can play an important role in checking the president. They may depend upon the president for the execution of their judgments, as Hamilton argued, but the president's legitimacy, popularity, and power may be deeply affected by the courts' judgments and exercises of reason. It is within this framework that judicial decisions have become an important determinant of presidential power and a potentially strong check upon its use. The remainder of this essay will outline the character of presidential powers in the realms of administration, domestic policymaking, and in foreign and defense affairs.

THE PRESIDENT AS "CHIEF ADMINISTRATOR"

It is undisputable that the president is the head of the executive branch and is charged with a wide responsibility for administrative matters. However, it is equally true that under the Constitution, Congress also has a great deal of authority for federal administration. For example, according to the Constitution, *all* governmental offices not established by the Constitution itself, must be created by law. Similarly, money for salaries and other expenditures can only be appropriated pursuant to law. Congress has the power to vest the appointment of lower level executive officials in the heads of departments, the president, or the courts. This allows the legislature to establish some of the conditions for appointment and to partly define federal personnel policy. Today, such basics as the federal merit system, equal employment opportunity, and labor relations are based on law. Agency missions and authority are also established by law, rather than by presidential fiat alone. Furthermore, Congress can require executive branch officers and employees to testify before its committees. For the most part, therefore, the president and Congress share authority and responsibility for federal administration.

Presidents have sometimes resisted the legislative role in executive branch operations. In so doing, they have provoked constitutional litigation that has enabled the courts to establish some of the outer boundaries of presidential power in administrative matters. One of the major examples has been the issue of the president's power to dismiss subordinate officials. The Constitution provides that the heads of departments must be appointed by the president with the advice and consent of the Senate. It also allows Congress to place responsibility for the appointment of other employees in the heads of departments, the president, or the courts, as mentioned above. However, with the exception of the impeachment clause, the Constitution is silent on the location of the power to dismiss appointees in the executive branch. On a few occasions, this issue has been at the center of a contest between Congress and the president for control of federal administration. In fact, whether the president had the inherent or implied power to dismiss department heads without the agreement of the Senate was a specific legal question in the impeachment proceedings against President Andrew Johnson in 1868.

The president's removal power seemed to be established definitively in *Myers* v. *United States* (1926).[17] An 1876 statute allowed the removal of postmasters ". . . by the President with the advice and consent of the Senate." But after Myers was removed pursuant to presidential directive alone, he sued. The Supreme Court's majority opinion was written by Chief Justice Taft, who was President Taft from 1909 to 1913. Despite having subscribed to a literalist interpretation earlier, Taft took an expansive view of presidential power. He argued that Article II gave the president the power to dismiss executive officers appointed by him and that Congress could not constitutionally interfere with that power. The Court's opinion seemed to endorse a broad view of inherent and implied powers, but it was very soon thereafter limited by another decision.

In *Humphrey's Executor* v. *United States* (1935),[18] the Court upheld the constitutionality of congressional limitations on the president's authority to dismiss members of the Federal Trade Commission (FTC). It reasoned that the FTC, an independent regulatory commission, was not solely part of the executive branch. In so doing, the Court reduced the application of Myers to "purely" executive officers, without further definition. This line of reasoning was also applied in *Wiener* v. *United States* (1958).[19] During the 1960s and 1970s, the power to dismiss ordinary public employees was further reduced by judicial decisions finding that they possess constitutional rights to procedural due process, equal protection, and civil rights and liberties such as freedom of speech, assembly, and privacy.[20]

Another set of issues concerning the president's role as administrative chief is whether he has independent executive power to negate the clear will of Congress. In the 1838 case of *Kendall* v. *United States*,[21] the Supreme Court held that Congress has the power to impose responsibilities and duties on executive branch officials. In the Court's words:

> It would be an alarming doctrine, that congress cannot impose upon any executive officer any duty they may think proper, which is not repugnant to any rights secured and protected by the constitution; and in such cases, the duty and responsibility grow out of and are subject to the control of law, and not to the direction of the President.

However alarming, though, circumstances sometimes arise in which the demands for effective and economical administration impel a president to attempt to circumvent legislative authority over the executive branch.

One such instance was the basis for *The American Federation of Government Employees* v. *Phillips* (1973).[22] Phillips was acting director of the Office of Economic Opportunity (OEO), a legacy of President Lyndon Johnson's Great Society program, which was not favored by President Nixon. In a budgetary message, Nixon indicated that he intended to eliminate the OEO. Based upon this clear directive from his administrative chief, Phillips began to cut back on spending the appropriations previously granted for the then current fiscal year. In Phillips view, it would be wasteful and administratively improper to go about spending money and building up a program that was likely to come to

an abrupt halt. A federal district court disagreed, however, citing the congressional role in appropriations and noting that the legislature was not bound by the president's budget message. Other instances of executive refusal to spend funds appropriated by legislative action (impoundments), without congressional agreement, have also been found illegal.

Executive privilege is another aspect of the president's role as administrative chief that has tested the limits of his constitutional powers. It consists of the putative right of the president not to divulge his confidential communications with his executive branch staff to other governmental officials. Generally, executive privilege is asserted against Congress on the grounds that the separation of powers principle prohibits the legislature from inserting itself too deeply into executive branch affairs. Conversely, the executive power in Article II has been claimed to include the authority to resist legislative encroachments. Ironically though, the leading case on executive privilege involved a dispute within the executive branch.

United States v. *Nixon* (1974)[23] concerned the president's refusal to supply the Watergate Special Prosecutor with some documents, including tapes of Nixon's conversations with his closest aides. In complex litigation, the tapes had been subpoenaed, but the president moved to squash this directive on the grounds of executive privilege. The Supreme Court recognized that a general executive privilege was ". . . fundamental to the operation of government and inextricably rooted in the separation of powers under the Constitution." Nevertheless, it held that the fundamental needs of the judicial process outweighed the claims of executive privilege in the specific instance at hand. In other words, Nixon was legally required to deliver the tapes, which he did and which resulted in his resignation. The Court suggested that the claims of executive privilege might be stronger where national security was involved.

THE PRESIDENT AS CHIEF DOMESTIC POLICYMAKER

The judiciary has also been centrally involved in determining the scope of the president's powers to formulate and to enforce domestic policy. The Constitution assigns federal domestic policymaking largely to the Congress, but provides for a presidential role as well. The president's veto power and State of the Union address are examples. Since the New Deal of the 1930s, however, the political community has looked increasingly toward the president as the initiator of federal policy. Indeed, the presidency was restructured in 1939, through the creation of the Executive Office of the President, largely in order to enable the president to fulfill this role more effectively. But the shifting responsibility for policymaking has raised at least three important constitutional issues: (1) How much responsibility for domestic policymaking can Congress delegate to the president? (2) Can Congress retain an effective check or control on the use of delegated legislative power? and (3) Do his vastly increased responsibilities provide a basis for the exercise of emergency powers by the president in domestic matters?

The constitutional principles regarding the legitimacy of delegations of legislative power to the executive are clear, though actual political practice is often at odds with them. The fundamental principles were perhaps best set forth in *Schecter Poultry Corporation* v. *United States* (1935).[24] The case involved a central aspect of the National Industrial Recovery Act of 1935, which was the na-

tion's major public policy hope for ending the Great Depression. The premise behind the act was that economic competition had to be *reduced* for recovery to take place. President Franklin Roosevelt asked Congress to provide ". . . for the machinery necessary for a great co-operative movement throughout all industry in order to obtain wide re-employment, to shorten the working week, to pay a decent wage for the shorter week, and to prevent unfair competition and disastrous overproduction."[25] Congress responded by authorizing the president to approve fair codes of competition for a wide variety of industries. The Schecter Poultry Corporation objected to enforcement of the Live Poultry Code, which regulated selling practices and the wages and hours of employees. These regulations were clearly legislative in character, though they had been established by the executive branch. The Supreme Court agreed with Schecter's contention that the delegation was unconstitutional and, therefore, that the code was unenforceable. The Court held that under the Constitution, "Congress is not permitted to abdicate or to transfer to others the essential functions with which it is . . . vested." Delegations of legislative authority could be valid only if Congress "has itself established the standards of legal obligation, thus performing its essential legislative function."

The Schecter principle is clear, though the precise meaning of the "standards of legal obligation" is inherently debatable. However, its meaning has become a moot point because in practice, while the courts pay lip service to Schecter, even very broad delegations of legislative authority, without clear standards, have been sustained. Consequently, the president is constitutionally free to exercise broad policymaking powers delegated to him by congressionally enacted statutes and resolutions.

Congress may have good reasons for delegating its legislative authority to the executive branch. The legislature is overburdened and the lawmaking process is cumbersome and subject to deadlock at many points. The executive branch may have greater expertise in several policy areas by virtue of its day-to-day administrative responsibilities. But Congress may understandably seek to check the discretionary use of the legislative authority it delegates. One way of doing this is to make the exercise of such discretion subject to congressional approval or disapproval. For example, the Reorganization Act of 1939 and several successor statutes authorized the president to propose reorganizations of the federal bureaucracy to Congress. These would go into effect if, within sixty days, the legislature did not pass a concurrent resolution of disapproval. This approach, called the *legislative veto*, became very common before it was declared unconstitutional by the Supreme Court in *Immigration and Naturalization Service v. Chadha* (1983).[26]

The legislative veto, which was found in over 200 federal statutory clauses, had broad but somewhat ambiguous effects on presidential power. On the one hand, it clearly restrained the president by making some of his actions and policy proposals subject to congressional veto. On the other hand, though, the legislative veto was part of a general shift of much legislative power to the executive—power that the Congress might prefer to retain in the absence of the veto. As Supreme Court Justice Byron White noted in Chadha:

> Without the legislative veto, Congress is faced with a Hobson's choice: either to refrain from delegating the necessary authority, leaving itself with a hopeless task of writing laws with the requisite

specificity to cover endless special circumstances across the entire policy landscape, or in the alternative, to abdicate its lawmaking function to the executive branch and independent agencies. To choose the former leaves major national problems unresolved; to opt for the latter risks unaccountable policy-making by those not elected to fill that role.

In Chadha, the majority of the Supreme Court may have agreed with White that the legislative veto was a useful political device. Nonetheless, the Court held it to be an unconstitutional one. In the majority's view, the specific veto at issue, which allowed the House of Representatives to overturn certain decisions of the Attorney General, violated the separation of powers, bicameralism, and the constitutional procedure whereby Congress must present legislation to the president for potential veto by him.

Delegations of legislative power to the executive are extremely important to the modern presidency. But the issue of the scope of inherent and implied executive constitutional powers in domestic policymaking remains to be considered. Not everything a president may find expeditious and desirable is likely to be pursuant to a specific grant of legislative power. Presidents may claim independent constitutional authority for their actions and the judiciary may be called upon to adjudicate them.

In the domestic sphere, the overall scope of inherent and implied powers seems quite limited. The Supreme Court accepted implied powers in *In re Neagle* and also a degree of inherent power in the Myers and Nixon cases. However, it resoundingly rejected them in *Youngstown Sheet and Tube v. Sawyer* (1952).[27] The case is often considered the Court's key statement on the subject. In Youngstown, as Justice Hugo Black put it for the majority, the Court was ". . . asked to decide whether the President was acting within his constitutional power when he issued an [executive] order directing the Secretary of Commerce to take possession of and operate most of the Nation's steel mills." The president's executive order was intended to avert a strike that would have been a "national catastrophe" and have complicated the country's war effort in Korea. The president claimed inherent and implied powers, as well as those derived from his constitutional role as commander-in-chief. The Court rejected all three bases for his action in declaring the executive order unconstitutional.

The Youngstown case prompted a concurring opinion by Justice Robert Jackson that put forth what has become the classic formulation of the scope of independent executive powers:

1. When the President acts pursuant to an express or implied authorization of Congress, his authority is at its maximum for it includes all that he possesses in his own right plus all that Congress can delegate. In these circumstances, and in these only, may he be said (for what it may be worth) to personify the federal sovereignty. . . .

2. When the President acts in the absence of either a congressional grant or denial of authority, he can only rely upon his own independent powers, but there is a zone of twilight in which he and Congress may have concurrent authority, or in which its distribution is uncertain. . . .

3. When the President takes measures incompatible with the expressed or implied will of Congress, his power is at its lowest ebb, for then he can rely only upon his own constitutional powers minus

any constitutional powers of Congress over the matter.

The Youngstown decision is an indicator of the gap between the all-powerful imaginary presidency and the judicially delimited real one. In the domestic policy arena, the president may be held politically responsible for far more than he can deliver relying upon his constitutional authority alone. Chief Justice Vinson, along with Justices Reed and Minton, vigorously attacked what they considered the majority's evisceration of the presidency in Youngstown: "The broad executive power granted by Article II to an officer on duty 365 days a year cannot, it is said, be invoked to avert disaster. Instead, the President must confine himself to sending a message to Congress recommending action. Under this messenger-boy concept of the Office, the President cannot even act to preserve legislative programs from destruction so that Congress will have something left to act upon. . . ." Their dissent is indicative of the fact that the debates over the proper scope of domestic constitutional executive power that were begun by the Framers in 1787 remain fundamentally unresolved.

FOREIGN AFFAIRS AND DEFENSE

The president derives a great deal of power from his roles as representative of the United States in foreign relations and his position as commander-in-chief. Historically, the courts have adopted a very broad interpretation of presidential powers in these arenas. Both inherent and implied powers of consequence have been accepted and legitimized by the courts. However, since the 1950s, the judiciary has clarified the status of claimed executive powers and, in the process has placed significant limits upon them.

United States v. *Curtiss-Wright Export Corp.* (1936)[28] is the basic modern articulation of the concept of inherent presidential powers in foreign affairs. In 1934, Congress passed a joint resolution providing that the president could prohibit the sale of arms and munitions in the United States to countries engaged in armed conflict in an area of South America. In assessing the constitutionality of the resolution, the Supreme Court set forth two propositions enabling the president constitutionally to assume a great deal of power in foreign affairs. First, the Court reasoned that the national government itself has inherent powers in foreign affairs: "The investment of the Federal government with powers of external sovereignty did not depend upon the affirmative grants of the Constitution," but rather such powers were "vested in the Federal government as necessary concomitants of nationality." Second, some of these inherent powers can be exercised by the president alone:

> It is important to bear in mind that we are here dealing not alone with an authority vested in the President by an exertion of legislative power, but with such an authority plus the very delicate, plenary and exclusive power of the President as the sole organ of the Federal government in the field of international relations—a power which does not require as a basis for its exercise an act of Congress. . . .

The Court went on to indicate the advantages the president had over Congress in carrying out foreign relations. Among those mentioned were knowledge of conditions in foreign nations, confidential sources of information, diplomatic agents under his authority, and a capacity to act with greater secrecy.

The Curtiss-Wright decision may have been somewhat vague as to the specific inherent powers vested in the president under the Court's interpretation of the Constitution. But in 1937, the Court accepted the presidential power to enter into executive agreements. In *United States* v. *Belmont* (1937),[29] it held that not all agreements between the United States and other nations were treaties and therefore some could be entered into by the president acting alone. Moreover, such an agreement could be binding on the *state* governments with respect to matters otherwise under their control. This line of reasoning was carried further in *United States* v. *Pink* (1942),[30] in which the Court held that the president's powers with regard to recognition of foreign nations can achieve the status of the supreme law of the land and, therefore, override state policies to the contrary.

Taken together, Curtiss-Wright, Belmont, and Pink develop the constitutional perspective that the federal government has inherent powers in foreign relations, that some of these powers can be exercised by the president alone, and that if otherwise valid, presidential use of these powers becomes the supreme law of the land. But since the federal government's inherent powers in foreign relations are not limited by the Constitution itself, conceivably treaties and executive agreements, which become the supreme law of the land, could be used to override specific constitutional limitations on the government, such as those contained in the Bill of Rights or Fourteenth Amendment. This line of reasoning is not as far-fetched as it may at first seem. At one time, it was subscribed to by John Foster Dulles, who later became Secretary of State under President Dwight D. Eisenhower.[31] However, it was put to rest by the Supreme Court in *Reid* v. *Covert* (1957),[32] in which it was emphasized that:

No agreement with a foreign nation can confer power on the Congress, or on any other branch of government, which is free from the restraints of the Constitution. . . . The prohibitions of the Constitution were designed to apply to all the branches of the National Government and they cannot be nullified by the Executive or by the Executive and the Senate combined.

Thus, the government's inherent powers in foreign affairs and the president's powers to enter into valid executive agreements are restrained by the multitude of constitutional provisions regarding individual rights, the separation of powers, and possibly federalism as well.

The president's role as commander-in-chief is closely related to his position as the leading, if not sole, organ of the government in foreign relations. As commander-in-chief, the president might find it expedient or necessary to act in ways that either go beyond the letter of the Constitution or clearly violate what would seem to be its express provisions. For example, President Abraham Lincoln proclaimed a blockade of the secessionist states, suspended the writ of habeas corpus in some areas, increased the size of the Union's military forces without congressional authorization, issued the Emancipation Proclamation, and authorized the military to try civilians in some cases even though the regular civilian courts were functioning.[33] In *Ex parte Milligan* (1866),[34] the Supreme Court denounced the latter practice in no uncertain terms, but with little long-term effect. It declared that

The Constitution of the United States is a law for rulers and people, equally in war and in peace, and covers with the shield of its protection all classes of men, at all times, and under all circumstances. No doctrine involving more pernicious consequences was ever invented by the wit of man than that any of its provisions can be suspended during any of the great exigencies of government.

The lofty idealism of the Milligan decision was belied by its subsequent lack of impact. Clinton Rossiter pointed out that, "As a restraint upon a President beset by martial crisis it was then [in 1866], and in 1950, of practically no value whatsoever."[35] In the case of *In re Debs* (1895),[36] the Supreme Court upheld the president's authority to use the armed forces domestically: "If the emergency arises, the army of the Nation, and all its militia, are at the service of the nation to compel obedience to its laws." The full import of the latter approach became evident during World War II.

In February 1942, President Roosevelt issued Executive Order 9066, authorizing the establishment of military areas, within the United States, from which "any or all persons" might be excluded as a means of preventing sabotage and espionage. Pursuant to the order, 112,000 persons of Japanese ancestry were forceably removed from their homes on the West Coast and in part of Arizona. Some 70,000 of these people were citizens of the United States. Although the relocation and a related curfew order looked like massive deprivations of constitutional rights, they were upheld by the Supreme Court. The curfew was accepted in *Hirabayashi* v. *United States* (1943)[37] and the more drastic relocation was found constitutionally legitimate in *Korematsu* v. *United States* (1944).[38] In the latter case, the Court found the president's power as commander-in-chief to expand in conjunction with the dangers faced by the nation: "But when under conditions of modern warfare our shores are threatened by hostile forces, the power to protect must be commensurate with the threatened danger." This was a far cry indeed from the "Milligan Constitution's" protection of "all classes of men, at all times, and under all circumstances."

Prior to the 1950s, the judiciary and Congress seem to have envisioned war as an event with a beginning and an end. As the Cold War evolved through the 1950s and the nation subsequently became used to a sense of permanent crisis in foreign relations, both of these branches of government sought ways of checking the president's over-arching powers. The Supreme Court's decision in the Youngstown case was part of this effort. Later, in *The New York Times* v. *United States* (1971)[39] a majority of the Court could agree that the president must bear a heavy burden of proof when relying upon inherent powers to prevent the publication of government documents in the nation's newspapers, even though the national security might be at stake. In *United States* v. *United States District Court* (1972),[40] the Court held that warrants were required to engage in electronic surveillance of purely domestic organizations, despite the executive branch's claim that the national security was under threat. A year later, Congress passed the War Powers Resolution in an effort to prevent the president from using his commander-in-chief powers to wage wars without congressional authorization.

CONCLUSION

There is no doubt that the judiciary has played an important role in defining the powers of the modern president. Inherent and implied powers have been accepted by the courts, but limits have also been placed upon their use. Cases like Youngstown, Nixon, *New York Times*, and U.S. District Court leave no doubt that the courts can constrain the use of presidential power. But cases such as Neagle, Debs, Curtiss-Wright, Belmont, Pink, Hirabayashi, and most prominently, Korematsu indicate that the Supreme Court may be inclined to grant broad discretion and great leeway to the president. As for a general theory of presidential power, the best effort to date remains Justice Jackson's formulation in Youngstown: Is the president acting with the consent or direction of Congress? Is he (or maybe in the not too distant future, she) acting alone? Does the action involved violate or circumvent the will of Congress? These questions along with the concepts of inherent and implied powers are likely to be employed while analyzing and deciding the constitutional issues involved in the exercise of presidential power in the future. Mentioning them here is a convenient means of concluding this chapter while recognizing that they are but a means of continuing the discourse begun by the Framers of the Constitution in 1787.

NOTES

1. Clinton Rossiter, ed., *The Federalist Papers* (New York: Mentor Books, 1961), No. 78, p. 465.

2. See David Nachmias and David H. Rosenbloom, *Bureaucratic Government, USA* (New York: St. Martin's Press, 1980), chapter 4 for a review.

3. Thomas I. Cronin, *The State of the Presidency* (Boston: Little, Brown, 1975), p. 33.

4. Ibid.

5. James D. Barber, "The Presidency: What Americans Want," in Pietro S. Nivola and David H. Rosenbloom, eds., *Classic Readings in American Politics* (New York: St. Martin's Press, 1986), p. 393.

6. Winton U. Solberg, ed., *The Federal Convention and the Formation of the Union of the American States* (Indianapolis: Bobbs-Merrill, 1958), pp. 145–46.

7. Quoted in Martin Diamond et al., *The Democratic Republic* (Chicago: Rand McNally, 1970), p. 220.

8. 135 U.S. 1 (1890).

9. 1 Cranch 137 (1803).

10. C. Herman Pritchett, *The American Constitution*, 3rd ed. (New York: McGraw-Hill, 1977), p. 83.

11. See Burton P. Sapin, *The Making of United States Foreign Policy* (Washington, D.C.: Brookings Institution, 1966), p. 90.

12. Richard Neustadt, *Presidential Power: The Politics of Leadership With Reflections on Johnson and Nixon* (New York: John Wiley & Sons, 1976).

13. Robert Sherrill, *Why They Call It Politics*, 2nd ed. (New York: Harcourt Brace Jovanovich, 1974), p. 8.

14. 418 U.S. 683 (1974).

15. 301 U.S. 324 (1937).

16. 315 U.S. 203 (1942).

17. 272 U.S. 52 (1926).

18. 295 U.S. 602 (1935).

19. 357 U.S. 349 (1958).

20. See David H. Rosenbloom, *Federal Service and the Constitution* (Ithaca, N.Y.: Cornell University Press, 1971) and Rosenbloom, *Public Administration and Law* (New York: Marcel Dekker, 1983), chapter 4.

21. 12 Peters 524 (1838).

22. 358 F. Supp. 60 (1973).

23. 418 U.S. 683 (1974).

24. 295 U.S. 495 (1935).

25. Robert H. Jackson, *The Struggle for Judicial Supremacy* (New York: Knopf, 1941), pp. 110–11.

26. 77 L. Ed. 2d 317 (1983).

27. 343 U.S. 579 (1952).

28. 299 U.S. 304 (1936).

29. 301 U.S. 324 (1937).

30. 315 U.S. 203 (1942).

31. Arthur S. Miller, *Presidential Power* (St. Paul, Minn.: West Publishing, 1977), p. 143.

32. 351 U.S. 487 (1956); 354 U.S. 1 (1957).

33. Clinton Rossiter, *The Supreme Court and the Commander in Chief*, expanded edition (Ithaca, N.Y.: Cornell University Press, 1976), p. 26.

34. 4 Wall. 2 (1866).

35. Rossiter, *Supreme Court and Commander in Chief*, p. 34.

36. 158 U.S. 564 (1895).

37. 320 U.S. 81 (1943).

38. 323 U.S. 214 (1944).

39. 403 U.S. 713 (1971).

40. 407 U.S. 297 (1972).

CHAPTER XII

The Presidential Personality

What kind of president do we want for our American democracy?[1] If we can determine the kind of president we want, how do we get that kind of president? A response to these questions comes from James David Barber in the form of a theory of presidential personalities, one of which, he argues, will serve Americans well.[2] More importantly, the theory proposes methods for predicting what the personalities are likely to be under a given set of circumstances.

The basic method of analysis in Barber's theory is that of biography. A person's early life is studied and psychological insights applied to that study for gaining insights and clues into how one coped with a number of developmental crises while growing up and how those coping experiences developed into adult styles of behavior toward oneself, others, and the world.

From this research, Barber has developed a four-part classification of presidents based on two dichotomized dimensions. The classifications are the active-positive, the active-negative, the passive-positive, and the passive-negative. The two dichotomized dimensions are the active-passive (how much or how little energy a president puts into the job) and the positive-negative (how much or how little enjoyment a president derives from the work).

Barber asserts that fundamental to his four-part classification are several variables that are basic to the personality of the president. These are character (one's view of oneself vis-à-vis life), worldview (one's view of human nature or others), and style (one's habitual way of getting things done).

Barber links these fundamental personality variables to two external variables: the public climate of expectations, that is, the demands thrust upon a candidate[3] or president by the people and the political or power situation determined by the support a president receives from the public, interest groups, Congress, the bureaucracy, the Supreme Court, etc. Barber concludes that the active-positive president is the democratic ideal.

Jeffrey Tulis writes that Barber's study is a valuable addition to the literature of political science because it is the first attempt to construct a generalized predictive theory of the presidency, the first systematic effort to apply personality theory to the task of assessing candidates for the presidency, and a pedagogy for presidents themselves, since they will try to be what their electorate expects.[4] It is also the first attempt to link character to policymaking.[5] William Lammers adds that Barber's analysis has the major advantage of identifying a category of behavior for the active and politically experienced personality, which had not received specific attention in previous studies.[6]

Barber's work has come under some criticism. On technical grounds it is argued, for example, that personality theory is insufficiently developed to carry the burden of prediction, that there is a need for mixed as well as dichotomous variables, that the two dimensions are not grounded in the specialized literature on personality, and that there are no footnotes to the psychological literature anywhere in the book.[7] On practical grounds, it is argued Barber's study places too much emphasis on personality at the expense of institutions.[8]

Bert Rockman, however, puts the Barber study in the most appropriate perspective when he writes, "Barber gives us clear hints, methodological issues aside, as to how we should search for those presidential prospects whose passion for power is mitigated by their passion for the enjoyment of political life. We need to read with care life histories in order to detect clues about character."[9] And therein lies the great value of Barber's pioneering research.

Barber's enduring study, as reflected in the growing number of applications of his model that have been published,[10] reminds us that it is individuals who work within institutions, in this case the presidency, who can and often do make a considerable difference. Barber's essay on "The Presidential Character" is reprinted here.

One of the recent applications of Barber's conceptual framework is Fred Greenstein's assessment of President Reagan's personality, worldview, and political style. Utilizing Barber's typology of presidential personalities, Greenstein questions whether, in light of Reagan's leadership and behavior in the presidency, he should be placed in the passive-positive category, which Barber once tentatively applied to him. Indeed, Greenstein argues that Reagan really fits the active-positive mold, albeit themes in Barber's passive-positive presidential personality type inform us of the compliant elements in Ronald Reagan's political psychology.

Greenstein's assessment (or reassessment, as the case may be) of the Reagan personality alerts us to the possibility that presidential observers may be misled by ideological biases against a particular president. One could, without great sensitivity to one's own predispositions, mistake a conservative political philosophy for a passive personality.[11] Fred Greenstein's essay on "The Reagan Personality" is reprinted here.

NOTES

1. For this sort of question raising, see Louis W. Koenig, *The Chief Executive*, 4th ed. (New York: Harcourt Brace Jovanovich, 1981), p. 344. Another study that asks what kind of presidential leadership we need is Erwin C. Hargrove, "What Manner of Man? The Crisis of the Contemporary Presidency," in *Choosing the President*, ed. James David Barber (Englewood Cliffs, N.J.: Prentice-Hall, 1974).

2. But see also Erwin Hargrove, *Presidential Leadership: Personality and Political Style* (New York: Macmillan, 1966) who made the first step beyond individual psycho-histories of presidents by classifying nine modern presidents as active or passive types.

3. On the relationship of the public climate of expectations to what sorts of presidential personalities may be elected by the people at a given time, see James David Barber, *The Pulse of Politics: Electing Presidents in the Media Age* (New York: W. W. Norton, 1980), especially pages 13–22.

4. See Jeffrey Tulis, "On Presidential Character," in *The Presidency in the Constitutional Order*, ed. Joseph M. Bessette and Jeffrey Tulis (Baton Rouge: Louisiana State University Press, 1981), pp. 285, 309.

5. See Jeffrey Tulis, "On Presidential Character and Abraham Lincoln," in *Rethinking the Presidency*, ed. Thomas E. Cronin (Boston: Little, Brown, 1982), p. 88.

6. See William W. Lammers, *Presidential Politics: Patterns and Prospects* (New York: Harper and Row, 1976), p. 79. Lammers' reference here is to the active-negative presidential personality.

7. See Alexander George, "Assessing Presidential Character," *World Politics* 26, no. 2 (1974), pp. 234–82. See also Michael Nelson, "James David Barber and the Psychological Presidency," *Virginia Quarterly Review* 56, no. 4 (1980), p. 658.

8. Martin Levin, "Ask Not What Our Presidents Are 'Really Like'; Ask What We and Our Politics Are Like: A Call for a Politics of Institutions Not Men," in *American Politics and Public Policy*, ed. Walter Dean Burnham and Martha Wagner Weinberg (Cambridge, Mass.: MIT Press, 1978), pp. 109–39. On the call for an institutional over an individual psychological approach see also Theodore Lowi, *The Personal President: Power Invested, Promise Unfulfilled* (Ithaca, N.Y.: Cornell University Press, 1985), pp. 136–37.

9. Bert A. Rockman, *The Leadership Question: The Presidency and the American System* (New York: Praeger Publishers, 1984), p. 12.

10. For applications of Barber's model, see William D. Pederson, "Amnesty and Presidential Behavior: A 'Barberian' Test," *Presidential Studies Quarterly* 7, no. 4 (Fall 1977), pp. 175–83; John S. Latcham, "President McKinley's Active-Positive Character: A Comparative Revision with Barber's Typology," *Presidential Studies Quarterly* 12, no. 4 (Fall 1982), pp. 491–521; and Eric B. Herzik and Mary L. Dodson, "Public Expectations and the Presidency: Barber's Climate of Expectations Examined," *Presidential Studies Quarterly* 12, no. 4 (Fall 1982), pp. 485–90. See also Bruce Buchanan, *The Citizen's Presidency* (Washington, D.C.: CQ Press, 1987), especially pp. 142–186, which examines Barber's concept of character as a basis for citizens choosing among candidates for the presidency.

11. On this point, see Benjamin I. Page and Mark P. Petracca, *The American Presidency* (New York: McGraw-Hill, 1983), p. 84; and Latcham, *McKinley's Character*, p. 492.

<u>29</u>
The Presidential Character

James David Barber

When a citizen votes for a Presidential candidate he makes, in effect, a prediction. He chooses from among the contenders the one he thinks (or feels, or guesses) would be the best President. He operates in a situation of immense uncertainty. If he has a long voting history, he can recall time and time again when he guessed wrong. He listens to the commentators, the politicians, and his friends, then adds it all up in some rough way to produce his prediction and his vote. Earlier in the game, his anticipations have been taken into account, either directly in the polls and primaries or indirectly in the minds of politicians who want to nominate someone he will like. But he must choose in the midst of a cloud of confusion, a rain of phony advertising, a storm of sermons, a hail of complex issues, a fog of charisma and boredom, and a thunder of accusation and defense. In the face of this chaos, a great many citizens fall back on the past, vote their old allegiances, and let it go at that. Nevertheless, the citizen's vote says that on balance he expects Mr. X would outshine Mr. Y in the Presidency.

This essay is meant to help citizens and those who advise them cut through the confusion and get at some clear criteria for choosing Presidents. To understand what actual Presidents do and what potential Presidents might do, the first need is to see the man whole—not as some abstract embodiment of civic virtue, some scorecard of issue stands,

or some reflection of a faction, but as a human being like the rest of us, a person trying to cope with a difficult environment. To that task he brings his own character, his own view of the world, his own political style. None of that is new for him. If we can see the pattern he has set for his political life we can, I contend, estimate much better his pattern as he confronts the stresses and chances of the Presidency.

The Presidency is a peculiar office. The Founding Fathers left it extraordinarily loose in definition, partly because they trusted George Washington to invent a tradition as he went along. It is an institution made a piece at a time by successive men in the White House. Jefferson reached out to Congress to put together the beginnings of political parties; Jackson's dramatic force extended electoral partisanship to its mass base; Lincoln vastly expanded the administrative reach of the office; Wilson and the Roosevelts showed its rhetorical possibilities—in fact every President's mind and demeanor has left its mark on a heritage still in lively development.

But the Presidency is much more than an institution. It is a focus of feelings. In general, popular feelings about politics are low-key, shallow, casual. For example, the vast majority of Americans know virtually nothing of what Congress is doing and care less. The Presidency is different. The Presidency is the focus for the most intense and persistent emotions in the American polity. The

Source: *The Presidential Character*, 3rd ed. (Englewood Cliffs, N.J.: Prentice-Hall, 1985). Reprinted with the permission of the author.

President is a symbolic leader, the one figure who draws together the people's hopes and fears for the political future. On top of all his routine duties, he has to carry that off—or fail.

Our emotional attachment to Presidents shows up when one dies in office. People were not just disappointed or worried when President Kennedy was killed; people wept at the loss of a man most had never even met. Kennedy was young and charismatic—but history shows that whenever a President dies in office, heroic Lincoln or debased Harding, McKinley or Garfield, the same wave of deep emotion sweeps across the country. On the other hand, the death of an ex-President brings forth no such intense emotional reaction.

The President is the first political figure children are aware of (later they add Congress, the Court, and others, as "helpers" of the President). With some exceptions among children in deprived circumstances, the President is seen as a "benevolent leader," one who nurtures, sustains, and inspires the citizenry. Presidents regularly show up among "most admired" contemporaries and forebears, and the President is the "best known" (in the sense of sheer name recognition) person in the Country. At inauguration time, even Presidents elected by close margins are supported by much larger majorities than the election returns show, for people rally round as he actually assumes office. There is a similar reaction when the people see their President threatened by crisis: if he takes action, there is a favorable spurt in the Gallup poll whether he succeeds or fails.

Obviously the President gets more attention in schoolbooks, press, and television than any other politician. He is one of very few who can make news by doing good things. *His* emotional state is a matter of continual public commentary, as is the manner in which his personal and official families conduct themselves. The media bring across the President not as some neutral administrator or corporate executive to be assessed by his production, but as a special being with mysterious dimensions.

We have no king. The sentiments English children—and adults—direct to the Queeen have no place to go in our system but to the President. Whatever his talents—Coolidge-type or Roosevelt-type—the President is the only available object for such national-religious-monarchical sentiments as Americans possess.

The President helps people make sense of politics. Congress is a tangle of committees, the bureaucracy is a maze of agencies. The President is one man trying to do a job—a picture much more understandable to the mass of people who find themselves in the same boat. Furthermore, he is the top man. He ought to know what is going on and set it right. So when the economy goes sour, or war drags on, or domestic violence erupts, the President is available to take the blame. Then when things go right, it seems the President must have had a hand in it. Indeed, the flow of political life is marked off by Presidents: the "Eisenhower Era," the "Kennedy Years."

What all this means is that the President's *main* responsibilities reach far beyond administering the Executive Branch or commanding the armed forces. The White House is first and foremost a place of public leadership. That inevitably brings to bear on the President intense moral, sentimental and quasi-religious pressures which can, if he lets them, distort his own thinking and feeling. If there is such a thing as extraordinary sanity, it is needed nowhere so much as in the White House.

Who the President is at a given time can make a profound difference in the whole thrust and direction of national politics. Since we have only one President at a time, we can never prove this by comparison, but even the most superficial speculation confirms the common-sense view that the man himself weighs heavily among other historical factors. A Wilson re-elected in 1920, a Hoover in 1932, a John F. Kennedy in 1964 would, it seems very likely, have guided the body politic along rather different paths from those their actual successors chose. Or try to imagine a Theodore Roosevelt ensconced behind today's "bully pulpit" of a Presidency, or Lyndon Johnson as President in the age of McKinley. Only someone mesmerized by the lures of historical inevitability can suppose that it would have made little or no difference to government policy had Alf Landon replaced FDR in 1936, had Dewey beaten Truman in 1948, or Adlai Stevenson reigned through the 1950s. Not only would these alternative Presidents have advocated different policies—they would have approached the office from very different psychological angles. It stretches credibility to think that Eugene McCarthy would have run the institution the way Lyndon Johnson did.

The crucial differences can be anticipated by an understanding of a potential President's character, his world view, and his style.[1] This kind of prediction is not easy; well-informed observers often have guessed wrong as they watched a man step toward the White House. One thinks of Woodrow Wilson, the scholar who would bring reason to politics; of Herbert Hoover, the Great Engineer who would organize chaos into progress; of Franklin D. Roosevelt, that champion of the balanced budget; of Harry Truman, whom the office would surely overwhelm; of Dwight D. Eisenhower, militant crusader; of John F. Kennedy, who would lead beyond moralisms to achievements; of Lyndon B. Johnson, the Southern conservative; and of Richard M. Nixon, conciliator. Spotting the errors is easy. Predicting with even approximate accuracy is going to require some sharp tools and close attention in their use. But the experiment is worth it because the question is critical and because it lends itself to correction by evidence.

My argument comes in layers.

First, a President's personality is an important shaper of his Presidential behavior on nontrivial matters.

Second, Presidential personality is patterned. His character, world view, and style fit together in a dynamic package understandable in psychological terms.

Third, a President's personality interacts with the power situation he faces and the national "climate of expectations" dominant at the time he serves. The tuning, the resonance—or lack of it—between these external factors and his personality sets in motion the dynamic of his Presidency.

Fourth, the best way to predict a President's character, world view, and style is to see how they were put together in the first place. That happened in his early life, culminating in his first independent political success.

But the core of the argument is that Presidential character—the basic stance a man takes toward his Presidential experience—comes in four varieties. The most important thing to know about a President or candidate is where he fits among these types, defined according to (a) how active he is and (b) whether or not he gives the impression he enjoys his political life.

Let me spell out these concepts briefly before getting down to cases.

PERSONALITY SHAPES PERFORMANCE

I am not about to argue that once you know a President's personality you know everything. But as the cases will demonstrate, the degree and quality of a President's emotional involvement in an issue are powerful influences on how he defines the issue itself, how much attention he pays to it, which facts and persons he sees as relevant to its resolution, and, finally, what principles and purposes he associates with the issue. Every story of Presidential decision-making is really two stories: an outer one in which a rational man calculates and an inner one in which an emotional man feels. The two are forever connected. Any real President is one whole man and his deeds reflect his wholeness.

As for personality, it is a matter of tendencies. It is not that one President "has" some basic characteristics that another President does not "have." That old way of treating a trait as a possession, like a rock in a basket, ignores the universality of aggressiveness, compliancy, detachment, and other human drives. We all have all of them, but in different amounts and in different combinations.

THE PATTERN OF CHARACTER, WORLD VIEW, AND STYLE

The most visible part of the pattern is style. *Style is the President's habitual way of performing his three political roles: rhetoric, personal relations, and homework.* Not to be confused with "stylishness," charisma, or appearance, style is how the President goes about doing what the office requires him to do—to speak, directly or through media, to large audiences; to deal face to face with other politicians, individually and in small, relatively private groups; and to read, write, and calculate by himself in order to manage the endless flow of details that stream onto his desk. No President can escape doing at least some of each. But there are marked differences in stylistic emphasis from President to President. The *balance* among the three style elements varies; one President may put most of himself into rhetoric, another may stress close, informal dealing, while still another may devote his energies mainly to study and cogitation. Beyond the balance, we want to see each President's peculiar habits of style, his mode of coping with and adapting to these Presidential demands. For example, I think both Calvin Coolidge and John F. Kennedy were primarily rhetoricians, but they went about it in contrasting ways.

A President's *world view* consists of his primary, politically relevant beliefs, particularly his conceptions of social causality, human nature, and the central moral conflicts of the time. This is how he sees the world and his lasting opinions about what he sees. Style is his way of acting; world view is his way of seeing. Like the rest of us, a President develops over a lifetime certain conceptions of reality—how things work in politics, what people are like, what the main purposes are. These assumptions or conceptions help him make sense of his world, give some semblance of order to the chaos of existence. Perhaps most important: a man's world view affects what he pays attention to, and a great deal of politics is about paying attention. The name of the game for many politicians is not so much "Do this, do that" as it is "Look here!"

"Character" comes from the Greek word for engraving; in one sense it is what life has marked into a man's being. As used here, *character is the way the*

President orients himself toward life—not for the moment, but enduringly. Character is the person's stance as he confronts experience. And at the core of character, a man confronts himself. The President's fundamental self-esteem is his prime personal resource; to defend and advance that, he will sacrifice much else he values. Down there in the privacy of his heart, does he find himself superb, or ordinary, or debased, or in some intermediate range? No President has been utterly paralyzed by self-doubt and none has been utterly free of midnight self-mockery. In between, the real Presidents move out on life from positions of relative strength or weakness. Equally important are the criteria by which they judge themselves. A President who rates himself by the standard of achievement, for instance, may be little affected by losses of affection.

Character, world view, and style are abstractions from the reality of the whole individual. In every case they form an integrated pattern: the man develops a combination which makes psychological sense for him, a dynamic arrangement of motives, beliefs, and habits in the service of his need for self-esteem.

THE POWER SITUATION AND "CLIMATE OF EXPECTATIONS"

Presidential character resonates with the political situation the President faces. It adapts him as he tries to adapt it. The support he has from the public and interest groups, the party balance in Congress, the thrust of Supreme Court opinion together set the basic power situation he must deal with. An activist President may run smack into a brick wall of resistance, then pull back and wait for a better moment. On the other hand, a President who sees himself as a quiet caretaker may not try to exploit even the most favorable power situation.

So it is the relationship between President and the political configuration that makes the system tick.

Even before public opinion polls, the President's real or supposed popularity was a large factor in his performance. Besides the power mix in Washington, the President has to deal with a national climate of expectations, the predominant needs thrust up to him by the people. There are at least three recurrent themes around which these needs are focused.

People look to the President for *reassurance*, a feeling that things will be all right, that the President will take care of his people. The psychological request is for a surcease of anxiety. Obviously, modern life in America involves considerable doses of fear, tension, anxiety, worry; from time to time, the public mood calls for a rest, a time of peace, a breathing space, a "return to normalcy."

Another theme is the demand for a *sense of progress and action.* The President ought to do something to direct the nation's course—or at least be in there pitching for the people. The President is looked to as a take-charge man, a doer, a turner of the wheels, a producer of progress—even if that means some sacrifice of serenity.

A third type of climate of expectations is the public need for a sense of *legitimacy* from, and in, the Presidency. The President should be a master politician who is above politics. He should have a right to his place and a rightful way of acting in it. The respectability—even religiosity—of the office has to be protected by a man who presents himself as defender of the faith. There is more to this than dignity, more than propriety. The President is expected to personify our betterness in an inspiring way, to express in what he does and is (not just in what he says) a moral idealism which, in much of the public mind, is the very opposite of "politics."

Over time the climate of expectations shifts and changes. Wars, depressions, and other national events contribute to that change, but there also is a rough cycle, from an emphasis on action (which begins to look too "political") to an emphasis on legitimacy (the moral uplift of which creates its own strains) to an emphasis on reassurance and rest (which comes to seem like drift) and back to action again. One need not be astrological about it. The point is that the climate of expectations at any given time is the political air the President has to breathe. Relating to this climate is a large part of his task.

PREDICTING PRESIDENTS

The best way to predict a President's character, world view, and style is to see how he constructed them in the first place. Especially in the early stages, life is experimental; consciously or not, a person tries out various ways of defining and maintaining and raising self-esteem. He looks to his environment for clues as to who he is and how well he is doing. These lessons of life slowly sink in: certain self-images and evaluations, certain ways of looking at the world, certain styles of action get confirmed by his experience and he gradually adopts them as his own. If we can see that process of development, we can understand the product. The features to note are those bearing on Presidential performance.

Experimental development continues all the way to death; we will not blind ourselves to midlife changes, particularly in the full-scale prediction cases. But it is often much easier to see the basic patterns in early life histories. Later on a whole host of distractions—especially the image-making all politicians learn to practice—clouds the picture.

In general, character has its *main* development in childhood, world view in adolescence, style in early adulthood. The stance toward life I call character grows out of the child's experiments in relating to parents, brothers and sisters, and peers at play and in school, as well as to his own body and the objects around it. Slowly the child defines an orientation toward experience; once established, that tends to last despite much subsequent contradiction. By adolescence, the child has been hearing and seeing how people make their worlds meaningful, and now he is moved to relate himself—his own meanings—to those around him. His focus of attention shifts toward the future; he senses that decisions about his fate are coming and he looks into the premises for those decisions. Thoughts about the way the world works and how one might work in it, about what people are like and how one might be like them or not, and about the values people share and how one might share in them too—these are typical concerns for the post-child, pre-adult mind of the adolescent.

These themes come together strongly in early adulthood, when the person moves from contemplation to responsible action and adopts a style. In most biographical accounts this period stands out in stark clarity—the time of emergence, the time the young man found himself. I call it his first independent political success. It was then he moved beyond the detailed guidance of his family; then his self-esteem was dramatically boosted; then he came forth as a person to be reckoned with by other people. The *way* he did that is profoundly important to him. Typically he grasps that style and hangs onto it. Much later, coming into the Presidency, something in him remembers this earlier victory and re-emphasizes the style that made it happen.

Character provides the main thrust and broad direction—but it does not *determine*, in any fixed sense, world view and style. The story of development does not end with the end of childhood. Thereafter, the culture one grows in and the ways that culture is translated by parents and peers shapes the meanings one makes of his character. The going world view gets learned and that learning helps channel character forces. Thus it will not necessarily be true that compulsive characters have reactionary beliefs, or that compliant characters believe in compromise. Similarly for style: historical accidents play a large part in furnishing special opportunities for action—and in blocking off alternatives. For example, however much anger a young man may feel, that anger will not be expressed in rhetoric unless and until his life situation provides a platform and an audience. Style thus has a stature and independence of its own. Those who would reduce all explanation to character neglect these highly significant later channelings. For beyond the root is the branch, above the foundation the superstructure, and starts do not prescribe finishes.

FOUR TYPES OF PRESIDENTIAL CHARACTER

The five concepts—character, world view, style, power situation, and climate of expectations—run through the accounts of Presidents which cluster the Presidents into four types. This is the fundamental scheme of the study. It offers a way to move past the complexities to the main contrasts and comparisons.

The first baseline in defining Presidential types is *activity-passivity*. How much energy does the man invest in his Presidency? Lyndon Johnson went at his day like a human cyclone, coming to rest long after the sun went down. Calvin Coolidge often slept eleven hours a night and still needed a nap in the middle of the day. In between the Presidents array themselves on the high or low side of the activity line.

The second baseline is *positive-negative affect* toward one's activity—that is, how he feels about what he does. Relatively speaking, does he seem to experience his political life as happy or sad, enjoyable or discouraging, positive or negative in its main effect. The feeling I am after here is not grim satisfaction in a job well done, not some philosophical conclusion. The idea is this: is he someone who, on the surfaces we can see, gives forth the feeling that he has *fun* in political life? Franklin Roosevelt's Secretary of War, Henry L. Stimson wrote that the Roosevelts "not only understood the *use* of power, they knew the *enjoyment* of power, too. . . . Whether a man is burdened by power or enjoys power; whether he is trapped by responsibility or made free by it; whether he is moved by other people and outer forces or moves them—that is the essence of leadership."

The positive-negative baseline, then, is a general symptom of the fit between the man and his experience, a kind of register of *felt* satisfaction.

Why might we expect these two simple dimensions to outline the main character types? Because they stand for two central features of anyone's orientation toward life. In nearly every study of personality, some form of the active-passive contrast is critical; the general tendency to act or be acted upon is evident in such concepts as dominancesubmission, extraversion-introversion, aggression-timidity, attack-defense, fight-flight, engagement-withdrawal, approach-avoidance. In everyday life we sense quickly the general energy output of the people we deal with. Similarly we catch on fairly quickly to the affect dimension—whether the person seems to be optimistic or pessimistic, hopeful or skeptical, happy or sad. The two baselines are clear and they are also independent of one another: all of us know people who are very active but seem discouraged, others who are quite passive but seem happy, and so forth. The activity baseline refers to what one does, the affect baseline to how one feels about what he does.

Both are crude clues to character. They are leads into four basic character patterns long familiar in psychological research. In summary form, these are the main configurations:

Active-Positive

There is a congruence, a consistency, between much activity and the enjoyment of it, indicating relatively high self-esteem and relative success in relating to the environment. The man shows an orientation toward productiveness as a value and an ability to use his styles flexibly, adaptively, suiting the dance to the music. He sees himself as developing over time toward relatively well defined personal goals—growing toward his image of himself as he might yet be. There is an emphasis on rational mastery, on using the brain to move the feet. This may get him into trouble; he may fail to take account of the irrational in politics. Not everyone he deals with sees things his way and he may find it hard to understand why.

Active-Negative

The contradiction here is between relatively intense effort and relatively low emotional reward for that effort. The activity has a compulsive quality, as if the man were trying to make up for something or to escape from anxiety into hard work. He seems ambitious, striving upward, power-seeking. His stance toward the environment is aggressive and he has a persistent problem in managing his aggressive feelings. His self-image is vague and discontinuous. Life is a hard struggle to achieve and hold power, hampered by the condemnations of a perfectionistic conscience. Active-negative types pour energy into the political system, but it is an energy distorted from within.

Passive-Positive

This is the receptive, compliant, other-directed character whose life is a search for affection as a reward for being agreeable and cooperative rather than personally assertive. The contradiction is between low self-esteem (on grounds of being unlovable, unattractive) and a superficial optimism. A hopeful attitude helps dispel doubt and elicits encouragement from others. Passive-positive types help soften the harsh edges of politics. But their dependence and the fragility of their hopes and enjoyments make disappointment in politics likely.

Passive-Negative

The factors are consistent—but how are we to account for the man's *political* role-taking? Why is someone who does little in politics and enjoys it less there at all? The answer lies in the passive-negative's character-rooted orientation toward doing dutiful service; this compensates for low self-esteem based on a sense of uselessness. Passive-negative types are in politics because they think they ought to be. They may be well adapted to certain nonpolitical roles, but they lack the experience and flexibility to perform effectively as political leaders. Their tendency is to withdraw, to escape from the conflict and uncertainty of politics by emphasizing vague principles (especially prohibitions) and procedural arrangements. They become guardians of the right and proper way, above the sordid politicking of lesser men.

Active-positive Presidents want most to achieve results. Active-negatives aim to get and keep power. Passive-positives are after love. Passive-negatives emphasize their civic virtue. The relation of activity to enjoyment in a President thus tends to outline a cluster of characteristics, to set apart the adapted from the compulsive, compliant, and withdrawn types.

The first four Presidents of the United States, conveniently, ran through this gamut of character types. (Remember, we are talking about tendencies, broad directions; no individual man exactly fits a category.) George Washington—clearly the most important President in the pantheon—established the fundamental legitimacy of an American government at a time when this was a matter in considerable question. Washington's dignity, judiciousness, his aloof air of reserve and dedication to duty fit the passive-negative or withdrawing type best. Washington did not seek innovation, he sought stability. He longed to retire to Mount Vernon, but fortunately was persuaded to stay on through a second term, in which, by rising above the political conflict between Hamilton and Jefferson and inspiring confidence in his own integrity, he gave the nation time to develop the organized means for peaceful change.

John Adams followed, a dour New England Puritan, much given to work and worry, an impatient and irascible man—an active-negative President, a compulsive type. Adams was far more partisan than Washington; the survival of the system through his Presidency demonstrated that the nation could tolerate, for a time, domination by one of its nascent political parties. As President, an angry Adams brought the United States to the brink of war with

France, and presided over the new nation's first experiment in political repression: the Alien and Sedition Acts, forbidding, among other things, unlawful combinations "with intent to oppose any measure or measures of the government of the United States," or "any false, scandalous, and malicious writing or writings against the United States, or the President of the United States, with intent to defame . . . or to bring them or either of them, into contempt or disrepute."

Then came Jefferson. He too had his troubles and failures—in the design of national defense, for example. As for his Presidential character (only one element in success or failure), Jefferson was clearly active-positive. A child of the Enlightenment, he applied his reason to organizing connections with Congress aimed at strengthening the more popular forces. A man of catholic interests and delightful humor, Jefferson combined a clear and open vision of what the country could be with a profound political sense, expressed in his famous phrase, "Every difference of opinion is not a difference of principle."

The fourth President was James Madison, "Little Jemmy," the constitutional philosopher thrown into the White House at a time of great international turmoil. Madison comes closest to the passive-positive, or compliant, type; he suffered from irresolution, tried to compromise his way out, and gave in too readily to the "war-hawks" urging combat with Britain. The nation drifted into war, and Madison wound up ineptly commanding his collection of amateur generals in the streets of Washington. General Jackson's victory at New Orleans saved the Madison administration's historical reputation; but he left the Presidency with the United States close to bankruptcy and secession.

These four Presidents—like all of the

Presidents—were persons trying to cope with the roles they had won by using the equipment they had built over a lifetime. The President is not some shapeless organism in a flood of novelties, but a man with a memory in a system with a history. Like all of us, he draws on his past to shape his future. The pathetic hope that the White House will turn a Caligula into a Marcus Aurelius is as naive as the fear that ultimate power inevitably corrupts. The problem is to understand—and to state understandably—what in the personal past foreshadows the Presidential future.

NOTE

1. The books' central concepts have grown on me through a series of previous studies. See: *The Lawmakers: Recruitment and Adaptation to* *Legislative Life* (New Haven, Yale University Press, 1965); "Peer Group Discussion and Recovery from the Kennedy Assassination," in Bradley A. Greenberg and Edwin B. Parker, eds., *The Kennedy Assassination and the American Public* (Stanford, Stanford University Press, 1965); *Power in Committees: An Experiment in the Governmental Process* (Chicago, Rand-McNally, 1966); "Leadership Strategies for Legislative Party Cohesion," *Journal of Politics*, Vol. 28, 1966; "Adult Identity and Presidential Style: The Rhetorical Emphasis," *Daedalus*, Summer 1968; "Classifying and Predicting Presidential Styles: Two 'Weak' Presidents," *Journal of Social Issues*, Vol. 24, 1968; *Citizen Politics* (Chicago, Markham, 1969); "The Interplay of Presidential Character and Style: A Paradigm and Five Illustrations," in Fred I. Greenstein and Michael Lerner, eds., *A Source Book for the Study of Personality and Politics* (Chicago, Markham, 1979); "The Presidency: What Americans Want," *The Center Magazine*, Vol. 4, 1971.

30
The Reagan Personality
Fred I. Greenstein

REAGAN AND TYPES OF PRESIDENTIAL PERSONALITY

James David Barber's account of presidential character and his general formulation of the array of elements (character, world view, style, and political context) that affect presidential performance are more often discussed than turned to analytic use.[1] When seen with some care against the most reliable reports of the qualities Reagan brings to his leadership, however, Barber's psychological contribution to the lore of the modern presidency illuminates and is illuminated by the Reagan experience. Moreover, his overall conceptualization of the elements of presidential performance provides a useful framework for identifying lessons of Reagan's presidency.

Barber, in research on state politicians done in the 1950s, provisionally identified four types of political actors with distinctive political styles, and by implication personality patterns, that could be detected by using two criteria.[2] One criterion is whether the emotional

Source: Excerpted from *The Reagan Presidency: An Early Assessment* edited by Fred I. Greenstein. Copyright © 1983 by the Johns Hopkins University Press. This article has been retitled; it originally appeared as "Reagan and the Lore of the Modern Presidency: What Have We Learned?" Notes have been renumbered.

energy leaders invest in political activity is positive or negative—whether they derive pleasure or pain from politics. The other is whether these energies are turned to active or passive role-performance.

Reagan manifestly participates in politics with relish.[3] In the title phrase of his 1965 memoir, politics enabled him to find "the rest of me." He seems cut out to fit Barber's positive type, in contrast to the relentlessly hard-working Carter and the periodically tormented Johnson and Nixon. But are his nine-to-five work habits, punctuated by vacations and midweek horseback rides, active or passive? Asking the question reveals the ambiguity of the terms "active" and "passive." When called upon to be active, largely in his additional roles as chief administration communicator and persuader, Reagan has been unstinting. Certainly he also has been an activist in the traditional policy sense of that ambiguous term. He knows what he wants and does everything he can to attain his goals. (Franklin Roosevelt, it may be added, is viewed as a classical activist, but he was no workaholic.) Thus, Reagan is not readily placed in a passive-active continuum.

Suppose, however, we use Barber's analysis as a sensitizer rather than as a predictor. Consider, for example, the political psychological insights Barber sought to condense in his use of the passive-positive category, which he once tentatively applied to Reagan.[4]

In *The Lawmakers*, Barber identifies through the use of the passive-positive category the traits that he found united in a political type he called the "spectator." This is the politician who, like the people identified in David Riesman's account of the other-directed character, seems more interested in the status derived from leadership than in policy accomplishment and who is highly compli-

ant to advisers.[5] As an issue-oriented ideologue, Reagan has *not* been an "easy sell"—indeed, according to some accounts he has been overly disposed to steer his advisers, signaling in advance the recommendations he wants. Furthermore, if presidential leadership has been fundamentally an occasion for Reagan to bask in a sense of exalted status, he has kept this need well concealed.

Nevertheless, the Barber category does fit certain other-directed qualities Reagan seems to manifest. For example, his beliefs clearly are not so deeply rooted in characterological needs that he refuses to bend them when compromises are necessary. Overall, his career and practices display other-directed, context-dependent qualities of the sort that cognitive psychologist Herman Witkin calls "field dependence."[6] Reagan's beliefs have followed a parabola from keen Roosevelt liberalism to enthusiastically strong conservatism in close synchronization with the changes in his own life circumstances from Depression child to big business spokesman. And while he is capable of overruling his advisers, he is widely said to be reluctant to discipline them or even to tolerate heated disagreement (in contrast to civil, measured debate) among them in his presence. Thus, although the "passive" Barber category does not work for Reagan, themes in Barber's account of passive-positive presidential personality alert us to compliant elements in Reagan's political psychology.

In his analyses of modern era presidents, Barber's overwhelming preoccupation is with the active types. (The only modern president Barber treats in *The Presidential Character* as passive is Eisenhower, who, he notes, does not easily fit his classification scheme.[7]) Underlying the distinction between the active-positive and -negative types in

Barber's analysis is a set of issues that derive from Harold D. Lasswell's work on political personality.[8] Lasswell was profoundly impressed by the danger that psychologically wounded leaders will use politics not only for seeking to influence the real world dilemmas of national and international politics, but also for giving vent to their inner distresses by means of "symptoms" such as irrational anger, rigidity, or grandiosity. At a minimum, the bulk of observers of the presidency have felt that neurotic needs of one type or another have influenced—indeed distorted in ways that undermined their own policies—the performance in office of at least two modern presidents, Nixon and Johnson, and (here there is the most agreement) one of the major precursively modern presidents, Woodrow Wilson.[9]

Reagan would never have rigidified in the face of a League of Nations conflict. On one often-quoted occasion as California governor, he announced that his feet were set in concrete. Later he accepted a compromise with a characteristically disarming one-liner: "You are hearing the sound of concrete cracking." Reagan also is no insomnia-haunted Johnson, waking to nightmares, and he cannot be imagined as a cornered Nixon denying that he is "a crook" and allowing himself to become immersed in self-destructive acts that culminate in a forced resignation from office. Yet the tension between ideological faith and pragmatic works has—as the preceding chapters make clear—been a continuing element in Reagan's leadership. Evidently Reagan's leadership is significantly influenced by his psychological "wiring," but by other aspects of it than are illuminated by Lasswell's and Barber's studies of presidents who "rigidify" because of neurotic motivations, such as compulsive power needs.

REAGAN AND THE MODERN PRESIDENCY: PARALLELS AND DEPARTURES

Although the typologies just discussed provide a partial perspective on Reagan and his presidency, it is now necessary to go beyond them, first examining additional aspects of his personality, then considering his beliefs and political style.

Personality

The official campaign photograph of Ronald Reagan portrays a rugged-faced westerner in modified cowboy attire. This public relations image, however, is clearly *not* the outward manifestation of a president with the impulses of a gunslinger. Reagan's anti-Soviet rhetoric and his commitment to increased military expenditures have understandably aroused antinuclear and more generally dovish concerns about dangers that may ensue from his leadership. Even his adversaries, however, recognize that he exhibits none of the personal insecurities that characterize the power-preoccupied leaders about whom Lasswell and Barber write.

In responding to being shot by a would-be assassin, Reagan revealed neither bravado nor panic. Instead, he displayed his almost reflexive proclivity to be ingratiating, including the familiar humor. ("I hope you fellows are Republicans," he said to the emergency room surgeons.) Reagan may be "militaristic," but he illustrates the fallacy in political psychology writings that treat all commitments to enhance military strength as "neurotic," rather than recognizing that a proarmaments position may stem from beliefs about the nature of world politics. The psychological roots of a leader's political beliefs are of profound significance. Neurotically rooted beliefs are less open to change when they lead to unproductive consequences than are beliefs that mainly serve to provide a map of the political universe. And it is instructive that throughout his political career this emotionally secure leader has been willing to adapt the positions he derives from doctrine if circumstances force him to recognize that they cannot be achieved or will not work.

Reagan's ability to be ingratiating, like many outward manifestations of his conduct of the presidency, stands in particularly distinct relief against the personal attributes that, according to many press, memoir, and research reports, flawed his predecessor's leadership. University of Maryland scholar Allen Schick, for example, interviewed a congressman who found the experience of meeting with Reagan strikingly more persuasive than that of consulting with Carter. In a meeting with Carter on proposed legislation, the congressman recalled that "we had barely got seated and Carter started lecturing us about the problems he had with one of the sections of the bill. He knew the details better than most of us, but somehow that caused more resentment than if he had left the specifics to us."[10] In his meeting with Reagan, the congressman reported admiringly that he was only in the president's office for "a couple of minutes, but I didn't feel rushed and I'm not quite sure how I was shown the door. A photographer shot the usual roll of pictures; the president gave me a firm, friendly handshake. He patted me on the back and told me how much he needed and appreciated my vote. He said that I should call if I needed anything."

All of the modern presidents, including Carter, have had successes in patting—and scratching—backs. All also have learned that charm is a marginal rather than a decisive political influ-

ence, especially in the long haul. After all, other political leaders are more responsive to their own convictions, their constituency interests, and such elements of external reality as the state of the economy than to personal niceties. Reagan, a "generic politician," does, however, illustrate the capacity of a chief executive, especially early in a presidency, to derive substantial benefits from being gifted at small-group persuasion. By extension, this side of Reagan's performance contributed to a general impression that post-Watergate assertions stressing the limits on presidents' capacities to achieve their goals have underplayed the potential of the Oval Office as a base for skillful politicking.

Reagan's adeptness at using the politics of persuasiveness in face-to-face settings is paralleled by his professionalism in projecting public messages through the broadcast media. Of the nine modern presidents, Reagan's capacity for what Hamilton in *Federalist* 68 cuttingly called "the little arts of flattery" most resembles that of the president he admired so greatly during his young adulthood—Franklin Roosevelt. Both are examples of political dramatists and charmers. Both spent more time than most modern presidents have in writing their speeches, not wholly delegating this task to speechwriters. Both also typify politicians who publicly exude confidence and optimism, qualities that can be extraordinarily important when inspirational leadership and morale building are needed.

In Roosevelt's case, however, optimism was not enough to end the Great Depression that had led to his election in 1932. The Depression ended when preparations for war stimulated the economy. Critics of the "fit" between Roosevelt's personality and the national needs of the time focus on the flaw in the cognitive side of his personality, echoing the oft-quoted description of him as a man whose temperament was first-rate, but whose mind was second-rate.[11] What they refer to is the tatterdemalion nature of the policies that Roosevelt supported. The Hundred-Days legislation included both public assistance programs and a federal pay cut—policies likely to cancel each other in their macro-economic consequences.[12]

Lou Cannon believes that Reagan's attraction to the painless remedy implicit in supply-side economics resonates with Reagan's own high-spirited optimism, a trait that has been reinforced continually throughout his career by lucky breaks—finding lucrative employment in the Depression, becoming a well-paid political spokesman just as his film career was about to end, unexpectedly achieving national political prominence through a single television broadcast, and the like. Cannon also portrays Reagan's approach to analyzing policy much as the media reports based on first- and second-hand personal contact with him do. He is said not to apply rigorous thought to policy issues; not to have a "hypothesis-testing" cast of mind. Rather, he defends his positions with anecdotes or highly selective statistics that support his initial predilections. Unlike Roosevelt, Reagan has long had difficulty using his sound political temperament to conceal any cognitive limitations he may have. Aides keep his press conferences to a minimum and at first did not schedule them at prime time. In general, his spontaneous discourse with the press has shown conspicuous gaps of information and flaws in reasoning when compared with the comportment of his predecessors in comparable unrehearsed circumstances.[13]

Reagan is like Roosevelt in being personally and politically flexible, even though he is unlike him in his ardent commitment to abstract beliefs. Discussing Reagan's conversion to conservatism in the 1950s, Cannon writes, "his views changed, as his views would change on other things, but he rarely became obsessive about his new opinions. . . . Reagan had changed his mind . . . not his personality."[14]

But the two obviously are not psychological clones. Roosevelt evinced extraordinary curiosity about people and programs and delighted in being personally at the center of an inordinately complex network of political intelligence. Reagan, for all of his outward bonhomie, is a private man. What and whom he knows are unclear. He seems to be an instinctive political strategist but is said to be bored with political tactics, just as he seems not to be interested in close analysis of his policies.

As usual, however, the qualifier "seems" is vital at this stage in assessment of Reagan's leadership. It is, after all, strategically advantageous for the president to keep public distance from the details of the policies his aides are advancing, thus retaining maneuverability for retreat, bargaining, and compromise. And Reagan manifestly does not seal himself off from criticisms of his policies and leadership. He follows the *Washington Post*, *New York Times*, selected regional newspapers, the White House press summary, and television news—a diet of communication scarcely calculated to induce the illusion that he and his policies only receive accolades. Again, he is like Roosevelt in ardently following the news media. The difference seems to be that Reagan's reading serves especially to inform his rhetoric. Roosevelt's reading also guided his leadership tactics and was more likely than Reagan's to lead him to make independent judgments about what policies to pursue, when, and how.

This speculative exercise in comparative Reagan-Roosevelt character analysis points to a type of politician better able to sell policies than to analyze them. In this respect, although Reagan's White House is seething with organizational entities (whereas Roosevelt's was still an extension in many respects of the presidential household), neither man has left a record of having addressed his aides to the task of systematically analyzing and anticipating the workability of alternative policies. In certain respects Reagan has more extended contacts with his official associates than Roosevelt did, meeting regularly with the cabinet and encouraging cabinet discussion (as long as it takes place in the spirit of discourse rather than combat) and also meeting regularly with a body that was not formed until the Truman years, the National Security Council. But both presidents and their practices may prove to be particularly instructive to students of the modern presidency because they illustrate the difficulties that arise when a president is so constituted that his political skills far exceed his skills at or impulses toward policy analysis.

Jimmy Carter gave policy analysis a bad name by immersing himself in policy content and failing to assess adequately the political feasibility of his programs. But the flaw was in Carter's analytic mode. Feasibility and substance both need analysis. Carter made the mistake of seeking to break complex issues into a multitude of technical components and attempting to evaluate them by politically neutral criteria. Effective policy analysis should be neither apolitical nor atomized. Rather, it should identify the grand contours of policies and project their consequences in order to weigh their substantive and political costs and benefits.

In Reagan's case, the most conspicuous time in which political skill was wedded to defective policy analysis was during the months leading up to the 1981 spending and tax cuts. Within the year, these enactments were haunting the administration by contributing to massive budgetary deficits. As budget politics proceeded in the course of 1983, the dilemma of massive projected deficits led to unusually intense disagreement among Reagan's advisers and between groups of them and Reagan himself.

Perhaps the most extreme modern display of short-run exercise of presidential skill in getting a result that had long-run catastrophic results for a president and his presidency was Lyndon Johnson's 1965 success in rallying his aides and other political leaders behind an open-ended commitment of American combat troops to Vietnam. Johnson himself sensed the danger in the decision. When a military adviser observed that "the Gallup Poll shows people are basically behind our commitment," Johnson presciently posed this parallel: "If you make a commitment to jump off a building and you find out how high it is, you may want to withdraw that commitment."[15]

Johnson's skepticism about the viability of a policy he was undertaking did not lead him to back off or even to apply analytically neutral staff resources to examining the consequences that were likely to ensue from escalation and exploring alternatives to such action. Reports of Reagan's style of thinking about policy consequences and employing advisers to extend his personal cognitive capacities suggest he does not find it natural even to worry about possible negative consequences of actions like the 1981 tax decrease.[16] And reports of the White House debates on the tax cut and about the views of others in Reagan's coalition, such as key congressional actors, suggest that in 1980 Reagan's personal political effectiveness (much augmented by presidential and other administration lobbying and successful efforts to manufacture a mandate out of the ambiguous 1980 Republican election victory) discouraged even skeptical advisers from bringing their views to his attention.[17] Here, Reagan has been especially resistant to reconsidering policies in the areas closest to his most central beliefs.

Belief System

In charting Ronald Reagan's political rise, I stressed that he is unique among the modern presidents in his depth—and one might add, duration—of ideological commitment. Some of the slogans he wove together in his 1950s public addresses, through which he perfected "The Speech" that won him acclaim in 1964, appeared again in his 1980 campaign pronouncements. Yet Reagan is less than the compleat ideologue in two senses. In an Eric Hoffer world of "true believers"—individuals who rely on detailed elaborations of doctrine to guide their day-to-day actions and even to lend meaning to their lives—Reagan is a tame specimen.[18] His beliefs are important to him, but so are his wife, his family, his friends, his avocations, and much else that keeps him from being a Savonarola descended upon Washington to purge it of evil. His beliefs did not stop him from making immediate, amiable contact with the old New Dealer and urban-machine politician, House Speaker Thomas O'Neill. Indeed, to the distress of his conservative supporters, one of Reagan's first postelection social gatherings in Washington was with a Nixon enemies-list liberal—*Washington Post* publisher Katherine Graham.

If Reagan's beliefs are not branded on his skin, neither are they highly specific in terms of their policy implica-

tions. One of the dilemmas of Reagan aides such as Budget Director David Stockman has been to translate Reagan's broad conservative aphorisms—some of them in conflict with one another (for example, cutting spending is not always the best way to "eliminate waste and fraud")—into policy. Turning the coin over, the generalized nature of his beliefs contributes to his public (and allegedly private) ability to rationalize the compromises he makes in terms of his overarching political philosophy. That Reagan does state broad precepts, albeit in general form, serves his political purposes in another fashion. His enunciation of a broadly conceived but unequivocal conservative commitment has enabled his administration to recruit a roughly like-minded core of committed supporters to staff White House and administrative branch positions, as well as to shape a bloc of local allies in Congress.

Basic agreement on broadly stated principles has helped promote overall cohesion in his forces and maintain solid relations with his main allies in the face of extremely sharp disagreements among his associates and allies as the hard budgeting and economic policy choices had to be made after 1982. When options are debated, the possibilities for reaching compromises are enhanced because all parties concerned have a good general idea of what kind of policy will or will not be acceptable to Reagan. Their task then is to convert his principles into legislation and executive orders, establishing what is politically feasible, but still plausibly susceptible to interpretation as Reagan orthodoxy.

Again comparisons with Carter are inescapable. Carter, his speechwriter James Fallows complained, knew an enormous amount about innumerable matters but had no general conceptions of the direction that public policy should take.[19] In Reagan's case the general direction is always identifiable, no small advantage for influencing the policy agenda.

Advisers have complained that it is difficult to bring Reagan's attention to bear on the specifics of converting the principle to the policy. Some of them have also told journalists that Reagan's ease at enunciating generalities, his broad commitment to them, and his resistance to the hard work of policy analysis foster a kind of duplicity among them that is the opposite of the "yea saying" George Reedy describes in *The Twilight of the Presidency*.[20] Rather than blindly adhering to Reagan's views, his advisers seem sometimes to develop new positions for him and privately apply to him the same kind of casuistry that is used publicly to keep him from being (in the cruel Reagan administration locution for vacillation) "Carterized." They seek to persuade him by providing him with the rationale that what in fact are policy changes really are reflections of his principles. Thus, for example, a tax increase may become a closed loophole in the tax code or a user's fee in his thinking as well as in his public rhetoric. The shortcomings of such advising are obvious. Relabeling programs in order to change them may blunt an already flawed presidential ability to assess policies, depending on whether the president is unaware of what he is doing or is merely participating in a face-saving political charade.

Political Style

If we provisionally draw on Lasswell and Barber to identify those presidents who in their leadership emphasize rhetoric, those who put self-conscious effort into their direct personal relations with aides and others, and those who devote substantial time to perusing documents and other sources of substantive information, we find that Reagan scores highest in his use of the first two elements of leadership. Compared with his predecessors, he is lowest in the third category.

On the matter of rhetorical facility, Anthony King[21] appropriately remarks on Reagan's career as an actor and on the other prepresidential activities that made oral communication second nature to him. Americans—politicians and scholars, as well as members of the general public—place a high premium on the chief executive's oratorical powers. The emphasis stems in part from the nation's egalitarian traditions that contribute to the widespread American distrust of parties and the other institutions that mediate between citizens and leaders in democracies.

It is taken for granted that the citizen should directly observe candidates and leaders and judge them by their words and actions. The premium on rhetoric has been much augmented in the era of the modern presidency. One of the characteristics of the expanded presidency that took shape during Franklin Roosevelt's incumbency was that citizens increasingly came to view the workings of the government in terms of the actions of the president. And his most conspicuous actions are his utterances. Not coincidentally, the evolution of the modern presidency roughly parallels the explosion of opportunity for direct presidential appeal to the public via radio, newsreels, television, and other forms of communication.[22]

Curiously, despite the weight scholars' and politicians' assessments of presidential effectiveness give to rhetorical skill, Reagan is only the third modern president (the others being Roosevelt and Kennedy) who could be said to have exhibited a professionally adept podium manner. Given the belief that rhetorical gifts are a major political resource, it is less surprising that a professional mass communicator made his way to the White House in 1981 than that such a figure did not become a serious presidential contender sooner. In 1982, immediately after Edward Kennedy announced he would not seek the 1984 Democratic nomination, one of the two foremost "obvious" Democratic candidates was Senator John Glenn. The crucial point made against Glenn by politicians and press commentators was not that his understanding of issues, political skills, or policy positions are deficient, but rather that he is an uninspiring public speaker.

Reagan, of course, has used his public speaking skill to the hilt. There have been accounts of the self-conscious attention he has given to perfecting his speaking technique—his fund of anecdotes and catchphrases, his insistence on rehearsing important presentations, his facility in using the teleprompter (quite unconvincingly turning blank pages on the podium as he makes eye contact through the television camera lens with his audience), and, above all, of his ability to convey a humble but eloquent image of sturdy middle-Americana. Although his mass media presentations are pitched to the public, their impact on other leaders is highly significant. As Neustadt suggests in *Presidential Power*, the Washington politicians who must be influenced if the chief executive is to achieve results are less impressed by their own response to the president than by their perception of their constituents' view of him. In the case of a rhetorically gifted president, however, they are likely to be persuaded that he has public support not only from standard sources such as polls and constituent mail, but also from observing how he makes his appeals to the public and intuiting that a presentation they feel *should* have been effective *must* have been.

But *is* Reagan as effective a communicator as has generally been assumed? Close analysis of the 1980 election results does not support Reagan's use of the inevitable claim of just-elected politicians—that their victory carries with it a mandate for their policy proposals. Although experienced politicians discount such presidential claims, members of Congress, bolstered by near uniformity in mass media accounts and by partially engineered constituency pressure, clearly were persuaded at the time of the 1981 Reagan tax and expenditure cuts that the president was riding high. One reason they were persuaded was that it was difficult to believe that such an effective communicator had not won the public over. It must be added that they also correctly perceived the general if short-lived national enthusiasm he aroused in the dramatic appearance before Congress that marked the end of his convalescence from the assassination attempt. He was confident and buoyant, radiating unpretentious self-assurance. From the good will he engendered, it was not hard to conclude that the legislators' constituents backed the specifics of his proposals and would be prepared to accept their consequences.

In retrospect, it is illuminating to look at Gallup support for Reagan from inauguration through the midterm elections. Table 1 shows public response to the question Gallup has regularly asked since the 1940s: "Generally speaking, how do you think President [name of incumbent] is doing his job?" During the key period in June and July 1981, when Reagan was the most visible performer in the brilliantly orchestrated legislative campaign that produced the tax and expenditure cuts, he had begun already to slip. His top Gallup rating of 68 percent approval in early May had followed his recovery from the attempted assassi-

TABLE 1 • APPROVAL/DISAPPROVAL OF HOW PRESIDENT
REAGAN IS DOING HIS JOB

| | | Gallup Poll Findings from Inauguration Day through 1982 Midterm Election | | |
		Approve	Disapprove	No Opinion
1981	Jan. 30–Feb. 2	51	13	36
	Feb. 13–16	55	18	27
	Mar. 13–16	60	24	16
	Apr. 3–6	67	18	15
	Apr. 10–13	67	19	14
	May 8–11	68	21	11
	June 5–8	59	28	13
	June 19–22	59	29	12
	June 26–29	58	30	12
	July 17–20	60	29	11
	July 24–27	56	30	14
	July 31–Aug. 3	60	28	12
	Aug. 14–17	60	29	11
	Sept. 18–21	52	37	11
	Oct. 2–5	56	35	9
	Oct. 30–Nov. 2	53	35	12
	Nov. 13–16	49	40	11
	Nov. 20–23	54	37	9
	Dec. 11–14	49	41	10
1982	Jan. 8–11	49	40	11
	Jan. 22–25	47	42	11
	Feb. 5–8	47	43	10
	Mar. 12–15	46	45	9
	Apr. 2–5	45	46	9
	Apr. 23–26	43	47	10
	Apr. 30–May 3	44	46	10
	May 14–17	45	44	11
	June 11–14	45	45	10
	June 25–28	44	46	10
	July 23–26	42	46	12
	July 30–Aug. 2	41	47	12
	Aug. 13–16	41	49	10
	Aug. 27–30	42	46	12
	Sept. 17–20	42	48	10
	Nov. 5–8	43	47	10

Source: Gallup Report No. 203 (August 1982), with later figures supplied by the Gallup organization.

nation and triumphant April 28 appearance before Congress. But by late spring his approval rate dropped to the upper 50 percent range. And just after he signed the tax and expenditure cuts in August, a steady erosion of support began. By the spring of 1982 more Gallup respondents disapproved than approved of his job performance. This continued through to the midterm election. As of early 1983 Reagan was running behind both John Glenn and Walter Mondale in "trial heat" polls of whom citizens would support in 1984. Reagan's approval rating at the end of his second year in office was lower than the second-year ratings of any of the presidents who initially reached the White House by election for the period during which Gallup has surveyed—lower, that is, than the ratings of Eisenhower, Kennedy, Nixon, and even Carter.

Reagan and his lieutenants found it far more necessary to bargain and form coalitions in 1982 policy-making than in 1981, just as the results of the midterm election pushed them even further toward the traditional mode of White House—congressional negotiation rather than White House dominance. Nevertheless, even in the midterm election, the Democrats took great pains to avoid personal attacks on the "popular" Reagan. The political wisdom was that attacks on such a well-meaning, personally liked president would backfire.

Midterm election Democratic political commercials stressed the links between Republican leadership in the 1980s and the Depression leadership of Herbert Hoover, barely recognizing Reagan's existence, in fear of encouraging a sympathy vote for him. In retrospect, we can see from the Gallup data on perceptions of Reagan (Table 2), that citizens were less impressed with Reagan than politicians thought they were.

He did score favorably (as Carter before him had, even in defeat) in such personal traits as likeability, loftiness of moral principles, and intelligence. But the single most common perception was that he "cares about the needs of upper-income or wealthy people" and the two least common were that he is "sympathetic to problems of the poor" and "sides with the average citizen." A mere 39 percent agreed that he "has well thought out, carefully considered solutions for national problems." In short, quite early in his presidency, Reagan was in trouble with the public, though he and his allies were able to limit opposition leaders' impulses to take advantage of his vulnerabilities for longer than might have been expected. The popular judgment of Reagan as "bright" un-

TABLE 2 · REAGAN PERSONALITY PROFILE—TREND

Question: "Here is a list of terms (respondents were handed a card)—shown as pairs of opposites—that have been used to describe Ronald Reagan. From each pair of opposites, would you select the term which you feel best describes Reagan? Just read off a number and letter from each pair."

	May 14–18, 1982	Sept. 12–15, 1980	June 27–30, 1980
Cares about the needs of upper-income or wealthy people	75	na	na
Bright, intelligent	70	73	65
A man of high moral principles	69	70	60

TABLE 2 *(concluded)*

	May 14–18, 1982	Sept. 12–15, 1980	June 27–30, 1980
A likeable person	65	na	61
Has strong leadership qualities	60	65	56
The kind of person who can get the job done	56	56	na
Would display good judgment in a crisis	54	55	58
A religious person	51	40	28
Has a clear understanding of the issues facing the country	46	55	na
Takes moderate, middle-of-the-road positions	43	48	46
Cares about the needs and problems of women	42	na	na
Cares about the needs and problems of middle-income people	41	na	na
Cares about the needs and problems of the elderly	41	na	na
Adaptable, willing to compromise on his positions	40	na	na
Has well thought out, carefully considered solutions for national problems	39	45	na
Cares about the needs and problems of people like yourself	39	na	na
Cares about the needs and problems of black people	37	na	na
Has modern, up-to-date solutions to national problems	36	51	na
Sides with the average citizen	28	43	40
Sympathetic to problems of the poor	24	41	35
A colorful, interesting personality	na	70	na
Decisive, sure of himself	na	69	60
Says what he believes even if unpopular	na	54	44
You know where he stands on issues	na	54	48
Has a well-defined program for the country ahead	na	53	41
Offers imaginative, innovative solutions to national problems	na	52	45
A man you can believe in	na	na	42
Puts country's interests ahead of politics	na	na	37
A person of exceptional abilities	na	na	35

na = not available

Source: Gallup Report No. 203 (August 1982).

doubtedly departed from the views many Washington professionals had begun to form precisely because they felt he lacked the initiative and capacity to do his homework. But even if citizens did not cast aspersions on Reagan's brain power, their sense that he lacked "carefully considered solutions" (Table 2) converged with Washington (and media) concerns about whether this president was seriously at work with his aides on devising coherent problem-solving strategies.

The emphasis on oratory in Reagan's political style adds to the lore of modern presidential leadership in several ways. One, specific to Reagan's performance, is the possibility that his oratory oversold political leaders on his popular appeal.[23] A second is that oratory without results is as dead as faith without works. But how then do we explain the success of another oratorical president—FDR—in an era when the economy was misperforming far more profoundly than now? Among the differences surely are low national expectations in the 1930s about the inevitability of expanding economic well-being; Roosevelt's efforts to provide direct assistance to victims of the Depression; and, most pertinent to Reagan's circumstances, Roosevelt's studious resistance to making precise predictions and specific promises about what results he would achieve when.

Reagan went much further than he had to in promising results. The promises were glowing. But as daily television news portrayals of soup kitchens and closed factories began to occupy public attention, the raised expectations were bound to engender disillusionment, exacerbated by the eloquence of the leader who raised them.

In general, as Ceaser, Thurow, Tulis, and Bessette suggest in "The Rise of the Rhetorical Presidency,"[24] there are costs to presidential reliance on address-

ing the public to get results. The greatest communicator among modern presidents, Roosevelt, was concerned in a way that Reagan evidently is not to avoid overexposing himself to the public and thus inducing indifference. He also was less disposed than Reagan has been to use his utterances as a direct means of placing pressure on Congress. Even so, the emphasis on rhetoric of both presidents early in their administrations contributed to congressional enactments that were passed without the customary degree of deliberation. Thus, on the one hand, without presidential rhetoric certain enactments would not have come to pass. But on the other, some legislation that was passed in the wake of presidential oratorical appeals later came under fire or, in the case of many New Deal measures, was repealed or invalidated on the ground that it had been ill-considered.

A final comment on rhetorical presidencies: even though an FDR may be sparing in making detailed promises, and even though the second of the three modern oratorical presidents, John F. Kennedy, addressed some of his oratory to the need for coolly rational policy-making, Henry Fairlie is persuasive in suggesting in *The Kennedy Promise*[25] that oratorical leadership fosters lack of realism in public political thinking and discourse. At a minimum, if the speech making is compelling, it encourages citizens to expect more of the same from other presidents and consequently adds to the personalization of the presidency and to preoccupation with the chief executive rather than with the full policy-making establishment. Further, even if they do not traffic in promises that cannot be kept, rhetorical presidents may be institutionally costly. In particular, they may weaken the presidency by being hard acts to follow. Truman suffered in part because he lacked FDR's histrionic gifts. Johnson had difficulties that arose from his failure to sway audiences as Kennedy had.

I have already touched on Reagan's political style in his direct personal relations with others and his use of documentary and other intelligence sources. Further observations are that he does not seek systematically staffed position papers with the contending views of his advisers carefully distinguished and defended, the practice Eisenhower used to prepare his associates for National Security Council meetings. His strength has been less in working with his aides to clarify policy than in rallying them around him and his policies. In general, with both Executive Office of the President staff and the cabinet he manages to delegate extensively but nevertheless keep administration members' actions in line with his political principles.

On the matter of the contention among foreign policy aides, if the Reagan presidency stretches to eight years, the first year—marked by feuding among the secretary of state, the secretary of defense, and (covertly) the assistant for national security—will seem no more than a ripple. After all, by 1982 the kind of harmony-without-groupthink that Reagan prizes had been achieved in foreign policy-making. William P. Clark had replaced Richard Allen as NSC assistant, providing the White House with a foreign policy aide who is a general policy broker and who reports directly to the president. And it would be difficult for any cabinet change to receive more favorable press than did the shift from Haig to Shultz in the State Department. Further, for whatever reasons, Shultz's accession was accompanied by an end to the Pentagon disagreements with the State Department. As Destler remarks, Reagan has been far more successful than a number of his predecessors in reshaping his for-

eign policy team when its initial members were working together inadequately.

In choosing his three top White House advisers—Meese, Deaver, and Baker—Reagan exhibited an ability unusual in presidents. Influential White House aides often get the reputation of being "yes men," or at any rate of being extensions of the president's own proclivities rather than complementary actors who compensate for the president's weaknesses and augment his strengths. H. R. Haldeman was as disposed as Richard Nixon to think the White House was surrounded by enemies. Harry Hopkins shared Roosevelt's love of manipulative leadership. However, in appointing his triumvirate, Reagan seems to have been sensitive to ways in which he, as communicator, overarching strategist, and proponent of broad doctrine, needs to be supplemented. He requires help in organizing his staff to transform political philosophy into policy and needs a tactician to establish what is or is not politically feasible. In addition, he clearly values a friend and confidant who empathizes with him and has an intuitive understanding of what demands on his time and requests for his approval will be personally congenial to him. Meese, Baker, and Deaver respectively have carried out these three roles.

In general, Reagan appears to have a good sense of how to judge personnel and motivate his associates. Although we have no account of his rationale in choosing this constellation of aides, it is difficult to believe that they came together without Reagan's conscious choice or stayed together without his continuing encouragement. He shows every sign of having a genuine gift for casting major supporting actors in positions that will back up the leading man.

As in his change of foreign policy teams, Reagan's White House staffing practices contribute to the lore of effective presidential leadership. In insisting neither on sycophants nor on aides who duplicate his own style, Reagan teaches future presidents that it is feasible and even desirable to shape their official family to their distinctive needs, whether or not in doing so they organize the White House in a manner that defies orthodox organization theory.

NOTES

1. James David Barber, *The Presidential Character: Predicting Performance in the White House* (Englewood Cliffs, N.J.: Prentice-Hall, 1972).

2. James David Barber, *The Lawmakers* (New Haven: Yale University Press, 1965).

3. My remarks on Reagan are inevitably speculative. They rely heavily on Lou Cannon's excellent *Reagan* (New York: G. P. Putnam's Sons, 1982), but also draw on extensive "Reaganology" in the mass media.

4. James David Barber, "Worrying about Reagan," *New York Times*, September 8, 1980, p. 19.

5. David Riesman, *The Lonely Crowd: A Study of the Changing American Character* (New Haven, Conn.: Yale University Press, 1950).

6. Herman A. Witkin and Donald R. Goodenough, *Cognitive Styles: Essence and Origins* (New York: Inter-Universities Press, 1981).

7. Moreover, the data on Eisenhower and his leadership that became available after Barber wrote clearly make it inappropriate to treat him as passive. Greenstein, *The Hidden-Hand Presidency*, ch. 2.

8. The seminal Lasswell book on personality and politics is Harold D. Lasswell, *Psychopathology and Politics* (Chicago: University of Chicago Press, 1930; reprinted with "afterthoughts" and a new preface by the same publisher in 1979). The following work reprints later key Lasswell writings on the topic and has a valuable introduction and a bibliography of Lasswell's writings: Dwaine Marvick, *Harold D. Lasswell on Political Sociology* (Chicago: University of Chicago Press, 1977).

9. Dorothy Ross, "Review Essay: Woodrow Wilson and the Case for Psychohistory," *Journal of American History* 64 (December 1982):659–68.

10. Allen Schick, "How the Budget Was Won and Lost," in Norman J. Ornstein, ed., *President and Congress: Assessing Reagan's First Year* (Washington, D.C.: American Enterprise Institute, 1982), pp. 14–43.

11. See, for example, James MacGregor Burns, *Roosevelt: The Lion and the Fox* (New York: Harcourt, Brace & Co., 1956).

12. Pendleton Herring, *Presidential Leadership: The Political Relations of Congress and the Chief Executive* (New York: Rinehart, 1940; reprint ed., Westport, Conn.: Greenwood Press, 1972).

13. Again, the qualification is necessary that I am writing from presently available information and echoing themes in current journalism. Eisenhower, who often seemed innocent of fundamental current information in his press conferences, can now be seen (on the basis of transcripts of pre-press conference briefings) to have deliberately feigned ignorance on controversial matters. His professions of ignorance, however, were not "bloopers," like Reagan's confusion about the circumstances that led to the creation of North and South Vietnam and, in general, his press conference texts, although full of fractured syntax, reveal a better informed, more clear-headed president than do Reagan's. See Greenstein, *The Hidden-Hand Presidency*.

14. Cannon, *Reagan*, p. 87.

15. Berman, *Planning a Tragedy*, p. 119.

16. For a typical example of such a report, see "How Reagan Decides: Intense Beliefs, Eternal Optimism and Precious Little Adaptability," *Time*, December 13, 1982, pp. 12–17.

17. Steve Weisman, "Reaganomics and the President's Men," *New York Times Magazine*, October 24, 1982, p. 26.

18. Eric Hoffer, *The True Believer: Thoughts on the Nature of Mass Movements* (New York: Harper, 1951), first ed.

19. James Fallows, "The Passionless Presidency: Part I," and "The Passionless Presidency: Part II," *Atlantic Monthly*, May and June 1979.

20. George Reedy, *The Twilight of the Presidency* (New York: World Publishing Co., 1970).

21. Anthony King, "How Not to Select Presidential Candidates: A View from Europe," in Austin Ranney, ed., *The American Elections of 1980* (Washington, D.C.: American Enterprise Institute, 1981), pp. 303–28.

22. See, for example, the essays and sources cited in Doris A. Graber, *The President and the Public* (Philadelphia: Institute for the Study of Human Issues, 1982).

23. Since an oratorical president may get results less by "going over the heads" of other leaders than by conveying the impression that he is succeeding in doing so, it would be instructive to have evidence about citizens' responses to Reagan the communicator that were more subtle than those allowed by standard public opinion polls. I have in mind such procedures as the market research discussion group technique of arranging "focus group" conversations between people who have just seen by live television or videotape a presidential communication. The essence of the procedure is to encourage "natural" discussion of *both* the president's specific television presentation and his leadership in general. My hypothesis is that in spite of Reagan's extensive reliance on polls to gauge the effects of his leadership, group interviews would show rather little public attention to Reagan's skill and persuasiveness as a communicator. Rather, the packaging of the message, especially in a controversial area such as economic policy, probably would be beside the point. Discussion would quickly move to his stewardship, especially of the economy, not the skill with which he justifies his policies or his attractive human qualities.

24. James Ceaser, Glen E. Thurow, Jeffrey Tullis, and Joseph M. Bessette, "The Rise of the Rhetorical Presidency," *Presidential Studies Quarterly*, Spring 1981, pp. 158–71.

25. Henry Fairlie, *The Kennedy Promise: The Politics of Expectation* (Garden City, N.Y.: Doubleday, 1973).

CHAPTER XIII

Perspectives on Presidential Power

The increasing complexities of our national and international political life have placed greater responsibilities and burdens upon the presidency for leadership far beyond anything anticipated by the Founders. Theirs was a much simpler time and place: a homogeneous population (for all intents and purposes)[1] of about four million, an agrarian economy, an Atlantic civilization living mostly along the seaboard of the eastern United States, and a population protected from the warring powers of Europe by thousands of miles of open sea. Moreover, there were no aircraft, no nuclear weapons, no space program, no social security program, no balance-of-trade problems, and no massive budget deficits. All of this has changed. And, in the process, the presidency has become the intense focus of political leadership, the central figure in American political life.

Early on in this book, we asked: In what ways have presidents themselves viewed their power role in office? Our responses pointed to the prerogative, stewardship, and literalist theories of presidential power articulated by each of three well-known presidents and subscribed to by many others. Those presidents who acted in terms of prerogative theory simply felt that there were some occasions when they might have to act, and did act, to preserve the nation, even though their actions violated the Constitution or congressional statutes. Those who allied themselves with the stewardship theory averred that they were free to do all they could for the people, so long as no provision in the Constitution precluded their actions. The literalists argued, essentially, that they were bound by the Constitution to take no actions unless authority for those actions could be traced to an enabling phrase in the Constitution.

In this modern era, where the nuances of policymaking and the exercise of power are far more complex and tentative, we now ask: What is it that shapes the probabilities of presidential power? For the answers we turn to several students of presidential power, the first of whom is Edward Corwin.

Corwin's *The President: Office and Powers,* first published in 1940, was hailed as the definitive explanation of presidential power.[2] Utilizing a public-law approach to assess the historical development of the presidency in its various roles—administrative chief, chief executive, foreign relations head, commander in chief, and legislative leader—Corwin located the power of the presidency in the Constitution.[3]

The problem, as Corwin saw it, was that the presidents had, under the double stimulation of economic and war crises, as well as an enlarged conception of the role of government in America, grown to such an extent that the civil liberties (including property rights) of American citizens were threatened.[4] Corwin inveighed against presidential excesses and even argued for a single term for the president in the hope of encouraging the president to adhere to the Constitution of the Founders.[5]

Unlike Corwin, Richard Neustadt was worried not so much by the possibility that the president would exceed the powers of government, but about the fragility and elusiveness of presidential power. Neustadt's *Presidential Power*, published in 1960 on the eve of John F. Kennedy taking office, was greeted as a pioneering addition to our understanding of presidential power. The exercise of power, Neustadt argued, is more than office holding, role enactment, or hat wearing; it is the power to persuade.[6] Neustadt went on to say that a president as mere office holder is so weak that he or she must persuade significant numbers of other political actors, especially members of Congress, that what the White House wants of them matches their appraisal of what their own responsibilities require them to do in their own interest and on their own authority.

The limits of command, Neustadt avers, suggest the structure of our government and the burden of the presidency. Thus, the essence of a president's power resides not in his capacity to issue directives, but rather in this ability to persuade. Neustadt concludes that a president's capacity to persuade will rest mightily on his bargaining skills, on his professional reputation, and on his popular prestige. Neustadt's essay, "The Power to Persuade," is reprinted here.

Neustadt's critics are numerous. One body of literature argues that Neustadt is essentially correct, but asks: Shouldn't he have considered at greater length the question: Persuasion for what purpose? The representative research here is the work of Peter Sperlich,[7] John Hart,[8] Thomas Cronin,[9] George Edwards,[10] and James MacGregor Burns.[11]

A second body of post-Neustadt research asserts that presidential power as persuasion is really off the mark, that persuasion is both insufficient and overemphasized, and that the realities of presidential power lie in the prerogatives the president can wrest from the Constitution. Articulated mainly by Richard Pious, this view, albeit more politically sensitive than Corwin's work, is reminiscent of the earlier Corwin studies, which adopted a constitutional and public-law approach to presidential power.[12]

A third body of literature argues that neither the persuasion-as-power nor the prerogatives-of-office-as-power models are alone sufficient for an understanding of presidential power. Rather, the two models are viewed as opposite sides of the same (power) coin. Presidential power thus finds its locus in both persuasion and prerogative. This view is represented mainly by Raymond Tatalovich and Byron Daynes. They write, "if Neustadt underestimated the impact of authority, Corwin ignored many behavioral conditions which affect power."[13]

Tatalovich and Daynes have developed a theoretical framework that analyzes the empirical foundations of presidential power. Included in this framework are five variables: authority, decisionmaking, public inputs, expertise, and crisis. These variables are seen as paramount in determining the amount of political resources available to a president in each of his five major roles: commander in chief, cheif diplomat, chief executive, legislative leader, and opinion/party leader. Tatalovich and Daynes show how each variable operates in the five presidential roles. They conclude that presidential power depends upon political resources and that some roles contain more resources than others. Their essay, "Toward a Framework to Explain Presidential Power," which empirically supports the contention that persuasion and prerogative represent two important faces of presidential power, is reprinted here.[14]

NOTES

1. The black slave population did not yet loom large in the calculus of political decisionmaking, albeit the Founders agonized over the issue and the Constitution banned the importation of slaves after 1808; see Article I, Section 9.

2. Edward S. Corwin, *The President: Office and Powers* (New York: New York University Press, 1940). The fourth revised edition of the book was published by the same press in 1957. The book went into a fifth edition in 1968.

3. For representative examples of other studies that located the power of the president in the Constitution, see Clinton Rossiter, *The American Presidency* (New York: Harcourt Brace Jovanovich, 1956); and Herman Finer, *The Presidency: Crisis and Regeneration* (Chicago: University of Chicago Press, 1960).

4. See Corwin, *President*, 4th rev. ed., pp. 29–30 and 312.

5. See Douglas T. Hoekstra, "Presidential Power and Presidential Purpose," *Review of Politics* 47, no. 4 (October 1985), p. 577.

6. Richard E. Neustadt, *Presidential Power: The Politics of Leadership* (New York: John Wiley & Sons, 1960), passim.

7. Peter W. Sperlich, "Bargaining and Overload: An Essay on Presidential Power," in *Perspectives on the Presidency*, ed. Aaron Wildavsky (Boston: Little, Brown, 1975), pp. 406–30.

8. John Hart, "Presidential Power Revisited," *Political Studies* 25 (March 1977), pp. 48–51.

9. Thomas E. Cronin, "Presidential Power Revised and Reappraised," *Western Political Quarterly* 32 (December 1979), pp. 381–95. See also Cronin, *The State of the Presidency*, 2nd ed. (Boston: Little, Brown, 1980), pp. 119–36.

10. George C. Edwards III, *Presidential Influence in Congress* (San Francisco: W. H. Freeman, 1980), passim, but see especially pp. 131–35 and 205.

11. See James MacGregor Burns, *Leadership* (New York: Harper & Row, 1978), especially pp. 388–89.

12. Richard M. Pious, *The American Presidency* (New York: Basic Books, 1979).

13. Raymond Tatalovich and Byron W. Daynes, "Toward a Paradigm to Explain Presidential Power," *Presidential Studies Quarterly* 9, no. 4 (Fall 1979), p. 429.

14. For an earlier assessment of the contributions of Tatalovich and Daynes to the question of presidential power, see Harry A. Bailey, Jr., "Neustadt's Thesis Revisited: Toward the Two Faces of Presidential Power," *Presidential Studies Quarterly* 11, no. 3 (Summer 1981), pp. 351–57.

31
The Power to Persuade
Richard E. Neustadt

The limits on command suggest the structure of our government. The constitutional convention of 1787 is supposed to have created a government of "separated powers." It did nothing of the sort. Rather, it created a government of separated institutions *sharing* powers.[1] "I am part of the legislative process," Eisenhower often said in 1959 as a reminder of his veto.[2] Congress, the dispenser of authority and funds, is no less part of the administrative process. Federalism adds another set of separated institutions. The Bill of Rights adds others. Many public purposes can only be achieved by voluntary acts of private institutions; the press, for one, in Douglass Cater's phrase, is a "fourth branch of government."[3] And with the coming of alliances abroad, the separate institutions of a London, or a Bonn, share in the making of American public policy.

What the Constitution separates our political parties do not combine. The parties are themselves composed of separated organizations sharing public authority. The authority consists of nominating powers. Our national parties are confederations of state and local party institutions, with a headquarters that represents the White House, more or less, if the party has a President in office. These confederacies manage presidential nominations. All other public offices depend upon electorates confined within the states.[4] All other nominations are controlled within the states. The President and congressmen who bear one party's label are divided by dependence upon different sets of voters. The differences are sharpest at the stage of nomination. The White House has too small a share in nominating congressmen, and Congress has too little weight in nominating Presidents for party to erase their constitutional separation. Party links are stronger than is frequently supposed, but nominating processes assure the separation.[5]

The separateness of institutions and the sharing of authority prescribe the terms on which a President persuades. When one man shares authority with another, but does not gain or lose his job upon the other's whim, his willingness to act upon the urging of the other turns on whether he conceives the action right for him. The essence of a President's persuasive task is to convince such men that what the White House wants of them is what they ought to do for their sake and on their authority.

Source: Material excerpted and reprinted with permission of Macmillan Publishing Company from *Presidential Power: The Politics of Leadership from FDR to Carter* by Richard E. Neustadt. New York: Macmillan Publishing Company, 1980.

Persuasive power, thus defined, amounts to more thqan charm or reasoned argument. These have their uses for a President, but these are not the whole of his resources. For the men he would induce to do what he wants done on their own responsibility will need or fear some acts by him on his responsibility. If they share his authority, he has some share in theirs. Presidential "powers" may be inconclusive when a President commands, but always remain relevant as he persuades. The status and authority inherent in his office reinforce his logic and his charm.

Status adds something to persuasiveness; authority adds still more. When Truman urged wage changes on his Secretary of Commerce while the latter was administering the steel mills, he and Secretary Sawyer were not just two men reasoning with one another. Had they been so, Sawyer probably would never have agreed to act. Truman's status gave him special claims to Sawyer's loyalty, or at least attention. In Walter Bagehot's charming phrase "No man can *argue* on his knees." Although there is no kneeling in this country, few men—and exceedingly few Cabinet officers—are immune to the impulse to say "yes" to the President of the United States. It grows harder to say "no" when they are seated in his oval office at the White House, or in his study on the second floor, where almost tangibly he partakes of the aura of his physical surroundings. In Sawyer's case, moreover, the President possessed formal authority to intervene in many matters of concern to the Secretary of Commerce. These matters ranged from jurisdictional disputes among the defense agencies to legislation pending before Congress and, ultimately, to the tenure of the Secretary, himself. There is nothing in the record to suggest that Truman voiced specific threats when they negotiated over wage

increases. But given his *formal* powers and their relevance to Sawyer's other interests, it is safe to assume that Truman's very advocacy of wage action conveyed an implicit threat.

A President's authority and status give him great advantages in dealing with the men he would persuade. Each "power" is a vantage point for him in the degree that other men have use for his authority. From the veto to appointments, from publicity to budgeting, and so down a long list, the White House now controls the most encompassing array of vantage points in the American political system. With hardly an exception, the men who share in governing this country are aware that at some time, in some degree, the doing of *their* jobs, the furthering of *their* ambitions, may depend upon the President of the United States. Their need for presidential action, or their fear of it, is bound to be recurrent if not actually continuous. Their need or fear is his advantage.

A President's advantages are greater than mere listing of his "powers" might suggest. The men with whom he deals must deal with him until the last day of his term. Because they have continuing relationships with him, his future, while it lasts, supports his present influence. Even though there is no need or fear of him today, what he could do tomorrow may supply today's advantage. Continuing relationships may convert any "power," any aspect of his status, into vantage points in almost any case. When he induces other men to do what he wants done, a President can trade on their dependence now *and* later.

The President's advantages are checked by the advantages of others. Continuing relationships will pull in both directions. These are relationships of mutual dependence. A President depends upon the men he would persuade; he has to reckon with his need or fear of them. They too will possess status, or authority, or both, else they would be of little use to him. Their vantage points confront his own; their power tempers his.

Persuasion is a two-way street. Sawyer, it will be recalled, did not respond at once to Truman's plan for wage increases at the steel mills. On the contrary, the Secretary hesitated and delayed and only acquiesced when he was satisfied that publicly he would not bear the onus of decision. Sawyer had some points of vantage all his own from which to resist presidential pressure. If he had to reckon with coercive implications in the President's "situations of strength," so had Truman to be mindful of the implications underlying Sawyer's place as a department head, as steel administrator, and as a Cabinet spokesman for business. Loyalty is reciprocal. Having taken on a dirty job in the steel crisis, Sawyer had strong claims to loyal support. Besides, he had authority to do some things that the White House could ill afford. Emulating Wilson, he might have resigned in a huff (the removal power also works two ways). Or emulating Ellis Arnall, he might have declined to sign necessary orders. Or, he might have let it be known publicly that he deplored what he was told to do and protested its doing. By following any of these courses Sawyer almost surely would have strengthened the position of management, weakened the position of the White House, and embittered the union. But the whole purpose of a wage increase was to enhance White House persuasiveness in urging settlement upon union and companies alike. Although Sawyer's status and authority did not give him the power to prevent an increase outright, they gave him capability to undermine its purpose. If his authority over wage rates had been vested by a statute, not by revocable presidential or-

der, his power of prevention might have been complete. So Harold Ickes demonstrated in the famous case of helium sales to Germany before the Second World War.[6]

The power to persuade is the power to bargain. Status and authority yield bargaining advantages. But in a government of "separated institutions sharing powers," they yield them to all sides. With the array of vantage points at his disposal, a President may be far more persuasive than his logic or his charm could make him. But outcomes are not guaranteed by his advantages. There remain the counter pressures those whom he would influence can bring to bear on him from vantage points at their disposal. Command has limited utility; persuasion becomes give-and-take. It is well that the White House holds the vantage points it does. In such a business any President may need them all—and more.

II

This view of power as akin to bargaining is one we commonly accept in the sphere of congressional relations. Every textbook states and every legislative session demonstrates that save in times like the extraordinary Hundred Days of 1933— times virtually ruled out by definition at mid-century—a President will often be unable to obtain congressional action on his terms or even to halt action he opposes. The reverse is equally accepted: Congress often is frustrated by the President. Their formal powers are so intertwined that neither will accomplish very much, for very long, without the acquiescence of the other. By the same token, though, what one demands the other can resist. The stage is set for that great game, much like collective bargaining, in which each seeks to profit from the other's needs and fears. It is a game played catch-as-catch-can, case by case. And everybody knows the game, observers and participants alike.

The concept of real power as a give-and-take is equally familiar when applied to presidential influence outside the formal structure of the Federal government. The Little Rock affair may be extreme, but Eisenhower's dealings with the Governor—and with the citizens—become a case in point. Less extreme but no less pertinent is the steel seizure case with respect to union leaders, and to workers, and to company executives as well. When he deals with such people a President draws bargaining advantage from his status or authority. By virtue of their public places or their private rights they have some capability to reply in kind.

In spheres of party politics the same thing follows, necessarily, from the confederal nature of our party organizations. Even in the case of national nominations a President's advantages are checked by those of others. In 1944 it is by no means clear that Roosevelt got his first choice as his running mate. In 1948 Truman, then the President, faced serious revolts against his nomination. In 1952 his intervention from the White House helped assure the choice of Adlai Stevenson, but it is far from clear that Truman could have done as much for any other candidate acceptable to him.[7] In 1956 when Eisenhower was President, the record leaves obscure just who backed Harold Stassen's efforts to block Richard Nixon's renomination as Vice-President. But evidently everything did not go quite as Eisenhower wanted, whatever his intentions may have been.[8] The outcomes in these instances bear all the marks of limits on command and of power checked by power that characterize congressional relations. Both in and out of politics these checks and limits seem to be quite widely understood.

Influence becomes still more a matter of give-and-take when Presidents attempt to deal with allied governments. A classic illustration is the long unhappy wrangle over Suez policy in 1956. In dealing with the British and the French before their military intervention, Eisenhower had his share of bargaining advantages but no effective power of command. His allies had their share of counter pressures, and they finally tried the most extreme of all: action despite him. His pressure then was instrumental in reversing them. But had the British government been on safe ground *at home*, Eisenhower's wishes might have made as little difference after intervention as before. Behind the decorum of diplomacy—which was not very decorous in the Suez affair—relationships among allies are not unlike relationships among state delegations at a national convention. Power is persuasion and persuasion becomes bargaining. The concept is familiar to everyone who watches foreign policy.

In only one sphere is the concept unfamiliar: the sphere of executive relations. Perhaps because of civics textbooks and teaching in our schools, Americans instinctively resist the view that power in this sphere resembles power in all others. Even Washington reporters, White House aides, and congressmen are not immune to the illusion that administrative agencies comprise a single structure, "the" Executive Branch, where presidential word is law, or ought to be. Yet when a President seeks something from executive officials his persuasiveness is subject to the same sorts of limitations as in the case of congressmen, or governors, or national committeemen, or private citizens, or foreign governments. There are no generic differences, no differences in kind and only sometimes in degree. The incidents preceding the dismissal of Mac-

Arthur and the incidents surrounding seizure of the steel mills make it plain that here as elsewhere influence derives from bargaining advantages; power is a give-and-take.

Like our governmental structure as a whole, the executive establishment consists of separated institutions sharing powers. The President heads one of these; Cabinet officers, agency administrators, and military commanders head others. Below the departmental level, virtually independent bureau chiefs head many more. Under mid-century conditions, Federal operations spill across dividing lines on organization charts; almost every policy entangles many agencies; almost every program calls for interagency collaboration. Everything somehow involves the President. But operating agencies owe their existence least of all to one another—and only in some part to him. Each has a separate statutory base; each has its statutes to administer; each deals with a different set of subcommittees at the Capitol. Each has its own peculiar set of clients, friends, and enemies outside the formal government. Each has a different set of specialized careerists inside its own bailiwick. Our Constitution gives the President the "take-care" clause and the appointive power. Our statutes give him central budgeting and a degree of personnel control. All agency administrators are responsible to him. But they *also* are responsible to Congress, to their clients, to their staffs, and to themselves. In short, they have five masters. Only after all of those do they owe any loyalty to each other.

"The members of the Cabinet," Charles G. Dawes used to remark, "are a President's natural enemies." Dawes had been Harding's Budget Director, Coolidge's Vice-President, and Hoover's Ambassador to London; he also had been General Pershing's chief assistant for supply in the First World War. The words are highly colored, but Dawes knew whereof he spoke. The men who have to serve so many masters cannot help but be somewhat the "enemy" of any one of them. By the same token, any master wanting service is in some degree the "enemy" of such a servant. A President is likely to want loyal support but not to relish trouble on his doorstep. Yet the more his Cabinet members cleave to him, the more they may need help from him in fending off the wrath of rival masters. Help, though, is synonymous with trouble. Many a Cabinet officer, with loyalty ill-rewarded by his lights and help withheld, has come to view the White House as innately hostile to department heads. Dawes's dictum can be turned around.

A senior presidential aide remarked to me in Eisenhower's time: "If some of these Cabinet members would just take time out to stop and ask themselves, 'What would I want if I were President?', they wouldn't give him all the trouble he's been having." But even if they asked themselves the question, such officials often could not act upon the answer. Their personal attachment to the President is all too often overwhelmed by duty to their other masters.

Executive officials are not equally advantaged in their dealings with a President. Nor are the same officials equally advantaged all the time. Not every officeholder can resist like a MacArthur, or like Arnall, Sawyer, Wilson, in a rough descending order of effective counter pressure. The vantage points conferred upon officials by their own authority and status vary enormously. The variance is heightened by particulars of time and circumstance. In mid-October 1950, Truman, at a press conference, remarked of the man he had considered firing in August and would fire the next April for intolerable insubordination:

Let me tell you something that will be good for your souls. It's a pity that you . . . can't understand the ideas of two intellectually honest men when they meet. General MacArthur . . . is a member of the Government of the United States. He is loyal to that Government. He is loyal to the President. He is loyal to the President in his foreign policy. . . . There is no disagreement between General MacArthur and myself. . . .[9]

MacArthur's status in and out of government was never higher than when Truman spoke those words. The words, once spoken, added to the General's credibility thereafter when he sought to use the press in his campaign against the President. And what had happened between August and October? Near-victory had happened, together with that premature conference on *post*-war plans, the meeting at Wake Island.

If the bargaining advantages of a MacArthur fluctuate with changing circumstances, this is bound to be so with subordinates who have at their disposal fewer "powers," lesser status, to fall back on. And when officials have no "powers" in their own right, or depend upon the President for status, their counter pressure may be limited indeed. White House aides, who fit both categories, are among the most responsive men of all, and for good reason. As a Director of the Budget once remarked to me, "Thank God I'm here and not across the street. If the President doesn't call me, I've got plenty I can do right here and plenty coming up to me, by rights, to justify my calling him. But those poor fellows over there, if the boss doesn't call them, doesn't ask them to do something, what *can* they do but sit?" Authority and status so conditional are frail reliances in resisting a President's own wants. Within the White House precincts, lifted eyebrows may suffice to set an aide in motion; command, coercion,

even charm aside. But even in the White House a President does not monopolize effective power. Even there persuasion is akin to bargaining. A former Roosevelt aide once wrote of Cabinet officers:

Half of a President's suggestions, which theoretically carry the weight of orders, can be safely forgotten by a Cabinet member. And if the president asks about a suggestion a second time, he can be told that it is being investigated. If he asks a third time, a wise Cabinet officer will give him at least part of what he suggests. But only occasionally, except about the most important matters, do Presidents ever get around to asking three times.[10]

The rule applies to staff as well as to the Cabinet, and certainly has been applied *by* staff in Truman's time and Eisenhower's.

Some aides will have more vantage points than a selective memory. Sherman Adams, for example, as The Assistant to the President under Eisenhower, scarcely deserved the appelation "White House aide" in the meaning of the term before his time or as applied to other members of the Eisenhower entourage. Although Adams was by no means "chief of staff" in any sense so sweeping—or so simple—as press commentaries often took for granted, he apparently became no more dependent on the President than Eisenhower on him. "I need him," said the President when Adams turned out to have been remarkably imprudent in the Goldfine case, and delegated to him even the decision on his own departure.[11] This instance is extreme, but the tendency it illustrates is common enough. Any aide who demonstrates to others that he has the President's consistent confidence and a consistent part in presidential business will acquire so much business on his own account that he becomes in some sense independent of his chief. Nothing in the Constitution keeps a well-placed aide from converting status into power of his own, usable in some degree even against the President—an outcome not unknown in Truman's regime or, by all accounts, in Eisenhower's.

The more an officeholder's status and his "powers" stem from sources independent of the President, the stronger will be his potential pressure on the President. Department heads in general have more bargaining power than do most members of the White House staff; but bureau chiefs may have still more, and specialists at upper levels of established career services may have almost unlimited reserves of the enormous power which consists of sitting still. As Franklin Roosevelt once remarked:

> The Treasury is so large and far-flung and ingrained in its practices that I find it almost impossible to get the action and results I want—even with Henry [Morgenthau] there. But the Treasury is not to be compared with the State Department. You should go through the experience of trying to get any changes in the thinking, policy, and action of the career diplomats and then you'd know what a real problem was. But the Treasury and the State Department put together are nothing compared with the Na-a-vy. The admirals are really something to cope with—and I should know. To change anything in the Na-a-vy is like punching a feather bed. You punch it with your right and you punch it with your left until you are finally exhausted, and then you find the damn bed just as it was before you started punching.[12]

In the right circumstances, of course, a President can have his way with any of these people. But one need only note the favorable factors giving those three orders their self-executing quality to recognize that as between a President and his "subordinates," no less than others on whom he depends, real power is reciprocal and varies markedly with organization, subject matter, personality,

and situation. The mere fact that persuasion is directed at executive officials signifies no necessary easing of his way. Any new congressman of the Administration's party, especially if narrowly elected, may turn out more amenable (though less useful) to the President than any seasoned bureau chief "downtown." *The probabilities of power do not derive from the literary theory of the Constitution.*

III

There is a widely held belief in the United States that were it not for folly or for knavery, a reasonable President would need no power other than the logic of his argument. No less a personage than Eisenhower has subscribed to that belief in many a campaign speech and press-conference remark. But faulty reasoning and bad intentions do not cause all quarrels with Presidents. The best of reasoning and of intent cannot compose them all. For in the first place, what the President wants will rarely seem a trifle to the men he wants it from. And in the second place, they will be bound to judge it by the standard of their own responsibilities, not his. However logical his argument according to his lights, their judgment may not bring them to his view.

The men who share in governing this country frequently appear to act as though they were in business for themselves. So, in a real though not entire sense, they are and have to be. When Truman and MacArthur fell to quarreling, for example, the stakes were no less than the substance of American foreign policy, the risks of greater war or military stalemate, the prerogatives of Presidents and field commanders, the pride of a pro-consul and his place in history. Intertwined, inevitably, were other stakes, as well: political stakes for men and factions of both parties; power stakes for interest groups with which they were or wished to be affiliated. And every stake was raised by the apparent discontent in the American public mood. There is no reason to suppose that in such circumstances men of large but differing responsibilities will see all things through the same glasses. On the contrary, it is to be expected that their views of what ought to be done and what they then should do will vary with the differing perspectives their particular responsibilities evoke. Since their duties are not vested in a "team" or a "collegium" but in themselves, as individuals, one must expect that they will see things *for* themselves. Moreover, when they are responsible to many masters and when an event or policy turns loyalty against loyalty—a day by day occurrence in the nature of the case—one must assume that those who have the duties to perform will choose the terms of reconciliation. This is the essence of their personal responsibility. When their own duties pull in opposite directions, who else but they can choose what they will do?

When Truman dismissed MacArthur, the latter lost three posts: the American command in the Far East, the Allied command for the occupation of Japan, and the United Nations command in Korea. He also lost his status as the senior officer on active duty in the United States armed forces. So long as he held those positions and that status, though, he had a duty to his troops, to his profession, to himself (the last is hard for any man to disentangle from the rest). As a public figure and a focus for men's hopes he had a duty to constituents at home, and in Korea and Japan. He owed a duty also to those other constituents, the UN governments contributing to his field forces. As a patriot he had a duty to his country. As an accountable official

and an expert guide he stood at the call of Congress. As a military officer he had, besides, a duty to the President, his constitutional commander. Some of these duties may have manifested themselves in terms more tangible or more direct than others. But it would be nonsense to argue that the last *negated* all the rest, however much it might be claimed to override them. And it makes no more sense to think that anybody but MacArthur was effectively empowered to decide how he, himself, would reconcile the competing demands his duties made upon him.

Similar observations could be made about the rest of the executive officials. Price Director Arnall, it will be recalled, refused in advance to sign a major price increase for steel if Mobilization Director Wilson or the White House should concede one before management had settled with the union. When Arnall did this, he took his stand, in substance, on his oath of office. He would do what he had sworn to do in *his* best judgment, so long as he was there to do it. This posture may have been assumed for purposes of bargaining and might have been abandoned had his challenge been accepted by the President. But no one could be sure and no one, certainly, could question Arnall's right to make the judgment for himself. As head of an agency and as a politician, with a program to defend and a future to advance, *he* had to decide what he had to do on matters that, from his perspective, were exceedingly important. Neither in policy nor in personal terms, nor in terms of agency survival, were the issues of a sort to be considered secondary by an Arnall, however much they might have seemed so to a Wilson (or a Truman). Nor were the merits likely to appear the same to a price stabilizer and to men with broader duties. Reasonable men, it is so often said, *ought* to be able to agree on the requirements of given situations. But when the outlook varies with the placement of each man, and the response required in his place is for each to decide, their reasoning may lead to disagreement quite as well—and quite as reasonably. Vanity, or vice, may weaken reason, to be sure, but it is idle to assign these as the cause of Arnall's threat or MacArthur's defiance. Secretary Sawyer's hesitations, cited earlier, are in the same category. One need not denigrate such men to explain their conduct. For the responsibilities they felt, the "facts" they saw, simply were not the same as those of their superiors; yet they, not the superiors, had to decide what they would do.

Outside the Executive Branch the situation is the same, except that loyalty to the President may often matter *less*. There is no need to spell out the comparison with Governors of Arkansas, steel company executives, trade union leaders, and the like. And when one comes to congressmen who can do nothing for themselves (or their constituents) save as they are elected, term by term, in districts and through party structures *differing* from those on which a President depends, the case is very clear. An able Eisenhower aide with long congressional experience remarked to me in 1958: "The people on the Hill don't do what they might *like* to do, they do what they think they *have* to do in their own interest as *they* see it." This states the case precisely.

The essence of a President's persuasive task with congressmen and everybody else, *is to induce them to believe that what he wants of them is what their own appraisal of their own responsibilities requires them to do in their interest, not his.* Because men may differ in their views on public policy, because differences in outlook stem from differences in duty—duty to one's office, one's constituents, oneself—that task is bound to be more like collective bargaining than like a reasoned argument among philosopher kings Overtly or implicitly, hard bargaining has characterized all illustrations offered up to now. This is the reason why: persuasion deals in the coin of self-interest with men who have some freedom to reject what they find counterfeit.

IV

A President draws influence from bargaining advantages. But does he always need them? There are instances where views on public policy diverged with special sharpness. Suppose such sharp divergences are lacking, suppose most players of the governmental game see policy objectives much alike, then can he not rely on logic (or on charm) to get him what he wants? The answer is that even then most outcomes turn on bargaining. The reason for this answer is a simple one: most men who share in governing have interests of their own beyond the realm of policy *objectives.* The sponsorship of policy, the form it takes, the conduct of it, and the credit for it separate their interest from the President's despite agreement on the end in view. In political government, the means can matter quite as much as ends; they often matter more. And there are always differences of interest in the means.

Let me introduce a case externally the opposite of my previous examples: the European Recovery Program of 1948, the so-called Marshall Plan. This is perhaps the greatest exercise in policy *agreement* since the cold war began. When the then Secretary of State, George Catlett Marshall, spoke at the Harvard commencement in June of 1947, he launched one of the most creative, most imaginative ventures in the history of American foreign relations.

What makes this policy most notable for present purposes, however, is that it became effective upon action by the 80th Congress, at the behest of Harry Truman, in the election year of 1948.[13]

Eight months before Marshall spoke at Harvard, the Democrats had lost control of both Houses of Congress for the first time in fourteen years. Truman, whom the Secretary represented, had just finished his second troubled year as President-by-succession. Truman was regarded with so little warmth in his own party that in 1946 he had been urged *not* to participate in the congressional campaign. At the opening of Congress in January 1947, Senator Robert A. Taft, "Mr. Republican," had somewhat the attitude of a President-elect. This was a vision widely shared in Washington, with Truman relegated, thereby, to the role of caretaker-on-term. Moreover, within just two weeks of Marshall's commencement address, Truman was to veto two prized accomplishments of Taft's congressional majority: the Taft-Hartley Act and tax reduction.[14] Yet scarcely ten months later the Marshall Plan was under way on terms to satisfy its sponsors, its authorization completed, its first-year funds in sight, its administering agency in being: all managed by as thorough a display of executive-congressional cooperation as any we have seen since the Second World War. For any President at any time this would have been a great accomplishment. In years before mid-century it would have been enough to make the future reputation of his term. And for a Truman, at this time, enactment of the Marshall Plan appears almost miraculous.

How was the miracle accomplished? How did a President so situated bring it off? In answer, the first thing to note is that he did not do it by himself. Truman had help of a sort no less extraordinary than the outcome. Although each stands for something more complex, the names of Marshall, Vandenberg, Patterson, Bevin, Stalin, tell the story of that help.

In 1947, two years after V-J Day, General Marshall was something more than Secretary of State. He was a man venerated by the President as "the greatest living American," literally an embodiment of Truman's ideals. He was honored at the Pentagon as an architect of victory. He was thoroughly respected by the Secretary of the Navy, James V. Forrestal, who that year became the first Secretary of Defense. On Capitol Hill Marshall had an enormous fund of respect stemming from his war record as Army Chief of Staff, and in the country generally no officer had come out of the war with a higher reputation for judgment, intellect, and probity. Besides, as Secretary of State, he had behind him the first generation of matured foreign service officers produced by the reforms of the 1920s, and mingled with them, in the departmental service, were some of the ablest of the men drawn by the war from private life to Washington. In terms both of staff talent and staff's use, Marshall's years began a State Department "golden age" which lasted until the era of McCarthy. Moreover, as his Under Secretary, Marshall had, successively, Dean Acheson and Robert Lovett, men who commanded the respect of the professionals and the regard of congressmen. (Acheson had been brilliantly successful at congressional relations as Assistant Secretary in the war and postwar years.) Finally, as a special undersecretary Marshall had Will Clayton, a man highly regarded, for good reason, at both ends of Pennsylvania Avenue.

Taken together, these are exceptional resources for a Secretary of State. In the circumstances, they were quite as necessary as they obviously are relevant. The Marshall Plan was launched by a "lame duck" Administration "scheduled" to leave office in eighteen months. Marshall's program faced a congressional leadership traditionally isolationist and currently intent upon economy. European aid was viewed with envy by a Pentagon distressed and virtually disarmed through budget cuts, and by domestic agencies intent on enlarged welfare programs. It was not viewed with liking by a Treasury intent on budget surpluses. The plan had need of every asset that could be extracted from the personal position of its nominal author and from the skills of his assistants.

Without the equally remarkable position of the senior Senator from Michigan, Arthur H. Vandenberg, it is hard to see how Marshall's assets could have been enough. Vandenberg was chairman of the Senate Foreign Relations Committee. Actually, he was much more than that. Twenty years a senator, he was the senior member of his party in the Chamber. Assiduously cultivated by F.D.R. and Truman, he was a chief Republican proponent of "bipartisanship" in foreign policy, and consciously conceived himself its living symbol to his party, to the country, and abroad. Moreover, by informal but entirely operative agreement with his colleague Taft, Vandenberg held the acknowledged lead among Senate Republicans in the whole field of international affairs. This acknowledgement meant more in 1947 than it might have meant at any other time. With confidence in the advent of a Republican administration two years hence, most of the gentlemen were in a mood to be responsive and responsible. The war was over, Roosevelt dead, Truman a caretaker, theirs the trust. That the Senator from Michigan saw matters in this light, his diaries make clear.[15] And this was not the outlook from the Senate side alone; the attitudes of House Republicans associated with the Herter Committee and its tours abroad suggest the same mood of responsibility. Vandenberg was not the only source of help on Capitol Hill. But relatively speaking, his position there was as exceptional as Marshall's was downtown.

Help of another sort was furnished by a group of dedicated private citizens who organized one of the most effective instruments for public information seen since the Second World War: the Committee for the Marshall Plan, headed by the eminent Republicans whom F.D.R., in 1940, had brought to the Department of War: Henry L. Stimson as honorary chairman and Robert P. Patterson as active spokesman. The remarkable array of bankers, lawyers, trade unionists, and editors, who had drawn together in defense of "internationalism" before Pearl Harbor and had joined their talents in the war itself, combined again to spark the work of this committee. Their efforts generated a great deal of vocal public support to buttress Marshall's arguments, and Vandenberg's, in Congress.

But before public support could be rallied, there had to be a purpose tangible enough, concrete enough, to provide a rallying ground. At Harvard, Marshall had voiced an idea in general terms. That this was turned into a hard program susceptible of presentation and support is due, in major part, to Ernest Bevin, the British Foreign Secretary. He well deserves the credit he has sometimes been assigned as, in effect, co-author of the Marshall Plan. For Bevin seized on Marshall's Harvard speech and organized a European response with promptness and concreteness beyond the State Department's expectations. What had been virtually a trial balloon to test reactions on both sides of the Atlantic was hailed in London as an invitation to the Europeans to send Washington a bill of particulars. This they promptly organized to do, and the American Administration then organized in turn for its reception without further argument internally about the pros and cons of issuing the "invitation" in the first place. But for Bevin there might have been trouble from the Secretary of the Treasury and others besides.[16]

If Bevin's help was useful at that early stage, Stalin's was vital from first to last. In a mood of self-deprecation Truman once remarked that without Moscow's "crazy" moves "we would never have had our foreign policy . . . we never could have got a thing from Congress."[17] George Kennan, among others, had deplored the anti-Soviet overtone of the case made for the Marshall Plan in Congress and the country, but there is no doubt that this clinched the argument for many segments of American opinion. There also is no doubt that Moscow made the crucial contributions to the case.

By 1947 events, far more than governmental prescience or open action, had given a variety of publics an impression of inimical Soviet intentions (and of Europe's weakness), and a growing urge to "do something about it." Three months before Marshall spoke at Harvard, Greek-Turkish aid and promulgation of the Truman Doctrine had seemed rather to crystallize than to create a public mood and a congressional response. The Marshall planners, be it said, were poorly placed to capitalize on that mood, nor had the Secretary wished to do so. Their object, indeed, was to cut across it, striking at the cause of European weakness rather than at Soviet aggressiveness, *per se*. A strong economy in Western Europe called, ideally, for restorative measures of continental scope. American assistance proffered in an anti-Soviet context would have been contra-

dictory in theory and unacceptable in fact to several of the governments that Washington was anxious to assist. As Marshall, himself, saw it, the logic of his purpose forbade him to play his strongest congressional card. The Russians then proceeded to play it for him. When the Europeans met in Paris, Molotov walked out. After the Czechs had shown continued interest in American aid, a communist coup overthrew their government while Soviet forces stood along their borders within easy reach of Prague. Molotov transformed the Marshall Plan's initial presentation; Czechoslovakia assured its final passage, which followed by a month the takeover in Prague.

Such was the help accorded Truman in obtaining action on the Marshall Plan. Considering his politically straightened circumstances he scarcely could have done with less. Conceivably, some part of Moscow's contribution might have been dispensable, but not Marshall's, or Vandenberg's, or Bevin's, or Patterson's, or that of the great many other men whose work is represented by their names in my account. Their aid was not extended to the President for his own sake. He was not favored in this fashion just because they liked him personally, or were spellbound by his intellect or charm. They might have been as helpful had all held him in disdain, which some of them certainly did. The Londoners who seized the ball, Vandenberg and Taft and the congressional majority, Marshall and his planners, the officials of other agencies who actively supported them or "went along," the host of influential private citizens who rallied to the cause—all these played the parts they did because they thought they had to, in their interest, given their responsibilities, not Truman's. Yet they hardly would have found it in their interest to collaborate with one another, or with him, had he not furnished them precisely what *they* needed from the White House. Truman could not do without their help, but he could not have had it without unremitting effort on his part.

The crucial thing to note about this case is that despite compatibility of views on public policy, Truman got no help he did not pay for (except Stalin's). Bevin scarcely could have seized on Marshall's words had Marshall not been plainly backed by Truman. Marshall's interest would not have comported with the exploitation of his prestige by a President who undercut him openly, or subtly, or even inadvertently, at any point. Vandenberg, presumably, could not have backed proposals by a White House which begrudged him deference and access gratifying to his fellow-partisans (and satisfying to himself). Prominent Republicans in private life would not have found it easy to promote a cause identified with Truman's claims on 1948—and neither would the prominent New Dealers then engaged in searching for a substitute.

Truman paid the price required for their services. So far as the record shows, the White House did not falter once in firm support for Marshall and the Marshall Plan. Truman backed his Secretary's gamble on an invitation to all Europe. He made the plan his own in a well-timed address to the Canadians. He lost no opportunity to widen the involvements of his own official family in the cause. Averell Harriman the Secretary of Commerce, Julius Krug the Secretary of the Interior, Edwin Nourse the Economic Council Chairman, James Webb the Director of the Budget—all were made responsible for studies and reports contributing directly to the legislative presentation. Thus these men were committed in advance. Besides, the President continually emphasized to

everyone in reach that he did not have doubts, did not desire complications and would foreclose all he could. Reportedly, his emphasis was felt at the Treasury, with good effect. And Truman was at special pains to smooth the way for Vandenberg. The Senator insisted on "no politics" from the Administration side; there was none. He thought a survey of American resources and capacity essential; he got it in the Krug and Harriman reports. Vandenberg expected advance consultation; he received it, step by step, in frequent meetings with the President and weekly conferences with Marshall. He asked for an effective liaison between Congress and agencies concerned; Lovett and others gave him what he wanted. When the Senator decided on the need to change financing and administrative features of the legislation, Truman disregarded Budget Bureau grumbling and acquiesced with grace. When, finally, Vandenberg desired a Republican to head the new administering agency, his candidate, Paul Hoffman, was appointed despite the President's own preference for another. In all of these ways Truman employed the sparse advantages his "powers" and his status then accorded him to gain the sort of help he had to have.

Truman helped himself in still another way. Traditionally and practically no one was placed as well as he to call public attention to the task of *Congress* (and its Republican leadership). Throughout the fall and winter of 1947 and on into the spring of 1948, he made repeated use of presidential "powers" to remind the country that congressional action was required. Messages, speeches, and an extra session were employed to make the point. Here, too, he drew advantage from his place. However, in his circumstances, Truman's public advocacy might have hurt, not helped, had his words seemed directed toward the forthcoming election. Truman gained advantage for his program only as his own endorsement of it stayed on the right side of that fine line between the "caretaker" in office and the would-be candidate. In public statements dealing with the Marshall Plan he seems to have risked blurring this distinction only once, when he called Congress into session in November 1947 asking both for interim aid to Europe *and* for peacetime price controls. The second request linked the then inflation with the current Congress (and with Taft), becoming a first step toward one of Truman's major themes in 1948. By calling for both measures at the extra session he could have been accused—and was—of mixing home-front politics with foreign aid. In the event no harm was done the European program (or his politics). But in advance a number of his own advisers feared that such a double call would jeopardize the Marshall Plan. Their fears are testimony to the narrowness of his advantage in employing his own "powers" for its benefit.[18]

It is symptomatic of Truman's situation that "bipartisan" accommodation by the White House then was thought to mean congressional consultation and conciliation on a scale unmatched in Eisenhower's time. Yet Eisenhower did about as well with opposition Congresses as Truman did, in terms of requests granted for defense and foreign aid. It may be said that Truman asked for more extraordinary measures. But it also may be said that Eisenhower never lacked for the prestige his predecessor had to borrow. It often was remarked, in Truman's time, that he seemed a "split-personality," so sharply did his conduct differentiate domestic politics from national security. But personality aside, how else could *he*, in his first term, gain ground for an evolving foreign policy?

The plain fact is that Truman had to play bipartisanship as he did or lose the game.

V

Had Truman lacked the personal advantages his "powers" and his status gave him, or if he had been maladroit in using them, there probably would not have been a massive European aid program in 1948. Something of the sort, perhaps quite different in its emphasis, would almost certainly have come to pass before the end of 1949. *Some* American response to European weakness and to Soviet expansion was as certain as such things can be. But in 1948 temptations to await a Taft Plan or a Dewey Plan might well have caused at least a year's postponement of response had the "outgoing" Administration bungled its congressional, or public, or allied, or executive relations. Quite aside from the specific virtues of their plan, Truman and his helpers gained that year, at least, in timing the American response. As European time was measured then, this was a precious gain. The President's own share in this accomplishment was vital. He made his contribution by exploiting his advantages. Truman, in effect, lent Marshall and the rest the perquisites and status of his office. In return they lent him their prestige and their own influence. The transfer multiplied *his* influence despite his limited authority in form and lack of strength politically. Without the wherewithal to make this bargain, Truman could not have contributed to European aid.

Bargaining advantages convey no guarantees. Influence remains a two-way street. In the fortunate instance of the Marshall Plan, what Truman needed was actually in the hands of men who were prepared to "trade" with him. He personally could deliver what they wanted in return. Marshall, Vandenberg, Harriman, *et al.*, possessed the prestige, energy, associations, staffs, essential to the legislative effort. Truman himself had a sufficient hold on presidential messages and speeches, on budget policy, on high-level appointments, and on his own time and temper to carry through all aspects of his necessary part. But it takes two to make a bargain. It takes those who have prestige to lend it on whatever terms. Suppose that Marshall had declined the Secretaryship of State in January 1947; Truman might not have found a substitute so well-equipped to furnish what he needed in the months ahead. Or suppose that Vandenberg had fallen victim to a cancer two years before he actually did; Senator Wiley of Wisconsin would not have seemed to Taft a man with whom the world need be divided. Or suppose that the Secretary of the Treasury had been possessed of stature, force, and charm commensurate with that of his successor in Eisenhower's time, the redoubtable George M. Humphrey. And what if Truman then had seemed to the Republicans what he turned out to be in 1948, a formidable candidate for President? It is unlikely that a single one of these "supposes" would have changed the final outcome; two or three, however, might have altered it entirely. Truman was not guaranteed more power than his "powers" just because he had continuing relationships with Cabinet secretaries and with senior senators. Here, as everywhere, the outcome was conditional on who they were and what he was and how each viewed events, and on their actual performance in response.

Granting that persuasion has no guarantee attached, how can a President reduce the risks of failing to persuade? How can he maximize his prospects for effectiveness by minimizing chances that his power will elude him? The Marshall Plan suggests an answer: he guards his power prospects in the course of making choices. Marshall himself, and Forrestal, and Harriman, and others of the sort held office on the President's appointment. Vandenberg had vast symbolic value partly because F.D.R. and Truman had done everything they could, since 1944, to build him up. The Treasury Department and the Budget Bureau—which together might have jeopardized the plans these others made—were headed by officials whose prestige depended wholly on their jobs. What Truman needed from those "givers" he received, in part, because of his past choice of men and measures. What they received in turn were actions taken or withheld by him, himself. The things they needed from him mostly involved his own conduct where his current choices ruled. The President's own actions in the past had cleared the way for current bargaining. His actions in the present were his trading stock. Behind each action lay a personal choice, and these together comprised *his* control over the give-and-take that gained him what he wanted. In the degree that Truman, personally, affected the advantages he drew from his relationships with other men in government, *his power was protected by his choices.*

By "choice" I mean no more than what is commonly referred to as "decision": a President's own act of doing or not doing. Decision is so often indecisive and indecision is so frequently conclusive, that choice becomes the preferable term. "Choice" has its share of undesired connotations. In common usage it implies a black-and-white alternative. Presidential choices are rarely of that character. It also may imply that the alternatives are set before the choice-maker by someone else. A President is often left to figure out his options for himself. Neither implication holds in any of the references to "choice" throughout this article.

If Presidents could count upon past choices to enhance their current influence, as Truman's choice of men had done for him, persuasion would pose fewer difficulties than it does. But Presidents can count on no such thing. Depending on the circumstances, prior choices can be as embarrassing as they were helpful in the instance of the Marshall Plan. Among others: Eisenhower's influence with Faubus was diminished by his earlier statements to the press and by his unconditional agreement to converse in friendly style at Newport. Truman's hold upon MacArthur was weakened by his deference toward him in the past.

Assuming that past choices have protected influence, not harmed it, present choices still may be inadequate. If Presidents could count on their own conduct to provide them *enough* bargaining advantages, as Truman's conduct did where Vandenberg and Marshall were concerned, effective bargaining might be much easier to manage than it often is. In the steel crisis, for instance, Truman's own persuasiveness with companies and union, both, was burdened by the conduct of an independent Wage Board and of government attorneys in the courts, to say nothing of Wilson, Arnall, Sawyer, and the like. Yet in practice, if not theory, many of *their* crucial choices never were the President's to make. Decisions that are legally in other's hands, or delegated past recall, have an unhappy way of proving just the trading stock most needed when the White House wants to trade. One reason why Truman was consistently more influential in the instance of the Marshall Plan than in the steel case, or the Mac-

Arthur case, is that the Marshall Plan directly involved Congress. In congressional relations there are some things that no one but the President can do. His chance to choose is higher when a message must be sent, or a nomination submitted, or a bill signed into law, than when the sphere of action is confined to the Executive, where all decisive tasks may have been delegated past recall.

But adequate or not, a President's own choices are the only means *in his own hands* of guarding his own prospects for effective influence. He can draw power from continuing relationships in the degree that he can capitalize upon the needs of others for the Presidency's status and authority. He helps himself to do so, though, by nothing save ability to recognize the pre-conditions and the chance advantages and to proceed accordingly in the course of the choice-making that comes his way. To ask how he can guard prospective influence is thus to raise a further question: what helps him guard his power stakes in his own acts of choice?

NOTES

1. The reader will want to keep in mind the distinction betwen two senses in which the word *power* is employed. When I have used the word (or its plural) to refer to formal constitutional, statutory, or customary authority, it is either qualified by the adjective "formal" or placed in quotation marks as "power(s)." Where I have used it in the sense of effective influence upon the conduct of others, it appears without quotation marks (and always in the singular). Where clarity and convenience permit, *authority* is substituted for "power" in the first sense and *influence* for power in the second sense.

2. See, for example, his press conference of July 22, 1959, as reported in the *New York Times* for July 23, 1959.

3. See Douglass Cater, *The Fourth Branch of Government*, Boston: Houghton-Mifflin, 1959.

4. With the exception of the Vice-Presidency, of course.

5. See David B. Truman's illuminating study of party relationships in the 81st Congress, *The Congressional Party*, New York: Wiley, 1959, especially chaps. 4, 6, and 8.

6. As Secretary of the Interior in 1939, Harold Ickes refused to approve the sale of helium to Germany despite the insistence of the State Department and the urging of President Roosevelt. Without the Secretary's approval, such sales were forbidden by statute. See *The Secret Diaries of Harold L. Ickes*, New York: Simon and Schuster, 1954, Vol. 2, especially pp. 391–393, 396–399. See also Michael J. Reagan. "The Helium Controversy," in the forthcoming case book on civil-military relations prepared for the Twentieth Century Fund under the editorial direction of Harold Stein.

   In this instance the statutory authority ran to the Secretary as a matter of *his* discretion. A President is unlikely to fire Cabinet officers for the conscientious exercise of such authority. If the president did so, their successors might well be embarrassed both publicly and at the Capitol were they to reverse decisions previously taken. As for a President's authority to set aside discretionary determinations of this sort, it rests, if it exists at all, on shaky legal ground not likely to be trod save in the gravest of situations.

7. Truman's *Memoirs* indicate that having tried and failed to make Stevenson an avowed candidate in the spring of 1952, the President decided to support the candidacy of Vice President Barkley. But Barkley withdrew early in the convention for lack of key northern support. Though Truman is silent on the matter, Barkley's active candidacy nearly was revived during the balloting, but the forces then aligning to revive it were led by opponents of Truman's Fair Deal, principally Southerners. As a practical matter, the President could not have lent his weight to *their* endeavors and could back no one but Stevenson to counter them. The latter's strength could not be shifted, then, to Harriman or Kefauver. Instead the other Northerners had to be withdrawn. Truman helped withdraw them. But he had no other option. See Memoirs by Harry S. Truman, Vol. 2, *Years of Trial and Hope*, Garden City, N.Y.: Doubleday, 1956, copr. 1956 Time Inc., pp. 495–496.

8. The reference is to Stassen's public statement of July 23, 1956, calling for Nixon's replacement on the Republican ticket by Governor Herter of Massachusetts, the later Secretary of State. Stassen's statement was issued after a conference with the President. Eisenhower's public statements on the vice-presidential nomination, both before and after Stassen's call, permit of alternative inferences: either that the President would have preferred another candidate, provided this could be arranged without a showing of White House dictation, or that he wanted Nixon on condition that the latter could show popular appeal. In the event, neither result was achieved. Eisenhower's own remarks lent strength to rapid party moves which smothered Stassen's effort. Nixon's nomination thus was guaranteed too quickly to appear the consequences of popular demand. For the public record on this matter see reported statements by Eisenhower, Nixon, Stassen, Herter, and Leonard Hall (the National Republican Chairman) in the *New York Times* for March, 1, 8, 15, 16; April 27; July 15, 16, 25–31; August 3, 4, 17, 23, 1956. See also the account from private sources by Earl Mazo in *Richard Nixon: A Personal and Political Portrait*, New York: Harper, 1959, pp. 158–187.

9. Stenographic transcript of presidential press conference, October 19, 1950, on file in the Truman Library at Independence, Missouri.

10. Jonathan Daniels, *Frontier on the Potomac*, New York: Macmillan, 1946, pp. 31–32.

11. Transcript of presidential press conference, June 18, 1958, in *Public Papers of the Presidents: Dwight D. Eisenhower, 1958*, Washington: The National Archives, 1959, p. 479. In the summer of 1958, a congressional investigation into the affairs of a New England textile manufacturer, Bernard Goldfine, revealed that Sherman Adams had accepted various gifts and favors from him (the most notoriety attached to a vicuña coat). Adams also had made inquiries about the status of a Federal Communications Commission proceeding in which Goldfine was involved. In September 1958, Adams was allowed to resign. The episode was highly publicized and much discussed in that year's congressional campaigns.

12. As reported in Marriner S. Eccles, *Beckoning Frontiers*, New York: Knopf, 1951, p. 336.

13. In drawing together these observations on the Marshall Plan, I have relied on the record of personal participation by Joseph M. Jones, *The Fifteen Weeks*, New York: Viking, 1955, especially pp. 89–256; on the recent study

by Harry Bayard Price, *The Marshall Plan and Its Meaning*, Ithaca, N.Y.: Cornell University Press, 1955, especially pp. 1–86; on the Truman Memoirs, Vol. 2, chaps. 7–9; on Arthur H. Vandenberg, Jr., editor, *The Private Papers of Senator Vandenberg*, Boston: Houghton Mifflin, 1952, especially pp. 373 ff.; and on notes of my own made at the time. This is an instance of policy development not covered, to my knowledge, by any of the university programs engaged in the production of case studies.

14. Secretary Marshall's speech, formally suggesting what became known as the Marshall Plan, was made at Harvard on June 5, 1947. On June 20 the President vetoed the Taft-Hartley Act; his veto was overridden three days later. On June 16 he vetoed the first of two tax reduction bills (HR 1) passed at the first session of the 80th Congress; the second of these (HR 3950), a replacement for the other, he also disapproved on July 18. In both instances his veto was narrowly sustained.

15. *Private Papers of Senator Vandenberg*, pp. 378–379 and 446.

16. The initial reluctance of Secretary of the Treasury, John Snyder, to support large-scale spending overseas became a matter of public knowledge on June 25, 1947. At a press conference on that day he interpreted Marshall's Harvard speech as a call on Europeans to help themselves, by themselves. At another press conference the same day, Marshall for his own part had indicated that the U.S. would consider helping programs on which Europeans agreed. The next day Truman held a press conference and was asked the inevitable question. He replied, "General Marshall and I are in complete agreement." When pressed further, Truman remarked sharply, "The Secretary of the Treasury and the Secretary of State and the President are in complete agreement." Thus the President cut Snyder off, but had programming gathered less momentum overseas, no doubt he would have been heard from again as time passed and opportunity offered.

The foregoing quotations are from the stenographic transcript of the presidential press conference June 26, 1947, on file in the Truman Library at Independence, Missouri.

17. A remark made in December 1955, three years after he left office, but not unrepresentative of views he expressed, on occasion, while he was President.

18. This might also be taken as testimony to the political timidity of officials in the State Department and the Budget Bureau where that fear seems to have been strongest. However, conversations at the time with White House aides incline me to believe that there, too, interjection of the price issue was thought a gamble and a risk. For further comment see my "Congress and the Fair Deal: A Legislative Balance Sheet," *Public Policy*, Cambridge, Mass.: Harvard University Press, 1954, Vol. 5, pp. 362–364.

32
Toward a Framework to Explain Presidential Power
Raymond Tatalovich & Byron W. Daynes

Students of the presidency and citizens alike must understand the nature of presidential power so that its promise as well as its dangers can be appreciated. This balanced perspective requires a theoretical framework that analyzes the empirical foundations of presidential power. In spite of the tremendous amount of

Source: Excerpted from *Presidential Power in the United States*, by Raymond Tatalovich and Byron W. Daynes. Copyright © 1984 by Wadsworth, Inc. Reprinted by permission of Brooks/Cole Publishing Company, Monterey, California 93940.

research done on the presidency by political scientists, historians, journalists, and scholars in related fields, compared with the literature on other sociopolitical topics (such as voting behavior), much less attention to empirical theory has guided analyses of the presidency. For this reason, it may not be obvious how the varied and specialized studies of the presidency interrelate in a coherent framework for analysis.

Any analysis of presidential power must necessarily draw on the discussions by many scholars, journalists, and political leaders. Their data is organized into a framework suggestive of a theory of presidential power. We will study the presidency in terms of role analysis. This article outlines the components of our framework. An important requirement of empirical theory is that it incorporate the requisite knowledge about a political phenomenon so that explanation, and ideally prediction, is achieved. Included in our framework are five variables which seem paramount to determining the power available to a president in his various roles. This approach has utility when applied to any incumbent, during most historical periods, and regardless of the scope of government activity; it provides a balanced and comprehensive theory of presidential power.[1]

FIVE PRESIDENTIAL ROLES

Our discussion is based on these five presidential roles: *commander-in-chief, chief diplomat, chief executive, legislative leader,* and *opinion/party leader*. A role is defined by Andrew McFarland as "a regularly recurring pattern of social interaction that can be described by (1) who expects (2) whom (3) to do what (4) in which situation."[2] The use of role analysis is prevalent in the literature on the presidency. Roles are central to the texts written by Clinton Rossiter, Ed-

ward Corwin, and Louis Koenig, among others.[3] A study by Thomas Bailey cites no fewer than forty-three presidential roles as measures of presidential responsibility. The scholars in this analytic tradition view roles as jobs or functions; they also agree that certain roles are specifically mentioned in the Constitution (commander-in-chief) whereas others have evolved upon the president with the passage of time (legislative leader).

For our purposes, therefore, *a role is that set of expectations by other political elites and the citizenry which defines the scope of presidential responsibilities within a given sphere of action*. Each of the five presidential roles can be identified with a general sphere of action, and over time added responsibilities have accrued to the president in all these roles. Commander-in-chief is the nation's highest military leader, just as the title chief diplomat suggests that our relationship to other nations is largely defined by the president. Chief executive refers to the complex and ever-changing relationship of the president to his bureaucracy, the advisory system, and to the administration of public policy. A president's relationship to Congress is demarcated by the role legislative leader, and the role of opinion/party leader points to the linkage between a president and the public, whether organized into interest groups or viewed as an unorganized mass. In this work the five roles are organized along a *continuum*, from the most powerful to the least powerful. The continuum is shown below:

COMMANDER- → CHIEF →
   IN-CHIEF   DIPLOMAT
(most powerful)
→ CHIEF   → LEGISLATIVE →
EXECUTIVE   LEADER
       → OPINION/PARTY
        LEADER
          (least powerful)

We maintain that any roles beyond these five are either subdivisions or amalgamations of these roles or misnomers for what essentially are *obligations*, not roles. For example, Clinton Rossiter defines the president as "World Leader," noting that he "has a much larger constituency than the American electorate; his words and deeds in behalf of our own survival as a free nation have a direct bearing upon the freedom and stability of at least several score other countries."[4] But the president as world leader is not a viable role in terms of theory building. At the outset, Rossiter admits that this role depends upon a president acting as commander-in-chief, chief of state, and chief diplomat, so clearly the resources available to the president as world leader must depend on the effective use of existing roles. Writing in the late 1950s Rossiter stated that the role of world leader was "not much more than a decade old," which implies that its definition is time-bound. Indeed, that particular role orientation reflected the tensions between the United States and the Soviet Union which became so exaggerated during the Cold War years following World War II. It is clear this role would have limited relevance to earlier historical periods. It appears in this instance what Rossiter calls a "role" is really an "obligation," for he is saying that the realities of international politics demand that the president be a leader of the "free" world. Thus, he is identifying a goal for the president to pursue.

As the previous example shows, authors who talk about a president's obligations are identifying an area of public policy requiring executive action, and they exhort the president to assume leadership in promoting those objectives.[5] Many writers on the presidency reflect the obligations approach by focusing on certain substantive policies that demand

a president's attention, such as the economy or civil rights. Their implication is that the president has a special obligation to the country to discharge his authority and responsibilities in these policy areas.

Obviously, the ability to fulfill any objective depends on which roles are involved; most often a president will have to act in many roles in order to advance such goals as racial justice and economic well-being. Consider the matter of civil rights. As commander-in-chief, President Truman issued an executive order that integrated the armed forces. The extraordinary success of Lyndon Johnson as legislative leader resulted in the enactment of the Civil Rights Acts of 1964, 1965, and 1968. When John F. Kennedy put the civil rights question on the public agenda, he tried as opinion/party leader to educate the American people to understand the morality of equal rights in our society. And as chief diplomat, Kennedy's efforts to recognize the aspirations of African nations, an area of the world long ignored by the United States, may have earned him the added respect of black Americans.

A president advancing the cause of civil rights acts in a variety of roles, and the same applies to his efforts to direct the economy. All presidents have exhorted the public to hold down wage demands and businesses to limit price increases; such persuasion by the use of one's office is called "jawboning." As chief executive, a president, for example Ronald Reagan, may limit pay raises for federal employees to reduce expenditures. In his budget message to Congress, the president as legislative leader is expected to define a fiscal policy that coordinates the levels of spending, taxation, and indebtedness. The price of food and goods may be affected by a president's policy on importation. For instance, when President Carter eased restrictions on the amount of beef being imported from Argentina, this action slowed the rise in domestic beef prices. So a president's effective leadership in promoting any goal—be it social justice, economic growth, or world peace—may require action in many roles. The problem is that his success depends upon the political resources available to him, and these are mainly determined by the roles in which he is operating. The probability of success, therefore, decreases markedly if a president has to rely exclusively on his influence as legislative leader and opinion/party leader, the two least powerful roles on the continuum, to achieve some desired goal.

FIVE DETERMINANTS OF PRESIDENTIAL POWER

The interrelationships among five variables—authority, decision making, public input, expertise, and crisis—determine the political resources available to a president in each role. The fact that these variables have *differential* impact on each role explains why a president is more powerful in some roles than in others. The determinants of presidential power may be subdivided into their component parts, as follows:

Authority
1. constitutional mandate
2. statutory delegation
3. judicial precedent
4. customary practice

Decision Making
5. separation of powers
6. federalism
7. political institutions (for example, parties)

Public Inputs
8. political mobilization
9. public deference

Expertise
10. monopoly of information
11. technocratic knowledge

Crisis
12. likelihood of crisis
13. need for decision making

Authority

Perhaps the chief determinant of presidential power is the degree of authority available to the president. We can speak of authority to the extent that power has been "routinized" by constitutional mandate, statutory delegations, judicial precedent, and customary practice. Moreover, such authority can be passed on from president to president, and enlarged upon, unless, that is, Congress enacts new legislation or the Supreme Court reinterprets existing law. As will be documented, in its effort to regain a stronger voice in policymaking during the period after Watergate and Vietnam, the Congress in many instances has undermined the president's authority by legislation. Two examples are its use of the War Powers Act of 1973 to limit presidential war making and its enactment of the Budget and Impoundment Control Act of 1974 to prevent the president from refusing to spend money appropriated by Congress. A substantial body of literature traces legislative/executive relationships in terms of how the law defines the roles of Congress and the president.[6] Other scholars are concerned about how presidential power is expanded or limited by decisions of the federal judiciary, especially the Supreme Court.[7]

Under certain conditions a president can make legally binding decisions. We can estimate how much authority he enjoys in each role by studying the Constitution, judicial precedent, statutory delegations, and customs as they have evolved historically. Customs are authoritative to the extent that they are accepted as legitimate by the people, opinion leaders, and the other branches of government. For example, the cabinet is not established by any statute, the Constitution, or a Supreme Court decision; its use is based upon a custom begun by George Washington.

Decision Making

The president's power is affected by the number of decision makers involved in formulating and implementing any policy. His power is strengthened when he shares decision making with few other political actors. This argument is predicated on E. E. Schattschneider's contention that, as the "scope of conflict" affecting an issue increases, the expansion in the number of participants in that dispute precludes its control by any small group of decision makers.[8] In terms of presidential power, the number of decision makers *formally* involved depends upon the role affected, One may conceptualize this variable as a series of concentric rings moving outward from the president, who is in the center (Figure 1). As one moves along the continuum of roles, from commander-in-chief to opinion/party leader, the number of decision makers increases because of three factors: separation of powers, federalism, and political institutions.

The commander-in-chief often is portrayed by scholars as a "constitutional dictator," suggesting that during wartime the normal, external checks on his power all but disappear and decision making is lodged in the office of president and his key advisers. As chief diplomat, a president must contend with the constitutional role given to Congress in foreign affairs. As a chief executive, however, a very different picture emerges. In addition to the president, his advisers, and Congress, government administration also involves the Supreme Court, the bureaucracy, subna-

tional political elites (for example, mayors, governors), and clientele groups. Why is this the case? First, the judiciary tends to defer less to the president in the realm of administration than with regard to his duties as commander-in-chief and as chief diplomat. Second, the implementation of federal laws often requires the assistance of federal, state, and local agencies as well as "private" groups, such as neighborhood organizations and professional associations.

As legislative leader, the president's major antagonist is Congress, which can exercise independent power over lawmaking. And there is always the possibility that the Supreme Court may declare a president's programs to be unconstitutional, as happened to Franklin Roosevelt several times. Furthermore, in this role a president must contend with political party organizations, or the lack thereof; perhaps the major reason presidents are so ineffective as legislative leaders is the decentralized nature of our party system. The recruitment, nomination, and election of congressmen and senators are controlled by state and local political elites and by party activists who may have no loyalty to the president's program.

As opinion/party leader, finally, a president confronts the entire gamut of decision makers. At this role level the mass media and the citizenry take on great importance. Virtually any actor in the political system can affect a president's popularity and electoral success. The ordinary citizen participates in this role when casting a vote in elections, by recording his or her preferences with opinion pollsters, or demonstrating for or against policy decisions.

Public Inputs

Besides studying the decision makers who formally share power with the president in each role, we must also consider those political actors who act as "veto

FIGURE 1 • DECISION MAKERS AFFECTING PRESIDENTIAL POWER IN FIVE ROLES

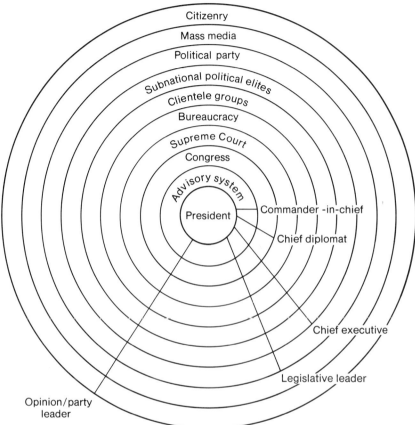

Citizenry

Mass media

Political party

Subnational political elites

Clientele groups

Bureaucracy

Supreme Court

Congress

Advisory system

President

Commander-in-chief

Chief diplomat

Chief executive

Legislative leader

Opinion/party leader

Source: Adapted from "Towards a Paradigm to Explain Presidential Power," by R. Tatalovich and B. W. Daynes. In *Presidential Studies Quarterly*, 9(4), Fall, 1979, p. 432. Copyright © 1979 by the Center for the Study of the Presidency.

groups," limiting the options available to a president. Proceeding along the continuum of roles, one may note that a president's policy options are restricted or opened up because (1) the level of political mobilization tends to fluctuate and (2) deference to the president's viewpoint by the people and various interest groups changes. Public opinion normally supports a president's policy initiatives when acting as commander-in-chief or as chief diplomat. In the role of chief executive, on the other hand,

public opinion as such is less important than the intrigues of special interests and clientele groups who jockey to maintain their privileged access to government. There is a substantial increase in public inputs of all kinds when we consider the role of legislative leader. Interest groups, political parties, social movements, and voter blocs all try to influence the legislative process. Similarly, our analysis of public inputs in the least powerful role of opinion/party leader suggests that the president's options are so limited that virtually no course of action can be implemented by him without incurring some political costs.

Expertise

A president's power is enhanced to the extent that decision making requires expertise. Of course, expertise is not equally available to everybody because it depends upon a monopoly of information sources and an understanding of technocratic knowledge. Here the expertise determinant refers to any use of information that prevents a president's critics from being able to evaluate his policies and actions, including secrecy, data manipulation, as well as expert testimony. Given its nature, expertise aids presidential power only insofar as other decision makers and citizens acknowledge its direct relevance to policy formation.

As commander-in-chief and chief diplomat, therefore, the expertise variable is very important; a president monopolizes information sources and is able to classify data or impose censorship to prevent their dissemination to the general public. As the facts about the Vietnam War became highly publicized in the media by journalists and commentators and in such documents as the Pentagon Papers, only then did we appreciate fully how often Presidents Johnson and Nixon had deceived the American people about the degree of our involvement there.

As chief executive and legislative leader, expertise is less beneficial. In the past, a president's reputed knowledge strengthened his position vis-à-vis Congress when he submitted the budget for the federal government, and no doubt expertise aids his position when Congress must approve highly technical programs, such as the space program or medical research. But Congress gets much

valuable and sophisticated information about proposed legislation from nongovernmental experts, from interest groups, and from its own committee staff.

In addition, the chief executive is very dependent upon public and private institutions beyond his immediate control for data the federal government needs to implement laws. A compelling argument can be made that a president's ability to manipulate our economy, to promote growth while reducing inflation, is severely limited by minimal knowledge about the multitude of social, political, and economic forces that shape our nation's economy. In trying to forge public opinion, similarly, a president's success is related less to expertise than to such factors as personality, historic events, patriotism, and partisan appeal. As was noted before, expertise aids presidential power only when others acknowledge its relevance, but in the role of opinion/party leader the citizenry rarely evaluates a president's performance or his policies in terms of his knowing what is best for us.

Crisis

As indicated before, crisis augments a president's power, especially in wartime and during periods of international turmoil. But the emergency variable should be viewed in its broadest sense: a crisis is a situation characterized by sudden, intense, and sometimes unexpected danger. It is manifested by wars, depressions, domestic violence, natural disasters, epidemics, and assassinations. In politics, crisis has the effect of undermining normal power relationships among the president, the Congress, and the Supreme Court because of the urgent need to mobilize a quick response to the danger. Couple the president's singular ability to act quickly with the urgency for action, and he gains leverage in whatever role is affected by crisis. In some nations constitutional provisions exist by which the chief executive may declare a state of national emergency and assume dictatorial powers. Such explicit authority is not given in our Constitution, but our political system does permit the extraordinary amplification of presidential power during crises.

Presidents are aware of the relationship between crisis and heightened executive power, and they try to use the crisis mentality for political advantage. William Mullen comments,

> In "doing what needs doing for the people," our chief executives have come to operate a crisis presidency as almost a routine way of doing business. Even relatively minor issues are now cased in terms of emergency.[9]

Thus, presidents refer to the oil crisis, the urban crisis, health care crisis, and the Middle East crisis in order to quickly mobilize resources but also to silence dissent. Lyndon Johnson declared "war" on poverty, and Jimmy Carter called the energy problem the moral equivalent of war. One might be tempted to perceive the crisis variable to be simply a facet of authority, since a president's powers often are based on statutory delegation. However, their use depends upon certain social, economic, and political conditions widely perceived to be crises. A president may routinely call any issue a crisis, but it is highly unlikely that the public will share that perception about all policy questions.

As commander-in-chief and chief diplomat, crises usually require a president to confront a threat to our national interest, if not our very survival. In these roles, therefore, a crisis quickly mobilizes a consensus behind the need for decisive action. As a chief executive, crisis augments presidential power during periods of domestic turmoil. Frequently the

Congress delegates to the president the required authority to deal with threats to the nation's well-being when they can be anticipated. For example, the Taft-Hartley Act (1947) permits a president to delay strikes for 80 days should they imperil the nation.

The crisis variable is less effective in the roles of legislative leader or opinion/party leader. The major difficulty seems to be that congressmen and citizens often disagree with the president's definition of a problem as a crisis; moreover, there may be differences of opinion about the appropriate remedy. In evaluating this variable, therefore, it is not enough to find a relationship between a social problem and a legislative enactment, for in a sense all laws reflect societal demands. Rather, crisis suggests that a common feeling of urgency or danger exists, with Congress ready to rapidly answer a presidential initiative.

Similar problems impede the operation of the crisis variable in the role of opinion/party leader. Some events, such as a president's injury, heart attack, or assassination quickly generate a climate of opinion that a serious emergency has happened. Obviously, such real threats do not happen every day. For this reason, crises cannot be relied on for leverage by the opinion/party leader in any systematic way; they occur at random, the public may or may not react uniformly, and therefore a president's actions may not necessarily lead to his increased political popularity.

Summary

An inventory of the five variables indicates the power potential of the president at any period in our history. By our calculation (Table 1), commander-in-chief and chief diplomat roles are very close in terms of the political resources available to the contemporary president; chief executive is a distant third in power

TABLE 1 · VARIABLES AFFECTING PRESIDENTIAL POWER*

	Presidential Role				
Variable	Commander-in-Chief	Chief Diplomat	Chief Executive	Legislative Leader	Opinion/Party Leader
Authority					
Constitutional mandate	very strong	strong	moderate	moderate	none
Statutory delegation	very strong	strong	strong	weak	none
Judicial precedent	very strong	very strong	weak	very weak	none
Customary practice	very strong	very strong	weak	moderate	moderate
Decision Making					
Separation of powers	very weak	moderate	strong	very strong	strong
Federalism	none	none	moderate	moderate	moderate
Political institutions	weak	weak	moderate	very strong	very strong
Public Inputs					
Political mobilization	very weak	weak	moderate	strong	very strong
Public deference	very strong	strong	weak	weak	very weak
Expertise					
Monopoly of information	very strong	strong	moderate	weak	weak
Technocratic knowledge	very strong	strong	strong	moderate	weak
Crisis					
Likelihood of crisis	very strong	strong	weak	weak	weak
Need for decision making	very strong	very strong	moderate	moderate	moderate

* These values reflect our judgment about how each variable operates in the five presidential roles. For example, whereas public deference to the commander-in-chief is "very strong," it is "very weak" in terms of opinion/party leadership. Similarly, the commander-in-chief has a "very strong" constitutional mandate but the president as opinion/party leader has none from which to operate.

potential, followed closely by the legislative leader role. Given the few resources available for opinion/party leadership, a president's power in this role would seem to be illusory, and essentially shaped by the incumbent's personality, political skills, and policy agenda, as well as the nature of the times. Although some very popular presidents have been elected to office, the acid test is that power as opinion/party leader cannot be routinized and passed on to a president's successor. The same drawback applies to the roles of legislative leader and chief executive. In relatively weaker roles, presidential power must be reestablished by each incumbent, for a president can rely on few antecedents established in these areas by his predecessors. In contrast, no president begins his term of office as commander-in-chief or chief diplomat with such a power vacuum.

Historic developments have affected the evolution of presidential roles; for example, the advent of mass media was essential to exploiting the full potential of opinion/party leadership. However, the relative position of each role on our continuum has changed very little over time. Any president acting as commander-in-chief and chief diplomat will be more powerful than when acting as chief executive, legislative leader, or opinion/party leader. Pointing out Thomas Jefferson as an extraordinary legislative leader supports this argument; in that role, Jefferson was one of few successful presidents. Moreover, was Jefferson any less effective as a commander-in-chief or chief diplomat? Presidential power depends upon political resources, and a president simply has more ammunition in some roles than in others.

Our analysis has implications for those reformers who seek to fundamentally alter the interrelationships between the presidency and the other branches of government, particularly Congress. It is doubtful that any single panacea will change the quality of executive/legislative relations. Enlarging Congress' formal authority over war making and foreign affairs may be inadequate if Congress lacks the information capability to evaluate presidential initiatives in these areas. It is unlikely that Congress can overcome the president's inherent advantages in conducting the day-to-day business of diplomacy, especially during an international crisis. On the other hand, presidential power has always been fragile, and vulnerable to assault by Congress, in the weaker roles in which the president lacks the requisite political resources: chief executive, legislative leader, and opinion/party leader. But in roles in which the president's power is firmly established, as commander-in-chief and chief diplomat, the composite of resources available to him is too great to be easily eclipsed by a few structural changes in executive/legislative relations. For the Congress to regain a meaningful say in foreign and

military policy, what is required is a sustained congressional commitment to oversee executive initiatives in a variety of policy areas, during periods of "normalcy" *and* crisis, and *in spite of* the public's apparent complacent attitude towards foreign affairs.

We suspect any judgment about the decline of presidential power today is premature. Earlier periods of "congressional government" (for example, post-Civil War) did not last indefinitely, so one must determine whether the modern era has witnessed a change in variables underlying presidential power that indicates a fundamental realignment from the president to Congress. Recent literature alluding to a reassertion of Congress' role, even in foreign affairs, tends to emphasize the legal (War Powers Act) and institutional ("legislative veto") changes made by Congress to reassert its role in diplomacy and war making.[10] But these studies deemphasize the effect of such "political" variables as public opinion, expertise, and crisis in sustaining presidential power. The intellectual argument about the relative importance of "legal" versus "political" resources to a president's power is a long-standing one. A major advantage of the framework used here is that in addressing this question it poses a balanced alternative which seems more productive than either point of view alone. The following section briefly reviews the debate over the nature of presidential power.

PRESIDENTIAL POWER: AUTHORITY OR INFLUENCE?

Two diametrically opposing views of presidential power are offered by Richard Neustadt and Edward Corwin.[11] In the tradition of Machiavelli, Neustadt is concerned about understanding the realities of power. In the first edition of *Presidential Power*, based on the experiences of Harry Truman and Dwight Eisenhower, Neustadt's original thesis was a straightforward one. Presidential power is not authority but rather *persuasion*, which derives from the effective use of (1) reputation, (2) prestige, and (3) bargaining. Neustadt begins his analysis with three case studies: Truman's seizure of the steel mills during the Korean War, Truman's dismissal of General Douglas MacArthur during the Korean War, and Eisenhower's decision to desegregate Little Rock, Arkansas High School by using federal troops. At first glance, all three decisions would seem to exemplify a president's use of "command" or formal authority to achieve results, but upon closer inspection Neustadt argues that all were "painful last resort" decisions suggestive more of failure than of success. Therefore, Neustadt doubts that any president acting within the confines of his formal powers can be any more than a "clerk"; to be a "leader" requires that the president use persuasion. Neustadt is clearly an advocate of the "heroic" or "textbook" president, for he prefers the active presidents such as Franklin D. Roosevelt and Harry Truman to the more passive ones, for example, Eisenhower. Neustadt implicitly recognizes the effect of a president's personality on his ability to exercise power. The cultivation of power requires an executive to be attuned to the needs of legislators, public opinion, civil servants, and other power brokers who can adversely affect a president's decision making.

Neustadt's research, while very influential, has been disputed by other political scientists on various grounds.[12] One criticism focuses on his neglect of formal authority as a source of presidential power. Peter Sperlich, for one, says Neustadt sees only two forms of presidential power, command or persuasion, and that "the former is underrated and

the latter is overrated in Neustadt's schema."[13] One reason for this imbalance, according to Sperlich, is that the very controversial issues chosen by Neustadt as case studies may have depreciated the overall importance of command as a resource: "Less dramatic examples or influence attempts in matters of less importance might have produced a more positive picture of the use of command."[14] Certainly the day-to-day operations of government function according to legal authority, bureaucratic procedures, and routine, with little need for a president to use massive amounts of prestige, reputation, and bargaining to achieve results.

Neustadt's thesis exemplifies political "statecraft," argues David Paletz, who contrasts it with the "anti-aggrandizement" perspective found in Edward S. Corwin's seminal work, *The President: Office and Powers.*[15] Where Neustadt contends that an effective president has to augment his formal authority by exploiting political resources, Corwin is concerned that a president could assume too much power in our governmental system. Therefore Paletz argues that writers in the Corwin tradition tend to be constitutionalists who respect the separation of powers arrangement. While they may understand why presidential power has grown historically, they remain concerned that its growth has been at the expense of Congress. Corwin wrote the first edition of his text in 1940, but his argument is very compatible with the "revisionist" position articulated by liberal historians and political scientists two decades later.

Unlike Neustadt's approach, Corwin's analysis is highly legalistic; his understanding of presidential power (or authority) relates to the office, not the man himself. The powers of the president, he says, derive from the Constitution, Supreme Court rulings, statutes, and custom. Corwin feels more comfortable in designating Dwight Eisenhower as his model president rather than Franklin D. Roosevelt. Corwin approves of the collective responsibility fostered by Eisenhower's use of his cabinet rather than Roosevelt's "cult of personality" because, in FDR's case, the office became indistinguishable from the man. Since Corwin would like to deemphasize personality and the behavioral factors that underly presidential power, presumably he believes that a president can govern effectively solely by using the formal powers at his disposal.

A recent text in the Corwin tradition is Richard Pious's *The American Presidency*.[16] Pious's analysis touches on the Neustadt/Corwin dichotomy insofar as he differentiates between a president's "political" power and his "prerogative" power. Pious clearly discounts the importance of political statecraft in favor of prerogative or authority as the basis for presidential power. Pious claims that "the fundamental and irreducible core of presidential power rests not on influence, persuasion, public opinion, elections, or party, but rather on the successful assertion of constitutional authority to resolve crises and significant domestic issues."[17]

Pious's view of prerogative (or authority) as the mainstay of a president's power can be defended in some instances. Harry Bailey observes, "Vietnam and Watergate made it clear that some domestic and foreign policies could be accomplished without persuasion."[18] On the other hand, Pious's analysis would be troubling to scholars who study the historical events and political conditions affecting a president's use of power. Though it may be true that many presidents, even a majority, were unable to exploit "political" resources consistently for their advantage, this does not deny the importance of such resources to a handful of truly great presidents. The extraordinary success of FDR's New Deal was tied not to his formal authority but to political variables: the crisis of the Great Depression, the Democratic party control of Congress, his electoral landslide in 1932, a realignment in public opinion favoring governmental intervention in the economy, and his own cunning use of personal power.[19] Moreover, adverse political conditions, rather than any void in their authority, prompted Lyndon Johnson not to seek reelection in 1968 and forced Richard Nixon to resign in 1974.

Pious apparently fails to acknowledge the vital role that political variables play in his analysis. Pious refers to a "frontlash effect" and a "backlash effect." By the frontlash effect he means that Congress and the Supreme Court will often acquiesce to a president's claim of prerogative when his actions have been successful in meeting a domestic crisis. But the backlash effect has the opposite effect; sometimes even though a president successfully confronts a major issue, the Congress, the judiciary, and public opinion resist the president's claim of prerogative. Harry Bailey notes that this inconsistency contains "an element of Neustadt's persuasion model to which Pious gives very little attention. Clearly some persuasion of someone is necessary or how else does one account for frontlash over backlash or vice versa?"[20] Pious's account gives little credence to the notion of statecraft, as developed by Neustadt, and evinces less appreciation for the quality of "democratic statesmanship." Thomas Engeman, in assessing the inadequacy of a theory based solely on prerogative, states:

> The Office of the President . . . is the finest institution of democratic statesmanship currently known to us, and perhaps of all time. As a constitutional office, it is bound by custom, precedent, and

statute; but, as the highest source of authority for a living people, it remains magnificently protean.

The successful President will be one who combines an understanding of the democratic principles of the regime with a prudent assessment of his moment's possibilities.[21]

Our framework based on roles and variables resolves this intellectual dispute by synthesizing Neustadt's and Corwin's views of presidential power. Each writer is correct with regard to particular roles. As will be shown, the power of the commander-in-chief and the chief diplomat is best understood by applying Corwin's emphasis on formal, legal authority. Neustadt's insights are essential in explaining why certain presidents are more effective in the roles of chief executive, legislative leader, and opinion/party leader. As the formal authority available to a president is reduced, as is the case in these weaker roles, he must necessarily draw upon informal, personal resources in order to achieve his objectives. Thus, while any president *may* resort to bargaining, prestige, and reputation to bolster his position over military policy and foreign affairs, he *must* rely on these techniques of political "persuasion" to succeed in administration, legislative relations, and in cultivating a supportive public. In these areas the option of relying on authority is not open to presidents; the Constitution, statutes, judicial precedent, and customs have only marginally routinized power in these roles and each incumbent must in effect begin anew.

In summary, presidential power is a complex, elusive phenomenon, not amenable to simple explanations. Our approach is eclectic; our framework focuses on five key variables affecting presidential power in each role. What varies across roles is not the components of presidential power but how each operates within different roles. For example, whereas public opinion tends to unite behind a wartime president, it is extremely difficult to mobilize the American people behind a chief executive's program for reforming the bureaucracy. Similarly, though we worry that a commander-in-chief may take the nation into war without a "declaration" by Congress, we know that an opinion/party leader cannot command our obedience to his program or his party. A *president's power depends upon the roles in which he is operating*, and our great presidents have been successful in all five presidential roles.

NOTES

1. For an interesting discussion of six approaches to studying the presidency see David L. Paletz, "Perspectives on the Presidency," *Law and Contemporary Problems* (Summer 1970), pp. 429–445.

2. Andrew S. McFarland, "Role and Role Conflict," in Aaron Wildavsky, ed., *The Presidency* (Boston: Little, Brown, 1969), p. 3.

3. Clinton Rossiter, *The American Presidency*, 2nd ed. (New York: Harcourt, Brace and World, 1960); Edward S. Corwin, *The President: Office and Powers*, 4th ed. (New York: New York University Press, 1957); Louis W. Koenig, *The Chief Executive*, 4th ed. (New York: Harcourt Brace Jovanovich, 1981). Also see Thomas A. Bailey, *Presidential Greatness: The Image and the Man from George Washington to the Present* (New York: Appleton-Century-Crofts, 1966).

4. Rossiter, *The American Presidency*, pp. 39–40.

5. A prominent example of the obligations approach is found in Richard Longaker, *The President and Individual Liberties* (Ithaca, N.Y.: Cornell University Press, 1963).

6. A recent example of this legalistic approach is found in Louis Fisher, *The Politics of Shared Power: Congress and the Executive* (Washington, D.C.: Congressional Quarterly Press, 1981).

7. Glendon A. Schubert, Jr., *The Presidency in the Courts* (Minneapolis: University of Minnesota Press, 1957); Arthur S. Miller,

Presidential Power in a Nutshell (St. Paul, Minn.: West Publishing, 1977).

8. E. E. Schattschneider, *The Semi-Sovereign People* (New York: Holt, Rinehart and Winston, 1960), chapter 1.

9. William F. Mullen, *Presidential Power and Politics* (New York: St. Martin's Press, 1976), p. 95.

10. See Thomas M. Franck, ed., *The Tethered Presidency* (New York: Columbia University Press, 1981); Thomas M. Franck and Edward Weisband, *Foreign Policy by Congress* (New York: Oxford University Press, 1979).

11. Richard E. Neustadt, *Presidential Power*, 3rd ed. (New York: Wiley, 1960); Edward S. Corwin, *The President: Office and Powers*, 4th ed. (New York: New York University Press, 1957).

12. For a good overview of this literature see Harry A. Bailey, "Neustadt's Thesis Revisited: Toward the Two Faces of Presidential Power," paper delivered at annual meeting, Midwest Political Science Association, April 24–26, 1980.

13. Peter W. Sperlich, "Bargaining and Overload: An Essay on Presidential Power," in Aaron Wildavsky, ed., *Perspectives on the Presidency* (Boston: Little, Brown, 1975), p. 185.

14. Ibid.

15. Paletz suggests that Corwin's volume could be viewed within the "role" perspective, except that his conservative argument on presidential power is more indicative of what he calls the "anti-aggrandizement" perspective. See Paletz, "Perspectives on the Presidency," p. 440.

16. Richard M. Pious, *The American Presidency* (New York: Basic Books, 1979).

17. Ibid., p. 17.

18. Bailey, "Neustadt's Thesis Revisited," p. 14.

19. The classic study of FDR during the New Deal is James MacGregor Burns, *Roosevelt: The Lion and the Fox* (New York: Harcourt, Brace, 1956).

20. Bailey, "Neustadt's Thesis Revisited," p. 10.

21. Thomas Engeman, "Presidential Statesmanship and the Constitution: The Limits of Presidential Studies," *Review of Politics* (April 1982), p. 281.

SUGGESTED READINGS

Bailey, Harry A., Jr. *Classics of the American Presidency*. Oak Park, Ill.: Moore Publishing, 1980.

Bailey, Thomas A. *Presidential Greatness: The Image and the Man from George Washington to the Present*. New York: Appleton-Century-Crofts, 1966.

Corwin, Edward S. *The President: Office and Powers*. 4th ed. New York: New York University Press, 1957.

Goldsmith, William M. *The Growth of Presidential Power: A Documented History*. New York: Chelsea House, 1974.

Haight, David E., and Johnson, Larry D., eds. *The President: Roles and Powers*. Chicago: Rand McNally, 1965.

Koenig, Louis. *The Chief Executive*, 4th ed. New York: Harcourt Brace Jovanovich, 1981.

Longaker, Richard. *The President and Individual Liberties*. Ithaca, N.Y.: Cornell University Press, 1963.

Lowi, Theodore J. *The End of Liberalism*. New York: W. W. Norton, 1969.

Miller, Arthur S. *Presidential Power in a Nutshell*. St. Paul, Minn.: West Publishing Company, 1977.

Mullen, William F. *Presidential Power and Politics*. New York: St. Martin's Press, 1976.

Neustadt, Richard E. *Presidential Power: The Politics of Leadership from FDR to Carter*, 3rd ed. New York: Wiley, 1980.

Paletz, David L. "Perspectives on the Presidency." *Law and Contemporary Problems* (Summer 1970), pp. 429–445.

Pious, Richard M. *The American Presidency*. New York: Basic Books, 1979.

Rossiter, Clinton, *The American Presidency*, 2nd ed. New York: Harcourt, Brace and World, 1960.

Schubert, Glendon A., Jr. *The Presidency in the Courts*. Minneapolis: University of Minnesota Press, 1957.

Wildavsky, Aaron, ed. *The Presidency*. Boston: Little, Brown, 1969.

———. *Perspectives on the Presidency*. Boston: Little, Brown, 1975.

About the Authors

Harry A. Bailey, Jr., Ph.D., University of Kansas, is professor and chairman of the graduate studies program in political science at Temple University where he specializes in the American presidency and state and local politics. Winner of the Christian and Mary F. Lindback Award for Distinguished Teaching conferred by the College of Liberal Arts Alumni Association, he is the editor of *Classics of the American Presidency* (Moore Publishing, 1980) and the author of numerous articles on the presidency. Professor Bailey is chairman of the City of Philadelphia Civil Service Commission that performs both an oversight and appellate role for the city's nearly 28,000 civil service employees.

Jay M. Shafritz is a professor of Public and International Affairs at the University of Pittsburgh. Previously he has taught at the University of Houston in Clear Lake City, the State University of New York in Albany, Rensselaer Polytechnic Institute, and the University of Colorado in Denver. He is the author, coauthor, and editor of more than two dozen books on public administration and related fields, including *The Facts on File Dictionary of Public Administration*, *Classics of Public Administration*, and *Classics of Organization Theory*. Dr. Shafritz received his M.P.A. from the Baruch College of the City University of New York and his Ph.D. in political science from Temple University.